Best Short Plays

of the World Theatre

1968–1973

Also by STANLEY RICHARDS

BOOKS:

BEST SHORT PLAYS OF THE WORLD THEATRE: 1958–1967

10 CLASSIC MYSTERY AND SUSPENSE PLAYS OF THE MODERN THEATRE

BEST MYSTERY AND SUSPENSE PLAYS OF THE MODERN THEATRE

BEST PLAYS OF THE SIXTIES

MODERN SHORT COMEDIES FROM BROADWAY AND LONDON

THE BEST SHORT PLAYS 1973

THE BEST SHORT PLAYS 1972

THE BEST SHORT PLAYS 1971

THE BEST SHORT PLAYS 1970

THE BEST SHORT PLAYS 1969

THE BEST SHORT PLAYS 1968

CANADA ON STAGE

PLAYS:

THROUGH A GLASS, DARKLY

AUGUST HEAT

SUN DECK

TUNNEL OF LOVE

JOURNEY TO BAHIA

O DISTANT LAND

MOOD PIECE

MR. BELL'S CREATION

THE PROUD AGE

ONCE TO EVERY BOY

HALF-HOUR, PLEASE

KNOW YOUR NEIGHBOR

GIN AND BITTERNESS

THE HILLS OF BATAAN

DISTRICT OF COLUMBIA

Best Short Plays
of the World Theatre

1968–1973

EDITED WITH AN INTRODUCTION
AND PREFACES TO THE PLAYS BY

Stanley Richards

Crown Publishers, Inc., NEW YORK

© 1973 BY STANLEY RICHARDS
LIBRARY OF CONGRESS CATALOG CARD NUMBER: 73-82936
ISBN: 0-517-505894
PRINTED IN THE UNITED STATES OF AMERICA

for Herbert Michelman

CONTENTS

INTRODUCTION

AN INTRODUCTION to an anthology is, ostensibly, as *de rigueur* as an *apéritif* is to a well-planned dinner party. Without either, there is a seeming air of inhospitality. At least, tradition promulgates this theory and practice and while, personally, I contend that plays in a collection ought to possess enough stamina and voice to stand up and speak for themselves, nonetheless, I am most pleased to have this opportunity to share the spotlight, at least momentarily, with the outstanding dramatists who dominate these pages.

Periodically we are reminded that through the centuries there has been no more fabulous an "invalid" than the living theatre. To historians and peripheral observers it has been an unyielding valetudinarian constantly on the verge of demise. Yet somehow the theatre perpetually manages to renew its flame and triumphantly rises from the ashes of sibyllic maunderings of imminent doom. In its arduous journey down through the centuries it has overcome plagues, armed conflicts, religious opposition, the wrath of monarchs and overheated statesmen, censorship, assorted calamities—both major and minor —and even stonings by audiences. In more proximate times, specifically in the twentieth century, it has overridden such formidable challengers for supremacy and audience lurement as vaudeville, motion pictures, radio and television. But like eternity, it seems to be inured to recurring reversals and the omnipresent shadows of defeat, and while, upon occasion, it temporarily may have lowered its curtain, never has it completely lowered the boom. The theatre, then, in fact and record of survival against all species of odds never truthfully has been (nor is) quite as infirm as the prognosticators would have us believe. As the noted scenic designer Jo Mielziner so aptly stated, "live theatre, from Sophocles to Miller, is still the dwelling place of wonder," and nothing short of a world holocaust ever can reduce it completely and irretrievably to dust and oblivion, for, seemingly, it has uncanny recuperative powers.

Perhaps Sir John Gielgud, one of the world's outstanding players, summed up best the enchantment of the stage when he declared: "Nothing can compare with the magic of the real occasion, which is to me the true glory of the art of the theatre— the living actor appearing before the living audience."

For more than half a century, the Broadway stage reigned unchallenged as the theatrical nerve center of the nation. It still does, but at a diminishing degree, for in the past decade or so, the living theatre in America has expanded—not only Off- and Off-Off-Broadway (still within the shadows of Times Square)—but in many other pivotal areas of the country. And with this geographical expansion there has been a broadening of the American theatre's activity, a refreshing renewal, a stimulating revitalization.

The playwright, unquestionably, forever will be the focal and motivating force in the theatre regardless of other evolutions, transmutations or regional relocations. Yet, I can just hear refuting murmurs in the wings about occasional performing groups that have eschewed, almost obliterated, the dramatist in favor of displaying some amorphous, pointless and narcissistic exercises that have been hailed in certain quarters as "significant theatre."

Equally, there have been innumerable attempts to regale us lately with some odd ambiguities that have masqueraded as "drama." To some, of course, the fuzzier the veil of communication, the more spiritedly divine the work. Well and good— for experimentation provides perpetual fertilization to the roots of the theatre— but there does come that moment when a creative artist must shed his swaddling clothes and convert his jejune put-ons into human, understandable terms. Maturity demands preciseness and communicative wavelengths, and audience receptivity *only* can be stirred and enhanced by understanding.

The British essayist T. C. Worsley once observed that "the ability to engage an audience is the hallmark of a true dramatist." Quite right, for without engaging the interest, absorption and emotional tides of an audience, there is little or no play. Notice, I am stressing drama, not dance or ritual, and that returns us to the sphere of the playwright, for it is he who sets the dramatic torch aglow. All other considerations may be emanating sparks, but the true torch, the *only* torch, is ignited by the playwright.

Ever mindful that no form of art attains total fulfillment until it embraces the spectator or listener, the late Sir Noël Coward set down these words of advice to the "new" dramatist more than a dozen years ago: "Consider the public. Treat it with tact and courtesy. It will accept much from you if you are clever enough to win it to your side. Never fear or despise it. Coax it, charm it, interest it, stimulate it, shock it now and then if you must, make it laugh, make it cry and make it think, but above all, dear pioneers, in spite of indiscriminate and largely ignorant critical acclaim, in spite of awards and prizes and other dubious accolades, never, never, never bore the living hell out of it."

As editor of *Best Short Plays of the World Theatre: 1968–1973,* I strongly share Sir Noël's precepts, for a collection of printed plays, too, must consider the reader as an integral member of the audience, involve, absorb and entertain him, just as does the staged work. This, of course, does not imply that an editor must slant his own judgment in making his selections or rearrange his personal standards and esthetics to fit into a wider, more general mold of acceptance. On the contrary, it is an admission that he respects his readers and is eager to share with them the pleasures of the dramatic experience that he encountered while working on the book.

Undeniably, form has to be broken, fresher visions pursued, more pertinent advancements made in the theatre just as in any other facet of modern life and culture. Since the stage mirrors the times, it is obligatory that it keep tempo with its period in history. Yet, and again, no matter how progressive the format, no mat-

ter how radical the concept and approach, it is both fundamental and peremptory that one never discount or lose sight of the audience, for whatever one's personal theories, however brisk the march forward, the constant remains as steadfast as it has through the centuries—without an audience there is no theatre.

The London drama critic Harold Hobson has wisely observed that "too much theory, though it makes a brave show in the textbooks and examination syllabuses, is out of place in the theatre." Thus cued and to personalize for a moment—and I sincerely hope that readers and audiences will be in accordance—I feel rather strongly that the plays included in *Best Short Plays of the World Theatre: 1968–1973* are theatre, pure theatre, on various levels, and speak for themselves, dramatically and effectively in various hues and tones, without extended introductory formalities or ornate embellishments.

At this point, perhaps it should be explained that originally I had planned to include plays from several other foreign nations, but, regrettably, the English-language translations were either inadequate or incomplete at the time of going to press. Once again, it is hoped that these and other omissions will be compensated for in succeeding volumes, ultimately bringing a more comprehensive international representation to the series.

Preparing this volume has been a most rewarding experience but the *true* gratification will come in *sharing* these plays, for the theatre is and always will remain a communal experience.

STANLEY RICHARDS

New York, New York

Best Short Plays

of the World Theatre

1968–1973

CONFESSIONAL

Tennessee Williams

LEONA

DOC

MONK

BILL

VIOLET

STEVE

YOUNG MAN

BOY FROM IOWA

A POLICEMAN

Reprinted by permission of New Directions Publishing Corporation.
From *Dragon Country* by Tennessee Williams.

THE LIFE and career of Tennessee Williams (born Thomas Lanier Williams in Columbus, Mississippi, on March 26, 1911) have been so thoroughly documented in countless periodicals and books, as well as in critical and biographical studies, that there seems little need for reiteration in the pages of this collection. Merely to list Mr. Williams' plays is sufficient for the evocation of many memorable moments in the theatre, for he has peopled the world's stages with characters so durably vibrant that their presences still stalk the corridors of a playgoer's memory.

Named by *Time* magazine as "the greatest living playwright in the Western World," Tennessee Williams, recipient of two Pulitzer Prizes and four New York Drama Critics' Circle Awards, remains, indisputably, a consummate master of theatre. His plays pulsate with the heart's blood of the drama: passion. When one reexamines Mr. Williams' predominant works, one cannot but be awed by the dazzling skill of a remarkable dramatist whose major plays no longer tend to be merely plays but, somehow, through the process of creative genius, have transcended into haunting realities.

Tennessee Williams is, at his best, an electrifying dramatist because, in the main, he creates people who are the sort who breathe fire into scenes, explosively and woundingly. His dialogue reverberates with a lilting eloquence far from the drab, disjunctive patterns of everyday speech and, above all, he is a master of mood. At times, it is hot, oppressive, simmering with catastrophe as in *A Streetcar Named Desire* and *Cat on a Hot Tin Roof;* at other times, it is sad, autumnal, elegiac as in *The Glass Menagerie* and *The Night of the Iguana*. To achieve it, he utilizes the full complement of theatrical instruments: setting, lighting, music, plus that most intangible of gifts, the genius for making an audience forget that any other world exists except the one onstage.

As Mr. Williams often has stated, his special compassion is for "the people who are not meant to win—the lost, the odd, the strange, the difficult people—fragile people who lack talons for the jungle." The clarion call of many, if not most, of his plays is loneliness. Just as the captured iguana in *The Night of the Iguana* symbolizes the bondage to which the people who populate the play are chained, so do his characters in other of his dramas yearn to break loose, out of the cell of the lonely self, to touch and reach another person. "Hell is yourself," Mr. Williams has said. "When you ignore other people completely, that is hell." The revelation toward which all of his plays aspire is that "moment of self-transcendence, when a person puts himself aside to feel deeply for another person."

The author first won general recognition with the 1945 production of *The Glass Menagerie,* starring Laurette Taylor. Thereafter, he attained worldwide repute with a succession of impressive plays, notably: *A Streetcar Named Desire* (1947); *Summer and Smoke* (1948); *The Rose Tattoo* (1951); *Cat on a Hot Tin Roof* (1955); and *The Night of the Iguana* (1961). Among his other plays, in nonchronological order: *Sweet Bird of Youth; Camino Real; Orpheus Descending; Period of Adjustment; The Milk Train Doesn't Stop Here Anymore; Kingdom of Earth* (known in its Broadway manifestation as *The Seven Descents of Myrtle*); and *In the Bar of a Tokyo Hotel*. His most recent play, *Out Cry,* opened in New York in March, 1973, and it was described in the press as "a haunting play full of ghosts, memories and outcries."

Mr. Williams also has written a number of short plays, including: *27 Wagons Full of Cotton; This Property Is Condemned; I Rise in Flame, Cried the Phoenix; The Lady of Larkspur Lotion; The Last of My Solid Gold Watches; Moony's Kid Don't Cry; Suddenly Last Summer; Slapstick Tragedy (The Mutilated and The Gnädiges Fräulein); I Can't Imagine Tomorrow; The Frosted Glass Coffin;* and *A Perfect Analysis Given by a Parrot*. Additionally, he has published several volumes of short stories, a book of poetry and a novella, *The Roman Spring of Mrs. Stone*.

Confessional was first published in 1970 in Tennessee Williams' *Dragon Country*—"the country of pain, an uninhabitable country which is inhabited, where there is endured but unendurable pain." The play in an expanded version—but not changing the essential part of it—and retitled *Small Craft Warnings* opened at the Off-Broadway Truck and Warehouse Theatre on April 2, 1972. It was greeted in the press as "a deeply human play" that is "eloquent and moving," a work that "must rank with the finest plays of our time" and which "conclusively affirms Williams' special power to hold and move audiences." In June of the same year, the play moved uptown to the New Theatre where it continued its successful run, occasionally with Mr. Williams performing the role of Doc.

A firm disciplinarian where his work is concerned, the dramatist dedicates four hours of each day—"year in, year out"—to writing and about every two years completes a new play. Before settling down to the actual task of writing, however, he "marinates impressions, characters, experiences."

In 1969, Tennessee Williams received a Gold Medal for Drama from the prestigious National Institute of Arts and Letters and, more recently, he was given the National Theatre Conference Annual Award honoring his "countless contributions to the American theatre spanning the past three decades."

SCENE ONE

The scene is a somewhat nonrealistic evocation of a bar on the beach-front in one of those coastal towns between Los Angeles and San Diego. It attracts a group of regular patrons who are nearly all so well known to one another that it is like a community club, and most of these regulars spend the whole evening there. Ideally, the walls of the bar, on all three sides, should have the effect of fog rolling in from the ocean. A blue neon outside the door says: "Monk's Place." The bar runs diagonally from upstage to down; over it is suspended a large varnished sailfish, whose gaping bill and goggle-eyes give it a constant look of amazement. There are about three tables, with hurricane lamps, each of which is turned on only when that particular table is being used in the play. Near the entrance is the juke box, and in the wall at left are doors to the ladies' and gents' lavatories. A flight of stairs ascends from behind the back table, giving access to the bar-owner's living quarters. The stairs should be "masked" above first few steps.

Ideally, there should be a forestage, projecting a few feet in front of the proscenium; if that isn't practical, then there should be an area in the downstage center that can be lighted in a way that sets it apart from the bar at those points in the play when a character disengages himself from the group to speak as if to himself. This area is the "confessional"; it is used by everyone in the bar at some time in the course of the play.

The first few minutes of the play are given over to a tirade by a drunk female patron named LEONA, *a large, ungainly woman who paces the floor in the slightly crouched, menacing posture of a "villain" wrestler. She wears white clam-digger slacks and a woolly pink sweater. On her head of dyed corkscrew curls is a sailor hat which she occasionally whips off her head to slap something with—the bar, a tabletop, somebody's back—to emphasize a point. A few moments before the curtain rose, she had apparently exchanged blows, or rather given a blow to another female "regular,"* VIOLET, *who has taken refuge in the locked ladies' room from which she keeps shouting for* MONK, *the owner and barman, to "call the wagon." This sobbing appeal should be repeated at intervals during* LEONA's *tirade. The "regulars" are a fairly raffish bunch.* LEONA *and* VIOLET *are in their late thirties.* STEVE, *and* MONK, *the bar-owner, and* DOC—*who lost his license for heavy drinking but still practices more or less clandestinely, are middle-aged.* BILL *is still in his twenties and is crudely attractive. At the rise of the curtain,* LEONA *is in the midst of a declamation against* VIOLET.

————

LEONA.—with no respect for herself, and that I don't blame her for. What could she possibly find to respect in herself? She lives like an animal in a room with no bath that's directly over the amusement arcade at the foot of the pier, yeah, right over the billiards, the pinball games, and the bowling alleys at the amusement arcade, it's bang, bang, bang, loud as a TV western all day and all night, it would drive a sane person crazy but she couldn't care less. I know, I been there, I seen it and I heard it, bang, bang, till two or three in the morning, then bang, bang, again at eight A.M. when it opens for the next day. She don't have a closet, she didn't have a bureau so she hangs her dresses on a piece of rope that hangs across a corner between two nails, and her other possessions she keeps on the floor in boxes.

BILL. What business is it of yours?

LEONA. None, not a goddam bit! When she was sick? I went there to bring her a chicken. I asked her, where is your silver? Get up, sit at the table, where's your silver? She didn't have any silver, not a fork, spoon, or knife, hell, not even a plate, but she ate the chicken, aw, yeah, she ate the chicken like a dog would eat it, she picked it up in her paws and gnawed at it just like a dog. Who came to see if she was living or dead? ME! ONLY! I got her a bureau, I got her a knife, fork, and spoon, I got her some china, I got her a change of bed linen for her broken-down cot, and ev'ry day after work I come by that goddam rat hole to see what she needed and bring it, and then one time I come by there to see what she needed and bring it. The bitch wasn't there. I thought my God she's died or they put her away. I run downstairs and I heard her screaming with joy in the amusement arcade; she was having herself a ball with a shipload of drunk sailor boys: she hardly had time to speak to me.

BILL. Maybe she'd gotten sick of you: that's a possible reason.

LEONA. It's a possible reason I was sick of her, too, but I'd thought that the bitch was dying of malnutrition so I'd come by her place ev'ry day with a bottle of hot beef bouillon or a chicken or meatloaf for her because I thought she was human and a human life is worth saving or what the shit *is* worth saving. But is she human? She's just a parasite creature, not even made out of flesh but out of wet biscuit dough, she always looks like the bones are dissolving in her, that's what she—

BILL (*Banging his beer bottle on the table*). DO YOU THINK I BELONG TO YOU? I BELONG TO MYSELF, I JUST BELONG TO MYSELF.

LEONA. Aw, you pitiful piece of—worthless—conceit! (*She addresses the bar.*)— Never done a lick of work in his life.—He has a name for his thing. He calls it Junior. He says he takes care of Junior and Junior takes care of him. How long is that gonna last? How long does he figure Junior is going to continue to provide for him, huh? HUH! —Forever or *less* than forever? —Thinks the sun rises and sets between his legs and that's the reason I put him in my trailer, feed him, give him beer money, pretend I don't notice there's five or ten bucks less in my pocketbook in the morning than my pocketbook had in it when I fell to sleep, night before.

BILL. Go out on the beach and tell that to the sea gulls, they'd be more int'rested in it.

VIOLET (*shrilly, from the ladies' room*). Help me, help me, somebody, somebody call the po-liiiiice!

LEONA. Is she howling out the ladies' room window?

VIOLET. How long do I have to stay in here before you get the police!?

LEONA. If that fink is howling out the ladies' room window, I'm going out back and throw a brick in at her.

MONK. Leona, now cool it, Leona.

LEONA. I'll pay the damage, I'll pay the hospital expenses.

MONK. Leona, why don't you play your

violin number on the multi-selector and settle down at a table and—

LEONA. When I been insulted by someone, I don't settle down at a table, or nowhere, NOWHERE!

(VIOLET *sobs and wails as* STEVE *comes into the bar.*)

STEVE. Is that Violet in there?

LEONA. Who else do you think would be howling out the ladies' room window but her, and you better keep out of this, this is between her and me.

STEVE. What happened? Did you hit Violet?

LEONA. You're goddam right I busted that filthy bitch in the kisser, and when she comes out of the ladies', if she ever comes out, I'm gonna bust her in the kisser again, and kiss my ass, I'm just the one that can do it! MONK! DRINK! BOURBON SWEET!

MONK. Leona, you're on a mean drunk, and I don't serve liquor to anyone on a mean drunk.

LEONA. Well, *you* can kiss it, too, you monkey-faced mother.

(*She slaps the bar top with her sailor hat.*)

STEVE. Hey, did you hit Violet?

(BILL *laughs at this anticlimactic question.*)

LEONA. Have you gone deaf, have you got wax in your ears, can't you hear her howling in there? Did I hit Violet? The answer is *yes,* and I'm not through with her yet. (LEONA *approaches the door of the ladies' room.*) COME ON OUT OF THERE, VIOLET, OR I'LL BREAK IN THE DOOR!

(*She bangs her fist on the door, then slaps it contemptuously with her cap, and resumes her pacing.* BILL *keeps grinning and chuckling.*)

STEVE. Why did she hit Violet?

LEONA. Why don't you ask *me* why?

STEVE. Why did you hit Violet?

LEONA. I hit Violet because she acted indecent with that son of a bitch I been supporting for six months in my trailer, that's the reason I hit her and I'll take another crack at her when she comes out of the ladies' if I have to wait here all night.

STEVE. What do you mean "indecent"?

LEONA. Jesus, don't you know her habits? Are you unconscious ev'ry night in this bar and in her rat hole over the amusement arcade? I mean she acted indecent with her dirty paws under the table, hell, and I'd even bought the mother a drink and told her to sit down with us. She sat down. I looked at her hands on the table. The red enamel had nearly all chipped off the nails and the fingernails, black, I mean *black,* like she'd spent every day for a month without washing her hands after making mud pies with filthy motherless kids, and I thought to myself, it's awful, the degradation a woman can sink down into without respect for herself, so I took her hand and pulled it up under the lamp on the table, and said to her, Violet, will you look at your hand, will you look at your fingernails, Violet?

STEVE. Is that why you hit Violet?

LEONA. Goddam it, NO! Will you listen? I told her to look at her nails and she said, oh, the enamel is peeling, I know. I mean the dirtiness of the nails was not a thing she could notice, just the chipped red enamel.

STEVE. Is that why you hit Violet?

LEONA. Shit, will you shut up till I tell you why I hit her? I wouldn't hit her just for being unclean, unsanitary, I wouldn't hit her for nothing that affected just her. And now, if you'll pay attention, I'm going to tell you exactly why I did hit her. I got up from the table to play "Souvenir."

STEVE. What is she talking about? What are you talking about?

LEONA. A violin number I like to play on the box. And when I come back to the table her hands had disappeared off it. I thought to myself, I'm sorry, I made her ashamed of her hands and she's hiding them now.

STEVE. Is that why you hit Violet?

LEONA. Why do you come in a bar when you're already drunk? No! Listen! It wasn't embarrassment over her filthy nails that had made her take her hands off the tabletop, it was her old habit, as filthy as her nails, and you know what I'm talking about if you've ever known her at all. The reason her pitiful hands had disappeared off the table was because under the table she was acting indecent with her hands in the lap of that ape that moved himself into my trailer and tonight will move himself out as fast as he moved him-

self in. And now do you know why I hit her? If you had balls, which it doesn't look like you do, you would've hit her yourself instead of making me do it.

STEVE. I wasn't here when it happened, but that's the reason you hit her?

LEONA. Yeah, now the reason has got through the fog in your head which is thick as the fog on the beach.

(VIOLET *wails from the ladies' room.*)

STEVE. I'm not married to Violet, I never was or will be. I just wanted to know who hit her and why you hit her.

LEONA (*slapping at him with her cap*). Annhh!

STEVE. Don't slap at me with that cap. What do I have to do with what she done or she does?

LEONA. No responsibility? No affection? No pity? You stand there hearing her wailing in the ladies' and deny there's any connection between you? Well, now I feel sorry for her. I regret that I hit her. She can come back out now and I won't hit her again. I see her life, the awfulness of her hands reaching out under a table, automatically creeping under a table into the lap of anything with a thing that she can catch hold of. Let her out of the ladies', I'll never hit her again. I feel too much pity for her, but I'm going out for a minute to breathe some clean air and to get me a drink where a barman's willing to serve me, and then I'll come back to pay up whatever I owe here and say good-bye to the sailfish, hooked and shellacked and strung up like a flag over— over—lesser, much lesser—creatures that never, ever sailed an inch in their—lives. . . . .

(*The pauses at the end of this speech are due to a shift of her attention toward a* YOUNG MAN *and a* BOY *who have entered the bar. Her eyes have followed them as they walked past her to a table in the front. She continues speaking, but now as if to herself.*)

LEONA.—When I leave here tonight, none of you will ever see me again.

BILL. Is anyone's heart breaking?

LEONA. Not mine, not mine.

BILL. The heartbreak of a slob makes a lot of noise over nothing.

LEONA. Over nothing is right, and the nothing is you. When I leave here tonight, I'm going to stop by the shop, let myself in with my passkey, and collect my own equipment, which is enough to open a shop of my own, write a good-bye note to Flo, she isn't a bad old bitch, I doubled her trade since I been there, she's going to miss me, poor Flo, then leave my passkey and cut back to my trailer and pack like lightning and move on to—

BILL.—Where?

LEONA. Where I go next. You won't know, but you'll know I went fast.

(*Now she forgets her stated intention of going out of the bar and crosses to the table taken by the* YOUNG MAN *and the* BOY. *The* BOY *wears khaki shorts, and a sweatshirt on the back of which is lettered "Iowa to Mexico." The* YOUNG MAN *is dressed effetely in a yachting jacket, maroon linen slacks, leather sandals, and a silk neck-scarf. Despite this costume, he has a quality of sexlessness, not effeminacy. Some years ago, he must have been remarkably handsome: now his face seems to have been burned thin by a fever that is not of the flesh.*)

LEONA (*suddenly very amiable*). Hi, boys!

YOUNG MAN. Oh, hello. Good evening.

BOY (*with shy friendliness*). Hello.

(BILL *is grinning and chuckling.* VIOLET'S *weeping in the ladies' room no longer seems to interest anyone in the bar.*)

LEONA (*to the* BOY). How's the corn growing out there where the tall corn grows?

BOY. Oh, it's still growing tall.

LEONA. Good for the corn. I'm from the corn country, too. What town or city are you from in Iowa?

BOY. Dubuque.

LEONA. Oh, from Dubuque, no shoot. I could recite the telephone book of Dubuque, but excuse me a minute, I want to play a selection on the box, and I'll come right back to discuss Dubuque with you. Huh? (*She moves as if totally pacified to the juke box and removes some coins from a pocket. They fall to the floor. She starts to bend over to pick them up, then decides not to bother, gives them a slight kick, gets a dollar bill out of a pocket, calling out—*) Monk, gimme change for a buck.

YOUNG MAN. Barman? —Barman? — What's necessary to get the barman's attention here, I wonder.

MONK. I heard you. You've come in the wrong place. You're looking for the Jungle Bar, half a mile up the beach.

YOUNG MAN. Does that mean you'd rather not serve us?

MONK. Let me see the kid's draft card.

BOY. I just want a coke.

YOUNG MAN. He wants a plain Coca-Cola, I'd like a vodka and tonic.

(BILL *has left his table and walked casually onto the forestage, the lighted confessional. As he begins to speak, the confessional is lighted and the rest of the bar is dimmed.*)

BILL. Y' can't insult 'em, there's no way to bring 'em down except to beat 'em and roll 'em. I noticed him stop at the door before he come in. He was about to go right back out when he caught sight of me. Then he decided to stay. A faggot that dresses like that is asking for it. After a while, say about fifteen minutes, I'll go in the gents' and he'll follow me in there for a look at Junior. Then I'll have him hooked. He'll ask me to meet him outside by his car or at the White Castle. It'll be a short wait and I don't think I'll have t'do more than scare him a little. I don't like beating 'em up. They can't help the way they are. Who can? Not me. Left home at fifteen, and like Leona says, I've never done a lick of work in my life and I never plan to, not as long as Junior keeps batting on the home team, but my time with Leona's run out. She means to pull out of here and I mean to stay. . . .

(*As he slouches back to his table, the forestage spot is dimmed out and the bar is brought up.* LEONA *is still at the multi-selector: she lights it up with a coin and selects a violin number, "Souvenir." A look of ineffable sweetness appears on her face, at the first note of music.*)

MONK (*rapping at the ladies'*). Violet, you can come out, now, she's playing that violin number.

(BILL *and* STEVE *laugh. As he laughs,* STEVE *leaves the barstool and walks to the confessional area where he is lighted as the bar is dimmed.*)

STEVE. I guess Violet's a pig, all right, and I ought to be ashamed to go around with her. But a man unmarried, forty-seven years old, employed as a short-order cook at a salary he can barely get by on alone, he can't be choosy. Nope, he has to be satisfied with the goddam scraps in this world, and Violet's one of those scraps. She's a pitiful scrap, but—(*He shrugs sadly and lifts the beer bottle to his mouth.*)—something's better than nothing and I had nothing before I took up with her. She gave me a clap once and tried to tell me I got it off a toilet seat. I asked the doctor, Is it possible to get a clap off a public toilet seat, and he said, Yes, you can get it that way but you *don't!* (*He grins sadly and drinks again, wobbling slightly.*) —Oh, my life, my miserable, cheap life! It's like a bone thrown to a dog! I'm the dog, she's the bone. Hell, I know her habits. She's always down there in that amusement arcade when I go to pick her up, she's down there as close as she can get to some navy kid, playing a pinball game, and one hand is out of sight. Hustling? I reckon that's it. I know I don't provide for her, just buy her a few beers here, and a hot dog on the way home. But Bill, why's he let her mess around with him? One night he was braggin' about the size of his tool, he said all he had to do to make a living was wear tight pants on the street. Life!—Throw it to a dog. I'm not a dog, I don't want it. I think I'll sit at the bar and pay no attention to her when she comes out. . . .

(He turns back upstage and takes a seat at the bar. During his speech in the confessional area, the violin number has been heard at a very low level. Now the light in the bar and the violin selection are brought up to a normal level. After a moment, VIOLET *comes out of the ladies' room slowly with a piteous expression. She is dabbing her nostrils with a bit of toilet tissue. She has large, liquid-looking eyes and her lips are pursed in sorrow so that she is like a travesty of a female saint under torture. Nothing said about her could prepare for her actual appearance. She has a kind of bizarre beauty although her two-piece velvety blue suit has endured several years—since its acquisition at a thrift shop—without darkening the door of a cleaner. She gasps and draws back a little at the sight of* LEONA; *then, discreetly sobbing, she edges onto a bar-*

stool and is served a beer. STEVE *glares at her. She avoids looking at him.* BILL *grins and chuckles at his table.* LEONA *ignores the fact that* VIOLET *has emerged from her retreat: she goes on pacing the bar but is enthralled by the music.)*

LEONA. My God, what an instrument, it's like a thing in your heart, it's a thing that's sad but better than being happy, in a— crazy drunk way. . . .

VIOLET (*piteously*). I don't know if I can drink, I feel sick at my stomach.

LEONA. Aw, shit, Violet. Who do you think you're kidding? You'll drink whatever is put in the reach of your paws.

(She slaps herself on the thigh with the sailor cap and laughs.)

VIOLET. I do feel sick at my stomach.

LEONA. You're lucky you're sick at your stomach because your stomach can vomit but when you're sick at your heart, that's when it's awful, because your heart can't vomit the memories of your lifetime. I wish my heart could vomit, I wish my heart could throw up the heartbreaks of my lifetime, my days in a beauty shop and my nights in a trailer. It wouldn't surprise me at all if I drove up to Sausalito alone this night. With no one . . .

(She glances at BILL, *who grins and chuckles.* VIOLET *sobs piteously again.* LEONA *gives* VIOLET *a fairly hard slap on the shoulders with her sailor cap.* VIOLET *cries out in affected terror.)*

Shuddup, I'm not gonna hit you. Steve, take her off that barstool and put her at a table, she's on a crying jag and it makes me sick.

STEVE (*to* VIOLET). Come off it, Violet, Sit over here at a table, before you fall off the barstool.

LEONA. She hasn't got a mark on her, not a mark, but she acts like I'd nearly kilt her, and turns to a weeping willow. But as for that ape that I put up in my trailer, him I could blast out of my trailer and out of my life and out of all memory of him. I took him in because a life in a trailer, going from place to place any way the wind blows you, gets to be lonely, sometimes, and you make the mistake of taking in somebody that don't respect you for anything but his tendency in your trailer, I mean the tenancy of it. . . .

STEVE. Violet, I told you to come over

to this table.

LEONA. Take her over before she falls off the stool.

(STEVE *supports* VIOLET'S *frail, weeping figure to a table.* MONK *receives a phone call.*)

MONK. Doc, it's for you.

DOC (*crossing to the end of the bar*). Thanks, Monk.

MONK. The old Doc's worked up a pretty good practice for a man in retirement.

LEONA. Retirement your ass, he was kicked out of the medical profession for performing operations when he was so loaded he couldn't tell the appendix from the gizzard.

MONK. Leona, go sit at your table.

LEONA. You want responsibility for a human life, do you?

MONK. Bill, I think she's ready to go home now.

LEONA. I'll go home when I'm ready and I'll do it alone.

BILL. I seen a circus with a polar bear in it that rode a three-wheel bicycle. That's what you make me think of tonight.

LEONA. You want to know something, McCorkle? I could beat the shit out of you.

BILL. Set down somewhere and shut up.

LEONA. I got a suggestion for you. Take this cab fare—(*She throws a handful of silver on the table.*)—And go get your stuff out of my trailer. Clear it all out, because when I go home tonight and find any stuff of yours there, I'll pitch it out of the trailer and bolt the door on you. I'm just in the right mood to do it.

BILL. Don't break my heart.

LEONA. What heart? We been in my trailer together for six months and you contributed nothing.

BILL. Shit, for six months I satisfied you in your trailer!

LEONA. You never satisfied nothing but my mother complex. Never mind, forget it, it's forgotten. Just do this. Take this quarter and punch number six three times on the juke box.

BILL. Nobody wants to hear that violin number again.

LEONA. I do, I'm somebody. My brother, my young brother, played it as good if not better than Heifetz on that box. Y'know, I look at you and I ask myself a question. How does it feel to've never

had anything beautiful in your life and not even know you've missed it? (*She crosses toward the multi-selector.*) Walking home with you some night, I've said, Bill, look at the sky, will you look at that sky? You never looked up, just grunted. In your life you've had no experiation—experience!—Appreciation!—of the beauty of God in the sky, so what is your life but a bottle of, can of, glass of—one, two, three!

(*She has punched the violin selection three times.*)

MONK. The Doc's still on the phone.

LEONA. "Souvenir" is a soft number.

DOC (*returning to the bar*). I've got to deliver a baby. Shot of brandy.

LEONA (*returning to* BILL'S *table*). It wouldn't be sad if you didn't know what you missed by coming into this world and going out of it some day without ever having a sense of, experience of, and memory of, a beautiful thing in your life such as I have in mine when I remember the violin of and the face of my young brother.

BILL. You told me your brother was a fruit.

LEONA. I told you privately something you're repeating in public with words as cheap as yourself. My brother who played this number had pernicious anemia from the age of thirteen and any fool knows a disease, a condition, like that would make any boy too weak to go with a woman, but he was so full of love he had to give it to someone like his music. And in my work, my profession as a beautician, I never seen skin or hair or eyes that could touch my brother's. His hair was a natural blond as soft as silk and his eyes were two pieces of heaven in a human face, and he played on the violin like he was making love to it. I cry! I cry! —No, I don't, I *don't* cry! —I'm proud that I've had something beautiful to remember as long as I live in my lifetime . . .

(VIOLET *sniffles softly.*)

LEONA. When they passed around the plate for the offering at church, they'd have him play in the choir stall and he played and he looked like an angel, standing under the light through the stained glass window. Um-hmmm. (*Her expression is rapt.*)—And people, even the tightwads, would drop paper money in the plates when he played. Yes, always before the service, I'd give him a shampoo-rinse so that his silky hair, the silkiest hair I've ever known on a human head in my lifetime as a beautician, would look like an angel's halo, touched with heavenly light. Why, people cried like I'm crying, why, I remember one Easter, the whole choir started crying like I'm crying and the preacher was still choked up when he delivered the sermon. "Angels of Light," that was it, the number he played that Easter . . . (*She sings a phrase of the song.*) Emotions of people can be worse than people but sometimes better than people, yes, superior to them, and Haley had that gift of making people's emotions uplifted, superior to them! But he got weaker and weaker and thinner and thinner till one Sunday he collapsed in the choir stall and after that he failed fast, just faded out of this world. Anemia—pernicious . . .

VIOLET (*sobbing*). Anemia, that's what I've got!

LEONA. Don't compare yourself to him, how dare you compare yourself to him! He was too beautiful to live and so he died. Otherwise we'd be living together in my trailer. I'd train him to be a beautician, to bring out the homeliness in—I mean the, I mean the—(*She is confused for a moment; she lurches into a barstool and knocks it over.*) I mean I'd train my young brother to lay his hands on the heads of the homely and lonely and bring some beauty out in them, at least for one night or one day or at least for an hour. We'd have our own shop, maybe two of 'em, and I wouldn't give you—(*She directs herself to* BILL.)—the time of the day, the time of the night, the time of the morning or afternoon, the sight of you never would have entered my sight to make me feel pity for you, no, *noooo!* (*She bends over* BILL's *table, resting her spread palms on it, to talk directly into his face.*) The companionship and the violin of my brother would be all I had any need for in my lifetime till my death-time! Remember this, Bill, if your brain *can* remember. Everyone needs! One beautiful thing! In the course of a lifetime! To save the heart from colluption!

BILL. What is "colluption," fat lady?

LEONA. *CORRUPTION!* —Without one beautiful thing in the course of a lifetime, it's all a death-time. A woman turns to a slob that lives with a slob, and life is disgusting to her and she's disgusting to life, and I'm just the one to—

BILL (*cutting in*). If you'd rather live with a fruit—

LEONA. Don't say it! Don't say it! (*She seizes hold of a chair and raises it mightily over her head.* VIOLET *screams.* LEONA *hurls the chair to the floor.*) Shit, he's not worth the price of a broken chair!

(*Suddenly she bursts into laughter that is prodigious as her anger or even more: it's like an unleashed element of nature. Several patrons of the bar, involuntarily, laugh with her. Abruptly as it started, the laughter stops short: there is total silence except for the ocean sound outside.*)

DOC (*rising from his barstool*). Well, I better be going. Somebody's about to be born at Treasure Island.

LEONA. That's my trailer court where I keep my trailer. A baby's about to be born there?

BILL. Naw, not a baby, a full-grown adult's about to be born there, and that's why the Doc had t'brace himself with a coupla shots of brandy.

DOC (*turning about on his barstool, glass in hand*). You can't make jokes about birth and you can't make jokes about death. They're miracles, holy miracles, both, yes, that's what both of them are, even though, now, they're usually surrounded by—expedients that seem to take away the dignity of them. Birth? Rubber gloves, boiled water, forceps, surgical shears. And death? —The wheeze of an oxygen tank, the jab of a hypodermic needle to put out the panic light in the dying-out eyes, tubes in the arms and the kidneys, absorbent cotton inserted in the rectum to hold back the bowels discharged when the—the *being* stops. (*During this speech, or possibly before it, he has moved into the pool of light, at the center front, which serves as a confessional for the characters.*)—It's hard to see back of this cloud of—irreverent—paraphernalia. But behind them both are the holy mysteries of—birth and—death. . . . They're dark as the face of God whose face is dark because it's the face of a black man; yes, that's right, a Negro, yes. I've always figured that God is a black man with no light on his face, He moves in the dark like a black man, a Negro miner in the pit of a lightless coal mine, obscured completely by the—irrelevancies and irreverencies of public worship—standing to sing, kneeling to pray, sitting to hear the banalities of a preacher—(*The pool of light dims out and he returns to the bar to put his glass down.*)

LEONA (*as light comes up on the bar*). I want to know: is nobody going to stop him from going out, in his condition, to deliver a baby? I want to know quick, or I'll stop him myself!

DOC. Monk, did I give you my—?

MONK. Bag? Yeah, here.

(MONK *hands a medical kit across the bar.*)

DOC. Thanks. And I'll have a shot of brandy to wash down a benzedrine tablet to steady my hands.

LEONA. NOBODY, HUH?

DOC. Tonight, as I drove down Canyon Road, I noticed a clear bright star in the sky, and it was right over that trailer court, Treasure Island, where I'm going to deliver a baby. So now I know: I'm going to deliver a new Messiah tonight.

LEONA. The hell you are, you criminal, murdering quack, leggo of that bag! (*She tries to snatch the bag from him.* BILL *and* STEVE *hold her back. The* DOC *leaves: the boom of surf is heard through the door left open after* DOC's *departure.*) You all, all of you, are responsible, too, if he murders that baby and the baby's mother. Is life worth nothing in here? I'm going out. I'm going to make a phone call!

(BILL *makes a move to stop her.*) DON'T!—you *dare* to!

MONK. Who're you going to call?

LEONA. That's my business, I'm not gonna use your phone.

(*She charges out of the bar, leaving the door open.*)

BILL. I know what she's up to. She's gonna call the office at Treasure Island and tell 'em the Doc's comin' out there to deliver a baby.

MONK. Go and stop her, she could get the Doc in serious trouble.

BILL. Shit, they know her too well to

pay her any attention when she calls.

VIOLET (*plaintively*). Last week she give me a perm and a rinse for nothing, and then tonight she turns on me, threatens to kill me.

BILL. Aw, she blows hot and cold, dependin' on whichever way her liquor hits her.

VIOLET. She's got two natures in her. Sometimes she couldn't be nicer. A minute later she—

MONK (*at the telephone*). Shut up a minute. Treasure Island? This is Monk speaking from Monk's Place. Just a minute. (*He turns to the table.*) Close that door, I can't hear the talk over the surf. (STEVE *shuts the door on the surf's boom.* BILL *takes* STEVE's *seat next to* VIOLET.)— Yeah. Now. If you get a phone call out there from Leona Dawson, you know her, she's got a trailer out there, don't listen to her; she's on a crazy mean drunk, out to make trouble for a capable doctor who's been called by someone out there, an emergency call. So I thought I'd warn you, thank you.

(MONK *hangs up the telephone.* VIOLET *comes downstage and the light is focused on her.*)

VIOLET. It's perfectly true that I have a room over the amusement arcade facing the pier. But it's not like Leona describes it. It took me a while to get it in shipshape condition because I was not a well girl when I moved in there, but now it's clean and attractive. It's not luxurious but it's clean and attractive and has an atmosphere to it. I don't see anything wrong with living upstairs from the amusement arcade, facing the pier. I don't have a bath or a toilet but I keep myself clean with a sponge bath at the washbasin and use the toilet in the amusement arcade. Anyhow, it's a temporary arrangement, that's all it is, a temporary arrangement ...

(LEONA *returns to the bar.* BILL *rises quickly and walks over to the bar.*)

LEONA. One, two, button my shoe, three, four, shut the door, five, six, pick up sticks ... (*No one speaks.*)—Silence, absolute silence. (*She goes to the table of the* YOUNG MAN *and the* BOY FROM IOWA.) Well, boys, what went wrong?

YOUNG MAN. I'm afraid I don't know what you mean.

LEONA. Sure you know what I mean. You're not talking to each other, you don't even look at each other. There's some kind of tension between you. What is it? Is it guilt feelings? Embarrassment with guilt feelings?

YOUNG MAN. I still don't know what you mean, but, uh—

LEONA. "But, uh" what?

YOUNG MAN. Don't you think you're being a little presumptuous?

LEONA. Naw, I know the gay scene. I learned it from my kid brother. He came out early, younger than this boy here. I know the gay scene and I know the language of it and I know how full it is of sickness and sadness; it's so full of sadness and sickness, I could almost be glad that my little brother died before he had time to be infected with all that sadness and sickness in the heart of a gay boy. This kid from Iowa, here, reminds me a little of how my brother was, and you, you remind me of how he might have become he's dead, then.

YOUNG MAN. Yes, you should be relieved he's dead, then.

(*She flops awkwardly into a chair at the table.*)

YOUNG MAN (*testily*). Excuse me, won't you sit down?

LEONA. D'ya think I'm still standing up?

YOUNG MAN. Perhaps we took your table.

LEONA. I don't have any table. I'm moving about tonight like an animal in a zoo because tonight is the night of the death-day of my brother and—Look, the barman won't serve me, he thinks I'm on a mean drunk, so do me a favor, order a double bourbon and pretend it's for you. Do that, I'll love you for it, and of course I'll pay you for it.

YOUNG MAN (*calling out*). Barman? I'd like a double bourbon.

MONK. If it's for the lady, I can't serve you.

(BILL *laughs heartily at the next table.*)

YOUNG MAN. It isn't for the lady, it's for me.

LEONA. How do you like that shit? (*She shrugs.*) Now what went wrong between you before you come in here, you can tell me and maybe I can advise you. I'm practically what they call a faggot's moll.

YOUNG MAN. Oh. Are you?

LEONA. Yes, I am. I always locate at least one gay bar in whatever city I'm in. I live in a home on wheels, I live in a trailer, so I been quite a few places. And have a few more to go. Now nobody's listening to us, they're having their own conversation about their own situations. What went wrong?

YOUNG MAN. Nothing, exactly. I just made a mistake, and he did, too.

LEONA. Oh. Mistakes. How did you make these mistakes? Nobody's listening, tell me.

YOUNG MAN. I passed him riding his bicycle up Canyon Road and I stopped my car and reversed it till I was right by his bike and I—spoke to him.

LEONA. What did you say to him?

BOY. Do you have to talk about it?

YOUNG MAN. Why not? I said: "Did you really ride that bike all the way from Iowa to the Pacific Coast," and he grinned and said, yes, he'd done that. And I said: "You must be tired?" and he said he was and I said: "Put your bike in the back seat of my car and come home with me for dinner."

LEONA. What went wrong? At dinner? You didn't *give* him the dinner?

YOUNG MAN. No, I gave him drinks, first, because I thought that after he'd had dinner, he might say: "Thank you, goodnight."

BOY. Let's shut up about that. I had dinner after.

LEONA. After what?

YOUNG MAN. After—

BOY. I guess to you people who live here it's just an old thing you're used to, I mean the ocean out there, the Pacific, it's not an *experience* to you any more like it is to me. You say it's the Pacific, but me, I say *THE PACIFIC!*

YOUNG MAN. Well, everything is in "caps" at your age, Bobby.

LEONA (*to the* YOUNG MAN). Do you work for the movies?

YOUNG MAN. Naturally, what else?

LEONA. Act in them, you're an actor?

YOUNG MAN. No. Scriptwriter.

LEONA (*vaguely*). Aw, you write movies, huh?

YOUNG MAN. *Rewrite* them. My specialty is sophisticated chatter at cocktail parties —*you* know . . .

LEONA (*still vaguely*). No, I don't know.

YOUNG MAN. Politely bitchy remarks between smartly gowned ladies such as—

LEONA. No. No, I don't know. Never mind. I've known many a bitch but no polite ones. I don't think that monkey-faced mother is gonna serve us that bourbon. — I've never left this bar without leaving a dollar tip on the table, and this is what thanks I get for it, just because it's the death-day of my brother and I showed a little human emotion about it. Now what's the trouble between you and this kid from Iowa where the tall corn blows, I mean grows?

YOUNG MAN. I only go for straight trade. But this boy—look at him! Would you guess he was gay? —I didn't, I thought he was straight. But I had an unpleasant surprise when he responded to my hand on his knee by putting his hand on mine.

BOY. I don't know the word *gay*. What does that word mean?

LEONA. Don't tell him—he's got plenty of time to learn the meanings of words and cynical attitudes. Why, he's got eyes like my brother's! Have you paid him?

YOUNG MAN. For disappointment?

LEONA. Don't be a mean-minded mother. Give him a five, a ten. If you picked up what you don't want, it's your mistake and pay for it.

BOY. I don't want money from him. I thought he was nice, I liked him.

LEONA. Your mistake, too. (*She turns to the* YOUNG MAN). Gimme your wallet. (*The* YOUNG MAN *hands her his wallet.*)

BOY. He's disappointed. I don't want anything from him.

LEONA. Don't be a fool. Fools aren't respected, you fool. (*She removes a bill from the wallet and stuffs it in the pocket of the* BOY's *shirt. The* BOY *starts to return it.*) OK, I'll hold it for you till he cuts out of here to make another pickup and remind me to give it back to you when he goes. He wants to pay you, it's part of his sad routine. It's like doing penance—penitence . . . (*She turns to the* YOUNG MAN.) Do you like being alone except for vicious pickups? The kind you go for? If I understood you correctly? —Christ, you have terrible eyes, the expression in them! What are you looking at?

YOUNG MAN. That fish over the bar . . .

LEONA. You're changing the subject.

YOUNG MAN. No, I'm not, not a bit — Now suppose some night I woke up and I found that fantastic fish—what is it?

LEONA. Sailfish. What about it?

YOUNG MAN. Suppose I woke up some midnight and found that peculiar thing swimming around in my bedroom? Up the Canyon.

LEONA. In a fishbowl? Aquarium?

YOUNG MAN. No, not in a bowl or aquarium: free, unconfined.

LEONA. Impossible.

YOUNG MAN. Granted: it's impossible. But suppose it occurred just the same as so many impossible things *do* occur just the same. Suppose I woke up and discovered it there, swimming round and round in the darkness over my bed, with a faint phosphorescent glow in its big goggle-eyes and its gorgeously iridescent fins and tail making a swishing sound as it circles around and about and around and about right over my head in my bed.

LEONA. Hah!

YOUNG MAN. Now suppose this admittedly preposterous thing did occur.

LEONA. All right. Suppose it occurred. What about it?

YOUNG MAN. What do you think I would say?

LEONA. Say to who? To the fish?

YOUNG MAN. To myself and the fish.

LEONA. I'll be raped by an ape if I can imagine what a person would say in a situation like that.

YOUNG MAN. I'll tell you what I would say, I would say: "Oh, well . . ."

LEONA. That's all you would say, just "Oh, well"?

YOUNG MAN. "Oh, well" is all I would say before I went back to sleep.

LEONA. What I would say is: "Get the hell out of here, you goggle-eyed monstrosity of a mother," that's what I'd say to it.

MONK. Leona, you got to quiet down.

LEONA. But what's the point of your story?

YOUNG MAN. You don't see the point of my story?

LEONA. Nope.

YOUNG MAN (*to the* BOY). Do *you* see the point of my story? (*The* BOY *shakes his head.*) Well, maybe I don't either.

LEONA. Then why'd you tell it?

YOUNG MAN. What is the thing that you mustn't lose in this world before you're ready to leave it? The one thing you mustn't lose ever?

LEONA. Love?

(*The* YOUNG MAN *laughs.*)

BOY. Interest?

YOUNG MAN. That's closer, much closer. Yes, that's almost it. The word that I had in mind is surprise, though. The capacity for being surprised. I've lost the capacity for being surprised, so completely lost it, that if I woke up in my bedroom late some night and saw that fantastic fish swimming right over my head, I wouldn't be really surprised.

LEONA. You mean you'd think you were dreaming?

YOUNG MAN. Oh, no. Wide awake. But not really surprised. (*He rises casually and moves to the confessional: the light concentrates on him.*) There's a coarseness, a deadening coarseness, in the experience of most homosexuals. The experiences are quick, and hard, and brutal, and the pattern of them is practically unchanging. Their act of love is like the jabbing of a hypodermic needle to which they're addicted but which is more and more empty of real interest and surprise. This lack of variation and surprise in their—"love life" —(*He smiles harshly.*) —spreads into other areas of—"sensibility?"—(*He smiles again.*) —Yes, once, quite a long while ago, I was often startled by the sense of being alive, of being *myself, living!* Present on earth, in the flesh, yes, for some completely mysterious reason, a single, separate, intensely conscious being, *myself: living!*—Whenever I would feel this— *feeling,* this—shock of—what?—self-realization?—I would be stunned, I would be thunderstruck by it. And by the existence of everything that exists, I'd be lightning-struck with astonishment . . . It would do more than astound me, it would give me a feeling of panic, the sudden sense of— I suppose it was like an epileptic seizure, except that I didn't fall to the ground in convulsions; no, I'd be more apt to try to lose myself in a crowd on a street until the seizure was finished. —They were dangerous seizures. One time I drove into the mountains and smashed the car into

a tree, and I'm not sure if I *meant* to do that, or . . . In a forest you'll sometimes see a giant tree, several hundred years old, that's scarred, that's blazed by lightning, and the wound is almost obscured by the obstinately still living and growing bark. I wonder if such a tree has learned the same lesson that I have, not to feel astonishment anymore but just go on, continue for two or three hundred years more? —This boy I picked up tonight, the kid from the tall corn country, still has the capacity for being surprised by what he sees, hears, and feels in this kingdom of earth. All the way up the canyon to my place, he kept saying, *I can't believe it, I'm here, I've come to the Pacific, the world's greatest ocean!*—as if nobody, Magellan or Balboa or even the Indians, had ever seen it before him; yes, like he'd discovered this ocean, the largest on earth, and so now, because he'd found it himself, it existed, now, for the first time, never before . . . And this excitement of his reminded me of my having lost the ability to say: "My God!" instead of just: "Oh, well." I've asked all the questions, shouted them at deaf heaven, till I was hoarse in the voice box and blue in the face, and gotten no answer, not the whisper of one, nothing at all, you see, but the sun coming up each morning and going down that night, and the galaxies of the night sky trooping onstage like chorines, robot chorines: one, two, three, kick; one, two, three, kick . . . Repeat any question too often and what do you get, what's given? —A big carved rock by the desert, a—monumental symbol of wornout passion and bewilderment in you, a stupid stone paralyzed Sphinx that knows no answers that you don't but comes on like the oracle of all time, waiting on her belly to give out some outcries of universal wisdom, and if she woke up some midnight at the edge of the desert and saw that fantastic fish swimming over her head— y'know what she'd say, too? She'd say: "Oh, well"—and go back to sleep for another five thousand years. (*He turns back; the confessional light fades out and the bar is relighted. He returns to the table and adjusts his neck-scarf as he speaks to the* BOY.)—Your bicycle's still in my car. Shall I put it on the sidewalk?

BOY. I'll go get it. (*He turns to* LEONA) Good-night.

LEONA. You could put your bike in my trailer and go up the Coast with me. I've got two bunks in my trailer.

BOY. Thank you, but I—

LEONA. Why not? It wouldn't cost you nothing and we'd be company for each other.

BOY. I, uh, I—

LEONA. Why *not?* Are you afraid I'd put the make on you, Sonny?

BOY. I, uh, I've got my trip planned. I'm headed for Mexico.

LEONA. Mexico's dangerous country for a kid that don't know the score, and you could get sick there. You'd be better off with me. I can teach you the gay scene if you want to learn it.

BOY. It's nice of you, but I—better get my bicycle.

BILL (*to* STEVE). She wants that young fruit in her stinking trailer but the offer has been turned down.

LEONA. You can't understand one person wanting to give protection to another, it's way past your understanding.

(*The* BOY *moves downstage, pulling on a sweater he carried into the bar. The bar is dimmed and the voices fade out. Light comes up in the confessional as the* BOY *enters that area.*)

BOY. In Goldenfield, Iowa, there was just one man like that. He ran a flower shop and I heard boys talk about him. They said you went in a back room of the flower shop and it was decorated Chinese with incense and naked pictures. I was afraid to go there. I was afraid to even walk down the street it was on. These kids made fun of the man, they said he was a—bad word—but he'd give 'em two dollars any time they went there. One time there was a discussion of what made a man like that and I remember Clay Rivers said that they had something in their throats, something different from normal throats, which made them need to—bad word—and I felt my face turning hot and my throat choked up so I couldn't say anything in that discussion, at all. One time, one winter night, I rode down the street the flower shop was on, and I saw it was closed—for rent—and I heard he'd been run out of town because he'd—bad word

—had immoral relations with a kid still in grade school. That's all I've known of that world until tonight. Tonight was— initiation. It scares me because I liked it, and liked him, too. I'll never turn into the —bad word—flower shop man, but I'll probably have an experience like that again, and next time I won't make the mistake of showing any excitement and pleasure. —I think I'll ride my bike all night tonight, I've got a lot to think over . . .

(*He leaves the area of the confessional and goes out of the bar.*)

LEONA (*suddenly*). *Aw, the money!* (*She rushes to the door.*) HEY, IOWA TO MEXICO, HEYYY!

BILL. He don't want a lousy five bucks, he wants everything in the wallet. He'll roll the faggot and hop back on his bike looking sweet and innocent as your brother fiddling in church.

(LEONA *rushes out, calling.*)

STEVE. The Coast is overrun with 'em they come running out here like animals out of a brushfire.

MONK (*crossing into the confessional*). I've got no moral objections to them as a part of humanity, but I don't encourage them here. One comes in, others follow. First thing you know you're operating what they call a gay bar and it sounds like a birdcage, they're standing three deep at the bar and lining up at the men's room. Business is terrific for a few months. Then in comes the law. The place is raided, the boys hauled off in the wagon, and your place is padlocked. And then a cop or a gangster pays you a social visit, big smile, all buddy-buddy. You had a good thing going, a real swinging place, he tells you, but you needed protection. He offers you protection and you buy it. The place is reopened and business is terrific a few months more. And then? It's raided again, and the next time it's reopened, you pay out of your nose, your ears, and your ass. Who wants it? I don't want it. I want a small steady place that I can handle alone, that brings in a small, steady profit. No buddy-buddy association with gangsters and the police. I want to know the people that come in my place so well I can serve them their brand of liquor or beer before they name it, soon as they come in the door. And all their personal problems, I want to know that, too.

(VIOLET *begins to hum softly, swaying to and fro like a water plant.*)

I'm fond of, I've got an affection for, a sincere interest in my regular customers here. They send me postcards from wherever they go and tell what's new in their lives and I am interested in it. Just last month one of them I hadn't seen in about five years, he died in Mexico City and I was notified of the death and that he'd willed me all he owned in the world, his personal effects and a two-hundred-fifty-dollar savings account in a bank. A thing like that is beautiful as music. These things, these people, take the place of a family in my life. I love to come down those steps from my room to open the place for the evening, and when I've closed for the night, I love climbing back up those steps with my can of Ballantine's ale, and the stories, the jokes, the confidences and confessions I've heard that night, it makes me feel not alone. —I've had heart attacks, and I'd be a liar to say they didn't scare me and don't still scare me. I'll die some night up those steps, I'll die in the night and I hope it don't wake me up, that I just slip away, quietly.

(*During his speech, the light has been concentrated on him, the rest of the bar very dim.* LEONA *has returned. The light in the bar comes up but remains at a low level.*)

LEONA.—Is there a steam engine in here? Did somebody drive in here on a steam engine while I was out?

MONK (*returning from his meditation*). —Did what?

LEONA. I hear something going huff-huff like an old locomotive pulling into a station. (*She is referring to a sound like a panting dog: it comes from the unlighted table where* VIOLET *is seated between* BILL *and* STEVE.)—Oh, well, my home is on wheels. —Bourbon sweet, Monk.

MONK. Leona, you don't need another.

LEONA. Monk, it's after midnight, my brother's death-day is over. I'll be all right, don't worry. (*She goes to the bar.*)— It was selfish of me to wish he was still alive.

(*A pin-spot of light picks up* VIOLET'S tear-stained and tranced face at the otherwise dark table.)—She's got some form of religion in her hands . . .

(*The lights dim slowly for a time passage.*)

SCENE TWO

An hour later. "Group singing" has been in progress at the back table. LEONA *is not participating. She is leaning moodily against the bar in front.*

VIOLET. I like the old numbers best. I bet none of you know this one, this one's a real, real oldie I learned from mother. (*She opens her eyes very wide and assumes a sentimental look.*)

"Lay me where sweet flowers blos-som,
Where the whitest lily blows
Where the pinks and violets min-gle,
Lay my head beneath the rose."

LEONA (*disparagingly*). Shit.

VIOLET. "Life is from me fastly fa-ding,
Soon I'll be in sweet re-pose.
Ere I die I ask this fa-vor—
Lay my head beneath the rose . . ."

—Now how is that for a sweet, sentimental old number?

(*No one offers any comment but* LEONA.)

LEONA. Y'don't need a rose to lay her, you could lay her under a cactus and she wouldn't notice the diff-rence. (BILL *crosses to the bar for a beer.*) I guess you don't think I'm serious about it, hitting the highway tonight. (BILL *shrugs and crosses to a downstage table.*) Well, I am, I'm serious about it. (*She sits at his table.*) An experienced expert beautician can always get work anywhere.

BILL. Your own appearance is a bad advertisement for your line of work.

LEONA. I don't care how I look as long as I'm clean and decent—and *self-supporting.* When I haul into a new town, I just look through the yellow pages of the telephone directory and pick out a beauty shop that's close to my trailer camp. I go to the shop and offer to work a couple of days for nothing, and after that couple of days I'm in like Flynn, and on my own terms which is fifty percent of charges for all I do, and my tips, of course, too. They like my work and they like my personality, my approach to customers. I keep them laughing.

BILL. You keep me laughing, too.

LEONA. —Of course, there's things about you I'll remember with pleasure, such as waking up sometimes in the night and looking over the edge of the upper bunk to see you asleep in the lower. (BILL *leaves the table. She raises her voice to address the bar-at-large.*) Yeah, he slept in the lower 'cause when he'd passed out or nearly, it would of taken a derrick to haul him into the upper bunk. So I gave him the lower bunk and took the upper myself.

BILL. As if you never pass out. Is that the idea you're selling?

LEONA. When I pass out I wake up in a chair or on the floor, but when you pass out, which is practically every night, I haul you onto your bunk. I never would dream of leaving you stoned on the floor, I'd get you into your bunk and out of your shoes when you passed out on the floor, and you know goddam well you never done that for me, oh, no, the floor was good enough for me in your opinion, and sometimes you stepped on me even, yeah, like I was a rug or a bug, and that's the God's truth and you know it, because your nature is selfish. You think because you've lived off one woman after another woman after eight or ten other women you're something superior, special. Well, you're special but not superior, baby. I'm going to worry about you after I've gone and I'm sure as hell leaving tonight, fog or no fog on the highway, but I'll worry about you because you refuse to grow up and that's a mistake that you make, because you can only refuse to grow up for a limited period in your lifetime and get by with it. —I *loved* you!—I'm not going to cry. (*Violet starts weeping for her.*) When I come to a new place, it takes me two or three weeks, that's all it takes me, to find somebody to live with in my home on wheels and to find a night spot to hang out in. Those first two or three weeks are rough, sometimes I wish I'd stayed where I was before, but I know from experience that I'll find somebody and locate a night spot to booze in, and get acquainted with —friends . . . (*The light has focused on her. She moves downstage with her hands in her pockets, her face and voice very grave as if she were less confident that things will be as she says.*) And then, all at once, something wonderful happens. All the past disappointments in people I left behind me, just disappear, evaporate from my mind, and I just remember the good things, such as their sleeping faces, and—Life! Life! I never just said, "Oh, well," I've always said "Life!" to life, like a song to God, and when I die, I'll say "death," like a song to God, too, because I've lived in my lifetime and not been afraid of—changes . . . (*She goes back to the table.*) —However, y'see, I've got this pride in my nature. When I live with a person I love and care for in my life, I expect his respect, and when I see I've lost it, I GO, GO! —So a home on wheels is the only right home for me. Now what is she doing here? VIOLET *has weaved to the table and taken a chair.*) Hey! What are *you* doing here?

VIOLET. You're the best friend I ever had, the best friend I—

(*She sways and sobs like a* religieuse *in the grip of a vision.*)

LEONA. What's that, what're you saying? (VIOLET *sobs.*) She can't talk. What was she saying?

VIOLET. —BEST—!

LEONA. WHAT?

VIOLET.—*Friend!*

LEONA. I'd go further than that, I'd be willing to bet I'm the *only* friend that you've had, and the next time you come down sick in that room upstairs from the amusement arcade, nobody will bring you nothing, no chicken, no hot beef bouillon, no chinaware, no silver, and no interest and concern about your condition, and you'll die in your rattrap with no human voice, just bang, bang, bang from the bowling alley and billiards. And when you die you should feel a relief from the conditions you lived in. Now I'm leaving you two suffering, bleeding hearts together, I'm going to sit at the bar. I had a Italian boyfriend that taught me a saying, "Meglior solo que mal accompanota," which means that you're better alone than in the company of a bad companion. (*She starts to the bar, as the* DOC *enters.*) Back already, huh? It didn't take you much time to deliver the baby. Or did you bury the baby? Or did you bury the mother? Or did you bury them both, the mother and baby?

DOC (*to* MONK). Can you shut up this woman?

LEONA. Nobody can shut up this woman. Quack, quack, quack, Doctor Duck, quack, quack, quack, quack, quack!

DOC. I'M A LICENSED PHYSICIAN!

LEONA. *SHOW* me your license. *I'll shut up when I see it!*

DOC. A doctor's license to practice isn't the size of a drunken driver's license, you don't put it in a wallet, you hang it on the wall of your office.

LEONA. Here is your office! Which wall is your license hung on? Beside the sailfish or where? Where is your license to practice hung up, in the gents', with other filthy scribbles?!

MONK. Leona, you said your brother's death-day was over and I thought you meant you were—

LEONA. THOUGHT I MEANT I WAS WHAT?

DOC. You were ready to cool it. BILL! —Take Leona home, now.

LEONA. Christ, do you think I'd let him come near me?! Or near my trailer?! Tonight?! (*She slaps the bar several times with her sailor cap, turning to right and left as if to ward off assailants, her great bosom heaving, a jungle look in her eyes.*)

VIOLET (*sweetly and sadly*). —Steve, it's time to leave.

(VIOLET, STEVE, *and* BILL *start out.*)

LEONA (*stomping the floor with a powerful foot*). Y'WANT YOUR ASS IN A SLING? BEFORE YOU'RE LAID UNDER THAT ROSE?

VIOLET (*shepherded past* LEONA *by* STEVE *and* BILL). If we don't see you again, good luck wherever you're going.

(*They go out the door.*)

LEONA (*rushing after them*). Yes, she does, she wants her ass in a sling!

(*She charges out of the door. A moment or two later are heard, above the boom of the surf, the shrill outcries of* VIOLET. MONK *crosses toward the door:* VIOLET *collides with him, screeching, blood flowing from her nose. She utters several wild cries, then dashes into the ladies' room and bolts the door.*)

VIOLET (*shrilly, from the ladies' room*). They're calling the wagon for her, she's like a wild animal out there! Lock the

door! Keep her out!

(MONK *closes and locks the bar entrance. There is a sudden quiet in the bar, except for the sobbing of* VIOLET *in the ladies' room, and a muted disturbance outside.* MONK *turns out the bar lights, all except the hurricane lamp on one table.*)

MONK. Doc, have a nightcap with me?

DOC. Yes, thanks, I could use one. (MONK *sets a bottle and two shot glasses at the one lighted table. They sit in profile on either side of the table.* DOC *speaks—as if answering a question.*) The birth of the baby was at least three months premature, so it was born dead, of course, and just beginning to look like a human baby. —The man living with the woman in the trailer said, "Don't let her see it, get it out of the trailer." I agreed with the man that she shouldn't see it, so I put this fetus in a shoe box . . . (*He speaks with difficulty, as if compelled to.*) The trailer was right by the beach, the tide was coming in with heavy surf, so I put the shoe box—and contents—where the tide would take it.

MONK. Are you sure that was legal?

DOC. Christ, no, it wasn't legal. —I'd barely set the box down when the man came out shouting for me. The woman had started to hemorrhage. When I went back in the trailer, she was bleeding to death. The man hollered at me, "Do something, can't you do something for her!"

MONK. Could you?

DOC. —I could have told the man to call an ambulance for her, but I thought of the probable consequences to me, and while I thought about that, the woman died. She was a small woman, but not small enough to fit in a shoe box, so I— I gave the man a fifty-dollar bill that I'd received today for performing an abortion. I gave it to him in return for his promise not to remember my name—(*He reaches for the bottle. His hand shakes so that he can't refill his shot glass:* MONK *fills it for him.*)—You see, I can't make out certificates of death, since I have no legal right any more to practice medicine, Monk.

MONK. —In the light of what happened, there's something I'd better tell you, Doc. Soon as you left here to deliver that baby, Leona ran out of the bar to make a phone call to the office at Treasure Island, warning them that you were on your way out there to deliver a baby. So, Doc, you may be in trouble. —If you stay here . . .

DOC. —I'll take a benzedrine tablet and pack up tonight and be on the road before morning.

(*The sound of a squad car siren is heard.* LEONA *appears at the door, shouting and pounding.*)

LEONA. MONK! THE PADDY WAGON IS SINGING MY SONG!

(MONK *lets her in and locks the door.*)

MONK. Go upstairs. Can you make it?

(*She clambers up the steps, slips, nearly falls. The squad car screams to a stop outside the bar. An* OFFICER *knocks at the door.* MONK *admits him.*) Hi, Tony.

OFFICER. Hi, Monk. What's this about a fight going on here, Monk?

MONK. Fight? Not here. It's been very peaceful tonight. The bar is closed. I'm sitting here having a nightcap with—(*He indicates the* DOC, *slumped over the table.*)

OFFICER. Who's that bawling back there?

MONK (*pouring a drink for the* OFFICER). Some dame disappointed in love, the usual thing. Try this and if it suits you, take the bottle.

OFFICER (*He drinks*).—OK. Good.

MONK. Take the bottle. Drop in more often. I miss you.

OFFICER. Thanks, g'night.

(*He goes out. As* MONK *puts another bottle on the table,* LEONA *comes awkwardly back down the stairs.*)

LEONA. Monk? Thanks, Monk. (*She and* MONK *sit at the table.* VIOLET *comes out of the ladies' room. She sees* LEONA *at the table and starts to retreat.*) Aw, hell, Violet. Come over and sit down with us, we're having a nightcap, all of us, my brother's death-day is over.

VIOLET. Why does everyone hate me? (*She sits at the table: drinks are poured from the bottle.* VIOLET *hitches her chair close to* MONK's. *In a few moments she will deliberately drop a matchbook under the table, bend to retrieve it, and the hand on* MONK's *side will not return to the table surface.*)

LEONA. Nobody hates you, Violet. It would be a compliment to you if they did.

VIOLET. I'd hate to think that I'd come between you and Bill.

LEONA. Don't torture yourself with an

awful thought like that. Two people living together is something you don't understand and since you don't understand it you don't respect it, but, Violet, this being our last conversation, I want to advise something to you. I think you need medical help in the mental department and I think this because you remind me of a—of a—of a plant of some kind . . .

VIOLET. Because my name is Violet?

LEONA. No, I wasn't thinking of violets, I was thinking of water plants, yeah, plants that don't grow in the ground but float on water. With you everything is such a—such a—well, you know what I mean: don't you?

VIOLET. Temporary arrangement?

LEONA. Yes, you could put it that way. Do you know how you got into that place upstairs from the amusement arcade?

VIOLET. —How?

LEONA. Yes, *how* or *why* or *when?*

VIOLET. —Why, I—

(*She obviously is uncertain on all three points.*)

LEONA. Take your time: and *think.* How, why, when?

VIOLET. Why, I was—in L.A., and—

LEONA. Are you sure you were in L.A.? Are you sure about even that? Or is everything foggy to you, is your mind in a cloud?

VIOLET. Yes, I was—

LEONA. I said take your time, don't push it. Can you come out of the fog?

MONK. Leona, take it easy, we all know Violet's got problems.

LEONA. Her problems are mental problems and I want her to face them, now, in our last conversation. Violet? Can you come out of the fog and tell us how, when, and why you're living out of a suitcase upstairs from the amusement arcade, can you just—

MONK (*cutting in*). She's left the amusement arcade, she left it tonight, she came here with her suitcase.

LEONA. Yeah, she's a water plant, with roots in water, drifting the way it takes her.

(VIOLET *weeps.*)

LEONA. And she cries too easy, the waterworks are back on. I'll give her some music to cry to before I go back to my home on wheels and get it cracking up the Old

Spanish Trail.

(*She rises from the table.*)

MONK. Not tonight, Leona. You have to sleep off your liquor before you get on the highway in this fog.

LEONA. That's what you think, not what I think, Monk. My time's run out in this place. (*She has walked to the multi-selector and started the violin piece.*) —How, when, and why, and her only answer is tears. Couldn't say how, couldn't say when, couldn't say why. And I don't think she's sure where she was before she come here, any more sure than she is where she'll go when she leaves here. She don't dare remember and she don't dare look forward, neither. Her mind floats on a cloud and her body floats on water. And her dirty-fingernail hands reach out to hold on to something she hopes can hold her together. (*She starts back toward the table, stops; the bar dims and light is focused on her.*) —Oh, my God, she's at it again, she's got a hand under the table. (LEONA *laughs sadly.*) Well, I guess she can't help it. It's sad, though. It's a pitiful thing to have to reach under a table to find some reason to live. You can always tell when she's about to do it. She gets a look that's almost unconscious in those big, wet eyes that're too big for her face and her mouth hangs open a little. Then she does it. She hitches her chair up closer to the man next to her: then she lets something drop on the floor, bends over to pick it up, and one of her hands comes up but the other stays down. The man slouches down in his chair and takes little sips of his drink with a faraway look like hers. Then you know she's worshipping her idea of God Almighty in her personal church. It's her kick, and like they say, don't knock another man's kick. Why the hell should I care she done it to a nowhere person that I put up in my trailer for a few months? Well, to be honest about it, I know I got some lonely weeks ahead of me before I find myself another companion in wherever I'm going. I wish that kid from I-oh-a with eyes like my lost brother had been willing to travel with me but I guess I scared him. What I think I'll do is turn back to a faggot's moll when I haul up to Sausalito or San Francisco. You always find one in the gay bars that needs a big

sister with him, to camp with and laugh and cry with, and I hope I'll find one soon—it scares me to be alone in my home on wheels built for two . . .

(*She turns as the bar is lighted and goes back to the table.*)

DOC. Have a drink with us, Leona.

LEONA. Thank you, no. I've had my quota, and I've got to haul-ass upstate in foggy weather. Well, I'll toss another shot down, then go to my home on wheels and get it moving up the Old Spanish Trail. Fog don't bother me unless it's fog in my head, and my head's completely clear now. —MONK, HEY, MONK! What's my tab here t'night?

MONK. Forget it, don't think about it, go home and sleep, Leona.

(*He and* VIOLET *appear to be in a state of trance together.*)

LEONA. I'm not going to sleep and I never leave debts behind me. This twenty ought to do it.

(*She places a bill on the table.*)

MONK. Uh-huh, sure, keep in touch. . . .

LEONA. Tell Bill he'll find his effects in the trailer-court office, and when he's hustled himself a new meal ticket, he'd better try and respect her, at least in public. —Well—(*She extends her hand slightly:* MONK *and* VIOLET *are sitting with closed eyes. The* DOC *is looking down at the table.*)—I guess I've already gone.

VIOLET (*dreamily*). G'bye, Leona.

MONK. G'bye. . . .

DOC. G'bye, Leona. (LEONA *lets herself out of the bar. The* DOC *rises unsteadily from the table.*) —G'bye, Monk.

MONK. G'bye, Doc. Keep in touch.

VIOLET. G'bye, Doc.

MONK. Take care.

(*The* DOC *departs.*)

VIOLET. —Monk? Let's go upstairs. Huh, Monk?

MONK. Hmm? Oh. Upstairs—Yeah, go on up and make yourself at home. Take a shower up there while I lock up the bar.

(VIOLET *crosses to the stairs and climbs a few steps.*)

VIOLET. Monk! —I'm scared of these stairs, they're almost steep as a ladder. I better take off my slippers. Take my slippers off for me. (*She holds out one leg from the steps, then the other.* MONK *removes her slippers. She goes on up, calling down to him.*) Bring up some beer with you, sweetheart.

MONK. Yeh, I'll bring some beer up. Don't forget your shower.

(*Alone in the bar,* MONK *opens the door on the boom of the ocean, then crosses to the confessional, pulling a chair with him.*)

—I always leave the door open for a few minutes to clear the smoke and liquor smell out of the place, and to hear the ocean. It sounds different this late than it does when people are on the beach front. It has a private sound to it, a sound that's just for itself. Just for itself and for me. I'm going to stay down here till I hear the shower running. I don't hear it running. She probably thinks she'd dissolve in a shower. I shouldn't have let her stay here. The Doc says she gave Steve the clap. I

better not touch her up there, have no contact with her, maybe not even go up. — Till she's asleep. (*He lets one of the slippers fall by the chair, turns the other slowly in his hands.*)—A dirty, worn-out slipper that's still being worn, sour smelling from sweat from being worn too long, but still set down by the bed to be worn again the next day, walked on here and there on—pointless—errands, till finally the sole of it's worn through. —But even then you can't be sure that it will be thrown away, no, it might be resoled or just padded with cardboard, and still be put on to walk on, till it's past all repair—all repair . . .

(*He goes on turning the slipper in his hands as the stage is dimmed out.*)

CURTAIN

VISITOR FROM FOREST HILLS

Neil Simon

NORMA HUBLEY
ROY HUBLEY

BORDEN EISLER
MIMSEY HUBLEY

EVER SINCE 1961, Neil Simon has reigned supreme as America's foremost writer of contemporary comedies. His gilt-edged chain of successes began with his initial Broadway play, *Come Blow Your Horn,* which ran for 677 performances. This was followed by the book for the musical *Little Me* (1962); *Barefoot in the Park* (1963); *The Odd Couple* (1965);the musical *Sweet Charity* (1966); and *The Star-Spangled Girl* (1966).

When *Plaza Suite* opened on February 14, 1968, it was immediately apparent that Mr. Simon once again had mined theatrical gold. The play was hailed as "a triple-barreled explosion of comedy" that provided "a wonderfully happy and gratifying evening of sheer entertainment." The production, which originally costarred Maureen Stapleton and George C. Scott, was directed by Mike Nichols and it had an engagement of 1,097 performances. It is the final play of this trio of short comedies (each transpires, at different times, in the identical suite at the Plaza Hotel, New York) that appears in this anthology.

In December of that same year, Mr. Simon unveiled another success, the musical *Promises, Promises* (with music by Burt Bacharach and lyrics by Hal David), and in 1969 his Broadway entry was *Last of the Red Hot Lovers,* followed in 1970 by *The Gingerbread Lady.*

The author was born in the Bronx, New York, on July 4, 1927. He attended New York University and the University of Denver. His first theatrical affiliation came as a sketch writer (in collaboration with his brother Danny) for resort revues at Camp Tamiment, Pennsylvania. From there he moved on to television, supplying comedy material for such personalities as Phil Silvers, Jackie Gleason, Red Buttons, Tallulah Bankhead and, notably, for Sid Caesar and Imogene Coca in *Your Show of Shows.* An accomplished hand at comedy, he later contributed sketches to two Broadway revues, *Catch a Star* (1955) and *New Faces of 1956.*

During the season of 1966–67, Mr. Simon had the phenomenal total of four hit shows (*Barefoot in the Park; The Odd Couple; Sweet Charity;* and *The Star-Spangled Girl*) running concurrently on Broadway—and as this is being written he is represented by two of New York's leading successes, *The Sunshine Boys* and *The Prisoner of Second Avenue.*

In 1965, the dramatist won an Antoinette Perry (Tony) Award as the year's best author for *The Odd Couple,* and in 1968 he was the recipient of the Sam S. Shubert Award in recognition of his outstanding contribution to the American theatre.

An acknowledged master of comedy technique, Mr. Simon recently was asked for his "prescription" for successful comedy writing. "The idea of a prescription for comedy," he replied, "is obviously ridiculous. What works for one playwright rarely works for another, and even the fact that a certain approach succeeded for a writer before does not mean that it will surely produce an amusing play for that same scribe a second time."

Mr. Simon, however, would be the first to agree that comedy, as with all forms of drama, must originate with the characters, for valid and appreciable humor only can emerge from their involvements in, and reactions to, a situation. "In the first of 112 versions of *Come Blow Your Horn,* the opening five minutes of the play were crammed with good jokes . . . in fact, some of the best I had ever written . . . and the scene was terrible. The audience, knowing nothing of the characters or situation, could not have cared less. Now I know enough to *start* with the *characters.*"

While Neil Simon's plays may be regarded by some as merely lighthearted entertainments, there is, if one digs deeply enough beyond the surface of laughter, an underlying element of human truths, particularly in his more recent works. As London's respected drama critic Herbert Kretzmer wrote in *The Daily Express:* "Mr. Simon's genius has been not only to write some of the funniest one-line gags now being spoken on the English-speaking stage, but to suggest also something of the pain, aspiration and panic behind all those flip phrases."

The author also has written a number of screenplays; the most recent, *The Heartbreak Kid,* called by Vincent Canby of *The New York Times* "the best and most original American comedy of 1972."

SCENE. *A suite at the Plaza Hotel on the seventh floor, overlooking Central Park. The set is divided into two rooms. The room at stage right is the living room. It is a well-appointed room, tastefully furnished with an entrance door at the extreme right and windows that look out over the park. A door leads into the bedroom, which has a large double bed, etc., and a door that leads to the bathroom.*

It is three o'clock on a warm Saturday afternoon in June.

The living room is bedecked with vases and baskets of flowers. In the bedroom one opened valise containing a young woman's street clothes rests on the floor. A very large box, which had held a wedding dress, rests on the luggage rack, and a man's suit lies on the bed. A fur wrap and gloves are thrown over the back of the sofa. Telegrams of congratulation and newspapers are strewn about. The suite today is being used more or less as a dressing room, since a wedding is about to occur downstairs in one of the reception rooms.

As the lights come up, NORMA HUBLEY *is at the phone in the bedroom, impatiently tapping the receiver. She is dressed in a formal cocktail dress and a large hat, looking her very best, as any woman would want to on her daughter's wedding day. But she is extremely nervous and harassed, and with good cause—as we'll soon find out.*

––––

NORMA (*on the phone*). Hello? . . . Hello, operator? . . . Can I have the Blue Room, please . . . The Blue Room . . . Is there a Pink Room? . . . I want the Hubley-Eisler wedding . . . The Green Room, that's it. Thank you . . . Could you please hurry, operator, it's an emergency . . . (*She looks over at the bathroom nervously. She paces back and forth*) Hello? . . . Who's this? . . . Mr. Eisler . . . It's Norma Hubley . . . No, everything's fine . . . Yes, we're coming right down . . . (*She is smiling and trying to act as pleasant and as calm as possible*) Yes, you're right, it certainly *is* the big day . . . Mr. Eisler, is my husband there? . . . Would you, please? . . . Oh! Well, I'd like to wish you the very best of luck, too . . . Borden's a wonderful boy . . . Well, they're *both* wonderful kids . . . No, no. She's as calm

as a cucumber . . . That's the younger generation, I guess . . . Yes, everything seems to be going along beautifully . . . Absolutely beautifully . . . Oh, thank you. (*Her husband has obviously just come on the other end, because the expression on her face changes violently and she screams a rasping whisper filled with doom. Sitting on the bed*) Roy? You'd better get up here right away, we're in big trouble . . . Don't ask questions, just get up here . . . I hope you're not drunk because I can't handle this alone . . . Don't say anything. Just smile and walk leisurely out the door . . . and then get the hell up here as fast as you can. (*She hangs up, putting the phone back on the night table. She crosses to the bathroom and then puts her head up against the door. Aloud through the bathroom door*) All right, Mimsey, your father's on his way up. Now, I want you to come out of that bathroom and get married. (*There is no answer*) Do you hear me? . . . I've had enough of this nonsense . . . Unlock that door! (*That's about the end of her authority She wilts and almost pleads.*) Mimsey, darling, please come downstairs and get married, you know your father's temper . . . I know what you're going through now, sweetheart, you're just nervous . . . Everyone goes through that on their wedding day . . . It's going to be all right, darling. You love Borden and he loves you. You're both going to have a wonderful future. So please come out of the bathroom! (*She listens; there is no answer.*) Mimsey, if you don't care about your life, think about mine. Your father'll kill me. (*The front doorbell rings.* NORMA *looks off nervously and moves to the other side of the bed.*) Oh, God, he's here! . . . Mimsey! Mimsey, please spare me this . . . If you want, I'll have it annulled next week, but please come out and get married! (*There is no answer from the bathroom but the front doorbell rings impatiently.*) All right, I'm letting your father in. And heaven help the three of us!

(*She crosses through the bedroom into the living room. She crosses to the door and opens it as* ROY HUBLEY *bursts into the room.* ROY *is dressed in striped trousers, black tail coat, the works. He looks elegant but he's not too happy in this attire. He is a volatile, explosive man equipped to handle the rigors of the competitive business world, but a nervous, frightened man when it comes to the business of marrying off his only daughter.)*

ROY. Why are you standing here? There are sixty-eight people down there drinking my liquor. If there's gonna be a wedding, let's have a wedding. Come on! *(He starts back out the door but sees that NORMA is not going anywhere. She sits on the sofa. He comes back in)* . . . Didn't you hear what I said? There's another couple waiting to use the Green Room. Come on, let's go!

(He makes a start out again.)

NORMA *(very calm)*. Roy, could you sit down a minute? I want to talk to you about something.

ROY. *(She must be mad.)* You want to talk *now*? You had twenty-one years to talk while she was growing up. I'll talk to you when they're in Bermuda. Can we please have a wedding?

NORMA. We can't have a wedding until you and I have a talk.

ROY. Are you crazy? While you and I are talking here, there are four musicians playing downstairs for seventy dollars an hour. I'll talk to you later when we're dancing. Come on, get Mimsey and let's go.

(He starts out again.)

NORMA. That's what I want to talk to you about.

ROY *(comes back)*. Mimsey?

NORMA. Sit down. You're not going to like this.

ROY. Is she sick?

NORMA. She's not sick . . . exactly.

ROY. What do you mean, she's not sick exactly? Either she's sick or she's not sick. Is she sick?

NORMA. She's not sick.

ROY. Then let's have a wedding! *(He crosses into the bedroom.)* Mimsey, there's two hundred dollars' worth of cocktail frankfurters getting cold downstairs . . . *(He looks around the empty room.)* Mimsey? *(He crosses back to the living room to the side of the sofa. He looks at NORMA.)* . . . Where's Mimsey?

NORMA. Promise you're not going to blame me.

ROY. Blame you for what? What did you do?

NORMA. I didn't do anything. But I don't want to get blamed for it.

ROY. What's going on here? Are you going to tell me where Mimsey is?

NORMA. Are you going to take an oath you're not going to blame me?

ROY. *I take it! I take it!* NOW WHERE THE HELL IS SHE?

NORMA. . . . She's locked herself in the bathroom. She's not coming out and she's not getting married.

(ROY looks at NORMA incredulously. Then, because it must be an insane joke, he smiles at her. There is even the faint glint of a chuckle.)

ROY *(softly)*. . . . No kidding, where is she?

NORMA *(turns away)*. He doesn't believe me. I'll kill myself.

(ROY turns and storms into the bedroom. He crosses to the bathroom and knocks on the door. It's locked. He tries again. He bangs on the door with his fist.)

ROY. Mimsey? . . . *MIMSEY?* *(There is no reply. Girding himself, he crosses back through the bedroom into the living room to the sofa. He glares at NORMA.)* . . . All right, what did you say to her?

NORMA *(jumping up and moving away)*. I knew it! I knew you'd blame me. You took an oath. God'll punish you.

ROY. I'm not blaming you. I just want to know what *stupid* thing you said to her that made her do this.

NORMA. I didn't say a word. I was putting on my lipstick, she was in the bathroom, I heard the door go click, it was locked, my whole life was over, what do you want from me?

ROY. And you didn't say a word?

NORMA. Nothing.

ROY *(ominously moving toward her as NORMA backs away)*. I see. In other words, you're trying to tell me that a normal, healthy, intelligent, twenty-one-year-old college graduate, who has driven me crazy the last eighteen months with wedding lists, floral arrangements, and choices of assorted hors d'oeuvres, has suddenly decided to spend this, the most important day of her life, locked in the Plaza Hotel john?

NORMA (*making her stand at the mantel*). Yes! Yes! Yes! Yes! Yes!

ROY (*vicious*). YOU MUSTA SAID SOMETHING!

(*He storms into the bedroom.* NORMA *goes after him.*)

NORMA. Roy . . . Roy . . . What are you going to do?

ROY (*stopping below the bed*). First I'm getting the college graduate out of the bathroom! Then we're gonna have a wedding and then you and I are gonna have a big talk! (*He crosses to the bathroom door and pounds on it.*) Mimsey! This is your father. I want you and your four-hundred-dollar wedding dress out of there in five seconds!

NORMA (*standing at the side of the bed*). Don't threaten her. She'll never come out if you threaten her.

ROY (*to* NORMA). I got sixty-eight guests, nine waiters, four musicians and a boy with a wedding license waiting downstairs. This is no time to be diplomatic. (*bangs on the door*) Mimsey! . . . Are you coming out or do we have the wedding in the bathroom?

NORMA. Will you lower your voice! Everyone will hear us.

ROY (*to* NORMA). How long you think we can keep this a secret? As soon as that boy says "I do" and there's no one standing next to him, they're going to suspect something. (*He bangs on the door.*) You can't stay in there forever, Mimsey. We only have the room until six o'clock . . . *You hear me?*

(*There is still no reply from the bathroom.*)

NORMA. Roy, will you please try to control yourself.

ROY. (*with great display of patience moves to the foot of the bed and sits*) All right, I'll stay here and control myself. You go downstairs and marry the short, skinny kid. (*exploding*) *What's the matter with you?* Don't you realize what's happening?

NORMA (*moving to him*). Yes. I realize what's happening. Our daughter is nervous, frightened and scared to death.

ROY. Of what? OF WHAT? She's been screaming for two years if he doesn't ask her to marry him, she'll throw herself off the Guggenheim Museum . . . What is she scared of?

NORMA. I don't know. Maybe she's had second thoughts about the whole thing.

ROY (*getting up and moving to the bathroom door*). Second thoughts? This is no time to be having *second thoughts.* It's costing me eight thousand dollars for the *first* thoughts. (*He bangs on the door.*) Mimsey, open this door.

NORMA. Is that all you care about? What it's costing you? Aren't you concerned about your daughter's happiness?

ROY (*moving back to her below the bed*). Yes! Yes, I'm concerned about my daughter's happiness. I'm also concerned about that boy waiting downstairs. A decent, respectable, intelligent young man . . . who I hope one day is going to teach that daughter of mine to grow up.

NORMA. You haven't the faintest idea of what's going through her mind right now.

ROY. Do you?

NORMA. It could be anything. I don't know, maybe she thinks she's not good enough for him.

ROY (*looks at her incredulously*). . . . Why? What is he? Some kind of Greek god? He's a plain kid, nothing . . . That's ridiculous. (*moves back to the door and bangs on it*) Mimsey! Mimsey, open this door. (*He turns to* NORMA.) Maybe she's not in there.

NORMA. She's in there. (*clutches her chest and sits on the side of the bed*) Oh, God, I think I'm having a heart attack.

ROY (*listening at the door*). I don't hear a peep out of her. Is there a window in there? Maybe she tried something crazy.

NORMA (*turning to him*). That's right. Tell a woman who's having a heart attack that her daughter jumped out the window.

ROY. Take a look through the keyhole. I want to make sure she's in there.

NORMA. She's in there, I tell you. Look at this, my hand keeps bouncing off my chest.

(*It does.*)

ROY. Are you gonna look in there and see if she's all right or am I gonna call the house detective?

NORMA (*getting up and moving below the bed*). Why don't *you* look?

ROY. Maybe she's taking a bath.

NORMA. Two minutes before her own

wedding?

ROY (*crossing to her*). What wedding? She just called it off.

NORMA. Wouldn't I have heard the water running?

ROY (*making a swipe at her hat*). With that hat you couldn't hear Niagara Falls! . . . Are you going to look to see what your daughter's doing in the bathroom or do I ask a stranger?

NORMA (*crossing to the door*). I'll look! I'll look! I'll look! (*Reluctantly she gets down on one knee and looks through the keyhole with one eye.*) Oh, my God!

ROY. What's the matter?

NORMA (*to him*). I ripped my stockings. (*getting up and examining her stockings.*)

ROY. Is she in there?

NORMA. She's in there! She's in there! (*hobbling to the far side of the bed and sitting down on the edge*) Where am I going to get another pair of stockings now? How am I going to go to the wedding with torn stockings?

ROY (*crossing to the bathroom*). If *she* doesn't show up, who's going to look at *you*? (*He kneels at the door and looks through the keyhole.*) There she is. Sitting there and crying.

NORMA. I *told* you she was in there . . . The only one in my family to have a daughter married in the Plaza and I have torn stockings.

ROY (*He is on his knees, his eye to the keyhole*). Mimsey, I can see you . . . Do you hear me? . . . Don't turn away from me when I'm talking to you.

NORMA. Maybe I could run across to Bergdorf's. They have nice stockings. (*crosses to her purse on the bureau in the bedroom and looks through it*)

ROY (*still through the keyhole*). Do you want me to break down the door, Mimsey, is that what you want? Because that's what I'm doing if you're not out of there in five seconds . . . Stop crying on your dress. Use the towel!

NORMA (*crossing to* ROY *at the door*). I don't have any money. Give me four dollars, I'll be back in ten minutes.

ROY (*gets up and moves below the bed*). In ten minutes she'll be a married woman, because I've had enough of this nonsense. (*yells in*) All right, Mimsey,

stand in the shower because I'm breaking down the door.

NORMA (*getting in front of the door*). Roy, don't get crazy.

ROY (*preparing himself for a run at the door*). Get out of my way.

NORMA. Roy, she'll come out. Just talk nicely to her.

ROY (*waving her away*). We already had nice talking. Now we're gonna have door breaking. (*Through the door*) All right, Mimsey, I'm coming in!

NORMA. No, Roy, don't! Don't!

(*She gets out of the way as* ROY *hurls his body, led by his shoulder, with full force against the door. It doesn't budge. He stays against the door silently a second; he doesn't react. Then he says calmly and softly*)

ROY. Get a doctor.

NORMA (*standing below the door*). I knew it. I knew it.

ROY (*drawing back from the door*). Don't tell me I knew it, just get a doctor. (*Through the door*) I'm not coming in, Mimsey, because my arm is broken.

NORMA. Let me see it. Can you move your fingers?

(*moves to him and examines his fingers*)

ROY (*through the door*). Are you happy now? Your mother has torn stockings and your father has a broken arm. How much longer is this gonna go on?

NORMA (*moving* ROY's *fingers*). It's not broken, you can move your fingers. Give me four dollars with your other hand, I have to get stockings.

(*She starts to go into his pockets. He slaps her hands away.*)

ROY. Are you crazy moving a broken arm?

NORMA. Two dollars, I'll get a cheap pair.

ROY (*as though she were a lunatic*). I'm not carrying any cash today. Rented, everything is rented.

NORMA. I can't rent stockings. Don't you even have a charge-plate?

(*starts to go through his pockets again*)

ROY (*slaps her hands away. Then pointing dramatically*). Wait in the Green Room! You're no use to me here, go wait in the Green Room!

NORMA. With torn stockings?

ROY. Stand behind the rented potted plant. (*takes her by the arm and leads her below the bed. Confidentially*) They're going to call from downstairs any second asking where the bride is. And *I'm* the one who's going to have to speak to them. *Me! Me! Me!* (*The phone rings. Pushing her toward the phone*) That's them. *You* speak to them!

NORMA. What happened to *me me me?* (*The phone rings again.*)

ROY (*moving to the bathroom door*). Answer it. Answer it.

(*The phone rings again.*)

NORMA (*moving to the phone*). What am I going to say to them?

ROY. I don't know. Maybe something'll come to you as you're talking.

NORMA (*moving to the phone*). What ... Oh, Mr. Eisler ... Yes, it certainly is the big moment.

(*She forces a merry laugh.*)

ROY. Stall 'em. Stall 'em. Just keep stalling him. Whatever you do, stall 'em!

(*turns to the door*)

NORMA (*on the phone*). Yes, we'll be down in two minutes.

(*hangs up*)

ROY (*turns back to her*). Are you crazy? What did you say that for? I told you to stall him.

NORMA. I stalled him. You got two minutes. What do you want from me?

ROY (*shakes his arm at her*). You always panic. The minute there's a little crisis, you always go to pieces and panic.

NORMA (*shaking her arm back at him*). Don't wave your broken arm at me. Why don't you use it to get your daughter out of the bathroom?

ROY (*very angry, kneeling to her on the bed*). I could say something to you now.

NORMA (*confronting him, kneels in turn on the bed*). Then why don't you say it?

ROY. Because it would lead to a fight. And I don't want to spoil this day for you. (*He gets up and crosses back to the bathroom door.*) Mimsey, this is your father speaking ... I think you know I'm not a violent man. I can be stern and strict, but I have never once been violent. Except when I'm angry. And I am really angry now, Mimsey. You can ask your mother.

(*moves away so NORMA can get to the door*)

NORMA (*crossing to the bathroom door*). Mimsey, this is your mother speaking. It's true, darling, your father is very angry.

ROY (*moving back to the door*). This is your father again, Mimsey. If you have a problem you want to discuss, unlock the door and we'll discuss it. I'm not going to ask you this again, Mimsey. I've reached the end of my patience. I'm gonna count to three ... and by God, I'm warning you, young lady, by the time I've reached three ... *this door better be open!* (*moving away to below the bed*) All right—One! ... Two! ... THREE! (*There is no reply or movement from behind the door. ROY helplessly sinks down on the foot of the bed.*) ... Where did we fail her?

NORMA (*crosses to the far side of the bed, consoling him as she goes, and sits on the edge*). We didn't fail her.

ROY. They're playing "Here Comes the Bride" downstairs and she's barricaded in a toilet—we must have failed her.

NORMA (*sighs*). All right, if it makes you any happier, we failed her.

ROY. You work and you dream and you hope and you save your whole life for this day, and in one click of a door, suddenly everything crumbles. Why? What's the answer?

NORMA. It's not your fault, Roy. Stop blaming yourself.

ROY. I'm not blaming myself. I know *I've* done my best.

NORMA (*turns and looks at him*). What does that mean?

ROY. It means we're not perfect. We make mistakes, we're only human. I've done my best and we failed her.

NORMA. Meaning *I* didn't do my best?

ROY (*turning to her*). I didn't say that. I don't know what your best is. Only *you* know what your best is. Did you do your best?

NORMA. Yes, I did my best.

ROY. And I did my best.

NORMA. Then we *both* did our best.

ROY. So it's not our fault.

NORMA. That's what I said before.

(*They turn away from each other. Then*)

ROY (*softly*). Unless one of us didn't do our best.

NORMA (*jumping up and moving away*). I don't want to discuss it any more.

ROY. All right, then what are we going

to do?

NORMA. I'm having a heart attack, *you* come up with something.

ROY. How? All right, I'll go down and tell them.

(*gets up and moves to the bedroom door*)

NORMA (*moving to the door in front of him*). Tell them? Tell them what?

(*As they move into the living room, she stops him above the sofa.*)

ROY. I don't know. Those people down there deserve some kind of an explanation. They got all dressed up, didn't they?

NORMA. What are you going to say? You're going to tell them that my daughter is not going to marry their son and that she's locked herself in the bathroom?

ROY. What do you want me to do, start off with two good jokes? They're going to find out *some* time, aren't they?

NORMA (*with great determination*). I'll tell you what you're going to do. If she's not out of there in five minutes, we're going to go out the back door and move to Seattle, Washington! . . . You don't think I'll be able to show my face in this city again, do you? (ROY *ponders this for a moment, then reassures her with a pat on the arm. Slowly he turns and moves into the bedroom. Suddenly, he loses control and lets his anger get the best of him. He grabs up the chair from the dresser, and brandishing it above his head, he dashes for the bathroom door, not even detouring around the bed but rather crossing right over it.* NORMA *screams and chases after him.*) ROY!

(*At the bathroom door,* ROY *manages to stop himself in time from smashing the chair against the door, trembling with frustration and anger. Finally, exhausted, he puts the chair down below the door and straddles it, sitting leaning on the back.* NORMA *sinks into the bedroom armchair.*)

ROY. . . . Would you believe it, last night I cried. Oh, yes. I turned my head into the pillow and lay there in the dark, crying, because today I was losing my little girl. Some stranger was coming and taking my little Mimsey away from me . . . so I turned my back to you—and cried . . . Wait'll you hear what goes on *tonight!*

NORMA (*lost in her own misery*). I should have invited your cousin Lillie. (*gestures to the heavens*) She wished this on me, I know it. (*Suddenly* ROY *begins to chuckle.* NORMA *looks at him. He chuckles louder, although there is clearly no joy in his laughter.*) Do you find something funny about this?

ROY. Yes, I find something funny about this. I find it funny that I hired a photographer for three hundred dollars. I find it hysterical that the wedding pictures are going to be you and me in front of a locked bathroom! (*gets up and puts the chair aside*) All right, I'm through sitting around waiting for that door to open.

(*He crosses to the bedroom window and tries to open it.*)

NORMA (*following after him*). What are you doing?

ROY. What do you think I'm doing?

(*Finding it impossible to open it, he crosses to the living room and opens a window there. The curtains begin to blow in the breeze.*)

NORMA (*crosses after him*). If you're jumping, I'm going with you. You're not leaving *me* here alone.

ROY (*looking out the window*). I'm gonna crawl out along that ledge and get in through the bathroom window.

(*He starts to climb out the window.*)

NORMA. Are you crazy? It's seven stories up. You'll kill yourself.

(*She grabs hold of him.*)

ROY. It's four steps, that's all. It's no problem, I'm telling you. Now will you let go of me.

NORMA (*struggling to keep him from getting out the window*). Roy, no! Don't do this. We'll leave her in the bathroom. Let the hotel worry about her. Don't go out on the ledge.

(*In desperation, she grabs hold of one of the tails of his coat.*)

ROY (*half out the window, trying to get out as she holds onto his coat*). You're gonna rip my coat. Let go or you're gonna rip my coat. (*As he tries to pull away from her, his coat rips completely up the back, right up to the collar. He stops and slowly comes back into the room.* NORMA *has frozen in misery by the bedroom door after letting go of the coat.* ROY *draws himself up with great dignity and control. He slowly turns and moves into the bed-*

room, stopping by the bed. With great patience, he calls toward the bathroom.) Hey, you in there . . . Are you happy now? Your mother's got torn stockings and your father's got a rented ripped coat. Some wedding it's gonna be. (*Exploding, he crosses back to the open window in the living room.*) Get out of my way!

NORMA (*puts hand to her head*). I'm getting dizzy. I think I'm going to pass out.

ROY (*getting her out of the way*). . . . You can pass out *after* the wedding . . . (*He goes out the window and onto the ledge.*) Call room service. I want a double Scotch the minute I get back.

(*And he disappears from view as he moves across the ledge.* NORMA *runs into the bedroom and catches a glimpse of him as he passes the bedroom window, but then he disappears once more.*)

NORMA (*bemoaning her fate*). . . . He'll kill himself. He'll fall and kill himself, that's the way my luck's been going all day. (*She staggers away from the window and leans on the bureau.*) I'm not going to look. I'll just wait until I hear a scream. (*The telephone rings and* NORMA *screams in fright.*) Aggghhh! . . . I thought it was him . . . (*She crosses to the phone by the bed. The telephone rings again.*) Oh, God, what am I going to say? (*She picks it up.*) Hello? . . . Oh, Mr. Eisler. Yes, we're coming . . . My husband's getting Mimsey now . . . We'll be right down. Have some more hors d'oeuvres . . . Oh, thank you. It certainly *is* the happiest day of my life. (*She hangs up.*) No, I'm going to tell him I've got a husband dangling over Fifty-ninth Street. (*As she crosses back to the opened window, a sudden torrent of rain begins to fall. As she gets to the window and sees it.*) I knew it! I knew it! It had to happen . . . (*She gets closer to the window and tries to look out.*) Are you all right, Roy? . . . Roy? (*There's no answer.*) He's not all right, he fell. (*She staggers into the bedroom.*) He fell, he fell, he fell, he fell . . . He's dead, I know it. (*She collapses onto the armchair.*) He's laying there in a puddle in front of Trader Vic's . . . I'm passing out. This time I'm really passing out! (*And she passes out on the chair, legs and arms spread-eagled. The doorbell rings; she*

jumps right up.) I'm coming! I'm coming! Help me, whoever you are, help me! (*She rushes through the bedroom into the living room and to the front door.*) Oh, please, somebody, help me, please!

(*She opens the front door and* ROY *stands there dripping wet, fuming, exhausted and with clothes disheveled and his hair mussed.*)

ROY (*staggering into the room and weakly leaning on the mantelpiece. It takes a moment for him to catch his breath.* NORMA, *concerned, follows him*). She locked the window, too. I had to climb in through a strange bedroom. There may be a lawsuit.

(*He weakly charges back into the bedroom, followed by* NORMA, *who grabs his coattails in an effort to stop him. The rain outside stops.*)

NORMA (*stopping him below the bed*). Don't yell at her. Don't get her more upset.

ROY (*turning back to her*). Don't get her *upset?* I'm hanging seven stories from a gargoyle in a pouring rain and you want me to worry about *her?* . . . You know what she's doing in there? She's playing with her false eyelashes. (*moves to bathroom door*) I'm out there fighting for my life with pigeons and she's playing with eyelashes . . . (*crossing back to* NORMA) . . . I already made up my mind. The minute I get my hands on her, I'm gonna kill her. (*moves back to the door*) Once I show them the wedding bills, no jury on earth would convict me . . . And if by some miracle she survives, let there be no talk of weddings . . . She can go into a convent. (*slowly moving back to* NORMA *below the bed*) . . . Let her become a librarian with thick glasses and a pencil in her hair, I'm not paying for any more canceled weddings . . . (*Working himself up into a frenzy, he rushes to the table by the armchair and grabs up some newspapers.*) Now get her out of there or I start to burn these newspapers and smoke her out.

(NORMA *stops him, soothes him, and manages to get him calmed down. She gently seats him on the foot of the bed.*)

NORMA (*really frightened*). I'll get her out! I'll get her out! (*She crosses to the door and knocks*) Mimsey! Mimsey, please! (*She knocks harder and harder*) Mimsey, you want to destroy a family? You want a scandal? You want a story in the *Daily News?* . . . Is that what you want? Is it? . . . Open this door! *Open it!* (*She bangs very hard, then stops and turns to* ROY.) . . . Promise you won't get hysterical.

ROY. What did you do?

(*Turns wearily to her*)

NORMA. I broke my diamond ring.

ROY (*letting the papers fall from his hand*). Your good diamond ring?

NORMA. How many do I have?

ROY (*yells through the door*). Hey, you with the false eyelashes! (*getting up and moving to the door*) . . . You want to see a broken diamond ring? You want to see eighteen hundred dollars' worth of crushed baguettes? . . . (*He grabs* NORMA's *hand and holds it to the keyhole.*) Here! Here! *This* is a worthless family heirloom— (*kicks the door*)—and *this* is a diamond bathroom door! (*controlling himself. To* NORMA) Do you know what I'm going to do now? Do you have any idea? (NORMA *puts her hand to her mouth, afraid to hear.* ROY *moves away from the door to the far side of the bed.*) I'm going to wash my hands of the entire Eisler-Hubley wedding. You can take all the Eislers and all the hors d'oeuvres and go to Central Park and have an eight-thousand-dollar picnic . . . (*stops and turns back to* NORMA) I'm going down to the Oak Room with my broken arm, with my drenched rented ripped suit —and I'm gonna get blind! . . . I don't mean drunk, I mean totally blind . . . (*erupting with great vehemence*) because I don't want to see you or your crazy daughter again, if I live to be a thousand. (*He turns and rushes from the bedroom, through the living room to the front door. As he tries to open it,* NORMA *catches up to him, grabs his tail coat and pulls him back into the room.*)

NORMA. That's right. Run out on me. Run out on your daughter. Run out on everybody just when they need you.

ROY. You don't need me. You need a rhinoceros with a blowtorch—because no one else can get into that bathroom.

NORMA (*with rising emotion*). I'll tell you who can get into that bathroom. Someone with love and understanding. Someone who cares about that poor kid who's going through some terrible decision now and needs help. Help that only *you* can give her and that *I* can give her. *That's* who can get into that bathroom now.

(ROY *looks at her solemnly . . . Then he crosses past her, hesitates and looks back at her, and then goes into the bedroom and to the bathroom door.* NORMA *follows him back in. He turns and looks at* NORMA *again. Then he knocks gently on the door and speaks softly and with some tenderness.*)

ROY. Mimsey! . . . This is Daddy . . . Is something wrong, dear? . . . (*He looks back at* NORMA, *who nods encouragement, happy about his new turn in character. Then he turns back to the door.*) . . . I want to help you, darling. Mother and I both do. But how can we help you if you won't talk to us? Mimsey, can you hear me?

(*There is no answer. He looks back at* NORMA.)

NORMA (*at the far side of the bed*). Maybe she's too choked up to talk.

ROY (*through the door*). Mimsey, if you can hear me, knock twice for yes, once for no. (*There are two knocks on the door. They look at each other encouragingly.*) Good. Good . . . Now, Mimsey, we want to ask you a very, very important question. Do you want to marry Borden or don't you?

(*They wait anxiously for the answer. We hear one knock, a pause, then another knock.*)

NORMA (*happily*). She said yes.

ROY (*despondently*). She said no.

(*moves away from the door to the foot of the bed*)

NORMA. It was two knocks. Two knocks is "yes." She wants to marry him.

ROY. It wasn't a double knock "yes." It was two single "no" knocks. She doesn't want to marry him.

NORMA. Don't tell me she doesn't want to marry him. I heard her distinctly knock "yes." She went (*knocks twice on the foot of the bed*) "Yes, I want to marry him."

ROY. It wasn't (*knocks twice on the foot of the bed*) . . . It was (*knocks once on the foot of the bed*) . . . and then another (*knocks once more on the foot of the bed*) . . . That's "no," twice, she's not marrying him.

(*sinks down on the side of the bed*)

NORMA (*crossing to the door*). Ask her again. (*Into the door*) Mimsey, what did you say? Yes or no? (*They listen. We hear two distinct loud knocks.* NORMA *turns to* ROY) . . . All right? There it is in plain English . . . You never *could* talk to your own daughter.

(*moves away from the door*)

ROY (*getting up wearily and moving to the door*). Mimsey, this is not a good way to have a conversation. You're gonna hurt your knuckles . . . Won't you come out and talk to us? . . . Mimsey?

NORMA (*leads* ROY *gently to the foot of the bed*). Don't you understand, it's probably something she can't discuss with her father. There are times a daughter wants to be alone with her mother. (*sits* ROY *down on the foot of the bed, and crosses back to the door*) Mimsey, do you want me to come in there and talk to you, just the two of us, sweetheart? Tell me, darling, is that what you want? (*There is no reply. A strip of toilet paper appears from under the bathroom door.* ROY *notices it, pushes* NORMA *aside, bends down, picks it up and reads it.*) What? What does it say? (ROY *solemnly hands it to her.* NORMA *reads it aloud.*) "I would rather talk to Daddy."

(NORMA *is crushed. He looks at her sympathetically. We hear the bathroom door unlock.* ROY *doesn't quite know what to say to* NORMA. *He gives her a quick hug.*)

ROY. I—I'll try not to be too long.

(*He opens the door and goes in, closing it behind him, quietly.* NORMA, *still with the strip of paper in her hand, walks slowly and sadly to the foot of the bed and sits. She looks glumly down at the paper.*)

NORMA (*aloud*). . . . "I would rather talk to Daddy" . . . Did she have to write it on this kind of paper? (*She wads up the paper.*) . . . Well—maybe I didn't do my best . . . I thought we had such a good relationship . . . Friends. Everyone thought we were friends, not mother and daughter . . . I tried to do everything right . . . I tried to teach her that there could be more than just love between a mother and daughter . . . There can be trust and respect and friendship and understanding . . . (*Getting angry, she turns and yells toward the closed door.*) Just because *I* don't speak to my mother doesn't mean *we* can't be different!

(*She wipes her eyes with the paper. The bathroom door opens. A solemn* ROY *steps out, and the door closes and locks behind him. He deliberately buttons his coat and crosses to the bedroom phone, wordlessly.* NORMA *has not taken her eyes off him. The pause seems interminable.*)

ROY (*into the phone*). The Green Room, please . . . Mr. Borden Eisler. Thank you. (*He waits.*)

NORMA (*getting up from the bed*). . . . I'm gonna have to guess, is that it? . . . It's so bad you can't even tell me . . . Words can't form in your mouth, it's so horrible, right? . . . Come on, I'm a strong person, Roy. Tell me quickly, I'll get over it. . . .

ROY (*into the phone*). Borden? Mr. Hubley . . . Can you come up to 719? . . . Yes, now . . . (*He hangs up and gestures for* NORMA *to follow him. He crosses into the living room and down to the ottoman, where he sits.* NORMA *follows and stands waiting behind him. Finally*) She wanted to talk to me because she couldn't bear to say it to both of us at the same time . . . The reason she's locked herself in the bathroom . . . is she's afraid.

NORMA. Afraid? What is she afraid of? That Borden doesn't love her?

ROY. Not that Borden doesn't love her.

NORMA. That she doesn't love Borden?

ROY. Not that she doesn't love Borden.

NORMA. Then what is she afraid of?

ROY. . . . She's afraid of what they're going to become.

NORMA. I don't understand.

ROY. Think about it.

NORMA (*crossing above the sofa*). What's there to think about? What are they going to become? They love each other, they'll get married, they'll have children, they'll grow older, they'll become like us—(*Comes the dawn. Stops by the side of the sofa and turns back to* ROY.)—I never thought about that.

ROY. Makes you stop and think, doesn't it?

NORMA. I don't think we're so bad, do

you . . . All right, so we yell and scream a little. So we fight and curse and aggravate each other. So you blame me for being a lousy mother and I accuse you of being a rotten husband. It doesn't mean we're not happy . . . does it? . . . (*her voice rising*) Well? . . . Does it? . . .

ROY (*looks at her*). . . . She wants something better. (*The doorbell rings. He crosses to open the door.* NORMA *follows.*) Hello, Borden.

BORDEN (*stepping into the room*). Hi.

NORMA. Hello, darling.

ROY (*gravely*). Borden, you're an intelligent young man, I'm not going to beat around the bush. We have a serious problem on our hands.

BORDEN. How so?

ROY. Mimsey—is worried. Worried about your future together. About the whole institution of marriage. We've tried to allay her fears, but obviously we haven't been a very good example. It seems you're the only one who can communicate with her. She's locked herself in the bathroom and is not coming out . . . It's up to you now.

(*Without a word,* BORDEN *crosses below the sofa and up to the bedroom, through the bedroom below the bed and right up to the bathroom door. He knocks.*)

BORDEN. Mimsey? . . . This is Borden . . . Cool it! (*Then he turns and crosses back to the living room. Crossing above the sofa, he passes the* HUBLEYS, *and without looking at them, says*) See you downstairs!

(*He exits without showing any more emotion. The* HUBLEYS *stare after him as he closes the door. But then the bathroom door opens and* NORMA *and* ROY *slowly turn to it as* MIMSEY, *a beautiful bride, in a formal wedding gown, with veil, comes out.*)

MIMSEY. I'm ready now!

(NORMA *turns and moves into the bedroom toward her.* ROY *follows slowly, shaking his head in amazement.*)

ROY. *Now* you're ready? *Now* you come out?

NORMA (*admiring* MIMSEY). Roy, please . . .

ROY (*getting angry, leans toward her over the bed*). I break every bone in my body and you come out for "Cool it"?

NORMA (*pushing* MIMSEY *toward* ROY). You're beautiful, darling. Walk with your father, I want to look at both of you.

ROY (*fuming. As she takes his arm, to* NORMA). That's how he communicates? That's the brilliant understanding between two people? "Cool it"?

NORMA (*gathering up* MIMSEY's *train as they move toward the living room*). Roy, don't start in.

ROY. What kind of a person is that to let your daughter marry?

(*They stop above the sofa.* MIMSEY *takes her bridal bouquet from the table behind the sofa, while* NORMA *puts on her wrap and takes her gloves from the back of the sofa.*)

NORMA. Roy, don't aggravate me. I'm warning you, don't spoil this day for me.

ROY. Kids today don't care. Not like they did in my day.

NORMA. Walk. Will you walk? In five minutes he'll marry one of the flower girls. Will you walk—

(MIMSEY *takes* ROY *by the arm and they move to the door, as* NORMA *follows.*)

ROY (*turning back to* NORMA). Crazy. I must be out of my mind, a boy like that. (*opens the door*) She was better off in the bathroom. You hear me? Better off in the bathroom . . . (*They are out the door . . .*)

CURTAIN

DAY OF ABSENCE

(A Satirical Fantasy)

Douglas Turner Ward

CLEM	INDUSTRIALIST
LUKE	BUSINESSMAN
JOHN	CLUBWOMAN
MARY	COURIER
FIRST OPERATOR	ANNOUNCER
SECOND OPERATOR	CLAN
THIRD OPERATOR	AIDE
SUPERVISOR	PIOUS
MAYOR	DOLL WOMAN
JACKSON	MOP MAN
FIRST CITIZEN	BRUSH MAN
SECOND CITIZEN	RASTUS
THIRD CITIZEN	

A MAN of multiple theatrical talents, Douglas Turner Ward was born on a plantation in Burnside, Louisiana, on May 5, 1930. He was educated at Wilberforce University and the University of Michigan. After a spell as a journalist, he turned to acting and first appeared on the New York stage in 1957 in the Circle-in-the-Square revival of Eugene O'Neill's *The Iceman Cometh.* Subsequently, he performed in a succession of plays including: *A Raisin in the Sun; The Blacks; One Flew Over the Cuckoo's Nest; The Blood Knot;* and *Coriolanus.*

As a dramatist, he made his professional debut at the Off-Broadway St. Marks Playhouse on November 15, 1965, with two short plays, *Happy Ending* and *Day of Absence.* The latter was conceived for performance by a Negro cast, "a reverse minstrel show done in whiteface" that takes place now, in an "unnamed southern town of medium population on a somnolent cracker morning—meaning no matter the early temperature, it's gonna get hot" and "the hamlet is just beginning to rouse itself from the sleepy lassitude of night." In the words of Loften Mitchell in his excellent book *Black Drama:* "In *Day of Absence,* Mr. Ward has Negroes of a southern city tire of white folks' treatment of them. They all vanish. The white town is left without vital services. Pandemonium breaks loose. And many a comment is made here. The play, performed by black actors in whiteface, brings a new dimension to the theatre" and "the question the author raises is: When will both groups learn the truth of their interrelationship and interdependence?"

The double bill ran for 504 performances and won for Mr. Ward both a Drama Desk–Vernon Rice Award and an "Obie" Award for outstanding Off-Broadway achievement. In March, 1970, *Day of Absence* was presented once again at the St. Marks Playhouse, this time with a new companion piece, *Brotherhood,* also written by Mr. Ward. The production was presented by the Negro Ensemble Company which was cofounded by Robert Hooks, Gerald S. Krone, and Mr. Ward, who continues to serve as its Artistic Director. The Negro Ensemble Company is one of the cornerstones of the flourishing black theatre movement and it stresses "relevant plays and players for tomorrow's black culture welfare." Since its first production in January 1968, the organization has emerged as a vital force in contemporary American theatre and has toured extensively both in the United States and in Europe.

In 1969, Douglas Turner Ward appeared in a prominent role in *Ceremonies in Dark Old Men* by Lonne Elder III, and in 1972 he directed the highly acclaimed production of Joseph A. Walker's *The River Niger.*

SCENE: Street.
TIME: Early morning.

CLEM (*sitting under a sign suspended by invisible wires and bold-printed with the lettering: "STORE"*). 'Morning, Luke . . .

LUKE (*sitting a few paces away under an identical sign*). 'Morning, Clem . . .

CLEM. Go'n' be a hot day.

LUKE. Looks that way . . .

CLEM. Might rain though . . .

LUKE. Might.

CLEM. Hope it does . . .

LUKE. Me, too . . .

CLEM. Farmers could use a little wet spell for a change . . . How's the Missis?

LUKE. Same.

CLEM. 'N' the kids?

LUKE. Them, too . . . How's yourns?

CLEM. Fine, thank you . . . (*They both lapse into drowsy silence, waving lethargically from time to time at imaginary passersby.*) Hi, Joe . . .

LUKE. Joe . . .

CLEM. . . . How'd it go yesterday, Luke?

LUKE. Fair.

CLEM. Same wit' me . . . Business don't seem to git no better or no worse. Guess we in a rut, Luke, don't it 'pear that way to you?—Morning, ma'am.

LUKE. Morning . . .

CLEM. Tried display, sales, advertisement, stamps—everything, yet merchandising stumbles 'round in the same old groove . . . But—that's better than plunging downwards, I reckon.

LUKE. Guess it is.

CLEM. Morning, Bret. How's the family? . . . That's good.

LUKE. Bret—

CLEM. Morning, Sue.

LUKE. How do, Sue.

CLEM (*staring after her*) . . . Fine hunk of woman.

LUKE. Sure is.

CLEM. Wonder if it's any good?

LUKE. Bet it is.

CLEM. Sure like to find out!

LUKE. So would I.

CLEM. You ever try?

LUKE. Never did . . .

CLEM. Morning, Gus . . .

LUKE. Howdy, Gus.

CLEM. Fine, thank you. (*They lapse into silence again.* CLEM *rouses himself slowly, begins to look around quizzically.*) Luke . . . ?

LUKE. Huh?

CLEM. Do you . . . er, er—feel anything —funny . . .?

LUKE. Like what?

CLEM. Like . . . er—something—strange?

LUKE. I dunno . . . haven't thought about it.

CLEM. I mean . . . like something's wrong—outta place, unusual?

LUKE. I don't know . . . What you got in mind?

CLEM. Nothing . . . just that—just that —like somp'ums outta kilter. I got a funny feeling somp'ums not up to snuff. Can't figger out what it is . . .

LUKE. Maybe it's in your haid?

CLEM. No, not like that . . . Like somp'ums happened—or happening—gone haywire, loony.

LUKE. Well, don't worry 'bout it, it'll pass.

CLEM. Guess you right. (*Attempts return to somnolence but doesn't succeed*) . . . I'm sorry, Luke, but you sure you don't feel nothing peculiar . . . ?

LUKE (*slightly irked*). Toss it out of your mind, Clem! We got a long day ahead of us. If something's wrong, you'll know 'bout it in due time. No use worrying about it 'til it comes and if it's coming, it will. Now, relax!

CLEM. All right, you right . . . Hi, Margie . . .

LUKE. Marge.

CLEM (*unable to control himself*). Luke, I don't give a damn what you say. Somp'ums topsy-turvy, I just know it!

LUKE (*increasingly irritated*). Now look here, Clem—it's a bright day, it looks like it's go'n' git hotter. You say the wife and kids are fine and the business is no better or no worse? Well, what else could be wrong? . . . If somp'ums go'n' happen, it's go'n' happen anyway and there ain't a damn fool thing you kin do to stop it! So you ain't helping me, yourself, or nobody else by thinking 'bout it. It's not go'n' be no better or no worse when it gits here. It'll come to you when it gits ready to come and it's go'n' be the same whether you worry about it or not. So stop letting it upset you! (LUKE *settles back in his chair.* CLEM *does likewise.* LUKE *shuts his eyes. After a few moments, they reopen. He forces them shut again. They reopen in greater curiosity. Finally, he rises slowly to an upright position in the chair, looks around frowningly. Turns slowly to* CLEM) . . . Clem? . . . You know something? . . . Somp'um is peculiar . . .

CLEM (*vindicated*). I knew it, Luke! I just knew it! Ever since we been sitting here, I been having that feeling!

(*Scene is blacked out abruptly. Lights rise on another section of the stage where a young couple lie in bed under an in-visible-wire-suspension-sign lettered: "HOME." Loud insistent sounds of baby yells are heard.* JOHN, *the husband, turns over trying to ignore the cries,* MARY, *the wife, is undisturbed.* JOHN's *efforts are futile, the cries continue until they cannot be denied. He bolts upright, jumps out of bed, and disappears off-stage. Returns quickly and tries to rouse* MARY)

JOHN. Mary . . . (*nudges her, pushes her, yells into her ear, but she fails to respond*). Mary, get up . . . Get up!

MARY. Ummm . . . (*shrugs away, still sleeping*)

JOHN. GET UP!

MARY. UMMMMMMMMM!

JOHN. Don't you hear the baby bawling! . . . NOW GET UP!

MARY (*mumbling drowsily*) . . . What baby . . . whose baby . . . ?

JOHN. Yours!

MARY. Mine? That's ridiculous . . . What'd you say . . . ? Somebody's baby bawling? . . . How could that be so? (*hearing screams*) Who's crying? Somebody's crying! . . . What's crying? . . . WHERE'S LULA?!

JOHN. I don't know. You better get up.

MARY. That's outrageous! . . . What time is it?

JOHN. Late 'nuff! Now rise up!

MARY. You must be joking . . . I'm sure I still have four or five hours sleep in store —even more after that head-splittin' blow-out last night . . . (*tumbles back under covers*)

JOHN. Nobody told you to gulp those last six bourbons—

MARY. Don't tell me how many bour-bons to swallow, not after you guzzled the whole stinking bar! . . . Get up? . . . You must be cracked . . . Where's Lula? She must be here, she always is . . .

JOHN. Well, she ain't here yet, so get up and muzzle that brat before she does drive me cuckoo!

MARY (*springing upright, finally realizing gravity of situation*). Whaddaya mean Lula's not here? She's always here, she must be here . . . Where else kin she be? She supposed to be . . . She just can't *not* be here—CALL HER!

(*blackout as* JOHN *rushes offstage. Scene shifts to a trio of* TELEPHONE OPERATORS *perched on stools before imaginary switchboards. Chaos and bedlam are taking place to the sound of buzzes. Effect of following dialogue should simulate rising pandemonium.*)

FIRST OPERATOR. The line is busy—

SECOND OPERATOR. Line is busy—

THIRD OPERATOR. Is busy—

FIRST OPERATOR. Doing best we can—

SECOND OPERATOR. Having difficulty.

THIRD OPERATOR. Soon as possible—

FIRST OPERATOR. Just one moment—

SECOND OPERATOR. Would you hold on—

THIRD OPERATOR. Awful sorry, madam—

FIRST OPERATOR. Would you hold on, please—

SECOND OPERATOR. Just a second, please—

THIRD OPERATOR. Please hold on, please—

FIRST OPERATOR. The line is busy—

SECOND OPERATOR. The line is busy—

THIRD OPERATOR. The line is busy—

FIRST OPERATOR. Doing best we can—

SECOND OPERATOR. Hold on please—

THIRD OPERATOR. Can't make connec-tions—

FIRST OPERATOR. Unable to put it in—

SECOND OPERATOR. Won't plug through—

THIRD OPERATOR. Sorry, madam—

FIRST OPERATOR. If you'd wait a mo-ment—

SECOND OPERATOR. Doing best we can—

THIRD OPERATOR. Sorry—

FIRST OPERATOR. One moment—

SECOND OPERATOR. Just a second—

THIRD OPERATOR. Hold on—

FIRST OPERATOR. YES—

SECOND OPERATOR. STOP IT!—

THIRD OPERATOR. HOW DO I KNOW—

FIRST OPERATOR. YOU ANOTHER ONE!

SECOND OPERATOR. HOLD ON, DAM-

MIT!

THIRD OPERATOR. UP YOURS, TOO!

FIRST OPERATOR. THE LINE IS BUSY—

SECOND OPERATOR. THE LINE IS BUSY—

THIRD OPERATOR. THE LINE IS BUSY— (*The switchboard clamors a cacophony of buzzes as* OPERATORS *plug connections with the frenzy of a Chaplin movie. Their replies degenerate into a babble of gibberish. At the height of the frenzy, the* SUPERVISOR *appears.*)

SUPERVISOR. WHAT'S THE SNARL-UP???!!!

FIRST OPERATOR. Everybody calling at the same time, ma'am!

SECOND OPERATOR. Board can't handle it!

THIRD OPERATOR. Like everybody in big New York City is trying to squeeze a call through to li'l' ole us!

SUPERVISOR. God! . . . Somp'um terrible musta happened! . . . Buzz the emergency frequency hookup to the Mayor's office and find out what the hell's going on! (*Scene blacks out quickly to* CLEM *and* LUKE.)

CLEM (*something slowly dawning on him*). Luke . . . ?

LUKE. Yes, Clem?

CLEM (*eyes roving around in puzzlement*). Luke . . . ?

LUKE (*irked*). I said what, Clem!

CLEM. Luke . . . ? Where—where is— the—the?

LUKE. THE WHAT?!

CLEM. Nigras . . . ?

LUKE. ?????What . . . ?

CLEM. Nigras . . . Where is the Nigras, where is they, Luke . . . ? ALL THE NIGRAS! . . . I don't see no Nigras . . .?!

LUKE. Whatcha mean . . . ?

CLEM (*agitatedly*). Luke, there ain't a darky in sight . . . And if you remember, we ain't spied a nappy hair all morning. . . . The Nigras, Luke! We ain't laid eyes on nary a coon this whole morning!!!

LUKE. You must be crazy or something, Clem!

CLEM. Think about it, Luke, we been sitting here for an hour or more—try and recollect if you remember seeing jist *one* go by?!!!

LUKE (*confused*). . . . I don't recall . . . . . . But . . . but there musta been some . . . The heat musta got you, Clem! How

in hell could that be so?!!!

CLEM (*triumphantly*). Just think, Luke! . . . Look around ya. . . . Now, every morning mosta people walkin' 'long this street is colored. They's strolling by going to work, they's waiting for the buses, they's sweeping sidewalks, cleaning stores, starting to shine shoes and wetting the mops —right?! . . . Well, look around you, Luke—where is they? (LUKE *paces up and down, checking.*) I told you, Luke, they ain't nowheres to be seen.

LUKE. ???? . . . This . . . this . . . some kind of holiday for 'em—or something?

CLEM. I don't know, Luke . . . but . . . but what I do know is they ain't here 'n' we haven't seen a solitary one . . . It's scaryfying, Luke . . . !

LUKE. Well . . . maybe they's jist standing 'n' walking and shining on other streets. —Let's go look! (*Scene blacks out to* JOHN *and* MARY. *Baby cries are as insistent as ever.*)

MARY (*at the end of her patience*). SMOTHER IT!

JOHN (*beyond his*). That's a hell of a thing to say 'bout your own child! You should know what to do to hush her up!

MARY. Why don't you try?!

JOHN. You had her!

MARY. You shared in borning her?!

JOHN. Possibly not!

MARY. Why, you lousy—!

JOHN. What good is a mother who can't shut up her own daughter?!

MARY. I told you she yells louder every time I try to lay hands on her.—Where's Lula? Didn't you call her?!

JOHN. I told you I can't get the call through!

MARY. Try ag'in—

JOHN. It's no use! I tried numerous times and can't even git through to the switchboard. You've got to quiet her down yourself. (*firmly*) Now, go in there and clam her up 'fore I lose my patience! (MARY *exits. Soon, we hear the yells increase. She rushes back in.*)

MARY. She won't let me touch her, just screams louder!

JOHN. Probably wet 'n' soppy!

MARY. Yes! Stinks something awful! Phooooey! I can't stand that filth and odor!

JOHN. That's why she's screaming! Needs her didee changed.—Go change it!

MARY. How do you 'spect me to when I don't know how?! Suppose I faint?!

JOHN. Well, let her blast away. I'm getting out of here.

MARY. You can't leave me here like this!

JOHN. Just watch me! . . . See this nice split-level cottage, peachy furniture, multi-colored teevee, hi-fi set 'n' the rest? . . . Well, how you think I scraped 'em together while you curled up on your fat li'l' fanny? . . . By gitting outta here—not only *on time* . . . but EARLIER!—Beating a frantic crew of nice young executives to the punch—gitting there fustest with the mostest brown-nosing you ever saw! Now if I goof one day—just ONE DAY!—You reckon I'd stay ahead? NO! . . . There'd be a wolf pack trampling over my prostrate body, racing to replace my smiling face against the boss' left rump! . . . NO, MA'M! I'm zooming outta here on time, just as I always have and what's more—you go'n' fix me some breakfast, I'M HUNGRY!

MARY. But—

JOHN. No buts about it! (*flash blackout as he gags on a mouthful of coffee*) What you trying to do, STRANGLE ME!!!

(*jumps up and starts putting on jacket*)

MARY (*sarcastically*). What did you expect?

JOHN (*in biting fury*). That you could possibly boil a pot of water, toast a few slices of bread and fry a coupler eggs! . . . It was a mistaken assumption!

MARY. So they aren't as good as Lula's!

JOHN. That is an overstatement. Your efforts don't result in anything that could possibly be digested by man, mammal, or insect! . . . When I married you, I thought I was fairly acquainted with your faults and weaknesses—I chalked 'em up to human imperfection . . . But now I know I was being extremely generous, overoptimistic and phenomenally deluded!—You have no idea how useless you really are!

MARY. Then why'd you marry me?!

JOHN. Decoration!

MARY. You shoulda married Lula!

JOHN. I might've if it wasn't 'gainst the segregation law! . . . But for the sake of my home, my child, and my sanity, I will even take a chance on sacrificing my slippery grip on the status pole and drive by her shanty to find out whether she or some-

one like her kin come over here and prevent some ultimate disaster. (*storms toward door, stopping abruptly at exit*) Are you sure you kin make it to the bathroom wit'out Lula backing you up?!!!

(*blackout. Scene shifts to* MAYOR's *office where a cluttered desk stands center amid papered debris.*)

MAYOR (*striding determinedly toward desk, stopping midways, bellowing*). WOODFENCE! . . . WOODFENCE! . . . WOODFENCE! (*receiving no reply, completes distance to desk*) JACKSON! . . . JACKSON!

JACKSON (*entering worriedly*). Yes, sir . . . ?

MAYOR. Where's Vice-Mayor Woodfence, that no-good brother-in-law of mine?!

JACKSON. Hasn't come in yet, sir.

MAYOR. HASN'T COME IN?!!! . . . Damn bastard! Knows we have a crucial conference. Soon as he staggers through that door, tell him to shoot in here! (*angrily focusing on his disorderly desk and littered surroundings*) And git Mandy here to straighten up this mess—Rufus too! You know he shoulda been waiting to knock dust off my shoes soon as I step in. Get 'em in here! . . . What's the matter wit' them lazy Nigras? . . . Already had to dress myself because of JC, fix my own coffee without Maybelle, drive myself to work 'counta Bubber, feel my old Hag's tits after Sapphi—NEVER MIND!—Git 'em in here—QUICK!

JACKSON (*meekly*). They aren't . . . they aren't here, sir . . .

MAYOR. Whaddaya mean they aren't here? Find out where they at. We got important business, man! You can't run a town wit' laxity like this. Can't allow things to git snafued jist because a bunch of lazy Nigras been out gitting drunk and living it up all night! Discipline, man, discipline!

JACKSON. That's what I'm trying to tell you, sir . . . they didn't come in, can't be found . . . none of 'em.

MAYOR. Ridiculous, boy! Scare 'em up and tell 'em scoot here in a hurry befo' I git mad and fire the whole goddamn lot of 'em!

JACKSON. But we can't find 'em, sir.

MAYOR. Hogwash! Can't nobody in this office do anything right?! Do I hafta

handle every piddling little matter myself?!
Git me their numbers, I'll have 'em here
befo' you kin shout to—

(*Three men burst into room in various
states of undress.*)

ONE. Henry—they vanished!

TWO. Disappeared into thin air!

THREE. Gone wit'out a trace!

TWO. Not a one on the street!

THREE. In the house!

ONE. On the job!

MAYOR. Wait a minute!! . . . Hold your
water! Calm down—!

ONE. But they've gone, Henry—GONE!
All of 'em!

MAYOR. What the hell you talking 'bout?
Gone? Who's gone—?

ONE. The Nigras, Henry! They gone!

MAYOR. Gone? . . . Gone where?

TWO. That's what we trying to tell ya—
they just disappeared! The Nigras have
disappeared, swallowed up, vanished! All
of 'em! Every last one!

MAYOR. Has everybody 'round here
gone batty? . . . That's impossible, how
could the Nigras vanish?

THREE. Beats me, but it's happened!

MAYOR. You mean a whole town of Nigras just evaporate like this—poof!—Overnight?

ONE. Right!

MAYOR. Y'all must be drunk! Why, half
this town is colored. How could they just
sneak out!

TWO. Don't ask me, but there ain't one
in sight!

MAYOR. Simmer down 'n' put it to me
easy-like.

ONE. Well . . . I first suspected somp'um
smelly when Sarah Jo didn't show up this
morning and I couldn't reach her—

TWO. Dorothy Jane didn't 'rive at my
house—

THREE. Georgia Mae wasn't at mine
neither—and SHE sleeps in!

ONE. When I reached the office, I realized I hadn't seen nary one Nigra all
morning! Nobody else had either—wait a
minute—Henry, have you?!

MAYOR. ???Now that you mention it . . .
no, I haven't . . .

ONE. They gone, Henry . . . Not a one
on the street, not a one in our homes, not
a single, last living one to be found nowheres in town. What we gon' do?!

MAYOR (*thinking*). Keep heads on your
shoulders 'n' put clothes on your back . . .
They can't be far . . . Must be 'round
somewheres . . . Probably playing hide
'n' seek, that's it! . . . JACKSON!

JACKSON. Yessir?

MAYOR. Immediately mobilize our Citizens Emergency Distress Committee!—
Order a fleet of sound trucks to patrol
streets urging the population to remain
calm—situation's not as bad as it looks—
everything's under control! Then, have another squadron of squawk buggies drive
slowly through all Nigra alleys, ordering
them to come out wherever they are. If
that don't git 'em, organize a vigilante
search squad to flush 'em outta hiding!
But most important of all, track down
that lazy goldbricker, Woodfence, and tell
him to git on top of the situation! By God,
we'll find 'em even if we hafta dig 'em
outta the ground!

(*blackout. Scene shifts back to* JOHN
and MARY *a few hours later. A funereal
solemnity pervades their mood.* JOHN
stands behind MARY *who sits, in a scene
duplicating the famous "American Goth-
ic" painting.*)

JOHN. . . . Walked up to the shack,
knocked on door, didn't git no answer.
Hollered: "LULA? LULA . . . ?"—Not a
thing. Went 'round the side, peeped in
window—nobody stirred. Next door—nobody there. Crossed other side of street
and banged on five or six other doors—
not a colored person could be found! Not
a man, neither woman or child—not even
a little black dog could be seen, smelt, or
heard for blocks around . . . They've gone,
Mary.

MARY. What does it all mean, John?

JOHN. I don't know, Mary . . .

MARY. I always had Lula, John. She
never missed a day at my side . . . That's
why I couldn't accept your wedding pro-
posal until I was sure you'd welcome me
and her together as a package. How am I
gonna git through the day? My baby don't
know *me*, I ain't acquainted wit' *it*. I've
never lifted cover off pot, swung a mop or
broom, dunked a dish, or even pushed a
dustrag. I'm lost wit'out Lula, I need her,
John, I need her. (*begins to weep softly.*
JOHN *pats her consolingly.*)

JOHN. Courage, honey . . . Everybody

in town is facing the same dilemma. We mustn't crack up . . .

(*blackout. Scene shifts back to* MAYOR'*s office later in day. Atmosphere and tone resemble a wartime headquarters at the front.* MAYOR *is poring over huge map.*)

INDUSTRIALIST. Half the day is gone already, Henry. On behalf of the factory owners of this town, you've got to bail us out! Seventy-five percent of all production is paralyzed. With the Nigras absent, men are waiting for machines to be cleaned, floors to be swept, crates lifted, equipment delivered, and bathrooms to be deodorized. Why, restrooms and toilets are so filthy until they not only cannot be sat in, but it's virtually impossible to get within hailing distance because of the stench!

MAYOR. Keep your shirt on, Jeb—

BUSINESSMAN. Business is even in worse condition, Henry. The volume of goods moving 'cross counters has slowed down to a trickle—almost negligible. Customers are not only not purchasing—but the absence of handymen, porters, sweepers, stock-movers, deliverers, and miscellaneous dirty-work doers is disrupting the smooth harmony of marketing!

CLUBWOMAN. Food poisoning, severe indigestitis, chronic diarrhea, advanced diaper chafings, and a plethora of unsanitary household disasters dangerous to life, limb, and property! . . . As a representative of the Federation of Ladies' Clubs, I must sadly report that unless the trend is reversed, a complete breakdown in family unity is imminent . . . Just as homosexuality and debauchery signalled the fall of Greece and Rome, the downgrading of Southern Bellesdom might very well prophesy the collapse of our indigenous institutions . . . Remember—it has always been pure, delicate, lily-white images of Dixie femininity which provided backbone, inspiration, and ideology for our male warriors in their defense against the onrushing black horde. If our gallant men are drained of this worship and idolatry —God knows! The cause won't be worth a Confederate nickel!

MAYOR. Stop this panicky defeatism, y'all hear me! All machinery at my disposal is being utilized. I assure you wit' great confidence the damage will soon repair itself.—Cheerful progress reports are expected any moment now.—Wait! See, here's Jackson . . . Well, Jackson?

JACKSON (*entering*). As of now, sir, all efforts are fruitless. Neither hide nor hair of them has been located. We have not unearthed a single one in our shack-to-shack search. Not a single one has heeded our appeal. Scoured every crick and cranny inside their hovels, turning furniture upside down and inside out, breaking down walls and tearing through ceilings. We made determined efforts to discover where'bouts of our faithful Uncle Toms and informers—but even *they* have vanished without a trace . . . Searching squads are on the verge of panic and hysteria, sir, wit' hotheads among 'em campaigning for scorched earth policies. Nigras on a whole lack cellars, but there's rising sentiment favoring burning to find out whether they're underground—DUG IN!

MAYOR. Absolutely counter such foolhardy suggestions! Suppose they are tombed in? We'd only accelerate the gravity of the situation using incendiary tactics! Besides, when they're rounded up where will we put 'em if we've already burned up their shacks—IN OUR OWN BED-ROOMS?!!!

JACKSON. I agree, sir, but the mood of the crowd is becoming irrational. In anger and frustration, they's forgetting their original purpose was to FIND the Nigras!

MAYOR. At all costs! Stamp out all burning proposals! Must prevent extremist notions from gaining ascendancy. Git wit' it . . . Wait—'n' for Jehovah's sake, find out where the hell is that trifling slacker, WOODFENCE!

COURIER (*rushing in*). Mr. Mayor! Mr. Mayor! . . . We've found some! We've found some!

MAYOR (*excitedly*). Where?!

COURIER. In the—in the—(can't catch *breath*)

MAYOR (*impatiently*). Where, man? Where?!!!

COURIER. In the colored wing of the city hospital!

MAYOR. The hos—? The hospital! I shoulda known! How could those helpless, crippled, cut, and shot Nigras disappear from a hospital! Shoulda thought of that! . . . Tell me more, man!

COURIER. I—I didn't wait, sir . . . I—I

ran in to report soon as I heard—

MAYOR. WELL, GIT BACK ON THE PHONE, YOU IDIOT, DON'T YOU KNOW WHAT THIS MEANS!

COURIER. Yes, sir. (*races out*)

MAYOR. Now we gitting somewhere! . . . Gentlemen, if one sole Nigra is among us, we're well on the road to rehabilitation! Those Nigras in the hospital must know somp'um 'bout the others where'bouts . . . Scat back to your colleagues, boost up their morale, and inform 'em that things will zip back to normal in a jiffy! (*They start to file out, then pause to observe the* COURIER *reentering dazedly.*) Well . . . ? Well, man . . . ? WHAT'S THE MATTER WIT' YOU, NINNY, TELL ME WHAT ELSE WAS SAID?!

COURIER. They all . . . they all . . . they all in a—in a—a coma, sir . . .

MAYOR. They all in a what . . . ?

COURIER. In a coma, sir . . .

MAYOR. Talk sense, man! . . . Whaddaya mean, they all in a coma?

COURIER. Doctor says every last one of the Nigras are jist laying in bed . . . STILL . . . not moving . . . neither live or dead . . . laying up there in a coma . . . every last one of 'em . . .

MAYOR (*sputters, then grabs phone*). Get me Confederate Memorial . . . Put me through to the Staff Chief . . . YES, this is the Mayor . . . Sam? . . . What's this I hear? . . . But how could they be in a coma, Sam? . . . You don't know! Well, what the hell you think the city's paying you for! . . . You've got 'nuff damn hacks and quacks there to find out! . . . How could it be somp'um unknown? You mean Nigras know somp'um 'bout drugs your damn butchers don't?! . . . Well, what the crap good are they! . . . All right, all right, I'll be calm . . . Now, tell me . . . Uh huh, uh huh . . . Well, can't you give 'em some injections or somp'um . . . ?—You did . . . uh huh . . . DID YOU TRY A LI'L ROUGH TREATMENT?—that too, huh . . . All right, Sam, keep trying . . . (*puts phone down delicately, continuing absently*) Can't wake 'em up. Just lay there. Them that's sick won't git no sicker, them that's half-well won't git no better, babies that's due won't be born and them that's come won't show no life. Nigras wit' cuts won't bleed and them which need blood

won't be transfused . . . He say dying Nigras is even refusing to pass away! (*is silently perplexed for a moment, then suddenly breaks into action*) JACKSON?! . . . Call up the police—THE JAIL! Find out what's going on there! Them Nigras are captives! If there's one place we got darkies under control, it's there! Them sonsabitches too ornery to act right either for colored or white! (JACKSON *exits. The* COURIER *follows.*) Keep your fingers crossed, citizens, them Nigras in jail are the most important Nigras we got!

(*All hands are raised conspicuously aloft, fingers prominently exed. Seconds tick by. Soon* JACKSON *returns crestfallen.*)

JACKSON. Sheriff Bull says they don't know whether they still on premises or not. When they went to rouse Nigra jailbirds this morning, cell-block doors refused to swing open. Tried everything— even exploded dynamite charges—but it just wouldn't budge—Then they hoisted guards up to peep through barred windows, but couldn't see good 'nuff to tell whether Nigras was inside or not. Finally, gitting desperate, they power-hosed the cells wit' water but had to cease 'cause Sheriff Bull said he didn't wanta jeopardize drowning the Nigras since it might spoil his chance of shipping a record load of cotton pickers to the State Penitentiary for cotton-snatching jubilee . . . Anyway —they ain't heard a Nigra-squeak all day.

MAYOR. ???That so . . . ? WHAT 'BOUT TRAINS 'N' BUSES PASSING THROUGH? There must be some dinges riding through?

JACKSON. We checked . . . not a one on board.

MAYOR. Did you hear whether any other towns lost their Nigras?

JACKSON. Things are status quo everywhere else.

MAYOR (*angrily*). Then what the hell they picking on us for!

COURIER (*rushing in*). MR. MAYOR! Your sister jist called—HYSTERICAL! She says Vice-Mayor Woodfence went to bed wit' her last night, but when she woke up this morning he was gone! Been missing all day!

MAYOR. ??? Could Nigras be holding brother-in-law Woodfence hostage?!

COURIER. No, sir. Besides him—investigations reveal that dozens or more prominent citizens—two City Council members, the chairman of the Junior Chamber of Commerce, our City College All-Southern halfback, the chairlady of the Daughters of the Confederate Rebellion, Miss Cotton-Sack Festival of the Year, and numerous other miscellaneous nobodies—are all absent wit'out leave. Dangerous evidence points to the conclusion that they have been infiltrating!

MAYOR. Infiltrating???

COURIER. Passing all along!

MAYOR. ???PASSING ALL ALONG???

COURIER. Secret Nigras all the while!

MAYOR. *NAW!* (CLUBWOMAN *keels over in faint.* JACKSON, BUSINESSMAN *and* INDUSTRIALIST *begin to eye each other suspiciously.*)

COURIER. Yessir!

MAYOR. PASSING???

COURIER. Yessir!

MAYOR. SECRET NIG—!???

COURIER. Yessir!

MAYOR (*momentarily stunned to silence*). The dirty mongrelizers! . . . Gentlemen, this is a grave predicament indeed . . . It pains me to surrender priority of our states' rights credo, but it is my solemn task and frightening duty to inform you that we have no other recourse but to seek outside help for our deliverance.

(*blackout. Lights rerise on Huntley-Brinkley - Murrow - Sevareid - Cronkite-Reasoner-type* ANNOUNCER *grasping a hand-held microphone* [*imaginary*] *a few hours later. He is vigorously, excitedly mouthing his commentary, but no sound escapes his lips . . . During this dumb, wordless section of his broadcast, a bedraggled assortment of figures marching with picket signs occupy his attention. On their picket signs are inscribed various appeals and slogans.* "CINDY LOU UNFAIR TO BABY JOE" . . . "CAP'N SAM MISS BIG BOY" . . . "RETURN LI'L' BLUE TO MARSE JIM" . . . "INFORMATION REQUESTED 'BOUT MAMMY GAIL" . . . "BOSS NATHAN PROTEST TO FAST LEROY." *Trailing behind the marchers, forcibly isolated, is a woman dressed in widow-black holding a placard which reads:*

"WHY DIDN'T YOU TELL US—YOUR DEFILED WIFE AND TWO ABSENT MONGRELS.")

ANNOUNCER (*who has been silently mouthing his delivery during the picketing procession, is suddenly heard as if caught in the midst of commentary*) . . . Factories standing idle from the loss of nonessential workers. Stores shuttered from the absconding of uncrucial personnel. Uncollected garbage threatening pestilence and pollution . . . Also, each second somewheres in this former utopia below the Mason and Dixon, dozens of decrepit old men and women usually tended by faithful nurses and servants are popping off like flies—abandoned by sons, daughters, and grandchildren whose refusal to provide their doddering relatives with bedpans and other soothing necessities results in their hasty, nasty, messy corpus delecties . . . But most critically affected of all by this complete drought of Afro-American resources are policemen and other public safety guardians denied their daily quota of Negro arrests. One officer known affectionately as "TWO-A-DAY-PETE" because of his unblemished record of TWO Negro headwhippings per day has already been carted off to the County Insane Asylum—straitjacketed, screaming, and biting, unable to withstand the shock of having his spotless slate sullied by interruption . . . It is feared that similar attacks are soon expected among municipal judges prevented for the first time in years of distinguished bench-sitting from sentencing one single Negro to a hoosegow or pokey . . . Ladies and gentlemen, as you trudge in from the joys and headaches of workday chores and dusk begins to descend on this sleepy Southern hamlet, we REPEAT—today—before early morning dew had dried upon magnolia blossoms, your comrade citizens of this lovely Dixie village awoke to the realization that some —pardon me! Not some—but ALL OF THEIR NEGROES were missing . . . absent, vamoosed, departed, at bay, fugitive, away, gone, and so far unretrieved . . . In order to dispel your incredulity, gauge the temper of your suffering compatriots, and just possibly prepare you for the likelihood of an equally nightmarish eventuality, we have gathered a cross-section of this city's most distinguished leaders for exclusive interviews . . . First, Mr. Council Clan, grand-dragoon of this area's most active civic organizations and staunch bellwether of the political opposition . . . Mr. Clan, how do you ACCOUNT for this incredible disappearance?

CLAN. A PLOT, plain and simple, that's what it is, as plain as the corns on your feet!

ANNOUNCER. Whom would you consider responsible?

CLAN. I could go on all night.

ANNOUNCER. Cite a few?

CLAN. Too numerous.

ANNOUNCER. Just one?

CLAN. Name names when time comes.

ANNOUNCER. Could you be referring to native Negroes?

CLAN. Ever try quarantining lepers from their spots?

ANNOUNCER. Their organizations?

CLAN. Could you slice a nose off a mouth and still keep a face?

ANNOUNCER. Commies?

CLAN. Would you lop off a titty from a chest and still have a breast?

ANNOUNCER. Your city government?

CLAN. Now you talkin'!

ANNOUNCER. State administration?

CLAN. Warming up!

ANNOUNCER. Federal?

CLAN. Kin a blind man see?!

ANNOUNCER. The Court?

CLAN. Is a pig clean?!

ANNOUNCER. Clergy?

CLAN. Do a polecat stink?!

ANNOUNCER. Well, Mr. Clan, with this massive complicity, how do you think the plot could've been prevented from succeeding?

CLAN. If I'da been in office, it never woulda happened.

ANNOUNCER. Then you're laying major blame at the doorstep of the present administration?

CLAN. Damn tooting!

ANNOUNCER. But from your oft-expressed views, Mr. Clan, shouldn't you and your followers be delighted at the turn of events? After all—isn't it one of the main policies of your society to *drive* the Negroes away? *Drive* 'em back where they came from?

CLAN. DRIVVVE, BOY! DRIIIIVVVE!

That's right! . . . When we say so and not befo'. Ain't supposed to do nothing 'til we tell 'em. Got to stay put until we exercise our God-given right to tell 'em when to git!

ANNOUNCER. But why argue if they've merely jumped the gun? Why not rejoice at this premature purging of undesirables?

CLAN. The time ain't ripe yet, boy . . . The time ain't ripe yet.

ANNOUNCER. Thank you for being so informative, Mr. Clan—Mrs. Aide? Mrs. Aide? Over here, Mrs. Aide . . . Ladies and gentlemen, this city's Social Welfare Commissioner, Mrs. Handy Anna Aide . . . Mrs. Aide, with all your Negroes *AWOL*, haven't developments alleviated the staggering demands made upon your Welfare Department? Reduction of relief requests, elimination of case loads, removal of chronic welfare dependents, et cetera?

AIDE. Quite the contrary. Disruption of our pilot projects among Nigras saddles our white community with extreme hardship . . . You see, historically, our agencies have always been foremost contributors to the Nigra Git-A-Job movement. We pioneered in enforcing social welfare theories which oppose coddling the fakers. We strenuously believe in helping Nigras help themselves by participating in meaningful labor. "Relief is Out, Work is In" is our motto. We place them as maids, cooks, butlers, and breast-feeders, cesspool diggers, washbasin maintainers, shoeshine boys, and so on—mostly on a volunteer self-work basis.

ANNOUNCER. Hired at prevailing salaried rates, of course?

AIDE. God forbid! Money is unimportant. Would only make 'em worse. Our main goal is to improve their ethical behavior. "Rehabilitation Through Positive Participation" is another motto of ours. All unwed mothers, loose-living malingering fathers, bastard children, and shiftless grandparents are kept occupied through constructive muscle therapy. This provides the Nigra with less opportunity to indulge his pleasure-loving amoral inclinations.

ANNOUNCER. They volunteer to participate in these pilot projects?

AIDE. Heavens, no! They're notorious shirkers. When I said the program is voluntary, I meant white citizens in overwhelming majorities do the volunteering. Placing their homes, offices, appliances, and persons at our disposal for use in "Operation Uplift" . . . We would never dare place such a decision in the hands of the Nigra. It would never get off the ground! . . . No, they have no choice in the matter. "Work or Starve" is the slogan we use to stimulate Nigra awareness of what's good for survival.

ANNOUNCER. Thank you, Mrs. Aide, and good luck . . . Rev? . . . Rev? . . . Ladies and gentlemen, this city's foremost spiritual guidance counselor, Reverend Reb Pious . . . How does it look to you, Reb Pious?

PIOUS (*gazing skyward*). It's in *His* hands, son, it's in *His* hands.

ANNOUNCER. How would you assess the disappearance, from a moral standpoint?

PIOUS. An immoral act, son, morally wrong and ethically indefensible. A perversion of Christian principles to be condemned from every pulpit of this nation.

ANNOUNCER. Can you account for its occurrence after the many decades of the Church's missionary activity among them?

PIOUS. It's basically a reversion of the Nigra to his deep-rooted primitivism . . . Now, at last, you can understand the difficulties of the Church in attempting to anchor God's kingdom among ungratefuls. It's a constant, unrelenting, no-holds-barred struggle against Satan to wrestle away souls locked in his possession for countless centuries! Despite all our aid, guidance, solace, and protection, Old Beezlebub still retains tenacious grips upon the Nigras' childish loyalty—comparable to the lure of bright flames to an infant.

ANNOUNCER. But actual physical departure, Reb Pious? How do you explain that?

PIOUS. Voodoo, my son, voodoo . . . With Satan's assist, they have probably employed some heathen magic which we cultivated, sophisticated Christians know absolutely nothing about. However, before long we are confident about counteracting this evil witch doctory and triumphing in our Holy Saviour's name. At this perilous juncture, true believers of all denominations are participating in joint, 'round-the-clock observances, offering prayers for our Master's swiftest intercession. I'm optimis-tic about the outcome of His intervention . . . Which prompts me—if I may, sir—to offer these words of counsel to our delinquent Nigras . . . I say to you without rancor or vengeance, quoting a phrase of one of your greatest prophets, Booker T. Washington: "Return your buckets to where they lay and all will be forgiven."

ANNOUNCER. A very inspirational appeal, Reb Pious. I'm certain they will find the tug of its magnetic sincerity irresistible. Thank you, Reb Pious . . . All in all—as you have witnessed, ladies and gentlemen—this town symbolizes the face of disaster. Suffering as severe a prostration as any city wrecked, ravaged, and devastated by the holocaust of war. A vital, lively, throbbing organism brought to a screeching halt by the strange enigma of the missing Negroes . . . We take you now to offices of the one man into whose hands has been thrust the final responsibility of rescuing this shuddering metropolis from the precipice of destruction . . . We give you the honorable Mayor, Henry R. E. Lee . . . Hello, Mayor Lee.

MAYOR (*jovially*). Hello, Jack.

ANNOUNCER. Mayor Lee, we have just concluded interviews with some of your city's leading spokesmen. If I may say so, sir, they don't sound too encouraging about the situation.

MAYOR. Nonsense, Jack! The situation's well in hand as it could be under the circumstances. Couldn't be better in hand. Underneath every dark cloud, Jack, there's always a ray of sunlight, ha, ha, ha.

ANNOUNCER. Have you discovered one, sir?

MAYOR. Well, Jack, I'll tell you . . . Of course we've been faced wit' a little crisis, but look at it like this—we've faced 'em befo': Sherman marched through Georgia —ONCE! Lincoln freed the slaves—MOMENTARILY! Carpetbaggers even put Nigras in the Governor's mansion, state legislature, Congress, and the Senate of the United States. But what happened?—Ole Dixie bounced right on back up . . . At this moment the Supreme Court's trying to put Nigras in our schools and the Nigra has got it in his haid to put hisself everywhere . . . But what you 'spect go'n happen?—Ole Dixie will kangaroo back even higher. Southern courage, fortitude, chivalry, and superiority always wins out . . . SHUCKS! We'll have us some Nigras befo' daylight is gone!

ANNOUNCER. Mr. Mayor, I hate to introduce this note, but in an earlier interview, one of your chief opponents, Mr. Clan, hinted at your own complicity in the affair—

MAYOR. A LOT OF POPPYCOCK! Clan is politicking! I've beaten him four times outta four and I'll beat him four more times outta four! This is no time for partisan politics! What we need now is level-headedness and across-the-board unity. This typical, rash, mealy-mouth, shooting-off-at-the-lip of Clan and his ilk proves their insincerity and voters will remember that in the next election! Won't you, voters?! (*has risen to the height of campaign oratory*)

ANNOUNCER. Mr. Mayor! . . . Mr. Mayor! . . . Please—

MAYOR. . . . I tell you, I promise you—

ANNOUNCER. PLEASE, MR. MAYOR!

MAYOR. Huh? . . . Oh—yes, carry on.

ANNOUNCER. Mr. Mayor, your cheerfulness and infectious good spirits lead me to conclude that startling new developments warrant fresh-found optimism. What concrete, declassified information do you have to support your claim that Negroes will reappear before nightfall?

MAYOR. Because we are presently awaiting the payoff of a masterful five-point suprarecovery program which can't help but reap us a bonanza of Nigras 'fore sundown! . . . First: Exhaustive efforts to pinpoint the where'bouts of our own missing darkies continue to zero in on the bullseye . . . Second: The President of the United States, following an emergency cabinet meeting, has designated us the prime disaster area of the century—National Guard is already on the way . . . Third: In an unusual, but bold maneuver, we have appealed to the NAACP 'n' all other Nigra conspirators to help us git to the bottom of the vanishing act . . . Fourth: We have exercised our nonreciprocal option and requested that all fraternal southern states express their solidarity by lending us some of their Nigras temporarily on credit . . . Fifth and foremost: We have already gotten consent of the Governor to round up all stray, excess, and incorrigible Nigras

to be shipped to us under escort of the State Militia . . . That's why we've stifled pessimism and are brimming wit' confidence that this full-scale concerted mobilization will ring down a jackpot of jigaboos 'fore light vanishes from the sky!—

ANNOUNCER. Congratulations! What happens if it fails?

MAYOR. Don't even think THAT! Absolutely no reason to suspect it will . . . (*peers over shoulder, then whispers confidentially while placing hand over mouth of* ANNOUNCER's *imaginary mike*) . . . But speculating on the dark side of your question—if we don't turn up some by nightfall, it may be all over. The harm has already been done. You see the South has always been glued together by the uninterrupted presence of its darkies. No telling how unstuck we might git if things keep on like they have—Wait a minute, it musta paid off already! Mission accomplished 'cause here's Jackson 'head a time wit' the word . . . Well, Jackson, what's new?

JACKSON. Situation on the home front remains static, sir—can't uncover scent or shadow. The NAACP and all other Nigra front groups 'n' plotters deny any knowledge or connection wit' the missing Nigras. Maintained this even after appearing befo' a Senate Emergency Investigating Committee which subpoenaed 'em to Washington posthaste and threw 'em in jail for contempt. A handful of Nigras who agreed to make spectacular appeals for ours to come back to us, have themselves mysteriously disappeared. But, worst news of all, sir, is our sister cities and counties, inside and outside the state, have changed their minds, fallen back on their promises and refused to lend us any Nigras, claiming they don't have 'nuff for themselves.

MAYOR. What 'bout Nigras promised by the Governor?!

JACKSON. Jailbirds and vagrants escorted here from chain gangs and other reservations either revolted and escaped en route or else vanished mysteriously on approaching our city limits . . . Deterioration rapidly escalates, sir. Estimates predict we kin hold out only one more hour before overtaken by anarchistic turmoil . . . Some citizens seeking haven elsewheres have already fled, but on last report were being forcibly turned back by armed sentinels in other cities who wanted no parts of 'em —claiming they carried a jinx.

MAYOR. That bad, huh?

JACKSON. Worse, sir . . . we've received at least five reports of plots on your life.

MAYOR. What?!—We've gotta act quickly then!

JACKSON. Run out of ideas, sir.

MAYOR. Think harder, boy!

JACKSON. Don't have much time, sir. One measly hour, then all hell go'n' break loose.

MAYOR. Gotta think of something drastic, Jackson!

JACKSON. I'm dry, sir.

MAYOR. Jackson! Is there any planes outta here in the next hour?

JACKSON. All transportation's been knocked out, sir.

MAYOR. I thought so!

JACKSON. What were you contemplating, sir?

MAYOR. Don't ask me what I was contemplating! I'm still boss 'round here! Don't forgit it!

JACKSON. Sorry, sir.

MAYOR. . . . Hold the wire! . . . Wait a minute . . . ! Waaaaait a minute—GOD-AMMIT! All this time crapping 'round, diddling and futsing wit' puny li'l' solutions—all the while neglecting our ace in the hole, our trump card! Most potent weapon for digging Nigras outta the woodpile!!! All the while right befo' our eyes! . . . Ass! Why didn't you remind me?!!!

JACKSON. What is it, sir?

MAYOR. . . . ME—THAT'S WHAT! ME! A personal appeal from ME! *Directly to them!* . . . Although we wouldn't let 'em march to the polls and express their affection for me through the ballot box, we've always known I'm held highest in their esteem. A direct address from their beloved Mayor! . . . If they's anywhere close within the sound of my voice, they'll shape up! Or let us know by a sign they's ready to!

JACKSON. You sure *that'll* turn the trick, sir?

MAYOR. As sure as my ancestors befo' me who knew that when they puckered their lips to whistle, ole Sambo was gonna

come a-lickety-splitting to answer the call! . . . That same chips-down blood courses through these Confederate gray veins of Henry R. E. Lee!!!

ANNOUNCER. I'm delighted to offer our network's facilities for such a crucial public interest address, sir. We'll arrange immediately for your appearance on an international hookup, placing you in the widest proximity to contact them wherever they may be.

MAYOR. Thank you, I'm very grateful . . . Jackson, regrease the machinery and set wheels in motion. Inform townspeople what's being done. Tell 'em we're all in this together. The next hour is countdown. I demand absolute cooperation, citywide silence and inactivity. I don't want the Nigras frightened if they's nearby. This is the most important hour in town's history. Tell 'em if one single Nigra shows up during hour of decision, victory is within sight. I'm gonna git 'em that one— maybe all! Hurry and crack to it! (AN-NOUNCER *rushes out, followed by* JACKSON. *Blackout. Scene reopens, with* MAYOR *seated, eyes front, spotlight illuminating him in semidarkness. Shadowy figures stand in the background, prepared to answer phones or aid in any other manner.* MAYOR *waits patiently until "GO!" signal is given. Then begins, his voice combining elements of confidence, tremolo, and gravity)* Good evening . . . Despite the fact that millions of you wonderful people throughout the nation are viewing and listening to this momentous broadcast—and I thank you for your concern and sympathy in this hour of our peril—I primarily want to concentrate my attention and address these remarks solely for the benefit of our departed Nigra friends who may be listening somewhere in our far-flung land to the sound of my voice . . . If you are—it is with heartfelt emotion and fond memories of our happy association that I ask— "Where are you . . . ?" Your absence has left a void in the bosom of every single man, woman, and child of our great city. I tell you—you don't know what it means for us to wake up in the morning and discover that your cheerful, grinning, happy-go-lucky faces are missing! . . . From the depths of my heart, I can only meekly, humbly suggest what it means to me per-

sonally . . . You see—the one face I will
never be able to erase from my memory is
the face—not of my Ma, not of Pa, neither
wife or child—but the image of the first
woman I came to love so well when just
a wee lad—the vision of the first human I
laid clear sight on at childbirth—the profile—better yet, the full face of my dear old
. . . Jemimah—God rest her soul . . . Yes!
My dear old mammy, wit' her round
ebony moonbeam gleaming down upon
me in the crib, teeth shining, blood-red
bandana standing starched, peaked, and
proud, gazing down upon me affectionately
as she crooned me a Southern lullaby . . .
OH! It's a memorable picture I will eter-
nally cherish in permanent treasure chambers of my heart, now and forever always
. . . Well, if this radiant image can remain
so infinitely vivid to me all these many
years after her unfortunate demise in the
Po' Folks Home—THINK of the misery
the rest of us must be suffering after being *freshly* denied your soothing presence?! We need ya. If you kin hear me,
just contact this station 'n' I will welcome
you back personally. Let me just tell you
that since you eloped, nothing has been
the same. How could it? You're part of us,
you belong to us. Just give us a sign and
we'll be contented that all is well . . . Now
if you've skipped away on a little fun-fest,
we understand, ha, ha. We know you like
a good time and we don't begrudge it to
ya. Hell—er, er, we like a good time ourselves—who doesn't? . . . In fact, think of
all the good times we've had together,
huh? We've had some real fun, you and
us, yesiree! . . . Nobody knows better than
you and I what fun we've had together.
You singing us those old Southern coon
songs and dancing those Nigra jigs and us
clapping, prodding 'n' spurring you on!
Lots of fun, huh?! . . . OH BOY! The
times we've had together . . . If you've
snucked away for a bit of fun by yourself,
we'll go long wit' ya—long as you let us
know where you at so we won't be worried
about you . . . We'll go 'long wit' you long
as you don't take the joke too far. I'll admit a joke is a joke and you've played a
LULU! . . . I'm warning you, we can't
stand much more horsing 'round from
you! Business is business 'n' fun is fun!
You've had your fun so now let's get

down to business! Come on back, YOU
HEAR ME!!! . . . If you been hoodwinked
by agents of some foreign government, I've
been authorized by the President of these
United States to inform you that this lib-
erty-loving Republic is prepared to rescue
you from their clutches. Don't pay no
'tention to their sireeen songs and atheistic
promises! You better off under our control
and you know it! . . . If you been bam-
boozled by rabble-rousing nonsense of your
own so-called leaders, we prepared to offer
same protection. Just call us up! Just give
us a sign! . . . Come on, give us a sign . . .
give us a sign—even a teeny-weeny one
. . . ??!! (*glances around checking on possible communications. A bevy of head-
shakes indicate no success.* MAYOR *returns
to address with desperate fervor.*) Now
look—you don't know what you doing! If
you persist in this disobedience, you know
all too well the consequences! We'll track
you to the end of the earth, beyond the
galaxy, across the stars! We'll capture you
and chastise you with all the vengeance
we command! 'N' you know only too well
how stern we kin be when double-crossed!
The city, the state, and the entire nation
will crucify you for this unpardonable de-
fiance! (*checks again*) No call . . . ? No
sign . . . ? Time is running out! Deadline
slipping past! They gotta respond! They
gotta! (*resuming*) Listen to me! I'm begging y'all, you've gotta come back . . . !
LOOK, GEORGE! (*waves dirty rag aloft*)
I brought the rag you wax the car wit'
. . . Don't this bring back memories,
George, of all the days you spent shining
that automobile to shimmering perfection
. . . ? And you, Rufus?! . . . Here's the
shoe polisher and the brush! . . . 'Member,
Rufus? . . . Remember the happy mornings you spent popping this rag and whisk-
ing this brush so furiously 'til it created
music that was sympho-nee to the ear
. . . ? And you—MANDY? . . . Here's the
wastebasket you didn't dump this morning. I saved it just for you! . . . LOOK, all
y'all out there . . . ? (*signals and a three-
person procession parades one after the
other before the imaginary camera*)

DOLL WOMAN (*brandishing a crying
baby* [*doll*] *as she strolls past and exits*).
She's been crying ever since you left,
Caldonia . . .

MOP MAN (*flashing mop*). It's been waiting in the same corner, Buster . . .

BRUSH MAN (*flagging toilet brush in one hand and toilet plunger in other*). It's been dry ever since you left, Washington . . .

MAYOR (*jumping in on the heels of the last exit*). Don't these things mean anything to y'all? By God! Are your memories so short?! Is there nothing sacred to ya? . . . Please come back, for my sake, please! All of you—even you questionable ones! I promise no harm will be done to you! Revenge is disallowed! We'll forgive everything! Just come on back and I'll git down on my knees— (*immediately drops to knees*). I'll be kneeling in the middle of Dixie Avenue to kiss the first shoe of the first one 'a you to show up . . . *I'll smooch any other spot you request* . . . Erase this nightmare 'n' we'll concede any demand you make, just come on back—please???!! . . . PLEEEEEEEZE?!!!

VOICE (*shouting*). TIME!!!

MAYOR (*remaining on knees, frozen in a pose of supplication. After a brief, deadly silence, he whispers almost inaudibly*). They wouldn't answer . . . they wouldn't answer . . .

(*blackout as bedlam erupts offstage. Total blackness holds during a sufficient interval where offstage sound effects create the illusion of complete pandemonium, followed by a diminution which trails off into an expressionistic simulation of a city coming to a stricken standstill: industrial machinery clanks to halt, traffic blares to silence, etc. . . . The stage remains dark and silent for a long moment, then lights rearise on the* ANNOUNCER.)

ANNOUNCER. A pitiful sight, ladies and gentlemen. Soon after his unsuccessful appeal, Mayor Lee suffered a vicious pummeling from the mob and barely escaped with his life. National Guardsmen and State Militia were impotent in quelling the fury of a town venting its frustration in an orgy of destruction—a frenzy of rioting, looting, and all other aberrations of a town gone berserk . . . Then—suddenly—as if a magic wand had been waved, madness evaporated and something more frightening replaced it: Submission . . . Even whimperings ceased. The city: exhausted, benumbed.—Slowly its occupants slinked off into shadows, and by midnight the town was occupied exclusively by zombies. The fight and life had been drained out . . . Pooped . . . Hope ebbed away as completely as the beloved, absent Negroes . . . As our crew packed gear and crept away silently, we treaded softly—as if we were stealing away from a mausoleum . . . The Face of a Defeated City.

(*blackout. Lights rise slowly at the sound of rooster-crowing, signalling the approach of a new day, the next morning. Scene is same as opening of play.* CLEM *and* LUKE *are huddled over dazedly, trancelike. They remain so for a long count. Finally, a figure drifts onstage, shuffling slowly.*)

LUKE (*gazing in silent fascination at the approaching figure.*) . . . Clem . . . ? Do you see what I see or am I dreaming . . . ?

CLEM. It's a . . . a Nigra, ain't it, Luke . . . ?

LUKE. Sure looks like one, Clem—but we better make sure—eyes could be playing tricks on us . . . Does he still look like one to you, Clem?

CLEM. He still does, Luke—but I'm scared to believe—

LUKE. . . . Why . . . ? It looks like Rastus, Clem!

CLEM. Sure does, Luke . . . but we better not jump to no hasty conclusion . . .

LUKE (*in timid softness*). That you, Rastus . . . ?

RASTUS (*Stepin Fetchit, Willie Best, Nicodemus, B. McQueen and all the rest rolled into one.*) Why . . . howdy . . . Mr. Luke . . . Mr. Clem . . .

CLEM. It is him, Luke! It is him!

LUKE. Rastus?

RASTUS. Yas . . . sah?

LUKE. Where was you yesterday?

RASTUS (*very, very puzzled*). Yes . . . ter . . . day? . . . Yester . . . day . . .? Why . . . right . . . here . . . Mr. Luke . . .

LUKE. No you warn't, Rastus, don't lie to me! Where was you yestiddy?

RASTUS. Why . . . I'm sure I was . . . Mr. Luke . . . Remember . . . I made . . that delivery for you . . .

LUKE. That was MONDAY, Rastus, yestiddy was TUESDAY.

RASTUS. Tues . . . day . . . ? You don't say . . . Well . . . well . . . well . . .

LUKE. Where was you 'n' all the other Nigras yesterday, Rastus?

RASTUS. I . . . thought . . . yestiddy . . . was . . . Monday, Mr. Luke—I coulda swore it . . . ! . . . See how . . . things . . . kin git all mixed up? . . . I coulda swore it . . .

LUKE. TODAY is WEDNESDAY, Rastus. Where was you TUESDAY?

RASTUS. Tuesday . . . huh? That's somp-'um . . . I . . . don't . . . remember . . . missing . . . a day . . . Mr. Luke . . . but I guess you right . . .

LUKE. Then where was you!!!???

RASTUS. Don't rightly know, Mr. Luke. I didn't know I had skipped a day.—But that jist goes to show you how time kin fly, don't it, Mr. Luke . . . Uuh, uuh, uuh . . .

(*He starts shuffling off, scratching head, a flicker of a smile playing across his lips.* CLEM *and* LUKE *gaze dumbfoundedly as he disappears.*)

LUKE (*eyes sweeping around in all directions.*) Well . . . There's the others, Clem . . . Back jist like they useta be . . . Everything's same as always . . .

CLEM. ??? . . . . Is it . . . Luke . . . !

(*Slow fade*)

CURTAIN

A SONG AT TWILIGHT

Noël Coward

HILDE LATYMER
FELIX, a Waiter

HUGO LATYMER
CARLOTTA GRAY

The time is the present. The action of the play passes in a private suite of the Hotel Beau Rivage, Lausanne-Ouchy, Switzerland.

ONE OF THE GIANTS of the modern theatre, Noël Coward (who was knighted by Queen Elizabeth II in 1970) was born in Teddington, England, on December 16, 1899. He made his acting debut at the age of twelve as Prince Mussel in a children's play, *The Goldfish*, and when he was twenty-one, his first produced play, *I'll Leave It to You*, opened in the West End. As he personally described the event: "The first night was a roaring success, and I made a boyish speech. The critics were mostly enthusiastic, and said a lot about it having been a great night, and that a new playwright had been discovered, etc., but unfortunately their praise was not potent enough to lure audiences to the New Theatre for more than five weeks; so the run ended miserably . . ."

It was in 1924, though, that Sir Noël sprang to international prominence with *The Vortex* and ever since that eventful year he symbolized glistening sophistication, trenchant wit, and impeccable style in the theatre. His originality and superb craftsmanship and the fact that he was one of the few playwrights to have created a world of his own and made one enter into it on his own terms made him a legendary figure and few indeed could match his prolificacy as dramatist, composer, lyricist, director, and performer.

In the five decades that followed *The Vortex*, the unique theatrical wizardry of Noël Coward lured hundreds of thousands into theatres throughout the world. Among his forty plays, musicals, and revues are such landmarks of their respective eras as: *Hay Fever, Easy Virtue, This Year of Grace, Bitter Sweet, Private Lives, Design for Living, Cavalcade, Words and Music, Conversation Piece, Set to Music, Present Laughter, This Happy Breed, Blithe Spirit, Sigh No More, Peace in Our Time,* and *Relative Values*. His memorable series of nine short plays, *Tonight at 8:30*, with himself and the radiant Gertrude Lawrence as costars, brightened a depression-clouded world in the mid-1930s.

A Renaissance man of the theatre, Sir Noël also made some notable contribuitons to films (*In Which We Serve, Brief Encounter, This Happy Breed*) and added substantially to international library shelves with four volumes of memoirs, five collections of short stories, three of revue sketches and lyrics, a popular novel, *Pomp and Circumstance*, and of course his forty or so published plays.

In spite of the fact that he occasionally came under critical fire from some disciples of the "new wave" for persistently clinging to traditional—and ignoring exploratory—forms in the theatre, Sir Noël maintained his undeniable status as the grand *padrone* of modern stage comedy. This was reaffirmed unequivocally in 1964 when Britain's celebrated National Theatre, under the leadership of Lord (Laurence) Olivier, triumphantly revived Sir Noël's indestructible comedy, *Hay Fever*, with Dame Edith Evans as star. Its success with press and public sparked an extraordinary resurgence of interest in the author and his works and summoned forth periodic revivals of his most successful plays. Additionally, two revues culled from his songs and writings, *Cowardy Custard* and *Oh, Coward!*, recently enjoyed lengthy engagements in, respectively, London and New York. ("People have constantly written me off and are surprised that I've come back," Sir Noël once wryly observed. "Now, I wish they would tell me where I am supposed to have been.")

In April 1966, Sir Noël once again brightened the West End as author and costar (with Lilli Palmer and Irene Worth) of *Suite in Three Keys*. Lauded by the London *Daily Express* as "Coward at his zenith," *Suite in Three Keys* represents the omnibus title for three individual plays: *A Song at Twilight, Shadows of the Evening,* and *Come into the Garden Maud*. And while they are entitative, they are designed to be performed by the same players and are linked together by a mutual frame of action: the sitting room of a private suite in a luxury hotel in Switzerland. In 1971, a shortened version of *A Song at Twilight* was presented in England and it appears in an anthology for the first time in *Best Short Plays of the World Theatre: 1968–1973*.

Sir Noël frequently was likened to an earlier master of "artificial comedy," Oscar Wilde, for he, too, was a supreme precisionist at entertainingly tearing away at social pretensions and beneath the surface of his characteristically witty, cutting and pointed dialogue, there was invariably a flow of pertinent commentary on contemporary society and its values.

Would his plays—particularly the early plays—have been different if he had started writing them later? Shortly before his death, in March 1973, at his home in Jamaica, Sir Noël Coward reflected: "I would continue to write what I wanted to write and about people who are interesting . . . and both peers and charwomen are interesting to me."

ACT ONE

The action of the play passes in a private suite in a luxurious hotel in Switzerland.

The scene is the sitting room. The suite is occupied for two or three months each year by SIR HUGO LATYMER, *an elderly writer of considerable eminence.*

The conventional hotel furnishing has been augmented by some of SIR HUGO's *personal possessions which include an impressive writing desk, a special armchair by the side of which is a small table. On this are books, bottles of medicine and pills, a small gold clock and a slim vase containing a number of ball-point pens. On the walls hang some of* SIR HUGO's *favourite Impressionist paintings.*

On stage left there is a door leading into the bedroom. There are double doors at the back which open onto a small lobby and then the corridor. HILDE's *room also opens off the lobby.*

HILDE LATYMER *is a faded woman in her early fifties. She has been married to* SIR HUGO *for nearly twenty years and was originally his secretary. Apart from being his official German translator, she is capable, dedicated, and orders his life with considerable efficiency.*

When the curtain rises she is seated at the writing desk. Standing near her is FELIX, *the floor-waiter. He is startlingly handsome young man of about twenty-eight and there is already in his manner that subtle blend of obsequiousness, authority, and charm which, if he does not allow his good looks to lead him astray, will ultimately carry him to the top of his profession. At the moment he is holding a notebook and listening to* HILDE *with polite attention.*

HILDE. That will be all for the moment, Felix. Sir Hugo's guest is due at eight o'clock, but it is possible that she might be a little late, so I think you should be prepared to serve the dinner at about eight-thirty, but not before.

FELIX. A touch of garlic in the salad dressing as usual?

HILDE. Yes. But only the smallest touch. We don't want a repetition of last Friday, do we?

FELIX. Friday night is much to be re-gretted, Milady. But if you will remember, I was off duty. Giovanni is a most willing boy, but he is not yet accustomed to Sir Hugo's tastes.

HILDE. You will warn him to be more careful next time.

FELIX. Very good, Milady.

(He bows and goes out.)

HILDE *(picking up the telephone and speaking with a rather heavy German accent)* 'Allo. Mademoiselle, j'ai demandé un préavis à Londres il-y-a presqu'une demi-heure. Est-ce que vous en avez des nouvelles? . . . Oui—oui merci, j'attendrai. (*She replaces the receiver, rises, goes to the bureau, takes a file from the top of it, and returns to the desk. The telephone rings. Answering it*) Hallo . . . Is that you Carl? This is Hilde Latymer speaking. I have been trying to get you all the afternoon. First of all, regarding the lecture tour in the States . . . Yes, I know, but Sir Hugo really isn't up to it . . . Oh, yes, he is much better, but the doctor insists that he must not undertake anything that is not absolutely necessary . . . Yes, he will accept the Doctorate at the University and make a speech as arranged, but nothing more than that. After it's over we will either come straight back here or go to Arizona for a rest . . . Next, regarding the film proposition for *The Winding River.* You will have to put in the contract that he has complete veto on the script and the adapter . . . Well, he certainly won't sign it unless that is confirmed in writing . . . On the contrary, I think it matters a great deal. It involves his name and reputation. . . .

(At this moment SIR HUGO LATYMER *enters from the bedroom. He is a distinguished-looking man of seventy. His figure is slim and erect. Sometimes, when he is in a good mood, he looks younger than he actually is by several years. At other times, when upset over some triviality or worried about his health, he becomes suddenly enfeebled and deliberately ancient. This, of course, is a pose, but it works like a charm on doctors and nurses or whoever happens to be looking after him at the moment. It even works on* HILDE *occasionally, notwithstanding the fact that she has had twenty years to grow accustomed to it.* SIR HUGO *is wear-*

ing a brocaded dressing gown, his white hair is slightly tousled and he looks irascible.)

HUGO. What involves my name and reputation?

HILDE (*putting her hand over the receiver*). It's Carl. We're talking about *The Winding River* contract.

HUGO. Then you are both wasting your time. I have no intention of signing it whatever concessions they make.

HILDE. But, Hugo dear, you did say that providing they gave you complete veto of script and adapter that . . .

HUGO (*snappily*). Well, I have changed my mind. I have had no less than three novels and five of my best short stories massacred by that cretinous medium. I refuse to have any more of it.

HILDE (*into the receiver*). I can't talk any more at the moment, Carl. Ring me in the morning at eleven o'clock . . . Very well, ten o'clock, but be sure to have it put through to my room . . . Yes, three five five. Good-bye.

(*She hangs up.*)

HUGO (*sitting*). Carl's getting out of hand. He needs a serious talking to. All he thinks about is his damned percentage.

HILDE. You can't altogether blame him for that. He *is* your agent.

HUGO. What time is it?

HILDE (*glancing at her watch*). Nearly half-past seven. Isn't that clock going?

HUGO. I haven't the faintest idea. It's so exquisitely made that I can't see it without my glasses.

HILDE. You said you were delighted with it when I gave it to you.

HUGO. Well, I'm not now.

HILDE. I'm sorry. I'll try and change it.

HUGO. And please don't look martyred. It draws your mouth down at the corners. Like a weary old camel.

HILDE. Thank you.

HUGO. With two unsymmetrical humps.

HILDE. That's a dromedary. (*She rises, moves to the bureau, and puts three books from it into the cupboard.*) Have you had your bath?

HUGO. No, I have not had my bath.

HILDE. Well, don't you think you should? She's due at eight.

HUGO. If I'm not ready, she can wait for me, can't she? An extra ten minutes tacked on to all those years can't matter all that much.

HILDE. You're in a very disagreeable mood.

HUGO. I'm nervous.

HILDE. It's your own fault if you are. You needn't have agreed to see her, and in fact, I still think it is a great mistake.

HUGO. Yes, I know you do. You've made that abundantly clear during the last three days. You've never been exactly adept at hiding your feelings.

HILDE. On the contrary, Hugo, that is one of the things I do best. Living with you for twenty years has been excellent training.

HUGO. Why are you so frightened of Carlotta?

HILDE (*calmly*). I am not in the least frightened of Carlotta.

HUGO. Oh, yes, you are. The very idea of her fills your soul with dread. Come on now, admit it.

HILDE. It is time for your blue pill. (*She exits abruptly, leaving the door open.*)

HUGO (*enjoying himself*). You'd better take a tranquillizer to calm your desperate fears.

(HILDE *returns with a pill on a dish, and a glass of water.*)

HILDE. Whatever fears I may have about Carlotta are entirely on your account. She is bound to upset you in some way or other. She wouldn't suddenly reappear in your life like this unless she wanted something. (*handing him the pill*) Here you are.

(HUGO *takes the pill, swallows it, and drinks.*)

HUGO. Perhaps she wants a reunion.

HILDE. Money, more likely. She has not been very successful during the last fifteen years.

HUGO. Have you been following her career?

HILDE (*taking the glass*) There hasn't been much career to follow lately.

(*She goes off into the bedroom again.*)

HUGO. Poor Carlotta!

(*He rises and takes a cigarette from the box on the drinks table.* HILDE *returns.* HUGO *replaces the cigarette.*)

HILDE. She will upset you. I feel it in my bones. It is like the weather. I can always tell when it is going to rain.

HUGO. That particular form of prescience is rheumatic rather than clairvoyant. In any case, it is within the bounds of possibility that I might upset her.

HILDE. She doesn't suffer from your particular form of nervous indigestion.

HUGO. I see you're determined to be tiresome.

HILDE. It's unfair of you to say that. It's you I'm thinking of. You've been so much better lately. Doctor Benoist says your blood pressure is back to normal, you're sleeping well and you haven't had any pains for three weeks. I just don't want you to have a relapse. You know that any sort of excitement is bad for you.

HUGO. Do you seriously believe that seeing Carlotta again will excite me to the extent of sending up my blood pressure?

HILDE. You've been giving every indication of it.

HUGO. Oh, Hilde, Hilde! What an egregious ass you are.

HILDE. You have now called me a camel, a dromedary and an ass within the last ten minutes. Your normal dialogue is less zoological. You have worked yourself up into a state about seeing Carlotta again and it's no use pretending you haven't. I know the symptoms. I haven't been with you for twenty years for nothing.

HUGO (*patiently*). Now listen to me, Hilde. My affair with Carlotta lasted exactly two years, and we parted in a blaze of mutual acrimony. That was centuries ago, and I haven't clapped eyes on her since, except once on the cinema screen when she appeared briefly as a Mother Superior in an excruciatingly bad film about a nun with a vast bust. Nor have we corresponded. This sudden request on her part to see me again has not unnaturally filled me with curiosity. It is quite possible that your surmise is right and that she wants to borrow money. If that is so, I will lend her some for old times' sake. On the other hand, she may merely want to see me for sentimental reasons. Time and the difficult years may have mellowed her, or she may even wish to gloat over my age and infirmity.

HILDE (*sharply*). You are *not* infirm.

HUGO. After all, you must remember that she was very much in love with me.

HILDE. And you with her?

HUGO. Of course. Even so, the chances of a passionate, physical reunion are remote.

HILDE. So I should hope. The very idea would be ridiculous.

HUGO. Not quite so ridiculous as all that. Anyhow, you cannot deny that the possibility crossed your mind.

HILDE (*hotly*). I most certainly do deny it.

HUGO. Quite frankly, I suspect you of being jealous.

HILDE (*quietly*). No, Hugo, I am not jealous. I realized many years ago that I had no right to be jealous.

HUGO. Since when has jealousy been so law-abiding? Is it an emotion that obediently sticks to the rules?

HILDE. I have no wish to argue with you.

HUGO. You are jealous of all my friends, of anyone who is close to me, and you always have been.

HILDE (*with a show of spirit*). You have not so many friends for me to be jealous of.

HUGO. You hate Mariette. You are barely civil to Cedric Marcombe and David when they come here.

HILDE. They are barely civil to me.

HUGO. Cedric Marcombe is a man of brilliant intelligence and exquisite taste. He is also the greatest connoisseur of modern art alive today.

HILDE. And what is David?

HUGO (*defensively*). David is one of the most promising young painters that England has produced in the last twenty years. He also happens to be the son of Lord Tenterden.

HILDE. In that case he should have better manners. And his paintings I do not care for at all. They are ugly and cruel.

HUGO (*viciously*). As a full-blooded German you are scarcely in a position to object to cruelty in art or anything else.

HILDE. It is wrong of you to speak to me like that, Hugo, and most unkind. When you are in a better mood you will see that this is so, and be sorry. In any case, this sort of argument is waste of time and energy. You cannot, after all these long years, seriously imagine that I am jealous of your friends or your heart. If I am jealous at all it is for your well-being. You really must try not to get cross so easily. You know what it does to your acids. Remember what Doctor Benoist said.

HUGO. Now you're talking like a district nurse.

HILDE. No district nurse would have had the endurance to put up with your sudden tempers for as long as I have.

HUGO. Do you wish to leave me? Are you giving me a month's notice?

HILDE. If I wished to leave you I should have done so long ago. Now it is too late.

HUGO. For God's sake stop looking hurt, Hilde. It infuriates me.

HILDE. If you do not wish me to look hurt you should not try so hard to hurt me. I do my best to help you with the business of your life, even to love you as far as you will allow me to. But you make it most difficult for me, sometimes almost too difficult to be borne.

HUGO. Oh Lord! Now I suppose you are going to cry.

HILDE (*rising*). No, Hugo. I am not going to cry. That, too, is waste of time and energy. I am going to put on my hat.

HUGO (*realizing he has gone too far*). Hilde . . .

HILDE. If you are determined to receive your long-lost love in a dressing gown with your hair all rumpled, that is entirely your affair.

HUGO. Hilde . . . I'm sorry. I'm sorry that I upset you.

HILDE. It is nothing new.

HUGO. I don't feel now that I can face her alone. You'd better stay, after all.

HILDE. Certainly not. I've already arranged to dine with Liesel at the Grappe d'Or and go to the cinema afterwards.

HUGO. Liesel is a weather-beaten old lesbian.

HILDE. She is also highly intelligent.

HUGO. Is she in love with you?

HILDE. Not in the least. She lives with a Chinese student who paints butterflies on glass.

HUGO. Whatever for?

HILDE. Actually she's very talented.

HUGO. Put Liesel off—don't go—stay with me. I need your support.

HILDE (*firmly*). No, Hugo. (*rising*) You've brought this situation on yourself and you will have to deal with it yourself.

HUGO. You have ordered the dinner?

HILDE. Yes. Felix will bring it when you ring.

HUGO. I think I should like a drink, to fortify me.

HILDE. I'll ring for some ice. (*She rings the service bell.*) It had better be vodka. You're having it with the caviar, anyhow.

HUGO. I never told you to order caviar.

HILDE. No. It was my own idea. I ordered pink champagne, too.

HUGO. Pink champagne! Good God, why?

HILDE. You're always accusing me of not having a sense of humor. I thought I'd like to prove you wrong.

HUGO. Is the rest of the menu equally plutocratic?

HILDE. No, comparatively simple. Steak Bearnaise, green salad, and a chocolate soufflé.

HUGO. I shan't sleep a wink.

HILDE. I shouldn't count too much on that, anyhow. The Maalox tablets are in the table drawer if you should need them. (FELIX *enters with a bucket of ice.*) Give Sir Hugo a vodka on the rocks, will you, Felix?

FELIX. Very good, Milady.

HILDE. I won't be more than a few minutes.

(HILDE *exits.* FELIX *pours a vodka on the rocks.*)

HUGO (*with charm*). I missed you sadly last evening, Felix. Where did you disappear to?

FELIX. It was my half-day off, sir.

HUGO. Your substitute lacked charm. He also breathed like an old locomotive.

FELIX. That was Giovanni, sir. He comes from Calabria.

HUGO. The railway journey must have made a profound impression on him.

FELIX. Your vodka, sir.

HUGO (*taking it*). Thank you. Did you enjoy your half-day off?

FELIX. Oh, yes, sir. We went to swim in the piscine at Vevey, it is not so crowded as the one here, and then we came back and went to a film.

HUGO. We?

FELIX. My friend and I. He is the assistant barman at the Hotel de la Paix. He is a champion swimmer and has won many trophies.

HUGO. You look as though you should be a good swimmer yourself, with those shoulders.

FELIX. Not as good as he is, but I myself love to water-ski. It is a great sport.

HUGO. It must be. Water-skiing was not invented when I was your age. (HILDE *enters, goes to the desk and sits.*) Thank you, Felix. You will bring the dinner when I ring?

FELIX. Very good, sir.

HUGO. It should be in about half an hour's time, depending on when my guest arrives.

FELIX. *Bien, monsieur.*

(FELIX *bows and exits, closing the doors.* HILDE *starts to stamp letters.*)

HILDE. Are you feeling more relaxed?

HUGO. More resigned, at any rate. That's quite a masculine-looking little hat, almost a bowler. Are you wearing it as a subtle gesture to your hostess?

HILDE. You know I dislike that sort of joke, Hugo. Liesel has been a good friend of mine for many years. I am very fond of her. The other side of her life is of no interest to me.

HUGO. Give me a cigarette.

HILDE. No, Hugo. You've already had too many today.

HUGO. I tell you I'm nervous. (*The telephone rings.*) There now!

HILDE (*answering the telephone*). Oui, Gaston. Demandez à Madame de monter toute de suite.

(*She hangs up.*)

HUGO. The tiresome woman is early.

HILDE. No. It is you who are late. Go quickly. It would be inelegant to receive an ex-mistress in your dressing gown, however old she is. I will talk to her until you are ready. Go along.

(*She puts the letters in a pile on the desk ready for posting.*)

HUGO. Promise me you'll cut the cinema and come straight back here after dinner.

HILDE. That all depends. I'll think about it. Go along—hurry. (HUGO *exits. There is a knock at the door.* HILDE *goes to open it.* CARLOTTA GRAY *comes into the room. She is an attractive woman who at first glance would appear to be in her late forties or early fifties. She is heavily made up and her hair is expertly tinted. She is wearing expensive costume jewelry, perhaps a little too much of it. Her dinner dress is simple and well cut. She carries a fur wrap over her arm.* HILDE *holds out her hand*) I am

Hilde Latymer. (HILDE *and* CARLOTTA *shake hands.*) How do you do.

CARLOTTA. How do you do. I recognize your voice. You were so kind on the telephone.

HILDE. My husband is dressing; he won't be more than a few minutes. May I? (*She takes* CARLOTTA's *fur.*)

CARLOTTA. Thank you.

HILDE. Please be so kind as to sit down and take a cigarette if you should care to smoke. They are in that tortoiseshell box.

(HILDE *exits with the fur.* CARLOTTA *takes a cigarette from the box on the drinks table, lights it, and looks around the room.*)

HILDE (*returns*). Would you care for a drink?

CARLOTTA. Perhaps not quite yet. I would rather wait a little. How is he—Hugo? (*She corrects herself.*) Sir Hugo?

HILDE. He is almost completely well again. He has, of course, to take care not to overdo things and not to become agitated or unduly excited.

CARLOTTA. He has certainly had a wonderful career. It wouldn't be surprising if he sometimes found the burden of his eminence a trifle nerve-racking.

HILDE (*not quite pleased with this either*). Nerve-racking?

CARLOTTA. The continual demands made upon his time, the constant strain of having to live up to the self-created image he has implanted in the public mind. How fortunate he is to have you to protect him.

HILDE (*stiffly*). He isn't, I think, in quite such urgent need of protection as you imagine.

CARLOTTA. You've been married for twenty years, haven't you?

HILDE. Yes. He engaged me as his secretary in January nineteen forty-five and a few months later we were married.

CARLOTTA (*smiling*). I remember the headlines. It caused quite a sensation.

HILDE (*turning away*). Yes, I know it did. There was much foolishness written in the papers.

CARLOTTA. How does he feel about seeing me again, after so long?

HILDE. I cannot say. He is curious, naturally.

CARLOTTA. And you? What are your reactions to this—this rather peculiar situation?

HILDE. I have no feelings about it one way or the other.

CARLOTTA. I will accept the snub, but I am not entirely convinced by it.

HILDE. It was not intended to be a snub. You will please forgive me?

CARLOTTA. There is nothing whatever to forgive. I find it perfectly understandable that you should be suspicious of me. It is the duty of even the kindest protective dragons to be wary of strangers. It is sad that we did not meet in earlier, different circumstances. (*stubbing out her cigarette*) We might have been friends.

HILDE (*melting a trifle*). Thank you, Miss Gray.

(HUGO *enters from the bedroom. He is wearing an emerald green velvet smoking jacket over dark trousers. He has a cream shirt, a black tie, and his slippers are monogrammed in gold.* CARLOTTA *looks at him for a moment, then moves slowly toward him.*)

CARLOTTA. Hugo! What a strange moment this is, isn't it? I had planned so many things to say and now they've gone clean out of my head. Do we embrace?

HUGO (*with a slightly self-conscious smile*). Why not?

(*He kisses her formally on both cheeks.*)

CARLOTTA (*drawing away*). How well you look! Slim as ever and so distinguished. White hair definitely becomes you.

HUGO (*with splendid chivalry*). The years seem to have forgotten you, Carlotta.

CARLOTTA. Oh, no, my dear. It isn't that they've forgotten me; it's that I have remembered them and taken the right precautions.

HUGO. You and Hilde have already made friends, I see.

CARLOTTA (*glancing swiftly at* HILDE). Yes. As a matter of fact, we have. It's been puzzling me where I could have seen you before, but now I remember. There's a photograph of you in Hugo's autobiography. You are leaning against a sort of pillar and shading your eyes with your hand as though you were worried about the weather.

HUGO. The sort of pillar was one of the columns of the Parthenon.

HILDE. The light was very strong.

CARLOTTA. Alas. There is no photograph of me in the book. At least, only a verbal one. (*looking at* HUGO) The light was a little strong in that, too.

HUGO. Can I offer you a drink?

CARLOTTA. Oh, yes, by all means. I should love one.

(HUGO *starts towards the drinks table, but* HILDE *moves there instead.*)

HILDE. Whisky, brandy, gin, vodka?

CARLOTTA. Vodka, please, on the rocks. (HILDE *pours the drink. Turning to* HUGO) I expected you to look much older. But that's beside the point nowadays, isn't it? I mean—people hardly ever look their real age any more. Time is learning to accept a few defeats. It's rather fun frustrating the old monster.

HILDE. Your vodka, Miss Gray.

CARLOTTA. Thank you so much.

HILDE (*moving to the desk for the letters*). I am afraid I must leave you now. I have a dinner engagement.

CARLOTTA. Oh, how disappointing. I had hoped to get to know you better.

HILDE. We shall probably meet again.

CARLOTTA. Of course. We're almost bound to. I have moved into this hotel.

HILDE (*caught unawares*). Oh!

CARLOTTA (*putting out her hand*). Don't be alarmed. I shall only be here for a few days. I am having a series of injections at the Clinique and it's more convenient to be here than in Vevey.

HILDE (*shaking* CARLOTTA'*s hand*). Au revoir, then, Miss Gray.

CARLOTTA. À bientôt, Lady Latymer. (HILDE *shoots an equivocal look at* HUGO *and goes swiftly out of the room.* CARLOTTA *strolls over to the window.*) How lovely it is with the lights glittering in the distance. I went over to Evian the other evening on the little steamer and won nearly a thousand francs.

HUGO (*slightly shocked*). Can you afford to play so high?

CARLOTTA. Oh, yes. I have a certain amount put by. I also still get alimony from my last husband.

HUGO. Have you had many others?

CARLOTTA. Two before this one. They both died. One in an air crash and the other in the war.

HUGO. Did you love them?

CARLOTTA. Oh, yes. I shouldn't have married them if I hadn't.

HUGO. Have you any children?

CARLOTTA. Yes. I had a son by my second husband. He's twenty-four now and very attractive. You'd love him. Am I to drink alone?

HUGO. Too much alcohol is bad for me.

CARLOTTA. Too much alcohol is bad for everyone. Just pour yourself a teeny weeny one to keep me company.

HUGO (*moving to the drinks table and pouring himself a vodka*). Really, Carlotta, you're too absurd.

CARLOTTA (*sitting on the sofa*). She's nice, your wife. I like her.

HUGO. I'm so glad.

CARLOTTA. In spite of the fact that she doesn't care for me much. I don't think you quite did her justice in your book. But then, you weren't very nice about anybody in your book, were you?

HUGO. You were under no obligation to read it.

CARLOTTA. There was no warning on the cover. You take a fairly jaundiced view of your fellow creatures, don't you, on the whole?

HUGO. Perhaps. I prefer to see people as they are rather than as more sentimental minds would wish them to be. However, I am a commentator, not a moralist. (*He sits.*) I state no preferences.

CARLOTTA. Admirable!

HUGO. I would hate you to imagine that I am unaware of the mocking expression in your eye.

CARLOTTA (*with a smile*). Don't worry. I would never suspect you of missing a trick. Except perhaps the most important one of all.

HUGO. And what might that be?

CARLOTTA. The knack of discovering the best in people's characters instead of the worst.

HUGO. Without wishing to undermine your radiant self-confidence, I must break it to you that that has been said often before. Usually by ardent lady journalists.

CARLOTTA. One two—one two—and through and through—the vorpal blade went snicker-snack.

HUGO. My dear Carlotta. I had no idea you had such a thorough grounding in the classics. You were virtually illiterate when we first met.

CARLOTTA (*laughing*). It was you who set my stumbling feet upon the path of literature, Hugo. It was you who opened my eyes to many wonders.

HUGO. Don't talk such nonsense.

CARLOTTA. You worked assiduously on my virgin mind. And now I come to think of it, you didn't do so badly with my virgin body.

HUGO (*turning away*). Please don't talk like that, Carlotta. I find it distasteful.

CARLOTTA (*gently*). Try not to be so easily cross with me. It's almost too reminiscent. You always told me I was vulgar. According to your lights, that is. But your lights are so bright and highly placed that they bring out the bags under my eyes and the guttersnipe in my character. They always did and they always will. There's really nothing I can do about it, except perhaps go away. Would you like me to go away, now, this very minute? I promise I will if you truly want me to. You don't even have to answer. A valedictory nod will be enough.

HUGO. Of course I don't want you to go away. With all my faults, and in spite of my "jaundiced" view of my fellow creatures, I am seldom discourteous.

CARLOTTA. I would like it to be something warmer than your courtesy that wishes me to stay.

HUGO. I fear I can offer you little more at the moment, Carlotta, except perhaps curiosity, which is even less complimentary. I am what is called "set in my ways," which at my age is not entirely to be wondered at.

CARLOTTA. It implies resignation.

HUGO. Resignation has much to recommend it. Dignity, for one thing—(*looking at her*) a quality, alas, that is fast disappearing from our world.

CARLOTTA. I think I know what you're up to.

HUGO (*still secure on Olympus*). I am open to any suggestions.

CARLOTTA. You are remodeling your public image. The witty, cynical author of so many best sellers is making way for the Grand Old Man of Letters.

HUGO. Supposing your surmise to be accurate, do you consider such a transition reprehensible?

CARLOTTA. Of course not, if the process

is inevitable and necessary. But aren't you jumping the gun a little?

HUGO (*patiently*). No, Carlotta. I am not jumping the gun, or grasping Time by the forelock, or rushing my fences.

CARLOTTA. You must be prepared for a few clichés if you invite retired actresses to dinner.

HUGO (*ignoring her interruption*). I am merely accepting, without undue dismay, the fact of my own mortality. I am an old man and I at least have the sense to realize it.

CARLOTTA. Don't be waspish, my dear. Just as we are getting along so nicely. At least you can congratulate yourself on having had a fabulously successful career. How wonderful to have been able to entertain and amuse so many millions of people for such a long time. No wonder you got a knighthood.

HUGO. I begin to suspect that you are here as an enemy. I hoped for a friend.

CARLOTTA. Did you, Hugo? Did you really?

HUGO. Perhaps I was wrong?

CARLOTTA. Why did you write so unkindly about me in your memoirs?

HUGO. Aha! Now I'm beginning to understand.

CARLOTTA (*cheerfully*). Oh, no, you're not. You're merely jumping to conclusions. That was always one of your most glaring defects.

HUGO. Why can't we concentrate for a moment on some of my glaring assets? It might lighten the atmosphere.

CARLOTTA. We will, when you've answered my question.

HUGO. My autobiography was the assessment of the events and experiences of my life up to the date of writing it. I endeavored to be as objective and truthful as possible. If in the process I happened to hurt your feelings, I apologize. There was no unkindness intended. I merely wrote what I thought to be true.

CARLOTTA. Your book may have been an assessment of the *outward* experiences of your life, but I cannot feel that you were entirely honest about your inner ones.

HUGO. Why should I be? My inner feelings are my own affair.

CARLOTTA. In that case the book was sailing under false colors.

HUGO (*nastily*). And all this because I described you as a mediocre actress.

CARLOTTA (*serenely, rising*). You don't happen to have any parchment lying about, do you?

HUGO. Parchment?

CARLOTTA. Yes. When zoological experts extract the venom from snakes they force them to bite on parchment.

HUGO (*with a thin smile*). I accept your rebuke.

CARLOTTA. How generous of you.

HUGO. It's curious that you should still be able to arouse hostility in me.

CARLOTTA. Not really. As a matter of fact, it was always there, just below the surface.

(*She sits.*)

HUGO. When two young people are passionately in love a certain amount of bickering is inevitable. It even has charm, up to a point. But when the old indulge in it, it is merely tiresome.

CARLOTTA. Speak for yourself. You are the one who has decided to be old. I haven't yet; maybe I never shall. Some people remain young until they're ninety.

HUGO. You see no point in dignified withdrawal, in growing old gracefully?

CARLOTTA. There is little grace in growing old, Hugo. It's a dreary process that we all have to deal with in our different ways. To outside observers my way may seem stupid and garish and, later on perhaps, even grotesque. But the opinion of outside observers has never troubled me unduly. I am really only accountable to myself. I like slapping on the make-up and having my body massaged and my hair tinted. You've no idea how much I enjoy my long, complicated mornings. I admit I'm liable to cave in a bit by the late afternoon, but a short snooze fixes that and then I have all the fun of getting ready again for the evening.

HUGO. And does the evening really justify so much effort?

CARLOTTA. As a general rule, yes. I have many friends, some of them quite young. They seem to enjoy my company. I like to watch them dancing.

HUGO. I detest the young of today. They are grubby, undisciplined and ill-mannered. They also make far too much noise.

CARLOTTA. Youth always makes too much

noise. Many of the ones I know are better informed and more intelligent than we were. Also their world is more shrill than ours was. You really must make allowances.

HUGO. I'm too old to make allowances.

CARLOTTA. Oh, Hugo! You are positively stampeding toward the quiet grave, aren't you?

HUGO (*rising*). Shall we change the subject? Shall we try to discover some general theme on which we can both agree?

(*He goes to the drinks table for a cigarette.*)

CARLOTTA. Your indestructible elegance is flustering me and making me talk too much.

HUGO (*without malice*). You always talked too much, Carlotta.

(*He lights his cigarette.*)

CARLOTTA. Ah, yes. It's a compulsive disease. Useful at dinner parties, but fatal in the home.

HUGO. As this is neither, you can afford to relax.

CARLOTTA. There's so much I want to know about you, about what's happened to you during these long years, and here I am talking you into the ground. Will you forgive me?

HUGO. Why is there so much that you want to know about me? Why are you so suddenly curious about what has happened to me during these long years? Some motive must have impelled you to come here, some spark must have been struck. What is it that you want of me?

CARLOTTA. At the moment, dinner.

HUGO (*with irritation*). Carlotta!

CARLOTTA. I only had a salad for lunch and I'm famished.

HUGO (*resigned.*) Very well. Have it your own way. I am prepared to play any game you wish to play, up to a point. But do remember, won't you, that I tire easily. (*He rings the bell.*) The dinner is ordered, anyhow. I even remembered that you liked caviar.

CARLOTTA. That was sweet of you. The first time I ever tasted it was with you. You took me to Ciro's for supper after the show.

HUGO. Was I still wooing you then, or had I won?

CARLOTTA. You'd already won, more or less, but I think the caviar clinched it. I can remember what we had after the caviar, too.

HUGO. What was it?

CARLOTTA. A filet mignon with sauce Bearnaise and a green salad, and then— (*She thinks for a moment.*) then a chocolate soufflé.

HUGO. Did we by any chance have pink champagne as well?

CARLOTTA. Yes. I believe we did.

HUGO. You will see in a moment with what nostalgic charm history can repeat itself.

CARLOTTA. Oh, Hugo! I don't believe you're really old at all.

(*There is a knock on the door.*)

HUGO. *Avanti.*

(*FELIX enters with the dinner-trolley. HUGO stubs out his cigarette at the desk.*)

FELIX. Good evening, madame.

CARLOTTA. Good evening.

FELIX. The table in the usual place, sir?

HUGO. Yes, please, Felix.

FELIX (*seating CARLOTTA at the table*). Madame.

CARLOTTA. Thank you.

(*FELIX starts to open the vodka bottle.*)

HUGO (*stopping him*). You can leave the vodka. We will serve ourselves.

FELIX. *Bien, monsieur.*

(*He gives a quick glance at the table to see that everything is all right, then bows and exits.*)

CARLOTTA. How handsome he is, isn't he? Greek or Italian?

HUGO (*pouring out two vodkas*). Half Italian and half Austrian, I believe.

CARLOTTA. He has just a slight look of my first husband, Peter. Poor Peter. (*HUGO serves two helpings of caviar.*) His feet trod the world lightly and, alas, all too briefly.

HUGO. He was the one who was killed in an aeroplane?

CARLOTTA. Yes. He was studying to be a pilot in San Diego. I was trying out a new play in San Francisco. They had the sense not to tell me until after the matinée.

(*She butters some toast.*)

HUGO (*a little embarrassed by tragedy*). How dreadful for you.

CARLOTTA. Yes. It was my first real sorrow. We'd only been married for eighteen months, too soon for the gold to rub away.

Then a little while afterwards I had a miscarriage. That was my second real sorrow. It was quite a year. San Francisco is a divine city and I love it, but I always seem to have bad luck when I play there. In nineteen fifty-seven I lost my last remaining tooth in the Curran Theatre.

HUGO (*banging down his fork with a shudder of distaste.*) Carlotta!

CARLOTTA. It was a gallant old stump that held my lower plate together. I remember saying to my understudy one day: "Lily, when this is out, you're on!" And sure enough, a week later, it was and she was.

HUGO. I don't wish to sound fussy, Carlotta, but I really don't care to discuss false teeth during dinner.

(*He starts eating again.*)

CARLOTTA (*cheerfully*). Why ever not? That's when they're a force most to be reckoned with.

HUGO. Nevertheless, I should welcome a change of subject.

CARLOTTA. Dear Hugo, I am so sorry. I remember now, you always hated spades being called spades. What shall we talk about? Perhaps you would like some further vignettes from my rather ramshackle career.

HUGO. Provided that they are general rather than clinical.

CARLOTTA. Well, let me see now. My second husband, Vernon Ritchie, was my leading man in a ghastly play about the Deep South which ran for ages.

HUGO (*without much interest*). Was he a good actor?

CARLOTTA. No, terrible. But he made up for his performances on the stage by his performances in— (*She hesitates.*) in the boudoir. I didn't say bed in order to spare your feelings.

HUGO. Thank you. I appreciate your delicacy.

CARLOTTA. He was a sweet man and I was very fond of him. He was the father of my son David, and then, soon after Pearl Harbor, when the war came to us in America, he joined the Navy and was killed in the Pacific in nineteen forty-four.

HUGO. Was that another "great sorrow"?

CARLOTTA. No. Just a sadness.

HUGO. What decided you to make your life in America rather than in Europe, where you were born?

CARLOTTA. Because I happened to be there, I suppose. I went there originally on account of you. It was your play, if you remember, that first deposited me on the Great White Way, where it ran exactly ten days.

HUGO (*loftily*). That was no surprise to me. I never thought they'd understand it.

CARLOTTA. Do you know, Hugo? I have a terrible feeling that they did.

HUGO. Let me help you to some more caviar.

(*He serves two more helpings.*)

CARLOTTA. Thank you.

HUGO. And you never appeared in the London theatre since—since my first play?

CARLOTTA. Yes, twice.

HUGO. I don't remember hearing about it.

CARLOTTA. Why should you? As a matter of fact, on each occasion you were away, in the Far East, I believe, on one of your excavating expeditions.

HUGO. Excavating expeditions?

CARLOTTA. Yes, digging for treasure trove in the trusting minds of the innocent.

HUGO. You have a malicious tongue, Carlotta.

CARLOTTA. Yes, I really should learn to keep it between my false teeth. Let's stop talking about me now. Tell me about Hilde.

HUGO. I really see no reason to discuss Hilde with you.

CARLOTTA. Your loyal reticence does you credit, but it is a little overdone, almost defensive. After all, I'm not a newspaper reporter.

HUGO. You might easily be, judging by the tastelessness of some of your questions.

CARLOTTA. It's no use trying to intimidate me, Hugo, because it won't work. If you remember, it never did work. You have asked me questions about my husbands and I didn't snap your head off. Why shouldn't I ask you about your wife?

HUGO. The analogy is a trifle strained.

CARLOTTA. I truly want to know, not from idle curiosity, but because I liked her. She has wisdom and repose and her eyes are kind, a little sad perhaps, but kind. I suspect tragedy in her life.

HUGO. Well, you're right; there was tragedy in her life. She managed to escape from Nazi Germany in nineteen forty, soon after the "phoney" war began. She left behind the love of her life, a young poet called Gerhardt Hendl. He died two years later in a concentration camp. Now, are you satisfied?

CARLOTTA. Satisfied is not quite the word I would have chosen. But I am pleased that you told me.

(FELIX *enters with the serving trolley.*)

FELIX. Am I too early, sir?

HUGO. No, we've quite finished. You'd better open the wine.

FELIX. *Bien, monsieur.*

(*He opens the champagne and pours some for* HUGO *to taste.*)

CARLOTTA. Champagne! Oh, Hugo, I have a feeling it is going to be pink.

HUGO. It is.

CARLOTTA. How disarming of you to be so sentimental.

HUGO (*tasting the wine*). Excellent.

(FELIX *pours* CARLOTTA *some champagne. Then he fills* HUGO's *glass, and puts the bottle and bucket on the floor.*)

CARLOTTA. Do you remember the cottage at Taplow and driving down together on summer nights after the show?

HUGO. Yes. Yes, I remember.

CARLOTTA. And how cross you were that night at the Grafton Galleries, when I appeared in a red sequin frock that Baby Briant had lent me? You said I looked like a Shaftesbury Avenue tart.

(FELIX *clears two caviar plates, the toast and butter plates to the trolley.*)

HUGO. You did.

(FELIX *clears the vodka and caviar dish to the trolley, then the vodka glasses, and places the salad bowls on the table.*)

CARLOTTA. And the weekend we went to Paris and I got back to the theatre on the Monday night exactly seven minutes before curtain time? My understudy was all dressed and ready to go on. I often wonder why you didn't write any more plays. Your dialogue was so pointed and witty.

HUGO. You flatter me, Carlotta.

CARLOTTA. I've read everything you've ever written.

HUGO. You flatter me more than ever.

(FELIX *dishes up two steaks at the trolley.*)

CARLOTTA. I only said that I'd *read* everything you've ever written. I ventured no opinion, flattering or otherwise.

HUGO. The statement alone is flattering enough.

CARLOTTA. Yes. Yes, I expect it is. I suppose Ciro's isn't there anymore?

(FELIX *serves the filet mignons, etc.*)

HUGO. Lots of things aren't there anymore.

CARLOTTA. How right you are, Hugo. How right you are! (*She sighs.*) Oh dear!

HUGO. That was a pensive sigh.

(FELIX *puts the sauce Bearnaise on the table.*)

CARLOTTA. I've been in America too long. It's so lovely to see a steak that doesn't look like a bedroom slipper. . .

FELIX. *Tout va bien, monsieur?*

HUGO. *Oui, excellent. Merci, Felix.*

FELIX. *À votre service, monsieur.*

(FELIX *bows and exits with the trolley.*)

CARLOTTA. He really is most attractive, isn't he? Those glorious shoulders.

HUGO. I've never noticed them.

(*He begins to eat his steak.*)

CARLOTTA. They're probably padded, anyhow. Life can be dreadfully treacherous.

HUGO (*sitting back*). You really are extraordinary, Carlotta. You don't look a day over fifty.

CARLOTTA. I should hope not. After three cellular injections and two face-lifts.

HUGO (*pained*). Carlotta!

CARLOTTA. It's wonderful how they do it now. You can hardly see the scars at all.

HUGO. What on earth possessed you to tell me that?

CARLOTTA. Oh dear. Now I've shocked you again.

HUGO. Aesthetically—yes, you have.

CARLOTTA. I am sorry. Just as we were making such progress.

HUGO. As the object of such operations is, presumably, to create an illusion, why destroy the illusion by telling everybody about it?

CARLOTTA. Quite right, Hugo. As a matter of fact, you could do with a little snip yourself. Just under the chin.

HUGO. I wouldn't dream of it.

CARLOTTA. It would do wonders for your morale.

HUGO. My morale is perfectly satisfactory as it is, thank you.

CARLOTTA (*gaily, raising her glass to him*). Long may it remain so.

HUGO (*after a slight pause*). Why did you come here, Carlotta?

CARLOTTA. I told you. I'm having a course of injections at Professor Boromelli's clinique.

HUGO (*frowning*). Professor Boromelli!

CARLOTTA. Yes. Do you know him?

HUGO. I know of him.

CARLOTTA. You look disapproving.

HUGO. His reputation is rather dubious.

CARLOTTA. In what way?

HUGO. The general consensus of opinion is that he's a quack.

CARLOTTA. Quack or no quack, he's an old duck.

HUGO. Don't be foolish, Carlotta.

CARLOTTA. There's no need to stamp on my little joke as though it were a cockroach.

HUGO. Well? (*He smiles a faintly strained smile.*) I'm still waiting to hear the reason that induced you suddenly to make this, shall we say, rather tardy reappearance in my life? It must be a fairly strong one.

CARLOTTA. Not so very strong, really. It's only actually an irrelevant little favor. Irrelevant to you, I mean, but important to me.

HUGO. What is it?

CARLOTTA. Prepare yourself for a tiny shock.

HUGO (*with a note of impatience*). I'm quite prepared. Go on.

CARLOTTA. I, too, have written an autobiography.

HUGO (*raising his eyebrows*). Have you? How interesting.

CARLOTTA. There's a distinct chill in your voice.

HUGO. I'm sorry. I was unaware of it.

CARLOTTA. It is to be published in the autumn.

HUGO. Congratulations. Who by?

CARLOTTA. Doubleday in New York and Heinemann in London.

HUGO (*concealing surprise*). Excellent. (*He drinks.*)

CARLOTTA (*with a trace of irony*). I am so glad you approve.

HUGO. And have you written it all yourself? Or have you employed what I believe is described as a "ghost writer"?

CARLOTTA. No, Hugo. I have written every word of it myself.

HUGO. Well done.

CARLOTTA. On an electric typewriter. You really should try one. It's a godsend.

HUGO. I have no need of it. Hilde does my typing for me.

CARLOTTA. Of course, yes—I'd forgotten. Then you can give her one for a birthday present.

HUGO (*after a slight pause*). I suppose you want me to write an introductory preface.

CARLOTTA. No. I've already done that myself.

HUGO (*with a tinge of irritation*). What is it, then? What is it you want of me?

CARLOTTA. Permission to publish your letters.

HUGO (*startled*). Letters! What letters?

CARLOTTA. The letters you wrote to me when we were lovers. I've kept them all.

HUGO. Whatever letters I wrote to you at that time were private. They concerned no one but you and me.

CARLOTTA. I agree. But that was a long time ago. Before we'd either of us become celebrated enough to write our memoirs.

HUGO. I cannot feel that you, Carlotta, have even yet achieved that particular distinction.

CARLOTTA (*unruffled*). Doubleday and Heinemann do.

HUGO (*sitting back*). I believe that some years ago Mrs. Patrick Campbell made a similar request to Mr. George Bernard Shaw, and his reply was: "Certainly not. I have no intention of playing the horse to your Lady Godiva."

CARLOTTA (*stopping eating*). How unkind.

HUGO. It would ill become me to attempt to improve on Mr. George Bernard Shaw.

CARLOTTA (*helping herself to some more salad*). You mean you refuse?

HUGO. Certainly. I most emphatically refuse.

CARLOTTA. I thought you would.

HUGO. In that case surely it was waste of time to take the trouble to ask me?

CARLOTTA. I just took a chance. After all, life can be full of surprises sometimes, can't it?

HUGO. If your forthcoming autobiography is to be peppered with that sort of bromide, it cannot fail to achieve the bestseller list.

CARLOTTA. You can turn nasty quickly, can't you? You were quite cozy and relaxed a moment ago.

HUGO. I am completely horrified by your suggestion. It's in the worst possible taste.

(FELIX *enters with the trolley, on which is a chocolate soufflé.*)

CARLOTTA. Perfect timing, Felix. I congratulate you.

FELIX. Thank you, madame.

(*He clears the two steak plates to the trolley, then the salad dishes, side plates, cruet and sauce boat.*)

CARLOTTA (*after a longish pause*). The lake is like glass. There'll be a moon presently.

HUGO. How clever of you to know.

CARLOTTA. There was a moon last night. I just put two and two together. (*To* FELIX, *as he serves the soufflé*) Sir Hugo tells me that you are half Austrian and half Italian, Felix.

FELIX. That is correct, madame.

CARLOTTA. Which half do you like best?

HUGO. Please, Carlotta . . .

FELIX. I find the two perfectly satisfactory, madame. (*He smiles.*)

CARLOTTA. I expect both the waltz and the tarantella come quite naturally to you.

HUGO (*testily*). That will be all for the moment, Felix. Please bring the coffee immediately.

FELIX. *Subito, signore!*

(*He bows, smiles at* CARLOTTA, *and exits with the trolley.*)

CARLOTTA. Chocolate soufflé!

HUGO. I hate familiarity with servants.

CARLOTTA. Oh, eat up your soufflé for God's sake and stop being so disagreeable.

HUGO (*outraged*). How dare you speak to me like that!

CARLOTTA. Dare? Really, Hugo. What have I to fear from you!

(*She continues eating.*)

HUGO. I consider your rudeness insufferable.

CARLOTTA. And I consider your pomposity insufferable.

HUGO (*icily*). I should like to remind you that you are my guest.

CARLOTTA. Of course I am. Don't be so silly.

HUGO. And as such I have the right to demand from you at least a semblance of good manners.

CARLOTTA. "Semblance of good manners"! Talk about clichés. That's a clanger if ever I heard one.

HUGO (*quivering with rage*). Once and for all, Carlotta . . .

CARLOTTA. For heaven's sake, calm down. Your wife told me earlier on that it was bad for you to overexcite yourself. You'll have a fit in a minute if you don't stop gibbering.

HUGO (*beside himself, shouting*). I am not gibbering! (*He puts his serviette on the table and rises to the window. There is silence for a moment.* CARLOTTA *continues to eat her soufflé.* HUGO *moves to the desk. With superb control.*) I think, Carlotta, that as we really haven't very much more to say to each other it would be considerate of you to leave as soon as you've finished eating. I am sorry if I appear to be discourteous, but after all it was you who forced us both into this—this rather unprofitable meeting. I have done my best to receive you kindly and make the evening a pleasant one. That I have failed is only too obvious. I am sorry also that I was unable to accede to your request. I am sure, after you have given yourself time to think it over, that you will realize how impertinent it was.

CARLOTTA. Why impertinent?

HUGO. Not having read your book, I have naturally no way of judging whether it is good, bad or indifferent. I am perfectly aware, however, that, whatever its merits, the inclusion of private letters from a man in my position would enhance its value considerably. The impertinence, I think, lies in your assuming for a moment that I should grant you permission to publish them. We met and parted many years ago. Since then we have neither of us communicated with each other. You have pursued your career, I have pursued mine. Mine, if I may say so without undue arrogance, has been eminently successful. Yours, perhaps less so. Doesn't it strike *you* as impertinent that, after so long a silence, you should suddenly ask me to provide you with my name as a stepping-stone?

CARLOTTA. The letters really are very good, Hugo. It's disappointing that you won't allow me to use them. They *are* love letters, of course, up to a point, and brilliantly written. The more ardent passages are exquisitely phrased, although they do give the impression that they were commissioned by your head rather than dictated by your heart.

HUGO. I have no wish to discuss the matter any further.

CARLOTTA. It seems a pity that posterity should be deprived of such an illuminating example of your earlier work

HUGO. I really am very tired, Carlotta. I feel that my age entitles me to ask you to leave me alone now. Perhaps we may meet and talk again within the next few days.

CARLOTTA. My wrap is in your bedroom. Hilde put it there. May I fetch it?

HUGO. By all means.

(CARLOTTA *goes into the bedroom.* HUGO *lights a cigarette and immediately stubs it out again. He is obviously seething with irritation. He opens the table drawer, takes two tablets out of a bottle and has a drink of water.* CARLOTTA *returns.*)

CARLOTTA. Good night, Hugo. I am sorry the evening has ended so—so uncozily.

HUGO. So am I, Carlotta. So am I

CARLOTTA (*turning, on her way to the door*). To revert for a moment to the unfortunate subject of the letters. You may have them if you like. They are of no further use to me.

HUGO. That is most generous of you.

CARLOTTA. I'm afraid I can't let you have the others, though. I would be betraying a sacred promise.

HUGO. Others? What others?

CARLOTTA. Your letters to Perry.

HUGO (*visibly shaken*). My letters to Perry! What do you mean?

CARLOTTA. Perry Sheldon. I happened to be with him when he died.

HUGO. What do you know about Perry Sheldon?

CARLOTTA. Among other things that he was the only true love of your life. Good night, Hugo. Sleep well.

(CARLOTTA *turns to exit as—*)

THE CURTAIN FALLS

ACT TWO

SCENE. *The same. A few minutes later. When the curtain rises,* HUGO *is dis-* covered sitting, with his head in his hand. *After a moment he rises, goes to the drinks table and pours himself a brandy which he drinks in one gulp. Then he moves below the sofa, crosses back to the desk, sits and picks up the telephone.*

HUGO. 'Allo—Gaston? *Je veux parler avec Madame Gray, Madame Carlotta Gray . . . Oui, elle est arrivée cet après-midi. . . Merci, j'attendrai.* (*He waits.*) Hallo, Carlotta? . . . Yes, it's I, Hugo. Don't pretend to be surprised. . . . Quite a lot is the matter and you know it. Will you please come back. I must talk to you. . . . . Please, Carlotta. . . . No, you know perfectly well it can't wait until tomorrow. You've won your point—for God's sake have the grace not to exult too much. Please come. . . . Yes, now—immediately. . . . Very well. Thank you Carlotta.

(*He hangs up the telephone and sits for a moment with his head buried in his hands. Then he rises, goes to the drinks table and lights a cigarette. He returns to the desk and sits on it, watching the doors. There is little energy in his movements. He is a worried, unhappy man. Presently there is a perfunctory knock on the door and* CARLOTTA *enters.* HUGO *rises. They stand looking at each other in silence for a moment.*)

CARLOTTA (*with a ghost of a smile*). I'm sorry, Hugo. That was an unkind trick. But you had it coming to you.

HUGO. I would like, if you don't mind, a little further explanation of what you said when you left me a few minutes ago.

CARLOTTA. Shall we sit down? Oh, by the way, I met that charming Felix in the corridor and ordered another bottle of champagne. I do hope you don't mind. I thought we might need it.

HUGO. I see you have decided to set the mood in a light vein.

CARLOTTA. You are the challenged. You may have the choice of weapons. We can send the champagne away again if you like.

(HUGO *moves to the drinks table. There is a knock on the door.*)

HUGO. *Avanti.*

(FELIX *enters with champagne in a bucket and two glasses on a tray.*)

FELIX. The champagne, monsieur.

HUGO. Thank you, Felix. You may put it

on the table.

(FELIX *puts the champagne on the table*).

FELIX. Would you wish me to open it?

CARLOTTA. Please do, Felix. I am sure that neither Sir Hugo nor I could manage it as efficiently as you.

FELIX. *Certainement, madame.*

(*He opens the champagne and pours two glasses which he places on a small salver.*)

CARLOTTA. I was right about the moon. Look, Hugo. It's making a path right across the lake. How sad for you, Felix, to have to rush about serving people in this stuffy hotel when you might be dancing your heart away in one of those little open-air cafés on the shore.

FELIX. There is a time for everything, madame.

CARLOTTA. But not for everybody, Felix. Not for everybody.

FELIX (*bringing* CARLOTTA *her glass*). Madame.

CARLOTTA (*taking it*). Thank you.

FELIX (*taking the other glass to* HUGO). Monsieur.

HUGO. Put it down, please. I will drink it later.

(FELIX *replaces the glass and salver on the tray.*)

FELIX. That will be all, monsieur?

HUGO (*irritably*). Yes, yes—that will be all. Good night.

FELIX (*to* CARLOTTA). I have put a bottle of Evian in your room, madame, as you requested.

CARLOTTA. Thank you, Felix. Good night.

FELIX. Good night, madame.

(*He bows and exits.*)

CARLOTTA. Well, I must say it's pleasant to have *one* request granted, even if it's only a bottle of Evian.

HUGO. I am finding the flippancy of your manner extremely trying.

CARLOTTA. Now that I come to think of it, you always did. In any case, this is not a tragic situation, Hugo. All the tragedy was drained out of it when Perry died. There's only comedy left now. Rather bitter comedy, I admit, but not entirely unenjoyable.

HUGO. You must forgive my lack of humor.

CARLOTTA. You never had much anyhow. Wit, yes, a brilliant talent for the sharp riposte, the swift, malicious phrase. But true humor lies in the capacity to laugh at oneself. That you could never do.

HUGO. I fear it is a little too late for me to change.

CARLOTTA. Ah, yes. Much too late. It's all too late now. That's the pity of it. I should have talked to you before. Who knows? I might have been able to do a little good.

HUGO. If you had, would blackmail have so strongly colored your missionary zeal?

CARLOTTA. Blackmail? Really, Hugo! I had no idea you had such a highly developed sense of melodrama.

HUGO. You said you were with Perry Sheldon when he died. Is that true?

CARLOTTA. Yes. (*She takes a sip of champagne.*)

HUGO. And you have in your possession letters written by me to him?

CARLOTTA. Yes. Love letters, most of them. They are less meticulously lyrical than the ones you wrote to me, but there is more genuine feeling in them. They were written in your earlier years, remember, before your mind had been corrupted by fame and your heart by caution. The last ones were written in the last years of his life. There are three of them. All refusals to help him when he was in desperate straits. They also are fascinating in their way, masterpieces of veiled invective. Pure gold for your future biographer.

HUGO (*controlling a quiver in his voice*). Did you steal these letters?

CARLOTTA. No, Hugo. I didn't steal them. He gave them to me three days before he died.

HUGO. What do you propose to do with them?

CARLOTTA. I haven't quite decided yet. I made him a promise.

HUGO. What sort of promise?

CARLOTTA. I promised him that if he gave them to me I would keep them safe until the time came when they could be used to the best advantage.

HUGO. Used? To the best advantage! Used in what way?

CARLOTTA. By a suitable biographer.

HUGO. Are you intending to be that biographer?

CARLOTTA. Oh, no. I am not experienced enough. It would require someone more detached and objective than I am to write an accurate and unbiased account of you. My personal feelings would be involved.

HUGO. Your personal feelings would still be involved after more than half a lifetime?

CARLOTTA. Memory is curiously implacable. It can forget joy, but it seldom forgets humiliation.

HUGO. Your emotional tenacity is remarkable.

CARLOTTA. There is no longer any emotion in my feelings for you, Hugo.

HUGO. Wouldn't you consider revenge an emotion?

CARLOTTA (*with a little laugh*). Revenge! You are jumping to the wrong conclusions again.

HUGO. I wouldn't expect you to admit it.

CARLOTTA. You're wrong. I'd admit it like a shot if it were true, but it isn't. As a matter of fact, my motives in all this are altruistic rather than vindictive. Suddenly, in my raddled old age I have seen the light. I find myself possessed with a desire to right wrongs, to see justice done, to snatch a brand from the burning.

HUGO. I am not impressed

CARLOTTA. Never mind. (*fetching her glass from the table.*) The night is young.

HUGO. To revert to the subject of my, as yet unnamed, biographer. Have you found one?

CARLOTTA. Of course.

HUGO (*still with admirable calm*). May I ask his name?

CARLOTTA. Certainly. His name is Justin Chandler. He used to be a professor at Harvard. I met him first when I was playing *Hedda Gabler* in Boston.

HUGO (*fury breaking through*). I don't give a damn what you were playing in Boston.

CARLOTTA. I know you don't, but it was *Hedda Gabler*.

HUGO. And is it your intention to hand over to this—this Justin Chandler private letters of mine which were written to somebody else over thirty years ago?

CARLOTTA. You must realize that they are exceedingly valuable documents. Your fame has made them so. Not only financially valuable, although I have no doubt that they'd fetch quite a fancy price at a public auction, but their importance to

anyone who wishes to make an analytical survey of your life and career is too obvious to be ignored. Owing to your own ceaseless vigilance your "bubble reputation" must be almost as solid as a football by now. You mustn't be surprised that certain people should wish to kick it about a bit.

HUGO. How much do you want?

CARLOTTA. Don't be *silly,* Hugo. Give me a little more champagne. (*She hands him her glass and sits.* HUGO *refills it.*) I suggest that you'd better have some, too, while you're at it. It might help clear your mind.

HUGO (*taking* CARLOTTA *her glass*). I have no alternative but to follow your lead, Carlotta. If your object in all this is to humiliate and embarrass me, you have so clearly succeeded that no further comment is necessary. What is the next move?

CARLOTTA (*taking her glass*). Thank you.

HUGO (*with an effort*). The knowledge that my letters to Perry Sheldon are still in existence has naturally come as a considerable shock to me. It would be foolish to deny it.

CARLOTTA (*sipping her champagne*). Also unconvincing.

HUGO. I presume you have taken the trouble to acquaint yourself with the legal aspects of the situation?

CARLOTTA. The legal aspects of the situation are fairly simple. Any letter from the moment it is posted, automatically becomes the property of the recipient. In this case Perry was the recipient. He made the letters over to me in a written statement which was witnessed by a public notary. They now legally belong to me and I am at liberty to do what I like with them.

HUGO. I fear you have been misinformed. The letters may indeed be your property, but according to law they may not be published without my permission or, when I die, the permission of my estate.

CARLOTTA. I am sure you are right, but so far there has been no question of them being published. The important fact is that they exist, and for so long as they continue to exist they will remain a potential menace to your carefully sculptured reputation.

HUGO. Where are the letters?

CARLOTTA. I have them with me.

HUGO. You have not yet told me what

you propose to do with them.

CARLOTTA. Because I have not yet decided. There is still what you describe as my "missionary zeal" to be taken into account.

HUGO. I don't know what you're talking about.

CARLOTTA. All in good time, Hugo. All in good time.

HUGO (*losing his temper*). This is intolerable!

CARLOTTA. Keep calm.

HUGO. I have been calm long enough. I am sick to death of this interminable witless skirmishing. Come to the point, if there is a point beyond your feline compulsion to torment me and insult me. The implications behind all the highfalutin rubbish you have been talking have not been lost on me. The veiled threat is perfectly clear.

CARLOTTA. What veiled threat?

HUGO. The threat to expose to the world the fact that I have had, in the past, homosexual tendencies.

CARLOTTA (*calmly*). Tendencies in the past! What nonsense! You've been a homosexual all your life and you know it.

HUGO (*shouting*). That is not true!

CARLOTTA. Don't shout. It's waste of adrenalin. You've no idea what it does to the inside of your stomach when you work yourself into a state like that. If you won't drink champagne, for God's sake have a little brandy and pull yourself together. (*She rises to the drinks table.*) Here, I'll get you some.

(*She pours one brandy.*)

HUGO (*near hysteria*). I don't care what you do—do you hear me? You can publish whatever letters you like, and be damned to you!

CARLOTTA (*holding out the glass*). Here, Hugo. Drink this and stop being hysterical.

HUGO (*knocking the glass out of her hand*). Go away—go away from me—leave me alone!

(*He sinks into his chair and puts his hand over his face.*)

CARLOTTA. There. Now look what you've done! Brandy stains all over that nice carpet. For shame, Hugo! You're behaving like a petulant little boy at a children's party.

HUGO. I am an old man, Carlotta, and, as I already told you, I have recently been ill, very ill. I have neither the strength nor the will to continue this—this embittered conflict that you have forced upon me. I am too tired.

CARLOTTA. If I poured you out another glass of brandy, would you again dash it to the ground, or would you drink it calmly and sensibly?

HUGO. I am not supposed to drink brandy. It is bad for my heart.

CARLOTTA (*going to the drinks table and pouring out another glass of brandy*). I feel on this particular occasion a little licence might be permitted. (*Taking it to him*) Here, I think that your heart, what there is of it, will survive—here!

HUGO (*taking the glass and looking at her*). Why do you hate me so? Is it because you once loved me?

CARLOTTA. You've got it all wrong, Hugo. I don't hate you, and loving you I only dimly remember.

HUGO. You underrate my intelligence. (*He drinks.*)

CARLOTTA. Oh, no. I may have overrated your stamina but I would never underrate your intelligence. Your intelligence is of a very high order indeed, up to a certain point. It is what happens over and above that point that arouses my curiosity.

HUGO. I don't know what you're talking about.

CARLOTTA. You flew into a fine theatrical passion just now when I said you had been homosexual all your life. (*Turning to him*) Did you consider that an insult?

HUGO. Wasn't it intended to be?

CARLOTTA. Of course not. We are living in the nineteen-sixties, not the eighteen-nineties.

HUGO (*nastily*). This sophisticated tolerance hardly fits in with the sneer in your voice when you accused me of it.

CARLOTTA. You are oversensitive. If there had been a sneer in my voice, which there wasn't, it would not have been a sneer at the fact, but at your lifelong repudiation of it. In any case, I did not accuse you of it, for the simple reason that I do not consider it a crime. What I am accusing you of is something far worse than that. Complacent cruelty and moral cowardice.

HUGO. On what evidence?

CARLOTTA. On the evidence of every book you've written and the dismal record of your personal relationships.

HUGO. You know nothing of my personal relationships. We are strangers.

CARLOTTA. On the contrary, I know a great deal about them. Your ivory tower is not nearly so sacrosanct as you imagine it to be. You cannot be half so naïve as to imagine that a man of your sustained eminence could ever be entirely immune from the breath of scandal, however gingerly you may have trodden your secret paths.

HUGO (*putting his glass down*). I am not interested in the scruffy surmises of the mediocre.

CARLOTTA. By no means all the people I discussed you with were mediocre; and by no means all the things I heard were surmises.

HUGO. Nor am I interested in your opinion nor anyone else's opinion of my character. What I am interested in is the motive that impelled you to come here.

CARLOTTA. I find it awfully difficult to explain even to myself. I suppose basically that it was irritation more than anything else.

HUGO (*outraged*). Irritation!

CARLOTTA. And don't minimize the force of that apparently trivial little emotion. It can be more powerful than anger and more devastating than hatred. It can wear away rocks and stones and human tissues. It can also play merry hell with the kindliest of dispositions. I am not by nature a vindictive character, but you have irritated me for years, and I am determined to put an end to it before my whole system is poisoned.

HUGO (*with decision*). How much do you want for those letters?

CARLOTTA. I really am sorry for you, Hugo.

HUGO. That is entirely irrelevant.

CARLOTTA. It must be truly horrible to have gone through life holding your fellow creatures in such bitter contempt.

HUGO. Your present behavior is hardly calculated to improve my outlook.

CARLOTTA. Bravo!

HUGO. Please stop prevaricating and name your price.

CARLOTTA. The letters are not for sale.

HUGO. I am beginning to think you must be a little unbalanced.

CARLOTTA. I see your point. That would explain away a lot of things, wouldn't it? Unfortunately, it isn't true.

HUGO. We seem to have reached an impasse.

CARLOTTA. Yes, we do rather, don't we? (*There is a pause.* CARLOTTA *takes her champagne glass from the table, refills it, and sits on the arm of the sofa. She sips her drink and watches him. Her face is quite expressionless.*)

HUGO (*meeting her eye*). What did Perry die of?

CARLOTTA. Leukemia. He suffered no pain.

HUGO. Oh, I'm glad.

CARLOTTA. He had had a very bad attack of hepatitis the year before.

HUGO. Brought on by drink?

CARLOTTA. Yes. Yes, I think so. But he didn't drink at all during the last months of his life.

HUGO. How old was he? When he died, I mean?

CARLOTTA. Late fifties, early sixties, I'm not quite sure. But he looked much older than that.

HUGO. Yes—yes—I expect he did.

CARLOTTA. He was painfully thin and he had become rather deaf. I bought him a hearing aid.

HUGO. That was generous of you.

CARLOTTA. It was comparatively inexpensive.

HUGO. When did he die?

CARLOTTA. About two years ago.

HUGO. I see.

CARLOTTA. The only vitality he had left was in his eyes, they still retained a glimmer of hope.

HUGO. How do you expect me to react to all this, Carlotta?

CARLOTTA. Exactly as you are reacting. For the moment you are manufacturing a little retrospective regret. It may even be quite genuine, but it isn't enough and it won't last. One swallow doesn't make a summer. You didn't even know that he had died.

HUGO. How could I have known? Two years ago I was a long way away, in West Africa, as a matter of fact. I returned to Rome in the spring. We were living in Rome at the time.

CARLOTTA. Yes. It was from Rome that you wrote your last three cruel letters to him.

HUGO (*quietly*). I want those letters back, Carlotta.

CARLOTTA. Just those three? Or the earlier ones as well?

HUGO. All of them, of course. You must see how important this is to me.

CARLOTTA. Certainly I do.

HUGO. Was it true, what you told me a while ago about this ex-Harvard professor wishing to write about me?

CARLOTTA. Justin Chandler. Yes—perfectly true.

HUGO (*with an effort*). I have no alternative but to throw myself on your mercy, Carlotta.

CARLOTTA. No. You haven't really, have you? I thought we should arrive at this point sooner or later.

HUGO (*after a pause*). Well?

CARLOTTA (*rising*). If you had the choice of having the earlier letters back or the later ones, which would you choose?

HUGO (*a little too quickly*). The earlier ones.

CARLOTTA. Yes. I was afraid you'd say that.

HUGO. You can also, I should imagine, understand my reasons.

CARLOTTA. Yes. I understand your reasons perfectly. You would prefer to be regarded as cynical, mean and unforgiving, rather than as a vulnerable human being, capable of tenderness.

HUGO. In these particular circumstances, yes.

CARLOTTA. Why?

HUGO. My private inclinations are not the concern of the reading public. I have no urge to martyr my reputation for the sake of self-indulgent exhibitionism.

CARLOTTA. Even that might be better than vitiating your considerable talent by dishonesty.

HUGO. Dishonesty? In what way have I been dishonest?

CARLOTTA. Subtly in all your novels and stories, but quite obviously in your autobiography.

HUGO. I have already explained to you that my autobiography was an objective survey of the events and experiences of my life in so far as they affected my career.

It was never intended to be an uninhibited exposé of my sexual adventures.

CARLOTTA. In that case why the constant implications of heterosexual ardor? Why those self-conscious, almost lascivious references to laughing-eyed damsels with scarlet lips and pointed breasts? And above all, why that contemptuous betrayal of Perry Sheldon?

HUGO (*with anger*). I forbid you to say any more. There was no betrayal.

CARLOTTA (*relentlessly*). He loved you, looked after you, and waited on you hand and foot. For years he traveled the wide world with you. And yet in your book you dismiss him in a few lines as an "adequate secretary."

HUGO (*losing his temper again*). My relationship with Perry Sheldon is none of your god-damned business!

CARLOTTA. Considering that I have in my possession a bundle of your highly compromising letters to him, that remark was plain silly.

HUGO (*with forced calm*). Once and for all, Carlotta, will you either sell me or give me those letters?

CARLOTTA. No. Not yet—perhaps never.

HUGO. Are you planning to continue this venomous cat-and-mouse procedure indefinitely?

CARLOTTA. No. Not indefinitely. Just until something happens.

HUGO. What in God's name do you mean by that! What *could* happen?

CARLOTTA. Unconditional surrender.

HUGO. Do you wish me to plead with you? To fall abjectly at your feet and weep for mercy? Would that assuage your female vanity?

CARLOTTA. No. That would get you nowhere at all.

HUGO. What, then? What do you want of me?

CARLOTTA. Oh, I don't know. A moment of truth, perhaps. A sudden dazzling flash of self-revelation. Even an act of contrition.

HUGO. That, if I may say so, is pretentious twaddle.

(*He goes to the drinks table and tops up his brandy.*)

CARLOTTA. The time has come for me to roll up some heavier ammunition.

HUGO (*evenly*). By all means. I find that I have got my second wind. Fire away.

CARLOTTA (*rising*). Has it ever occurred to you that you were indirectly responsible for Perry's death?

HUGO. If I had murdered him with my bare hands, it would still have nothing to do with you.

CARLOTTA (*ignoring this*). You discarded him ruthlessly, without a shred of gratitude or compassion. Having corrupted his character, destroyed his ambition and deprived him of hope. You wrote him off like a bad debt.

HUGO. He was a bad debt. He became an alcoholic. And alcoholics bore me.

CARLOTTA. And whose fault was it that he became an alcoholic?

HUGO. His own.

CARLOTTA. Do you really think you can shrug off the responsibility as casually as that?

HUGO. You are implying that my tyranny drove him to it.

CARLOTTA. Not your tyranny. Your indifference.

HUGO. Rubbish. Perry took to the bottle because he liked it and because he was a weak and feckless character.

CARLOTTA. And yet you loved him. You loved him for quite a long while. Your letters prove it.

HUGO. I should have thought that even your cheap magazine mentality would have learnt by now that it is seldom with people's characters that one falls in love.

CARLOTTA. Granted. But when the first blind rapture begins to fade, most people have the instinctive grace to accept the situation without rancor; to make adjustments, to settle for a gentler climate.

HUGO. I seem to hear the sound of violins.

CARLOTTA. If they didn't, very few human relationships based initially on physical attraction would survive.

HUGO. I must frankly confess, Carlotta, that I am beginning to find your recurrent lapses into tabloid philosophy inexpressibly tedious. You spoke just now, rather grandiloquently I thought, of "rolling up heavier ammunition." Is this it? Am I expected to stagger to my knees, bloody and defeated, under a hail of simpering platitudes? If, for some reason best known to yourself, you feel it your bounden duty to chastise me, to destroy my reputation, to batter me to the dust and to lay bare the quivering secrets of my evil soul, I have no means of preventing you. So get on with it. Attack as much as you like. But for Christ's sake don't bore me. It is long past my bedtime.

CARLOTTA. Are you throwing me out again?

HUGO. Yes I am. The "impasse" remains.

CARLOTTA (*sitting in the chair*). You're bluffing.

HUGO. So are you.

CARLOTTA. I have no need. I hold the cards.

HUGO. For one thing I don't believe that this Justin Chandler exists.

CARLOTTA. He exists all right. But even in fact, a "regular guy."

HUGO. You must forgive me if I seem obtuse, but if you have no intention of selling me the letters or giving them to me, what do you hope to gain and why are you here? There must be something that impelled you, out of the blue, to launch this gratuitous attack upon my peace of mind. Is it perhaps a long-cherished, stale revenge for some imagined wrong I did you in the past?

CARLOTTA. No. It isn't that. Although the wrong you did me in the past was not imagined.

HUGO. Through your relationship with me you acquired a leading part which up to then nobody else had offered you, reasonably good press notices and, for the time being at any rate, an assured position in the theatre. You were praised and photographed and paid attention to for the first time in your life, and you finally went off to the United States in a blaze of gratifying publicity. You cannot blame me for the fact that from then on you did not quite achieve the dazzling prospects that had been predicted for you.

CARLOTTA. I did well enough. I have no complaints. What I am interested in is what you got out of the deal.

HUGO (*witheringly*). In the first place I didn't regard our affair as a "deal."

CARLOTTA. Very well, I'll put it more delicately. Let's say a profitable experiment.

HUGO. In what way profitable?

CARLOTTA. That old bubble reputation again.

HUGO. What are you implying by that?

CARLOTTA. I'm not implying anything. Just recapitulating a few facts.

HUGO (*with irritation*). Unfortunately I seem to have no way of stopping you.

CARLOTTA. I was twenty-one, and, curiously enough, considering that I had been involved with the theatre since I was fourteen, I was a virgin.

HUGO. Are you now casting me in the role of the vile seducer?

CARLOTTA. Oh, not at all. We were both virgins. That is, from the heterosexual point of view.

(*She pauses.*)

HUGO. Very well. I've registered that. Go on.

CARLOTTA. I didn't realize it at the time, of course. You were my first love. I loved you deeply and passionately. I had your photograph on the table by my bed. I used to kiss it every night before I turned out the light. Sometimes I even went to sleep with it under my pillow.

HUGO. I hope you had the sense to take it out of its frame.

CARLOTTA. We had been together for well over a year before I began to realize my exact status in the cautious pattern of your life.

HUGO (*turning away*). Really, Carlotta, do you consider it entirely relevant to continue this musty, ancient soul-searching?

CARLOTTA. Yes, I do. I most emphatically do. (*Rising.*) It was your dishonesty and lack of moral courage in those far-off days that set you on the wrong road for the rest of your life.

HUGO. It is hardly for you to decide whether the course of my life has been wrong or right.

CARLOTTA. You might have been a great writer instead of merely a successful one, and you might also have been a far happier man.

HUGO. And what bearing has all this on that dreadful wound I inflicted on your feminine vanity in the nineteen-twenties?

CARLOTTA. Because you have consistently, through all your glittering years, behaved with the same callous cruelty to everyone who has been foolish enough to put their trust in your heart.

HUGO (*near violence again*). In what way was I so callous and cruel to you?

CARLOTTA. You used me. You used me

and betrayed me as you've always used and betrayed every human being who has ever shown you the slightest sign of true affection.

HUGO. In what way did I use you any more than you used me?

CARLOTTA. You waved me like a flag to prove a fallacy.

HUGO. What fallacy?

CARLOTTA. That you were normal, that your morals were orderly, that you were, in fact, a "regular guy."

HUGO. Was that so unpardonable? I was young, ambitious and already almost a public figure. Was it so base of me to try to show to the world that I was capable of playing the game according to the rules?

CARLOTTA. It wasn't your deception of the world that I found so unpardonable; it was your betrayal of me, and all the love and respect and admiration I felt for you. If you had had the courage to trust me, to let me share your uneasy secret, not in the first year perhaps, but later on, when things were becoming strained and difficult between us, if then you had told me the truth, I would very possibly have been your loyal and devoted friend until this very minute. As it was you let me gradually, bit by bit, discover what my instincts had already half-guessed. You elbowed me out of your life vulgarly and without grace, Hugo, and I can even now remember the relief in your voice when you said good-bye and packed me off to America.

HUGO. I didn't pack you off to America. You went with an excellent contract in a first class stateroom.

CARLOTTA (*with a sigh*). I see clearly that I am wasting my time.

HUGO. You most certainly are. And mine. The only interesting fact that has emerged from your impassioned tirades this evening is that, in spite of a full life, three husbands, and an excessive amount of plastic surgery, you have managed to keep this ancient wound so freshly bleeding. You must be suffering from a sort of emotional hemophilia.

CARLOTTA. I salute you. You're an unregenerate old bitch!

(HILDE *enters quietly. She is still wearing her hat. There is something subtly strange in her manner. It is not that she is actually drunk, but she undoubtedly is what is described colloquially as a little "high." She is, of course, aware of this and is making a gallant effort to conceal it. She stands by the door for a moment, conscious of the oppressive silence, then comes forward.)*

HILDE *(tentatively).* I do hope I haven't come back at an awkward moment. Were you discussing anything of importance?

HUGO. No. Nothing of the least importance.

CARLOTTA. We were just reminiscing.

HILDE. How nice. It's always fun talking over old times, isn't it?

CARLOTTA. Enormous fun. Hugo and I have been in stitches, haven't we, Hugo? *(She sits on the sofa.)*

HUGO. I wish you'd take off that hat, Hilde, it makes you look like a cabdriver.

HILDE *(with a little giggle).* Certainly, dear. *(She takes off her hat, puts it on the bureau with her bag, and tidies her hair in the mirror.)* I don't really care for it very much myself.

HUGO. I see that you decided not to go to the cinema after all.

HILDE. Yes. Liesel and I just sat on after dinner, gossiping. *(to CARLOTTA)* You have never met Liesel Kessler?

CARLOTTA. No, I'm afraid I haven't.

HILDE. She is a great friend of mine. Hugo always laughs at her, but she is most intelligent.

CARLOTTA. Why does he always laugh at her?

HILDE *(with another little giggle).* I think because he disapproves of her. *(She sits on the sofa.)* Hugo is quite old-fashioned in some ways.

HUGO *(irritably).* Please, Hilde.

HILDE. But it doesn't really matter. Actually she disapproves of him, too.

CARLOTTA. Sacrilege.

HILDE *(laughing).* Forgive me, Hugo, but that is very, very funny.

HUGO *(looking at her searchingly).* Hilde, what's the matter with you?

HILDE. Nothing. Why do you ask?

HUGO *(sternly).* Have you been drinking?

HILDE. Oh, yes. We had a bottle of vin rosé at dinner and two stingers afterwards.

HUGO *(angrily).* Hilde!

CARLOTTA *(sweetly, to HUGO).* You seem to have a positive genius for driving those who love you to the bottle.

HILDE. Oh, it wasn't Hugo's fault, not really. I just felt like it.

HUGO. You'd better ring for some black coffee.

HILDE. No, thank you, Hugo. I do not want any black coffee; it would keep me awake. But now that my wicked secret has been discovered, I think I will take another little drink. *(She smiles conspiratorially at CARLOTTA.)* It is as good to be hung for a sheep as for a lamb.

HUGO *(warningly).* Hilde!

HILDE *(rising to the drinks table and pouring herself a brandy).* I would have liked it to have been a stinger, because they are so delicious, but we have no crème de menthe and it is too much trouble to send for any at this time of night, so I will make do with just the brandy alone.

HUGO. I absolutely forbid you to drink any more brandy, Hilde. I think you had better go to bed.

HILDE. *"Entbehren sollst Du! Sollst entbehren! Das ist der ewige Gesang."* *(She looks at them both blandly.)* *Das ist von Goethe.* He was a great genius.

CARLOTTA *(amused).* What does it mean?

HILDE. "Deny yourself! You must deny yourself! That is the song that never ends." *(She takes a swig of brandy and sighs contentedly.)* *Ach das ist besser, das ist sehr gut.*

HUGO *(frigidly).* You are perfectly aware that I do not like you to speak German in my presence. It is a language that I detest.

HILDE. The language of Goethe is not merely German, it is universal. You must not forget, Hugo, that my translations of your books have earned you a great deal of money in Germany. It is ungrateful of you to turn up your nose. *(To CARLOTTA)* You have no idea of his popularity in my country, Miss Gray. *The Winding River* went into three editions in five months.

HUGO. I cannot feel that the subject of my foreign royalties can be of the smallest interest to Miss Gray.

HILDE. But why are you so suddenly formal, Hugo? You were calling her Carlotta when she first arrived.

CARLOTTA. I hope you will call me Carlotta, too.

HILDE. But of course. With the utmost

pleasure.

HUGO (*turning away*). Oh, my God!

HILDE (*cheerfully oblivious of undertones*). Liesel was so amused when I told her about this strange, unexpected reunion you are having with Carlotta tonight, after so many years.

HUGO. She must have a very warped sense of humor.

CARLOTTA. What was it about the situation that so amused her?

HILDE (*a little giggly again*). Oh, I don't know. I expect I was a little indiscreet. But it was such a long, long time ago, wasn't it? I mean, it couldn't really matter speaking of it now.

HUGO. You had no right to speak of it at all. How dare you discuss my private affairs with Liesel or anybody else!

CARLOTTA. You mean you told your friend that Hugo and I had once been lovers?

HILDE. Not in so many words. . . .

CARLOTTA. Was that why she laughed?

HILDE (*a little uneasy*). I don't remember. We were just talking. She has always been most admiring of Hugo as a writer, although I must admit she doesn't care for him very much as a man. But that is largely his own fault, because he has now and then been a little offish with her. We were talking in German, naturally, and she quoted some lines of Heinrich Heine:
"*Ich weiss nicht, was soll es bedeuten*
Dass ich so traurig bin;
Ein Märchen aus alten Zeiten,
Das kommt mir nicht aus dem Sinn."

CARLOTTA. Please translate.

HILDE (*with a furtive look at* HUGO). "I know not why I am so sad; I cannot get out of my head a fairy tale of olden times." That was when she laughed.

CARLOTTA (*glancing at* HUGO *and laughing herself*). I wonder why.

HILDE. You are not angry, I hope?

CARLOTTA. Of course I'm not.

HUGO. You may not be. But I am.

HILDE. Please don't be, Hugo. You know how bad it is for you. You have been looking angry ever since I came into the room. Is there anything wrong—between you and Carlotta, I mean? Has something bad happened?

HUGO. Oh, no. It has all been delightful. Carlotta came here this evening either to blackmail me or reform me. I have not yet discovered which.

HILDE (*apprehensively*). Blackmail! What do you mean? I do not understand.

HUGO. She is a very remarkable character, a mixture of adventuress and evangelist. Her strongly developed sense of moral rectitude has impelled her to span the vast grey wastes of the Atlantic Ocean in order to confront me with my past demeanors and upbraid me for my lack of conscience. The fact that she has an ex-husband living from whom she extorts a regular income on condition that she no longer share his hearth and home, she apparently finds in no way inconsistent with her ethical principles. All of which goes to prove what I have always contended, that the capacity of the female mind for convenient rationalization is unlimited.

CARLOTTA. And what makes you imagine that the male mind is so vastly superior?

HUGO. I don't imagine it. I know it.

HILDE. I do not understand. I do not understand at all what is happening.

HUGO (*savagely*). If you had spent less time guzzling down stingers with that leather-skinned old Sapphist your perceptions might be clearer!

HILDE (*with spirit*). You will *not* speak of Liesel like that. She is my close friend and I am devoted to her.

HUGO. Then you should have more discrimination.

HILDE. Nor will I permit you to speak to me in that tone in front of a stranger. It is in very bad taste and makes me ashamed of you.

CARLOTTA (*enjoying herself*). Hurray! A "sudden flood of mutiny"!

HILDE (*in full spate*). When you are ill and in discomfort, I am willing to endure your rudeness to me, but now you are no longer ill, you are perfectly well, and I will stand no more of it. This very evening you accused me of being jealous of your friends and of anyone who is close to you; you even said I was jealous of Carlotta. But the truth of the matter is you have no friends; you have driven them all away with your bitter tongue, and the only one who is close to you in the world is me. And I will say one thing more. I will choose whatever friends I like and I will drink as many stingers as I like, and so that there shall be no further misunderstanding between us I am at this moment going to have some more brandy.

(*She goes purposefully to the drinks table and pours herself more brandy.*)

CARLOTTA. This is certainly not your evening, Hugo.

HILDE. Now, then. I should like to know what all this is about, this talk of blackmail. What does it mean? What has been taking place?

CARLOTTA. Shall I explain, Hugo, or will you?

HUGO. No explanation is necessary. I do not wish Hilde to be involved in anything we have discussed tonight. It is none of her concern.

CARLOTTA. On the contrary, I should say that it concerned her most vitally.

HUGO. In addition to which I do not consider her to be in a fit state to do anything but go to bed.

HILDE. What nonsense. My mind is perfectly clear. Perhaps a lot clearer than it usually is. It is only my legs that are a little uncertain; therefore I shall sit down.

(*She sits.*)

HUGO (*crossing toward the bedroom*). In that case I shall retire to bed myself.

CARLOTTA. And leave me in command of the field? (HUGO *stops and turns.*) I cannot feel that even for the sake of making a majestic exit you would be as foolish as that.

HILDE (*with quiet determination*). I am waiting.

CARLOTTA. Well, Hugo?

HUGO. Carlotta is about to publish a book of her memoirs, and she asked my permission to include in it some love letters I wrote to her in the nineteen-twenties. I refused my permission.

HILDE. Why? It seems a most reasonable request. (*to* CARLOTTA) Are they nice letters?

CARLOTTA. Charming. They make up in style for what they lack in passionate intensity.

HUGO (*loudly*). I will explain why if you will stop interrupting and allow me to. May I go on?

HILDE. Yes, dear, please do.

(*She takes a sip of brandy.*)

HUGO (*glaring at them both*). A little later it transpired that Carlotta has in her possession some other letters, written by me to someone else. These she threatens to hand over to an ex-Harvard professor called Justin Chandler, who is apparently planning to write an analytical survey of my life and works.

HILDE. He'll do it very well. He's a very clever man and a brilliant writer.

(*She takes another sip of brandy.*)

HUGO (*thunderstruck*). What do you mean?

HILDE. Exactly what I say.

HUGO. You mean that you know him?

HILDE. Not personally, but we have corresponded quite a lot over the last three years. He wrote a monograph on you for the *Atlantic Monthly*. I didn't show it to you, because I thought it might make you cross.

HUGO. Do you mean to say that you have been corresponding with this man about me behind my back, without saying a word about it?

HILDE. There is no need to look so agitated. I have said nothing indiscreet. He asked politely for certain information and I saw no harm in giving it to him.

HUGO (*through clenched teeth*). What sort of information?

HILDE. Oh, dates of publication, lists of places you have visited in your travels, a few small biographical details. He really is one of your greatest admirers. It should be an excellent book when he gets around to writing it. At the moment he is only assembling material and making notes.

HUGO (*furiously*). How dared you! How dared you! You have no earthly right to give out details of my private life to strangers without consulting me first. You have been guilty of the most shameful disloyalty.

HILDE (*rising*). I have never been guilty of disloyalty to you, Hugo. Never in my whole life. And you will please never say such a thing to me again. Nor did I give Mr. Chandler any details of your private life, and you know that I would never do so in a million years. (*She turns to* CARLOTTA.) These other letters, Carlotta—are they love letters?

CARLOTTA (*extremely embarrassed.*) I think I would rather not say.

HILDE. That means they are. Please tell me. It is important for me to know.

CARLOTTA. Very well. Yes—they are.

HILDE. Who are they written to?

CARLOTTA. I really cannot tell you that.

HILDE. Hugo, will you tell me?

HUGO. There would be nothing to be gained by my telling you. They were written many years ago, long before I married you.

HILDE (*with a sigh*). It is of no consequence. I think I can guess anyhow. (HILDE *catches* HUGO's *eye*.) But I would have liked you to tell me yourself. As a matter of fact, I would have liked you to have told me long ago; it would have shown me that even if you didn't love me, you at least were fond enough of me to trust me.

HUGO (*obviously disturbed*). They were no concern of yours. They belonged to a part of my life that was over and done with.

HILDE (*with a sad little smile*). Over and done with! Oh, Hugo! Earlier this evening you called me a camel, a dromedary and an ass, but I would like to point out to you that all those three animals are more sensible than an ostrich.

HUGO (*only a little bluster left*). And pray what do you mean by that?

HILDE. For twenty years I have looked after your business affairs, dealt with your correspondence, typed your manuscripts and shared, at least, the outward aspects of your life. You cannot seriously imagine that in all that time you have been able to withhold many secrets from me. The letters were written to Perry Sheldon, weren't they? (*To* CARLOTTA) And these letters you have from Hugo to Perry—you wish us to buy them from you?

CARLOTTA. No. I have already explained to Hugo that they are not for sale.

HILDE. You intend to give them to Mr. Justin Chandler?

CARLOTTA. Possibly. I have not yet decided.

HILDE. As you know Hugo's feelings in the matter, Miss Gray, that would be a malicious and unforgivable thing to do.

CARLOTTA. I notice that you no longer call me Carlotta.

HILDE. I called you Carlotta when I thought we were to be friends. But I cannot possibly be friends with anyone who sets out deliberately to hurt my husband.

CARLOTTA. You are certainly magnani-mous.

HILDE. It has nothing to do with magnanimity. It is a statement of fact.

CARLOTTA. I was thinking of Hugo's treatment of you.

HILDE. As you have only seen Hugo and me together this evening for the first time in your life, you cannot know anything about his treatment of me one way or the other.

CARLOTTA. You don't find it humiliating to have been used by him for twenty years not only as an unpaid secretary, manager and housekeeper, but as a social camouflage as well?

HUGO (*violently*). Once and for all, Carlotta, I forbid you to talk like that!

HILDE. You are a very forceful woman, Miss Gray, and Hugo is a complex and brilliant man, but it is beginning to dawn on me that I have a great deal more common sense than either of you. Your visit actually has little or nothing to do with permission to publish letters or threats of blackmail, has it?

CARLOTTA. No. No, it hasn't. I genuinely wanted to prove something to him. Something that, with all his brilliance and talent and eminence, he has never yet taken into account.

HILDE. What is it that he has failed to take into account?

CARLOTTA. You, being the closest to him, should know better than anybody. He has never taken into account the value of kindness and the importance of compassion. He has never had the courage or the humility to face the fact that it was not whom he loved in his life that really mattered but his own capacity for loving.

HUGO. Hark the Herald Angels Sing!

HILDE. Stop behaving like that, Hugo. You should be ashamed.

HUGO. I see that in addition to being my unpaid secretary, manager and housekeeper, you have now elected to become my dear old Nanny.

CARLOTTA. It is clear that my mission has most dismally failed.

HILDE. It could never have succeeded. You are a sentimentalist. Hugo is not. I, too, am a sentimentalist, but then I happen to be a German, and sentimentality is ingrained in the German character.

CARLOTTA. There is a wide gulf between

sentiment and sentimentality.

HUGO. Turgid mysticism, Santa Claus, Christmas trees and gas chambers.

HILDE. You see. He is quite incapable of recognizing people as individuals. His mind classifies all human beings in groups and races and types. Whenever he is angry with me he punishes me for my country's sins. He is a profound cynic, which is one of the reasons he has been proclaimed as the greatest satirical writer of our time.

CARLOTTA. Why does he mean so much to you? Why are you so loyal to him?

HILDE. Because he is all I have. (*She sits on the arm of the sofa.*) You have lived so differently from me, Miss Gray, that I quite see why you must find my attitude difficult to understand. I have only loved one man in my life, one of my own countrymen, who was destroyed by my own countrymen in nineteen forty-two. When I came to Hugo as secretary I was desolate and without hope, and when, a little later, he asked me to marry him, it seemed like a sudden miracle. Please do not misunderstand me. I was not in love with him and I knew that he could never be in love with me. I also knew why and was not deceived as to his reasons for asking me. I recognized his need for a "façade" and was quite content to supply it. I thought that it was a most realistic and sensible arrangement, and, what is more, I think so still. I am not pretending that our married life has been twenty years of undiluted happiness. He is frequently sarcastic and disagreeable to me and I have often been unhappy and lonely. But then, so has he. The conflict within him between his natural instincts and the laws of society has been for the most of his life a perpetual problem that he has had to grapple with alone.

CARLOTTA. Wouldn't it at least have eased the problem if he had trusted you enough to share it with you?

HILDE. Possibly. But it would have been out of character. He has made his career and lived his life in his own way according to the rules he has laid down for himself. Now, when the passing years have diminished the conflict, he is growing to rely on me more and to need me more, and that, with my sentimental, Teutonic mentality, is the reward that I have been waiting for.

HUGO (*very gently*). Hilde . . .

HILDE (*rising*). Don't interrupt for a moment, Hugo; I have not quite finished. (*She turns back to* CARLOTTA.) To revert to the Perry Sheldon letters. You must, of course, dispose of them as you see fit. If Mr. Justin Chandler wishes for them and you wish to give them to him, there is nothing we can do to prevent you. But I must warn you that, according to law, he will not be allowed to publish them without Hugo's written permission. He may possibly quote them and paraphrase them to a certain extent, I believe, but I cannot feel that a really good writer would waste time in referring to them at all. If Perry Sheldon had been in any way significant as a human being; if he had been in any way worthy of attention on his own account, apart from the fact of his early relationship with Hugo, there might be some point in disclosing them. But he wasn't. He was a creature of little merit; foolish, conceited, dishonest and self-indulgent.

CARLOTTA. How do you know?

HILDE. Through Liesel. Curiously enough, we were talking about him this evening. She knew him for years when she was a scriptwriter in Hollywood. She lent him money on several occasions, but, as she said, it is no use lending money to the morally defeated. They only spend it on further defeat.

(CARLOTTA *rises slowly, takes her handbag from the table and walks thoughtfully about the room for a moment or two.* HILDE *and* HUGO *watch her in silence. Finally she opens her handbag, takes from it a bundle of letters, and holds them out to* HUGO.)

CARLOTTA. Here they are, Hugo. Here are the letters. They can be no practical use to me or to Mr. Justin Chandler. They might conceivably, however, be of service to you.

HUGO *takes the letters. His face is expressionless.*)

HUGO. Thank you.

CARLOTTA. I cannot say that I entirely regret this evening. It has been most interesting, and almost embarrassingly revealing. If many of the things I have said have hurt you, I'm sorry. (*She gives a slight smile.*) I don't apologize, I'm just sorry. I am also sorry for having kept you up so late.

HUGO. I will see that the permission you asked for earlier in the evening is delivered to you in the morning. Good night, Carlotta.

CARLOTTA (*looking at him, still with a quizzical smile*). Good night, Hugo. (*She turns to* HILDE.) Good night, Lady Latymer.

HILDE. Good night, Carlotta. I will see you out.

CARLOTTA. There is no necessity for that. My room is only just along the corridor.

HILDE. Nevertheless, I should like to. (HILDE *takes* CARLOTTA *by the arm and they go out.* HUGO *looks at the bundle of letters, then puts on his glasses, se-lects one at random and reads it. He puts the pile on the little table, takes another and starts to read it. After a moment he frowns slightly and looks up. It is apparent from his expression that he is deeply moved. He takes off his glasses, wipes away a tear, replaces the glasses and goes on reading. As he replaces his glasses,* HILDE *comes quietly back into the room. She stands looking at him for a moment, then sits down silently on the edge of the sofa.*)

HUGO (*after a long pause*). I heard you come in.

HILDE (*almost in a whisper*). Yes. I thought you did.

(HUGO *continues reading the letter, as:*)
    THE CURTAIN SLOWLY FALLS

LINE

Israel Horovitz

STEPHEN   DOLAN
FLEMING   ARNALL
MOLLY

THE PLACE OF THE PLAY: A LINE.
THE TIME OF THE PLAY: NOW.

ISRAEL HOROVITZ first came to international attention in 1968 with *The Indian Wants the Bronx,* a powerful and terrifying study of violence on a New York street. A striking Off-Broadway success, it also scored heavily in other major American cities, at the Spoleto (Italy) Festival, and in numerous foreign countries. The play won a 1968 Drama Desk–Vernon Rice Award and three "Obies," as well as a commendation from *Newsweek* magazine citing the author as one of the three most original dramatists of the year.

Mr. Horovitz was born on March 31, 1939, in Wakefield, Massachusetts. After completing his studies at Harvard College, he journeyed to London to continue his education at the Royal Academy of Dramatic Art and in 1965 became the first American to be chosen as playwright-in-residence with Britain's celebrated Royal Shakespeare Company.

The author's first play, *The Comeback,* was written when he was seventeen; it was produced in Boston in 1960. In the decade that followed, Mr. Horovitz's plays tenanted many stages of the world. Among them: *It's Called the Sugar Plum* (paired with *The Indian Wants the Bronx* on the New York stage); *The Death of Bernard the Believer; Rats, Morning* (as *Chiaroscuro* it was produced on a triple bill, *Morning, Noon and Night,* Henry Miller's Theatre, New York, 1968); *Trees; Acrobats;* and *The Honest-to-God-Schnozzola,* for which he won a 1969 Off-Broadway "Obie" Award.

Line was presented at the Theatre de Lys, New York, on February 15, 1971, and once again Israel Horovitz received critical plaudits. Walter Kerr of *The New York Times* found the play to be "a brilliantly imagined conceit executed with wit and an almost inexhaustible inventiveness." Others proclaimed it as "an amusing commentary on the American success story" and commended the author for employing "an ingenious metaphor to examine life in microcosm, in all its purposelessness and futility . . . it has implications and nuances about the way we live that are funny and pertinent."

Mr. Horovitz's newest works for the stage include: *Shooting Gallery; Alfred the Great* (part of a projected trilogy); and *Dr. Hero,* which is scheduled for New York production in 1973.

A collection of his plays, *First Season,* was published in 1968 and he has twice been a recipient of a Rockefeller Foundation Playwriting Fellowship.

The author, who lives in New York City, also has written several screenplays, notably *The Strawberry Statement,* which won the *Prix de Jury,* Cannes Film Festival, 1970.

Mr. Horovitz has just published his first novel, *Cappella,* and is now at work on a criticism of Samuel Beckett's early fiction.

As the audience enters the theatre, FLEMING *is standing behind a fat, white strip of adhesive tape that is fixed to the stage floor. The play has begun.*

He is waiting . . . waiting . . . waiting. The stage is without decoration other than FLEMING *and the line. The lighting is of that moment when late night turns to early morning: all pinks and oranges and, finally, steel-gray blue.*

FLEMING *checks and rechecks his feet in relation to the line. He is clearly first there, in first place.*

He steps straight back now and again, testing his legs and the straightness of the line that will follow.

FLEMING *has carried a large war-surplus duffle with him, full of beer, potato chips, whatever he might need for a long-awaited long wait.*

Back to the audience, he reaches into the bag and takes something out. He stands, hands penis-high, in a small pantomime of urination. He turns again to the line and reveals that he has peeled a banana. He eats it.

His feet are planted solidly at the line now, yet his body breaks the rigidity, revealing his exhaustion. He is waiting . . . waiting . . . waiting.

He dips again into the bag and produces a bag of potato chips, a can of beer (flip-top) and a rather nice cloth napkin, which he tucks into his shirt top. He opens the beer, eats the chips, drinks, belches and does it all again.

His feet never move from the mark now.

He leans back and sings, softly at first, "Take Me Out to the Ball Game," possibly confusing the lyrics. He drinks, belches, and spills potato chips all over the place, then continues singing again to end of song. STEPHEN *enters quietly. He watches* FLEMING *carefully.* FLEMING *senses* STEPHEN's *presence. He stops singing and, waiting for* STEPHEN *to speak, does nothing. Neither does* STEPHEN. FLEMING *gets on with it. Singing carefully now.* STEPHEN *cuts him off with a soft question.*

STEPHEN. Is this a line? (FLEMING *stares directly into* STEPHEN's *eyes, but doesn't answer.*) Excuse me, mister. Is this a line? (*After studying* STEPHEN's *clothing and manner,* FLEMING *rechecks his feet and turns from* STEPHEN, *facing straight ahead.*) Is this a line, huh?

FLEMING (*does a long, false take*). What's it look like?

STEPHEN (*walking over, leaning between* FLEMING's *legs, he literally caresses the tape*). Oh, yeah. There it is. It's a line all right. It's a beautiful line, isn't it? I couldn't tell from back there. I would have been earlier if I had started out earlier. You wouldn't think anyone would be damn fool enough to get up this early. Or not go to bed. Depending on how you look at it. (FLEMING *stares at* STEPHEN *incredulously.*) Oh, I didn't mean you were a damn fool. (*pauses*) Not yet. Nice line. Just the two of us, huh?

FLEMING. What's it look like? What's it look like?

STEPHEN. That's all you ever say, huh? "What's it look like?"—"What's it look like?" (*pause*) Must be nice.

FLEMING. Huh?

STEPHEN. Being first. Right up front of the line like that. Singing away. Singing your damn fool heart out. I could hear you from back there. Singing your damn fool heart out. You like music?

STEPHEN (*walking over, leaning begins to talk with incredible speed.*) I'm a music nut myself. Mozart. He's the one. I've got all his records. Started out on seventy-eight. Moved on up to forty-fives. Then I moved on to thirty-three and a third when I got to be thirteen or so. Now I've got him on hi-fi, stereo and transistorized snap-in cartridges. (*displays a portable cartridge tape recorder*) I've got him on everything he's on. (*pause*) Must be nice. (*pauses*) Want to trade places?

FLEMING. You yak like that all the time?

STEPHEN (*peeks over* FLEMING's *shoulder at the line*). That's a good solid line. I've seen some skimpy little lines in my day, but that one's a beauty. (*whistles a strain from* The Magic Flute) That's Mozart. Want me to whistle some more? Or we could sing your song. "Take Me Out to the Ball Game." I know most of your pop songs from your twenties, your thirties and your forties. I'm bad on your fifties and your sixties. That's when *I* started composing. And, of course, that's when Mozart really started getting in the way. But, have it like you will—just name the tune. 'Course, don't get me wrong. I'd rather be whistling my own songs any day of the week. Any night, for that matter. Or whistle Mozart. *The Magic Flute. Marriage of Figaro."* Go on. Just "Name That Tune." I can sing it in Italian, German, French, or your Basic English. Hell, if he could knock them out at seven, I should be able to whistle at thirty, right? Christ, I am thirty, too. Not thirty-two. Thirty *also.* Three-o. Thirty. He was thirty-five. Around the age of Christ. What hath God wrought? (*pauses, arms out and feet pinned together as in crucifixion*) God hath wrought iron! (*pauses. Waits to see if* FLEMING *has crumbled yet. Sees* FLEMING *is confused, but still on his feet, so* STEPHEN *continues*) Thirty-five. That's how old he was. He thought he was writing his funeral music all right. He was, too. Isn't that something, to have that kind of premonition? That's what you call your young genius. The only real genius ever to walk on this earth, mister. Wolfgang Amadeus Mozart. W-A-M. (*Yells at* FLEMING'S *face.*) WAM! WAM! WAM! (FLEMING, *thunderstruck, turns and overtly snubs* STEPHEN, *who is perched, ready to take first position, if* FLEMING *falls.* FLEMING *stays afloat, so* STEPHEN *takes his wallet out of his pocket and studies its contents carefully. He pokes* FLEMING.) You want to read my wallet?

FLEMING. Huh?

STEPHEN (*begins to unfold an enormous credit card case*). You want to read my wallet? You can read my wallet and I'll read your wallet. You can learn a lot about people from their wallets. Avis cards. Hertz cards. American Express. Air Travel. Bloomingdale's. Saks. Old phone numbers. Bits and scraps. Contraceptives. Locks of hair. Baby pictures. Calendars. Business cards. And the ladies. Business ladies have cards. ID cards. Not the ladies, I mean. I mean the men who own the wallets who you're learning about, right? (FLEMING *sings two bars of "Take Me Out to the Ball Game."*) Hey. Don't turn your back on me, huh? Let me read your wallet. I've read mine before. I read my wallet all the time. Hey, will you? Here. Take my wallet, then. You don't even have to let me read yours. (*forces his wallet into* FLEMING'S *hands.* FLEMING *is*

absolutely astonished.) That's it. Go on. Read. (FLEMING *obeys, wide-eyed.*) There. See that ID card? That lets you know who I am, right away. See? Stephen. Steve. Or Stevie. Gives you a choice, even. And where I work. See that? Now look at the pictures. My kids. That one's dead. That one's dead. That one's dead. That one's dead. There are more. Don't stop. More pictures.

(STEPHEN *leaves the wallet in* FLEMING'S *hand and begins a wide circle around him, almost forcing* FLEMING *out of line.*)

FLEMING. How'd you lose all those kids?

STEPHEN. Lose the kids?

FLEMING. Dead. All these dead kids? (*Sees that the pictures are lithographs of Mozart*) Hey! Those are drawings!

STEPHEN. Who said they were kids?

FLEMING (*waits, staring*). Oh, boy. Here we go.

(*Sings three bars of "Take Me Out to the Ball Game," after jamming* STEPHEN'S *wallet back into* STEPHEN'S *pocket.* STEPHEN *joins in for one bar. In unison.* FLEMING *stops.*)

STEPHEN (*sings another bar, then stops, asks*). Do you really think this line is for a ball game? Huh? There's no ball game around here. I mean, I wouldn't be here if there was a ball game. Ball games aren't my kind of stuff. I loathe ball games, myself. You like ball games?

FLEMING (*at this point, the situation has gone beyond* FLEMING'S *comprehension, and his confusion surfaces like a rubber duck*). Who are you?

STEPHEN. That's why I gave you my wallet. If everybody would just pass their wallets around, sooner or later something would happen, right?

FLEMING. Yeah.

STEPHEN. Can you imagine if you met the President and he gave you his wallet to read? You'd know everything about him. Or the mayor. Kings. Ballplayers, even. Read *their* wallets. Boy, would you know it all soon enough. Scraps of paper that held secrets they forgot were secrets. Meetings they were supposed to make. Locks of hair. Pictures of babies they forgot they had. Names. Addresses. ID cards. Secret money hidden in secret places. You'd know everything, wouldn't you? (STEPHEN *has* FLEMING *going now. He in-*

creases the speed of his delivery, eyes flickering, hands waving, watching FLEM-ING's *terrified responses.*) You see, friend, all those up-front people are fakes. Fakes. There's never been a real first place . . . never a real leader. Except you know *who*.

FLEMING. Who?

STEPHEN. War heroes? All frauds. If there had been one really efficient war, we wouldn't be here, would we?

FLEMING. I'm first. All I know is I'm first.

STEPHEN. First. It's just a word. Twist the letters around, you get strif. God backwards. Dog. Split the first three letters off the word therapist, you get two words: the rapist. Spell Hannah backwards, you get Hannah. Spell backwards backwards, you get sdrawkcab. I tell you, show me one of your so-called winners, and let me have one look at his wallet; just one. I'll never have to count the money, either. There's never been a real first before. Never. I know, friend. I know. See that line? Turn it on end, you know what you've got? A number one. But how do you hang on to it? How do you really hold it, so you're not one of those wallet-carrying, secret compartment fakes like all of them? Answer that question and I'd let you follow me in. You could be second.

FLEMING. What do you mean "second"? I'm first. I'm right at the front.

STEPHEN. For the moment.

FLEMING. Don't get any smart ideas.

STEPHEN. The only conclusions I draw are on men's-room walls. Now if you'd shut up for a while, I'll sing my wallet. (STEPHEN *sings his Hertz card lyric to* "Eine Kleine Nachtmusik.") "This non-transferable Hertz charge card entitles the person named to use Hertz Rent A Car service under the terms of the Hertz Rental Agreement on a credit basis. Where you desire to make immediate payments, the card enables you to rent without deposit. Payment for rentals charged is due within ten days after the billing date. This card is subject to invalidation and modification without notice and is the property of the Hertz system . . ." (MOLLY, *a plump woman, wanders onto the stage. When he sees her, he continues to sing the Hertz lyric, but*

changes the melody to a tacky love song. STEPHEN *stops* MOLLY *as she crosses the stage.*) Hey. You looking for a line, lady?

MOLLY. Line?

STEPHEN. That's right. This is a line. You're third. Number three. There used to be just two of us here. Me and Fleming. This is Fleming. Who are you?

FLEMING. How'd you know my name, huh? How'd you know my name?

STEPHEN (to FLEMING). I read your wallet. (*to* MOLLY) You're third. That's not too bad. You won't have to wait long.

FLEMING (*checks to see if* STEPHEN *has stolen his wallet, then screams*). You didn't read my wallet! Nobody's read my wallet, except me!

MOLLY (*joining the line*). Third? I'm third, huh? How long have you been waiting?

STEPHEN. About nine and a half minutes. Fleming must have been here all night. Were you here all night, Fleming? He looks it, huh?

FLEMING. How the hell did you know my name? How'd you know?

MOLLY. Third place. How soon do they open?

STEPHEN. You'll probably see a crowd before that. There's always a crowd. The crowd that says, "Maybe there won't be a crowd, let's go anyway." That crowd. You'll see that crowd, won't she, Fleming?

FLEMING. How'd you know my name? How'd you know my name?

STEPHEN. Fleming, don't be a bore! What's your name? Mine's Stephen.

MOLLY. Molly. I'm Molly.

STEPHEN. Hello, Molly. Glad you're third. Fleming, this is Molly.

MOLLY. Hello.

FLEMING. Hey, kid. Hold our places in line. Come here, ma'am. (*takes her aside whispers*) That kid's crazy. Watch out. He's one of them freaky weirdos. He's been saying crazy things to me.

STEPHEN (*moves into first position*). I can't guarantee your places. The crowd's going to come sure as hell and I can't guarantee anybody's place. The fact is, Fleming, I'm first now.

FLEMING. What?

STEPHEN. I'm first. (*straddles the line*) Look at me. I'm up first. Up front. Front of the line. (MOLLY *jumps into second position*.)

MOLLY. You could have held our places. Nobody else is here.

STEPHEN. It's just not right. Besides, Fleming wouldn't hold anybody's place. You can tell that just from looking at him. He's never held anybody's place in his life.

FLEMING (*enraged, but trying to maintain control*). Kid, I've been standing there all night. All night. Waiting. Waiting in the front of the line. The very front. Now I think you'd better let me get right back up there. (*As* FLEMING *continues,* DOLAN *enters and walks toward the line. He carries a canvas-topped, artist's portable stool.*) Just step back one pace and let me in there. (DOLAN *quietly steps into line behind* MOLLY. *To* DOLAN) I'm up front.

DOLAN (*sitting*). Huh?

FLEMING. I'm first. That kid just took my spot. You're fourth.

DOLAN. I don't mean to argue, but I count third. You're fourth.

FLEMING. Hey. Listen. That kid grabbed my place. I waited all night up front. Right at the front of the line.

DOLAN. I don't want to argue, but you're not getting in front of me, pal, so skip it.

FLEMING. Skip it? Bull, I'll skip it. (*walks up to* STEPHEN) Give me back my place, kid, or I'll knock you out of it. (STEPHEN *drops to the floor in a lotus-position.* FLEMING *stares, again astonished.*) Get up!

DOLAN. I hate to argue, but get out of the front, mac! The kid was up front and I'm third. The lady's second.

MOLLY. He *was* up front, actually.

DOLAN. Well, he can go second if you want him to, lady. I'm third.

(ARNALL *enters and walks directly into the line.*)

ARNALL. Molly?

MOLLY. Arnall. Here I am.

ARNALL. You think I can't see you? You saved my place?

MOLLY (*to* DOLAN). I was saving his place, sir. We had an arrangement.

DOLAN. Not that I want to run things, but that's too bad. No place was saved. He can go fourth.

FLEMING. I'm fourth! For Christ's sake what am I saying? I'm *first*.

ARNALL (*jumps into fourth position*). I'm fourth.

MOLLY. I'm second.

DOLAN. I'm third.

STEPHEN (*after the stampede, to* DOLAN). Obviously, I'm first. My name's Stephen. Who are you?

DOLAN (*shaking* STEPHEN'S *hand*). Dolan's what they call me. How long you been waiting?

STEPHEN. About twelve and a half minutes.

ARNALL. Jesus. If I could have found my clean shirts, Molly . . . If I could have found where you hid them . . . I would have been here half an hour ago. I would have been first.

FLEMING. I've been here all night.

ARNALL (*considers it*). How come you're fifth? (*pause for a "take" from* FLEMING) You're not even in line. Why aren't you first?

FLEMING. I *am* first. God damn it! I *am* first. That crazy kid grabbed my place. How'd you know my name, kid?

ARNALL. Fleming?

FLEMING. How the hell do you know?

ARNALL (*pulls* FLEMING'S *T-shirt neck to his eyes*). It's written on your undershirt.

(FLEMING *spins around trying to read the label.*)

STEPHEN. I read your undershirt.

FLEMING (*to* DOLAN). Look, I've been here all night. I've been standing right at the front of the line all night. You know that's true. (*to* MOLLY) You saw me here, lady. You know I was first.

MOLLY. You stepped out of line. (*to* ARNALL) He stepped out of line, Arnall.

ARNALL. Serves you right, then, Fleming. If I could have found my clean shirt, I would have been first. My dumb wife hides my dumb shirts. Isn't that terrific? She hides my shirts. I could have been first by half an hour. But she hid my shirt. You know where I found it? (*simply*) I couldn't find it.

FLEMING (*after rapt attention to* ARNALL'S *shaggy-shirt story. Furiously*). This is ridiculous. I was first. All night. (*to* ARNALL) I just took your wife aside to warn her about that crazy kid. He jumped the line. He jumped in front. That's not fair, is it? I was here all night.

DOLAN. You're fifth. There's plenty here for five. You'll get your chance.

FLEMING (*to* ARNALL). That's not the point. God damn it! There's only one first and I waited up all night. All night in the line all by myself. And he took it away from me. Now that is definitely unfair.

ARNALL (*completely against* FLEMING'*s problem*). I hate to go anywhere at night with the shirt from the day still on. You never know what kind of germs you come in contact with during the day. You never can tell, can you?

STEPHEN. Life's full of dirt.

ARNALL. Our place is full of dirt. My wife never cleans. If it were up to her, we'd be up to our lips in dirt. Day and night. That's why I'm late. What movie's playing?

FLEMING (*he's had it!*). Movie?

ARNALL. I thought we were going to the movies, Molly?

MOLLY. Arnall, don't cause a scene!

STEPHEN. Your shirt looks terrific, Arnall.

ARNALL. Looks are deceptive. Hospitals look clean, don't they? But if you ever ran a check for germ count, oh, boy, wouldn't you get a score? After all, people come there—to hospitals—because they're ridden with germs. Take an old building full of germ-ridden people, paint it stark white, you got yourself a place that looks clean, but underneath that look, there's just a white hospital—full of germ-ridden people.

STEPHEN. How do you feel about that, Fleming? Do germ-ridden people disturb you, too?

FLEMING. Don't get smart with me, kid. I was waiting here a long time before you, and you know it. (*to* DOLAN) He's trying to distract your attention from the fact that he *took* first place . . . he didn't earn it. No, sir. *I* earned it. I waited up for that place. He took it!

DOLAN. Well, I don't want to be the one who starts any arguments, but he *is* in first place, and he was in first place when I first got here.

STEPHEN. Fair is fair, Fleming!

FLEMING (*yells*). Don't "fair" me, kid, or you'll have a fat lip to worry about!

DOLAN. Now listen to me, Fleming.

FLEMING (*screams*). What do *you* want?

DOLAN (*screams*). Lower your voice!

ARNALL. Easy, Dolan, easy.

DOLAN (*to* FLEMING). Look, I don't want to start any trouble, but it seems to me if you want to be first, be first. Move the kid. If you want to be second, be second. Move his old lady. (*And with that,* DOLAN [*Mister Niceguy*] *nearly strangles* ARNALL. *He catches himself before* ARNALL *dies. He brushes* ARNALL'*s jacket and smiles. To* ARNALL) And don't you—God damn it!—"easy" me. I'm nice and easy all the time. I'm Mister Niceguy. Get it? Mister Niceguy.

ARNALL. Move *who*?

DOLAN. Your old lady.

FLEMING. Your old lady.

ARNALL. You can't do that.

DOLAN. And why not?

FLEMING. And "why not" is right.

ARNALL (*archly*). She's second. She's in line. That's the way things are. She's in second place. She can beat you there.

FLEMING (*has an original thought*). Hell, she did! I spent the night in first. Right up there at the white line. Got my sack here with food and drink. I'm prepared. Prepared to be first. God damn it! Not second. Not third. Not fifth. I'm prepared for first. But, mind you, if I want to move your old lady and be second, I'll just move your old lady and be second. Just like that.

(ARNALL *steps out of line into* FLEMING'*s way, as* FLEMING *pretends to move toward* MOLLY. FLEMING *quickly jumps into line in* ARNALL'*s spot.* FLEMING *is now fourth.*)

ARNALL (*stunned*). Hey. Hey, you dirty sonofabitch! Sonofabitch! You took my place. He took my place. What the hell is this? Get out of line, Fleming. Move out, Fleming. You took my place!

FLEMING (*laughing*). That's what a woman does to you, what'syourname. That's what a woman does.

ARNALL (*humiliated*). Stop laughing, you sonofabitch!

FLEMING (*a mule giggling*). That's what a woman does to you.

ARNALL (*walks up to* MOLLY, *squares off*). He's right! (*He slaps* MOLLY *on the hand.*)

MOLLY (*amazed and furious*). Arnall! Arnall! Damn you! How could you?

(*She chases him, slapping his head.*
DOLAN *and* FLEMING *quickly move up
one space, laughing.*)
DOLAN (*a jock's scream of victory*).
I'm second. I'm second.
FLEMING (*a neat imitation*). I'm right
behind you.
ARNALL (*giving the proof of the pud-
ding*). Now look, you bitch! Now look.
We're both out. They moved up. You
moved up, you sons of bitches! You snuck
up.
DOLAN. You stepped out.
STEPHEN (*whispers*). Out of line, out of
luck!
DOLAN (*picks it up*). Out of line, out
of luck!
FLEMING (*instinct*). Out of line, out of
luck.
ARNALL. Out of line, out of luck? That
supposed to be funny, huh? That's sup-
posed to be a joke? Out of line, out of
luck?
FLEMING. Who said that?
ARNALL. You said that. "Out of line,
out of luck!"
FLEMING (*a bit boggled, but giddy*).
Well, then . . . that's right! That's what
a woman does to you, Arnall. You lose
your place.
MOLLY. You made me do that, Arnall.
You made me do that.
ARNALL (*too heavy for him*). Shut up,
you bitch! You start first with the shirts,
now my place, now your place. Just shut
up . . . I've got to think.
STEPHEN (*sings*). "Se vuol venire nella
—" I'm first.
FLEMING. Don't be smart, kid. I don't
forget easily. You'll get yours.
STEPHEN. I got mine. I'm first! (*sings*)
   Se vuol venire nella mia scuola,
      La capriolo le insegnero.
That's a song my mother taught me. I'll
never forget it, either. (*sings*)
      Se vuol venire . . . etc.
FLEMING. Forget it.
MOLLY (*sidling up to* STEPHEN). Your
mother?
ARNALL. Stay away from him, Molly.
MOLLY. Shut your dumb mouth, Arnall!
Just shut up. (*to* STEPHEN) Is she young?
(*She puts a foot on* FLEMING's *bag.*)
STEPHEN (*a sweaty Benjamin*). "Metza-
Metz."

(*He sings.*)
      Se vuol venire nella mia . . .
MOLLY (*interrupts*). You've got a
pretty face, you know that?
ARNALL. Molly! For crying out loud.
MOLLY (*to* STEPHEN). Don't pay any
attention to him.
(ARNALL *walks to the other side of the
stage and sits.*)
STEPHEN. I'll pay attention to whom I
choose. To *who* I choose? Whatever I
choose. You know what I mean.
MOLLY. I was saying that you have a
pretty face.
STEPHEN. Yes, you were.
MOLLY. Good bones. Strong bones in
your face. Like James Dean.
STEPHEN. James Dean?
MOLLY. The movie star. The one who
got killed in his Porsche. That's who you
look like. James Dean.
FLEMING. Who's James Dean? A movie
star?
DOLAN. Killed in his what?
STEPHEN. Is James Dean still dead?
MOLLY. Don't make jokes about James
Dean. He was a beautiful boy. And I'm
telling you that you remind me of him.
STEPHEN. I wasn't trying to be funny.
MOLLY. I always wanted to make love
with James Dean.
FLEMING. Holy Jesus!
DOLAN. Shut up!
(*He wants to hear.*)
STEPHEN. Why didn't you?
MOLLY. I never met him, silly. He's a
movie star. And then he got killed. If I
could have met him, I would have made
love to him. If I had been Marilyn Mon-
roe, I'd have played with him.
FLEMING. Monroe? Joltin' Joe's missus?
MOLLY. I could have made him happy.
(*pauses*) I could make you happy.
STEPHEN. I don't have a Porsche.
MOLLY. It's very warm here, don't you
think? Don't you think it's very warm
here?
STEPHEN (*unbuttoning his shirt, just a
few buttons*). Yeah. I can't remember a
time this hot. It makes you want to take
all your clothes off, doesn't it?
MOLLY (*she takes his hand in hers*).
All your clothes.
STEPHEN. Unbearable.
MOLLY. Unbearable.

MOLLY and STEPHEN. Torture.

(*They kiss, a long, deep, passionate kiss. Suddenly, they break apart and dance off, in a comically insane minuet.*)

STEPHEN (*sings. Optional: he sings in German, French, Italian, or English*).
Should he, for instance, wish to go dancing,
He'll face the music, I'll lead the band, yes.
I'll lead the band.
And then I'll take my cue, without ado,
And slyly, very, very, very, very, very slyly.
Using discretion, I shall uncover his secret plan.
Subtly outwitting, innocent seeming,
Cleverly hitting, planning and scheming,
I'll get the best of the hypocrite yet,
I'll beat him yet!

(*As STEPHEN sings, DOLAN and FLEMING talk. ARNALL walks forward quickly to watch MOLLY and STEPHEN as they dance. All are astonished.*)

FLEMING (*almost a whisper*). You've got to hand it to that kid.

DOLAN. Shh! Her old man's watching.

FLEMING. It's disgusting.

DOLAN (*watching the lovers*). What's disgusting?

FLEMING. Her old man watching like that. It ain't natural.

DOLAN. Yeah. It certainly ain't natural.

FLEMING. Sonofabitch! You've got to hand it to that kid. I never would have guessed.

DOLAN. I had a woman once in a car.

FLEMING. What happened?

(*By now, their attitudes should reveal that Molly and Stephen are copulating-by-dance.*)

DOLAN. The usual thing.

FLEMING. That's all?

DOLAN. Yeah.

FLEMING. Oh.

DOLAN. I've never had a woman in a line.

FLEMING. Me neither.

DOLAN. It's funny watching like this, ain't it?

FLEMING. Yeah.

DOLAN. I'd rather be doing it.

FLEMING. Yeah.

(*They both continue to stare goggle-eyed.*)

DOLAN. I'm getting horny.

FLEMING. Yeah.

DOLAN. Yeah.

FLEMING. Yeah.

(*The "yeahs" start to build in a crescendo as the lovers reach their first climax.*)

ARNALL (*from nowhere*). Yeah.

DOLAN. Yeah. Yeah.

ALL. Yeah! Yeah! Yeah! *Yeah!!! Yeah!!!!*

STEPHEN (*sings his orgasm*).
"Piano . . . Piano . . . Piano . . ."!

(*After they dance, MOLLY takes first! STEPHEN sings again, exhausted, but "dances her" out of first place, tired, but not to be undone.*)

FLEMING. He's doing it again!

DOLAN. I can't take much more of this!

FLEMING. What are we going to do?

DOLAN. You figure it out, pal. I know what I want.

(*He jumps forward and grabs MOLLY. Sings "I Want a Girl Just Like the Girl That Married Dear Old Dad." ARNALL tries to jump into first position, but STEPHEN does a terrific baseball slide into first. ARNALL is forced into the slot DOLAN vacated: second. FLEMING is stunned.*)

STEPHEN. I'm still first. I'm still first!

ARNALL (*to MOLLY*). Bitch! Bitch! You bitch!

STEPHEN (*to ARNALL*). You're second. You were nowhere. You were nowhere.

FLEMING. What happened?

ARNALL. He slid into first.

FLEMING. Yeah. But what happened? (*In the meantime, DOLAN and MOLLY are dancing as DOLAN sings. After each "dance," MOLLY calmly attempts to return to first and brush her hair. DOLAN continues singing happily. Over his song, the dialogue continues. FLEMING, finally realizing*) This is terrible. I forgot to move up.

STEPHEN. You didn't move up. You didn't move in. Fleming, you disappoint me. (*He lies down on the floor, goes to sleep.*)

FLEMING (*to ARNALL*). You just let your old lady do that? I mean, does she do it all the time?

ARNALL. All the time. All the time.

FLEMING. That's terrible. That's a terrible thing. You must get embarrassed.

ARNALL. It doesn't hurt any more. Not after all these years.

FLEMING. Why don't you throw her out?

ARNALL. Why? She's predictable.

FLEMING. Predictable?

ARNALL. Consistent. I never have any surprises with Molly. She's pure. All bad.

FLEMING. That's good?

ARNALL. Surprises hurt. You should know that. Look how hurt you were when you didn't move up. Or "move in." You were surprised and hurt, right?

FLEMING. That's bad.

ARNALL. Right. My philosophy is quite simple. Never ever leave yourself open for surprises, and you'll never be surprised. Surprise brings pain, pain is bad. No surprise, no pain. No pain, no bad. No bad, all good. (*proudly*) I've got it made.

DOLAN. Da-ah-aahd!

ARNALL (*after a pause*). They're finished now. Want to take a whack at it?

FLEMING. What?

ARNALL. Go on. Go ahead. Have a bash. Have a go at it. It'll do you good. Go on. I don't mind.

FLEMING. You sure?

ARNALL. Positive.

FLEMING. Do you mind if Dolan holds my place in line?

ARNALL. Of course not.

FLEMING. Hey, Dolan.

DOLAN. What?

FLEMING. Hold my place in line, will you. I'd like to have a bash.

DOLAN. Have a what?

FLEMING. Have a go at it. That's what her old man calls it. Hey, Dolan. Hold my place, will you?

DOLAN (*slides into* FLEMING's *place and falls there*). Go get it.

(FLEMING *stares at* DOLAN, MOLLY, ARNALL, *and the lot again. He grabs* MOLLY *and drags her upstage slightly, he "counts" a foxtrot beat. He sings his song and they dance.*)

FLEMING. One two three—one two three—one two three—and—

(*Sings "Take Me Out to the Ball Game." As he continues his song, the dialogue does not stop.*)

DOLAN. I like the way you think, Arnold.

ARNALL. You mean my little philosophy?

DOLAN (*a bit confused*). Yeah, I guess you could call it that. Your little philosophy. I like the way you think, Arnold.

ARNALL. *Arnall.* (*spells it, then goes on like a house-on-fire*) A-R-N-A-L-L. My mother wanted to call me Arthur. My father liked Nathan. Thought it was strong. My grandmother liked Lloyd, after Harold Lloyd. So they took the A-R from Arthur, the N-A from Nathan, the L-L from Lloyd, and called me Arnall. What do you want?

DOLAN. I like the way you think, Arnold. I want to tell you how touched I am. I have a little philosophy myself; I call it the Under*dog* philosophy.

ARNALL. Under*dog*?

DOLAN. Did you ever hear of Arnold Palmer? Arnold Palmer is the world's richest golfer. He always looks like he is going to lose, but he almost never loses. He's the world's richest golfer.

ARNALL. I don't get it.

DOLAN. Everybody wants to be first, right?

ARNALL. Right.

DOLAN. Now you can be obvious about it. Just jump in like the kid and yell and brag about being first. Or about deserving to be first. What I mean is you got to stand back a little. (DOLAN *has walked* ARNALL *around in a circle and is about to take second place.*) Maybe in second place for a while. Then when nobody's looking, you kind of sneak into first place. But first you got to build up everybody's confidence that you're really one hell of a nice guy. You smile a lot. You say nice things all the time like, "Great night for a line," or, "Terrific wife you've got there, Arnall, kid." Then, when everybody likes you . . . you sneak up.

ARNALL. I still don't get it.

DOLAN (*now in second place*). You notice I'm second in line? You notice I was second to make it with your wife. Second in this line to make it . . . right?

ARNALL. Right.

DOLAN. There you are.

ARNALL. Why do you call that Under*dog*?

DOLAN. The easiest way to kick a dog in the balls is to be underneath him. Let him walk on top of you for a while. Take good aim. And . . .

ARNALL. I get it.

(FLEMING *and* MOLLY *waltz into view, and then off.*)

DOLAN. Good boy. Terrific wife you got there, Arnall. Kid. Great night for a line. (ARNALL *is crying.*) What's the matter?

ARNALL. My philosophy is quite simple. Never ever leave yourself open for surprise and you'll never be surprised. Surprise brings pain. Pain is bad. No pain, no bad. No bad all good. I've got it made. (*weeping now*) I've got it made.

DOLAN. You've got to learn to take it easy, Arnall. You're making a wreck of yourself with all that unhappiness. You got to get happy.

ARNALL. I have a real philosophy, real philosophy. I'm supposed to be gleeful. All the time. I didn't know. I really didn't know. I knew she had friends.

DOLAN. Certainly she had friends. She's very friendly.

ARNALL. But I thought they were just friends.

DOLAN (*checking* FLEMING). They'll be done soon.

ARNALL. I can't stand it! I can't stand it!

(ARNALL *rushes to* FLEMING *and* MOLLY. *He taps* FLEMING *on the shoulder, "cutting in."* FLEMING *nods and moves into line.*)

FLEMING (*realizing*). Hey, I didn't finish. I didn't finish. I didn't finish. I didn't finish.

DOLAN. Hop in line. You can be third.

FLEMING. But I didn't finish! Didn't you see?

DOLAN. See? Of course I saw. You were doing it with his old lady. Right in front of his eyes!!!

FLEMING. *You* did it in front of his eyes.

DOLAN. Jesus, don't remind me.

FLEMING. I didn't finish. For Christ's sake, I'm hornier than ever.

STEPHEN. What took you so long?

FLEMING. Shut up, kid. Shut up before I finish with *you.*

ARNALL (*tapping out a bunny hop beat*). Molly. It's me, Arnall. Your husband.

MOLLY (*shocked*). Arnall? What the hell are you doing?

ARNALL (*dancing the bunny hop*). I'm doing it. With you. My wife. A surprise, Molly! A surprise!

MOLLY. You've lost your place in line. You stepped out of line!

ARNALL (*tapping away*). I couldn't stand it. Watching all those others doing it with you. It drove me crazy. It made me want you, Molly. I really want you.

MOLLY (*tapping with him*). Oh, Arnall. You're such a bore.

ARNALL (*humming "Tiptoe Through the Tulips" before he speaks*). Please, Molly. Please.

MOLLY (*They're dancing now.*) Well, you're doing it, aren't you?

ARNALL (*hums "Tiptoe" and dances a bit*). I am. Oh. I am. Oh, I like it, Molly. I like it.

MOLLY (*bored sick*). Hurry up, Arnall. Hurry up.

ARNALL (*stops*). Shall I sing?

MOLLY (*angry*). Just hurry up, Arnall. Just hurry up.

(ARNALL *sings "Tiptoe Through the Tulips," picking it up in the middle and continuing to end of song. Exits.*)

DOLAN (*pauses*). Now that's the way it should be. A man and his wife. That's a beautiful thing. Great night, huh?

(STEPHEN, *helping* ARNALL *and* MOLLY *gain speed, sings his wallet.*)

STEPHEN (*to "Tiptoe" tune*).
Saks' card and a Hertz card and an Avis card
And a Un-ih-Card Card
Diners Club and a Chemical New York.

DOLAN. That's a beautiful sight, isn't it?

FLEMING. It's terrible. *Terrible.* I never finished.

DOLAN. Just wait, Fleming. Let the husband finish first. That's decent enough. Then you can finish. You can start from scratch.

MOLLY. Hurry up, Arnall.

FLEMING. Yeah, Arnall. Hurry up.

(ARNALL'S *erection and song begin to "die" offstage.*)

STEPHEN (*a dirge, sings*).
That's one's dead. That one's dead.
That's one's dead. That one's dead.

DOLAN. Sing a happy song, kid. For Christ's sake. That part of your wallet depresses the hell out of me.

STEPHEN (*He sings again.*)
Henry Brown, insurance man.

Harry Schwartz, the tailor.
Alvin Krantz, delivery service.
My Uncle Max, the sailor.
Franklin National Saving Bank.
(MOLLY *and* ARNALL *bunny hop onto stage with gusto.*)
Doyle, and Dane and Bernbach
DOLAN. That's nice. That's got a beat.
STEPHEN (*stops. Speaks*). He's ready! He's ready!
ARNALL (*screams*). Surprise, Molly! Surprise!
DOLAN. That's a beautiful thing.
(ARNALL *collapses in* MOLLY'S *arms.*)
ARNALL. Were you surprised, Molly?
MOLLY. Let me go, Arnall.
FLEMING. No. Not yet. Not yet. I never finished.
(FLEMING *grabs* MOLLY.)
MOLLY. Hey.
FLEMING (*explaining, a whiny child*). I never finished.
MOLLY. Take the gum out of your mouth.
FLEMING. Oh.
ARNALL. What place am I in?
DOLAN. Third.
STEPHEN. Last.
ARNALL. I'd rather be third.
STEPHEN. You're in last place.
DOLAN. Shut up, kid. Don't listen to the kid. You're third. Two from the front. You did very well. I watched you all the way.
ARNALL. It's been a long time. My legs are all rubbery. I'm very nauseous. I've got to practice up a little, maybe. A little practice and I'd be better.
DOLAN. You did good.
ARNALL. I'll practice up some. (FLEMING *sings "Take Me Out to the Ball Game." They dance off.*) Oh, God! Him again.
DOLAN. Don't watch. You'll feel better. (*Pours beer into* ARNALL'S *mouth.* FLEMING, *offstage, continues song at a more rapid speed.*) You feeling any better now?
ARNALL (*screams*). I want it again.
DOLAN. You what?
ARNALL. I want it again. Molly's mine. I want it again. I liked it.
DOLAN. You'll get sick again, pal. You know it makes you sick.
ARNALL. I like it. I like it. (FLEMING *and* MOLLY *dance back on—past* ARNALL. *They stop in front of* DOLAN.)

DOLAN. Fleming. (*no answer*) Fleming! (*no answer*) Fleming.
(DOLAN *reaches over with his foot and kicks* FLEMING *a hard one in the behind.* FLEMING *wheels around, dazzled.*)
FLEMING. What's the matter?
DOLAN (*flatly*). Her old man wants it again.
FLEMING (*overlapping*). He had it already.
DOLAN (*overlapping*). He wants it again.
STEPHEN (*wise ass*). He wants it again.
FLEMING (*angrily*). I heard Dolan!
DOLAN (*flatly*). He wants it again.
ARNALL (*cockily*). I want it again.
FLEMING (*as though no one knows. To* MOLLY). Your old man wants it again.
MOLLY (*a solid pronouncement*). I want the boy.
DOLAN (*senses the unjust*). But your old man wants it.
MOLLY (*a solid pronouncement*). I want the boy.
DOLAN (*realizes he might move up to the Big Space*). She wants you.
STEPHEN (*exhausted with the understanding of this complicated moment*). I heard her.
MOLLY (*moving in*). I want you, boy.
STEPHEN (*holding his eyes*). I heard you.
ARNALL (*overlapping*). She likes them young.
FLEMING (*overlapping*). What about me?
DOLAN. You had two chances.
FLEMING. I didn't finish.
DOLAN. You had two chances.
FLEMING. I was almost finished. Some bastard kicked me!
DOLAN. Two chances. I only had one. The kid only had one.
FLEMING. The kid took two.
DOLAN. Two on one chance. *He's a kid.*
ARNALL. She likes the young ones. She always likes the young ones.
MOLLY. Come here, boy.
STEPHEN (*pretends to be engrossed in his wallet*). American Express. Chemical New York. Unicard. My library card!
(STEPHEN *is pulled out by* MOLLY. DOLAN *jumps up into first position.* FLEMING *jumps over* ARNALL.)
DOLAN. I'm first! I'm first.

STEPHEN. You've made me lose my place.

MOLLY. You have such a wonderful bone structure.

ARNALL. She always always likes them young. (STEPHEN *knows he's out for now. He laughs. He and* MOLLY *dance off, singing together in harmony.*) I'm last, last, last. *Last dammit!*

DOLAN. You're third. (*to* FLEMING) Tell him he's third.

FLEMING. You're third.

ARNALL. I'm last. There are only three of us. One, two, three. Three is me. I'm last.

DOLAN. Two over there. Those two. The kid and your terrific wife.

FLEMING (*counting on his fingers*). That makes five.

DOLAN. You're two from the front and two from the back. Two from the first and two from last. You're the average.

(STEPHEN *sings lightly now as he and* MOLLY *dance.* ARNALL *tells his story to the world.*)

ARNALL. I would like to tell the story of my marriage. I worked hard every night. I knew she had friends, but I never knew they were doing it. (*pauses*) That's the story of my marriage.

(*There is a shaggy-dog silence.*)

DOLAN. As first man, I say that Arnall gets a chance to do it again as soon as the kid is finished. (STEPHEN *screams the ending of his song, "Piano."*) The kid is finished.

FLEMING. Have a bash, Arnall.

ARNALL. I'll lose my place in line. Never mind.

DOLAN. Stay put, then. Fleming? You want a whack at it? You want a third, uh, try?

FLEMING. I'm second. It ain't worth it now. You want another one, Dolan? Huh? Why don't you have a go at it? Give it another bash.

DOLAN. You're pretty obvious, Fleming. Pretty obvious. Did anybody ever tell you how dumb you are? Did anybody ever take the time to tell you just how really dumb and stupid you really are?

FLEMING (*after a hideously long pause*). You think I don't know? You think I'm too stupid to know how dumb I am? Brains ain't everything, you know? I

ain't exactly at the end of the line. It ain't over yet.

(STEPHEN *walks to the opposite side of the line and squares off with* DOLAN, *eye to eye.* STEPHEN *speaks with simple authority.*)

STEPHEN. The line's facing the wrong way.

DOLAN (*incredulously*). What the hell are you talking about, kid?

STEPHEN (*to all; an announcement*). The line's facing the wrong way. (*to* DOLAN) The line's facing the wrong way. I'm first.

(STEPHEN *and* DOLAN *eye each other for a full half minute with terrifying tension. Nobody moves.* STEPHEN *smiles a frozen smile.* DOLAN *wipes his hands with a handkerchief, checking everyone in line. As* DOLAN *checks to one side,* MOLLY *quickly sneaks around into second place, behind* STEPHEN. DOLAN *does a take.* ARNALL *quickly slides around, following* MOLLY. *He's now third in* STEPHEN's *line.* DOLAN *does a full take. Then* DOLAN *turns to* FLEMING *and signals* FLEMING *to "take it easy," to wait, to rest.* FLEMING *nods agreement. Suddenly, as soon as* FLEMING's *settled down,* DOLAN *races into fourth place in* STEPHEN's *line.* FLEMING *sees and races after him, ending up last. When* STEPHEN's *line is settled; the very instant, in fact, that* STEPHEN's *line is full,* STEPHEN *steps over the line into the true first position. He smiles. All others freeze, staring at him.* MOLLY *breaks and jumps into second*)

MOLLY. I'm second!

(DOLAN *bolts into third*)

DOLAN. I'm third!

FLEMING (*leaping into fourth*). I'm fourth!

ARNALL (*limping into last*). I'm last. Bitch-damn-crap! I'm really last now.

DOLAN (*overlapping*). Oh, man. That was rotten, kid. Really and truly filthy rotten.

FLEMING (*overlapping*). That kid is no good. I told you that kid was no good.

ARNALL (*overlapping*). Always the young ones. I'm sick of it. Sick of it. Sick of the young ones getting to be first.

DOLAN (*screams*). We'll get him, Arnall.

FLEMING. Not finished. Not first! We'll

get him. (*screams*) We're gonna' get you, kid!

ARNALL (*whining*). Cuckolded. Cuckolded. I'm a buffoon. (*screams*) A buffoon!!!

MOLLY (*desperately sexual, caressing with her voice*). You have the face of a president. A movie star. A senator. You have a Kennedy's face. A beautiful face.

FLEMING (*overlapping*). Breathe the air now, kid. Breathe it deep! We're gonna' get you!

DOLAN (*overlapping*). Third. First to goddam third!

ARNALL (*overlapping*). Last. Really last. This time there's no question.

STEPHEN (*a maniacal scream*). SHUT UP, IDIOTS!!!

FLEMING. Who the hell are you calling "idiot"????

STEPHEN. All of you. Idiots. Fools. Lemmings. Pigs. Lint.

DOLAN. Lint?

MOLLY. Lint?

ARNALL. Lint?

FLEMING. Lint?

STEPHEN. Lint!

FLEMING. Oh, boy. Oh, boy. That's the limit. We're gonna' have your ass, kid.

STEPHEN. It's too late, idiots. I've won. I'm in first and anyone who isn't in first is an idiot. We've got nothing in common, so why talk about it?

DOLAN. We've all got something in common, kid. And don't you forget it, either.

STEPHEN. What's that, Dolan????

DOLAN. We've all been at his terrific wife. Whatever she's got, we've got.

FLEMING. That's true. We're like a club. Whatever she's got, we've got. (*does a huge "take" to* ARNALL) What's she got?

STEPHEN. They're right, damn you! You let them all have you. Even your husband.

ARNALL (*hopefully*). Molly?

MOLLY. Nobody had me.

FLEMING. Nobody but all of us!

MOLLY. Nobody had me.

STEPHEN (*turns sharply about to* MOLLY). Everybody had you . . . everybody.

MOLLY. Nobody had me.

DOLAN. She's crazy, too. (*to* ARNALL) You've got a crazy wife, mister.

MOLLY. Nobody had me, get it? Nobody. *I* had all of you. *I* did the doing. Not you. *I* made the choices. You all

wanted to be first, what kept you from it, huh? What kept you? (*pushes* STEPHEN *over the line, out of first place, viciously. He falls to one side, shocked.*) I'm first now. *Me!*

STEPHEN (*wandering, confused*). You pushed me. She pushed me.

MOLLY. I'm first now!

DOLAN. She's crazy. You've got a crazy wife, mister. This is a terrible night.

STEPHEN. Don't flatter yourself, Molly. Not for a second. You've screwed your way to first and you'll be screwed right out of first. That's the way it's always been and that's the way it's always going to be. This line's my last, Molly. You really think I'm going to let you come in first?

MOLLY. I am first. I am first. And I'm not moving. I screwed my way to first and now I'm resting. Maybe this is my last line, too. Look who's first. Just look who's first. Me! Molly. Just where I knew I'd be from the moment I saw this line.

FLEMING. You got yourself a real bitch for a wife there, Arnall. A real bitch.

ARNALL. I know. I know.

MOLLY. I know what you've been thinking all night. Here we are, four big shots. One woman in line. Might as well roll her over, just to kill time. That's what you're always thinking. That's what every line's about, right? And you think in any other place you'd never give me a look . . . but . . . as long as we're all killing time together . . . why not? 'Course, under *normal* conditions, she'd never be good enough for me. Well, I've got a piece of news for you all: under any conditions, none of you is good enough for me. Not a one of you!

STEPHEN (*crosses to her*). Molly. You're good enough for me.

MOLLY. Go to the back of the line, boy. You didn't satisfy me. You didn't make it. You didn't thrill me. You need experience. You make love like a child.

STEPHEN. What about my beautiful bones?

MOLLY. Go to the back of the line.

DOLAN. That's telling the wise-ass kid. Go to the back of the line, kid. You heard the lady.

MOLLY. Don't gloat. Don't lick your lips. I could have done better with an ape than with you.

FLEMING. Terrific, Molly. An ape, Dolan. An ape.

MOLLY. Are you the one with the beer and the gum who's too old and tired to finish?

FLEMING. What's that supposed to mean?

ARNALL. Molly? Molly? Is it me?

MOLLY. Don't be a bore, Arnall. You couldn't satisfy a canary.

DOLAN. You've run out. If none of us satisfied you, who did?

MOLLY. None of you. Simple as that. I am an unsatisfied woman still looking for a man. You all failed.

DOLAN. I've had better than you, tubby, and I mean some real beauties. And they've screamed for more. Screamed for more!

MOLLY. More money? Okay. Sure. I can understand that.

FLEMING. I've had models.

DOLAN. Screw your models. I had one in a car once.

FLEMING. Yeah. You told me.

MOLLY. I'm first. I'm unsatisfied. I've had four men. One three times. One unfinished. And I'm unsatisfied.

ARNALL. Don't let her get to you. Don't let her get you going. She'll drive you all crazy. Make surprises. Ruin all your philosophies. She'll hide your shirts.

MOLLY. Arnall, you're such a bore.

STEPHEN (*crosses to her, whispers*). I've got something to tell you.

MOLLY. To the back of the line, sonny. You lost. You're last . . . move.

DOLAN. You're out of line completely, kid. She's right. When the crowds come, you'll be left out altogether.

(STEPHEN *wanders to portal.*)

MOLLY. I hope there's a man in the *crowd.* One man.

ARNALL. You see what I mean? She won't let up now. Now that she's first, she'll just keep pouring it on.

DOLAN. She's worse than *my* old lady. Much worse. My old lady's a dog, but nothing like yours. Yours is the biggest dog of all. Queen dog. Yeah. She's the biggest dog of all. How'd you get stuck with her, anyway?

ARNALL. She picked me up at a party. I was at a party. The lights were dim. I felt a hand sneak between my legs. I was

only fifteen. It was Molly. She taught me everything I know. I don't know anything either.

STEPHEN (*a proclamation*). When I make love to a woman, I never shut my eyes. Never. I watch. I watch and I listen to every movement she makes.

FLEMING (*embarrassed*). Shut up!

DOLAN (*wants to hear* STEPHEN's *"secret"*). You shut up, Fleming.

STEPHEN. I listen to every movement she makes. So that every time I move, I understand her response. One little wiggle to the left, one little wiggle to the right and I get a response I remember. I make notes. I have a whole loose-leaf binder filled with notes and half another filled as well. All kinds of notes. How to wiggle front and back. How short women respond. How tall women respond. How certain ethnic groups respond.

MOLLY. What did you learn from me, little boy?

STEPHEN (*his guile has worked. He knows it. He sets up his next line carefully, ready to strike. He moves into position close to* MOLLY). Never screw an ugly, greedy, slob like you. Always to follow my natural desire. Only screw who I want, when I want. If I had followed my natural desire, I never would have screwed you. Not once. Not twice, certainly. Not three times. It was all an incredible waste of my incredibly valuable time. That's what I wanted to tell you.

MOLLY (*explodes*). You little squirt! You little jerk!

(*She charges at him in a rage. He knocks her aside and regains first position . . .*
MOLLY *is out of line.*)

STEPHEN (*with a flourish*). Gentlemen, I am first again.

FLEMING. You've really got to hand it to that kid. Go on, Dolan. Hand it to the kid.

DOLAN (*he is standing on* STEPHEN's *toes*). Nice work, kid.

ARNALL (*a small bitch*). I'm not last. You're last, Molly. I'm ahead of you. You're last.

DOLAN (*ruefully*). Nice work, kid.

STEPHEN. Say it again, Dolan.

DOLAN. Nice work, kid. (*He pushes* STEPHEN *violently offstage.* DOLAN *takes first.* STEPHEN *falls into the audience.*)

Look who's first now, will you?

STEPHEN. You pushed me. He pushed me. Hey, he pushed. Did you see him??? That's not fair, Dolan.

DOLAN. I'm first.

FLEMING (*jumps forward*). I'm second.

ARNALL (*jumps forward*). I'm third.

MOLLY. I'm fourth.

STEPHEN (*starts walking up the aisle*). I'm out.

DOLAN. In every crowd, there's a winner. A winner. I waited back there. I hung in. Look at me now.

STEPHEN (*from the back of the theatre*). You broke the rules, Dolan.

DOLAN. What rules?

STEPHEN (*from another aisle*). He pushed me.

DOLAN. She pushed you.

STEPHEN (*screaming*). She's a woman. That's different.

FLEMING. That's true, Dolan. It's different when it's a woman. Especially *that* woman.

ARNALL. You see, Molly's always breaking rules. She breaks everything. Dishes. Cups. Saucers.

MOLLY. Just shut your dumb mouth, Arnall!

FLEMING. Yeah. Shut up, Arnall. We got to figure this out.

DOLAN. What's to figure out? I'm up front. Head of the line. I won. That's pretty simple.

FLEMING. Yeah, but you pushed the kid. We sort of had an unwritten rule here. I mean, none of us did any pushing.

DOLAN. You want to push me, Fleming?

FLEMING. Hey, look. Don't start that stuff! I'm a hell of a lot tougher than you, pal. You want to start that stuff and that's the kind of stuff you'll get. You know what I mean?

STEPHEN (*walking back to the stage*). I'd hate to see you start a fight over me, Fleming. It's probably better that I just stay right out of line. You people can handle things on your own. You don't need me.

FLEMING. Yeah, I suppose.

DOLAN. What the hell are you trying to do, kid? You're gonna' just *let* me stay in first? You ain't gonna' trick me out of it?

STEPHEN (*standing, facing the stage*).

You don't trust people. That's your trouble, Dolan. You think everybody's out to get you all the time, don't you?

DOLAN. I don't think of anybody but NUMBER ONE. I hung in back there in second all that time. I knew what I was doing. I've watched you up there. I knew when to strike. I knew when my iron was hot. I waited it out. I'm first. That's simple, isn't it?

STEPHEN (*leaning on the stage*). There are ways of getting to first that are acceptable and ways of getting to first that are unacceptable. Women and children excluded, of course.

FLEMING. That's right.

DOLAN. What's right?

FLEMING. The thing he said about women and children. That's always the way about women and children.

STEPHEN. Women and children first.

FLEMING. Women and children first.

STEPHEN. Dolan's not a women.

FLEMING. Dolan's not a children.

ARNALL. Dolan's none of those things.

MOLLY. Dolan's nothing.

STEPHEN. Everybody's something.

FLEMING. Not Dolan!!! (FLEMING *pushes* DOLAN *violently offstage, and takes first.*) Holy Christ! I'm in first place!

ARNALL. I'm second.

MOLLY (*jumping up*). I'm third.

DOLAN (*crawling back on stage*). For Christ's sakes! For crying out loud! Fleming pushed me.

STEPHEN. You changed the rules. You pushed first.

DOLAN. She pushed first.

FLEMING. Holy Christ! I'm really in first place. I'm first guy. Top dog. (*And he pushes* DOLAN *offstage again*).

DOLAN. He pushed me right out of first place.

MOLLY (*she pushes* ARNALL). Be a winner, Arnall.

(*She pushes* ARNALL *so hard, he clobbers* FLEMING *right out of first place.* ARNALL *is first now.*)

FLEMING. Hey! Hey! Hey!

(DOLAN *crawls back onto the stage and* FLEMING *crashes into him—*DOLAN *flies offstage again.*)

ARNALL. I didn't do that. She did that. She pushed me so hard I pushed you. I didn't push you. Honest to God, I didn't push you. Here. Take it back.

(ARNALL *walks right out of first place, trembling. He leads* FLEMING *by the hand back into first place.* MOLLY *stands frozen. Astonished.* DOLAN *crawls back on stage and into second.*)

FLEMING. I'm first again.

DOLAN. I'm second. Hah! I'm second.

ARNALL (*slipping, mincing into third, in front of an astonished* MOLLY, *he says simply:*) I'm third.

MOLLY. Arnall, you damn dumb fool! Look what you did. Look what you did, you damn dumb dummy.

ARNALL. I gave that to you, Fleming. I gave you first. But you've got to protect me!

FLEMING. From what?

ARNALL. Her.

FLEMING. Why?

ARNALL. Please, Fleming?

FLEMING. Why?

MOLLY. Damn you, Arnall! Damn you! (*She beats him, like a child swatting a mosquito.*)

ARNALL. See? See what I mean? I need help, Fleming. Help me, Fleming.

FLEMING (*he walks to* MOLLY *and talks to her, reasonably*). Now look, ma'am. I don't want to hurt a lady. I've never hurt a lady.

ARNALL. She's no lady.

DOLAN *jumps into first, incredulously*). I'm first again!

(*Everybody freezes, out of line, as* DOLAN *stands alone.*)

FLEMING. Now just wait a goddamned minute!

DOLAN. I'm first, first!

(FLEMING *clobbers* DOLAN.)

ARNALL. This is awful. (*jumps in first*).

MOLLY. This is your fault, Arnall. (*Pushes* ARNALL *out*)

STEPHEN (*from the audience, giggling*). I'd say it was Dolan's fault.

DOLAN. Knock it off, kid!

STEPHEN. Hell, I'll knock it off. If you hadn't broken the rules and pushed me, we'd be in a perfectly straight line. This is chaos, friends! Chaos.

(ARNALL *dashes into first place.*)

ARNALL. I'm first. I'm first!

(DOLAN *slams* ARNALL *to the ground.*)

DOLAN. No, you're not. I am. I'm first.

MOLLY (*attacking* DOLAN, *she kicks his testicles*). Move out of there. Move. (*They all end up in a horrible fistfight, ending with* DOLAN *hitting* MOLLY *fiercely . . .* ARNALL *crawls in and bites* MOLLY's *leg.*)

FLEMING (*astonished*). You hit her. You hit her!

STEPHEN. See? See what you have? Chaos. Pure, plain and simple. Chaos.

FLEMING. You're goddamned right it is, kid. Goddamned right. (FLEMING *has* DOLAN's *arm pinned.*) Help the kid back in the line. Go on.

DOLAN. Are you crazy?

FLEMING. I've seen this happen before. Help him back!

STEPHEN (*walking into line, into first*). Anybody mind my being first?

DOLAN. I held back, dammit! I waited! What is this? ? ? ?

FLEMING (*screams at* DOLAN). Don't!

DOLAN (*frightened*). Okay. Okay. (DOLAN *suddenly lurches for first.* FLEMING *grabs him and beats him with three quick terrifying punches.*) Ughhh. Ahhh. Ughhh.

FLEMING. I said "don't" and I mean "don't"! Everybody hear me? Huh? Everybody hear me clear.

DOLAN (*whipped*). I'm second.

FLEMING. Okay. I'll stay in third. 'Til we get straightened out. You, Arnall. You get fourth. And you, you fat bitch, you started this pushing business. You get in fifth.

ARNALL (*like a three-year-old child*). I'm not last. You're last, Molly. I'm ahead of you. You're last.

FLEMING. Everybody shut up! (*pauses*) Okay, kid. What do we do now?

STEPHEN. Shut up and listen. (*He presses the "on" button on his tape recorder and Mozart's "Eine Kleine Nachtmusik" fills the theatre.*) Can you feel him? Mozart. "Eine Kleine Nachtmusik." The Allegro. He was younger than me when he wrote this. A baby. The Allegro. Then Andante. Then Minuet. Then Rondo.

ARNALL. Austrian, right? Isn't he Austrian, Stephen?

STEPHEN. That's Mozart, for Christ's sakes! It's Mozart. I'm not first. I'm second. Stop. Please. This is crazy. This is a crazy thing. (STEPHEN *turns off the re-*

corder.)

FLEMING. You're the crazy thing.

ARNALL (*really spooky*). You know how he died, Stephen? Singers came in and sang him to death. His Requiem, Stephen. They sang while he died.

STEPHEN (*staring at the Mozart he sees ahead of him*). It's not true. It's not true.

ARNALL. But I was there, Stephen. I saw it. I heard it.

STEPHEN (*weeping*). Stop it. Stop it.

ARNALL. I was there, Stephen. He was writing the percussion up until the last. Boom-boom. Boom-boom. (ARNALL *marches singing "boom-boom."*)

STEPHEN. I'm losing my mind.

MOLLY. Arnall. You weasel, Arnall.

ARNALL. Boom-boom. Just shut up, you bitch! Just shut up. Boom-boom.

STEPHEN. No! This isn't happening! I'm first. Look at me. I'm first. I earned this, I know I did!

FLEMING. Bullshit, you did! We'll get you, kid.

DOLAN. We'll get you, kid.

ARNALL. Want me to sing it, Stephen? The Requiem? Want me to sing The Requiem now? (*He sings like a choirboy: "La-ah cree-mo-sa, Ita-es-eela. etc." He continues The Requiem and* STEPHEN *seems totally hypnotized. He walks toward* STEPHEN *and then past him. He moves around past* DOLAN *and* FLEMING, *who stare wide-eyed. He swings around again, softly singing, heading straight for first place.*) Boom-boom. Boom-boom. It could be lovely, Stephen. Lovely. I'll sing . . . (*checks, sees*) . . . and Dolan . . . boom-boom . . .

DOLAN (*taking a nod from* ARNALL). Boom-boom . . . boom-boom . . .

ARNALL . . . and Fleming . . . boom-boom . . .

FLEMING (*confused, follows with his voice*). Boom-boom . . . boom-boom . . .

ARNALL . . . will do their work . . . BOOM BOOM . . . BOOM BOOM . . . BOOM BOOM . . .

DOLAN and FLEMING. BOOM BOOM . . . BOOM BOOM . . .

ARNALL. BOOM BOOM . . . BOOM . . . BOOM . . . BOOM BOOM . . .

(STEPHEN *grabs his neck in anguished pain. He screams a most hideous scream and falls forward onto his face. He writhes on the floor, sobbing in agony.* ARNALL *walks quietly into first place.*)

FLEMING (*after a huge pause*). That's terrible. I'll never sing with you again, Arnall.

DOLAN. Holy Jesus Christ!! Will you look at that????

(STEPHEN *is silently staring from the floor. He sees* ARNALL. *He stands slowly, almost berserk now. He lunges at* ARNALL, *grabbing his throat.*)

STEPHEN. You little twirp! You little plucked chicken. You step back, Arnall. You're playing with fire, Arnall. Fire. You move now or I'm going to strangle you, Arnall. You'll be dead, Arnall.

ARNALL. Please, Stephen. Please. I only want Molly. I don't want first. Only Molly. Please, Stephen. Please???

(*But* STEPHEN's *too far gone. He squeezes* ARNALL's *throat.*)

STEPHEN. You move or I'll kill you, Arnall! Do you believe me?

(ARNALL *and* STEPHEN *stare at each other. A long hold.*)

ARNALL (*defeated*). Yes.

STEPHEN. Back of the line, Arnall.

FLEMING. Yeah, Arnall. Back of the line. I can't see what the kid is saying when you're standing there. You're blocking me from the kid.

DOLAN. That ain't right, Arnall. Move back, Arnall.

FLEMING. Move back, Arnall.

MOLLY (*fiercely*). You heard them! Move!!!

(ARNALL *walks slowly to the end of the line. Broken. Defeated*)

FLEMING (*breaking the horrific silence of* ARNALL's *total humiliation*). What's next, kid?

STEPHEN. The end. I beat all of you, not with luck, but with genius. There's only one person to beat, and you can't see him in this line. *I* can see him in this line. (STEPHEN *is now screaming at the place in front of him.*) I'll beat you. I'll die youngest, the best. And after I'm gone you'll see I can take it with me!

(STEPHEN *turns on the recorder to an unbearable volume and slides the machine across the stage. It lands, blaring and staring up at a startled* ARNALL. *Slowly, carefully,* STEPHEN *picks up the line—that white piece of tape that is first place itself—and eats it, as a berserk strand of spaghetti.* ARNALL *picks up the tape recorder and smashes the "off" button: killing it, as though he were swatting an insect.*)

ARNALL (*in the now-deafening silence; carefully*). You *are* crazy! You are an insane, horrible child. (ARNALL *draws a deep, deep breath.*)

STEPHEN (*He's swallowed the tape by now*). How dare you, you cuckolded little nothing!!! You let your wife—your fat horrible wife—screw on the street while you do nothing more than watch. She screws and you watch. And tomorrow you'll crawl in bed beside her with your chubby clean-but-sweaty little body begging for a whore's kisses!!!

MOLLY. You animal! You animal! Hit him, Arnall! Hit him!

ARNALL. We're much older than you are, son. You could show some respect.

STEPHEN (*The final insult follows*). Maybe I hate you most, Arnall. Just maybe. (*like a bullet*) You're a loser, Arnall.

FLEMING. It's okay, Arnall, you can hit him. Boom Boom. Boom Boom.

STEPHEN. I won! I did it! I did it! I did it. I won. I won. (*chasing them all*) Come on, Arnall. It's okay now. Hit me. Scratch my eyes out. Kill me.

ARNALL. Me?

STEPHEN. You. Anybody. Come on. Let's get on with it.

DOLAN. We're gonna get you, kid.

STEPHEN. Do it, Dolan. Do it.

FLEMING. Go on, Arnall. Get him. Boom Boom.

MOLLY. Hit him, Arnall. Boom Boom. (MOLLY *gets the recorder and gives it to* ARNALL.)

ARNALL. Me?

DOLAN. Kill him, Arnall. Boom Boom.

ARNALL. Me?

DOLAN *and* FLEMING. Kill him, Arnall. Boom Boom.

STEPHEN (*He laughs maniacally*). *I* can take it with me. I finally won!

(STEPHEN *kneels; head up, eyes closed— waiting to be killed.* DOLAN, FLEMING, *and* MOLLY *chant "Boom Boom" over and over, urging* ARNALL *to kill* STEPHEN.)

ARNALL. You son of a bitch! You son of

a bitch!!!

(ARNALL *takes tape recorder and raises it to kill* STEPHEN. *He stops, as* MOLLY *shrieks. They all stop and jump back one step.*)

STEPHEN (*opens his eyes; stands, amazed*). What's wrong? Why are you stopping? Somebody's got to kill me.

ARNALL. Us?

FLEMING. Kill him?

MOLLY. Kill him?

STEPHEN. You've got to kill me. I've got to die first. Please . . . please . . . please . . . please . . . please . . .

(*Dolan walks into first position, but of course the line is gone.* DOLAN *is astonished.*)

DOLAN (*a whine*). Where's the line?

FLEMING. The line! Where is it?

ARNALL. The line!

MOLLY. Arnall! The line's gone.

ARNALL. Where'd it go?

STEPHEN (*burps a little, smiles*). I ate it.

FLEMING. What?

STEPHEN. I ate it. (*He groans.*)

MOLLY. He ate it. He ate it?

FLEMING. He ate it. He ate it?

DOLAN. He ate it?

ARNALL. He ate it?

STEPHEN. I ate it.

MOLLY. See? I'm right. He *is* crazy. He's really crazy.

FLEMING. I told you that, lady. I told you that the second you walked up. He's really crazy.

STEPHEN. What is this? I'm supposed to die!

(*He's stunned, as it appears that he isn't going to die after all*)

MOLLY. He wanted us to beat him so he'd die so there'd be a dead kid in first. And we were supposed to just watch.

ARNALL. How could we watch a thing like that?

FLEMING. Why not? We've been watching everything else.

MOLLY. Oh, my God! What if I'm pregnant?

ARNALL. Pregnant? Molly. A son? A son, Molly?

FLEMING (*thrilled; laughs a relieved laugh*). I never finished

MOLLY. He finished. The way it counts.

FLEMING (*pointing to* STEPHEN). You see, Arnall? They never really forget the first one.

ARNALL. What?

DOLAN. Jesus! What a wife you've got there. What a rotten night! (*to* STEPHEN) Give us back the line, kid. They're going to open soon and we need a line.

MOLLY. They'll open and we won't have a line. (*steps behind* STEPHEN) And I'm only second.

ARNALL. I'm right beside you.

FLEMING. Me, too.

DOLAN. For crying out loud! We're all second!

FLEMING. This looks very phoney. Give us back our line, Steve.

MOLLY. Please, Stevie. Please.

ARNALL. Give it back, Steven.

DOLAN. Cough it up, Stephen. Steve, Stevie. Cough it up.

(STEPHEN *begins to gag and choke. The line begins to appear.*)

FLEMING. Hey! The line!

DOLAN. There it is!

MOLLY. The line!

ARNALL. He *did* eat it.

(DOLAN *grabs the line from* STEPHEN's *mouth and runs across stage.*)

DOLAN. He took it with him.

(STEPHEN *rises, dazzled.* DOLAN *runs downstage.* FLEMING *runs to* STEPHEN.)

STEPHEN. I didn't take it with me. I didn't go anywhere. Damn it all! I'm not dead.

(STEPHEN *begins to go through a series of contortions like a woman in labor.*)

DOLAN (*standing victoriously, his own line on the floor*). I'm first. I had to wait for my chance, but I'm first. Had to wait. Wait. Hang back. But I'm first.

(STEPHEN *gags again and a second piece of tape appears: another line.* FLEMING *grabs the line and stares at it as a moron might, then follows* DOLAN's *example, setting his line downstage right*)

FLEMING. I'm first! Finally, I'm first! I should be first. I was the first one here. Fair's fair.

(STEPHEN *retches as he stands up.* MOLLY *steps forward and kisses* STEPHEN *full on the lips. She comes away with a piece of line as her reward, between her teeth.* STEPHEN *is now a dispenser. He walks mechanically, emitting sounds like a berserk Coca-Cola machine.*)

MOLLY (*setting her line down: her first*). He gave me first. He made me first. He gave me first place.

(FLEMING, MOLLY, *and* DOLAN *now stare, dreamy-eyed with victory. All of them will continue repeating their victory speeches until* ARNALL's *final line, which he will repeat alone in the silence.* ARNALL *slaps* STEPHEN *on the back and a line falls into his hands.*)

ARNALL (*after placing his line upstage right*). Molly. Darling. I'm first. I didn't want to be first. I never wanted first. But I'm first. And I like it, Molly! First is good.

(STEPHEN *still walks like a machine, puking up a final scrap of line. He grabs it and just as he places it on the floor downstage center, he sees the others in their victory. He understands and casually throws his line away. As he turns to leave, the lights switch off.*)

THE PLAY IS OVER

LOU GEHRIG DID NOT DIE OF CANCER

Jason Miller

BARBARA SPINNILLI
HELEN MARTIN
VICTOR SPINNILLI

ONE OF THE more memorable events of the 1971–72 New York theatre season was the emergence of a major new dramatist, Jason Miller. Rarely had a young writer earned such a cascade of superlatives from the critics or flashed as meteorically from near anonymity to the forefront of American playwrights as did Mr. Miller with *That Championship Season.* The drama, which deals with the twentieth annual reunion of a high school basketball coach, now retired, and four members of the team that he guided to the state championship two decades earlier, originally opened on May 2, 1972, at Off-Broadway's New York Shakespeare Festival Public Theatre. In September it was transferred by producer Joseph Papp to Broadway where it settled into a lengthy run at the Booth Theatre. Described by the press as "a drama of searing intensity, agonized compassion and consummate craftsmanship" and its author as "a towering new dramatist," *That Championship Season* won the 1972 New York Drama Critics' Circle Award as the best play of the year while Mr. Miller garnered a Drama Desk citation for outstanding playwright of the year. The play is scheduled for early filming by a major studio, with the screenplay to be written by Mr. Miller.

Prior to the opening of *That Championship Season,* the author was represented Off-Broadway in 1970 by *Nobody Hears a Broken Drum,* which tarried briefly, and a bill of three short plays bearing the overall title of *The Circus Theatre.* A newly revised version of one of the triumvirate dramas, *Circus Lady,* is included in this editor's collection, *The Best Short Plays 1973.*

Jason Miller was born in Scranton, Pennsylvania, in 1939. While a student at the University of Scranton, he began writing short plays and winning prizes for his efforts. He then became interested in acting, which he pursued as a graduate student at Catholic University. He subsequently appeared at the Champlain and Cincinnati Shakespeare festivals as well as Off-Broadway in *Subject to Fits* and in Washington, D.C., with Helen Hayes in Eugene O'Neill's *Long Day's Journey Into Night* and Geraldine Fitzgerald in Sean O'Casey's *Juno and the Paycock.* Presently, he is costarring in the film version of William Peter Blatty's novel, *The Exorcist.*

Lou Gehrig Did Not Die of Cancer originally was presented in New York in March, 1970, as an Equity Theatre Informal and its inclusion in *Best Short Plays of the World Theatre: 1968–1973* marks its first appearance in an anthology.

The author, his wife, and their three children live in Neponsit, New York.

Note: Since the above was written, Jason Miller also became the recipient of a Pulitzer Prize (1973) and an Antoinette Perry (Tony) Award for *That Championship Season.*   •

SCENE: *The suburban living room of* VICTOR SPINILLI. *The furnishings should suggest a comfortable, if not financially secure home. The furniture is modern, a hi-fi sound system rings the living room, some modern paintings adorn the wall. In short, the room is tastefully done in the style which has become known as mortgaged middle class.*

BARBARA SPINILLI, VICTOR'S *wife, lean, tanned, twenty-eight, large breasted, is sitting rather rigidly on the edge of the couch. She is rehearsing lines, out loud from* Hedda Gabler, *a play she will star in this evening at the local community theatre.*

BARBARA (*said to imaginary actor on her left*). "At ten o'clock—he will be here. I can see him already—with vine leaves in his hair—flushed and fearless. (*waits for imaginary actor's reply*) And then, you see—then he will have regained control over himself. Then he will be a free man for all his days. (*waits for reply. Rises and moves toward imaginary actor. By the way, she isn't a bad actress at all. Pause*) I want for once in all my life to have the power to mold a human destiny. (*She repeats this line, not satisfied with her delivery.*) I have never had the power and now I want it desperately . . ."

(*Phone rings while* BARBARA *is in the middle of this line.*) Damn it! (*answers phone*) Barbara speaking! . . . No, he is not, Phil. I expected him over an hour ago . . . Did the team lose? . . . Well then, you know he's probably at the lounge drowning his sorrow . . . I know. And you know, and everybody with rational sense knows, they're only kids and it's only a little league team, but Victor isn't too rational these days . . . What? (*pauses*) The umpire is going to sue him! . . . Victor hit him in the mouth with the catcher's mitt! (*pauses*) How can he sue us for that? . . . A front tooth? . . . I know it's a bad example for the kids, but he just gets so involved . . . OK. Call him about seven and you can catch him before we go to the theatre . . . *Hedda Gabler* . . . No, it's not a racy play . . . I play Hedda, of course . . . It's not a funny name in Norwegian. Yes, tonight's opening night . . . two dollars. Alright, call! Call at seven, Phil, he should be here . . . 'bye.

(*hangs up phone*) Moron!

(BARBARA *sits on edge of sofa and resumes her lines.*) For once in my life I want the power to mold a human destiny! (*repeats this again when the phone rings*) Damn it! (*answers phone*) . . . No, I'm sorry, Mr. Weiner, my husband is not here. (*to herself*) God almighty! . . . I know I'm sure your son's as good a hitter as anyone on the team, but I'm sorry, I don't know why Victor doesn't play him more . . . Now, Mr. Weiner, calm down . . . that is not true . . . that's simply ridiculous . . . my husband's not anti-Semitic. Good God, you're acting like a child, Mr. Weiner . . . Look, I am very busy. Call him tomorrow and talk to him yourself because I have to hang up now . . . Yes . . . I know . . . Yes . . . 'Bye, 'bye, Mr. Weiner.

(*She hangs up phone in the middle of* MR. WEINER'S *conversation, sits on couch and begins to recite lines again.*) "First you shall have a cup of tea, you little stupid. And then at ten o'clock Eilert Lovberg will be here, with vine leaves in his hair. Like a young Greek god, power incarnate! (*doorbell rings*) Give me patience!

(*She goes to door and opens it.* MRS. MARTIN *enters. She is an attractive woman, in her mid-thirties. A naturally shy woman, she possesses a taste and sensitivity that give her a quiet grace in contrast to* BARBARA'S *controlled but ever-present hysteria.*)

BARBARA. Oh! Hello, won't you come in and sit down.

MRS. MARTIN. I'm very sorry to barge in here like this, Mrs. Spinilli, especially since we've never been introduced. My name is Helen Martin and I live down the street. I feel very foolish coming here like this. But I would like to talk to your husband concerning my son Jeffrey. Jeffrey plays on your husband's little league team, you see.

BARBARA. I see! Well, at least you're civilized about it; usually the parents come frothing at the mouth. Can I get you something to drink? My husband should be here momentarily.

MRS. MARTIN. No, thank you. I assure you, Mrs. Spinilli, I am not going to lose my temper. And I hope I'm not intruding . . .

BARBARA. Oh, please don't feel that way. My God! Parents usually arrive at the door ready to crucify Victor on the nearest telephone pole.

MRS. MARTIN. Well, I certainly did not come here to cause you or Mr. Spinilli any discomfort. I just think there are some things he should know in regard to Jeffrey. I mean, Jeffrey is the type of boy . . . I'm not asking for favoritism, Mrs. Spinilli, I'm afraid it sounds as if I am, but my son Jeffrey is rather . . . unaggressive. Oh, he loves to play, but I'm afraid he's not one to throw himself fiercely into the fray. I encouraged him to use his mind and completely neglected his body.

BARBARA. Well, that certainly wasn't the improper thing to do. I mean, most of the children around here seem to be rather mindless.

MRS. MARTIN. But, you see, I had forgotten the value competitive sports have for a boy. What I'm trying to say is, since we moved here, I've encouraged him to become part of a team; in fact, I encouraged him to join your husband's group. You know, Mrs. Spinilli, he adores your husband, he really does. And it hurts him very much . . . when . . . the problem is . . . Jeffrey never plays. I know because I go to all the games and he just sits way down at the end of the bench alone. And it just hurts me to see him so miserable. And children can be very cruel, you know, and because he's not really equal, because he really doesn't belong, he's become an object of ridicule. They refer to Jeffrey as . . . the other boys call him . . . Mary Jane. He's terribly hurt and ashamed and I don't know what to do. He has no father to turn to and he refuses to talk to me now. I was hoping your husband could find time to pay just a tiny bit of attention to Jeffrey. It needn't be much, just a pat on the head or a friendly word now and then. I'm sure if the other boys see that Mr. Spinilli accepts him, it will make it much easier for Jeffrey (*pause*). Good Lord, I have been giving a lecture, haven't I? You know, when you get an ex-schoolteacher started you have to ring a bell to shut her up.

BARBARA. There is no need for apologies, Mrs. Martin. I understand your problem, believe me I do. My husband, as you prob-ably have gathered from seeing the games, is a great big, giant-sized little boy.

MRS. MARTIN. But he's so passionately involved, Mrs. Spinilli. I mean, watching him, I get the feeling he really, he deeply, cares about the boys.

BARBARA. Sure, he cared so much today he knocked out some man's tooth and now we just might get slapped with a law suit.

MRS. MARTIN. I was there and the man did, it seemed to me, provoke your husband . . . he called Mr. Spinilli, in a loud voice, a dumb wop. I think your husband was more embarrassed than angry, because everyone started to laugh when the man said it and so . . . he just hit him with that big round thing.

BARBARA. The catcher's mitt.

MRS. MARTIN. And also considering that the play in question was disputable, I don't think your husband was entirely wrong.

BARBARA. I don't think it's a good example for these boys to see Victor assaulting people, do you?

MRS. MARTIN. No, I don't. But these young boys are surrounded by so many neutral people today, I mean so many people just straddle the fence, taking absolutely no side with anything, that I think it's good for them to see a man who believes in his convictions. Even defends them if necessary.

BARBARA. But it's only a game, it's not Victor's profession or vocation. He just gets so . . . volcanic over the whole thing.

MRS. MARTIN. Yes, he does put on quite a show. Just between ourselves, I sometimes think he's better than the game.

BARBARA. Speaking of shows, I have to make one in about an hour. We open tonight.

MRS. MARTIN. Yes, I see you're playing Hedda Gabler with the community group.

BARBARA. And it is without a doubt the most exhausting role I've ever undertaken.

MRS. MARTIN. I saw you, you know, in *Summer and Smoke*. I thought you were superb, really.

BARBARA. Why, thank you. I give Stephen Frankel, he's the director, marvelous talent, should be on Broadway, really too much integrity though, Broadway commercialism disgusts him, I give him credit for that performance. I was lost, just lost, he pulled me through.

MRS. MARTIN. I'd better be off. Maybe I can call your husband later this evening.

BARBARA. You'd better make it tomorrow. He'll be at the theatre tonight. And then the cast party, which is simply a mad affair and never ends before five.

MRS. MARTIN. Well, I'll call tomorrow. You've been very kind.

BARBARA. Not at all. I really enjoyed talking to you, and I hope you can make the show some evening.

MRS. MARTIN. I certainly will, maybe Sunday night.

BARBARA. Good. We can have a few drinks afterwards and you can tell me just what you thought about the show . . . as long as it's complimentary.

(*They laugh.*)

MRS. MARTIN. I'd love to. Well, what is it they say, break an arm?

BARBARA. Leg.

MRS. MARTIN. Leg. It just shows you how out of contact I am with things. Oh, I must tell you that your husband's company makes the best spaghetti sauce I've ever tasted, really.

BARBARA. "Spaghetti is Spinilli."

MRS. MARTIN. Yes, it certainly is. Well, I really must run . . . Good-bye again; I may see you Sunday.

BARBARA. Fine and dandy. 'Bye now. (MRS. MARTIN exits. BARBARA *starts for the kitchen off left and phone rings. She answers it.*)

Barbara speaking! . . . No, Mr. Toomey, my husband is not here and I don't know when he'll be in . . . I gathered it was in relation to your son . . . Is that so? Really! I don't know why he only plays your son two innings a game, maybe he's afraid your son will have a heart attack if he plays him any more than two innings.

(VICTOR SPINILLI *enters. He's about thirty-two. He's a sad little clown underneath his coarse and sometimes volatile temperament. He wears a sweatshirt with "Spinilli Spaghetti" printed on the back. He's a bit high.*)

BARBARA (*handing him phone*). A friend. I've had it up to here!

VICTOR. Hello! . . . Yeah, Mr. Toomey . . . Yeah . . . Yeah . . . Oh, yeah? Well, let me tell you something, your son cracks under pressure, he can't take the pressure.

He's a two-inning ballplayer. After that his nerves go to pieces.

BARBARA. Oh, God!

VICTOR. Yeah . . . well, none of us likes to hear the truth, Mr. Toomey . . . Fine, you do that, take him off the team . . . send him to the tennis courts . . . Yeah . . . yeah. Send him to dance school, he's very graceful . . . Nobody's casting aspersions on anything. I said he'd be a better dancer than ballplayer, that's all . . . Mr. Toomey, go to hell!

(*He hangs up, goes to bar, makes a drink.*)

BARBARA. Nerves going to pieces! Victor, he's only an eleven-year-old child.

VICTOR. He's a shaky kid . . . doesn't have it in here.

BARBARA. He's just a baby.

VICTOR. By the time he's sixteen he'll be on tranquilizers.

BARBARA. You are hard to believe, Victor Spinilli. You're just too much.

VICTOR. Am I? Look, Greta, save the acting for the stage, alright?

BARBARA. I will, I certainly will. If you'll save your antics for the boxing ring.

VICTOR. Oh! Who called?

BARBARA. That moron Phil. The man is going to sue us, Victor.

VICTOR. Let him sue. Honey, I really laid one on that loud mouth. Bam! His ears almost fell off.

BARBARA. There are other ways of settling disputes than hitting someone in the mouth with a catcher's mitt.

VICTOR. What catcher's mitt? I hit him with my fist . . . this fist, closed just like this . . . and I hit him like so.

(*He slowly demonstrates on* BARBARA's *chin.*)

BARBARA. Really? Then Phil must have made a mistake because he said you hit him with a catcher's mitt.

VICTOR. Listen, sweetie, I don't need weapons.

BARBARA. Mrs. Martin must be mistaken, too. She said you hit him with a catcher's mitt and she was there.

VICTOR. Who's Mrs. Martin?

BARBARA. Her son plays on your team. I believe he's the one who sits on the end of the bench alone.

VICTOR. Oh, Mary Jane . . . Mrs. Martin is Mary Jane's mother?

BARBARA. No, she's Jeffrey's mother. That boy adores you and you won't even give him the time of day. He's deeply hurt by all this juvenile name calling. Mrs. Martin came here to talk to you about it. She's very upset.

VICTOR. You want to know the truth? I gave the kid a suit, right? A gift. Because he's so bad it's unbelievable, but I felt sorry for this skinny bloodless kid and I put him on the team. And I let him bat once, just once, the first game I let him bat and I thought that kid would pee all over home plate . . . one . . . two . . . three. He came back and sat at the end of the bench and that's where he's staying until the end of the season.

BARBARA. She's going to call you tomorrow; use a little tact when you talk to her, please.

VICTOR. I'll charm the pants right off her.

BARBARA. Figuratively speaking, of course.

VICTOR. Is there any other way?

BARBARA. Put a little juice in you and you're just a wit.

VICTOR. You know, I think I'll try out for one of your plays, I'd probably electrify everyone.

BARBARA. Well, Stephen was thinking of doing *The Hairy Ape.*

VICTOR. Is it a good role? Would I be the hero?

BARBARA. Victor, you wouldn't have to memorize a line. Just walk out there and burp and belch and scratch.

VICTOR. Forget it, I don't think I'd get along with that faggoty friend of yours.

BARBARA. Stephen is not a faggot. He's a gentleman and an excellent director.

VICTOR. He's also an excellent faggot.

BARBARA. Don't tell me, I worked with the man for six months and . . .

VICTOR. I saw the guy for six minutes and I'm telling you he's sweet . . . Come on, that tight-assed little walk, holding his cigarette like a baton, ascots, lisping . . . Baby, he's three feet off the ground. Flies like a birdie looking for a nest . . .

BARBARA. It's just so *you,* Victor, to mistake breeding and culture for something crude.

VICTOR. Fine. So he's read a few books. Went to NYU. . . uses hundred dollar words. Fine. Live and let live, that's my philosophy. But I wouldn't take a shower with him, that's all I'm saying.

BARBARA. You're just jealous of him.

VICTOR. Jealous of him? Come on. Look . . . Stop, look, listen. If he was Adam and you were ever Eve, you'd still be in the Garden of Eden, alone.

BARBARA. Why do you resent people with intelligence and ability and class? People who have exciting minds. People who can think and feel beyond all the rest of your ordinary, drab, beer-belly friends.

VICTOR. Because my beer-belly friends are not phony. They don't have fake smiles, fake laughs, fake words. And they don't wear pants five sizes too small. Does that answer your question?

BARBARA. I know what it is. I know why the people from the theatre bother you so.

VICTOR. Oh, yeah!

BARBARA. Because they make you feel stupid. They make you feel awkward and nervous and stupid. They make you feel just like that little Martin boy because you almost pee in your pants every time I have them over here.

VICTOR. Are you serious? Come *on.*

BARBARA. It's true. Last week when the group was here and we were talking about books and Stephen asked you if you had ever read Proust and you said sure all the time, he was one of your favorite writers. Everybody just froze with embarrassment. Just absolutely went rigid with embarrassment, because they knew you never even heard of Proust let alone read him. God, it was humiliating!

VICTOR. I went to college. I know who Proust is, Proost, Prusti!

BARBARA. You graduated with a business degree from NYU! I don't call that going to college. And that even took you six years to get.

VICTOR. Well, that's just too goddamn bad about you and your intellectual friends. Sitting around talking about Proust, drinking all my liquor, sitting around drinking all my booze and talking about . . . what's his name, the guy that ended up a drunk? You know they made a movie about him, the guy that . . .

BARBARA. F. Scott Fitzgerald had terrifying problems.

VICTOR. Sure he did and one of them was

alcohol. And the other guy, the one who shot himself in the mouth with a shotgun . . . Hemingway. There you are sitting around for two hours talking about a drunk and a suicide. Talking like crazy, "Oh, he was marvelous." "What perception, what depth . . ." Depth? Ah fongo, depth! Those two guys couldn't even face life. One drowns in Scotch and the other scatters his brains all over the living room. So, what's all the cheering about?

BARBARA. Please don't use yourself as a model of life-facing, Victor.

VICTOR. I stare it right in the face, baby. I don't sit around talking about how other people face it because I face it every day of my life. I think my thoughts, I don't steal them from books. I don't pick dead men's brains for ideas so I can impress a bunch of people who aren't going to be impressed because they are too busy trying to impress me. You know what I noticed about your little sewing circle the other night? Everybody talked but nobody listened. Everybody sat around doing monologues and nobody gave a good goddamn what anyone else was saying.

BARBARA. And you just sat back there like Buddha, like a big fat Buddha, silly grin and all, and said nothing.

VICTOR. Right.

BARBARA. Just like you sit back and say nothing every time your father comes to this house.

(*Pause*)

VICTOR. Let's leave my father out of this, Barbara.

BARBARA. No, let's not. Let's really clear the air. You can face anything, right? Old King Kong Spinilli can face a little thing like the truth. Do you know you are terrified of your father just as you are terrified of my friends?

(VICTOR *puts a Caruso record on the phonograph.*)

VICTOR. You're going to say that once too often and I'm going to knock you right on your fat bitchy ass.

BARBARA. Do you have your catcher's mitt ready?

VICTOR. Keep it up, mouth! My relationship with my father is *my* business, not yours.

BARBARA. It's very much my business when he comes in here telling me how

to run my house.

VICTOR. He tells you nothing.

(VICTOR, *during* BARBARA'S *speech, starts to sing in a mock-Caruso manner, very loudly*)

BARBARA. No? How come every time he arrives here for his semimonthly visit he has the nerve to ask me if I'm pregnant? He doesn't ask anymore, he demands it. "Are you pregnant yet?" He gives me that Neanderthal look and I'm afraid to say no.

VICTOR. He wants a grandchild, so what?

BARBARA. He's got two from your sister and one from your brother. What does he want, an army of grandchildren?

VICTOR. He wants a boy . . . he wants the name continued . . . he's from the old country, alright?

BARBARA. He's from the old country, alright . . .

VICTOR. Alright, you've said enough!

BARBARA. I just want to tell him we are living our lives separate from him. He is not going to terrorize me into having a child before I want one.

VICTOR. How can you have a child, Barbara, you've got a little piece of steel up there between your legs, remember?

BARBARA. Tell him then about the coil.

VICTOR. He wouldn't understand. He's old-fashioned about that.

BARBARA. Well, your father and I are going to come to an understanding. What's he going to do, stop his annual donation to us? Cut you out of your share of the company? Fire you?

VICTOR. He'd be very hurt.

BARBARA. He had the nerve to ask me to go to a specialist to see if I could make babies, make babies . . .

VICTOR. We've been married for five years, it's a legitimate question, for Christsake!

BARBARA. The man owns us.

VICTOR. I do a good job for him. We're paying our own way.

BARBARA (*quietly*). Victor, that is not true, not really.

VICTOR. Look, they've accepted my new advertising line, "Spinilli gives you the sauciest spaghetti." The old man was delighted with that line. We might even put it to music.

BARBARA. Accepting it and using it are

two different things.

VICTOR. He'll use it, I know it.

BARBARA. He accepted "Spinilli, the sauce that made spaghetti famous," but did he use it? No! He used "Spinilli is spaghetti" instead, which was Bob's suggestion. But I tell everybody it was yours.

VICTOR. You don't have to do that.

BARBARA (sad). Victor, all you're doing is collecting your check every Friday.

VICTOR. I sold them on the idea of sponsoring the little league team, didn't I? He bought the uniforms, jackets, everything.

BARBARA. Only because he loves baseball. He didn't even ask you about the team the last time he was here.

VICTOR. It bothers him because we're in last place.

BARBARA. Victor, this is insane, honey. I'd leave here tomorrow with you if you'd go back to the city and start with Harry again. Face the facts, Victor, here with your father's firm you will always be a lackey, the son of the boss.

VICTOR. I face the facts, but I am going to prove to the old man that I can carry the weight of my share of the company.

BARBARA. For God's sake! You've been trying to prove something to your father for the last thirty years. You thought he wanted you to be a baseball player. You tried it, you know what happened. He wanted you to be a doctor, you flunked out. You did everything he wanted you to and nothing you wanted. You keep telling yourself lies, pretending you're important to the company.

VICTOR. Let's not talk about lying to ourselves. Don't tell *me* about daydreams.

BARBARA. And what does that mean?

VICTOR. It means that this stupid community play acting has gone straight to your head. Dancing lessons on Thursday, speech lessons on Monday. And you're not going to New York with any faggot, to see any agent, about any commercials, understand?

BARBARA. That agent is coming to the show tonight, at Stephen's request, and if he likes my work, I'm going to New York and read for anything that might come up.

VICTOR. He's coming to see the play tonight, huh . . . Well, forget about New York, baby, wake up, because tonight the

dream's over. Bye-bye, big city.

BARBARA. You saw a dress rehearsal last week. Dress rehearsals are never very good.

VICTOR. Do you know that it was so rotten, everybody was so terrible that I almost puked. Everybody falling all over everybody else. The guy that plays your old lover or something opens the door and the goddamn door falls down . . . he's just standing there with a doorknob in his hand. That agent will die laughing.

BARBARA. If he doesn't die of laughter, if by some small miracle he wants to get me work, I am going to New York. Do you understand?

VICTOR. Hey, you know where your talent is? Your talent is in your boobs. Everybody goes to see your enormous boobs. I'm not kidding. Your boobs come on stage first, and then you follow. That should be your stage name, Barbara Boobs. Old Bullet Breasts.

BARBARA. Thank you for your confidence in me, Victor. But I'm still going to work in New York.

VICTOR. You better move out of my house then.

BARBARA. Whose house?

VICTOR. Mine, this house is mine. My house!

BARBARA. You know, this play acting started as just a simple diversion, an escape from all the sterility that surrounds me. Just a little exercise of female vanity, but now it's become all I have, it's become a necessity. And you're right, Victor, it's a daydream, but it's mine and nobody gave it to me and so I'm not afraid of anyone taking it away. And as things stand now, it may very well be the most important thing in my life.

VICTOR. I swear to you, if you go to New York, never come back to this house again.

BARBARA. I am through sitting with your father and you every third Thursday like clockwork, sitting in this living room, listening to the goddamn grieving voice of Caruso for three hours. I am done inflicting that torture upon myself! And now I shall go upstairs and finish dressing for the theatre.

(*She exits. Phone rings. He answers.*)

VICTOR. What! . . . Hello, Phil . . . yeah . . . Look, Phil, nobody calls me a wop . . . No, with my fist, Phil, the mitt was in the other hand . . . I know it doesn't look good for the league . . . What . . . what do you mean fired? . . . You can't fire me, I'm the sponsor, remember? My old man bought the suits, balls, and bats, I own the team . . . You did . . . my old man said what? . . . (*unbelieving*) . . . Are you serious, my old man said that!? . . . No, I do not want to coach the eight-to-ten-year-olds, Christ, that's like being shipped to the minors . . . No, no hard feelings, I'll see you around.

(*He hangs up phone. Goes to record player, puts on a Caruso record, a sad mournful one, fixes a drink.* BARBARA *enters.* VICTOR *is pretty high by now.*)

BARBARA. If you drive me down to the theatre now, you'll still have time to come back and get dressed.

VICTOR. I'm not going to the theatre.

BARBARA. Where are the keys? (VICTOR *hands them to her.*) You know what I think? We've simply outgrown each other. After five years together I have to remind myself.

VICTOR (*quietly*). Hey, I never made love to you without getting the feeling that you were defending yourself against something, and that's not booze talking, either!

BARBARA. I'm going to the party, I'll be very late.

VICTOR. Have a nice time.

(BARBARA *exits.* VICTOR *throws a cushion at the door. He is quite high but he can hold his drinks with a certain grace; he is not a sloppy, staggering kind of drunk. The only indication of his heavy drinking is a slowness of speech and lengthy pauses between thoughts, as he drifts occasionally into himself and becomes oblivious to his surroundings. He turns on the record player, mixes a drink and starts to sing with Caruso. He walks around the room, now singing loudly. He stops when he comes to the bookcase on the far wall. He sings aloud some of the names of the authors, in grand operatic manner.*)

VICTOR. O'Neill, Mailer Stanislavski, Hemingway, Proust . . . Burn the books . . . the big book burning. Where's a match? (*he loads his arms with books and starts toward kitchen. The doorbell rings. He opens the door.*) Who are . . . don't tell me, I know, I have it. You are Mrs. Martin. Mother of Jeffrey Martin, boy baseball player.

(*He turns off record player.*)

MRS. MARTIN (*startled*). Why, yes, I am, how did you know?

VICTOR. It's a secret!

MRS. MARTIN. Well, I promise only to take a little of your time. Your wife was coming down the street in the car as I was coming up. She stopped and said you were home and available to talk about Jeffrey. So, here I am.

VICTOR. Isn't my wife a charitable person, Mrs. Martin? She is just the little flower of Pleasant Hills.

MRS. MARTIN. She's a lovely person, Mr. Spinilli.

VICTOR. Broke the mold. Just threw the old mold right into the old polluted river. Come in, let me fix you a drink. Excuse me for just a moment . . . the great purge is just beginning. I'm just going to the incinerator and burn some subversive books. Be right back . . . Do you have a match? . . . Never mind, I have some.

(*He exits.* MRS. MARTIN *sits in chair, rather confused, waiting for* VICTOR. *He returns, goes into the bedroom, comes out with three trophies, puts them in the bookcase.*) The crisis is over . . . this is my trophy case, Mrs. Martin (*imitating W. C. Fields*). I shall take you on a little tour of my trophy case. This little gold gentleman here I received the night of September tenth, 1953. Most valuable player of the American Legion Baseball Tournament, hit three home runs in that tournament, two doubles, and stole home. "Number Twelve on your score cards but number one in your hearts, Victor Spinilli." And this little gold gentleman here represents the home run championship of the year 1953. Thirty-eight home runs, Victor Spinilli, same night, September tenth, 1953. And this one here, ah, this one here's the king of the little gold gentlemen, because it represents the award given by the American Legion to the best ballplayer on the East Coast, Mrs. Martin, the most promising young baseball player on the whole Eastern seaboard, and the name reads, Victor Spinilli, September tenth, 1953 (*pause*). I just realized, I never won a goddamned thing after September tenth, 1953 (*pause*). My day of doom. One brief night of glory and wham, obscurity . . . Oh, let me fix you a drink.

MRS. MARTIN. Scotch and soda, please.

VICTOR (*singing the song, "Scotch and Soda"*). Scotch and soda . . . etc . . . One Scotch and soda . . . (*he sits*). Now, Mrs. Martin, you're here to discuss Jeffrey.

MRS. MARTIN. Yes, I am. I talked at length, I'm afraid at very great length, about . . .

VICTOR. Wonderful woman, my wife, cries at the fall of a sparrow. Almost divorced me last winter when I had to drown the four kittens. Terrible mess . . . Sorry, go on.

MRS. MARTIN. Yes, well, you see . . . I don't mean to sound . . .

VICTOR. Like a bitch? Don't be silly, believe me, that is not my impression of you at all, Mrs. Martin, believe me. I know you are not a bitch. There's not a bitchy bone in your body. My impression of you is of a mother who is sad because her son is sad and feels on the outside of everything and everybody.

MRS. MARTIN. That just about sums it up.

VICTOR. I understand about these things, Mrs. Martin. I mean, about being on the outside looking in at that circle of importance, you know what I mean? I mean, I feel for the poor slob who can't find the handle . . . not that your son is a slob, Mrs. Martin, but, when it comes to baseball, he can't find the handle. I'm going to be very blunt, your son is a rotten baseball player . . .

MRS. MARTIN. I know that, Mr. Spinilli, I can see that for myself. But that's really not what's bothering him so much. Really. All he wants is to be included and respected and not made a scapegoat for the other boys.

VICTOR. Isn't that what we all want? I want it, you want it, everybody wants it. We really don't change that much, do we? (*pause*)

MRS. MARTIN. Mr. Spinilli . . . Ah, Mr. Spinilli . . .

VICTOR. What . . . Oh, oh . . . I was just thinking of something. (*pause*) You are a very pretty woman, Mrs. Martin.

MRS. MARTIN. Why, thank you.

VICTOR. I think beauty should be complimented. (*pause*) I am a great complimenter of beauty . . . so let me fill you up.

(MRS. MARTIN *protests*.) Drink up, you can trust me.

(*He goes to record player, puts on Caruso. Sits on couch. Long pause*)

MRS. MARTIN. I gather you're a fan of Caruso.

VICTOR. Actually, he bores the hell out of me. I'm Italian but I don't understand a word he's saying. My old man likes him . . . I listen to him out of habit, I guess.

MRS. MARTIN. He has an unbelievable voice.

VICTOR. To the Italians he's a *magnifico*. A national hero.

MRS. MARTIN. I think he must be *magnifico* to anyone that ever heard him. A voice like that is not of this world, if you know what I mean.

VICTOR. Well, we gotta have somebody besides Capone.

MRS. MARTIN. Capone?

VICTOR (*giving her drink*). Al Capone . . . the gangster. He's an Italian hero, too.

MRS. MARTIN. I always thought he was Jewish!

VICTOR (*laughs*). No! Listen, to the Italians, Capone and Valentino are more popular than the Pope.

MRS. MARTIN. And Caruso, too?

VICTOR. Yeah, and Caruso, too. (*pause*) Look, I won't be coaching the team anymore, so I don't know what help I can be.

MRS. MARTIN. You've been replaced?

VICTOR. Yeah! Got my walking papers.

MRS. MARTIN. Was it because of what you did this afternoon?

VICTOR. Yeah. Bad for the boys to see me punching people around. Bad for "Spinilli Spaghetti" image.

MRS. MARTIN. But, you were insulted. To see a man stand up for his honor is a good example for the boys, I should think.

VICTOR. Do you really believe that?

MRS. MARTIN. I most certainly do.

VICTOR. My wife thinks I'm crazy.

MRS. MARTIN. Well . . . you did the only thing a man could do after being crudely provoked and I'm very sorry you've been replaced.

VICTOR. You know, Jeffrey's a very—kind of quiet—kid. He's not the athletic type.

MRS. MARTIN. Yes, he is more like me than his father. His father was very athletic. He loved to hunt and he loved to ski.

VICTOR. You're a widow, Mrs. Martin?

MRS. MARTIN. Not really.

VICTOR. What do you mean? You're either a widow or you're not a widow, there's no in-between.

MRS. MARTIN. I feel like a widow, but my husband is very much alive. And I'm not divorced, nor am I legally separated. It sounds confusing, doesn't it?

VICTOR. Sounds in-between.

MRS. MARTIN. You see, Jeffrey's father, when Jeffrey was very young, decided that married life was too confining. So, he left. Anyway, Jeffrey now is in the habit of adopting fathers for himself, you know, teachers, instructors, etc. . . . You were his idol since the first day you let him on the team. And even when he didn't make a hit with the other boys, and although he didn't play much, he never blamed you or said anything unkind about you. I think he felt he let you down. He admired your spirit. The way you fought and demanded justice for your little team. Respect and justice and fair play are very important to Jeffrey.

VICTOR. Well, it wasn't anything that eloquent, Mrs. Martin, I just get mad very easily. Especially when I'm in last place.

MRS. MARTIN (*getting up*). I'd better run and let you get to your wife's play.

VICTOR. It's alright. I'm going tomorrow night. Tomorrow night they'll know at least half their lines.

MRS. MARTIN. Oh.

(*pause*)

VICTOR. Sit down, have another Scotch . . . You just moved here recently?

MRS. MARTIN. About six months ago.

VICTOR. You work in town?

MRS. MARTIN. I taught school in New York up until last year. I am now on what you might call an extended sabbatical. Actually, I sought refuge up here from the city, which can be very frightening to a single woman.

VICTOR. You don't have many friends up here, huh?

MRS. MARTIN. Oh, some. I prefer the quiet pace now. If you know what I mean. I've had the carnival side of life with my husband . . . Now I just want to take . . . a rest, a kind of inventory of myself, if you know what I mean.

VICTOR (*handing her a drink*). You know what I think? I think you're still waiting for your husband to come back.

(*pause*)

MRS. MARTIN. I might have agreed with you three years ago. Right now I don't know, maybe that's why I'm here in my suburban retreat.

VICTOR. You want some advice? Advice from the original Ann Landers? I think he's gone and he's not coming back. He's going to fly right past the sun and not come back. And you're still a good-looking woman and it's time for Jeffrey to have a father, so I'd start hunting if I were you. I'm a blunt bastard, so you'll have to excuse me. I'm very good at telling other people how to put out their own fires while my own house is burning to the ground . . . that's an inside joke, Mrs. Martin.

MRS. MARTIN. Strange as it may seem, Mr. Spinilli, I don't know if I can love anyone but my husband. I have tried and failed. I've gone through the sordid politics of manhunting and almost convinced myself one or two times that I had found someone that I could be happy with. But, inevitably, my wandering husband would write, just a short note, saying nothing really, or he would call from some strange little town whose name I never heard of, and talk to me in the middle of the night and we would become nostalgic and I would cry and he would cry and he would promise and swear on all the gods that ever existed that he loved me and was coming home to stay for good. Well, after one of those midnight scenes the other man just never existed. I may be old-fashioned, but I'm getting very tired of waiting.

VICTOR. You're alright, Mrs. Martin, a little strange but you're alright.

MRS. MARTIN. You're right, I'm afraid I am a little strange.

VICTOR. I'm just kidding, you're a good woman.

MRS. MARTIN. Sometimes I think I was born two hundred years too late . . . Mary Shelley and I would have a lot in common.

(*phone rings.*)

VICTOR. Hello . . . No, this is the ex-coach! (*hangs up. Goes to bar*) You're a strong woman . . . a little strange but strong . . . Tell you what I'm going to do. I just got an idea. Since I am now the retired ex-coach of the Spinilli Spoilers, I have a little memento, souvenir my father gave me, a little gift for Jeffrey. (*goes to desk, takes out baseball with signature on it*) This is a baseball. It is a very special baseball. It is a special baseball because it was hit by Lou Gehrig on Sunday, June 14, 1939, into the left field D Box seats at Yankee Stadium, present, among the other thirty thousand people, were me and my father. You see, my father loved baseball and he loved Lou Gehrig. And on that Sunday, Lou Gehrig, not even knowing my father loved him like a son, not even knowing my father was at the game, Lou Gehrig, hit this baseball right into my father's lap. It was the first and last time I ever believed in God. My father was in a trance. It was a miracle. After the game, my father and me waited outside until it was almost dark and the stadium was empty. My father said not one word. We waited alone in the darkness for Lou Gehrig. Finally, he came out and my father went over and spoke to him in Italian. Then, he did the most incredible thing, Lou Gehrig did the most amazing thing, he hugged my father and then they were laughing together and I remember I started to cry, standing there watching Lou Gehrig hug my father. I don't know why to this day. They didn't notice me, though, and when he came over and shook my hand and handed me the autographed ball I just smiled up at him . . . and to this day I don't know what my father said to Lou Gehrig in the dark outside of Yankee Stadium. It's a strange feeling even now, you know.

MRS. MARTIN. Yes, I do.

VICTOR. And when Lou Gehrig died, a few years later, the day Lou Gehrig died, my father cried. And that was the first and last time I ever saw my father cry. Even when they lowered my mother in the ground, his face was dry. Even when the Scouts came to see me play, even when the Big League Scouts came to see me play and I struck out three times and they wanted nothing to do with me, he said nothing. But, the day Lou Gehrig died, when he heard the news, he said one thing, "Lou Gehrig did not die of cancer, he died of a broken heart." Those are the exact and only words he said on that day . . . Isn't it incredible, that my father could be hurt so much by the death of a stranger. Someone he never even . . . Give this ball to Jeffrey . . . I've had it too long.

MRS. MARTIN. Are you sure you want Jeffrey to have this?

VICTOR. Things like this mean a lot to a boy and I don't need it anymore. I've outgrown it. You know what I like about you, Mrs. Martin? You listen, you really listen to someone. It makes someone want to talk.

MRS. MARTIN. Thank you!

VICTOR. Maybe someday, when I have some time, I'll come up and just talk to him, Jeffrey, I mean. Hit a few balls, stuff like that.

MRS. MARTIN. I'm sure he'd appreciate that . . . My, it's late and I'm sure I'm keeping you from something important.

VICTOR. The only important thing I have to do is make sure I don't get so drunk that I burn about six holes in the new couch . . . Stay a little while, Mrs. Martin. You see, my wife will be home very late. You see, they have a party after the show and that's where the best acting is, at the party. When they start to tell each other how good they are. It's better than any play they ever put on . . . Don't go, Mrs. Martin, stay awhile.

(*pause*)

MRS. MARTIN. Perhaps I could make you some coffee, you seem a little tired.

VICTOR. The word is drunk, Mrs. Martin, but I hold my liquor well, right?

MRS. MARTIN. Yes, remarkable.

VICTOR (*facing her*). I'm going to be blunt again. We are both waiting for sure defeat to turn into sudden victory, Mrs. Martin, and it ain't going to happen. Do you know that there are people who die waiting for something that might not even exist?

(*long pause*)

MRS. MARTIN. Yes.

VICTOR. Don't hold on to hope, Mrs. Martin, hold on to another human being, it's better.

MRS. MARTIN. I don't know if I can.

VICTOR. You won't know if you don't try.

MRS. MARTIN. Do you take cream in your coffee?

VICTOR. One cream and two sugars.

CURTAIN

EPISODE IN THE LIFE OF AN AUTHOR

(*Épisode de la Vie d'un Auteur*)

Jean Anouilh

Translated by MIRIAM JOHN

THE AUTHOR	THE MOTHER
ARDÈLE	THE FRIEND
MADAME BESSARABO	A WOMAN
THE PHOTOGRAPHER	LA SURETTE, *a tramp*
THE MAID	THE HOUSING INSPECTOR
TWO PLUMBERS	GONTRAN

THE PLAYS of Jean Anouilh, France's most esteemed contemporary dramatist and one of the titans of the modern theatre, have been translated into many languages and have been produced in every conceivable theatrical corner of the world. Yet, in striking contrast to other notables of the international theatre, comparatively little is known about the man personally. Adamantly reticent about private divulgences, M. Anouilh has immunized himself from most journalistic questionings and the granting of interviews: "I shall keep the details of my life to myself."

Nonetheless, some facts have managed to seep through the scrim curtain that separates the man from the dramatist. The son of a skilled tailor, Jean Anouilh was born on June 23, 1910, in Bordeaux, and while he was still quite young, his family moved to Paris. There he attended the Ecole Colbert and, later, the Collège Chaptal.

After a year and a half of studying law (at the Université de Paris à la Sorbonne), Anouilh washed his hands of briefs and legal documents and joined forces with an advertising firm "where I learned to be ingenious and exact, lessons that took for me the place of literary studies." In one of his rare press interviews, the dramatist reflected: "For three years I wrote copy for products ranging from noodles to automobiles. I consider advertising a great school for playwriting. The precision, conciseness and agility of expression necessary in writing advertisements helped me enormously." Eventually, though, Anouilh and advertising came to a parting of the ways and his passionate interest in the theatre propelled him toward Louis Jouvet, the celebrated actor-manager, and in 1931 he became his secretary.

Whether by destiny or proximity to the great man of the theatre, one year later, Jean Anouilh himself was to become a public figure in France. The occasion: the presentation of his first play, *L'Hermine,* starring Pierre Fresnay. Though it vanished from the boards after only thirty-seven performances, critics welcomed the young writer as "a promising avant-garde talent"; the play's *succès d'estime* launched him on his career.

The next five years were not exactly auspicious ones for M. Anouilh, but in 1937 he scored heavily with *Le Voyageur sans bagages (Traveler Without Luggage).* Performed by the enormously influential theatre couple Georges and Ludmilla Pitoëff, the play transcended Jean Anouilh's erstwhile "avant-garde" status and became the inaugural link in a long chain of successes. To list some, in nonchronological order: *The Waltz of the Toreadors, The Lark, The Rehearsal, Legend of Lovers, Antigone, Ring Round the Moon, Romeo and Jeannette, Médée, Mademoiselle Colombe, Ardèle, The Fighting Cock, Thieves' Carnival, Time Remembered, Poor Bitos, The Cavern,* and *Becket.*

M. Anouilh also has written a number of short plays, notably *The Orchestra* and *Madame de . . .* (both are included in *Best Short Plays of the World Theatre: 1958–1967*); *Cécile, or The School for Fathers,* and his earliest work, *Humulus le muet.* The latter, known in its English version as *Augustus,* was written in collaboration with Jean Aurenche, one of France's most distinguished scenarists, and was published for the first time in the United States in this editor's collection, *The Best Short Plays 1969.*

The primary function of the theatre is, was and forever will be entertainment. Even the most sublime poetry, the noblest of thoughts, could not exist onstage without a concomitant quota of entertainment. If we strip bare the basic elements of drama, then we are left with nothing more stimulating or revealing than disembodied speeches, routine polemics and platitudinous lectures. And Jean Anouilh fully realized this.

After serving two masters, Luigi Pirandello and Jean Giraudoux, Anouilh began to develop and perfect an individualistic style that even in its most bitter moments was eminently entertaining and irresistibly theatrical. The recurring theme of his many plays—the related axis upon which they dazzlingly revolve—is the quest for purity and happiness, deterred or frustrated by either a moral flaw in the central character's own nature or by the corruption of society. A subtle, witty and sardonic writer, Anouilh has classified his plays in two groups: *Pièces roses,* in which the theme is surveyed with illumining wit and comedy, and *Pièces noires,* where it is interpreted through a bitter eye. Whichever mold he happens to select for his interpretation, invariably his technical virtuosity and theatrical brilliance give stunning life to his premise, people and plot.

The décor is as nonrealistic as possible, but the AUTHOR's *study should be distinguishable center, with three doors, a lobby stage left, the bottom of the staircase, and the front door. It is morning. The* AUTHOR *and* ARDÈLE *are discovered on stage in the study, both in dressing gowns. Standing face to face and both extremely agitated, they are shouting and banging on the desk. All the characters in this sketch are realistic, the women charming, but—and this production detail is indispensable—everyone is wearing a false nose.*

———

AUTHOR (*banging on the desk*). Exactly!
ARDÈLE (*also banging on the desk*). Exactly!
AUTHOR (*as above*). Exactly!
ARDÈLE (*as above*). Exactly!
AUTHOR (*suddenly icy*). Good. The play's over. We've no more to say to each other.
ARDÈLE (*no less loftily*). I hope not.
AUTHOR. Just one thing. That letter was not from your sister.
ARDÈLE. So you're rummaging in my drawers now. It's humiliating.
AUTHOR. Your sister's fond of you, of course, but hardly to the point of calling you "my own love."
ARDÈLE. So I'm not enough. You have to smear my sister.
AUTHOR. I'm not smearing your sister. I'm simply making an observation. Your sister isn't overloaded with culture, but after all she can spell. She wouldn't have systematically left out *all* the feminine endings on her past participles.
ARDÈLE. The things you pick on!
AUTHOR. That letter was from a man.
ARDÈLE. You're despicable. Might I be allowed to put one question?
AUTHOR. Put away.
ARDÈLE. Supposing it was all your fault?
AUTHOR (*laughing nastily*). Ah-ha ha!
ARDÈLE. What are you doing?
AUTHOR. I'm laughing nastily.
ARDÈLE. How horrible! I deceive you and you laugh. You're not even capable of suffering. I've given you my youth and you rummage in my drawers.
AUTHOR. The letter was on the floor. In the closet.
ARDÈLE. Rummaging in closets. In two hours I shall have gone. I'm going back to my mother.

AUTHOR. She died in 1922.
ARDÈLE. Try—go on, *try* to make me more miserable by reminding me that my poor mother is dead and that I've nothing left in the world. All the same, she did leave a house. One twenty-two rue des Retaillons in Saint-Malo. My illiterate sister's living there. I'm going to her.
AUTHOR. Splendid.
ARDÈLE. You're delighted, of course. At last you'll be able to be unfaithful to me. For twelve years you've been waiting for this moment, and you've arranged it so that I'm the one that looks guilty.
AUTHOR (*yelling suddenly*). For God's sake! Who sent you that letter?
ARDÈLE (*with marblelike contempt*). What *can* be the matter? I suppose my sister can't write.
(*At that moment someone rings. They listen. In the lobby, the* MAID, *young and pleasant, but dissolved in tears, opens the door.*)
MADAME BESSARABO. I've come to see the Master. I have an appointment. Madame Bessarabo. This gentleman is the photographer.
AUTHOR. She's a Rumanian journalist. I sent her packing a week ago. We'll continue with this conversation later. And I'm not even shaved!
ARDÈLE (*sneering as she goes out*). That makes twelve years you haven't been shaved.
AUTHOR (*passing his hand over his face*). You exaggerate. It would have shown. Am I at least clean?
ARDÈLE (*slamming the door so hard that a picture falls down and the* AUTHOR *picks it up*). NO!
(*The* MAID, *still in tears, introduces* MADAME BESSARABO *and the* PHOTOGRAPHER, *who is weighed down with equipment.*)
MADAME B. Master! I am overwhelmed by the tremendous favor. This gentleman is the photographer.
AUTHOR. Do sit down, madame. Excuse my receiving you in these clothes. I was working.
MADAME B. Oh, Master! How very disturbing. I have interrupted a scene perhaps?
AUTHOR. Precisely. (*recovering himself*) I mean, er—no. It's of no importance. It wasn't my scene.

MADAME B. (*embarrassed*). Oh! Please forgive me, I have been indiscreet. I shall go, Master; I shall go immediately. (*She installs herself.*) Do you mind if I smoke? I smoke like a—how do you say it?—like a chimney sweep.

AUTHOR. Like a chimney. Sweeps don't smoke—at least not on duty. In fact it's their job to stop the chimney smoking.

MADAME B. What a fascinating detail! Everything French is quite extraordinary. Now, in Rumania we are all slaves. Master, I've come to talk to you about your last play. You know, of course, that *La Marguerite* had an enormous success in Bucharest. Three performances—for us that is much.

AUTHOR. Really?

MADAME B. We have such a small theatre public. But very enthusiastic, too! We are traditionally devoted to anything French. The play made a great impression. The press was unanimous—we almost reached the fourth performance. The general opinion was that it was a little *dur* as you say —a little hard. We Rumanians are such great idealists. We believe enormously in sentiment. In fact, this explains why I am here. We want to know in my country what you really think about love. Our two cultures are so closely linked you cannot refuse us this. (*Someone rings.*) Well, Master, what do you say? I swear to you I shall be absolutely faithful.

AUTHOR (*suspicious*). Why do you say that?

MADAME B. Because there are journalists who betray. I shall never betray.

AUTHOR. Er . . . well, madame, truth to tell I feel somewhat embarrassed . . . What shall I say about love and *La Marguerite*? I think you have caught the subtle hint in the title. "Marguerite"—I love you, I love you not, I love you, I love you not.

(*The* MAID, *still weeping, has been to open the door. She lets in* TWO PLUMBERS.)

PLUMBER. How do, gorgeous! We're here for the leak.

(*The* MAID *knocks on the door of the study.*)

AUTHOR. Excuse me. Come in . . . what is it?

MAID. It's the plumbers, sir, for the leak.

AUTHOR. Well, let them look for it. You can see I'm busy.

PLUMBER (*shouting from the doorway*). Where is it?

MAID. They're asking where it is.

AUTHOR. Why should we have sent for them if we knew where it was? Let them start in the attic and check the whole house.

PLUMBER. Okay, mister. We'll start with the attic. Which way, gorgeous?

MAID (*sobbing*). This way.

PLUMBER (*going upstairs with her and his mate*). What's up, gorgeous? Love's wonderful really, you know.

AUTHOR (*who has shut the door again*). Please excuse me. Curious phenomenon. Water trickling about all over the place and nobody knows where from.

MADAME B. How strange. You know, almost the same thing happened in the house of my great-uncle, the Archimandrite, in Rumania. I wake up one morning and there is water all over the drawing room.

AUTHOR. Same here!

MADAME B. In the drawing room where there are no pipes.

AUTHOR. Same here!

MADAME B. And the ceiling absolutely intact. As it was the house of a holy man, we thought for a moment it must be a miracle.

AUTHOR. Same here! Or rather, no, I wouldn't go that far. Now, "Marguerite" —I love you, I love you not, I love you, I love you not.

(*The forestage left lights up and a* WOMAN *dials a number on the telephone. Almost immediately, the telephone rings in the study.*)

AUTHOR. Please excuse me. Hello!

WOMAN. Is that you, Léon?

AUTHOR. I'm sorry, madame, whom did you wish to speak to?

WOMAN. Oh, Léon, it's you. Why are you disguising your voice?

AUTHOR. No, madame, it's not me. Which number did you want?

WOMAN. Jasmin one two, one two.

AUTHOR. I am Jasmin one two, one two, madame, but I regret to say that I am not Léon.

WOMAN. But listen, monsieur, Jasmin one two, one two is the number of my first husband!

AUTHOR. I'm sorry, madame. There's

been a mistake. (*He hangs up and the light goes out forestage left.*) Some woman had the wrong number. It's very strange —they must make a habit of giving people my number.

MADAME B. Do you know, exactly the same thing has happened to me in Rumania. You are aware, of course, that unlike yours in France, our numbers are very long . . . mine was seven, eighty-three, one, one two six two one four.

MAID (*bounding in*). Monsieur, monsieur!

AUTHOR. What is it? I'm busy!

MAID (*tragically*). They're asking if they can cut off the water.

AUTHOR. Certainly. But if they cut off the water, how will they find the leak? (*noticing that she is weeping*) What is the matter with you?

MAID. Oh! Monsieur, it's terrible what's going on.

AUTHOR. You mean, the leak?

MAID. Oh no. Not the leak.

AUTHOR. Madame, perhaps?

MAID. Oh, no. Not madame. (*She goes out, crying even more bitterly.*)

AUTHOR (*turning hesitantly back to* MADAME BESSARABO). Strange.

MADAME B. She's charming. Quite like one of Molière's.

AUTHOR (*smirking*). You exaggerate, really! That's too high a compliment.

MADAME B. I say what I think, Master, I have such an admiration for all your work—and for Molière's too, of course.

AUTHOR. Thank you. But we were saying—about the water in your drawing room . . .

MADAME B. No—about my telephone number. But let us talk about *La Marguerite* instead.

(*The* WOMAN *has redialed the number forestage.*)

AUTHOR. Well, I was saying that the title contains a subtle allusion. "Marguerite"—I love you, I love you not . . .

(*The telephone rings.*)

WOMAN. Hello! Léon?

AUTHOR. Madame, you have the wrong number again. Are you dialing Jasmin one two, one two?

WOMAN. Of course, monsieur. I told you it is my first husband's number. Can you explain to me what you are doing on the line?

AUTHOR. What do you mean, what am I doing on the line? I'm waiting for someone to ring me on the line, madame; it happens to be mine! (*He hangs up.*) This is insane. I love you, I love you not, I love you, I love you not.

(*There is a knock. It is* ARDÈLE, *with nothing on but a bathrobe.*)

ARDÈLE. So that's how it is. You're starting that?

AUTHOR. Starting what? Do excuse me madame.

ARDÈLE. Your oafish practical jokes. Cutting off the water just as I'm taking my shower. You know I'm leaving you, and as if that isn't enough, you want to put the blame on me. After what you've done!

AUTHOR. What *have* I done?

ARDÈLE. Don't play innocent—you know as well as I do!

(*She goes out, banging the door. A picture falls down. The* AUTHOR *picks it up.*)

AUTHOR. I'm so sorry. Now, we were talking about love and *La Marguerite*.

MADAME B. Quite. The rest is incidental. My great-uncle's leak, the telephone—I can tell you all about these things later when you come to Rumania. But, Master, you were so *dur*, so hard in *La Marguerite*. Tell me you were lying; confess that you believe in love just the same.

AUTHOR (*embarking*). Well now, madame, to tell the truth, love, like the marguerite, has leaves, or rather petals . . .

(*A man has dialed a number forestage right. The* AUTHOR *picks up the receiver and yells into it.*)

AUTHOR. No, madame, I am not Léon!

FRIEND. What on earth's come over you, old thing? I know you're not Léon. This is Gustave. How are things, dear boy?

AUTHOR. Oh. It's you. Fine, thanks, fine. (*to* MADAME B.) One moment, please, I'm so sorry. How are things with you?

FRIEND. That's just it, they're not at all good, dear boy. You remember I had a simply fabulous idea for a scenario. I told you about it, I think?

AUTHOR. Yes, yes. I remember. (*to* MADAME B.) Please excuse me—a colleague of mine.

FRIEND. "The Woman with the Boas," I was calling it. You know, it's the story of a madly beautiful woman who meets a man in a train and falls in love with him.

AUTHOR. Yes, yes, I remember. Very original . . .

FRIEND. Paul Zed bought it from me. He was going to film it in the spring for Bourbanski. They'd got Liliane Trésor lined up. She'd accepted, and now she's refused.

AUTHOR (*politely*). Oh, Lord, what a bore. Why was that? (*to* MADAME B.) I'm so sorry.

FRIEND. She doesn't want to die at the end.

AUTHOR. That's reasonable. Listen, old man, I'm so sorry, but I have someone with me.

FRIEND. How do you mean, it's reasonable? Look at it from my point of view. If I want to kill her off, who's going to stop me? After all, *I'm* the author. Anyway, it doesn't make sense. First of all, who's ever heard of an actress refusing to die? They usually fall over themselves for a good death agony. What's more, dear boy, if you remember the story, you'll see that she can't not die. Damn it, here's a woman who's deceived her husband with two men; she then falls in love on a train with a third man who turns out to be an ex-convict who was a counterspy in the war and takes drugs. That was the whole point. Producers can say what they like about happy endings—life is like that, dear boy, life is like that. I ask you, is life supposed to be a picnic?

AUTHOR. No, it isn't a picnic, but listen, old man, I've got someone here in my study—a journalist come specially from Rumania to see me about a leak in the water pipe.

FRIEND. About what?

AUTHOR. Oh—no—I mean about love, but there was a leak as well. I'll explain later. Call me again, do you mind?

FRIEND. Oh, all right, I'll call you in ten minutes.

(*He hangs up. The forestage goes dark. Someone rings. The* MAID *opens the door. This time it is an elderly woman, flowerily dressed.*)

MOTHER. Is my son at home?

MAID. Yes, madame.

AUTHOR. Do forgive me, what was I saying?

MADAME B. That love had petals.

AUTHOR (*who has lost the drift*). Petals.

MADAME B. Yes, Master, you remember —the subtle allusion.

AUTHOR. Oh yes! The marguerite. So love, like the marguerite, has petals . . .

MADAME B. (*takes notes feverishly*). How moving. I have the feeling no one has ever said that before.

MAID (*knocking at the study door*). It's your mother, monsieur.

AUTHOR. Tell her I'm busy and ask her if she'd kindly call again.

MOTHER (*calling*). It's very urgent, darling. I must have a word with you at once.

AUTHOR. Would you excuse me? All right, I'm coming. (*He goes out into the hall.*) What is it?

MOTHER. Aren't you going to kiss me? When you were little, you always used to kiss me.

AUTHOR. Yes, yes, I'm going to kiss you. What is it, now? I'm busy.

MOTHER. The pet. You know, for me, you'll always be a little boy. Now, it's about the apartment. I've been told about one that's up for exchange. I have to let them have my answer this morning.

AUTHOR. Just wait for me a second. I've someone with me from Rumania. She's going back any minute now.

MOTHER. Is Ardèle at home?

AUTHOR. Yes, but do please leave her where she is. Things aren't going so well this morning. No scenes between you, please.

MOTHER. How dare you say such a thing to your mother! Was I ever one to start anything? Don't you think it's painful enough already to see one's only son married to someone who hates one?

AUTHOR. Yes, I know it's rather painful. So don't stand about. Do sit down. Read the paper. I'll be back.

MOTHER (*holding him back*). But you really must give me an answer about this flat. You know I've lost my lawsuit. That means I don't know how much in lawyers' fees and I may be thrown out on the street at any minute. If only you had a different wife—then I could come and live with you.

AUTHOR (*making her sit down and calmly but firmly placing a paper in her hands*). Read the paper! (*He goes back into the study.*) So. Love has petals. Excuse me, I must be brief, I've so much to do. You've asked me a straight question, and I'll give you a straight answer. I believe in love.

MADAME B. (*with a cry of relief*). Ah! At last! I shall send a cable at once, Master. It will be a great relief to the whole of Rumania!

(*At this moment the door opens behind the* AUTHOR *and the* TWO PLUMBERS *come in. They feel along the walls in silence, with an air of great mystery, weaving around everyone and putting the* PHOTOGRAPHER *in terror for his equipment. They then go out by another door without a word.*)

AUTHOR (*curtly*). Man is alone, madame—left to himself, with his ridiculous freedom, and no one to call out to him in the desert!

(*At this moment the* FRIEND *has dialed the number and the telephone rings.*)

AUTHOR. Excuse me, please. Hello!

FRIEND. Hello! Can I talk to you now, dear boy? Do you know what's happened to me? A phone call from Liliane Trésor. She agrees to die, provided it's consumption. The idea came to her when she had a bit of a cold. But now it's Paul Zed who won't play because he says it would be depressing. He says for Canada and the Channel Islands it would be better if she turned religious and went into a convent. He says that would make it sell better.

AUTHOR. Listen. I haven't finished with my visitor. Could you call me back later?

FRIEND. Right. Fine. I'll call you back. (*He hangs up.*)

(*While they are speaking, someone rings. It is* LA SURETTE, *a tramp, still quite young.*)

LA SURETTE. Is he in?

MAID (*who has opened the door to him, still sniffing*). You again? But he gave you something only a week ago.

LA SURETTE. They're going to cut off the gas.

MAID (*at the door of the study*). It's Monsieur La Surette, monsieur. He says they're going to cut off his gas.

AUTHOR (*getting up, furious, and coming into the hall*). No! Do you hear me, man—no! I know we served together in the army. I know you saved me from being court-martialed the time I mislaid my bayonet, but damn it all! I gave you seven thousand last week!

LA SURETTE. That was for the potatoes.

AUTHOR. And you've eaten seven thousand francs' worth of potatoes in a week?

LA SURETTE. They're cutting off the gas. I can't cook them.

AUTHOR (*weakening*). How much behind are you with the gas?

LA SURETTE. Nine months. They say if I pay half they won't cut me off. Better take the opportunity, hadn't I?

AUTHOR. How much?

LA SURETTE (*waving a hand*). Oh! I don't know—here, here's the bill. You see I wasn't lying. Plus expenses, of course. They always add that. And then, I wanted to tell you—I think I've found a place. Only I can't go there with these boots. Maybe you've got an old pair.

AUTHOR. God in heaven! Wait there! I'll see in a minute.

(*He turns to go back into the study when the* MOTHER *comes out from behind the paper and seizes him.*)

MOTHER. Darling, do you know what I've just come across in the paper? Another flat. Eight rooms. At the Trocadéro. Furniture for sale, too. Only they don't say the price. What does it mean when they don't say the price?

AUTHOR (*going out*). It means a million francs. Let's talk about it later.

MOTHER. A million francs for furniture? When I married, do you know how much an Empire commode was worth?

AUTHOR. I don't want to know. It's too late. (*He goes back into the study.*) I'm all yours, madame. Now, the marguerite . . .

(*At this moment the* WOMAN *has dialed the number. He takes off the receiver.*)

WOMAN. Hello, Léon?

AUTHOR (*howling*). No!

(*He hangs up. There is a ring at the bell.* LA SURETTE *opens the door. It is a serious-looking man in black. He greets the* MOTHER *and* LA SURETTE *and sits down to wait, having noticed that he is not the first. Meanwhile, the* AUTHOR *is addressing* MADAME B.)

AUTHOR. What was I saying?

MADAME B. Man is alone, Master, man is desperately alone.

(*The door at the back opens and* ARDÈLE *comes in, dressed this time and wearing an outrageous hat.*)

ARDÈLE (*standing on the threshold, tragic*). And what about the cats?

AUTHOR. You can see I'm busy.

ARDÈLE. Who's going to look after the cats now that I'm leaving?

AUTHOR. There's Léonie.

ARDÈLE. The maid! You'd leave the cats to the maid. You really mean that? Am I to believe my ears?

AUTHOR. Yes.

ARDÈLE. You monster! Clothaire's ill!

AUTHOR. What's the matter with him?

ARDÈLE. He's miaowing.

AUTHOR. All cats miaow. It's normal.

ARDÈLE. Insensitive brute. He's miaowing hoarsely. He suspects something.

AUTHOR. Talk to him then. Make him see reason. You see I'm busy. Open a tin of sardines.

ARDÈLE. Brute. Insensitive brute. That animal has more heart than you have. He'll refuse your old sardines. He's sad because I'm going.

(*The man in black, tired of waiting, has come to knock on the study door.*)

MAN IN BLACK. Excuse me, monsieur. I see there are several people waiting to see you and I have to have a word with you urgently.

AUTHOR. What about, monsieur?

INSPECTOR. I am the housing inspector. A complaint has been lodged against you for insufficient occupation of the premises and you are under threat of a requisition order for your surplus accommodation.

AUTHOR. Requisition order? But I occupy the entire house, monsieur. Who do you want to put in?

INSPECTOR. A police officer, monsieur. Father of eight. Brigadier Lapomme. Top priority.

AUTHOR. I object, monsieur. The premises are legally occupied.

INSPECTOR. That's what I've come to find out. (*He glances at* MADAME BESSARABO.) Is madame one of the family?

AUTHOR. Madame is a Rumanian journalist.

INSPECTOR (*taking notes*). Premises occupied by foreign *émigrés*. Have you a regular permit, madame?

MADAME. Monsieur, I am the Princess Bessarabo and I am staying at the Hotel Ritz.

INSPECTOR (*still taking notes*). I see. Illegal occupation of further premises in Paris.

AUTHOR. Please don't confuse matters, monsieur! Madame has absolutely nothing to do with this house. Would you be so good as to wait next door for a moment, madame? (*to the* PHOTOGRAPHER) You, too, please. And take your scrap iron with you.

INSPECTOR. Also one of the family?

AUTHOR. No, you can see perfectly well he's a phtotographer.

INSPECTOR. Doesn't stop him being one of the family. I've got an uncle who's a painter.

(*While the* AUTHOR *is easing the other two into the adjoining room,* ARDÈLE *has come up to the* INSPECTOR *gleefully.*)

ARDÈLE. You can send that policeman right along with his eight children. Let him make another one in the next nine months too if he wants to. He'll have plenty of room here because *I* am going, let me tell you, monsieur.

INSPECTOR (*taking more notes*). You're vacating part of the property? I'll make a note of that.

ARDÈLE. Please do.

AUTHOR (*separating them*). Ardèle! Inspector! Please. Let's keep calm.

(*The* MOTHER *come in, brandishing the paper.*)

MOTHER. A flat! Another flat! Darling, this time you'll be able to give your old mother a real treat. Twelve rooms in the Avenue Lamartine, just next door to dear Mademoiselle Pinocle. And for a song—only two million. And shall I tell you something? If I win my lawsuit, I shall keep my little flat at Asnières.

INSPECTOR (*noting*). Twelve rooms, Avenue Lamartine, and you say you also have a small flat at Asnières? How many rooms?

MOTHER (*mutinous*). Four, but I've been crafty and only declared two!

AUTHOR (*bawling*). Mother, I order you to be quiet! And you—stop scribbling down everything people say to you. It's not normal. Damn it all, we're talking about *this* house, aren't we? You'll see that everything's in order here. I have my study on the ground floor, with my secretary's office, a drawing room and dining room, and this is the lobby.

LA SURETTE (*still in the lobby*). Listen, the gas can wait, but about the boots—I've got to go there this afternoon.

AUTHOR. In a minute.

INSPECTOR (*taking a look at the staircase*). What about the second floor? What have you got there?

AUTHOR. Three rooms. All occupied.

INSPECTOR. Is there a third floor?

AUTHOR. Only a trompe-l'oeil façade. There's no third floor really. It's just a sort of optical illusion.

(*At this moment the* PLUMBERS *gallop down the stairs triumphantly.*)

PLUMBER. We've got it, mister. We've got it!

AUTHOR. What?

PLUMBER. The leak! It starts at the two big empty rooms on the third floor, runs right across the table tennis room, the winter garden, and the two libraries, and finishes up in that big room where you've got your collection of toy soldiers!

INSPECTOR (*rubbing his hands and mounting the staircase brandishing his notebook*). Splendid! I'm going to have a look at all this.

AUTHOR (*somewhat discouraged*). We've had it, now.

LA SURETTE. Look, do make an effort. When I lent you my bayonet so as to save you that court-martial, I didn't keep you waiting this long.

AUTHOR (*beside himself, suddenly rips off his shoes and throws them at* LA SURETTE). Here you are, then! Take mine! But get out!

LA SURETTE (*putting them on immediately*). Very well. But giving isn't everything. It's the way you do it. One may be poor, but one has one's dignity. (*He hands him the old boots.*) Do you want these? At least you can afford to have them mended. What have you decided about the gas?

AUTHOR (*who no longer knows what he is saying*). Go and get mine, it's in the kitchen.

MOTHER (*plucking at him*). Well, darling, what do you think about the flat? The twelve rooms at Avenue Lamartine or the eight at the Trocadéro? In a pinch I could make do with that, you know. I'm old now and I don't entertain much anymore.

ARDÈLE (*hooking him from the other side*). So it's agreed, you're going to let me go, but it isn't going to be as easy as you're hoping. I demand, you hear me, I demand now to know the name of this woman.

AUTHOR. What woman?

ARDÈLE. Your mistress.

AUTHOR. What *do* you mean, my mistress?

ARDÈLE. Exactly what I said. Do you think I can be fooled by that letter? Let me tell you I can't. I knew all the time that letter was concealing something.

AUTHOR. Ah, you knew all the time? How clever of you. So what was it concealing, may I ask?

ARDÈLE. You may not! I'm asking you. You've discovered that I'm deceiving you. Why should you choose today to discover I'm deceiving you unless you're deceiving me?

AUTHOR (*taking her by the arm*). Listen to me, Ardèle, I'm quite calm. I'm absolutely calm, and no matter what happens I shall stay calm.

ARDÈLE. You're molesting me! Deceiving me and molesting me! Look at him, your darling boy, look at the dear, sweet cherub.

MOTHER. Before he knew you, my son was sweetness itself. He has never failed his mother.

LA SURETTE (*putting his head through the door*). What have you decided about the gas? You're not going to leave me with two hundred and fifty kilos of raw potatoes on my hands, are you?

AUTHOR (*disengaging himself from the two women and storming*). Keep calm, everybody. We must keep exceedingly calm.

(*At this moment the* WOMAN *dials his number.*)

WOMAN. Hello! Is that you, Léon?

AUTHOR (*smoothly*). Yes, this is Léon speaking. I'd like to be Léon. Why shouldn't I be Léon?

WOMAN. Well then, why are you disguising your voice?

AUTHOR (*gloomily*). Just to make you laugh.

WOMAN. Don't be cruel, Léon. I know you love another woman. But I'm ringing you because something terrible has happened to me. I can't stay here. I must find a flat.

AUTHOR (*very calmly*). Oh, good. In that case I'll put you on to someone. One moment. Mother. There's a woman here telephoning about a flat.

MOTHER (*rushing to the phone*). A flat? A flat? Isn't he a darling? You see what a good son he is. Hello! Hello! Madame? Hello! Hello! You say you're ringing about a flat?

AUTHOR. That's one. Now—two: you. (*to* LA SURETTE) To the kitchen. Eat everything you can find in the icebox. Empty all the bottles in sight.

LA SURETTE. What about the maid?

AUTHOR. Comfort her. Now, number three: you. (*to* ARDÈLE) Listen to me carefully. Look me straight in the eye.

ARDÈLE. Oh, no! Don't start that. It's not fair. You know whenever you look me in the face I tell everything.

MOTHER (*at the telephone*). So you really want to talk about a flat?

WOMAN. Yes, madame, I do, indeed.

MOTHER. How many rooms?

WOMAN. Oh, three or four, madame . . .

MOTHER. But that would be perfect, madame . . .

WOMAN. Really, would it really be suitable, do you think, madame? I cannot tell you how glad I am . . .

MOTHER. But it is I who am glad, madame . . . I don't wish to be indiscreet, of course, but about the furniture and fittings . . .

WOMAN. It's a little embarrassing, but . . . to tell the truth . . . I'd been hoping we needn't discuss furniture and fittings . . .

MOTHER. Ah! So had I, madame!

WOMAN. So, shall we say without furniture and fittings, then, madame? Do you agree?

MOTHER. Certainly, madame, without furniture and fittings. . . . It is so much easier to come to an agreement with people of one's own kind? When may I come along to see you madame?

WOMAN. At once, madame, if that is possible. You can imagine I simply can't wait . . .

MOTHER. But it is I who cannot wait, madame. Please, what is your address?

WOMAN. One eighteen Boulevard Ravachol. Madame Fripon-Minet.

MOTHER. I shall wing my way, madame! I'll be with you immediately. (*She hangs up.*) Darling! Thank you! It's marvelous. Let me kiss you. Four rooms on the Boulevard Ravachol! A lovely quarter. And no furniture and fittings. Really one has only to deal with the right people. They are much less grasping than one thinks. Goodby now, good-by. Don't come with me, my turtledoves.

(*She flies to the door, younger by fifty years. As she opens it, there is* GONTRAN *on the threshold. He is a giant of a man.*)

GONTRAN. Is Jacques at home?

MOTHER. Yes, Gontran, yes. Come in, my little one. I adore you! (*She disappears.*)

AUTHOR (*left in the study with* ARDÈLE). Now, listen to me carefully. I realize one may suffer a momentary lapse.

ARDÈLE. So you admit it?

AUTHOR. God almighty! Admit what?

ARDÈLE. Let me go, then. Your dishonesty sickens me. My mind's made up. I'm going.

GONTRAN (*coming in*). So there you are, both of you!

AUTHOR (*somewhat ill-tempered*). Yes, here we are. As you can see. What is it?

GONTRAN. I must say I didn't expect that sort of welcome from you on a day like this.

ARDÈLE. What's the matter, Gontran? You're so pale, little one.

GONTRAN (*sitting down suddenly*). It's all over. Have you got a gun?

AUTHOR. Hell, no! I could do with one, though. Why a gun?

GONTRAN. Oh, never mind. I'd have preferred one, that's all. I'll get by.

ARDÈLE. But what on earth is the matter?

GONTRAN. You know I've left Lucienne?

AUTHOR (*embarrassed, as though it were himself*). Oh, yes, I never told you; he's left Lucienne.

ARDÈLE. You mean he's left Lucienne? And you never told me? I suppose you thought it would put ideas into my head. Go on, admit that you were thinking of leaving me, too!

AUTHOR. Let's keep calm. He left Lucienne more than three months ago.

GONTRAN. I'm in love with Léa.

ARDÈLE. That stick!

GONTRAN. Please make your wife be

quiet!

ARDÈLE. That shriveled prune? She hasn't even got any hair!

GONTRAN. I order you to make your wife be quiet, do you hear me?

AUTHOR. He's right. Be quiet. You have absolutely no right . . .

ARDÈLE. To say that she's a prune?

GONTRAN. Léa, a prune? She's blonde—well, anyway, now.

AUTHOR. Now you shut up, too! Let's all shut up. Don't let's ever say another word. Sign language only.

GONTRAN (in tears). In any case, who said anything about Léa? I'm not talking about Léa.

ARDÈLE. That's better. At least I'm glad I don't know this . . . this . . . tart.

GONTRAN. I'm talking about Lucienne! That's what's so awful.

ARDÈLE. What has she done? Killed herself? I bet she's killed herself. Ring her up at once.

AUTHOR. Do be calm. What's the good if she's killed herself.

GONTRAN. She doesn't answer the phone. She doesn't answer my letters. (He falls weeping into the AUTHOR's arms.) She's deceiving me, old man; she's been deceiving me ever since I left her!

(He begins to sob like a child in the arms of the AUTHOR, who supports his gigantic body as best he can. ARDÈLE meanwhile paces up and down the room laughing hysterically and breaking all the vases she can lay hands on.)

GONTRAN. To do that to me! To do that to me! To do that to me!

AUTHOR (yelling like a mad thing). Do let's be calm. Let's be absolutely calm. Let's try to be more and more calm.

(While all this is going on, the FRIEND dials, forestage. The telephone rings. The AUTHOR drags himself to the telephone, loaded down by the dead weight of GONTRAN, who has fainted away.)

AUTHOR. Hello!

FRIEND (he, at least, is calm). Is that you, dear boy? Your line was busy. I've had a marvelous idea for the end of my film story.

AUTHOR (not knowing what he is saying). Later, darling, later. The main thing is to keep calm. Please keep quite calm.

FRIEND. What do you mean, later dar-

ling? What on earth's come over you? Hello! Hello! Hello! Swine. (He hangs up.)

ARDÈLE (bearing down on the AUTHOR). Caught in the act! Who were you talking to? I demand to know who you were talking to, you great coward. To your girl friend—weren't you? Deny it. You've just given yourself away. Take that! And that!

(She slaps his face. He lets go of GONTRAN's inert body and it crumples on the floor.)

AUTHOR (bending over him). He's fainted. We must call a doctor. Maybe he's taken poison. I'll go and look for some tincture of iodine.

(He goes off to the kitchen. ARDÈLE calmly steps over the body and makes for the telephone.)

ARDÈLE. Hello! Mademoiselle! This is Jasmin one two, one two. I've just had a call and I must find out immediately the number of my caller. Oh, you say it's difficult. Call the supervisor then, please. It's for security reasons. Your job and the whole future of the country depends upon it. You say I'll be in for it if I'm not speaking the truth? Do as I say, please, and check the facts afterward. Hello! Hello! Hello! Thank you, mademoiselle, you're a good Frenchwoman. I'll mention you to the Minister. You'll certainly be promoted.

(She dials a number. The WOMAN takes off the receiver, forestage.)

WOMAN. Hello!

ARDÈLE. Hello. This is Jasmin one two, one two.

WOMAN. So you're Léon's new wife?

ARDÈLE. Oh, so he calls himself Léon these days? Coward!

WOMAN. I must confess I would like a word with you, madame! Was it you that sent this lunatic who wanted to snatch my flat from me?

ARDÈLE. Your flat? What in heaven's name do I care about your flat? You're trying to snatch my husband.

WOMAN. Let me remind you, madame, that it was you who snatched him from me! Léon adores me.

ARDÈLE. You! With that face? I can see it from here!

WOMAN. And yours, do you think I can't

see that, too? I assure you I shall come and get him if you don't give him back to me.

ARDÈLE. Who, me?

WOMAN. Yes, you.

ARDÈLE. Yes, me.

(*They continue with this incomprehensible exchange of "What, me?" "Yes, you," etc., while the* AUTHOR *comes back from the kitchen, dragging* LA SURETTE *roughly by the collar.*)

AUTHOR. Parasite! Scrounger! Ill-bred boor! I'll teach you to monkey with the maid.

LA SURETTE. I lent you my rifle, didn't I, in time for that parade? Just because you've become a success in life, it doesn't mean you can grab everything for yourself. Anyway, you told me to comfort her.

AUTHOR. Not that way!

LA SURETTE. After all, she's only your maid!

AUTHOR. Scum! Leave her alone! (*turning to the* MAID) And you—stop crying like that. You've been irritating me all the morning!

MAID. But monsieur doesn't know. It's terrible.

AUTHOR. What is it that's so terrible still? Tell me. Like Oedipus, I want to know everything.

MAID. I'm pregnant.

AUTHOR (*sitting down, quietly*). Whatever the case, we must keep calm.

MADAME B. (*bursting in*). Master, Master, I can't wait any longer. The Rumanian intelligentsia is burning to know what you think of love . . .

AUTHOR (*getting up and going to her*). Get out of here, you! Get the hell back to Rumania instantly!

MADAME B. He's gone mad. It's terrific! (*She calls out to the* PHOTOGRAPHER.) We'll have to photograph him like that. It'll make sensational headlines.

AUTHOR. Madame, I don't know how these things are done in Rumania, but I warn you that if you have me photographed in these clothes I shall kill the photographer.

MADAME B. That doesn't matter, we'll find another! Come along now, come along!

INSPECTOR (*looming*). Ah, there you are, monsieur. I've made my inspection. A

fine thing! A very fine thing! Twelve rooms to spare. You'll get your policeman all right. In fact, you'll probably get two!

ARDÈLE (*who has hung up a moment ago and has been listening, advances quietly*). What do I hear? What were you saying while I was on the telephone? Well, *I've* got a revolver.

(*She goes out, slamming the door. The picture falls down. The* AUTHOR *picks it up.*)

AUTHOR. Let's keep calm. Let's keep calm to the end. Very well, monsieur. Gentlemen don't lose their heads.

INSPECTOR. Ah, so you want to be funny, my fine fellow? Sarcasm into the bargain. Right, you can have three policemen. A brigadier and two recruits. All of them fathers. And when their children are grown up, they'll make some more and they'll all live here until their children's children marry and make you some more!

AUTHOR. I'm quite calm. Yoga. Remember Yoga.

INSPECTOR. Remember what you like! You're certainly not going to forget me. I'll send you along some old-age pensioners—none under a hundred.

AUTHOR (*having attained a certain degree of concentration, chants*). I am quite calm. Quite calm. I am becoming more and more calm.

MADAME B. Admirable! Admirable! He really looks like a madman! What genius. What enormous genius. Another picture please, my friend.

(*At this moment the* PLUMBERS *come in, shouting.*)

PLUMBERS. Look out, everyone! Look out! Look out!

AUTHOR. What's this?

PLUMBERS. The leak. The real one. We were wrong about the other one. We've only just found the real trouble, but something's gone wrong. There is water trickling all over the place. We can't control it anymore. It's everyone for himself now!

(*At this very moment cascades of water begin to fall from the ceiling while* MADAME BESSARABO, *the* MAID, *and the* MOTHER, *who has just returned, rush around in a panic, bellowing with fright.*)

MOTHER. A flat, indeed. A fine flat, I

must say. No one in this family will ever get a flat again!

(*The* FRIEND *takes up his receiver. The* AUTHOR, *who has knocked the telephone over in passing, picks it up and says mechanically:*)

AUTHOR. Hello!

FRIEND. Hello, dear boy, am I disturbing you?

AUTHOR (*trying to bring* GONTRAN *to by slapping his face*). Not at all.

FRIEND. Ah! So you finally condescend to listen to me! I must say I've hit on a splendid idea for the end, old thing—a fire. Just like that. Everything ends in a fire.

(*The* AUTHOR *is standing calmly beneath the waterfall while the others are running in all directions trying to catch the pictures as they fall. Only the* INSPECTOR *has opened his umbrella and begins quietly making his report under the deluge.*)

AUTHOR. That's an excellent idea!

FRIEND. At the same time, you can hear gunfire. Do you follow me? Gunfire and fire—can you imagine the effect?

AUTHOR (*somewhat agitated, since he has just seen* ARDÈLE *come in with a pistol in her hand*) Indeed!

(ARDÈLE *begins to shoot. He dodges the bullets and the water, at the same time trying to protect* GONTRAN'S *body.*)

AUTHOR. Indeed! I can well imagine it! (*dodging a bullet*) That'll be hilarious!

FRIEND (*pained*). I don't think you can be paying attention, dear boy. One mustn't be selfish in this life, you know. There you are sitting quietly in your study, without a thought for the agony I've been going through trying to find an ending.

(*During this time the* WOMAN *has been nervously dialing the number, forestage. As the last shot is fired,* ARDÈLE *screams:*)

ARDÈLE. Darling! Tell me you're not hurt at least!

AUTHOR. No, my love. Everything's all right.

ARDÈLE. Oh, I was so frightened.

(*She throws herself into his arms and and falls limply in a faint.*)

AUTHOR (*shouting hysterically into the telephone*). Everything's all right, do you hear me, everything's all right!

FRIEND (*furious*). Do you want me to tell you something? You're impossible. You're just saying anything to keep me quiet. You're not even listening. Be honest, for once; tell me straight you don't think this ending's a good one.

AUTHOR. (*holding up* ARDÈLE *and endeavoring to hoist up* GONTRAN). Listen, dear boy, I'll be frank with you. I agree with Paul Zed. I know I wrote *La Marguerite*, but all the same I prefer a story to end happily.

FRIEND (*suddenly venomous*). You're nothing but a cabaret turn! Just a piddling little unambitious cabaret turn! A lot of water'll flow under the bridge before I call you again!

(*He hangs up furiously at this, while the waterfall brings down the ceiling. The* WOMAN, *who has dialed the number for the tenth time, gives a cry of triumph*).

WOMAN. Hello! Léon?

(*She will go on shouting this until the curtain falls, while the* AUTHOR *comes forward dragging with him* ARDÈLE *and* GONTRAN. *There is general panic in the background, and the décor falls to pieces as the* AUTHOR *addresses the public.*)

AUTHOR. Ladies and gentlemen—one does what one can. . . And there are so many serious writers in the theatre today, I am sure you will forgive the author's failings if he has only made you laugh.

CURTAIN

MOJO

A Black Love Story

Alice Childress

TEDDY   IRENE

ALICE CHILDRESS was born in Charleston, South Carolina, and raised in Harlem, New York City, where she began her career with the American Negro Theatre. During the twelve years that she was associated with the history-making group, Miss Childress functioned as drama coach, director, writer and actress. She appeared in an important role in their production of *Anna Lucasta*, which initially was presented in Harlem and later transferred to Broadway (1944) where it ran for 957 performances.

Her first play, *Florence*, was written for and produced by the American Negro Theatre in 1954. This was followed by *Gold Thru the Trees* and *Just a Little Simple* (an adaptation of Langston Hughes' *Simple Speaks His Mind*), both presented in 1955 at the Club Baron Theatre in Harlem. Subsequently, Miss Childress moved downtown to the Greenwich Mews Theatre with her drama, *Trouble in Mind*, and it received the "Obie" Award for the best original Off-Broadway play of the 1955–56 season. The same play was produced twice by the B.B.C. in London.

Miss Childress received a Harvard appointment as scholar-writer to The Radcliffe Institute for 1966–68, and the University of Michigan presented her play, *Wedding Band*, as their professional theatre production of 1966, with Ruby Dee, Abbey Lincoln and Jack Harkins. The play was given its New York premiere in 1972 at the New York Shakespeare Festival Public Theatre. With Miss Dee once again starred, the production was codirected by the author and Joseph Papp.

Mojo originally was performed by the New Heritage Theatre in Harlem in November, 1970, and another of her short dramas, *Wine in the Wilderness*, was seen on television in 1969 as the first play in a series, *On Being Black*, produced under a Ford Foundation grant.

Miss Childress also is the author of *Martin Luther King at Montgomery, Alabama*, which toured schools and colleges from 1969 through 1971; *The African Garden*; and two published novels, *A Short Walk* and *The Habit*, the latter dealing with the problem of dope addiction and intended for young readers. She also has contributed articles to several major periodicals and is the editor of *Black Scenes*, a collection of fifteen scenes culled from the works of black playwrights.

As an actress, Alice Childress has appeared in many plays both on and off Broadway, on television and in films.

SCENE. TEDDY's *apartment. An overdone room . . . too much crystal, too many telephones and jacks, figurines, satiny, overstuffed furniture . . . ostentatious display of all the expensive junk and gadgetry that money can buy. The place is overneat and well-kept.*

TIME. *Fall—1969. The sound of African bells and stringed instruments . . . fading into a telephone ringing. The phone rings through the sound of shower water running.* TEDDY *enters . . . fortyish, black, and roughly good-looking. He is dripping wet, wears a terry-cloth robe and a man's shower cap.*

———

TEDDY. Hello? . . . I'm catchin double pneumonia. Who's callin? Yeah, yeah, yeah, I'm getting ready. Yeah, yeah, I'm late. A half hour late. Baby, you always measurin time. The Chinese people . . . listen now . . . the Chinese people . . . I'm giving you a fact . . . the Chinese people got a tradition . . . leisurely livin . . . you get there when you get there. Okay, all right, I apologize. Now, the reason you always measurin time is cause you a Got-dam-white-Anglo-Saxon-Protestant-American. Yall woulda held a stopwatch on God-all-mighty . . . Never woulda give him no seven damn days to make the world . . . cause you too fuckin impatient. I did apologize . . . in front. Okay, I apologize some more . . . No, I don't get no kick outta buggin you. You buggin your damn self. Wait, hold on. If your momma's in town, you *oughtta* be with her . . . *should* be with her, playin tiddley-winks or canasta or whatever other ass-draggin games you white folks like to play *(laughs)*. Ahhhhhhha . . . Aw, baby, I ain't callin you white folks, you wild, yaller-headed, fine thing, you! They all white folks *but* you . . . you somethin else. I'll be there. How I'm gonna get there if you keep talkin? Berniece, Berniece . . . keep cool . . . Aw, you sweet, vanilla ice-cream cone, you. Dammit, Berniece, I'm ketchin cold . . . Yeah, yeah, soon as I can *(hangs up phone)*. Women, women. *(looks in the mirror and gently removes the shower cap)* Aw, you good-lookin, black, heart-breakin, son-of-a-bitch, whoo! *(Phone rings again. He picks it up.)* Ber-

niece . . . whats-a-matta with you . . . Oh, yeah, yeah, right back at you, man. What *you* know? . . . Chicago? You tell Gut Wilson I ain't lost nothin in Chicago. New York's my hole card. Trouble with Gut Wilson is Gut's a liar. Lotta big talk, but when you get there nothin is happenin. How come he didn't call me hisself . . . Yeah, sure, he got you to do it and don't I know why. The last time he called about a big game, I got there, nothin was happenin. Yeah, had me takin off for Tampa, Florida, in a jet plane, nothin there but a lotta peanut guys and chili-parlor pimps with fifty or a hundred dollars apiece, all of em hopin to luck up on a few grand by hittin on me. What you call killin time. Business is business, after all. How is ole, ugly Gut? They tell me his ole lady shot him square in the ass! *(laughs)* Took the doctor a week fore he could find the bullet. Ole, four-flushin, tub-a-lard. But he's all right. Tell him um sorry I can't make it . . . Yeah, man, right back at you, you take it easy too. *(hangs up)* Chicago, shit. *(He turns on the radio to cool jazz and exits to the bedroom.* IRENE *opens the front door with her key. She is a brown woman, a little older than* TEDDY *. . . wearing a mink coat, a very ordinary blouse and skirt . . . comfort shoes. She is neat but looks a bit thrown together. She is carrying several packages and a suitcase.* TEDDY, *from offstage)* Who's that?

IRENE. Who the hell you think, nigger? How many people got keys to this door?

TEDDY. Irene? That you, Irene?

IRENE. Yeah, Irene. Not Mary or Susie, or Helen or Miss Ann or Aunt Jemima either. Did I leave anybody out? Who else is here? *(rests her packages and coat)* I couldn't find no parkin space and had to bribe the garage fella to let me in. What the hell is the matter with New York City! Traffic bumper to bumper. I brought you presents . . . and you don't deserve a damn one . . . not a one. Who else is here?

TEDDY. Not a soul, baby!

IRENE. Where you?

TEDDY. In here dressin.

IRENE *(surveying the room with hostility)*. Did that Berniece pick out your new drapes?

TEDDY. Yeah, yeah, yeah.

IRENE. I don't like um.

TEDDY. Okay!

IRENE (*smooths her hair and goes around the room, looking into cigarette boxes, straightening chairs, etc.*). I don't like the color. They cheap lookin too.

TEDDY. All right, darlin.

IRENE. Fact is . . . I don't like nothin about um. Lotta simple-minded bad taste.

TEDDY. I hear you, sugar.

IRENE. Damn, I sure wish youda told me you was gonna buy new drapes.

TEDDY. I wish so too, baby-doll, I really do. Whatcha lookin for out there?

IRENE (*opening the liquor cabinet*). Gettin me a drink.

TEDDY. You kiddin.

IRENE. No, I'm not. (*pours a small drink and steps out of her shoes*) Life is a dog. This life is somethin. Ain't one thing . . . it's another. (*Garbled announcement comes over radio.*) Mmmmmmmm, well, how bout that. Hey, Teddy! They passed some kinda civil rights!

TEDDY. Did what?

IRENE (*yelling*). I say they passed some kinda civil rights!

TEDDY. What was it?

IRENE. I don't know but whatever it was . . . it got passed.

TEDDY. Don't make me no damn difference!

IRENE. Well, it don't make me none either, but it's still nice. It's nice for those it make a difference to. It's nice for anybody whose taste runs in that direction. That's what I mean.

TEDDY (*enters wearing a splendid dark suit, pleated, white shirt . . . tie with pearl stickpin. He is fastening a cuff link*). A lotta crap, alla that prayin and crawlin all over the ground, kneelin whilst the police dogs be snappin at your ass. Singin while whitey throw tear gas. You lost your mind or somethin? Carryin on bout "civil rights."

IRENE. But if somebody's taste run in that direction, then . . . dammit . . . civil rights is their bag . . . that's all I say.

TEDDY. You losin your mind?

IRENE. The civil rights don't mean a father-grabbin thing to me. But to some people it do. Why you got to jump me about it?

TEDDY. Reenie, you sick? You don't sound like yourself.

IRENE. Why you jumpin your own kind? You don't like the civil rights . . . kill me! Hell, it's all my fault, huh?

TEDDY. No, baby, all I'm sayin is you don't have to go through alla that just to eat at some dirty, greasy hamburger joint.

IRENE. I'm with you. But some feel our way and some don't . . . and all ain't fools, dammit-to-hell. Don't you mess with me, Teddy, not today.

TEDDY (*wondering about her attitude*). Guess you right, Irene. Make yourself comfortable. I got a little run to make.

IRENE. Where you goin?

TEDDY. Gotta go see a fella name Shorty . . . bout settin up a poker session for me.

IRENE (*looking over his outfit*). Mmmm, Shorty must be a flyin faggot . . . way you all got up.

TEDDY. Don't gimmie a hard time. Where's my present?

IRENE. In that box. Don't go way and leave me, Teddy. Talk to me.

TEDDY. Business is business, baby. I ain't seen you for a couple months, you drop in unexpected. After all, I didn't know you were comin. Tell you what . . . I'll be gone for two hours . . . then be right back and talk to you. Okay?

IRENE. No. Stay here with me awhile . . . then go on and see Berniece or whoever. How is Berniece?

TEDDY. Still her same, simple self.

IRENE. She's all right, I guess . . . Don't leave me.

TEDDY (*picks up the mink coat and strokes it. He is uneasy about her attitude*). Mink . . . mink . . . alla this pretty mink. Go girl.

IRENE. Aw . . . ain't nothin but a animal's backside. They knock them in the head and slit their throat and sew em together . . . Who the hell cares.

TEDDY. You the one bought it.

IRENE. I bought it off a junky. He was shiverin and shakin from head to toe . . . like at the North Pole . . . I gave him three hundred and fifty dollars. I ain't never enjoyed that coat . . . keep seein him shiverin and shakin . . . needin a fix.

TEDDY. Reenie, you didn't sell him the junk, you didn't make him take it.

IRENE. But I know he had to lift that to buy junk . . . had to boost it and sell it to me to keep his habit goin.

TEDDY. Well, damn, look what they did to the mink . . . knocked him in the head and slit his throat . . . and all like you say. That's life.

IRENE. You make me feel better. Don't go out.

TEDDY. You unreasonable, baby. I'd do anything in the world for you . . . you my buddy-girl, you know that. Ain't you my buddy-girl?

IRENE. No, I'm your wife. Well, anyway . . . your divorced wife. I'm the only wife you ever had.

TEDDY (*gets a dark trench coat from closet, examines it for any stray piece of lint which might be found; of course it is lintless*). Why you wanta throw that in my face? You say . . . "I wanta be married . . . marry me." I married you . . . didn't see you no more for a year and a half . . . then you pop up with some paper . . . you want a divorce. I sign the paper. There's somethin about a colored woman that makes her a self-willed, non-understandable; but I been your buddy-boy through it all. Now I'm gonna cut my little run down to a hour or forty-five minutes . . . then I be right back . . . (*He has one arm in the coat.*)

IRENE. When I first met you . . . you wasn't nothin but a dinin car waiter.

TEDDY (*pauses*). Right.

IRENE. I taught you just about everything you know.

TEDDY. Just about, almost.

IRENE. I set you up in business . . . bought you a number wheel . . showed you where it was at . . . and I never asked much in return. (*He now has the coat on.*) I say don't go out . . . don't go out, dammit . . . I say that . . . don't go out!

TEDDY (*sits down but still wears coat*). I'm still here. Now tell me what you was doin when I met you.

IRENE. I got a good memory. I was attendant in the ofay ladies lounge . . . washin toilets, handin out toilet paper . . . A little saucer of change on the dressin table . . . a sign pasted on the mirror . . . *"Ladies, your tips are my livelihood"* . . . *"Towel, honey?"* Pinnin up torn dress hems, wipin up the floor behind sick drunks . . . laughin at their "Jew" and "darky" jokes, wipin away their tears. Each one of em tellin me how much they

loved the colored woman who raised em or cook the meals or whatever, tellin me how I must or must not feel about the race problem . . . and how I must not hate . . . The same jokes, the same advice from one damn rest room to another. Rest room attendant!

TEDDY. Yeah, well . . . I'm not soundin on you . . . even though you was the one soundin first. We been through some hard days together. Reenie, all that you ever did for me . . . I tried to thank you (*looks at her suitcase*).

IRENE. I'm gonna camp here for a couple of days.

TEDDY. Crazy. How is Philadelphia?

IRENE. That's one sad-ass city . . . bout to sink into the ground . . . but a little money is changin hands now and then. You don't come to see me like you used to.

TEDDY. Aw, you know, first one thing then another (*leans over the back of her chair and presses his cheek to hers*). What you know? Sweet thing.

IRENE. Don't know. What you know, daddy? You good-lookin, two-timin, black, sweet-lovin-man, you.

TEDDY. Welcome home, it's been a long time.

IRENE. So good to hear the sounda your voice.

TEDDY. I've broken three dates with Berniece.

IRENE. What I care? Make it four . . . she'll forgive you. Call her and say somethin came up. If I ain't somethin, what is? I'm bein bad about it.

TEDDY (*unbuttons coat*). I'm still here. You in some kinda trouble?

IRENE. Those damn doctors, what the hell they know. I gotta go in the hospital next Monday . . . God knows what all they plannin, but I said to myself . . . I'm goin to see my buddy-boy first, no matter what.

TEDDY. Somethin serious? They say it's serious?

IRENE. Yes, serious, and don't make me name it . . . gives me the creeps.

TEDDY. Oh . . . well, you can't really know bout these things till you take alla the tests.

IRENE. I took the tests and they gave me the results . . . and it's serious. That's bout all I got to say on that.

TEDDY. Sweetheart, you know . . . they got all kindsa things goin on now with these operations and what you call . . . er, you call . . .

IRENE. Radiation.

TEDDY. That's right. Radiation.

IRENE. Radiation therapy. I know that. I'm not plannin to curl up and die. Much as I been through in life . . . live or die . . . this ain nothin.

TEDDY. There you go . . . everything's gonna end up happy . . . just like a Sidney Potenay movie.

IRENE. Makes you think . . . you get to summin up your whole life . . . that is, after your first feelings. I was shook . . . it shook me. I put up a good front . . . brave, strong and cool . . . but on the inside I was shook . . . it shook me. I recall goin in the bathroom . . . a place full of echoes . . . there I was feelin light-headed in the middle of nowhere . . . high up . . . lookin down on myself. That must be how it feels to be a mountain climber, I'll bet. I leaned my head against the cold, tile wall . . . it was yellow tile . . . big, square, yellow tiles . . . and I cried out the fullness of my feeling . . . never cried like that before . . . never in this life. I got scared that I'd never stop . . . chokin and sobbin . . . and wonderin if I was chicken-hearted. Well, it seemed forever . . . but I stopped. They set the day for me to face the music . . . next Monday. I kept thinkin bout you and me and any unfinished business we might have. So I got on the highway and here I am.

TEDDY (*removing his coat*). Thank you. I'm sure glad you thought about me. Glad you got here, too. This where you belong. We gonna see this through together . . . and everything's gonna end up a Sidney Potenay movie. To what hospital you goin?

IRENE. Back down in Philly. I'll write everything down for you.

TEDDY. Philly . . . that where you wanta be?

IRENE. Yes. It's all one anyway . . . no matter where. Stay with me.

TEDDY (*hanging up his things and hers*). You couldn't chase me out. I wanta be here with you . . . I'm the one . . . it's you and me.

IRENE. You've always been good to me

. . . most of the time . . . except for once or twice . . .

TEDDY. Reenie, why bring up the once or twice?

IRENE. You knocked me down once . . . and my eye was swole . . . I remember how you sapped me up somethin awful.

TEDDY. But why? Why would I do somethin like that? Think. What had you done?

IRENE. Not a thing . . . that I can recall. I shoulda hollered for the law and had you hauled off to jail . . . that's what.

TEDDY. You whipped on my girlfriend. You almost kill Sadie.

IRENE. Aw . . . she was just puttin on.

TEDDY. Aw, no she wasn't. You hit her with a chair leg. And for what? You didn't have no right to mess with that poor girl.

IRENE. She got on my nerves.

TEDDY. You and me wasn't together. You busted that up . . . yet you was always runnin down my women to pick a quarrel.

IRENE. Not all of em . . . just the ones I didn't like.

TEDDY. But who did you ever like? Name one.

IRENE. Mmmmmmmmm, lemmie see . . . You remember Sugar? I liked Sugar very much.

TEDDY (*looking in her empty glass*). You liked Sugar cause she was homely.

IRENE. Maybe you right . . . Now tell me why *you* liked her. Maybe her beauty was not to be seen.

TEDDY (*with a proud, self-conscious grin*). Aw, come on . . . cut it out . . . S'matter with you! How bout the time you hit me in the head with the apple juice bottle? . . . The blood runnin down and had to have stitches . . . look, look-a-there (*kneels and leans his head in her lap*).

IRENE. Oh, the hair don't even grow there no more. (*She laughs.*) I almost knocked you into the next world.

TEDDY. You a mean, old bitch . . . just lookin at it gives you the jollies.

IRENE. You musta done somethin turble to aggravate me like that.

TEDDY. You done me awful.

IRENE. And you me.

TEDDY. You don't want another drink . . . do you?

IRENE. Yes, I do. Mix one and hand it to me.

TEDDY. Okay, whatcha want?

IRENE. Don't make me no difference. Drink is a drink.

TEDDY (*as he makes a fresh drink*). Reenie, why did you make me marry you?

IRENE. How could I make you? You was a full-grown man.

TEDDY. That was the craziest thing. Why?

IRENE. I had my reasons.

TEDDY. Was about seventeen years ago.

IRENE. Eighteen.

TEDDY. "Teddy," you said . . . "I want you to marry me cause every woman oughta be married one time." Two . . . three weeks of cuttin up, lovin and laughin . . . then bam! You cut out on me. Looka here . . . still in the frame . . . damn postcard from Atlanta-damn-Georgia . . .

(*He looks at framed card over the bar.*)

IRENE (*reciting the message from memory*). "Hey there, Teddy. Life is too short for you to be tied down . . . or me either. Forget it . . . Love . . . Reenie."

TEDDY. One year later you come walkin in on me with a double order of barbecued ribs. I made you welcome . . . glad to see you. There we was sittin in the kitchen eatin our ribs, havin one ha-ha after another . . . and you say . . . "Teddy, I gotta take you to court and charge you with adultery cause it's proper for the man to be the guilty one."

IRENE. *That's* why I liked Sugar so much! She was so gracious bout helpin' us out. Lord, yall looked funny when me and the witnesses knocked on the door. You had on a red satin robe and she was in my black lace nightie . . . and the camera goin off . . . yall was too funny. I still got one-a-them pictures somewhere. Look just like a Forty-second Street movie.

TEDDY (*hands her the drink*). When last you been to a movie, baby?

IRENE. I really don't remember.

TEDDY. They don't wear clothes in Forty-second Street movies. And people no longer got to bust into bedrooms to get a divorce.

IRENE. The world turns . . . don't it?

TEDDY. "Let's get married, let's divorce." Why you do like that? Why?

IRENE. Teddy, did you ever love me?

TEDDY. You know it.

IRENE. Not that buddy-love . . .

(*Phone rings.* TEDDY *picks it up.*)

TEDDY. Uh-huh, yeah, you right. I certainly do apologize. Listen . . . I say *listen* . . . this is a *bad* time. The wrong day. Well, I got a fella here and we goin over some Philadelphia business, tryin to get somethin set up. No need to holler. Let's leave it that I'll call tomorrow and we make it definite. Aww, now, course I do. You know I do. Sure I do. Yeah, I know you do too.

(*smacks his lips to send a kiss*).

IRENE. Mmmmmmph . . . nothin makes him sick (*smacks her lips in imitation.*)

TEDDY (*hangs phone up*). Aw, why you wanta act ugly? Now . . . what was we talkin about?

IRENE. Why did you marry me? You coulda said no.

TEDDY. I did it cause I thought that much of you. (*He opens drawers of a chest.*) Your things can go in here . . . plenty space (*opens the suitcase on a bench*). If marryin meant somethin to you I was glad to oblige. That's the same way I felt bout that damn fool divorce business. It was somethin you wanted and I could give it to you. Woman, I think a whole lotta you.

IRENE (*suddenly solemn*). Teddy, I want you to stay over there and keep unpackin that bag for me so I don't haveta look you in the face . . . and I want you to listen good . . . listen hard and let me say it all.

TEDDY. Right.

IRENE. The reason I asked you to be my husband was . . . I wanted to have a baby . . . and I wanted you for the father . . . I didn't want the child to be outta wedlock . . . I didn't think it was too much any of your business . . . because you didn't seem to love me like I loved you . . . I went on off and had the baby . . . (*dead silence for a few seconds*).

TEDDY. I don't believe you.

IRENE. It's true. We got a daughter. Her name used to be Teddi . . . T-e-d-d-i. It was that for a few weeks.

TEDDY. What's her name now?

IRENE. I don't know.

TEDDY. Where is she?

IRENE. I . . . I don't know . . . truly I

don't.

TEDDY. Why don't you know, Reenie?

IRENE. I got scared bout leavin her around here and there . . . I got to bein sorry that I brought a child here who might be like us . . . knocked about. The doctor saw how it was with my mind . . .

TEDDY. Your mind?

IRENE. Felt like I was goin stone-crazy . . . no sleep . . . pacin the floor . . . up and down, down and up. Such a pretty baby . . . I was afraid I might hurt her . . . Rest-broken and pacin the floor and no way to turn . . . I didn't want to hurt her.

TEDDY. You couldn't turn to me?

IRENE. No, somehow I couldn't. The doctor told me bout some folks who were well off . . . "Professional," he said. Maybe a lawyer or another doctor . . . or a teacher. I got to seein her in my mind's eye . . . livin nicely and havin a pretty home and a mama and a papa . . . and bein proud of em . . . Out of it, Teddy! free as black can be, free to get in some school, and live right. So I signed the papers and turned her over.

TEDDY. To who?

IRENE. They don't like you to know cause you might turn up and make trouble. They don't tell.

TEDDY. I'm sorry. We got a very sad story. Everytime I see you . . . you be laughin and pokin fun at yourself . . . always makin fun of yourself . . .

IRENE. Just tryin to beat the next fella to it. If you laugh at yourself . . . Well, that's how it was.

TEDDY. Is this her picture? (*takes a framed picture out of case*)

IRENE. No. That's a baby picture of one of Martin Luther King's children. I cut it outta the *Ebony* magazine . . . and framed it . . . Just cause it's cute.

TEDDY. Sorry . . . sorry to my heart. I'm sorry.

IRENE. I had to come and tell you, Teddy . . . As hurtful as it is . . . it's your business . . . ain't nobody got the right to keep your business from you . . . even if it's painful.

TEDDY. You right. At least it put your mind . . . at rest.

IRENE. Oh, dear heart . . . it ain't that easy. Instead of one child . . . I had thousands. When she was two . . . I looked at every two-year-old I passed . . . "Is that her . . . this one . . . that one?" When she was five . . . "There's one look just like Teddy." Years of lookin at strange, rag-gedy-ass children runnin round the streets . . . "That her?" Gets worse as the years pass . . . Now I look at some baby-face hooker standin on the corner with her mouth fulla that tough talk . . . "Come on home with me, baby." I stand there won-derin . . . "Is that my daughter?" The hooker see me starin and say . . . "What you lookin at, bitch?"

TEDDY (*trying to believe*). That wasn't her. She's with some lawyer or school-teacher. That's what . . . a civil rights law-yer and his wife.

IRENE (*unpacking as he fixes drink for himself*). I loved you so much, Teddy. I came here to let you know that much. I'm sorry I wasn't able to say it before. When we were around each other . . . it was all fightin and pokin fun . . . mockin our-selves. I believe niggers think it's dis-graceful to love one another . . . fightin like hell to cover up what's in the heart. My daddy once said to mama . . . "Sheeeeet . . . what's love, what's that? Better git yourself some money." Sayin them things right in fronta me. I'm tryin to eat the little bitta grits and bacon and make out that I don't hear what I'm hearin. She say . . . "Nigger, get the hell out." He slam the door and gone. She sit down and cry . . . then look at me and say . . . "Gal, you a millstone round my neck." Ain't like no Teevee story with us . . . Love is hard to live round when a woman is washin out her last raggy pair-a-drawers . . . and her man ain't got a quarter to put in her hand. When it's like that it's embarrassin to love each other . . . If you stop laughin at your-self for too long a time . . . they'll have to put you away in a straightjacket. I passed through this world . . . and for what? I don't even know who I am.

TEDDY. You're my Irene. Don't let no damn-ass doctor crack you up. I'm gonna take you to another doctor who knows what he's talkin about . . . and don't be handin people a lotta bad news. Our daughter is with a civil rights lawyer and his schoolteacher wife.

IRENE. How you know?

TEDDY. I'm the seventh child of a seventh

child.

IRENE (*shaking her head*). You in the number business and I been dealin in the hot goods these junkies bring in. Why would our daughter be in a lawyer's home? Do we deserve it?

TEDDY. Cause I say. My papa didn't walk out on Mom, but I'm tellin you . . . the family what's stayin together . . . ain't always prayin together. Pop pulled garbage in a old-law tenement building. Hot-dam . . . every night after supper . . . he drink down a pint-a wine and say, "Come on, boy . . . let's pull garbage." He's tanked, dig? I ain't had no wine cause I'm nine years old . . . and stone sober. Open the dumbwaiter shaft . . . great-day-in-the-mornin . . . a big rat be walkin straight up the pulley rope . . . Rat stop and look down on you like . . . whatchoo want . . . (*imitating the rat*). Then he walk *slower* . . . actin like . . . "Who you think you bluffin?" Pull garbage? We *shovelin* it out where folks pitch it down the shaft cause they scareda rats too. At night . . . when I'm sleepin . . . they runnin between the walls and the ceilin . . . bloom-bloom-bloom. Rats on the run. That ain't no place for love talk bout moonlight and butterflies and all that shit the white folks write stories bout. Openin up that stinkin, rotten garbage shaft took more heart than havin some damn "mutiny on the bounty" (*freshening his drink because of the chilling memory*). Them rats congregatin, baby, all along the basement steam pipes. Talkin bout werewolf and space saucer . . . sheeeeet. Try pullin garbage.

IRENE. This liquor is strong.

TEDDY. Ain't strong enough . . . whooo!

IRENE (*placing gift boxes to one side. Shaking out chiffon nightie from the suitcase. She is slightly feeling the liquor*). Over halfa my life spent in white folks' toilets, smellin their funk and grinnin in their face . . . what for? To hear the sound of a quarter hittin against a saucer. Bible say you got threescore and ten years to live . . . right?

TEDDY. Right.

IRENE. Some ain't got that . . . and some got a few more. Whatcha doin with these precious days, Teddy?

TEDDY. Don't go there no more. What's

done is done. You makin me feel bad, you makin yourself feel bad. Get yourself together so you can come through this thing in good shape.

IRENE (*removes a record from a bag*). In that Philadelphia where I live . . . there's this African-American something or other . . . on the corner. It's these kids on the poverty thing . . . program . . . poverty program they call it.

TEDDY. I don't need no poverty program . . . I need a *prosperity* program. (*sets up record player*) This my present?

IRENE. One of em. Kids hang out round this poverty program . . . seventeen, eighteen . . . wearin alla that *yaller* and red African print. Once a lady took care-a me when I was a child . . . mama off workin . . . Woman wouldn't let me wear a red hair ribbon. She say . . . "You too black to wear red. Dark people oughtta wear dark clothes." (*laughs*) Them poverty program kids wearin red and green and orange. Round the corner from my house . . . a soul-brother got a shop sellin Africa . . . you can *buy* Africa . . . robes, dresses, sandals, beads, mats, baskets, drums . . . every kinda Africa.

TEDDY. Mosta that stuff made in England. Whitey is gettin rich offa us wearin that mess . . .

IRENE. He gettin rich offa everything else we wear too . . . Also offa what you eat, drink, the liquor, wine, beer . . . the cameras, he gettin rich off all of it.

TEDDY. Whitey is still trickin you. They own Africa factories. They turnin out statues and robes and incense by the billion.

IRENE. Maybe they trickin theyself. Suppose you only had a few months to live, Teddy. What would you do? How would you spend the time?

TEDDY. I'm not gonna help you play them games. What kinda talk is that?

IRENE. Suppose you had a month to live? Suppose you had a year?

TEDDY. Aw, Reenie, damn . . . I'd do all the things I meant to do but been puttin off.

IRENE. And if you had ten years . . . twenty, thirty . . . seventy-five . . . ? Dontcha see, Teddy, the answer is the same. No matter how long or short the time . . . you oughta do all the things you mean to do. Never put it off. I discovered that all by myself while cryin in the room with yellow tile walls. The time we know is short. If you make seventy . . . that'll be seventy times to spend Christmas Day . . . seventy Thanksgivings . . . seventy chances to see springtime . . . Teddy, don't put off anything you want to do until later. Ain't no later. Later for later. It's all now.

TEDDY (*plays record*). What I wanta do right this minute . . . is whatever you wanta do.

IRENE (*opens box and takes out African robes and book*). I bought some of Africa in that shop. A robe for you and one for me.

TEDDY (*a bit uncomfortable*). Mmmmm, er . . . well, aw, gee . . . that was nice of you. Thank you very much.

IRENE. I know it don't gas you too much . . . but put it on and keep me company.

TEDDY (*puts on the robe*). When you come outta that jive hospital . . . we gonna get us some change together and take off for Africa . . . so you can eyeball it for yourself.

IRENE. I ain't lost nothin in Africa.

TEDDY. For a minute I thought you was bout to dig Marcus Garvey and run out on us. (*African record is playing.*) Street corner speakers out here hollerin how we come from kings and queens. Hell . . . everybody wasn't a king or a queen . . . Who would they rule over if all was kings and queens?

IRENE. Don't talk so damn ignorant. Fact is . . . you *coulda* been a king . . . but you *know* you not descended from any American Presidents . . . at least none of em ever claimed you (*keeping time to the music*). You descended from that. Look at you . . . pattin your foot . . . it's all in your face. This book tells how there was no orphan children in Africa . . . anybody die away from their children . . . or don't want em . . . some other is right there to take em in and love em. I read that.

TEDDY. Yeah . . . well, I read where they urinate in ditches over there in Africa, Reenie.

IRENE. So what! Slave labor built this country!

TEDDY. Right. And slave labor gonna tear it down!

IRENE. For years . . . I spent eight hours out of each day in toilets . . . places where I couldn't go in if I didn't work there. *They* piss all over the pink toilet seats! Ditch or marble floor . . . piss is piss.

TEDDY. Some-a them Africans sold us to the white folks, Reenie.

IRENE (*passing a box to him*). Salt peanuts? (*He opens the box.*) Some-a the niggers over here still sellin each other out . . . and robbin and muggin and hittin on the head and ransackin . . . (*significantly*) and also *racketeerin* . . .

TEDDY. Signify . . . go ahead . . . but I don't go to anybody's damn house and say . . . yall just gotta play the numbers . . . do I do that?

IRENE. Ain't just you. I done my share, you done yours and some did even worse. Holdin down your own people . . . for what?

TEDDY. For the money, that's what. When I run a game it's *racketeerin* . . . When New York State run a game it's patriotic. They can even put ads in the paper . . . BUY YOURSELF A LOTTERY TICKET . . . And when you ride the bus they got pitchers of people laughin and grinnin cause they had a hit. But they throw me in jail for takin a ten-cent bet. I served time twice . . . yes, I did . . . so hush the hell on up and listen to your damn African music. Git offa my back, Reenie . . . that's one thing bout that simple Berniece . . . she make you *feel* like a man. She's white, but she make you feel like . . .

IRENE. Feel like . . . feel like . . . I been hearing that all my days . . . sound like my poppa . . . "I wanta *feel like* a man." You wanta *be* a man . . . forget that *feel like* . . . *feel like* . . . Fix me another drink.

TEDDY. If you wasn't on your way to the hospital I'd knock the hell out of you, for underminin me. Berniece knows how to make you feel pleasant.

IRENE. You ain't had to watch her rinse out her last pair of raggy drawers . . . or pull garbage . . . Y'all busy poppin champagne by candlelight . . .

TEDDY. Yeah, yeah, yeah, you the best. (*putting away bottles*) Bar shut down . . . before the joint gets outta control.

IRENE (*near tears*). Oh, Lord, God . . . what is it all about? Suppose my girl is in jail on accounta the civil rights? Suppose she's out in the demonstration bein beat? God oughtta kill me for my sins! (*waves book at him and throws it to him*) I want you to have my Africa book. Know what they do with dice in Africa? They tell fortunes, read the future . . . call it rollin the bones . . . then they read what they rolled for you. Here they shoot dice to get at each other's rent money! (*She takes off her dress and unfolds her African robe to put it on*).

TEDDY (*takes out dice . . . rattles them and throws on the floor*). I told you I was a seventh child. Gotcha fortune right here. (*picks up, warms them in his hand . . . throws again*) Six . . . six is my point . . .

IRENE (*takes a roll of money out of her bosom*). Yeah? I got fifty that say you don't six. Nother fifty say you'll ten fore you crap out.

TEDDY. No you don't . . . put your money back in the bank . . . I'm tellin *fortune* this evenin . . . no gamblin . . . just fortune. (*surveying her robe*) Damn . . . don't she look pretty. (*throws dice*) Two spots . . . snake eyes lookin at you. The evil eye is always lookin but . . . (*throws dice*) Them boxcars signify that our daughter rides in style . . .

IRENE. Might could be so.

TEDDY. Six-ace . . . Lord, Lord, Lord, our little girl is a winner all around . . .

IRENE. You crapped out!

TEDDY. We not gamblin, baby . . . all these are signs for the fortune-tellin . . .

IRENE. That's right . . . tell it . . . I believe you . . .

TEDDY (*throws dice*). Her days are all comin up sevens and elevens . . . (*throws dice*) Little Joe . . . that's her boyfriend . . . maybe it's her husband . . . her . . . her . . . her what you call . . . guardian . . . (*throws dice*) . . . But he is . . . buyin them new shoes . . . with a seven . . . (*throws again*) Another seven . . . (*throws again*) Another seven . . .

IRENE. That's a streaka luck . . . you hot, baby.

TEDDY. And a seven again! Our daughter is a real gone girl . . . she's outta sight . . . her mind is together . . . her pocketbook is together . . . her soul is together . . . (*He starts to throw again and* IRENE *grabs his hands.*)

IRENE. That's enough, don't press your luck.

TEDDY. But, baby, I was bout to read you outta the hospital and back here with me overlookin the Harlem River.

IRENE (*puts dice in her bosom*). That's enough. I'll keep these. I'm feelin great. I'm ready to go in that all-white room . . . and let a white man in a white mask put me to sleep . . . And another white man in a white suit is gonna stick a knife in me . . . White dresses and white masks all around me . . . And I'm laid out on a white sheet . . . And they'll cut out a part of me . . . I'm wonderin if they could ever trust us that much.

TEDDY (*turns away from her a moment*). Hey, this record is a gas. The guy is drummin his ass off. Reenie, people got to trust each other in some strange ways.

IRENE. I want somethin else black in that room . . . besides me. I want a good blackness like some of the young people feel . . . clean black—a blackness I never knew . . .

TEDDY. Out on the coast one time . . . my car broke down in this little town . . . on the way to L. A. from Frisco. Didn't see a soul-brother or sister for two days. Folks were friendly in an offhand way . . . but by time to go . . . I needed to *see* Black . . . didn't need to even *talk* to Black, just want to *see* it, see Black walkin or workin in a store . . . or waitin for a train.

IRENE (*indicating the record*). That's what I got to take to the hospital with me . . . a little of this Africa . . . It'll be like a . . . like a . . .

TEDDY. A Mojo . . . a Mojo workin for you . . . yeah. Berniece say we can't go back to Africa . . . that the Africans don't know us anymore.

IRENE. When Black get to longin for Black . . . it bugs em. Black hate Black . . . it kicks em.

TEDDY. Later . . . later . . . later for what she say.

IRENE. You are Africa . . . Do you remember me, daddy? Will we ever love one another? If I go in that white room without some Black in my soul . . . I won't make it.

TEDDY. Don't say that.

IRENE. I got to take Africa in there with me . . . When they knock me out with gas or ether or whatever the hell . . . I got to be hearin that drum in one corner of my mind . . . so my heart can beat . . .

(TEDDY *turns the record up louder.*)

TEDDY. Dance it, Reenie . . . dance up on some BLACK . . . Africa for Reenie! (*She joins him in dancing. They improvise sweeping grand steps.*) That fool Gut Wilson . . . you know they say his ole lady shot him . . . but he's up and out now.

IRENE. Where's he at?

TEDDY. Out tryin to hustle up a poker game for Chicago.

IRENE. Don't you go no place till I get through this that I'm goin through.

TEDDY. Not even thinkin bout it. Never gonna leave . . . never . . . (*They continue dancing.* TEDDY *is overdoing the beat, stamping it out.*) Dig the beat . . . I love you, Reenie . . . dig the beat . . . I love you, baby . . . I love you . . . I love you . . . I love you . . . Dig the beat . . . I love you . . . I love you, Reenie . . .

(*They continue to dance and whirl.*)

CURTAIN

THE GIFT

Ronald Duncan

PERCY WORSTHORNE, *fifty-nine, a bank clerk*
MADELAINE WORSTHORNE, *fifty, his wife*
ERNEST TREMLETT, *seventy-three, her father*

TONY WORSTHORNE, *twenty-five, their son*
GERALDINE WORSTHORNE, *twenty-three, their daughter*

A PROMINENT British poet and playwright, Ronald Duncan was born in Salisbury, Rhodesia, on August 6, 1914, of an English mother and a father who was an illegitimate son of Crown Prince Rudolph of Bavaria. Mr. Duncan's great-great-uncle was Ludwig II of Bavaria, whose "passion for horses and music" he admittedly has inherited.

He was educated in Switzerland and at Downing College, Cambridge University. Between 1938 and 1946, he published and edited the magazine, *The Townsman,* and among its illustrious contributors were Igor Stravinsky, T. S. Eliot and Ezra Pound, the latter a staunch friend who once described Duncan as "the lone wolf of English letters."

In 1945, the author scored heavily with his poetic drama, *This Way to the Tomb,* produced at the Mercury Theatre, Notting Hill, and afterward transferred to the Garrick Theatre in the West End. According to one reviewer: "The author very skillfully contrasted the spiritual richness of medieval days with the inanities of modern civilization. It takes its place with the best of modern dramas as a work of literary quality which has contributed not a little to the movement to restore poetry to the English stage."

In 1946, Mr. Duncan created the libretto for *The Rape of Lucretia* (with music by Benjamin Britten) which has since become a classic of contemporary opera. It was during that same year that he also brought another challenging vehicle to the British stage—his adaptation of Jean Cocteau's *The Eagle Has Two Heads.* The play originally opened at the Lyric Theatre, Hammersmith, and on February 12, 1947, it was brought to the West End with Eileen Herlie as star. The play, in a somewhat distorted version, later was produced in New York with Tallulah Bankhead, but it lingered only briefly.

A cofounder of the famed English Stage Company at the Royal Court Theatre, Mr. Duncan's two verse plays, *Don Juan* and *The Death of Satan,* were successfully presented there on a double bill in 1957. Among his other plays are: *Stratton, The Catalyst, Abelard and Héloïse,* and *The Seven Deadly Virtues.*

The author, who also has published many books, including two volumes of autobiography, *All Men Are Islands* and *How to Make Enemies,* lives with his wife in Devonshire, close by the sea in a farmhouse which he helped rebuild, surrounded by land he has tended himself. In a recent interview, it was said of him: "He is incurably energetic and one has the impression that on a good day he could finish a poem, feed the pigs, ride his horse to a lather, mend the lavatory cistern, reread some favorite lines of Cavalcanti, Pound or Pope, put in some work on a libretto and then sit down to lunch (cooked by himself if necessary). He says he would wish to be remembered as somebody who was interested in making things and he doesn't regard writing as separate from making."

What has occupied him for the past decade or so is a poem, *Man,* which he declares is "already longer than *Paradise Lost* and almost as long as the *Inferno,*" and on which he probably will spend another ten years. He doesn't know—or care—if it even will be published: "It's something I have to do."

The Gift is one of Ronald Duncan's most recent plays and it is published for the first time in the United States in this anthology.

TIME: Now.
PLACE: Any place
SCENE. *What is known as a living room. But there is no window: just a door, a few uncomfortable chairs, a radio and a television set which are placed on either side of the proscenium in the style of a Greek chorus. No walls are necessary for the set: a hung picture or two will define the room's limits.*

The only essential prop is an enormous parcel which stands on the left side of the room: it measures six feet long by three feet high and two feet wide. This is wrapped in brown paper.

A small birthday cake with one candle is also conspicuous on a side table.

Throughout the action, the television and radio pursue their irrelevant and frivolous commentaries—or, at least, they do so at times as counterpoint.

When the curtain rises, MRS. WORSTHORNE *is tying a large blue ribbon around the parcel: the others watch her from the other side of the room.*

———

TV Set:

Leeds United	3	Chelsea	2
Manchester City	1	Bolton Wanderers	0
Bradford City	3	Liverpool	2
Charlton Athletic	4	Hull City	3
Fulham	2	Tottenham H'spur	2
Arsenal	1	Southampton	1

MADELAINE.
Doesn't it look pretty? I think it looks very pretty.
Percy will like this, blue's his favorite color.
Did you know blue was his favorite color?

Blackpool	1	York City	6
Aston Villa	5	Coventry	2

(*etc.*)

Well, there it is. Doesn't it look magnificent?
Doesn't it?
TONY.
Yes.
GERALDINE.
It does.
MADELAINE.
Don't you think so, Daddy?
                    (*The two women begin to set the tea.*)
TREMLETT.
(*marking football pools*) What?
TONY.
Mother said: doesn't it look magnificent?

TV Set:

Woolwich	2	Middlesboro	2

TREMLETT.
That's another draw: And on their home ground.
Yes. It does. It looks magnificent but . . .
MADELAINE.
But? . . .
TREMLETT.
But I think it is too big.
I suppose there will be another week, next week.

MADELAINE.
As it couldn't be any smaller
It is not very helpful of you
To remark that it is too big.

Radio:
Today for our program "Any Questions," the team consists of . . . (*etc.*)

GERALDINE.
(*to her mother*) You've got a point there.

TV Set:
Worthington makes you worthier and worthier . . . (*etc.*)

TREMLETT.
No, only six this week. Twelve draws.
TONY.
Yes, Mother is right. It isn't meaningful
To discuss the size of a thing
Without relating the size to the function.
Some people might say that the Pacific Ocean was big,
But it is not big when you consider
The amount of water it has to contain.
TREMLETT.
I still say it is big, too big.
TONY.
Yet it may prove too small.
GERALDINE.
That would be a pity.
TONY.
After the expense we've all been put to.
MADELAINE.
(*to Tony*). Don't worry. Your mother may not be a Bachelor of Science
As we all know you are.
(*to Geraldine*) Nor is she about to take her diploma
in psychiatric nursing. But your mother is practical.
She took precautions: I used a tape measure.
GERALDINE.
Must we go into details?
TREMLETT.
Too big for this room, I mean.
MADELAINE.
I am sure Percy will be pleased with it.
Eventually. I am sure no man has ever received
A more appropriate birthday present.
Or one to which his family has given so much thought.
Now what shall we put on the card?
GERALDINE.
(*impulsively*). Many happy returns . . . (*They look shocked.*) Sorry.
TONY.
"For Percy. With our undying love". Then all of us sign it.
MADELAINE.
Splendid. That's it. (*She writes.*) "Undying love". I'll underline that.
He'll like that.
There now, sign it.
                    (*They all do so, then she ties the card on to the parcel.*)
Percy will never guess what it is.

Last year I gave him an electric razor
Or was·that the year before last? I forget.
Now Tony, help me to put this screen round it
Your father enjoys a surprise.

(*They do so.*)

TREMLETT.

The year you'll remember.

MADELAINE.

We'll all remember. We all subscribed to it.
As a family what else could we do:
Once we had realized what he really wanted or needed?

TREMLETT.

I could have given him an ounce of tobacco.

MADELAINE.

You could have given him an ounce of tobacco,
And I could have given him a handknitted tie.
They could have given him a book token
Or a long-playing gramophone record.
But those would have been frivolous gestures of affection
And what we have given him here is something more than a casual gift.
It is a real token of love, our undying love.

GERALDINE.

Something he needed, but couldn't give himself.

TONY.

Something he needed, but didn't know he wanted.
What else could we do?

MADELAINE.

Nothing.

GERALDINE.

Nothing. He's certainly not certifiable.
You have my word for that.

TONY.

But assuredly as mad as a hatter.

MADELAINE.

Tony, don't speak of your father like that!
Though I admit his behavior is far from sane
Ever since he resigned from his job at the bank
(*bitterly*) Only four months before his pension!

TONY.

I still can't believe it.

TREMLETT.

After thirty years: four months before his pension!

MADELAINE.

To be precise: three months and seventeen days.

(*a pause*)

Ever since that day, when he marched in here one afternoon,
With his valise full of poems which he blandly admitted
That he had written in the bank's time and on the tills
And announced that he had resigned his job
Because he had suddenly realized that he'd misspent his life
Counting bits of paper there,
And that he was now going to devote the rest of his days
To important things such as persuading people to read poetry
          —which they will never do—
And urging them to love one another
          —which they can never do—

As I say, ever since that dreadful day, we have all known
That he would soon need more than a handknitted tie
Or an ounce of tobacco.

TREMLETT.

Two ounces. I always gave him two for his birthday.

GERALDINE.

Yes. What else could we do? I didn't mind
His sudden enthusiasm for poetry.
A lot of people write poetry,
Some people even read poetry.
And some people keep bees; others tropical fish in aereated tanks;
There's no accounting for tastes.
But what I thought indicated that he's gone over the top
        —and I'm not without professional experience—
Was when his manic-depressive moods
Fluctuated between such irrational and irreconcilable extremities.

TONY.

Precisely.

GERALDINE

His moments of despair were reasonable enough
Few of us can see any hope.
To me it's his moods of joyful optimism
Which prove he's now completely ga-ga.

MADELAINE.

Geraldine! A spade's a spade
You don't have to call it a bloody shovel!
He is your father.

GERALDINE.

That's why I'm so concerned for his future
And why I've contributed to that.
Do you know, Mother, I actually caught him at it yesterday.

MADELAINE.

Where?

GERALDINE.

In Chelsham Road. I had been to see Betty . . .

TONY.

Does it matter whom you'd been to see?
Keep to the point. What was father doing?

GERALDINE.

Going from house to house like a self-employed postman
Without any letters. He was singing gaily
And skipping over the railings which divide the front gardens.
You can guess what he was doing.
He was popping a copy of Keats's "Ode to a Nightingale" into every letter box.
I asked him what good he thought that would do!
And d'you know what he said?
He said: "I'm blowing their indifference up.
        Poetry is more powerful than an atom bomb".

TONY.

It's sad.

TREMLETT.

Very.

GERALDINE.

And clear that he is no longer in touch with reality.

MADELAINE.

Very clear. Think of the cost of printing all those copies.

TREMLETT.

What convinced me he was barmy was when he turned the greenhouse
Into a carpenter's shop
And started to make those boards he carries,
Better if they'd been used for a straitjacket.

(*Singing is heard off*)

MADELAINE.

Ssh! Here he comes.

(PERCY *enters, still singing gaily. He is wearing a sandwich board
which reads "Love One Another".*)

Have you had a good day, dear?

(PERCY *nods, takes the sandwich board off and props it up. We now see the other side:
it reads "Read Donne. Listen to Schubert".*)

GERALDINE.

(*going to embrace him*). Many happy . . .

TONY.

(*ditto*). I hope you have a happy day, Father.

PERCY.

Thank you, my boy, I have,
I am having the happiest day of my life.
D'you know what I've done today?

MADELAINE.

(*fearfully*). No, Percy. What have you done?

PERCY.

I stood all the afternoon in the High Street
Outside the bank, my bank.
And I sang: Schubert, of course.
And I gave a five-pound note to everybody who stopped to give me a penny.
It was wonderful business. You should have seen their faces.
Two women kissed me from gratitude.

MADELAINE.

Expensive kisses. How much did you give away?

PERCY.

Two hundred pounds or so.
It made my colleagues in the bank look pretty foolish.

MADELAINE.

So I can imagine, dear. Half our savings.

PERCY.

Not quite. I've enough for tomorrow, too.
People seemed most grateful. I daresay they'd overspent
On their summer holidays. Of course some thought my notes were counterfeit.
They took them into the bank and were soon disabused
Because I'd drawn them out from there this morning.
And there were one or two who paused before they folded the note into their wallet.
These may, in time, realize that I was not merely giving away fivers
But values.

TONY.

New lamps for old.

PERCY.

Exactly. I'm hoping one or two others will join me at it tomorrow.
We must cast our bread upon the water,
And if we haven't any bread, then paper has to do.
There's no alternative, otherwise it turns to stone; we turn to stone.
It's simple.

MADELAINE.

Yes, dear.

PERCY.
(*looking at table*). Well, where is it? I've been looking forward all day to my present.
Let me guess what it is. Don't tell me.
Some tobacco from Dad?

MADELAINE.
Not this year, dear.
This year we all clubbed together.
To give you something special,
Something you needed.

PERCY.
A screwdriver and a plane?

MADELAINE.
No.

PERCY.
A handknitted tie? Perhaps two?

GERALDINE.
No.

PERCY.
Clubbed together. That's a clue.
A Schubert Song Cycle?

GERALDINE.
It's not fair, Mummy. He'll never guess. Remove the screen.
(*They do so.*)

MADELAINE.
There!

TREMLETT.
Big. I say it's too big.
(PERCY *walks round it, then reads the attached card.*)

PERCY.
I was right, you see:
Generosity is more contagious than measles.
But I can't think what it is.

GERALDINE.
Try.

PERCY.
Something I need? . . . A printing press?

TREMLETT.
For fivers?

PERCY.
Poetry.

MADELAINE.
Cold.

PERCY.
A loudspeaker outfit?

MADELAINE.
Still cold.
(PERCY *walks round it again.*)

PERCY.
A coffin?

MADELAINE.
No. But you're getting warm.

GERALDINE.
Mother, Daddy will never guess.
(*She goes and undoes the ribbon, then rips the paper.*)
It's a deep-freeze.

MADELAINE.

The latest model. Made in Sweden.
    PERCY.
(*peering into it*). It's magnificent. Thank you.
But we have a refrigerator already.
We bought it only last year. It was alright this morning.
    TONY.
A deep-freeze is not the same thing as a refrigerator.
    PERCY.
Similar, surely?
    TONY.
A model like that will keep things indefinitely.
I knew a man who put a whole salmon in one.
After ten years, after ten years, it came out
As the day he'd poached it.
    PERCY.
A pity I don't fish or poach.
    TONY.
Indefinitely. Or you can put peas, beans, and raspberries in them.
At fifty degrees below zero decomposition is arrested.
    PERCY.
But I haven't a vegetable garden.
    TONY.
Pheasants. Some people put pheasants in them.
    PERCY.
So would I if I owned a shoot.
    GERALDINE.
You don't understand, Daddy.
Any meat will keep in them forever.
    PERCY.
A marvelous thing if I were a butcher or a farmer.
As it is, I hope you won't be offended
If I exchange it for a printing press, or something.
(*to* MADELAINE) I can't think what I could put in it, can you, dear?
    MADELAINE.
Yes, Percy. I can.
    PERCY.
What?
    MADELAINE.
Yourself, dear.
    PERCY.
Myself?
    MADELAINE.
You've talked so much recently about permanent values
And immortal life. This can give these to you.
    TONY.
It certainly can. Suspended animation.
    GERALDINE.
Indefinitely, Daddy.
    PERCY.
I see you are joking. (*He laughs alone.*)
I see you are *not* joking.
    MADELAINE.
No, dear.
Of course we thought of several things we could have given you.
At first, Geraldine suggested a carpentry set with an electric drill
And Tony proposed a press for your trousers

But we discarded these ideas as frivolous
Because we all realized that you were no longer interested
In things or in appearances . . .

TONY.

. . . either sartorially or philosophically
But only in the reality behind things.
And so, Mother suggested we should give you something you needed . . .

MADELAINE.

Something you really wanted
And this can give you immortal life
In a way no religion can.
The manufacturers guarantee it.

PERCY.

I must say, I've never had such a big present before.
All the same, I feel a little depressed by it.

GERALDINE.

You shouldn't be, Daddy. Think of the mammoths.

PERCY.

Why? I don't hunt mammoths either.

GERALDINE.

Because a few years ago they unearthed an entire mammoth in Siberia
I read about it in one of the Sunday papers.
Apparently the beast had been overtaken by the last Ice Age
And frozen to death while grazing on the steppes.
Its mouth was still full of grass. And d'you know
When it thawed out, it was still so fresh
That it bled when they cut steaks from it
Which they found succulent after ten thousand years?
Think of that, Daddy, ten thousand years
Of assumed preservation.

PERCY.

Which of you wants to eat me?

TREMLETT.

It's big, but not that big.
You wouldn't get much of a mammoth in that one.

MADELAINE.

(*pacifying* TREMLETT). It will be the time for the news soon, Dad.
Just you sit quiet and wait.

PERCY.

This must have cost you all a great deal
I can't countenance such extravagance . . .

MADELAINE.

You should talk!

PERCY.

. . . For myself. I'm sure the shop will exchange it
For some modest necessity or indulgence.
I really do need a set square, and some screws.

TONY.

Nonsense, Dad. Think of Cleopatra, or Helen of Troy.

PERCY.

Why, Tony?

TONY.

Think how you would have liked to have made love
To either or both of them.

MADELAINE.

Tony!

PERCY.

Since they are both dead and since I am both a realist and a monogamist,
At least in practice, I have never considered such liaisons.

TONY

No, but what I'm trying to tell you is:
Suspended animation makes such unlikely unions possible.
At least theoretically. If Cleopatra had stepped into a model like that
Instead of suckling an asp, she could have skipped two thousand years
And woken to embrace you as another Antony
In your strong toil of grace.

PERCY.

A somewhat unlikely hypothesis.

TONY.

Maybe. But they've proved that the male seed
When frozen to eighty degrees can remain potent indefinitely.

GERALDINE.

I can't see where this is getting us.

TONY.

Don't you? This deep freeze assures physical immortality
Completely.
Theoretically, Dad could, if he takes this step
Father a child five centuries from now.
—By artificial insemination if need be
Not of course from Cleopatra, but on some unborn film star.
You could say that a deep-freeze like that
Is a sort of savings bank
For a man's generative potential . . .

MADELAINE.

I don't think that description will appeal to your father
But I believe I know what will persuade him.
Percy, you threw up your job
Because you became interested in real and permanent values in life,
Didn't you?

PERCY.

Yes.

MADELAINE.

Then surely it's reasonable for you to take steps
To preserve those values permanently.
You explained that your enthusiasm for poetry
Was because you saw it as the highest point of human consciousness,
And you said that we should love one another
As being the only way to express that consciousness, didn't you?
You were right. None of us could disagree with you there.
But, Percy, you are before your time, a thousand years
Before your time, maybe even more.
Today nobody will even listen to you, even if you give them fivers.
The golden age of poetry is passed
And nowadays people don't love one another, but occasionally
Hate each other intimately and passionately in corners.
In spite of what they say, they are only interested in appearances
And in labels, not in realities.
So you see, if you value your values, Percy, you must wait
You must preserve yourself and them
Then wake to an Age that will listen to your message:
That poetry is the way to consciousness
As love is the way to joy.

GERALDINE.

Mother, I've never known you so articulate before
The occasion has inspired you. .
She is right, Daddy. Logically, there is no alternative for you:
If you continue as you are, you will die, as we all die,
With your values tarnished and your hopes dead with you.
You will eventually become as hopeless as we are.
Can't you see we want you to do this, not for your good
But for ours?
It's true that today poets and priests look hopeless and ridiculous figures
But for all that, they are our only points of hope.
We must preserve you somehow.

PERCY.

Your logic closes in on me like a prison.

GERALDINE.

(*running to embrace him*). Daddy, you know I love you: you know I shall miss you
And miss the poem you write especially for me
Every Christmas . . .
I couldn't bear the thought of you dying
And what you stand for dying, too.
That's why I want to preserve you
That's why I want you to step in there.

MADELAINE.

(*to* TONY). If anybody can persuade him, she will
He'll do anything for her.

TONY.

(*bitterly*). I know.

PERCY.

(*to* GERALDINE). I've already started to write something for you for next Christmas
But it's not finished.

TONY.

A poem never is finished
A poem is a point of growth.

MADELAINE.

(*Aside to* TONY). Clever! (*to* PERCY) Well, Percy?
                              (*She gets a pillow.*)
Shall we make you comfortable?

PERCY.

It will be cold in there.

MADELAINE.

(*taking his hand*). Colder for us outside when you can no longer warm us.

PERCY.

(*looking at her hand*). That was your best argument.
But I will not get in this thing to preserve myself
Or anything which I stand for:
Either the bad poem I am writing
Or the good poem I hope one day to write.

GERALDINE.

(*petulantly*). Oh, Daddy. How disappointing.

MADELAINE.

(*angrily*). What a waste of money!

PERCY.

Nor will I get into it to escape from the loneliness
Of growing old, or from the humiliation
Of being old. Or to evade the paralytic stroke,
The fatal motor accident or the cancer we nurture

That takes us unaware: though these fears are real fears
I will not get into it because I am dying
Because that it is what we are all doing
Dying as we wear a new handknitted tie.

TONY.

Most disappointing. We shall drop twenty percent on it.

PERCY.

(*taking his coat off*). But I will get into it because it was a gift from your love
It is that love alone which is worth preserving.
If I stand here, I reject that love

(*He steps in.*)

But in here, I accept it.
It's cold; but not so cold as I feared
Perhaps it was only my fear that was cold?

MADELAINE.

(*handing a scarf to him*). Put this on, dear.

GERALDINE.

Don't be silly, Mother.

MADELAINE.

And he never had a slice of his cake.

(*She goes to cut a piece.*)

PERCY.

(*almost to himself*). I can't feel my hands: I cannot feel my feet
My closest friends are lost:
It is in our extremities that we are vulnerable
But what matter, if in our hearts we are secure?

(*They gather round.*)

GERALDINE.

Is the thermostat switched on?

TONY.

Full.

TREMLETT.

Not too big, I was wrong there.

GERALDINE.

Oh, Daddy, first recite something to me
Like you used to do when you came to sit on my bed
When I was a girl. Please, Daddy.
Oh, his lips are going blue!

PERCY.

(*sitting up*). What, darling—one of the odes?
The "Ode to a Nightingale"?

GERALDINE.

No. Something of your own—
The poem you were writing for me for Christmas.

PERCY.

If love is made of words
  Who can love more than I?
If love is all self-love
  Who's more beloved than I?

If love is made of faith
  Who can love less than I?
If love is to submit
  Who's less beloved than I?

If love is made of tears

Who could love more than she?
If love is to betray
Who . . .
(*His lips move, completing the poem, but no sound is emitted. They lie him down.*)

TV Set:

| Bolton Wanderers | 2 | Sheffield United | 3 |
| Leeds United | 4 | Liverpool City | 3 |

(*etc.*)

(*The family now turn to face the audience as though looking through a window.*)
TONY.
Strange: I see they are playing tennis next door
And sitting out in deck chairs: but I feel cold: very.
TREMLETT.
Me, too. There the roses lean upon the evening
But frost feathers my brain, icicles nail my heart
Now I know what you meant by them mammoths.
MADELAINE.
I see my Michaelmas daisies need tying up
That proves it is summer still
Though winter is within us.
GERALDINE.
His greenhouse door needs mending.

(*to herself*)

"If love is to betray
Who was more loved than He?"

TV Set:

| Blackpool | I | Exeter | 2 |

(*etc.*)

CURTAIN

THE CHINESE

Murray Schisgal

MR. LEE
MRS. LEE
CHESTER LEE

GLADYS HOFFMAN
PU PING CHOW

MURRAY SCHISGAL was born in the East New York section of Brooklyn, on November 25, 1926. He attended Thomas Jefferson High School but left when he was seventeen to serve in the United States Navy during World War II. After his discharge in 1946, he worked at a number of odd jobs (including playing saxophone and clarinet with a small jazz band) and pursued his education at night. He earned his high school diploma, took classes at Long Island University and studied law at Brooklyn Law School. In 1953, he received his LL.B. degree and went into law practice in an office on Delancey Street in lower Manhattan. He relinquished the legal profession in 1956 and turned to teaching in New York City's public school system. While teaching, he worked for his B.A. degree at the New School for Social Research. Between classroom activities, Mr. Schisgal also devoted much time to writing, first fiction, then plays. As he once explained in an interview: "I write because I need to. I've written four novels and many short stories, all unpublished. I seem to write more effectively for the stage. I write about things that disturb me and which only can be placated by my writing of them."

In 1960, after completing five short plays, Mr. Schisgal quit teaching, and set off for Spain "to do nothing but write." En route, he stopped in London and, at the suggestion of a friend, took his plays to the British Drama League. The ruling powers of that organization were duly impressed and decided to produce two of the plays, *The Typists* and *The Postman* (later renamed *The Tiger*). The double bill opened in December, 1960, and its reception prompted the staging of his full-length work, *Ducks and Lovers,* at the Arts Theatre, London, in October, 1961.

The Typists and *The Tiger* opened at the Off-Broadway Orpheum Theatre on February 4, 1963, with Eli Wallach and Anne Jackson as the principals in both plays. Well received, the production ran for 200 performances and won several awards including the Drama Desk–Vernon Rice Award for outstanding achievement in the Off-Broadway theatre. *The Tiger* later was filmed under the title of *The Tiger Makes Out,* with Mr. Wallach and Miss Jackson re-creating their stage roles.

Mr. Schisgal's greatest success came on November 11, 1964, when his comedy, *Luv,* opened at the Booth Theatre, New York. Directed by Mike Nichols and with Eli Wallach, Anne Jackson and Alan Arkin comprising the cast, it ran for 901 performances on Broadway, had two national tours, and was translated into nineteen languages for presentation in twenty-six countries. It was subsequently filmed with Jack Lemmon, Peter Falk and Elaine May.

In 1967, the author was represented once again Off-Broadway by the double bill of *Basement* and *Fragments* (with James Coco and Gene Hackman) and this was followed in 1968 by the Broadway production of his comedy, *Jimmy Shine,* which starred Dustin Hoffman.

The Chinese (and its companion piece, *Dr. Fish*) had its New York premiere on March 10, 1970, at the Ethel Barrymore Theatre. Clive Barnes of *The New York Times* declared that the play, which deals with the comically frantic identity search of one Chester Lee, "does have a kind of instant facetiousness and quickly blissful sense of the ridiculous." Other drama assessors found the comedy "outrageously funny . . . wonderfully theatrical and altogether grand." George Oppenheimer, writing in *Newsday,* admitted that "Murray Schisgal continues to amaze me with his constant originality of themes and his gift of comic dialogue and of warm and rich characterizations."

Frequently described as an avant-garde author with black comedy tendencies, Mr. Schisgal has readily conceded that he has been enormously influenced by the works of Antonin Artaud, Luigi Pirandello, Jean Genet, and Eugene Ionesco, among others. His plays seem, on the surface, to be "a sort of pop-art theatre of the absurd," but beneath the comic surface, "there is always pathos, particularly the pathos of those who do not know the meaning of love." And in *The Chinese,* as he amuses us, he also reminds us of our pretensions and self-deceptions.

SCENE: *A Chinese laundry. Street window on right with block letters on it reading:* HO HING CHINESE LAUNDRY; *glass-paneled door also on right, leading into street. In the rear right to center is a work counter. There is a hinged shelf on left side of work counter; behind it and along left wall are wooden shelves on which there are stacked brown paper-wrapped packages of shirts and linen with colored tickets attached to them; bundles of dirty linen are on the floor; left, a rectangular table and chairs; a door leading into the kitchen is in the rear wall, right, next to it is a bureau; a doorless doorframe leading to bedrooms is in left wall.*

It is early afternoon.

MR. HO HING LEE *is ironing shirts at work counter. He wears a white shirt, open at the neck, dark trousers, and slippers.*

His wife, MRS. TING TOY LEE, *is seated at the table numbering shirt collars with pen. She also wears dark trousers, slippers, but has on a mandarin-style blouse that hangs over her trousers.*

It is suggested that MR. *and* MRS. LEE *are played by Caucasians. It is also suggested that* GLADYS HOFFMAN *and* PU PING CHOW *are played by the same actress.*

CHESTER *enters the laundry, a bell tinkles above the door; he moves to table; he is sullen, his posture is somewhat slouched. He turns neither right nor left but moves directly to table, sit opposite his mother, and thumbs through a Chinese newspaper.* CHESTER *is about twenty-five. His physical appearance is in no way Oriental. He wears tan pants, a striped shirt, canvas sneakers, and a shapeless cotton rain hat.*

MR. LEE (*as* CHESTER *moves to table, speaking to* MRS. LEE. *It is obvious, however, that his remarks are directed toward* CHESTER; *in Chinese.* CHESTER *tosses rain hat into bedroom area*). Ah, keu do le. Ngo day hai mm hai ying goy quai lok lai do dzieh keu fan lay, heh! Keu heng lay nee do, tsen hai teu ngo day tai ho le! Keu seang yut hai been do, ah? Keu deem gai mm hai po tou pong ngo day sai yeh tong yeh, dzo dee kung dzok? Keu yee wai tsien hai shu sheung dzak lok lai ge me? Keu yee wai fan tung yee fuk hai teen deet lok lai ge me? Keu yut go seen sou yup do mo, dan hai keu gum hai nee do

hang lay heu dong ngo day hai keu ge gung yun, keu wah dzo mut yeh ngo day dzou mut yeh, do dzieh yut siang do mm sai. (Oh, he's here. Well, I guess we should get down on our knees and thank him for making an appearance. It is so kind of him to reveal himself to us! Where was he all day? Why is he not in the store helping us wash and iron and do the work that's necessary? Does he think money grows on trees? Does he think food and clothes fall from the sky? He doesn't contribute a penny and yet he has the nerve to walk around as if we were in his employment, as if we are merely his household slaves to do his bidding for which he does not even show us the slightest sign of gratitude!)

(*There is a pause.* CHESTER *continues thumbing through newspaper, indifferently.*)

MRS. LEE (*in Chinese*). Chester, nay baba tung nay gong gun. Nay ying goy dop keu. Baba tung nay gong go dzun see, nay ying goy dop keu ge. (Chester, your dear father is speaking to you. You must answer him. It is only proper to answer your father when he speaks to you.)

(*Another pause.* CHESTER *turns pages of newspaper.*)

CHESTER (*grimly*). Tell him to speak in English. This is America, not China. We speak English in this country.

MRS. LEE (*to* MR. LEE, *in Chinese*). Jeung fu, nay dzee go ngo day ge dzai Chester hai deem yeung ge la. Gum yut mm ho ngai gow. Mm goy nay. Tung keu gong ying mun. (My dear husband, you know how our son Chester is, let us not quarrel today. I beg you. Speak to him in English.)

MR. LEE (*shouting angrily in Chinese*). Ying mun! Ying mun! Keu . . . keu gum dai dom gum geel ngo gong ying mun! Ngo yeel yung ying mun lay gong ngo dzou yung ying lai gong. Dan hai ngo mm yeel! Ngo sik ge ying mun tung keu ge yut yeung gum ho! (English! English! He . . . he has the outrageous nerve to ask me to speak in English! If I wished to I would speak in English! But I do not wish to! I know English as well as he does and I can speak English as well as he does!)

CHESTER (*answers him, in Chinese*). Gum may deem gai mm gong ne? Deem gai nay dzee hai gong jumg mun ge ne?

Deem gai nee gan nguk leu been mut yeh do hai jung gwok ge? Ngo day hai may gwok yun, ying goy ho tsee may gwok yun gong ying mun! (Then why don't you? Why do you always have to speak Chinese? Why does everything in this house have to be Chinese? We're Americans and we should speak English like Americans!)

MR. LEE (*shouts back in Chinese*). Nee do hai go jung gwok sai gwon jung gwok ge gah ting! (This is a Chinese laundry and a Chinese family!)

(CHESTER *turns his back to his father, crossing his legs and folding his arms, sulking.*)

MRS. LEE (*importunately, with Chinese accent*). Chester, my son, my precious child, for my sake, for your mother's sake, let this quarrel with your father be finished now. He has been standing on his feet all day. Let the rest of the afternoon pass pleasantly between us. Do it for me, Chester.

CHESTER (*to* MR. LEE *moving to door, looking out*). I . . .I'm sorry, Dad. I didn't mean to yell like that.

MR. LEE (*with Chinese accent*). That's all right, my son. I know that this is a difficult time for you. Is the young lady coming today to meet us?

CHESTER (*nods*). She's coming. She'll be here. I think you'll like Gladys. I really think your gonna be glad I'm getting serious about her.

MR. LEE. I would be more glad if you were serious with Pu Ping Chow. She is . . .

MRS. LEE (*interrupts him to prevent another quarrel*). Where did you meet this girl, Chester?

CHESTER (*staring grimly at his father at the mention of* PU PING CHOW). Oh, about five years ago. In high school. (*now turns to his mother, losing his grimness*) That's the funny thing, Ma. Gladys was in almost all my classes and I never looked at her twice. But then when I saw her a couple of months ago at Marvin Brockman's party, wow! what a difference. I was astonished at the difference!

MRS. LEE. Does she know you're getting serious?

CHESTER. She knows. That's why she's coming over. She's an exceptional girl. And she has a fantastic job, Dad.

MR. LEE. Still, my son, if you are thinking of marriage, you will have to find a job and support her.

CHESTER. I know, Dad. I know that. I'll find a job. I was over at Madison Square Garden yesterday. They got the Ice Follies there now. I met this man, Mr. Donleavy, and he said he'd put me to work tomorrow if I wanted.

MR. LEE. Doing what?

CHESTER. Cleaning the ice.

MR. LEE. Cleaning the ice?

CHESTER. After they skate on it. It gets all chopped up. So three or four fellows put on ice skates and go skating around, cleaning the ice. (*demonstrates, moving left*)

MR. LEE. What kind of job is that, cleaning the ice?

CHESTER. It happens to be a good job. It happens to be a union job, so don't knock it. But it would only be temporary. I know there's no future in it. But the thing is, if I married Gladys, we'd move in and live with her parents. Talk about a deal. That's what I call a deal.

MR. LEE. And it wouldn't bother the girl's parents that you are without money and have no job?

CHESTER. Look, Dad, I spoke to her father already. I'm not playing games here. He's brilliant. Some people, he said, it takes a little longer than other people to find themselves, to know what they wanna do with themselves. Especially today, when all the kids my age have the same problem, what with the wars and the armament race and the pressures they put on us. He said, "If you and Gladys decide to get married, Chester, take your time; go back to school if you want, work at different jobs if you want, nobody's putting any pressure on you; we'll do what we can to help." I tell you, Dad, after speaking to that man for five minutes, I felt so good I didn't care if I never found another job again!

MRS. LEE. And the woman who would be your mother-in-law? Is she a nice woman, Chester?

(*She starts to pick up huge laundry bag.* CHESTER *stops her, picks up bag, puts it in her arms, then moves to work counter and raises hinged counter shelf for* MRS. LEE *to enter.*)

CHESTER. My mother-in-law? Now I'm gonna surprise you, Ma. Now I'm really gonna surprise you because, as a matter of fact, I happen to be more in love with the woman who's gonna be my mother-in-law than I am with the woman who's gonna be my wife.

MRS. LEE. You love the mother more than Gladys?

CHESTER (*nods*). More than Gladys even. The truth. My mother-in-law to-be is not only good looking, not only intelligent and sensitive, but she has a figure on her that'll pop the eyes right out of your head!

MR. LEE. Chester!

MRS. LEE. With a young lady, you must be careful, my son. She is like a bud on a tree branch that needs sunshine and warmth to open up into a lovely blossom.

CHESTER. Gladys and me, we get along fine, Ma. Really. I don't think we're gonna have any trouble, unless it's . . . unless . . . (*a slight pause; he raises hinged shelf; exits; lowers shelf*). Dad, before I plan seriously about getting married, is there . . . is there anything you wanna tell me?

MR. LEE. Tell you?

CHESTER. About me, about . . . (MR. *and* MRS. LEE *exchange puzzled glances.*) You know I wouldn't go into this unless I had to. I stay away from this particular subject as much as I can. But now I have to go into it. I have to. Gladys'll be here soon and she'll wanna know and her parents'll wanna know . . .

MR. LEE. Know what? Why are you shouting? Why do you raise your voice?

CHESTER. Because you're both pretending you don't understand what I'm talking about when you both understand perfectly what I'm talking about!

MRS. LEE. Chester, my son, listen to me, please. It's best we don't go into . . .

CHESTER. Ma, I'm not going to disown anybody. I'll always love you. And I'll always love Dad. And I'll always be grateful to the both of you for bringing me up. But I have a right to know who my real biological parents are, that's all!

MR. LEE (*furiously; in Chinese*). Nah! Ngo dzee do keu wui gum lay ge! Ngo day ng fen jung ge ngon ding do mo. Keu dzou wui . . . keu dzou hov see . . . (There! I knew it would happen! We can't have five minutes of peace in this house! He has to start . . . He has to begin . . .)

MRS. LEE (*in Chinese*). Mm ho gun gun jeung. Mm goy nay. Mo ban fat ge. Mm ho gum gun jeung. (Don't get excited, my dear husband. Please. It does no good. Don't get excited.)

MR. LEE (*in Chinese*). Gun jeung! Been go gun jeung ah! Ngo mo gun jeung ah! Keu dzou wui . . . keu dzou hov see . . . (Excited! Who's excited! I'm not excited! He has to start . . . He has to begin . . .)

CHESTER (*angrily; in Chinese*). Ngo mui tsee mun nay go dzing dong hup lay get mun tai, nay dzou lun ngup yah sai, dzow lai now ngo! (Every time I ask you a perfectly legitimate and reasonable question, I get double-talk, I get yelled at and insulted.)

MRS. LEE (*in Chinese*). Aiya. Aiya. Nay leung go. Mm goy nay, mm ho gum le. Ngai gow been do you yung ge ne. (Please. Please. Both of you. I implore you. Be calm. Nothing is accomplished by quarreling.)

CHESTER. Somebody's hiding something, that's all I'm saying.

MRS. LEE. My dear son, my sweetheart, no one is hiding anything from you.

CHESTER. Then why does he always start yelling at me when I ask a perfectly legitimate and reasonable question?

MRS. LEE. It causes him great pain, my son. For you to deny Ho Hing as your father and me as your real mother, and this is not the first time you have done so, Chester, is very painful and humiliating to both of us.

CHESTER. That's not the point, Ma. If you told me right now that you weren't my real biological parents, that you adopted me or . . . or got me somewhere . . . Do you think I'd go running out of here looking for my real biological parents? No. I wouldn't. I don't even care who my real biological parents are. I just wanna know where you found me, that's all.

MR. LEE (*in Chinese, pointing to door*). You keu heu! Nah, moon hai go do! (Let him go! There's the door!)

MRS. LEE. Chester, we told you a thousand times, a thousand and one times . . . Would you like to hear it all again?

CHESTER (*stiffly*). Yes, Mother, I would. I definitely would.

(*sits at table*)

MR. LEE (*in Chinese*). Yow lay la! (Again!)

MRS. LEE (*with a sigh; sits at table*). Your father and I were born in Macao, off the coast of Southern China. We were childhood sweethearts and when we came to the United States we lived in Los Angeles for a brief period of time and then we moved here, to the Brownsville section of Brooklyn to buy this laundry which was advertised in a Chinese newspaper. You were born here, Chester. Doctor Thomas Wong, a general practitioner, delivered you. He was a wise old man who was of great help to us when we first moved into this neighborhood where very few Chinese families lived. But you grew up here, Chester. You played in the streets with the other children, and you went to school with the other children. If we seem strange to you, my son, it is because of this: we were not born in this country, we were not raised in this country, while you were, as were most of the people you grew up with.

CHESTER (*sulking*). There are other things, Ma. There are things you didn't go into.

MRS. LEE. Your appearance?

CHESTER. Yeah!

MRS. LEE. The fact that you do not look as we do?

CHESTER. Yeah!

MRS. LEE. That your skin is not the same color as ours and your eyes are not as small?

CHESTER. Yeah! That's right!

MRS. LEE. That, too, Chester, can be explained. On both sides of the family, on your father's side and mine, there has been intermarriage. I myself can count two great-uncles and a great-grandparent who are European, while your father's father came from . . . (*She turns to* MR. LEE; *in Chinese.*) Nay lo tai po hai been do lay ge? (*Where did you father come from, dear?*)

MR. LEE. Montgomery, Alabama.

MRS. LEE (*to* CHESTER). Montgomery, Alabama.

CHESTER (*rises*). Look, Ma, like you said, we've been over this a thousand times already but . . . Let me ask you one or two questions. Then I'll be quiet. I swear. I'll never open my mouth on this subject again. All right? All right, Dad?

MR. LEE. I will not tolerate rudeness or disrespect to me or your mother.

CHESTER. All right. Ma . . . You say Doctor Thomas Wong delivered me, is that right?

MRS. LEE. Yes. Doctor Thomas Wong. He was a wise old man.

CHESTER. And if I remember, if I remember correctly, you once said that Doctor Wong died six months after I was born, right?

MRS. LEE. Yes. About six months. We attended funeral services for him.

CHESTER. Now, think carefully, before you answer this, think very, very carefully. Ma . . . Was there anyone else present besides Doctor Thomas Wong on the day I was born?

(MRS. LEE *looks to* MR. LEE.)

MR. LEE. No. As far as we can remember he was the only one. It was in the bedroom that you were born. Early in the morning. At five o'clock. I ran to Doctor Wong's house and brought him back with me.

CHESTER (*softly*). Ma. (*She looks up at him.*) Why did you look at Dad then?

MRS. LEE. Look . . .?

CHESTER (*raising voice*). At Dad! Just then! I saw you look at Dad at the exact minute I asked you if anyone else was in this house besides Doctor Thomas Wong on the day I was born!

MRS. LEE. I couldn't remember. I was . . .

CHESTER. You couldn't remember or you didn't want to remember!

MR. LEE. Chester!

CHESTER. Dad, I have a right to know if there was anyone else in this house besides Doctor Thomas Wong at five o'clock in the morning on the day I was born. Will you or will you not answer that question!

(MRS. LEE *looks to* MR. LEE *again.*)

MR. LEE (*softly*). Yes, Chester. There was someone else.

CHESTER. Who?

MR. LEE. Madame Ching from Belmont Avenue.

CHESTER. Madame Ching from Belmont Avenue! Who's Madame Ching from Belmont Avenue?

MR. LEE. Madame Fannie Ching. You did not know her. And your mother did not want you to know anything about her because Madame Ching was a woman of . . . of loose ways, a bad woman, Chester.

CHESTER. So what does all that mean?

MR. LEE. That means she was here, with your mother, when I ran to get Doctor Wong. We did not like her to be here at your birth but we had no choice. Someone had to stay with your mother, and she was in the street when I opened the door. It is something your mother and I did not wish you to know.

CHESTER. Where is Madame Ching now?

MRS. LEE. Dead.

MR. LEE. Dead.

CHESTER. She's dead too, huh?

MR. LEE. She died soon after Doctor Wong.

MRS. LEE. That is the truth, Chester.

CHESTER. What did she die of?

MR. LEE. Hepatitis.

MRS. LEE. Yes, hepatitis.

CHESTER. And Doctor Wong, what did he die of?

MR. LEE. Inflammation of the lungs.

MRS. LEE. Yes, inflammation of the lungs.

CHESTER. And there was no one else who saw me on the day I was born except Madame Ching who died of hepatitis and Doctor Wong who died of inflammation of the lungs?

MR. LEE (nods). Now you know everything, Chester.

CHESTER. Now I know everything! Now I know there was an epidemic in this city the day I was born, that's all I know!

MRS. LEE. It's the truth, Chester.

CHESTER. Didn't you have one single friend or one single neighbor or even one single stranger who saw me on the day I was born who didn't die of hepatitis or inflammation of the lungs?

MR. LEE (wagging his finger). Chester, it's not for you to . . .

CHESTER (moves to door). Boy, this is all very convenient for you, isn't it? Like losing my birth certificate, that was also convenient. Gladys'll be here soon and I don't know how long I'm gonna explain . . .

(He stops himself. A pause.)

MRS. LEE. She does not know we are Chinese?

MR. LEE (in Chinese). Keu mm dzee? (She does not know?)

(Chester shakes his head.)

MRS. LEE. What did you tell her?

CHESTER. What's the difference.

MRS. LEE (rises). Chester, I want to know what you told her!

MR. LEE (in Chinese). Nay wah dzo bay keu teng mut yeh ah! (Tell us what you told her!)

CHESTER (slight pause). I told her we were Jewish.

MR. LEE (screams). Jewish! (He takes off his slipper and chases CHESTER through secret opening in work counter; in Chinese.) Chu tai! Keu fat sun ging ge me? Hai ma? Keu fat sun ging ge me? Ngo deem ho yee dzou ngo ge gung dzok, dan hai teang keu gong duk gum bum gum sun ging mm sheung sat keu ne! (Jewish! Is he out of his mind? Is he? Is he out of his mind? How can I get my work done and not want to kill him when I am forced to listen to him speak so . . . stupidly and insanely!)

MRS. LEE. Please, please, my husband. Let me take care of this. For once. Please. (To CHESTER) Chester, my son, my only child, why did you tell the young lady we were Jewish? Are you so ashamed of us and of all our ancestors?

CHESTER. It's not that, Ma. You don't understand what it was like growing up in this neighborhood and going to school here and everything. Everybody here was Jewish. I just got into the habit, that's all. People used to stop me and ask me what I was, so I'd say, "I'm Jewish," and right away they'd pat me on the head and they'd give me things. Flags, hats, candles, raisins. Once I even got a chopped herring sandwich.

MR. LEE. You think you're mother and I are such fools? You never brought home any of your friends to introduce to us. You never invited us to visit you in your school like other parents. But we kept our mouths closed. We said nothing. We did not wish to embarrass you despite your shameful conduct.

CHESTER. I didn't tell you to move into this neighborhood, did I? What did you want me to do? Explain to them something I didn't believe myself?

MR. LEE. That we are your parents?

CHESTER. I was only a kid, Dad.

MRS. LEE. But what will you tell the young lady when she comes here?

MR. LEE. Chester, if you would be interested in Pu Ping Chow . . .

CHESTER (*shouts at him*). But I'm not interested in Pu Ping Chow!

MRS. LEE. She is a lovely girl, Chester.

CHESTER. She's a foreigner, that's what she is. She's been in this country only three months. She can hardly speak two words of English yet. Every time I meet her in the street she bows down in front of me as if she just had a hernia operation!

MR. LEE. Don't speak ill of Pu Ping Chow!

MRS. LEE. Chester, Pu Ping Chow . . .

CHESTER. I don't want to hear any more about Pu Ping Chow. I got Pu Ping Chow coming out of my ears already! She's not gonna help me out of my predicament. Gladys'll be here any minute and I still don't know what I'm gonna tell her! If you could just give me the name of anyone who was . . .

(GLADYS *enters, interrupting* CHESTER *in mid-speech. She is a girl in her twenties, mini-skirted, brown tights.*)

GLADYS. Hello, Chester. (*looking around*) Why did you want to meet me in a Chinese laundry?

CHESTER (*turns to her*). Hi, Gladys.

GLADYS. Is this where you bring your shirts?

CHESTER. Come on in. Come on in. I . . . (*takes a deep breath*)

GLADYS (*sniffing*). I think I smell rice burning.

MRS. LEE (*sniffs at air, runs into kitchen, mumbling in Chinese*). Fan, fan, fan. (Rice, rice, rice.)

GLADYS (*takes* CHESTER'S *arm*). Let's go Chester. There's a lot I have to tell you. I ran into Marvin Brockman this morning and he told me . . . (*as they move toward the door, suddenly stops*) Aren't you taking your shirts?

CHESTER. My shirts? That's right. My shirts. I almost forgot. (*moves to counter, to* MR. LEE. *Deep formal voice*). I'd like to have my shirts, please.

MR. LEE (*in Chinese*). Ngo bay sut sam bay nay. Ngo bay nay da yut bah! (I'll give you your shirts. A broken head I'll give you!)

CHESTER (*turned away from* GLADYS, *in Chinese*). Baba, mm goy nay. Bay gay geen sut sam bay ngo. Nog tsee dee dzoy dai Gladys fan lay. (Dad, please. Give me some shirts. I'll bring Gladys back later.)

MR. LEE (*mutters; in Chinese*). Ngo mm lay nay dai mm dai keu fan lay. (I don't care if you never bring her back.)

CHESTER (*in Chinese*). Baba, mm goy nay. Ngo seen tung keu gong gui wah. (Please, Dad, I wanna speak to her alone first.)

MR. LEE (*in Chinese*). Dzou hoy! Dzou hoy! (Go! Go!)

(GLADYS *moves up to them.*)

CHESTER (*in Chinese*). Ngo day tsee . . . (We'll come back . . .)

GLADYS (*tapping* CHESTER *on the shoulder, interrupting him in mid-speech*). Are you speaking Chinese to him, Chester?

CHESTER. I . . .(*He nods vigorously.*)

GLADYS. Why, that's wonderful. When did you learn to speak Chinese?

CHESTER. I . . . I could speak it since I was a kid.

GLADYS. You could?

(CHESTER *nods.*)

CHESTER. Gladys, there's something I have to tell you.

GLADYS. Let me hear you say this in Chinese: The rain in Spain stays mainly in the plain.

CHESTER (*in Chinese; unhappily*). Sai ban nga yu lok hai ping day.

GLADYS (*delighted*). Now let me hear: Jack and Jill went up the hill, They each had a buck and a quarter.

CHESTER (*in Chinese*). Jack tung Jill pa sheung san Mui yun you yut go yee ho boon.

GLADYS (*pleased*). Jill came down with two-and-a-half. Do you think they went up for water? (MR. LEE *bangs down the iron, angrily mumbling in Chinese, and turns his back to them.*) What's wrong with him?

CHESTER. Gladys . . .

GLADYS. Is he crazy?

CHESTER. Gladys, listen . . .

GLADYS. Tell him to give you your shirts and let's get out of here.

CHESTER. Gladys . . .

GLADYS (*knocking on counter*). Hey! Are you deaf behind there?

CHESTER (*turning her toward him*). Gladys, listen to me, will you?

GLADYS. Don't you want your . . .

CHESTER. Forget that! There's a lot I didn't tell you that I wanna straighten out right now! (*He looks over at his parents.*)

Gladys . . . (*takes a deep breath*) Gladys, I want you to meet my mother and father.

GLADYS (*looks around the room, then at* MR. *and* MRS. LEE *and finally at* CHESTER). Where are they?

CHESTER (*moves between parents*). Dad, this is my friend, Gladys Hoffman. Ma, this is Gladys.

MRS. LEE. We are delighted to have you visit with us, Gladys.

GLADYS. I . . . I . . .

(*She stares dumbly at* CHESTER.)

MR. LEE. We welcome you to our home.

GLADYS (*turns to him*). I . . . Thank you. Thank you very much. I . . . Chester, may I speak to you privately for a minute? (*to parents as she moves backward to right with* CHESTER; *in confusion; bowing almost to floor*) Your pardon. I beg your pardon. Your forgiveness. I beg your pardon and your forgiveness and your forgiveness and your . . . (*grabbing* CHESTER, *pulling him close to her*) Chester, you're kidding. Tell me you're kidding.

CHESTER (*whispers*). I'm not kidding.

GLADYS. They're your parents?

CHESTER. They're my parents.

GLADYS. You're Chinese- (CHESTER *nods.*) Why did you tell me you were Jewish?

CHESTER. It was a habit.

GLADYS. A habit? What kind of habit is it to tell people you're Jewish?

CHESTER. I guess I just wanted to be like everybody else.

GLADYS. Lee. Chester Lee. It never occurred to me . . . Now I remember seeing you in school once wearing a black hat and carrying a Jewish flag. I thought that was peculiar.

CHESTER. People kept giving me those things. I didn't ask for them.

GLADYS. I know. I did it myself. I once gave you my chopped herring sandwich!

CHESTER. Was it you?

GLADYS. It was me.

CHESTER. Chopped herring on pumpernickel, right?

GLADYS. I think it was pumpernickel.

CHESTER. It was. I remember. And it was delicious. I bet your mother chopped the herring.

GLADYS (*angrily*). Will you stop talking about my mother so much! I'm the one who's suffering here! (*She glances toward* MR. *and* MRS. LEE.) I still can't believe they're your parents.

CHESTER. You wanna know something, Gladys?

(*He moves to other side; pulls her with him.*)

GLADYS. What?

CHESTER. I can't believe they're my parents, either.

GLADYS (*slight pause*). Who do you think they are?

CHESTER. I don't know.

GLADYS. Do you have any idea?

CHESTER. Maybe they adopted me or found me someplace.

GLADYS. Couldn't you take blood tests? Wouldn't that prove if they're your real parents or not?

CHESTER. I couldn't ask them to do that.

GLADYS. There must be some way you can find out.

(MRS. LEE *enters kitchen, returns shortly with tray on which there are a pot of tea, four cups, and a dish of cakes, all of which she sets out on the table.*)

CHESTER. And you wonder why I can't get a job. Try spending your whole life with something like this inside you and see how far you'd go!

GLADYS (*snaps her fingers*). I got it! I got it, Chester! (*tapping his shoulder*). The birthmark on your shoulder. The big brown one. Those are inherited characteristics. One of your real parents has the exact same birthmark.

CHESTER. Are you sure?

GLADYS. I'm sure. I'm sure. (*glances toward* MR. *and* MRS. LEE *out of the corner of her eye*). Did you ever see them naked?

CHESTER (*shakes his head*). They always walk around fully dressed.

GLADYS. How about on the beach?

CHESTER. On the beach, too.

GLADYS. They're always fully dressed on the beach?

CHESTER. What d'you want from me, Gladys? I can't tell them to walk around naked, can I?

GLADYS. All right, look, leave this to me. I think I have a way of finding out.

CHESTER. But be tactful. Don't just come out and say they're not my real biological parents to their face. I've been doing that all my life.

GLADYS. Okay. I'll be tactful. Let's go.

(*They move to parents.*)

CHESTER (*to parents*). Gladys was just telling me how glad she is to meet the both of you, finally.

GLADYS. I've been looking forward to it for a long, long time.

(*She looks to* CHESTER *who nods approvingly.*)

MRS. LEE. And we are pleased to meet you, Gladys. Will you have some tea with us?

GLADYS. It would be my pleasure, Mrs. Lee. Tea is one of my favorite beverages.

(*She looks to* CHESTER *who nods approvingly.*)

MRS. LEE (*to* MR. LEE). My dear husband, please join us. You have worked enough for now.

MR. LEE. There's still plenty to do but I will stop for a little while. (*moves out from behind counter.*)

GLADYS. It must be very interesting working in a Chinese laundry, Mr. Lee.

(MR. LEE *turns away from her with an expression of dismay.* CHESTER *changes the subject.*)

CHESTER (*to* GLADYS). The tea is good, isn't it?

GLADYS. Yes, yes, it looks delicious. Really delicious, Mrs. Lee. And so do the cakes. And that blouse you're wearing. I haven't been able to take my eyes off it since I walked in. Where did you get it?

MRS. LEE. I don't think I remember . . . I have it for years.

GLADYS. I'd love to get one like it. (*rises.*) Do you mind if I look and see if the store label is still on it? I really like it and if I can find out where you bought it . . .

(*She stands behind* MRS. LEE *and pushes her hand under the blouse.*)

MRS. LEE (*squirming, arching her back*). No, no, that tickles, Gladys . . .

(*She squeals with laughter.*)

GLADYS. Chester, why don't you see if there's a store label on your father's shirt so you can get one, and I'll get this blouse . . .

(*She hits* CHESTER *on the arm.*)

CHESTER (*rises*). Good idea, Glad. Excellent idea. Gladys is right. I should get one just like it. It's a beaut. (*starting to unbutton* MR. LEE's *shirt.*) Let me unbutton it so I can . . .

MR. LEE (*slaps* CHESTER's *hand, snaps*). Get your hand off me!

CHESTER. All right, all right, you don't have to get sore . . . If you don't want me to unbutton it, I won't unbutton it. I'll get a look at it from under here, it doesn't make any difference. Sit still, Dad, I'll just get under here and see what it says on the label so I can go out and get the same shirt for myself and we'll both have . . .

(CHESTER *pulls* MR. LEE's *shirt out at the waist and pushes his head under it.*)

MR. LEE (*in Chinese*). Nai ta me kwai? (What the hell are you doing?) (MR. LEE *rises, struggles to free himself of* CHESTER *who is caught under his shirt. He slaps at him as they turn around in a circle.* CHESTER *frees himself and runs behind the counter.* MR. LEE, *slipper off and in hand, pursues him. In Chinese*) Cheun choy, wai dan! Yeuk gwo ngo jook do nay . . . Nay dzou mo hong le! (Idiot! Imbecile! If I get my hands on you . . . It will be the end!)

CHESTER. I don't know what he has to get so excited about! What did I do that was so terrible?

MR. LEE (*in Chinese; moving toward* CHESTER). Ngo dzou wui dah bung nay ge tou, ngo mm hai tung may gong seel ge! (One more word from you, and I will split your head open, snot-nose!)

GLADYS (*to* CHESTER). What did your father say to you?

CHESTER. He called me a snot-nose!

MRS. LEE. Forgive us, Gladys. My husband and Chester have been quarreling about one thing or another all day.

GLADYS. I understand, Mrs. Lee. (*clapping her hands*). Say, I got an idea, everybody! Why don't we play cards? We're all so wrought up and anxious . . .

CHESTER (*shaking his head*). I don't wanna play.

GLADYS. With your parents. Chester. Poker. Strip poker.

CHESTER. Strip poker! What an idea! That's a great idea, Gladys. I'll get the cards . . . Don't move, anybody . . . Dad, you'll like this. It's not for money. It's not gambling. Ma, you'll love this game too. It's really a lot of fun. (*getting a deck of cards from the bureau*) You explain it to them, Glad.

GLADYS. It's simple. Chester will give us each one card and the person who gets the lowest card loses and has to remove one piece of clothing or jewelry, but shoes or socks or gloves or earrings will count as one thing. (*to* CHESTER, *who has been shuffling the cards*). Is that okay? It'll go quicker.

CHESTER. Good. Excellent. Here we go. (*He deals the cards: first to* GLADYS, *then to* MR. LEE, MRS. LEE, *and finally to himself. His parents watch everything with mouth slightly open, eyes wide and uncomprehending.*) Four, nine, jack, six. (*picking up dealt cards at once, putting them underneath deck*). You lose, Gladys.

GLADYS (*removes her boots*). This game is lots of fun. When I went to high school I used to play it almost every day.

CHESTER. All right. Here we go again. Five, nine, six, three. I lose. (*He kicks off his sneakers; he wears no socks.*) It starts off slow but it gets more interesting as it goes along. (*He deals.*) Seven, nine, queen, ten. You lose, Glad.

GLADYS (*takes off her wristwatch*). My parents bought me this watch for my last birthday. $59.95 downtown. You know what you would pay for this watch uptown?

CHESTER. Gladys!

GLADYS. Go ahead, go ahead!

CHESTER (*deals*). Seven, jack, eight, queen. You lose again, Glad.

GLADYS. This is becoming ridiculous. (*She removes her blouse without a pause. She is wearing an extraordinarily small and tight red brassiere, the rest of her torso is bare.* CHESTER, MR. *and* MRS. LEE *stare at her bosom. Aware of their intense staring,* GLADYS *flips her pigtails over her bosom.*)

CHESTER (*dealing again*). Nine, eight, jack, four. Damn it! (*He rises, pulls off his shirt.*) You're not gonna believe this but I never lose at this game.

GLADYS (*gathering cards together*). You had your chance. It's my turn to deal. (*She deals to* MR. LEE, MRS. LEE, CHESTER, *then to herself.*) Three, three, three, two. For cryin'-out-loud!

(*She stands, removes her skirt, and places it on the work counter. She is in tights.*)

MR. LEE (*in Chinese*). Mm dzee been go sai keu ge yee fuk ne? (I wonder who does her laundry?)

MRS. LEE (*in Chinese*). Mm dzee. (I wonder.)

GLADYS (*clutching her rear end; turning about quickly*). What? What did they say?

CHESTER. They wanna know who does your laundry.

GLADYS. Oh. (*sits down; deals*). Once again. Nine, queen, three, eight. You, Chester.

(CHESTER *pauses a moment, then he removes his pants. He is naked save for his jockey undershorts.*)

CHESTER (*sits, embarrassed by his parents' presence; tries to cover himself*). Let me deal now, huh?

GLADYS. No. I'm still dealing. You're getting mad because you're losing, aren't you?

CHESTER. *I'm* losing! You're not doing so hot yourself.

GLADYS. I'm doing as well as you are.

CHESTER. We'll see about that. Now if you're gonna deal, deal; come on!

GLADYS (*deals*). King, nine, ace . . . (*gives herself a card but is silent*).

CHESTER (*jumps up, hits table*). Six! Six! All right, Gladys, take it off!

GLADYS. Chester . . .

CHESTER. I don't wanna hear any excuses, Gladys. You lost. Now take it off, come on!

(GLADYS *turns to* CHESTER's *parents who stare back at her dumbly. She rises, quickly slips out of her brown tights: she is wearing a pair of red tights underneath.*)

GLADYS (*sits down; stiffly*). Shall we continue now?

CHESTER (*picking up the cards*). I'm dealing.

GLADYS. Deal.

CHESTER. Since when did you start wearing two pairs of leotards?

GLADYS. Since I started going out with you.

CHESTER. Thanks.

GLADYS. For nothing.

CHESTER (*deals*). Here we go. This is it now. Ten, nine, jack . . .

(*He hesitates a moment.*)

GLADYS. Go ahead, Chester, deal it. And not from the bottom either. (CHESTER *slowly throws out a card for himself.* GLADYS *claps her hands, shrieks.*) Seven!

It's a seven! He loses. Chester loses. Oh, I'm dying! This is a riot! (*She doubles over with laughter. Points at* CHESTER'*s jockey shorts.*) A seven! He's got a seven! (CHESTER *stares at her, sick-looking.*) We're waiting, Chester. (*pause*) Go ahead, Chester.

(CHESTER *removes a bandaid from his leg, holds it up hopefully.* GLADYS *shakes her head.* CHESTER *picks shyly at his undershorts.*)

MR. LEE (*in Chinese*). Ngo day wan yun le. (I think this game has gone far enough.)

MRS. LEE (*in Chinese*). Hai. Yeet lay yuet so. (Yes. It's becoming silly.)

GLADYS. What? What did they say?

CHESTER (*picking up his pants quickly*). They said the game's over. They're afraid the police are going to raid the joint.

GLADYS. Oh, now the game's over. But when *I* was losing, it wasn't over, was it?

CHESTER. What's the difference. We're not getting any place.

(MR. LEE *returns to ironing shirts;* GLADYS *starts to get dressed;* MRS. LEE *clears the table.*)

GLADYS. Did you want to get any place?

CHESTER. What does that mean?

GLADYS. It just seems to me that somebody isn't as anxious to prove something as he says he is.

CHESTER. I'm as anxious as you are, Gladys.

GLADYS. We'll see about that. (*She suddenly grabs* CHESTER *by the hair and pulls him down on the table before he can get his shirt on.*) Mr. Lee! Mrs. Lee! Look! Look what's on Chester's back!

(MR. *and* MRS. LEE *hurry to the table.* MR. LEE *is carrying a large flyswatter.*)

MRS. LEE. What is it, Gladys?

GLADYS. Look at this!

(*She points to the birthmark on* CHESTER'*s shoulder.* MRS. LEE *breaks into a smile.* MR. LEE *returns to the work counter, mumbling under his breath.*)

MRS. LEE. Oh, that. It's a birthmark, Gladys. Chester can have it removed if he wishes.

GLADYS. I . . . I got scared for a minute. Did he get it from you, Mrs. Lee?

MRS. LEE. From me?

CHESTER (*trying to get up*). Forget it, Gladys.

GLADYS (*pushing him down*). Things like that are inherited characteristics, Mrs. Lee. You get them from your parents.

MRS. LEE. I don't think that's so, Gladys. Neither Mr. Lee nor I have a birthmark like Chester's. And we're . . .

GLADYS. Mrs. Lee, are you and Mr. Lee Chester's real biological parents?

(MR. LEE *angrily tosses pieces of laundry up in the air.*)

MR. LEE (*in Chinese*). Nee go du lay! Geel deu dzou. Moon hai go do! (This one, too! Tell her to go. The door is there!)

MRS. LEE (*in Chinese; placating* MR. LEE). Jeung fu, mm ho gum yeung, mm goy nay. Sai mun dzai mm sik see. (My sweet husband, control yourself, please. She is a young girl. She doesn't know better.

(MR. *and* MRS. LEE *continue to talk in Chinese.* CHESTER *puts on his shirt;* GLADYS *puts on blouse, boots, knotting brown tights around her throat like a scarf.*)

CHESTER. I asked you not to say that, Gladys. I especially asked you not to say it!

GLADYS. I don't care. I can't be tactful or beat around the bush when something as important as this comes up. I'm the one who's on the spot. If we ever got married and had a wedding I wouldn't know what table to put them at.

CHESTER. So why are you making such a big deal out of it for? So my parents are Chinese. So I'm Chinese. So what's the big deal?

GLADYS. You lied to me, that's the big deal.

CHESTER. You never lied?

GLADYS. Not about something like this.

CHESTER. Why don't we just forget it, Gladys.

GLADYS. Because I can't. Because this is too important to me and just shows there's no honest relationship between us.

CHESTER. So there's no honest relationship between us.

GLADYS. So let's not pretend.

CHESTER. So let's not!

GLADYS. So you can take your problems and solve them yourself, Chester Lee! And stay away from my mother! (*To* MR. *and* MRS. LEE *as she exits, grabbing skirt from counter covering herself in confusion with skirt, bowing.*) I beg your pardon and your forgiveness . . . your pardon and your forgiveness . . . your forgiveness and your pardon . . .

(*She exits, slamming the door behind her. A pause.* MR. *and* MRS. LEE *move to* CHESTER.)

MRS. LEE. Chester, your father and I are sorry that you quarreled with the young lady.

(CHESTER *nods.*)

MR. LEE. You know that your mother and I are very fond of Pu Ping Chow.

(CHESTER *nods.*)

MRS. LEE. She is a lovely girl who is well brought up. She would be a wonderful wife to someone who . . .

CHESTER. Ma!

MRS. LEE. Only speak to her. That is all your father and I ask. And it would be good for you to do it now. While the memory of Gladys is fresh in your mind so that you can see the virtues of Pu Ping Chow.

MR. LEE. Only speak to her, Chester.

MRS. LEE. That is all we ask.

MR. LEE. Do it for us.

MRS. LEE. For your dear father and me.

CHESTER (*rises*). All right, I'll speak to her. I'll speak to her! But I'm not promising anything else. She's such a creepy weirdo.

MRS. LEE (*to* MR. LEE). My dear husband, please call Pu Ping Chow down. I know she's at home. I will prepare more tea.

CHESTER. Do me a favor, Ma, and don't bother with the tea. This is gonna be short and sweet.

MR. LEE (*goes out into street and calls upstairs in Chinese*). Chow Pu Ping, tsean nay lok lay yut dzun. Chester seang tung nay gong gay geu wah! (Pu Ping Chow, do us the honor of visiting with us. Chester would like to speak to you!)

PU PING (*from upstairs we hear* PU PING's *voice answering; in Chinese*). To jieh. Lay pok. (I will be honored.)

MR. LEE (*enters*). She is coming. She'll be right down.

MRS. LEE (*carries a shirt and tie to* CHESTER). Here put these on, Chester.

CHESTER. What's that?

MRS. LEE. A fresh shirt and tie.

CHESTER. Why do I have to wear a fresh shirt and tie?

MRS. LEE. Chester, Pu Ping Chow . . .

CHESTER (*takes shirt and tie from her*). Boy, what am I letting myself in for!

(*He exits into the bedroom. Both parents busily prepare the room for* PU PING. *From the kitchen area,* MR. LEE *produces an upholstered chair,* MRS. LEE *bring out a small Chinese tea table.*)

MRS. LEE (*in Chinese, as she goes behind the work counter to get a Chinese lantern*). Gum ho dee ge. Keu geel dzee gay fat kok Chow Pu Ping hai sik hup keu ge. (It is better this way. He must discover for himself that Pu Ping Chow is the one who will make him happy.)

(MRS. LEE *turns on the light switch, which illuminates the overhead bulb.* MR. LEE *goes into the kitchen and returns with an ornamental screen which he sets up.*)

MR. LEE (*in Chinese*). Hai me, hai me. Gladys . . . Gladys . . . Chester ngan hai mm hai you dee mo bang. (Yes, yes. Gladys . . . Gladys . . . Chester has a defect in his eyes.) (MR. LEE *covers the naked light bulb with the Chinese lantern. She and* MR. LEE *admire the effect.* CHESTER *returns from the bedroom. Moving to the work counter*) Dong yun-zun . . . dong yun-zun! (Wait . . . wait!) (*as he lowers the window blind*) Lai taiee. (Watch.)

(*The room is transformed.*)

MR. *and* MRS. LEE (*in Chinese*). Dhun long. (How pretty.)

(PU PING *enters from street, closing door behind her. She wears black trousers, a gold mandarin blouse. Her hair is long and black. She carries a large colorful shopping bag.*)

PU PING (*in Chinese; taking a deep bow in a singsong voice*). To jeah nay day foon ying ngo do nay ga ting. (I thank you for welcoming me to your home.)

MR. LEE (*in Chinese*). Mm sai, Pu Ping. (You are welcome, Pu Ping.)

PU PING (*in Chinese; bowing to* MRS. LEE). To jeah nay day foon ying ngo do nay ga ting. (I thank you for welcoming me to your home.)

MRS. LEE (*in Chinese*). Mm sai, Pu Ping. (You are welcome, Pu Ping.)

PU PING (*in Chinese; bowing to* CHES-

TER). To jeah nay day foon ying ngo do nay ga ting. (I thank you for welcoming me to your home.)

CHESTER (*without bowing; curtly*). Terrific!

MR. LEE (*in Chinese; motioning for* PU PING *to sit in the chair*). Tseang tso, tseang tso, Pu Ping. (Sit down, Pu Ping. Make yourself comfortable.)

PU PING (*in Chinese; sits in chair which faces front*). Do jeah. (Thank you.)

MRS. LEE. Your father and I have work to do, Chester. We will leave you alone.

CHESTER. Thanks a lot!

MRS. LEE (*in Chinese; to* PU PING). Tui mm ju, Pu Ping. (Excuse us, Pu Ping.)

PU PING (*in Chinese*). To jeah nay day foon ying ngo do nay ga ting. (I thank you for welcoming me to your home.)

MR. LEE (*in Chinese*). Ho foon hay. (It is our joy.) (MR. *and* MRS. LEE *start for the kitchen.* MR. LEE *notes that* CHESTER *makes no attempt to approach* PU PING. *In Chinese; indicating place beside* PU PING.) Choree she, Chester. (Sit over here, Chester.)

(CHESTER *turns his back.* MR. LEE *moves to him, pinches him on the rear.* CHESTER *jumps up,* MR. LEE *takes the stool he's been sitting on and places it beside the tea table. He and* MRS. LEE *exit into the kitchen.*)

CHESTER (*looking over at* PU PING). Hi.

PU PING (*in Chinese*). Ngo ho go hing you gay wui lay nee do. (I am delighted to be here.)

CHESTER. Hi again.

PU PING (*in Chinese*). Ngo hay mong ngo mm wui man fan nay. Ngo hay mong nay jung yee ngo lay nee do. (I hope that I do not cause you any unhappiness. I hope you like my being here.)

(*She removes a castanet and a small bell from her shopping bag. Then, she starts to sing, in Chinese. The song is taken from a recording by the Chinese Opera Company. First* PU PING *clicks the castanets, then, suddenly, she howls an improbably long and loud note: "Tse nooooooooo . . ." And proceeds to sing two more bars, improvising vowels on any pentatonic scale. Castanets click. Again she howls: "Tse nooooooooo . . ." And two more bars. She tinkles bell. Then starts a third time: "Tse nooooooo*

oo . . ." But CHESTER *has had enough. He shouts at her.*)

CHESTER. All right, that's enough singing, Pu Ping! Did you come here to sing or to talk to me?

PU PING (*in Chinese; returning the castanet and bell to shopping bag*). Nay seung dzou mut yeh ngo dzou dzo. (I come to do whatever is your desire.)

CHESTER. That's very nice of you, but I don't know what I'd like to do myself. (*calling*) Dad?

MR. LEE (*off*). Yes, Chester?

CHESTER. What would you like me to do with Pu Ping?

MR. LEE (*off; in Chinese*). Aiya! (Good heavens!)

(*He hurls a dish against the wall.*)

CHESTER. Never mind. Nobody around here helps me. (*He turns to* PU PING. *She is weaving straws together to complete a straw basket she has taken out of shopping bag. She hums song as she weaves.*) What are you doing?

PU PING (*in Chinese*). Ngo jik gun tso lam. (I am weaving a straw basket.)

CHESTER. What are you weaving a straw basket for? Will you put that thing away! Nobody weaves straw baskets in this country. It just isn't done, Pu Ping!

PU PING (*putting straw basket into shopping bag; in Chinese*). Tu mm ju, Chester. (I am sorry, Chester.)

CHESTER. Can't you just sit there and talk to me like a human being?

PU PING (*in Chinese; rapidly*). Ngo ho seung. Nay yeel deem . . . (I would be delighted to. Whatever you wish . . .)

CHESTER. In English! In English!

PU PING (*with an accent*). My English is . . . very bad. (*Pulls out small fan from under right sleeve; covers her face with it.*)

CHESTER. That's all right. Get used to it. My English isn't so hot either.

PU PING. You're English is . . . lovely.

CHESTER (*moving about*). That's because I use it all the time. Pu Ping, you have to get with it. You can't just sit back and live the way you did in Hong Kong. The kids today swing. They don't follow in their fathers' footsteps. They make up their own rules. Everything's wide open. You have to learn how to . . . (PU PING *has removed a large orange from shopping bag and is peeling it with her fingernails.*

Her back is to CHESTER.) What are you doing now?

PU PING (*holding out the orange to him*). I prepare an orange for you.

CHESTER. Who asked you to prepare an orange for me? You're a nut, Pu Ping!

PU PING. I put it away. (*She throws orange into shopping bag; folds her arms, angrily.*)

CHESTER (*sitting beside her*). I'm trying to explain something to you. We have nothing in common. I don't know how we're supposed to get together. I really don't.

PU PING. I will do . . . whatever you desire.

CHESTER. You mean that?

PU PING. Yes.

CHESTER. How about you and me making out?

PU PING. Making out? What is that?

CHESTER. You don't know? (PU PING *shakes her head.*) Wait. I'll show you. (*He rises.*) Stand up. Come on. Now get up on this table. Go ahead. Get up on the table. (*She does so.*) Now turn over on your back and lie flat, your arms at your sides.

PU PING (*on her back on table*). Like this?

CHESTER. Lik-a-dat! Very good. Now right arm, right leg up . . . (*She does so.*) Right arm, right leg down. Left arm, left leg up . . . Left arm, left leg down. (*She does so. And hereafter when she raises one side she mechanically lowers the other side.*) Very good. Now. Right side up. Left side up. (*He claps his hands rhythmically, interrupts to wave his hand as though leading a band.* PU PING *performs the bizarre exercise in tempo.*) Right-side up. Left-side up. I-make-out. You-make-out. We-make-out. They-make-out. Da-da-da. Da-da-da, etc. (CHESTER *continues to perform.* MR. *and* MRS. LEE *appear at the top of the screen. Shouting at his parents*) Do you mind if I have a little privacy! (*Their heads disappear behind the screen.*) Boy, I can't do anything in my own house. (*He turns, sees* PU PING *still throwing her arms and legs into the air. He moves to her.*) All right, Pu Ping. Stop it already or you'll have to get another hernia operation.

PU PING (*breathlessly*). Is making out finished, Chester?

CHESTER. Yeah, it's finished. Pretty good,

wasn't it?

PU PING. It was very . . . pleasant. I feel . . . happy now.

CHESTER. The man who marries you isn't gonna have much trouble. I'll tell you that, Pu Ping. (PU PING *sings.* CHESTER, *shouting*) All right already, Pu Ping! I don't know what I'm going to do with you. I really don't.

PU PING. You do not like me?

CHESTER. It's not you. It's me. You're a good kid, but I got so much on my mind . . . We'll just have to let it go for now. (*shouts*) Ma! Dad!

(MR. *and* MRS. LEE *suddenly appear from behind the screen.*)

MR. *and* MRS. LEE. Yes, Chester?

CHESTER. Pu Ping is going.

(PU PING *hastily picks up her shopping bag.*)

MRS. LEE (*in Chinese; to* PU PING). Ngo hay mong wui see see geen nay, Pu Ping. (I hope you enjoyed your visit, Pu Ping.)

PU PING (*in Chinese; bowing to* MR. LEE). To jeah nay day foon ying ngo do nay ga ting. (I thank you for welcoming me to your home.) (*to* CHESTER) Chester, there is an old Chinese proverb that says: "Man who puts girl on table, ends up on floor." (*She locks her left foot behind* CHESTER'*s right foot, pushes him, and sends him tumbling to the floor.*) Goodbye, Chester.

(*She exits.*)

MRS. LEE (*in Chinese*). Tai ee hoy. (See what she did.)

MR. LEE (*in Chinese; laughing, flexing his arm*). Wah Pu Ping chung hai chong. (I didn't know Pu Ping was so strong.)

MRS. LEE (*in Chinese*). Lou a sai Chester. (Chester will be angry.)

MR. LEE (*in Chinese*). Yow hoy lou. Yun why ngo fu tan eego kah. (Let him be angry. I pay the bills in this family.) (MR. LEE *goes behind the work counter and raises the window blind.* CHESTER *rises, exits into the bedroom and returns immediately with a suitcase, which he places on the table. He is wearing rain hat. Referring to the suitcase*) What is that for, Chester?

CHESTER (*getting shirts, shorts, undershirts, etc., from the bureau*). I'm packing.

MRS. LEE. Why? Where are you going?

CHESTER. Marvin Brockman. I'll stay with him for a while. He's got plenty of room and he's invited me to stay with him plenty of times.

MRS. LEE. But why?

CHESTER. Because I have to straighten things out in my mind. Because I can't do it here, that's why.

MR. LEE. Chester, anything I said to you before in anger was not meant to be taken seriously.

CHESTER. I know that. It has nothing to do with you. I'll be better off at Marvin's.

MRS. LEE. And Gladys, Chester? Will you be seeing her?

CHESTER. I guess so. I don't know. That's one of the things I have to think out by myself.

MR. LEE. Chester. (CHESTER *turns to him.*) Can we say or do anything that will make you change your mind?

CHESTER. No, Dad. It's about time I stood on my own two feet, anyway. (MR. LEE *pulls some bills from his pocket.* CHESTER *takes the money, slipping it in his pocket.*) Thanks, Dad. (*to both of them*) I'll give you a ring later in the day and tell you what's happening so let's make this clean and quick and no hysterics. Ma . . . (*He kisses her on cheek.*) Take care of yourself. I'll be all right. (*to* MR. LEE) Dad . . . Stop working so hard. And try to get out a little more. I'll call you both this afternoon.

(*He moves toward the door*).

MRS. LEE. We can tell him now, my dear husband.

MR. LEE. Yes, my lovely wife, we can tell him.

CHESTER (*puts suitcase down at door, turns to them*). Tell me? What can you tell me?

MRS. LEE. We were not allowed to do so before, my son.

MR. LEE. Not until you left our home.

MRS. LEE. Not until you left us of your own accord.

CHESTER (*shouting jubilantly; removes rain hat*). I knew it! I knew it! Didn't I say so? For how many years did I say so? I felt it inside, since I was a kid. I knew it all along.

MR. LEE. You tell him, dear.

MRS. LEE. No, my sweetheart. It is only right for you to tell him.

(*She sits.*)

CHESTER. Tell me, somebody! Did you promise my real parents you wouldn't tell me who they are until I left the house, is that it, Dad?

MR. LEE. No, no, that is not it, Chester. Doctor Thomas Wong. We promised him. On the day you were born.

CHESTER. Was he the in-between man?

MRS. LEE. Doctor Thomas Wong. He was a wise old man.

CHESTER. All right. Fine. I'm glad. Now will you please tell me who my real biological parents are?

MR. LEE (*stands beside* MRS. LEE). Your real biological parents?

CHESTER. My real biological parents! Who are they?

MR. LEE. Why, we are, Chester.

CHESTER. You are?

MR. LEE. We are, but . . . (*He nods to* MRS. LEE. *She nods.*) On the day you were born . . . Your mother and I . . . We were not man and wife.

CHESTER. You're kidding.

MRS. LEE. No, Chester. We did not marry until after you were born. That is why we threw away your birth certificate.

CHESTER. Then I'm really Chinese?

MR. LEE. Yes, Chester. Legally speaking, you are a Chinese bastard.

CHESTER. I knew you were hiding something from me.

MRS. LEE. We would have told you sooner, but we promised Doctor Wong to say nothing until you left us of your own accord.

MR. LEE. That is the truth.

MRS. LEE. We have no more secrets from you.

MR. LEE. Now go my son. Go into the world and take upon yourself the responsibilities of a man. Marry the woman you love, whoever she is, and do not be ashamed of your ancestors, do not be ashamed of your parents who love you very much . . . and above all else, for everyone's sake, get yourself a regular job.

CHESTER. Thanks, Dad. Thanks for telling me. Well, I guess I should be going . . .

(MR. *and* MRS. LEE *nod. Puts on rain hat. Picking up his suitcase.*) I think I can handle the future now. I think so.

(*He starts out the door.* MR. *and* MRS. LEE *watch him. He stands outside the window, looking in. They wave at him.*)

CURTAIN

ORANGE SOUFFLÉ

Saul Bellow

HILDA, a middle-aged prostitute in
Indiana Harbor, Indiana

PENNINGTON, a very ancient millionaire

AN EMINENT NOVELIST (as well as dramatist and university professor), Saul Bellow was born in Lachine, Quebec, on July 10, 1915. He learned four languages as he grew up—English, Hebrew, Yiddish and French—and his childhood was immersed in the Old Testament. In 1924, the Bellow family moved to Chicago. ("I grew up there and consider myself a Chicagoan, out and out.") In 1933, he graduated from Tuley High School and entered the University of Chicago, then transferred to Northwestern University in 1935. He obtained his B.S. degree from Northwestern in 1937, graduating with honors in anthropology and sociology. Then, under a scholarship, he enrolled in the University of Wisconsin in Madison, but found himself unsuited to graduate study in anthropology. "Every time I worked on my thesis," he once told an interviewer, "it turned out to be a story. I disappeared for the Christmas holidays and I never came back." At this point, he also had made up his mind to be a writer.

In 1943, he became a member of the editorial department of the *Encyclopædia Britannica* and at some time during World War II, he served in the Merchant Marine. His first novel, *Dangling Man,* was issued in 1944. The distinguished critic, Edmund Wilson, who promptly recognized Bellow's talent, praised the book as "one of the most honest pieces of testimony on the psychology of a whole generation who have grown up during the depression and the war."

While teaching English at the University of Minnesota and contributing essays and short stories to magazines, Mr. Bellow was awarded a Guggenheim Fellowship, enabling him to go to Paris and Rome to work on *The Adventures of Augie March,* a novel that brought him his first National Book Award (1954).

His second National Book Award came in 1964 for *Herzog* and it also won for him the *Prix International de Littérature.* "Herzog," wrote Granville Hicks in the *Saturday Review,* "reenforces my conviction that Bellow is the leading figure in American fiction today." Most other reviewers acknowledged that "his intellectual brilliance, comic gifts, and craftsmanship made him an exciting writer who had dared to cope in an unfashionably affirmative way with the prevailing theme of the suffering individual and his encounter with the times."

In 1970, Mr. Bellow came away with his third National Book Award for *Mr. Sammler's Planet,* a work of exceptional fiction that "mixes comedy and sadness, along with superb character drawing and a strain of speculation, both daring and serene, on the future of life."

The author's other books include: *The Victim, Seize the Day,* and *Henderson the Rain King.*

Mr. Bellow's first produced play, *The Last Analysis,* opened at the Belasco Theatre, New York, in October, 1964, and it starred Sam Levene. Although its engagement was brief, it was considered by many one of the funniest comedies of the period. In 1971, the comedy, in a somewhat revised version, was revived at the Off-Broadway Circle-in-the-Square in a production by Theodore Mann.

Orange Soufflé, published for the first time in the United States in this collection, originally was produced in London in 1966. Later in that same year, it was presented at the Cort Theatre, New York, as part of *Under the Weather.* The two characters were portrayed by Shelley Winters and Harry Towb.

In 1971, Saul Bellow was elected to membership in the nation's highest honor society of arts and letters—The American Academy of Arts and Letters.

SCENE. HILDA's *apartment, a kitchenette bedroom. A counter or room divider separates the kitchen from the sleeping quarters cum living room. The furniture is old-fashioned; by contrast, what can be seen of the kitchen is quite modern. A wintry afternoon.*

HILDA *is dressing old* PENNINGTON. *At curtain she has already gotten him into his long johns. She is treating him with special care; he is evidently puzzled by this unusual solicitude, and as he sits on the bed, tousled and feeble, he tries to penetrate her motive with his sharp, clear eyes.*

HILDA. Please sit straight, Mr. Pennington. How can I button your chest if you slump? I know you get so relaxed, you droop.

PENNINGTON. Ha! Relaxed!

HILDA. Up, chin, till I get the top button. That's it. I often wondered, Mr. Pennington, do you import these garments?

PENNINGTON. Italian. Tailored for me in Milan. Since 1909.

HILDA. A far cry from Montgomery Ward. (*feels the collar with her finger, first from the left, then the right*) Silk trim. All your accessories are so elegant.

PENNINGTON. Why are you so talkative?

HILDA. Oh, why not? Why be so formal after all these years? Ten years.

PENNINGTON. Since my seventy-eighth birthday.

HILDA. Once a month. That makes . . .

PENNINGTON. That makes only one hundred and twenty times.

HILDA. If I were one of your regular employees, I'd have plenty of seniority by now.

(*Rising, she takes a whisk broom and begins to brush his jacket.*)

PENNINGTON. You never did that before, brushing my clothes.

HILDA. Yes, often, unless you were in a terrific hurry. I've always been extra attentive. You just never noticed.

PENNINGTON. My powers of observation are famous throughout the financial world.

HILDA. Then maybe you've seen how good I've been for you.

PENNINGTON. I never complained.

HILDA. Why, the first time you had to be carried up the stairs.

PENNINGTON. Carried? Nonsense. Helped a little. My trick knee was acting up. I was the only man hurt in the Battle of Manila Bay. I was just a young gob, I lied to enlist. As I ran along the deck with a message for Admiral Dewey I fell on a winch.

HILDA. Poor Monty!

(*She opens an ironing board and begins to iron his necktie.*)

PENNINGTON (*stiffly*). Monty?

HILDA. What was the message?

PENNINGTON. You've never called me that.

HILDA. Well, perhaps it's time. You get very familiar with me.

PENNINGTON. That's different.

HILDA. The things you expect me to do— and say. The old-fashioned expressions you made me learn.

PENNINGTON (*fairly proud of himself*). I get carried away.

HILDA. A woman in my position is supposed to hold back nothing, allow anything. Here, put your arm into this shirt.

PENNINGTON. You see what I mean? Usually you just pull it over my head.

HILDA. What? Never. You're mistaken. You always get the most classy treatment here.

PENNINGTON. Madame Hilda, during the first year you behaved like a member of the bomb squad with a suspicious parcel.

HILDA. That's not true.

PENNINGTON. Would I forget it? When I said "Undress me," you bit your lip and had tears in your eyes . . .

HILDA. The pollen count is the real explanation. That was the worst hay fever season since 1951.

PENNINGTON. . . . And treated me like a mummy afterwards. You couldn't wrap me up fast enough. When I got home, my valet couldn't understand how I got so screwed up.

HILDA. It was only a matter of practice.

PENNINGTON. Perhaps my physique took some getting used to. Honestly, did my big bones scare you? (*no answer*) Pressing a tie with a hot iron makes the silk shiny. It'll smell peculiar, too. Hand it over.

(*She gives it to him. He passes the tie nearsightedly before his eyes.*)

HILDA (*sits beside him and helps him into the shirt*). It wasn't a weak knee, you were weak all over. The chauffeur brought you in his arms and put you on this bed.

PENNINGTON (*joyously, almost hooting*). Not all over! Not all over!

HILDA. If you're still going strong ten years later, it's no accident. You must admit it.

PENNINGTON (*looks about as she puts in his cuff links*). You're like me. You don't like to change or move. It's a nice little place, for what it is. Except the location.

HILDA. Surrounded by the steel mills, the coke ovens, the gas refineries, the brewery on the right and the soap factory behind. It's bright as day at midnight, and I hear the freights and cattle cars. And I never once even asked you . . .

PENNINGTON. Asked what?

HILDA. Whether you're a major stockholder in any of these companies.

PENNINGTON (*surprised*). What do you know about such things?

HILDA. Why shouldn't I? I read the papers, and that includes the society page, the financial section.

PENNINGTON. Aren't you peculiar today! Now what about my socks? All this talk! And the way you're acting.

HILDA. Politics, too. I wrote a letter to Congress about reapportionment.

PENNINGTON. The first eight, nine years you didn't get personal at all.

HILDA (*takes his stiff leg on her lap and puts on one of his garters*). No, you didn't encourage it.

PENNINGTON. And I don't encourage it now.

HILDA (*her nostrils flare*). No, you pay good dough. You even gave me a raise. I started at fifty an afternoon.

PENNINGTON. One hundred, in cash, and you don't have to report it.

HILDA. Neither do you. (*She buckles the second garter.*) I don't want to argue with you.

PENNINGTON. Aren't we running a little early this afternoon?

HILDA (*putting on his socks*). It's the same as always.

PENNINGTON. No, it isn't. (*betrays some agitation*) You've got me all twisted around today, and I don't like it. I've never been a troublemaker. I never asked for anything unusual. Did I ever make one single peculiar request? (*She is silent.*)

And I know what people are. Me, I only need a little assistance. I'm slightly feeble, and that's only natural at my time of life . . . Don't rush things.

HILDA. I never can get your long underwear to lie flat under your stockings.

PENNINGTON. My mother had the same problem.

(HILDA *quickly wriggles on the second sock, her hair falling over her eyes, and hurries to the counter, on the kitchen side. There she opens a large French cookbook.*)

HILDA. Flour, salt, sugar, baking powder.

PENNINGTON. What are you doing?

HILDA. Shortening, eggs, orange rind.

PENNINGTON. You rushed me through it. You think I didn't notice.

HILDA. Measuring spoons, and cups. All laid out.

(*She rubs her hands.*)

PENNINGTON. The timetable is off by as much as twenty minutes. Well, at least finish dressing me.

HILDA. I'm making something nice.

PENNINGTON. What are you pulling, Madame!

HILDA. It's time you knew some of my other talents, Sir! I'm cooking something.

PENNINGTON (*hooting angrily*). Come here and put on my pants!

HILDA. Just one second. Make yourself comfortable. The stove is heating. That's so pleasant on a winter day.

PENNINGTON. If it's for me, I don't want any. What do people cook in Indiana Harbor—pigs' knuckles and kapusta? I can't digest cabbage.

HILDA. Something you might enjoy—very—very light. An orange soufflé.

PENNINGTON (*tries feebly to rise; his voice is somewhat stifled*). Soufflé! Where is my chauffeur? He should be back. What time is it?

HILDA. He'll be back at five P.M. as usual. I know what you must be thinking, what does a Polack whore from Indiana Harbor know about soufflé? You think I spend my whole life in the sack with rough trade. Well, try to adjust your mind to the reality-situation. I have dozens and dozens of interests. I got a certificate from the Cordon Bloo school.

PENNINGTON. When were you in Paris?

HILDA. Not Paris. They have a branch

in Gary, Indiana. Only one thing, now, where's the bottle of Cointreau? Orange soufflé without Cointreau you can't make.

PENNINGTON. I won't eat it. I'm on a diet.

HILDA. Don't pay attention to doctors, they gave you up years ago. After a few visits, I had you leaping up the stairs and knocking down the door. You stopped going to Hot Springs.

PENNINGTON. Those stinking mucky baths.

HILDA. By the feel of the thing, I know what's good for you. Where's that little dish . . . (*rattling sheets of wax paper*) Where the Christ is it . . . excuse me. Ah, here.

PENNINGTON. All that kitchen stuff is new. It's still got labels on it.

HILDA. Once a year I throw my old stuff out and buy new colors. (*poring over the cookbook, holds her hair out of her eyes*) Sift—I did it before. Add a spoon of this, a crumb of that. So far so good. Meantime the eggs.

PENNINGTON. What do you know about kitchens, baking, eggs! It's winter. Hand me my pants!

HILDA. I go shopping like other women. You don't think they don't let whores in the supermarket? Or maybe they've got segregated steel carts? Go and look at all those broads in slacks, with curlers and eye makeup and pale lipstick, smoking, and figure out who's the married woman. Maybe *you* don't read the papers. To make ends meet some of those little married chicks do a trick or two and the husband sits for the kids and knows all about it. If wives can hustle, whores can bake.

(*She rapidly beats the eggs.*)

PENNINGTON (*wraps his legs in the blanket*). For ten years everything was smooth.

HILDA. Ten years, twelve days in the year.

PENNINGTON. I do the best I can.

HILDA. And the rest of the time?

PENNINGTON. I don't interfere with *you*.

HILDA (*making angry noises with the bowls*). You don't bother yourself about me. If you got enough dough, you can make the world stand still. You can tie it up like a horse and it'll be waiting when you get back. You never took any personal interest in me.

PENNINGTON. Is that so bad? People want

to be *seen*. Sometimes they're better off invisible. Anyhow, that's me. I'm old enough to be myself. In fact, too old to be anybody else.

HILDA. And rich enough so you don't have to be a hypocrite— That is a nice thing about you. I appreciate your character.

PENNINGTON (*interested now*). Do you?

HILDA. What's a whore good for if you can't be yourself with her either? What's the whole point of a whore? Her opinions don't worry you. She frees your mind. If you flunk, she doesn't get sore. She doesn't cripple you with a lot of stupid love.

PENNINGTON. Till today, you've been perfect. (*He seems moved.*) You may not know it, but these visits mean a lot to me. Sometimes I count the days. So why spoil things?

HILDA. Why, because I bake you something nice? You don't want to expand a little? I want you to know I have a lot of sides to me. I can cook and bake and serve and keep up a conversation with anybody. Wait till you see what kind of china I've got, and linen and silverware. To you a soufflé belongs in the Pump Room where the colored wear a turban. Why shouldn't we know each other better?

PENNINGTON. I know you plenty.

HILDA. Because of sex? I ought to know best how important it is. I never bum-rap it. But . . . (*Shaking her head, she studies the oven thermometer.*)

PENNINGTON. What I was as a captain of industry, what I was on the board of directors, what I was on the stock market, that's what I've been here. That's the best of me there is, the truest, anyway. Not what I was with my wife and sons. With them I did what I had to do, not what I wanted. (*with a strange emotion*) Why do people have to pry! The secret truth is the best, and let it to hell alone!

HILDA. But you could be a lot more free now. With me you're clinging to old habits.

PENNINGTON. Leave it to a woman to free a man. Heh! heh!

HILDA. I like you, Mr. Pennington. I've always liked you—Let me check now. The rind, the Cointreau, the nutmeg, the stiffener.

PENNINGTON. Stiffener?

HILDA. In she goes. (*puts dish in oven*) I'll set the timer. I'm really famous for my soufflé.

PENNINGTON (*too weak to sound tart*). In the gas-tank set.

HILDA. Don't be upset. You look so ruffled. You've got your feathers up. Don't you worry. Let's put on your pants. (*She brushes his trousers.*)

PENNINGTON. I liked it better when things were businesslike. It's upsetting this way.

HILDA. Who knows, things might become even better.

PENNINGTON. Or I might lose something valuable by tampering. I know what works. As long as it works, let it be.

HILDA. Tell me, Mr. Pennington, what's my name? What's the address here?

PENNINGTON. Your name is Hilda . . . (*He hesitates.*)

HILDA. Hilda what? Come on. If you can't pronounce it, spell it. You can't. You don't know what street this is. You couldn't get here if Otto quit. I'm just an old Polack broad from Indiana Harbor. You arrive in the Rolls, and she undresses you, she lays for you and dresses you and you go away for another month. Lots of people would try to find out who am I, where do I come from, did I have a father or mother or a husband or a kid, and how did I ever get into this racket . . .

PENNINGTON. But not me.

HILDA. You should have asked once, anyway, even if you didn't listen to the answer. Do you think I'm just a poor tramp? Well, I'm not. This building belongs to me.

PENNINGTON (*struck by this*). This is your own property?

HILDA. The mortgage is paid off, too.

PENNINGTON. Then why do you . . . ?

HILDA. Financially, I've been independent since 1959. For six years you've been my only client.

PENNINGTON (*as she puts on his pants he gives a cry from the soul, or its neighborhood*). Oh Lord, Lord, Lord! I always wanted things so simple.

HILDA. What's so simple? To arrive on this street in a Rolls-Royce to see a dumb Polack broad? What do you think I tell the neighbors? It isn't simple.

PENNINGTON. You tell them I'm your stock broker?

HILDA. *They* don't think I'm a dumb Polack. I have lots of refined friends, I go all over. At the Cordon Bloo I rubbed elbows with the best people on the South Shore, country club people, politicians' wives. You think I hang around with scrubwomen?

PENNINGTON. I knew you were discreet. We had one conversation.

HILDA (*she has brought up a little table and now begins to set it*). Yes, the first time. Did you think I'd phone the gossip columns? I'd say, Mr. Montgomery G. Pennington of Lakeshore Drive, Eagle River, and Palm Beach, President of the Tower Club, Chairman of the Board, and once a member of President Wilson's cabinet . . .

PENNINGTON. Stop, stop! I knew you wouldn't. I thought if I died in your bed, naked, a heart attack . . . I felt we should talk it over.

HILDA. I had to promise to dress you and call the chauffeur.

PENNINGTON. Yes. For some reason, I wouldn't want him to see me naked. And I still say . . .

HILDA. The scandal bothers you.

PENNINGTON. Scandal? Nonsense! I was thinking about my wife. She'd have given my body to a medical school. She threatened me with it. She'd let the students cut me up. She was insanely jealous.

HILDA. But she passed away first.

PENNINGTON. Yes. (*brief silence*) You read it in the papers?

HILDA. Four years ago. I wondered if you'd come that month.

PENNINGTON. I did come.

HILDA. Why shouldn't you? She'd have gone to the hairdresser, wouldn't she? She'd have her nails done.

PENNINGTON. No doubt.

HILDA. You miss her?

PENNINGTON (*hesitant*). She's much missed by everybody.

HILDA. I'm sure the Garden Club misses her. The zoo. The museum.

PENNINGTON. She gave that great collection of South American lizards to the museum.

HILDA. Do you believe in an afterlife?

PENNINGTON. I worry about it . . . What's that I smell?

HILDA (*starting violently*). My soufflé! Where's your watch? (*finds his large old-fashioned gold watch which hangs on a thick chain*) How long has it been in? (*darts to the timer*) It's only halfway. (*Her heart is beating. She presses it with both hands.*)

PENNINGTON. Hilda, why did you give up all your clients except me . . . ? Am I . . . Am I so special? (*leans toward her*) What is there about me?

HILDA (*smiling to herself*). You don't have to ask.

PENNINGTON (*takes her hand*). Terrific, eh? I hoped it was like that. I had the feeling. Everything about me is wearing out, except. With other men *it* goes first, they say. Not me. But sometimes I worried that you didn't care about me, really.

HILDA. No!

PENNINGTON. Yes. When I was young, up in Wisconsin, I was like an Indian—strong, husky, big, straight, tanned.

HILDA. Were you actually in the Battle of Manila?

PENNINGTON. I'm not one hundred percent sure.

HILDA. But you were in the navy?

PENNINGTON. It seems so, often. I've had so many lives. But I believe I can remember how it was as a young sailor in Hong Kong. And Admiral Dewey was a sportsman. He played golf. Ike wasn't the first. Then I think I can smell the battle—the explosives. Dewey steamed away from the Spanish fleet. He thought he had only fifteen rounds left. A miscount! I was sent with the message. There were forty-five. It started to be dawn, with one of those tropical flashes. But the deck was like a coal tunnel. It smelled like a mine. And suddenly, when I fell, the sun, like sparkling spumoni, chocolate, green, white and orange, like flamingoes.

HILDA (*plugging in an electric coffeepot, has her back to audience*). But why wouldn't I care for you?

PENNINGTON. I never liked old age, myself. It's loathsome. And now I'm *it*. Eyes coated, ears filled with old hair, big hollow kneebones, paunch and shanks, veins like bayous. (*raises his chin*) The elevens are up. Those two big sinews like one and one, right here in my neck.

HILDA. You don't realize how a woman looks at things. I've seen guys come and go, all kinds. I know what counts.

PENNINGTON. A strange thing. I was always virile. It showed in business, too.

HILDA. You break all the records.

PENNINGTON. You don't mean it!

HILDA. I mean, a man like you can do what he likes, write his own ticket.

PENNINGTON. You're very clever, Hilda. I wouldn't have known it.

HILDA (*setting out dishes*). Did you ever see more beautiful bone china? And look at these napkins. (PENNINGTON *looks nearsightedly.*) I put a lot of time into thinking to myself . . . (*abruptly*) The soufflé! (*consults the enormous watch again*) It's okay.

PENNINGTON (*catching at watch*). Otto should be here. (*tries to rise*)

HILDA (*forces him back on bed*). Hold still, I'll put on your necktie.

PENNINGTON. You pulled it too tight last time.

HILDA. I'll be careful.

PENNINGTON. Just knot it. I'll pull it into place myself. I couldn't breathe when you did it. And I couldn't loosen it.

HILDA. There we are. (*stands back to admire her work*) Look, Mr. Pennington . . . why should we see each other only a dozen times a year?

PENNINGTON. I might be able to manage every two weeks. I heard of a fellow who gives injections.

HILDA. It's not what I have in mind.

PENNINGTON. All this . . . mixing, egg-beating, pressing, brushing, china, and silverware . . . (*startled*) Marriage?

HILDA. No, what do you think I am, a lousy schemer?

PENNINGTON. I'm a little reassured. But some complicated idea is rotting your mind. I can tell.

HILDA. Why should I lie? There *is* something.

PENNINGTON (*exclaiming*). I guessed! I guessed! I guessed!

HILDA. How marvelous it would be to broaden our relationship.

PENNINGTON. Relationship!

HILDA. There's a side to me you haven't seen.

PENNINGTON. I haven't seen both sides of the moon, either, and it's all right with me. It's just more craters, I'm sure of it.

HILDA. When I say there is something, why do you think it's a scheme?

PENNINGTON. Listen, my dear, you read the papers, you say?

HILDA. Sure I do, and also the magazines.

PENNINGTON. Then you know about the Gemini capsule.

HILDA. Those two astronauts going up together, you mean?

PENNINGTON. Yes, and listen: when they reach outer space, they're going to open the hatch, did you know? Then one of them will sit in the doorway and let his feet hang. He'll be wearing his space suit, of course. Then, if conditions are right, he'll float outside on a wire or something. He'll glide along with the ship. They say he will. Oh, imagine! Hundreds of miles above the earth. Hundreds of degrees below zero. The earth under him. (*He strikes his chest with the back of his fist.*) That's what I've been through in my spirit. Floating on a tether through empty space, and each time making it back inside the capsule after my visit to death and nothing. It's very peculiar! (*tries to rise*) Where is my chauffeur? I'll fire that man!

HILDA (*holds his frail arm, putting his suspenders over his shoulders*). You can't go without tasting the soufflé. It smells delicious. What an aroma! So listen, the fellow floats in the air and that's marvelous. But then he comes back to earth and eats some soufflé. Isn't that kind of a beautiful mystery, too?

PENNINGTON. Where do you get your ideas!

HILDA. I don't know. I came out of the orphanage, and before I knew where I was, I was hustling.

PENNINGTON. What's that to me?

HILDA. My sister got married, but I always was on my own. Now it's my turn to tell you something peculiar. I have this sister, she lives in a slum, in urban renewal.

PENNINGTON. Well?

HILDA. Some time back, a truck fell on her. A trailer truck skidded on greasy pavement, she was standing at the bus stop, and boom!

PENNINGTON. Killed?

HILDA. Pinned. The fire department worked hours, and two doctors, one on the belly, one putting together her hip and legs. Skin grafts. Six months on her back. She got some money out of it. The lawyer took one-third, the doctor, plenty, but there was still enough from the settlement so she could be comfortable the rest of her life. However . . .

PENNINGTON. I knew that was coming.

HILDA. Along comes her son—he was a son, then—and says he wants to be the daughter, not the son.

PENNINGTON. You said peculiar.

HILDA. Queer. He wants to be a female out and out. He says, Mother, I want to have an operation in Denmark. And he takes the twenty thousand dollars she was going to retire on. You follow?

PENNINGTON. I wish I could say no.

HILDA. Archie comes back a young lady. Now they're opening a dress shop together, in Indiana Harbor.

PENNINGTON. Outer space is better.

HILDA. You're right, Mr. Pennington. Do I have to be hemmed in by freaks. They took the shop in this building.

PENNINGTON. On the corner?

HILDA. The same. My sister and her former son, now a daughter. Now I appeal to you . . .

PENNINGTON. No, no, leave me out of it. I've got a date at my club.

HILDA. After a little soufflé. You never even asked for a glass of water in this house.

(*The coffee begins to percolate with a loud squeak.*)

PENNINGTON. What have you got in mind?

HILDA. You hear strange things all the time. Is it nine-tenths normal like an iceberg, and one-tenth strange? Or the reverse? I don't know. My life has been very peculiar, Mr. Pennington. You think that when people sit at home and hear strange news on the TV and read Believe It or Not—you think they aren't doing anything themselves? Well, you're wrong. They're working hard. By nodding or smiling or lifting brows they're sitting it out for normalcy. They're like regular soldiers, taking orders from the world. They fight on their behinds, but they fight, believe me. They force everything irregular through their minds and through their flesh, and they try to make everything irregular regular again. They do it till they wear out and die. They have a duty to the normal version of how life is!

PENNINGTON. Okay, Madame, to the point.

HILDA (*rising*). I have to see is it browning yet. (*runs to oven*) It isn't doing what it's supposed to . . . but it'll be okay.

PENNINGTON. You don't know what you're doing.

HILDA. I do so. (*returns*) Just a little longer. Have a little coffee first.

PENNINGTON. I don't want any. Will you finally tell me what you're up to?

HILDA. You have that big place at Palm Beach, I read about it. I'd like to go there.

PENNINGTON. What!

HILDA. I'd be like a hostess. A chatelaine. (*She mispronounces the word.*) You think I can't do it? I could surprise you. I'm terrific with people. They love me. God, they do! They're happy to see me. Oh, Pennington, get me out of here. My sister and her daughter Archie are moving in next month and I'll be trapped.

PENNINGTON. I thought life had no more surprises.

HILDA. I'd run that place like a dream. Soufflé isn't all I can make. Duck with oranges. Bouillabaisse. Karsky Shashlik. Barcelona Paella with lobster claws and capers. Five kinds of mousse. Wine, I know all about. Flower arrangements. Your guests would be wild for me. I bet they need a little new interest. Just like you. Us American minorities are the spice of life. And to show I'm on the level I'll sign any kind of paper.

PENNINGTON. I have to go. I just can't listen.

HILDA. You have to listen. I'll make over my property so it'll go to your estate when I kick off. I don't want to leave it to my niece.

PENNINGTON. For once a man works out a good thing. For once! At last! After years of trying. A good thing. Naturally, it has to be ruined.

HILDA. A thing has got to be just the way you want it. Couldn't it be even a little bit the way *I* want it? Give a guy a little chance, Pennington. Try me at Palm Beach. If I don't work out what do you lose? You can trust me.

PENNINGTON (*His indignation is so great that he finds the strength to rise and reach for his jacket*). Take this table out of the way!

HILDA. No pay. On approval, how's that?

PENNINGTON. Where's my coat! My stick! (*Finding his cane, he stands straighter.*) Nobody has ever forced me out of character—not in the last sixty years anyway.

HILDA. Wait, it's ready.

PENNINGTON. That kind of stuff disagrees with me. What is this, February? I'll see you in March. (*walks slowly toward closet*) My overcoat's in there.

HILDA (*quickly goes to closet and takes out his fur-collared coat*). Here, put it on and sit down. (*Timer buzzes.*) It's ready, it's ready. You never tasted such soufflé. It'd be the rage of Palm Beach.

(*She drapes the coat over him quickly and runs to stove. He leans on cane, waiting. She bends out of sight as he peers over the counter. Then she rises, wearing asbestos stove mittens. In the round baking dish is nothing resembling a soufflé.*)

PENNINGTON. Is that it?

HILDA. I can't understand what went wrong.

PENNINGTON. You couldn't get it up.

(*After a short pause the rich tones of a Rolls-Royce horn are heard.*)

Ah, there's Otto with the car. I often wonder where he goes. (*thinking*) No, not Otto. (*sets Homburg on his head with trembling hands, puts on gloves*) About time, too. (*leans on counter, the better to point at* HILDA *with his cane*) Stick to what you know!

(*He exits.*)

HILDA (*wailing as the curtain begins to come down*). Ooooh! Ooooh! (*With mittened hands she hurls the dish to the floor. She seizes a skillet and menaces the vanished* PENNINGTON.) Oh, I could hit him! (*She strikes the oven.*) Once they get you down, they never let you up! (*striking the oven with the skillet*) Never, never!

CURTAIN

MALE OF THE SPECIES

Alun Owen

Part 1: MacNeil

BILLY

DAVID MACNEIL

FIRST BARMAID

SECOND BARMAID

MISS SAVILLE

WOMAN

MARY MACNEIL

"Playwrights who can make dialogue flow like Alun Owen, who can create characters and make one pay attention to them, and who can hold one's interest in what is going on seem to be at a premium," declared an editorial in the British trade publication, *The Stage and Television Today,* a conviction that was indisputably upheld in 1969 when his three part drama, *Male of the Species,* was seen on American television. Hosted by Lord (Laurence) Olivier and performed by a flawless cast headed by Sean Connery, Michael Caine, Paul Scofield and Anna Calder-Marshall, the presentation evoked lavish praise from the nation's press. It was unanimously hailed as "a smashing triumph on all counts" that provided "a moment of rare maturity and matchless quality" on the television screen, "a superior work . . . literate and articulate and filled with earthy, pungent humor." Its enormous success prompted the television network to repeat the show later in the year, and now *Male of the Species* appears in print for the first time in *Best Short Plays of the World Theatre: 1968–1973.*

Alun Owen was born on November 24, 1926, in Menai, North Wales, and was educated at Cardigan and Liverpool. He began his stage career at fifteen when he joined the Perth Repertory as a bit-part actor and assistant stage manager. During World War II, he was a "Bevin Boy" (one who worked in the mines as a public service, as an alternative to conscription during the war) in the pits in South Wales before a mining accident led to his discharge. An assortment of jobs followed. He worked as a waiter, a lorry driver's mate, a warehouse hand, a seaman in the Merchant Navy, for two trips; and then as an actor in repertory, pantomime, and on the West End stage and television He had meanwhile published poems in the United States and Wales and had gradually become interested in dramatic writing.

After five radio scripts had been accepted by the British Broadcasting Corporation, his first stage play, *Progress to the Park,* was presented as a Sunday night production at the Royal Court Theatre in 1959, was then produced for a run at the Theatre Royal, Stratford East, and subsequently transferred to the Saville in the West End. His other plays include *The Rough and Ready Lot,* produced at the Lyric in Hammersmith, and *A Little Winter Love,* which premiered at the Gaiety Theatre, Dublin.

In 1964, Mr. Owen's musical, *Maggie May* (with music and lyrics by Lionel Bart and starring Rachel Roberts), was an overnight success at the Adelphi Theatre, London, where it enjoyed a run of sixteen months.

A prolific author who transfers his allegiance from stage to television to films with equal facility, Mr. Owen received the 1960 award as Best Scriptwriter of the Year from the Guild of Television Producers and Directors, and was the recipient of the Television and Screenwriters' Guild citation for the Best Original Television Play of 1961 in England—*The Rose Affair.* Additional honors subsequently came to him when he was nominated for a Hollywood Academy Award for his screenplay, *A Hard Day's Night* (The Beatles' first feature film) and acquired the 1967 Gold Star Award from Britain's Associated Television for his play *George's Room,* which was published in this editor's collection of *Modern Short Comedies from Broadway and London.*

During the seasons of 1969 and 1970, Mr. Owen was represented by three separate offerings on British stages: as a contributor (along with Harold Pinter, John Bowen, and others) to *Mixed Doubles* (Comedy Theatre, London), nine short plays about marriage; *No Trams to Lime Street* (Richmond Theatre), a musical based on his television play; and *There'll Be Some Changes Made* (Fortune Theatre, London).

Alun Owen lives with his wife and children "mostly" in a large Victorian house in Cardigan, West Wales, on the banks of the River Teify.

PART ONE

MacNEIL

SCENE. *An old-fashioned furniture workshop. Early evening. Furniture, either made or half made, is piled neatly around the workshop to indicate that the day's work is over. The floor is covered with sawdust and shavings which* BILLY *is sweeping up in a lackadaisical manner.* BILLY *is a ratty, nervous, little Scotsman.*

From time to time BILLY *looks up a flight of open wooden stairs that lead to an office on the floor above.*

We hear a sharp cry from the office, a woman's cry.

BILLY *looks up and after a moment* DAVID MACNEIL *comes out of the office, slamming the door behind him.* DAVID MACNEIL *is a tall man, also a Scot. He has a hard look but he has a fine hand in irony which is his manifestation of humor.*

He pauses on the balcony outside the office and smiles with grim satisfaction before coming rapidly down the stairs, crossing the workshop floor toward the door.

BILLY *runs after him, agog for details.*

BILLY. What happened? (MACNEIL *ignores him consciously and gets his coat from a corner.*) What happened . . . what happened? (MACNEIL *looks at* BILLY *in disgust, again ignores him and leaves the workshop.* BILLY *runs after the swiftly disappearing* MACNEIL). (*Bleating at him*) What happened . . . what happened?

——

SCENE. *A public bar. Early evening. The bar is practically empty. Behind the bar are two attractive barmaids, one slightly older than the other. After a moment,* MACNEIL *enters, followed by a breathless* BILLY. MACNEIL *looks neither to left or right but crosses straight to the bar. The barmaids perk up when they see who it is. By this time* BILLY *is almost dancing with impatience and nervous anticipation.*

BILLY. Please . . . what happened? What happened, Mr. MacNeil?

MACNEIL. Nothing happened.

BILLY (*insistently*). Oh, something must have happened.

MACNEIL (*amused*). Nothing happened, Billy.

BILLY. Oh, it must have, it must have!

MACNEIL. Are we here to talk only?

BILLY (*abashed*). A pint?

MACNEIL. I believe that is the purpose of the establishment.

BILLY. Miss, a pint.

(*They wait for the barmaid to draw* MACNEIL *a pint, the barmaid looks inquiringly at* MACNEIL *who gives her a confirming look and nod.* BILLY *is in a fret of impatience while* MACNEIL *is quietly amused by his companion's sweaty curiosity. The pint is placed before* MACNEIL, BILLY *pays and turns to* MACNEIL.)

BILLY. Now, tell me. (*But* MACNEIL *has moved to an alcove and is sitting down at a small round table.* BILLY *joins him.*) Man, will you not tell me what happened?

(MACNEIL *takes a deep drink before speaking.*)

MACNEIL. I don't like London beer, I never will.

BILLY. Mr. MacNeil!

MACNEIL. It's overpriced.

BILLY. I expected more from you, Mr. MacNeil.

(MACNEIL *grins at him.*)

MACNEIL. Well . . . (*He pauses.*) . . . I went up to the office. She was there.

BILLY. Yes, Miss Saville.

MACNEIL (*silencing him*). She went into playing the madame from the off. "MacNeil, I'm seriously disturbed about your attitude," she says. She had that silky suit on.

BILLY. Morgeschell.

MACNEIL. What?

BILLY. The material—"Morgeschell" they call it.

MACNEIL. Do they? It does nothing but good for her.

(BILLY *brays a nervous laugh.*)

MACNEIL. Control yourself, Billy, do you want to give the place a bad name? Well, that's the setup, the grand lady, all vinegar and ice water, ready to give two barrels worth of dressing down to the lout, but before she'd time to get into her terah I was in like a flash. "Miss Saville, have you any complaints about my work?" I said.

BILLY. Good, good!

MACNEIL. That threw her.

BILLY. It would, it would.

(*Again* MACNEIL *silences him with a look*.)

MACNEIL. "Or are you suggesting I've been rude to you?" "No," she admitted, she had to.

BILLY (*delighted*). You had her, oh you had her!

MACNEIL. Not yet, Billy, but I was close. "Well, if I've not been rude to you and my work's fine, what ails you, woman?"

BILLY (*impressed*). That was a bold one.

MACNEIL (*ignoring him*). And out it came, as foolish as froth, "You look at me." "I do what?" I said. "You look at me all the time—whenever you see me, you look at me." "I look at you when you're there because you are there." "Well, it's got to stop," she says.

BILLY. She never did.

MACNEIL (*warningly*). Are you calling me a liar?

BILLY. No, of course not, I'm only enjoying you. What happened next?

MACNEIL. "I want to make myself clear," she said. "If this looking goes on, there'll be trouble." Well, I thought, in for a penny I might as well play for the bank— so I slapped her across the backside.

BILLY. You what?

MACNEIL. Not too hard, mind. (*He laughs.*) Then she let me have one right across the face so I gave her another one and left.

BILLY (*terrified*). You'll get the sack! She's an executive.

MACNEIL. I bet you say your prayers to that word. Billy, she's a woman—a damn fine one but only a woman. Anyway it's only her word against mine, and I don't tell lies, do I, Billy?

BILLY. She'll have you up in front of them.

MACNEIL. Who?

BILLY. All of them—the big fellas. You can't go around slapping executives' bottoms—it's tampering with authority—it's anarchy.

MACNEIL. I'd have called it maintaining mutual respect between a skilled craftsman and an officious female administrator. Anyway, she'll not report. It was too hard for frivolity and not hard enough for industrial unrest—apart from the fact she enjoyed it.

BILLY. Aye, but you don't know that. (MACNEIL *gives him a knowing look*.)

MACNEIL. Want to take a bet? (*He finishes his drink*.) Away up to the bar and get us a couple of refills.

(BILLY *takes the pound he is offered and scampers off leaving* MACNEIL *smiling to himself, with distinct satisfaction.* MISS SAVILLE *stands before him. She is in her late twenties, very attractive although at the moment she is nervous and unsure, a woman alone in a bar reserved for men*.)

MACNEIL. Miss Saville. Were you looking for me?

MISS SAVILLE (*impatiently*). I most certainly was.

(MACNEIL *makes no attempt to rise*.)

MACNEIL (*lazily*). Well, I'm here. (*He goes no further*.)

MISS SAVILLE. I think we should talk.

MACNEIL. No doubt, but I'm in company.

MISS SAVILLE. We could go into the lounge bar . . .

MACNEIL (*cutting in*). I prefer it here.

MISS SAVILLE. I see—well—I've got to talk to you.

MACNEIL (*playing with her*). Have we something to say? And before you climb up on the back of your status, I've finished for the day, I'm my own man.

MISS SAVILLE. You resent me because I'm a woman, don't you, MacNeil?

MACNEIL. I'm delighted you're a woman and I don't intend to let you forget it— mind, I've a few reservations when you start trying too hard to prove you're my boss.

MISS SAVILLE (*simply*). I am your immediate boss.

MACNEIL. What kind of a boss, an immediate boss, is it that objects to his workers looking at him?

MISS SAVILLE (*impatiently*). Oh, you know what I mean, MacNeil.

MACNEIL. Look, I'm a master carpenter and there isn't a man on the job, bosses included, that doesn't call me "Mister MacNeil" and when you call me MacNeil you're making me a plain man again so I decided you're a plain woman and I look at you. Will you have a drink?

MISS SAVILLE. Alright.

(MACNEIL *turns away and calls over to*

BILLY *at the bar.*)

MACNEIL. Billy—a gin and tonic—send 'em over and you stay where you are, do you hear me?

BILLY. I hear you.

(MACNEIL *turns back to* MISS SAVILLE *who is still standing.*)

MACNEIL. Are you not sitting down then?

MISS SAVILLE. You're not a married man?

MACNEIL (*amused*). If you'd read my file right the way through you'd have seen I was a widower with a wee daughter.

MISS SAVILLE. I'm sorry.

MACNEIL. You needn't be—my daughter's healthy, she lacks for nothing and the wife was no good, she'd run away with another man before she died. She was no loss to me—of course, that's not in the file.

MISS SAVILLE. I haven't been looking in your file, I was judging by your manners.

(MACNEIL *grins.*)

MACNEIL. Here's your drink.

(*One of the barmaids brings the drinks and he picks up the change.*)

MACNEIL. Now, Miss Saville, I promise not to hit out if you promise to . . .

MISS SAVILLE. You struck me.

MACNEIL. You've a pretty useful right there yourself but I'm prepared to let bygones be bygones.

MISS SAVILLE. Big of you.

MACNEIL (*enjoying himself*). I was always generous.

MISS SAVILLE. You're an arrogant man for a tradesman.

MACNEIL. It's because I have a trade I'm arrogant. (*He looks at her.*) I'll tell you how to humble me for nothing. You bring me a mortice or a dovetailed joint that's botched or show me a job where I've wasted so much as half a plank of timber and I'll give you the whip myself to crack over me, do you understand? Fellas like me—master carpenters—are hard to come by, we're the last of the good wine. Your sort—executives, male, female or neuter —you can get by the dozen at any cut-price shop and still have change out of a pound. If I work you can see the results, pick it up, use it. You see, Miss Saville, as long as I've got my tools I can earn my porridge.

MISS SAVILLE. Is that what's meant by the dignity of labor?

MACNEIL. I neither know nor care—just respect me and my function and we'll get on fine.

MISS SAVILLE. Alright, Mister MacNeil. (*He grins at her.*)

MACNEIL. That's my lassie . . . I'll miss looking at you though.

MISS SAVILLE. Do you have to stop?

MACNEIL (*confidingly*). As a matter of fact I didn't intend to, I'll just have to use a wee bit more discretion.

MISS SAVILLE. Let's shake hands on that. (*She extends her hand.*)

MACNEIL. I was brought up to believe shaking hands was only for tinkers. (MISS SAVILLE *starts to withdraw her hand*, MAC-NEIL *takes it.*) But I'm sure I was wrong. (*He is holding her hand but he doesn't shake it. Simply holds it too long before releasing it.*)

MISS SAVILLE. You know you embarrass me, don't you?

MACNEIL. Do I now?

MISS SAVILLE (*quietly*). I'm quite free.

MACNEIL. Good.

MISS SAVILLE. I'm going home now. (*She gets up.*) I think we understand each other.

(*She is very self-conscious.*)

MACNEIL. I think so and I'm glad.

MISS SAVILLE (*strained*). Come round and see me.

MACNEIL. Yes, I'll have to go and change first.

MISS SAVILLE. I'm not sure I like you.

MACNEIL (*gently*). There's nothing in the book says you have to. We can talk.

MISS SAVILLE. I'm not used to this sort of thing.

MACNEIL. Of course you're not.

MISS SAVILLE. You are, though?

MACNEIL. That way you're hurting yourself. Is that what you want?

MISS SAVILLE. No. Here's the address. (*She gives him a card.*) You don't have to come.

MACNEIL. I know.

MISS SAVILLE. Well, I am making a fool of myself, aren't I?

(*She stands indecisively for a moment then goes hurriedly out of the bar.* MAC-NEIL *smiles before getting up and returning to the bar with the empty glasses.* BILLY *is bursting with curiosity and the* SECOND BARMAID *is hanging on to the fringe of the conversation.*)

BILLY. Has she gone?

(MACNEIL *looks around the barroom and examines it. He then turns back to* BILLY.)

MACNEIL. You're very observant.

(*He solemnly winks at* BILLY *who sniggers heartily.* MACNEIL *joins in with a big laugh. The* SECOND BARMAID *can't help but smile at him. The other barmaid sees this and moves toward them. She is the girl that* MACNEIL *exchanged looks with on his arrival in the pub. The other barmaid moves away.*)

FIRST BARMAID (*overcasually*). You off then?

MACNEIL. I am.

FIRST BARMAID. Suppose I'll see you usual time, will I?

MACNEIL (*pleasantly*). Not tonight you won't.

FIRST BARMAID. What you mean—you nodded when you first come in.

MACNEIL. Something came up.

FIRST BARMAID. Yeah and I saw her.

MACNEIL (*coolly*). Watch your mouth.

FIRST BARMAID. If you think you're going to play me up, mate, you're over.

(MACNEIL *looks at her before speaking, with a sigh.*)

MACNEIL. Well, it was a fair run.

FIRST BARMAID (*sharply*). What you mean?

MACNEIL. You said it was over.

FIRST BARMAID. Well, I didn't mean it, I meant . . .

MACNEIL (*firmly*). Then think before you speak, dearie, it stops misunderstandings.

FIRST BARMAID. I'm sorry . . . tomorrow night?

MACNEIL. We'll see.

(*She is about to answer but bites her tongue knowing she can't win.*)

MACNEIL. I'm away. Mary will be waiting . . . my daughter.

FIRST BARMAID. Oh, yeah. (*as he goes*) Give her my love.

MACNEIL. Goodnight, Billy.

(*And looking to neither left or right he goes as he came—single-mindedly.*)

SECOND BARMAID. That big fella got a little girl then?

BILLY. He has.

SECOND BARMAID. Don't have a married look though, does he?

FIRST BARMAID (*sharply*). He isn't married, he's a widower.

SECOND BARMAID. Pity for the little girl —how old's she then?

FIRST BARMAID. Eight or nine, little like.

BILLY (*slyly*). What? She'll have twenty candles on her next cake.

FIRST BARMAID (*spluttering*). But . . . he told me . . . the lying pig!

SECOND BARMAID. I know, gel, I fancy him, too.

(*She and* BILLY *both laugh at the* FIRST BARMAID'S *discomfort.*)

FIRST BARMAID. The rotten liar!

The stairway of a house that is let in separate flats. Night.

A middle-aged woman is coming down the stairs. The front door at the foot of the stairs opens and MACNEIL *enters and starts to mount the stairs. The woman is back-lit and her own shadow obscures her face,* MACNEIL *couldn't possibly distinguish her face.* MACNEIL *stands aside to let her pass. She inclines her head away as she passes him.*

WOMAN. Thank you . . . Mr. MacNeil.

(MACNEIL *makes a slight movement to try and identify her but she already has her back to him.*)

MACNEIL. Not at all . . . Mrs. . . . .

(*He thinks no more about it and resumes his way to his flat. He opens the door and goes in.*)

Hallway/bedroom

The flat consists of a hallway, bathroom, two bedrooms, and a kitchen/living room. As he enters, MACNEIL *calls out. He is in high spirits.*

MACNEIL. Mary, are you there?

(*We see* MARY, *his daughter, sitting in her bedroom in front of her dressing table. On the table is a jumble of photographs, letters, and jewelry. She hears him but doesn't answer.*)

MACNEIL. Are you home, Mary?

MARY. Yes, Father.

MACNEIL. I'll wash before I eat.

(*There is again no answer.*)

MACNEIL (*slightly impatiently*) Did you hear me, Mary, I'll wash before I eat.

MARY. I heard.

MACNEIL (*goodhumoredly*). Well, answer when I talk to you, good girl.

Bathroom/Bedroom
(*He goes into the bathroom stripping off his shirt as he goes.*)
(MARY *is sitting motionless in front of her mirror. We hear the sound of running water.*)
(*Cut back to* MACNEIL)
MACNEIL. Did you have a good day?
(*Cut back to* MARY. *A spasm of violence twitches on her face but it doesn't come to anything.*)
MARY. Pretty usual.
(*Cut back to* MACNEIL.)
MACNEIL (*drying himself*). Well, you can't complain about that, can you?
MARY (*voice off*). I wasn't complaining.
MACNEIL (*laughing*). I didn't say you were, I said you couldn't. Did I not teach you to listen and answer accordingly? Is there a clean shirt for me?
(*Cut back to* MARY.)
MARY. Are you going out?
(*Cut back to* MACNEIL).
MACNEIL. You don't answer a question with a question, girl, that's for tinkers. (*He grins at himself in the bathroom mirror then says quietly:*) Isn't that right, Miss Saville? (*aloud*) Have I a clean shirt?
(*Cut to* MARY.)
MARY. It's on the sideboard.
MACNEIL (*voice off*). Well, get it for me, good girl.
(*She picks up a photograph from the pile.*)
MARY. It's on the sideboard.
MACNEIL (*voice off, insistently*). I heard you . . . bring it to me.
Living room/bathroom
(MARY *sighs and rises, she leaves her room, photo in hand, and goes into the living room/kitchen and takes a freshly ironed shirt from the sideboard and carries it to* MACNEIL *who is standing in the bathroom doorway.*)
MARY. Why couldn't you get it yourself?
MACNEIL. Oh, I could have done but I like being spoilt by pretty women.
(*He expects this to be taken as a joke but* MARY *says nothing and goes, leaving* MACNEIL *vaguely puzzled. He puts on the clean shirt and goes into the living room. The table is laid for one.* MARY *is taking his meal from the oven.* MACNEIL *sits at the table.*)

MACNEIL. Is there a new woman in the house?
MARY. I don't know.
MACNEIL. I passed a woman on the stairs, she used my name.
(MARY *sits down opposite him.*)
MARY (*carefully*). What was she like?
MACNEIL. I didn't get the proper look at her . . . she knew my name though . . . what's that in your hand?
(MARY *puts the photograph in her dress pocket.*)
MARY. A photograph.
MACNEIL. I could see that but what is it?
MARY. A photograph of my mother.
MACNEIL. Oh.
(*He addresses himself to his meal.*)
MACNEIL. Have you eaten?
MARY. Yes. She was very pretty.
MACNEIL. I'm going out tonight.
MARY. You usually do.
(*He ignores this.*)
MACNEIL (*indicating the dinner.*) This is good.
MARY. Thank you.
MACNEIL. Is there anything the matter?
MARY. Should there be?
MACNEIL. I told you, don't answer questions with questions. Is there something up with you?
MARY. No, no, nothing.
MACNEIL. Well, you'd not know it from here, you've a face like an open grave, take a look at yourself in the mirror.
MARY. I have been doing.
MACNEIL. Well . . . what did you see?
MARY. Me . . . and someone else.
(MACNEIL *looks at her coldly.*)
MACNEIL. You don't look like her.
MARY (*deliberately*). Who?
MACNEIL (*quietly*). Don't play swords with your father—you're a MacNeil like me.
MARY. I'm a girl like her.
MACNEIL. No, you're a good girl, you're nothing like the dead woman.
(MARY *flinches.*)
MACNEIL (*unrelenting*). You started this. That's all she is to me—the dead woman. I'm not going to let you kid yourself into believing she was some sort of misunderstood Sunday school teacher, all honey and talcum powder, because that mare wouldn't measure up for it.
MARY. How did you know when she

died?

MACNEIL (*sharply*). Are you out to give me indigestion. (*He pushes his plate away.*) I heard, I read it in a paper, she died, I was told—anything—I don't remember, alright?

MARY. Didn't you ever love her?

MACNEIL. I may have done but it's a long time ago and I was young.

MARY. She was younger . . .

MACNEIL. A nineteen-year-old girl from where she came was a woman, I was still a boy.

MARY. Did you ever love her?

MACNEIL. I could have gone on to a college—been an engineer. I became a husband and a father, isn't that enough for you?

MARY. I only want to know if you ever loved her?

MACNEIL. I've loved you all your life.

MARY. Have you?

MACNEIL. That's a daft question. I've fed you, looked after you and told you what to do, what else is there? I never raised my hand to you, did I?

MARY. Is that love?

MACNEIL. Well, until you get a man of your own that's all you're entitled to. Look, good girl, I'm not the man to go flinging love about all the time but I love you as best I can, maybe you went short of a mother, well, you'll have to take my word for it, you were better off without one.

(*He crosses to the door and exits to his bedroom to clean his shoes.*)

MARY (*goes to his bedroom door; quietly*) Who are you going out with to-night?

MACNEIL. A friend.

MARY. Billy?

MACNEIL. No, not Billy, what's it got to do with you anyway?

MARY. I just wanted to know.

MACNEIL. Well, if you must know it's one of the bosses—Mr. Saville. It's a private job on my own time.

MARY. I don't know Mr. Saville.

MACNEIL. He's a new chap—nice fella, we get on fine.

MARY. And you're wearing your suit?

MACNEIL. Yes, I am, why?

MARY (*deliberately*). The one you wear for women?

MACNEIL. What did you say?

MARY. The one that smells of scent.

MACNEIL. That'll be all, Miss.

MARY. I'll get it out.

MACNEIL. You'll not.

MARY. Why not?

MACNEIL. Because I said so.

MARY. Mr. Saville is Miss Saville.

MACNEIL. I see.

MARY. She phoned up just before you came in.

MACNEIL. Did she leave a message?

MARY. No, just her name.

MACNEIL. Well, I didn't want to bother you.

MARY. It didn't.

MACNEIL. That's part of a man's life that's nothing to do with his daughter.

MARY. A secret?

MACNEIL. No—but—

MARY. What?

MACNEIL. You'll have to take my word for it.

MARY. I don't know if I can take your word for things anymore.

MACNEIL. Are you calling me a liar?

MARY. I don't know—I don't know anything anymore.

(MARY *goes to living room to clear away meal.*)

MACNEIL (*following her*). Is all this because some woman phoned up?

MARY. She sounded upset.

MACNEIL. What did she say?

MARY. Nothing much, I think it was costing her a great deal to phone you, that's all.

(MARY *goes to kitchen.*)

MACNEIL (*following her*). No doubt she's a foolish woman.

MARY. Like my mother?

MACNEIL. No.

MARY. Like me.

MACNEIL. No—she's just a foolish woman who needs to be taught a lesson; you're my daughter, I hope you've more sense.

MARY. The lady you met on the stairs . . .

MACNEIL. Yes . . . well, what about her?

MARY. She said she was my aunt.

MACNEIL. What name did she give?

MARY. Sara Hellings.

MACNEIL. That'ud be her. Well, you needn't believe a word she said, she owes me a spite.

MARY. She's been looking for me.

MACNEIL. Why?

MARY. My mother died, *really* died, last month.

MACNEIL (*impatiently*). Oh, aye, what did she say?

MARY. What's the point of repeating it if it's all lies?

MACNEIL. I'd like to hear it all the same.

MARY. So you'd know just how much she told me?

MACNEIL (*blustering*). You believed her, didn't you? A woman you met for the first time in your life but you'd believe her before your own father!

MARY (*coolly*). I haven't believed you for years.

MACNEIL. What?

MARY. You've been telling me lies about your women—lies that I knew were lies, I mean—since I was thirteen.

MACNEIL. I don't believe you.

MARY. And it's been consistent.

MACNEIL. It has not.

MARY. "Mr." Saville?

MACNEIL. That wasn't important.

MARY. None of them were 'cos I knew the truth all the time.

MACNEIL. How?

MARY. You're not much good at it. Anyway, all the girls at school told me about you.

MACNEIL. What about me?

MARY. They said, "Where was your dad last night then, Mary?" I'd say, working late, at so and so, they'd all laugh and say, "He was working late in the back row of the Roxy." I laughed too, well, it was the only way to stop them.

MACNEIL. I'm entitled to go about with women.

MARY. Yes, but you lie about it. Why?

MACNEIL. Because you were a young girl and I thought it better you shouldn't know, maybe it was wrong.

MARY. It was.

MACNEIL. Well, it got into a habit.

MARY. Are you ashamed of it—the way you carry on?

MACNEIL. I'll not be questioned by you, Mary.

MARY. Why not? When I go out with a boy you give both of us the third degree.

MACNEIL. That's different.

MARY. How?

MACNEIL. I know about boys.

MARY. I'd have said you know about boys who were like yourself. You were a bad boy, weren't you?

MACNEIL. I was not.

MARY. Sara says you were.

MACNEIL. She'd say anything to get even with me.

MARY. Why would she do that?

MACNEIL. Use your brains, is it likely she'd be on my side?

MARY. Sara said you were both from the same village.

MACNEIL. I never said otherwise.

MARY. You implied otherwise, you always said her people were rubbish.

MACNEIL (*coldly*). Did I say that?

MARY. Their father was a doctor with a large house.

MACNEIL (*indifferently*). A drunkard.

MARY. But a doctor.

MACNEIL. Aye, if you want it that way.

MARY. Well, it's a bit different from the slum you said she came from and my grandfather, the drunkard, is still alive and still the local doctor. She said . . .

(*She pauses.*)

MACNEIL (*lazily*). She said what? Go on . . .

MARY. No. You tell me.

MACNEIL. She told you I was born in a ditch tent by the side of the road. I was a tinker's bairn, not too sure who my father was and not much bothered. I could barely read and just about sign my name and she and your mother used to lend me books and read to me on the cairnside. I paid them back by giving the "nicest" one a baby so we had to marry. I was a fancy man so your mother left me. I wouldn't let them keep you and before they could stop me, shanked it to England and became a master carpenter. Is there anything I left out?

MARY. Yes. My mother loved you.

MACNEIL. I never noticed.

MARY. You never noticed!

MACNEIL. You don't know anything about where I came out of and I never wanted to explain to my own daughter, I preferred what you called lies, I'm a tinker still.

MARY. But you tell lies about everything.

MACNEIL. Is that a fact?

MARY. I didn't mind about the women— you're right, it didn't matter because I didn't really know what it meant, besides, the girls all thought you were a dish and I liked that. But up till now I never realized you tell lies all the time and about the really important things, not just the trifles.

MACNEIL. You're talking like a fool.

MARY. Yes, you made a *fool* out of me, a mug, a muggins, a charley. You got me to believe my mother was an evil slut from a problem family who ran off and left her husband and child, and it wasn't true. Nothing ever has been between you and me. You've never told me the truth once, have you?

(MARY *runs to her bedroom, sobbing.*)

MACNEIL (*goes to her*). You're taking it too seriously. I told you what was fitting for a child. Look, you don't always tell women the truth, they'd never understand it, but if that's what you want—if that's what you think you want—you shall have it from now on—alright?

MARY. I don't trust you anymore.

MACNEIL. It'll be different from now on. (*He gives her a hug of reassurance and smiles at her.*) You'll see.

(*He goes out of the bedroom, closing the door behind him.* MARY *is left alone. She crosses to the door, opens it and makes for the living room.*)

Hall

(*As she goes she hears* MACNEIL'*s voice, quietly on the telephone. His voice is persuasive and gentle, he is unaware he is being overheard.*)

MACNEIL. I'm sorry but I'll be a bit late —what?—oh, no, my wee girl's had an accident—sprained her ankle on the stairs —oh, no, just a twist but it's swollen up— anyway I've seen to her—a doctor?—No, I didn't need a doctor—I bandaged it myself—oh, she trusts her daddy and he knows how to handle her.

(MARY *is leaning against the wall crying to herself.*)

MARY. Liar, liar, liar, liar, liar, . . .

(*As* MACNEIL'*s voice drones on soothingly*)

FADE

PART TWO

CORNY

FRED   MARY MACNEIL
CORNELIUS DOOLEY   SALLY

SCENE. *An office in a modern block. Day.*

It is a large room for draftsmen. Long— well-lit, big windows, low shaded lights over the slanting drawing boards. By the door is a unit for two men, further back is a much larger unit with several people busily working on their drawing boards.

Two men are working at the smaller unit. During the scene, now and again, they remember there are other people in the room and lower their voices accordingly. FRED, *tall and skinny, is obviously preoccupied with a problem and he keeps on looking at the other young man,* CORNELIUS DOOLEY, *a tall fair man who is absorbed in what he is doing, i.e., reading through some papers and making notes in a small book. They are both Londoners. After a moment* FRED *speaks.*

———

FRED. Corny.

CORNY (*without looking up*). No.

FRED. But, Corny . . .

CORNY. No, Fred, and don't call me Corny—you only call me Corny like that when you want a favor.

FRED. You don't know what you're missing.

CORNY. That's good, it won't bleed then, will it?

FRED. Where's your sense of adventure?

CORNY (*happily*). Lying dead doggo, I'm pleased to say.

FRED. Of course, it doesn't matter that she's a touch gorgeous, does it?

CORNY. Well, apart from the fact I'm truly glad for her—not a mouse's eyelid.

FRED. Don't just take my word, ask anyone.

CORNY. Well, she's certainly mudded your waters, I'll say that for her—what was her name again—Harold?

FRED. It's Mary—Mary MacNeil and she's all coolness and starched linen.

CORNY. Honest, you haven't been the same since you came out of that hospital.

FRED. What's that mean?

CORNY. Look at you, it's nurses, nurses all the way with you now.

FRED. No—she's very fresh looking, that's all.

CORNY. Pass us the swab and surgical spirit, Matron.

FRED. She's a typist and why you knocking her? You haven't even seen her.

CORNY. No, but I've got a feeling.

FRED. Your woman's intuition acting up again?

CORNY. You could say that but *I'd* have said it was more like an ingrowing nail on me gouty big toe. Hold that—half of us are working to help stabilize the pound sterling in spite of the dronelike resistance of the other half.

FRED. Flowery this morning, aren't we?

CORNY. I'm a martyr to English literature, it's me Irish blood.

(*There is a pause while* CORNY *works on and* FRED *watches.*)

FRED. You'd like her.

CORNY. I'd hate her.

FRED. And of course you'd be doing me a great favor.

CORNY (*looks up at him*). Well, go on.

FRED. What?

CORNY. You've tried "Corny" (*he whines it*)—isn't it about time we had your lovable cockney bit, you know, where you call me "me old darling."

FRED. And I thought we were mates.

CORNY. We are but you're such an emotional liberty taker. You've got a bit of trouble and you want to dump her right in my lap.

FRED. Just go and look at her.

CORNY. Fred—I've got enough bother of my own without invoicing for some of yours. I've been overstaffed with she all through a long hard winter so I'm lying fallow for a season, so I don't need anymore of your dropouts.

FRED. You could make room for a little 'un.

CORNY (*firmly*). No, they're money and time and I need both for spiritual and financial restocking. You weed your own garden.

FRED (*gloomily*). I started with her by accident—lent her me penknife to sharpen her pencil.

CORNY. You're still a boy scout underneath it all, aren't you? Got her in your tent yet?

FRED. Oh—there's nothing like that—I'm not in that deep—but she's bound to find out I'm married, she's that sort of girl (*hastily*). But lovable.

CORNY. Oh, yeah—dead lovable.

FRED. No, I thought I'd be doing you a favor—row you in, sort of thing.

CORNY. While you drift off on the ebb tide back to the marital harbor, leaving me holding two oars and a rowlock—you're very brassy for a husband, aren't you?

FRED. Well, it was an idea.

CORNY. Well, I promise you it won't be catching on around here.

(*There is a pause while* CORNY *resumes work.*)

FRED. But what am I going to do?

CORNY. Cut your throat.

FRED. I've got dependents.

CORNY. Of course you have and you had 'em when you were lending that penknife, didn't you?

FRED. Yeah, but . . .

CORNY. You know what you are, don't you?—a sexual opportunist.

FRED. Steady.

CORNY. What? Look, mate, I'll tell you about your pattern, shall I? A girl comes to you and legitimately asks you to fill her in on the basic principles of algebra and straight off you mentally strip her to the buff. A lady policeman asks you for your driver's license and quick as a trombone slide you say, "Hang about, darling, fancy a coffee and a cuddle?" You've no control, and look at you, scrawny, spotty, and the dandruff's heavy underfoot on your collar even on your better days but you can't see a woman without trying, can you?

FRED. I'm game, that's all.

CORNY. Game—you're match point, mate!

FRED. What's that mean?

CORNY. I dunno, but it sounds right.

FRED (*moodily*). I crave affection.

CORNY. You what?

FRED (*doubtfully*). I crave affection . . . don't I?

CORNY. Well, that's one way of putting it. I'd have said you were getting into training to be a dirty old man. Don't you know once you're married you're supposed to pack all that in?

FRED. All what in?

CORNY. Tomcatting — nannygoating — chasing nasty—all of it— what's the matter with your old woman anyway—she frigid or something?

FRED. 'Course not—she's got thin blood, that's all.

CORNY. Well, yours must be as thick as clotted cream, mate. Listen, Freddy, how many times in the last year have I got you down the creek?

FRED (*cautiously*). Not that many.

CORNY. What? How about that supervisor from the packing department?

FRED. You liked her.

CORNY. Yeah, but you forgot to tell me about her brother, the homicidal maniac, who was kinky for hatchets.

FRED (*lamely*). Well . . .

CORNY. And then there was that weeper in accounts with all that bad dialogue and climbing roses. I had hay fever for weeks. And how about that Indian student—Miss Sari, the Bombay duck.

FRED. I thought you liked curries.

CORNY. Yeah, but not for breakfast, it's a horrible way to start the day. No, my old son, one way and another you've given me a pretty rough passage over the past few months and enough's as good as a . . .

(*He searches for the word.*)

FRED (*obligingly*). A feast?

CORNY. None of them has been exactly a feast, more your sort of prepacked snack —the meat curling in its own congealed gravy and now you're only offering me a little haggis—well, I'm on a diet.

FRED. A haggis?

CORNY. Well, Mary MacNeil don't sound any too kosher to me.

FRED. Look, I told you she was Scotch but it doesn't show.

CORNY. No bagpipes hanging on her sporran, eh?

FRED. No. She sounds just like me and you.

CORNY. Oh, another illiterate.

FRED. No, but she hasn't got an accent or anything.

CORNY. How's she on warts?

FRED. What warts?

CORNY. Or is it blackheads and acne she goes in for?

FRED. No, she's lovely, I told you.

CORNY. Yeah, but what's her drawback 'cos I know she's got one. Is she a kleptomaniac or has she got marriage on her mind?

FRED. She's as honest as the day is long.

CORNY (*it comes in a flash to him*). Hello, you've only proposed to her, haven't you?

FRED. I have not.

CORNY. You've been looking at rings in jewelers' windows again, haven't you?

FRED (*guiltily*). Well . . .

CORNY (*triumphantly*). I knew it! You're just like my mum, you are, you love the idea of marriage. She stands outside a different church every Saturday— she's morbid about it, just like you.

FRED. I respect marriage.

CORNY. Well, why don't you start respecting your own then?

FRED. I do.

CORNY. Is that why you're always proposing to any stray wiggle that passes by? Listen, son, you've got to come to terms with the fact you're already married and you're not a Muslim.

FRED. I get carried away.

CORNY. You will be, mate, in a dirty great police van, 'cos they don't half lock you up for it.

FRED. What?

CORNY. Bigamy.

FRED. But that's why I need your help.

CORNY. Alright, you nasty thing, you. But this is the last time—final—finale— finito—got it?

FRED (*meekly*). Yes, Corny.

CORNY. And don't call me Corny!

FRED. Yes, Cornelius.

CORNY. That's better. (*looks at watch*) 'Ere coffee time. I'm having it away to the canteen.

FRED. Good. She's meeting us there.

CORNY. You're a right brass-faced article you are.

FRED. Why? I knew you'd stand by me in the death.

CORNY. Well, this is your funeral, son, this is the last time.

FRED (*hastily*). Of course.

CORNY. Never again.

FRED. Never.

CORNY. Oh, I give up.

Canteen

We see a queue of people waiting for coffee. FRED *and* CORNY *enter. They look toward* MARY.

FRED. There she is.

(*They move to* MARY.)

FRED. Hello, Mary.

MARY. Hello, Fred.

FRED. This is Mr. Dooley—Cornelius, the one I told you about.

MARY. Oh, yes, how are you, Mr. Dooley?

CORNY. How can I complain, I've just met you.

(MARY *gives him an amused but pained look.*)

CORNY. I'll do better next time around —Miss MacCloud.

MARY (*correcting*). MacNeil.

CORNY. Well, I was only a clan or two out, wasn't I?

FRED. I'll slip along and get the coffee.

CORNY. No, let me.

FRED. I'll get 'em.

(*And he disappears so rapidly that* MARY *and* CORNY *have to laugh.*)

CORNY. He was always a bit of a slow-coach was our Fred.

MARY (*amused*). I'd never noticed.

CORNY. Well now, where are you in this vast complex, Miss MacGregor?

MARY. One floor down and the name's MacCloud.

CORNY. It's MacNeil and you're from the incubator, aren't you?

MARY. The incubator? Oh, yeah . . .

MARY. ⎫
⎬ Where all the chicks are.
CORNY. ⎭

MARY. I see, well, don't mess about, when are you going to start?

CORNY. Start what?

MARY. The process.

CORNY. What process?

MARY. Where you wean me away from Fred and get me hung up on you and all that.

CORNY. What are you on about?

MARY. The dreaded Dooley devastator, you turn on the irresistible charm, I wilt for you, forgetting happily all about old Fred.

CORNY (*innocently*). Who's Fred?

MARY (*approvingly*). I like that—then you romance me for a couple of weeks until one night we have this adult conver-

sation about the impracticability of our relationship and with a few gentle, suave regrets from you I'm out on my ear.

CORNY. It's a lovely ear, mind.

MARY. That is the usual ploy, isn't it?

CORNY. It's a pleasure to do business with an educated gel, I always say, and I must admit I've been getting into a fair old rut lately, but there's been a terrible sameness in the material I've been supplied with and the situation—Fred wheels 'em in, I wheel 'em out . . .

MARY. Monotonous really.

CORNY. Dead humdrum but you seem to hint at something a little more offbeat . . . like originality and a fresh approach to those rusty old sex-mechanics.

MARY. I think you're tired of the staked-out lambs that Fred provides—your jaded palate needs the titillation of a challenge.

CORNY. That's the language to bring on a Dooley. I take it you don't give a monkey's toss about Fred?

MARY. He's pathetic.

CORNY. That can be an aphrodisiac to some ladies.

MARY. He's married.

CORNY. Lots of girls climb on the "other people's husbands" syndrome nowadays.

MARY (*primly*). I'm Scots and much too perceptive for that caper.

CORNY. But you've been out with him.

MARY. A girl must eat.

CORNY. Naughty.

MARY. Not at all, we only had lunch, I never compromised myself by so much as an evening meal.

CORNY. I wondered why old Fred has been giving the lunchtime pub a miss lately.

MARY. Who's Fred?

CORNY. You move well . . . but if it wasn't Fred in the first place, how do I arrive in the second place?

MARY. Oh, simple, it's you I'm after.

CORNY (*surprised*). Oh.

MARY. Well, I think I am—we'll have to wait and see though.

(CORNY *is more than a little surprised at this but before anything else can happen* FRED *enters with a tray of coffee and biscuits.*)

FRED. Well, here we are, anyone want a bite?

(*He proffers the plate of biscuits.* MARY

smiles at CORNY *who is still suffering from mild shock.*)

CORNY. You know, I rather think I've been bitten already.

(MARY *and* CORNY *smile at each other, much to* FRED's *mystification.*)

CORNY's *living room. Night.*

MARY *is seated at one end of the settee* —CORNY, *furious, right at the other end.*

MARY (*primly*). Well, alright, you can if you want to.

CORNY. Don't put yourself out, I'll manage.

MARY (*amused*). Don't be silly.

CORNY. I don't want to anymore—suddenly, I don't want to anymore.

MARY. You were pretty worked up a moment ago.

CORNY (*airily*). I could take it or leave it alone—I was in complete control.

MARY. Your hands weren't.

CORNY. Oh, them, well, they lead a life of their own, I'm glad to say—(*He looks down at his hands.*) Good old hands.

MARY. Horrid old hands.

CORNY. Oh, do leave off—it was only a bijou cuddle and you're coming on like it was the steamier part of the Kama-Sutra.

MARY. I don't like being mauled.

CORNY. Well, you haven't got much to look forward to then, have you?

MARY. We were having a nice comfy talk . . .

CORNY. I'm a martyr to your comfy talks.

MARY (*continuing*). . . . but you had to spoil it by . . .

CORNY. By what? I put my lousy arm round you, gave you a lousy tentative squeeze and closed in a lousy bit and you're making out it was the first three moves in the unarmed combat manual.

MARY. I don't like being rushed.

CORNY (*in despair*). Three weeks I've been at it and she talks about being rushed —I suppose you'd call a five-year engagement a whirlwind romance?

MARY. If we were engaged it would be different.

CORNY. Oh, I've heard about Scotch caution but we're in the right doldrums here.

MARY. Well, I've kissed you.

CORNY (*indignantly*). When? When? Go on, tell me when?

MARY. Every time we say good-night.

CORNY (*bitterly*). Oh, that stab with those two ribbons of ice you call lips is a kiss, is it? Well, south of the border we call that frostbite.

MARY. I'm sorry.

CORNY. Don't be, it's *you* I should be sorry for 'cos if you really think that was a kiss you were dishing out, you're living in a kid's dream world where mud pies are tutti-frutti ice cream.

MARY. Well, you're the expert—what do you mean by a kiss?

CORNY. Well, first of all you've got to *mean* it and it's certainly not that frozen chicken peck you've perfected, I can tell you.

MARY. Go on.

CORNY. You don't want to hear.

MARY. But I do, I love expertise.

CORNY. And in your case that "tease" is very important. Alright, you're sitting together, you turn to each other and melt into each other's arms, got it? (MARY *nods.*) Your faces are very close.

MARY. How about your noses?

CORNY. Don't worry about noses, in my experience they can look after themselves —not many people with broken noses got 'em from kissing—anyway, you close your eyes . . .

MARY. Why?

CORNY (*long-suffering*). Anyone who's got to ask why at that stage of the game should be disqualified for life. You'll just have to put it down to me and take my word for it—where was I?

MARY. Melting with closed eyes.

CORNY. Oh, yeah, that sounds like it— well, your lips get caught up together and you press gently—no pecking and . . . (*He breaks off sadly.*) . . . and have you ever tried to describe the ocean to a blind man?

MARY. How do you mean?

CORNY. I don't think it's your sort of exercise somehow. No, when it comes to kissing I think you're tone-deaf.

MARY. But I can be fond of you without kissing—what's so important about kissing?

CORNY. It's a token,
a gesture,
it's a vote of confidence,
it's a latchkey,

it's better than rubbing noses
and less painful than thumping
    you
over the head with a club.
It's a reassurance,
it does you good,
it's a tonic,
it's private but millions of people
are doing it right now and they
    don't
tax it—yet.
It's kind,
it's hello,
it's good-bye,
it's peace,
it's "here we go again,"
it's natural,
it's people,
and it's what I like doing 'cos it
don't half beat the egg and
    spoon race . . .
    . . . Any questions?

MARY. What time is it?

CORNY. It's bound to be time for you to go.

MARY (*rising*). I rather think it is, I'm afraid, and I was so enjoying your company.

CORNY (*rising*). I'll see you home.

MARY. Thank you.

CORNY. But only on one condition.

MARY (*primly*). What's that, Cornelius?

CORNY. You promise not to glacial scrape me with your lips when we say goodnight?

MARY. Silly boy.

(*She turns on her heels and daintily leaves the room.* CORNY *calls after her.*)

CORNY. I'll just get half a gallon of antifreeze out of the pantry to be on the safe side.

(*He follows after her miserably.*)

Lunchtime. City pub. Day.
The pub is old-fashioned with various sections partitioned off from each other. CORNY *and* FRED *are seated on high stools in their partition, beer in front of them.* FRED *is steadily demolishing sandwiches, potato crisps, etc . . . He eats all the way through the scene.* CORNY *is moodily toying with his beer glass. After a pause he listlessly turns to* FRED.

CORNY. Well, what am I going to do?

FRED (*munching*). I don't know.

CORNY (*impatiently*). No, don't mess us about, what am I going to do?

FRED. Cut your throat.

CORNY. Don't be silly, me head'ud drop off, wouldn't it?

FRED. Well, it's a fair corker.

CORNY. A corker? Where you find your words—Boy's Own Paper—1911? She's only driving me potty, isn't she?

FRED (*amazed*). Potty?

CORNY. Blimey, you've got me at it now. What am I going to do about her?

FRED (*helpfully*). Abandon her.

CORNY. She's not the one who's sinking, mate, it's me!

FRED. You tried getting her tight?

CORNY. Yeah, I was sick.

FRED. How about, "little boy lost"?

CORNY. She didn't bother to look for me.

FRED. Big brother?

CORNY. She's an only child, isn't she?

FRED. Father figure?

CORNY. He's a hairy great clan and she doesn't even want to know him. No, she's got me over a barrel, she's laughing up her kilt.

FRED. She sounds a right mare.

CORNY. Like you didn't know already? Who got me under starter's orders in the first place? Nosher Fred, the carbohydrate king.

FRED. Well, I'm sorry, I didn't know you'd lost your touch, did I?

CORNY (*indignant*). Lost me touch! I'm up against a governor here. That kid's only a natural man cracker, she's got me by the short bootstraps, I'm a shambles, I've got the knocks and the only fella I can turn to is having it away with half a crusty loaf and two pounds of stodge and brewer's yeast. You skinny glutton, you!

(FRED *has been preoccupied during the last speech. He now grabs hold of* CORNY's *arm.*)

FRED. Shush!

CORNY. Don't tell me to . . .

(FRED *is straining to hear something.*)

FRED. Shush!

CORNY. You brass-faced article, you!

FRED (*urgently*). Listen—in the next trough!

(*They both lean against the partition and listen. We cut to the ladies' bar on the other side of the partition. We see* MARY *and a girl friend,* SALLY, *taking their seats at the counter.*)

SALLY. Well, what happened next?

MARY. He was looking all gooey-eyed and moving in for the kill, the snake.

SALLY. Yeah, I remember that look—super.

MARY. So I said, "Your hands are all sweaty, do you mind not holding mine?"

SALLY. You never!

MARY. I did.

SALLY. That must have stung.

MARY. Oh, his eyes filled with pain—it was great. He was so hurt, on anyone else you'd have felt sorry for him.

(*They both laugh.*)

(*Cut back to* CORNY *and* FRED.)

FRED. It sounds like Mary?

CORNY (*grimly*). It is, I'd know that sexual death rattle anywhere.

(CORNY *moves his bar stool against the wall and climbs up in order to look over the partition into the next booth.*)

(*Cut back to* MARY *and* SALLY.)

SALLY. You're really giving him a good going over, aren't you?

MARY. I haven't started on that snake yet but I'll have him groveling by the time I've finished.

(CORNY'S *face appears above the partition. He looks down on them balefully.*)

SALLY. Well, it was about time someone brought him down, mind, I'm glad I wasn't elected.

MARY. You'd have given in again like the first time around. No, the girls were right to choose me—someone he didn't know and wouldn't relent, 'cos when it comes to the Cornelius Dooleys of this world I'm an unrelenter of the first water.

SALLY. Why?

MARY. Let's say I was scarred at an early age, and giving him one in the eye for every girl in the building is my idea of ten out of ten.

(CORNY *disappears down into his own part of the bar.*)

FRED. How about that? The biter bit.

CORNY. No, son, she doesn't know it yet but she's just handed me the old porcelain choppers—well, this afternoon she's for the chop!

(*He grins happily to himself.*)

Office. Typists' section. Day.
(MARY *is seated at her desk typing, so*

is her friend SALLY. FRED *enters the office.*

MARY (*briefly*). Hello, Fred, what can we do for you?

FRED (*accusingly*). You might well ask.

MARY. I just did, well?

FRED (*dignified*). I've got an urgent message for you from Cornelius. He says if you could manage it, could you sneak up to the roof garden and have a word with him?

MARY. What for?

FRED. I dunno, but then he doesn't speak to me much anymore, for that matter he doesn't talk to anyone much nowadays and if you speak to him he flinches—flinches something horrible.

MARY (*coolly*). Yes?

FRED. Oh, yes, he's become a right flincher.

MARY. Tough bananas.

FRED. No, he's a changed man—no bounce, no snap, and have you noticed that fine tracery of lines round his eyes?

MARY. Not really.

FRED. Funny, they've become his prominent feature. (*He starts to go.*) Well, mustn't keep you, but if you could manage it—he would be grateful.

MARY. Just a minute, why didn't he come himself?

FRED (*at the door*). You might well ask.
(*He goes out of the office.*)

Roof garden on top of the office block. Day.

CORNY *is seated on a small bench by a little pool looking at the goldfish.*

CORNY. Cor, what a sex life just swimming over each other's eggs—you poor little sods—still, it takes all sorts.

(MARY *appears and he immediately assumes a doleful expression.*)

MARY. Ah, there you are, Cornelius.

CORNY. Yeah, or so it would appear.

(*There is a pause while he gazes at her.*)

MARY. Well, what do you want?

CORNY. Seemingly the unobtainable but I'll settle for the chance to kiss the hem of your skirt.

(*He does so.*)

MARY. Don't be silly.

CORNY (*sadly*). Yes, I suppose I must seem so to you in the full confidence of your peerless beauty.

MARY. I beg your pardon?

CORNY (*continuing*). Look at me. (*He looks into the pool.*) Pale and wan, off me provender and three quarters off me chump. Oh, you heartless jade, you. Name and address? (*reproachfully*) Miss Mary Cruelty, Rejection Manor, Lesser Lovington, Despair County.

MARY (*slightly alarmed*). What are you talking about?

CORNY. You might well ask.

MARY. Wait a minute, that's what Fred said.

CORNY. That lucky swine.

MARY. Lucky?

CORNY. Married with a little cottage full of kids out in Rickmansworth, while me? —pining away in my bachelor sty in West Kensington. (*loudly*) Oh, Mary, I can't stand it any longer!

(*He flops on his knees in front of her much to her embarrassment.*)

MARY. Get up this minute!

CORNY (*kissing her hem*). You proud temptress, can't you see I love you?

(MARY *grabs her skirt from him and moves*).

MARY. You do nothing of the sort . . .

(CORNY *shuffles after her quickly, still on his knees.*)

CORNY. Oh, yes I do! I love you with a total passion that makes Scarlett and Rhett look like Laurel and Hardy.

MARY. Stop being disgusting and get up at once!

CORNY. Not until you say you're mine and this grass turns brown and withers from soil erosion.

MARY. You'll have a long wait, it's a plastic lawn carpet, thirteen shillings and ninepence a square yard and of guaranteed durability.

CORNY (*extravagantly*). You heartless, cruel queen, how can you compute so impeccably while my aching heart is on the rack?

MARY. You haven't got a heart.

CORNY. I have, you know, and it's sagging and spilling all over the place from the weight of my love for you.

MARY. Oh, yes, and what about all those girls?

CORNY. My only regret is that I didn't keep myself pure and unstained for you, my darling.

MARY. Shopworn's the expression.

CORNY. You flay me with the truth but give us a chance and I'll make it up to you! I'll love you silly while you're young and when you're old and gray I'll be your footrest. Oh, when I think of all those hearts I've dallied with I'm shamed, now I've found my true vocation at last.

MARY (*in spite of herself*). What's that?

CORNY. To shelter you from life's dirty great buffets and sunshine up all your darker days. Mary, I'm asking you to take those magic steps with me up to the wee kirk in the heather, aren't I?

MARY. What?

CORNY. I want you to be Mrs. Cornelius Dooley, the potential mum to ten little Dooleys—think of the fun we'd have in the long winter evenings—picking their names and that.

MARY. How many?

CORNY. Alright, twelve, I can't deny you anything, I love you, I can't live without you, say you'll be mine.

MARY. I certainly will not!

(*Quick as a flash* CORNY *is standing on his feet. He is his old self again.*)

CORNY (*briskly*). Alright then, you've had your chance, so push off out of my life while you can still walk.

(MARY *is about to answer when she realizes he has turned the tables on her.* CORNY *grins.*)

MARY. You knew—all the time you knew!

CORNY. Let's say I knew anyway.

MARY (*bitterly*). Congratulations, snake.

CORNY (*amused*). I love a good loser.

(MARY *starts to go but he stops her.*)

CORNY. Here, hang about, why did you do it? (MARY *glares at him.*) And don't give me all that bric-a-brac about seeing me off for all the other girls 'cos I know enough about your mob to know sex-solidarity just isn't in your book. So why did you do it?

(MARY *looks at him before she speaks.*)

MARY. I wanted to hurt you.

(CORNY *is completely taken aback.*)

CORNY. Me?

MARY. Yes—you.

CORNY. What for?

MARY. I don't like men who operate like you do, it's too easy for you, you needed to be hurt, I was elected.

CORNY. Sorry, love, I won't buy that—

have a bit of fun with me—why not?—a giggle for the rest of the girls in the ladies' loo—sure, fine, but I'm not evil—nobody ever reckoned me to be evil, you ask all over. And as for hurting, that's something else. I mean, it's not the game I play, is it? Your lady mates'll tell you I'm in first for a naughty but it's got to be willing. I don't hold with hurting, I mean, you got to be full of hurt yourself to want to go in for that lot, haven't you—and are you?

MARY. What?

CORNY. Full of hurt . . . and that?

MARY. I'm sorry, Corny, I seem to have been mixing you up with some other fellow.

CORNY. Anyone I know?

MARY. No, anyway, it's all over.

CORNY. Don't you believe it, gel.

MARY. Do you want to try again?

(CORNY *looks at her for a moment before speaking kindly.*)

CORNY. Better not, eh?

MARY. I suppose not.

(*She is about to go.*)

CORNY. Tread carefully, the grass is full of real snakes.

MARY. You're a nice man, sorry.

(*She kisses him briefly and goes.* CORNY *stands looking into the artificial pool.*)

CORNY. Well . . . it couldn't have worked out now, anyway . . . maybe swimming over eggs is safer . . . (*He answers himself.*) . . . but not as much fun as the other, is it?

(*As his face is wreathed in an enormous grin*)

FADE

PART THREE

EMLYN

MARY MACNEIL	JUDGE
TOBY PEARS	CHARLES
SIR EMLYN BOWEN, Q. C.	STEWARDESS

A courtroom. Day.

MARY MACNEIL *comes through the door of the courtroom carrying a folder of papers. She sees* TOBY PEARS, *and approaches him.*

MARY *leans against the wall next to him and listens.*

In the well of the court SIR EMLYN BOWEN, Q. C., *is making his defense speech to the jury.*

———

EMLYN. So much for the police evidence, and indeed that would seem to be a factual review of the salient features of the case, but there is of course more to this case than a mere recitation and chroniclising of events. There is an ancient judicial principle involved which I must crave his Lordship's indulgence to explore.

(*He pauses, looking into the distance.*)

MARY. Mr. Pears.

TOBY. Shush . . . Sir Emlyn is putting on his peek-a-boos.

(EMLYN *is putting on a pair of old-fashioned, half-lensed glasses in simple gold frames. The* JUDGE *is getting a little impatient.*)

JUDGE. Yes, Sir Emlyn.

EMLYN. Your Lordship will forgive me, I'm sure, when I explain that once again the enormity of the responsibility of the jury came crowding in on me and for a moment I was in awe of that responsibility. (*to jury*) Yours will be the decision and the resultant verdict. And there are many ways you can arrive at that verdict but may I commend your attention to one of the humbler clichés of our language, "benefit of the doubt." "Oh, give him the benefit of the doubt," we say when we are not sure. This is normal practice in social relationships. And so rooted and automatic is this benign attitude in our national life, we sometimes forget that it is also the one thing that stands between the legal procedure, of which the jury system is a pivotal part, on the one hand and the accused man on the other. Doubt . . . (*He looks about him.*) When you hear a man, on oath, swear to his having witnessed certain events but you have to admit to yourself misgivings, a troublesome unease, that is doubt and as an advocate I must claim that doubt for my client. (*The* JUDGE *moves to interrupt but* SIR EMLYN *presses on.*) Doubt is what helps to cushion the responsibility of the juror and he must not stifle that doubt but let it rise up within him because that doubt is my client's strongest advocate. Doubt is the ultimate safeguard that any accused man, woman, or child has the right to demand the benefit of and if there is, and I am totally convinced there is, doubt in this case, my client is entitled to the fullest benefit of it. (*abruptly*) My Lord, may I request at this time an adjournment?

(*The court is completely surprised.*)

MARY. What's he up to?

TOBY. Shush!

JUDGE (*surprised*). An adjournment, Sir Emlyn?

EMLYN. For luncheon, M'Lud.

JUDGE. You surprise me, Sir Emlyn.

EMLYN. M'Lud, in an excess of zeal on my client's behalf I fear I was about to encroach upon your Lordship's prerogatives in my address to the jury. I thought therefore, with your Lordship's permission, a break might enable me to avoid that presumption.

JUDGE (*dryly*). Your point is taken and accepted, Sir Emlyn. The court will rise for one hour.

MARY. What was that all in aid of?

TOBY. Simple. Our Welshman has just stopped the old boy giving him a bit of stick.

A restaurant. Day.
The restaurant is full of barristers and their entourages. SIR EMLYN *is seated at a small table. He is examining the menu while a distinguished waiter hovers over him. They play an elaborate game called "ordering the meal."*

EMLYN. Really, Charles, I can't make up my mind.

CHARLES. Yes, sir.

EMLYN. All your goodies tempt me.

CHARLES. Yes, sir.

EMLYN. Today this is hardly a menu, more an incitement to the pleasures of gluttony.

CHARLES. Yes, sir.

EMLYN. You ought to be ashamed to put this anthology of table poems into the debile hands of a mere dieter.

CHARLES. Yes, sir.

EMLYN. But I think I can resist its blandishments and be safe with a glass of hock and an omelette aux fine herbes followed by a peach and a single portion of Bel Paese.

(*The waiter looks up from his order tablet.*)

CHARLES (*reprovingly*). Bel Paese, sir?

EMLYN. Quite right, Charles, altogether too ostentatious—a little Cheshire cheese.

CHARLES (*delighted*). Yes, sir.

(*He is about to go.*)

EMLYN. Oh, Charles, I'm expecting my secretary.

CHARLES. Yes, sir.

EMLYN. She won't be eating with me.

(CHARLES *indicates he is shocked at the very idea.*)

CHARLES. Of course not, sir.

EMLYN. Quite, so it might be as well if you removed the cutlery to save any . . .

(*He leaves off vaguely.*)

CHARLES. Of course, sir.

(*The waiter collects the knives, forks and plate from the place opposite and leaves.* EMLYN *looks casually around him, aware that people are looking at him trying to catch his eye. He acknowledges greetings from various acquaintances. In the background we see* MARY MACNEIL *enter the restaurant. She is still carrying the folder of papers. She is dressed in a simple black costume, the female equivalent to the respectable garb of a city gent's clerk. This makes her seem a little older than when we saw her last. She speaks to* CHARLES, *the waiter, who points to* SIR EMLYN. *She approaches him.*)

MARY. Sir Emlyn.

(SIR EMLYN *turns to her; he is surprised to see her.*)

EMLYN. Yes?

(*He rises.* MARY *speaks rapidly.*)

MARY. Miss Leatherhead wasn't able to come to the court so she sent me instead.

EMLYN. Did she? I see, well, do sit down, Miss . . . er . . . ?

MARY. MacNeil, I'm the typist.

EMLYN. Oh, yes, the typist, in that little . . .

MARY. . . . room at the end . . .

EMLYN. . . . . of the corridor. Of course.

(*He waits for her to give him the folder.*)

MARY. Miss Leatherhead thought you wouldn't mind.

EMLYN. I don't

MARY. She had an urgent appointment.

EMLYN. Hard to imagine Miss Leatherhead with anything urgent.

MARY. Her dentist.

EMLYN. Ah.

MARY. So she sent me.

EMLYN. So it would appear.

(*He is amused by her mounting confusion.*)

MARY. So I'm here.

EMLYN. You are indeed and do you remember why you're here?

MARY. Oh, I'm terribly sorry, I've brought some papers for you to sign.

EMLYN. I thought you might have done. (MARY *looks at him sharply but he disarms her with a playful smile.* MARY *hands him the folder.*)

EMLYN. Thank you.

(MARY *now starts to hand him her pen but knocks over an empty glass.*)

MARY. I'm sorry.

EMLYN (*reassuringly*). That's alright, I've got my own pen, Miss MacNeil.

(*He busies himself signing the papers while* MARY *looks around the restaurant, fascinated by it all.* EMLYN *looks across at her when her face is caught in a beam of light and she looks young, fresh and dewy. He is taken by her and looks intently at her face; she becomes aware of his gaze.*)

MARY. I'm sorry.

EMLYN. Why?

MARY. What?

EMLYN. Why are you sorry?

MARY. I was being nosey.

EMLYN. I see . . . well, don't be.

MARY (*defensively*). Nosey?

EMLYN. No, sorry.

(*He smiles at her again.*)

MARY. Alright, I won't be.

(*She relaxes. A thought occurs to* EMLYN.)

EMLYN. Is this your lunch hour?

MARY. Yes.

EMLYN. Oh, this is absurd, my dear child, you must have some lunch. Charles!

MARY. Here?

EMLYN. Of course. Charles!

(*The waiter is at his elbow.*)

EMLYN. Charles, set a place for this young lady, she's given up her lunch hour to bring me these ridiculous papers.

CHARLES. Of course, sir.

MARY. This is very kind of you, Sir Emlyn, but . . .

EMLYN (*cutting in*). Is it? Well, if you say so it must be, I really wouldn't like to see myself contradicting a lady.

MARY. But I'm not a lady, I'm only a girl.

EMLYN. I suppose you are, must be delicious for you. (*She is nonplussed by him and again he reassures her.*) Miss MacNeil, it's alright, I'm flirting with you, that's all.

(*The waiter is setting her place.*)

MARY. Oh, well, that's alri . . . what did you say?

EMLYN. You heard me, I'm proposing to have a happy little lunchtime flirtation with a very pretty gel, I hope we'll enjoy it. Charles, bring us some sparkling wine.

CHARLES. They say you were splendid in court this morning, sir.

EMLYN. Do they?

CHARLES. Yes, sir.

(*He goes.*)

MARY. That was nice of him.

EMLYN. Oh, he meant it, Charles is a dear man and thank goodness he never tells lies.

MARY. I saw you in court and you were splendid.

EMLYN. Do you tell lies, Miss MacNeil?

MARY. No, sir, do you?

EMLYN (*amused*). Only to myself.

(*He laughs and* MARY *has to join in with him.*)

EMLYN's *office. Day.*

EMLYN *is seated behind his desk, his face a mask, completely expressionless. After a moment,* TOBY *enters.* EMLYN's *face at once comes to life with his charming smile.*

EMLYN. Ah, Toby, you don't knock anymore.

TOBY. No, Emlyn, I don't. What can I do for you?

EMLYN. What I always admire about you English is your refusal to waste time on the nicety of incidentals and address yourselves to the earnest immediate.

(TOBY *is in no way put out by his remarks.*)

TOBY. And what I find irritating about the Welsh is their convoluted sentences and oriental manners.

EMLYN. Oh, you see us as the Japanese of Europe, do you?

TOBY (*firmly*). Emlyn, what is it you want?

EMLYN (*blandly*). A little administration

matter that you with your mania for minutiae will solve in a trice.

TOBY. Why don't you talk to Turner? After all, he's the Clerk of the Chambers, those sort of things are his job.

EMLYN. But you're so much better at "things" than I am.

TOBY (*ironically*). Oh, really . . . and by the way, congratulations on yesterday.

EMLYN. What?

TOBY. Your victory in court.

EMLYN. Oh, that.

TOBY. Why, was there something else?

EMLYN. Isn't there always? But thank you, it was a bit naughty but worth the risk.

TOBY. Quite . . . now, about your problem.

EMLYN. Oh, yes, well, you know how busy one has been lately, yes, of course you do, you must have noticed poor Miss Leatherhead's tensions, she's my barometer and she's overworked.

TOBY. Is she?

(EMLYN *is faintly irritated by* TOBY's *refusal to help him.*)

EMLYN. Poor girl, it worries me.

TOBY. So?

EMLYN. She should have a rest, wouldn't you agree?

TOBY. Whatever you say.

EMLYN. Well, I'm proposing to give her a couple of weeks' holiday.

TOBY. Then you'll need a temp. sec.

EMLYN. A what?

TOBY. Temporary secretary.

EMLYN. I may well have done until a moment ago but I can tell you now no "temp. sec" is coming into my life. Haven't they got someone to spare?

TOBY (*infuriatingly*). Depends on who you had in mind.

EMLYN. There must be a spare gel, the place is teeming with them.

TOBY. Don't think so.

EMLYN. Well, how about . . .

(*He breaks off.*)

TOBY. Yes?

EMLYN. Well, there's a girl in the little room at the end of the corridor.

TOBY. Oh, Miss MacNeil, but she's the typist.

EMLYN. I daresay she is.

TOBY. And that's who you want?

EMLYN. Well, in preference to a temp.

sec, yes.

TOBY. I'll never for the life of me understand why you can't come out with things in a straightforward manner, Emlyn.

EMLYN. What's that mean?

TOBY. "I'm fed up with plain, spotty Nelly Leatherhead and there's a pretty little thing called Mary MacNeil who could brighten up my room better than a bunch of roses so I'll thank you to tell Turner to get her in here as quick as yesterday."

EMLYN. Her name's Mary, is it? Nice name.

TOBY (*rising*). You're too much, Emlyn.

EMLYN. All the same, you seem to be learning to live with it.

TOBY (*going*). You're too much, you really are.

(*He has gone.* EMLYN's *face loses all its expression. After a moment, he speaks to himself.*)

EMLYN. Mary MacNeil, I want you—
No, I don't—
Yes, I do.
Oh, I don't know what I want—
   unless it's Mary MacNeil and
   to be
twenty-four with Mary Mac-
   Neil—
Oh, who wants to be twenty-
   four,
It's Mary MacNeil and buying
   her
things, expensive things . . .
   (*He grins.*)
that cost me nothing and being
   dignified
and bringing her to my will, or
   letting her
or maybe I just like the idea of
   Mary MacNeil,
Mary MacNeil,
Mary MacNeil,
Mary MacNeil.

(*There is a knock at the door.*)

EMLYN. Come in.

(MARY *enters.*)

MARY. Mr. Turner said you wanted to talk to me.

EMLYN. Well, if Mr. Turner said that he must be right. Sit down, Miss MacNeil, while I think of something to say to you. (MARY *sits opposite him not knowing what is happening.*) And of course a special way of saying it.

(She is perplexed but once more he smiles at her to reassure her and she relaxes.)

EMLYN's *office. Evening.*
EMLYN *is standing at the window looking out. The glass pane is opaque with beating rain. After a moment,* MARY *knocks and enters the room. She has some papers in her hand. She puts them on the desk.*
MARY. They're finished, would you like to sign them?
EMLYN. It's raining very hard.
MARY. I thought it must be.
EMLYN *(turning to her)*. You hadn't noticed?
MARY. I'm afraid not, I've been too busy
EMLYN. Am I a slave driver?
MARY. Oh, no, you just make everything seem so urgent I want to get on with it.
EMLYN. Is that good?
MARY. I don't know about being good but it makes me feel very important.
EMLYN. You are.
MARY. No, not really but it's marvelous to be conned painlessly into thinking I am.
EMLYN. I don't know if I like you thinking of me as a confidence trickster, Miss MacNeil.
MARY *(hastily)*. Oh, I don't, Sir Emlyn.
EMLYN. Then how do you see me?
*(*MARY *looks him straight in the eye.)*
MARY. A Welsh Wizard, a strict descendant from Merlin.
*(*EMLYN *is delighted but manages to conceal it.)*
EMLYN. Is Mr. Pears still here?
MARY. Nobody's here—they all went over an hour ago.
EMLYN *(surprised)*. Did they?
MARY. Yes, I've got the office key.
EMLYN *(crossing to her)*. Then there's only you and me left.
MARY *(guardedly)*. Yes.
EMLYN. Intriguing—I know, let's be wicked and have a large drink each.
(They move to a part of the office where there are two comfortable armchairs. EMLYN *opens the drink cabinet.)*
EMLYN. What will you take?
MARY. Oh, anything.
EMLYN. You certainly will not, you'll decide and tell me. I've driven you hard all day but now you are being entertained and your any caprice will be my duty, madame.
MARY *(amused)*. Any suggestions?
EMLYN. You're a Scot, have some Scotch.
MARY. I'm not particularly pro-Scots.
EMLYN. I'm afraid the Welsh don't make a whiskey but we could try a compromise.
MARY. Yes?
EMLYN. Irish?
MARY. Yes, please.
EMLYN. That was quick.
MARY. I knew an Irishman once—a Cockney Irishman but Irish.
EMLYN. It's not very tactful of you to drink with one man a drink that reminds you of another.
MARY. I'm sorry.
EMLYN. I've told you about that before, *you* must never say you're sorry.
MARY. Even when I am?
EMLYN. Particularly when you are.
(He hands her the drink.)
MARY. You love playing games, don't you?
EMLYN. It's an occupational hazard. I enjoy playing games because I'm a barrister—although maybe I'm a barrister because I enjoy elaborate games. Either way I'm a gamester.
MARY. But your trials aren't games.
EMLYN. They have to be—it's like a surgeon, he cuts flesh, he daren't allow himself to think of that flesh as being a person, it could be literally fatal. I play intellectual games with the legal system, not justice, the actual written law, I'm involved with rules, circumnavigations and technicalities. And like really all good games I enjoy them for the game's sake and it's lovely when you win.
MARY. That seems so cynical.
EMLYN. No, practical and unromantic maybe but I should regret cynical. You are an enormous pleasure to look at.
MARY. You're flirting again.
EMLYN. I'm doing my damnedest, do you mind?
MARY. No, not really, it's very pleasant and you make me feel very grown-up, but why me?
(He considers then, looking at her, speaks simply.)

EMLYN. I suppose because you came in-to that restaurant at precisely the right moment on the right day and I looked up and saw your hair in a slant of light and it was perfect.

MARY. Your voice, oh, your voice, it's too much.

EMLYN (slightly edgy). What's the matter with it?

MARY. Nothing, it's too reassuring.

EMLYN. Yes, you do alarm easily, don't you?

MARY. Do I?

EMLYN. And you're guarded.

MARY. It's not unnatural—after all—

(She breaks off.)

EMLYN. Yes?

MARY. You're a very famous man, you're titled, probably rich.

EMLYN. I think I am.

MARY. And very dolly to look at and I'm worried about it.

EMLYN. Why?

MARY. I don't really know what you want from me.

EMLYN. What are you prepared to give?

MARY. I've got to go.

EMLYN. Don't.

(As he speaks he moves closer to her.)

MARY. I'm afraid of you.

EMLYN. Don't be.

MARY. You've got under my guard and I don't like men who can do that.

EMLYN. Are you so experienced? I'd have thought not.

MARY. I want to go.

EMLYN. Why?

MARY. Because my calves are trembling and I'm . . .

(She stops.)

EMLYN. . . . about to be kissed.

(He is holding her in his arms. She is trembling a little.)

MARY. Am I?

EMLYN (reassuringly). Oh, yes. I think so.

(He kisses her and then holds her in his arms.)

EMLYN. Oh, darling.

MARY (softly). I love you.

EMLYN. I love you.

(The moment after he says it we see that he is annoyed with himself for saying it.)

MARY. Yes?

(EMLYN pats her reassuringly.)

EMLYN (ruefully). I love you, too.

EMLYN's office. Day.

EMLYN is sitting behind his desk. He is in great spirits and chuckles to himself as he does the Times crossword puzzle. There is a knock.

EMLYN. Adelante!

(TOBY enters the room.)

EMLYN. Toby, my dear fellow, you've resumed the knock!

TOBY. I thought it better.

EMLYN. Toby, I'm going down to the West Country today for the Assizes.

TOBY. So I gather, why so early?

EMLYN. I thought it would be a pleasant little weekend before a lot of unpleasant work. I don't like sex cases.

TOBY. I see. Are you taking Miss Mac-Neil with you?

EMLYN. My secretary? What a very good idea, Toby. If I drove her down with me it'll save her train fare on Monday.

TOBY. Well, that is one way of looking at it.

EMLYN. Come now, Toby, you're the one who's always querying the Chambers' expenses.

TOBY (nettled). Somebody has to.

EMLYN. Of course. Well, that's settled.

TOBY. Just a point, who'll be paying for her weekend?

EMLYN. I've got quite a little preparatory work to clear up before Monday, you know.

TOBY. I'm sorry.

EMLYN. What's that mean?

TOBY. Work does tend to spoil pleasant little weekends before a lot of work. Well, I'll see you when you get back.

(He starts to go out but turns to EMLYN instead.)

TOBY. Emlyn.

EMLYN. Toby?

TOBY. She seems a very nice kid.

EMLYN. She is.

TOBY. So you're suited.

EMLYN. We'll see how it goes, eh?

TOBY. Oh.

EMLYN. After all, she is only a temp. sec. I don't know how permanent she could become . . . yet, but you will tell Turner, won't you?

(TOBY *is suddenly angry but checks himself and accepts* EMYLN's *charming smile.* TOBY *goes.* EMYLN *switches on the office intercom on his desk.*)

EMLYN. Miss MacNeil, I've just had a word with Mr. Pears and he thinks it would be a good idea if you came down to the West Country with me today. Don't bother about a ticket, we'll be driving down. I hope that won't inconvenience you too much, Miss MacNeil?

(*There is a pause.*)

MARY's voice. Not at all, Sir Emlyn.

(*On an impulse he leans close to the intercom.*)

EMLYN. I love you.

(*He regrets it immediately and flicks the machine off.*)

EMLYN. Why do I have to say things like that?

(*He sighs before he smiles wickedly.*) Emlyn, my boy, I'm afraid you're very vulgar.

Back of a Rolls-Royce. Night.

MARY *and* EMLYN *are sitting in the back of his Rolls-Royce.* MARY *is talking.*

MARY. Oh, I don't hate my father anymore, I haven't the time to waste in hating. Anyway, lots of times it was very funny, but so boring.

EMLYN. Boring?

MARY. Predictably boring. "Never tell the truth when a lie is just as easy" was my dad's motto.

EMLYN. He lied about everything then?

MARY. Oh, yes, not just the facts of life, the milk bill, the weather, anything, it was as if he could only keep us under control by puttting a useless string of lies between him and people.

EMLYN. Rather sad.

MARY. I was his daughter, not just people.

EMLYN. The young are very intolerant. (*He laughs.*) That was as pompous a statement as you're liable to gather with the nuts in May. And the Cockney Irishman?

MARY. That was something else, he was alright. I just wasn't ready for him.

EMLYN. And me?

MARY. Oh, you're different.

EMLYN (*delighted*). How clever of you

to say the one thing I wanted to hear.

MARY. Well, you are.

EMLYN (*luxuriously*). Tell me about me.

MARY. You're lovely, you make me laugh, you make me feel important, you make me feel a glamorous part of the grand world. You dazzle me.

EMLYN. Dazzle you, how?

MARY. I'm beginning to expect things again.

EMLYN. Kindly explain that curious statement, Miss.

MARY. When I left home I made up my mind that I was owed nothing—you know how people, when they get angry with things . . .

EMLYN (*cutting in*). Things? Life?

MARY. Yes, things. They say the world owes me and I'm going to collect and it's all very dramatic and bitter and rather silly. Well, I haven't felt like that since I left my first job. I decided I was owed nothing and the way things looked I wouldn't get anything so there'd be no disappointment—only—since you—it's all changed.

EMLYN. Oh, dear.

MARY. It's alright, Emlyn, knowing you is enough, without doing much you make me feel very safe (*She laughs.*) if a temp. sec. can ever feel safe.

EMLYN. Yes, we must do something about that.

(*He draws her to him.*)

Secretary's office. Day.

MARY *is busy sorting some papers in the office, she is obviously very happy. After a moment,* TOBY *enters.* MARY *looks up, expecting* SIR EMLYN. TOBY *is careful, formal, but embarrassed.*

MARY. Hello. (*She sees who it is.*) Oh.

TOBY. Hello, Miss MacNeil.

MARY. Hello, Mr. Pears.

TOBY. Yes, hello.

MARY. Can I do anything for you?

TOBY. Not really. Did you enjoy yourself in the West?

MARY. Oh, yes, it was the best week.

TOBY. I'm glad—oh, Mary . . .

MARY. Yes.

TOBY. Sir Emlyn isn't coming into the office today.

MARY. What?

TOBY. No, he's had to go to Geneva.

MARY. But he never . . .

TOBY (*cutting in*). His wife is there with the children—you didn't know—no, of course you didn't.

MARY. He didn't mention it last night.

TOBY. He's been booked on the plane for several days.

MARY. No.

TOBY. Oh, yes—how long have you known Sir Emlyn?

MARY. Why?

TOBY. I've known him since we were at Oxford.

MARY. Yes, I know.

TOBY. He's a strange man.

MARY. Yes.

TOBY. No, Mary, he's worse than that, he's not very nice.

MARY. I beg your pardon?

TOBY. Oh, he's brilliant but he kids himself and he only means it when he says it, he plays games and he enjoys winning them but he—well, he isn't really very nice, I'm afraid.

MARY. Where's all this going?

TOBY. Emlyn has this habit of walking out on things he can't or won't cope with and that's when Old Toby or Miss Leatherhead and even his wife come onto the scene.

MARY (*flatly*). Say it.

TOBY. Emlyn isn't here and it appears Miss Leatherhead is coming back tomorrow so . . .

MARY. I don't believe you!

TOBY. I'm afraid I, unlike Emlyn, make a habit of the truth in my dealings with people.

MARY. But he loves me.

TOBY. No, you love him but, you see,

Emlyn doesn't really want that, it happens all the time.

MARY. But . . .

TOBY. Of course, there's a letter and . . .

MARY. . . . . the little room at the end of the corridor.

TOBY. I'm really only the messenger boy. (*He puts the letter down on the desk.*)

MARY. Go away!

(TOBY *gives a regretful shrug and goes out.* MARY *picks up the letter and opens it. She reads aloud disjointedly.*)

MARY. I know it won't—

for the best—

try to underst—

but it couldn't—

Emlyn—

P.S. I'm sorry.

(*We go in close on her bleak young face.*)

MARY. Sorry.

First class air flight. Day.

SIR EMLYN *is the only passenger. He is expressionless and remote.*

STEWARDESS. Champagne, Sir Emlyn?

EMLYN. At this hour of the morning, young lady. (*He "tut tuts".*)

STEWARDESS. Oh, I'm sorry, sir.

(*He looks up at her.*)

EMLYN. Don't be sorry—do you know, I think you've persuaded me.

(*The girl looks worried, nevertheless she pours him a glass.*)

STEWARDESS. Of course, sir.

EMLYN. It's alright, I'm only flirting with you.

(*As he smiles his charming smile.*)

FADE

MARGUERITE

Armand Salacrou

Translated and Adapted by MICHAEL VOYSEY

MARGUERITE	THE FATHER
THE DOCTOR	THE STRANGER

ONE OF THE august figures of the French theatre, Armand Salacrou was born in Rouen, France, on August 9, 1899. He was regarded from the outset as an avant-garde dramatist "who wrote realistic plays in such fantastic terms as to depart very largely from naturalism." His work attracted the attention of the great director, Charles Dullin who, in 1921, founded L'Atelier, an avant-garde theatre in Montmartre, which continued until 1938. Basing his productions on the assumption that realism is not a natural part of the theatre, Dullin "emphasized the mysterious, poetic, and fantastic qualities of the literary text." He was the discoverer and mentor of many front-rank talents and was responsible for the first productions of such playwrights as Marcel Achard, Jean Anouilh, and Jean-Paul Sartre as well as Armand Salacrou.

Among M. Salacrou's plays are: *Tour à terre, Le Pont de l'Europe, Atlas Hôtel, La Terre est ronde, Histoire de rire,* (presented in the United States as *No Laughing Matter*), *Les Nuits de la colère* (produced in New York in 1947 by Erwin Piscator under the title *Nights of Wrath*), *L'Archipel Lenoir, Une Femme trop honnête, Le Miroir* and *Boulevard Durand.* He also has written a number of screenplays and many television dramas.

Armand Salacrou is a member of the Académie Goncourt and president of the Société des Auteurs Dramatiques de France.

Marguerite is one of the author's most translated and produced plays. The new English version, which appears in this collection, was made by Michael Voysey whose own plays have been widely seen on British stages and on television.

In 1966, Mr. Voysey devised and produced *By George,* a dramatized biography of George Bernard Shaw taken from his nontheatrical writings. The presentation first was seen at the Edinburgh Festival, later in London, and in 1967 it was brought to New York with Max Adrian impersonating Shaw in various stages of his life from age thirty-eight to age ninety-three.

In 1969, Michael Voysey received a Screenwriters' Guild Award for his screenplay of Arnold Bennett's *Imperial Palace.* One of his most recent works is a dramatization of Emile Zola's *Thérèse Raquin* which was performed in 1970 in several leading German cities.

SCENE. *The dining room of a farmer's cottage. A door leads to the rest of the house, and another opens on to the road. There is a curtained window in the angle up right and a dresser up left. Above the fireplace is a high-backed armchair. A table is at right center with chairs on either side. Other chairs are about the room. There is a grandfather clock right of the back door. On the walls are seascapes, and on the mantelpiece and elsewhere models of ships.*

The time is the present, early evening.

MARGUERITE, *a young woman of twenty-three, is discovered standing above the table pressing a black suit with an iron. The* DOCTOR, *a young man, comes in with his professional bag.*

———

MARGUERITE (*in a loud, cheerful voice, so as to be heard in the bedroom*). Well, Doctor?

DOCTOR (*in a doctor's conventional manner*). Well, I am very satisfied.

(*He closes the door.*)

MARGUERITE (*in a low voice*). How do you really find him?

DOCTOR (*a little irritated by his patient, who is condemned*). His blood pressure is still high; he can go on for months like this, or he could have another attack within the hour.

MARGUERITE. Thank you, Doctor.

DOCTOR. You look tired.

MARGUERITE. I am tired.

DOCTOR. You'll have to take care, or else I shall be having to nurse you, too. What are you doing?

MARGUERITE (*folding up the suit*). He ordered me to clean and prepare Paul's black suit.

DOCTOR (*bewildered*). But why?

MARGUERITE (*wearily, putting the suit on the chair*). He wants Paul's suit to be ready.

DOCTOR. Ready for what?

MARGUERITE. Ready for Paul to wear. (*exasperated*) He's got it into his head that Paul will arrive today. Paul, who is dead, must return, return just one hour, just one hour before his last attack, to help him die. (*She puts the iron on a metal tray on the floor by the window.*) So he wants his son's mourning suit to be ready to be worn at church at his funeral.

DOCTOR (*with quiet sympathy*). I'll come back and see you after dinner.

MARGUERITE. Then come in quietly. He hears everything, and gets up at the least excuse.

DOCTOR. I have forbidden him to.

MARGUERITE. He's very stubborn.

DOCTOR (*taking her in his arms*). Do you love me?

MARGUERITE. If I'd not had you . . . Thanks to you, for the last six months I've been nearly happy.

DOCTOR (*reproachfully*). Nearly?

MARGUERITE. He knows that we love each other—I don't know how.

DOCTOR. How can he know?

MARGUERITE. He knows, he's guessed it.

DOCTOR. I'll come back straight after dinner.

MARGUERITE. Thank you. Where are you going now?

DOCTOR. The young Pellerin has whooping cough.

MARGUERITE. Quiet, I heard him walking about.

DOCTOR. I've ordered him not to.

MARGUERITE. Please go.

DOCTOR. Make him get back to bed.

MARGUERITE (*wryly*). Make him?

DOCTOR. Try.

MARGUERITE. I'll try. Please go.

DOCTOR (*opening the door*). Until tonight.

MARGUERITE. Until tonight.

(*The* DOCTOR *goes.* MARGUERITE *closes the door behind him. The* FATHER, *a very old man wearing a dressing gown, enters. He is blind.*)

FATHER. Is that you, Paul?

MARGUERITE (*moving up to him*). You shouldn't be out of bed.

FATHER. I heard someone talking.

MARGUERITE. The doctor has just left.

FATHER. He stays a long time, that one.

MARGUERITE. He was making out a new prescription.

FATHER. You forget too quickly, Marguerite, that you are Paul's wife.

MARGUERITE. The doctor was just telling me not to let you get out of bed.

FATHER. He's a fool. (*He takes a couple of paces.*)

MARGUERITE. Would you like a little soup?

FATHER. Soup? You think you can save

your conscience with a bowl of soup?

MARGUERITE. You must eat something.

FATHER. Your soup is more honest than your heart, but I've had enough of your soup.

MARGUERITE. You shouldn't be out of bed. The doctor says your blood pressure . . .

FATHER. Blood pressure! An excuse to call the doctor here every day.

MARGUERITE. Well, if you won't go back to bed, do sit down. (*She moves to help him.*)

FATHER. Don't touch me!

MARGUERITE. I'm sorry.

FATHER. Women! From the time I was young they used to come smelling round, just like you round your doctor, and I took them. And now that my life is nearly over, they disgust me. You all disgust me.

MARGUERITE. You shouldn't excite yourself. Why don't you go back to bed and try to sleep?

FATHER. When I could see and when Paul lived here, I thought well of you. Even when he went away, you seemed honest.

MARGUERITE. Please, Father.

FATHER (*sitting in the armchair*). I am not your father, but his.

MARGUERITE. Please . . .

FATHER. Paul will come back, I tell you that. I tell you that because I know. Drowned? My son drowned!

MARGUERITE. For pity's sake, not again.

FATHER. I tell you he is not drowned, sons must not die before fathers. He'll come back. I won't die till he comes back.

MARGUERITE. Please, Father, you'll only tire yourself.

FATHER. Don't think I enjoy staying here! After he comes back, I shall leave. Aren't you ashamed? Three years—couldn't you have waited three years?

MARGUERITE. Wait? Wait for what?

FATHER. For my son. But it was not Paul that you loved.

MARGUERITE (*violently*). And who else?

FATHER. It was a man. You always need a man in your bed. In your bed, in the fields, on the roadside.

MARGUERITE (*indignant but calm*). You have no right to talk to me like that.

FATHER. Once, for a laugh, I had a woman in a muddy field in the rain. She didn't care, none of you care as long as you get it.

MARGUERITE (*unable to take much more*). I must go and have a look at the child. I'm worried, there's talk of whooping cough.

FATHER. Yes, look to your son. You can leave me to rot in the corner. But I wait for Paul. I could still see when he went away. I shan't see him again, but I shall hear his voice. The sea is not like the desert. One can live in the sea. One ship passes, and another may pass, too. They see my Paul. And the ships come into port where there are trains. (*A train whistles in the distance.*) That's the eight fourteen. (*He rises.*) Paul could be on that train. He gets off the train. Old Prevost collects his ticket. (*moving across to door*) It's Paul, he says, the lad Paul—hurry—run . . . Listen—the garden gate . . .

MARGUERITE. Father, please!

FATHER (*opening the door and calling out into the night*). Paul! Paul! Is that you? No. He will not come tonight.

(*The clock strikes.*)

MARGUERITE. You should lie down.

FATHER (*shutting the door*). No.

MARGUERITE. You should be in bed, and it's time for your medicine.

FATHER (*moving back to the fire*). You would poison me if you could, but even you wouldn't dare.

MARGUERITE. Oh!

FATHER. You can hide your doctor in your room, you have the courage for that.

MARGUERITE. I must go to Pierre.

FATHER. You forget that I'm a blind man. I can see in the dark. (MARGUERITE *exits.*) Her son! Her son! Does God think that I accept him in exchange for mine? (*He sits.*) Die, yes, I shall die. Paul's ship has sunk, but Paul wouldn't let himself be drowned. He doesn't know that I'm blind. He knows that I am old. And I'm tired of waiting for him, because I am tired and I want to die. Paul, where are you? Did some ship find you and take you far away? Come back to me, Paul. Paul, listen to me, you will climb into the train which will stop at the station at eight fourteen. Old Prevost will take your ticket, he will recognize you, it's the old man's lad, it's Paul. (*rising*) Run, Paul, run, your father is waiting for you. He might die tonight. Your black suit is ready—run! Paul runs—he sees the church where the bells will toll for the old man tomorrow. Hurry, Paul, hurry. I hear him running along the road—you push open the garden gate— (*The doorbell rings.*) —you ring the bell—(*He takes a step.*) you open the door . . . (*The door opens. A* MAN *enters, shabbily dressed, tired and restless*) My son—my son . . .

STRANGER (*taken aback by such hospitality*). Good evening.

FATHER. Good evening! Is that all you can say?

STRANGER. Well, yes.

FATHER. You open the door, you come in and say good evening as if you came home after only one hour's absence.

STRANGER (*perplexed*). An hour's absence— I've come from a long distance.

FATHER. Sure, sure.

STRANGER. And I'm very tired.

FATHER. You shouldn't have stayed so long on the roads. But if you are tired, sit down.

STRANGER. Thank you. (*He sits.*)

FATHER. You don't sound sorry.

STRANGER. Why should I be?

FATHER. Why should you be! (*He suddenly realizes he is not alone—he had thought he had been imagining the dialogue.*) You are there—answer me, answer me, I say!

STRANGER. I have been answering you.

FATHER (*calling*). Marguerite! Marguerite! Paul has come back, Paul's here— Paul . . . Marguerite, I can die now. Paul —Paul . . .

(*He makes to go to Paul and collapses,*) (*The* STRANGER *rises and bends down over the* FATHER, *to raise him.*)

STRANGER. Hey, old man, old man . . . (MARGUERITE *enters.*)

MARGUERITE. My God, what's happened?

STRANGER. I don't know.

(MARGUERITE *pulls the armchair out.*)

MARGUERITE. Please help me!

(MARGUERITE *and the* STRANGER *put the old man into the armchair.*)

STRANGER. I called in because I was hungry and . . .

MARGUERITE. He said Paul had returned.

STRANGER. Yes.

MARGUERITE. Are you sure you're alone?

STRANGER (*thinking he is suspect*). Of course I'm alone. I'm not a thief, if that's what you think.

MARGUERITE (*feeling the* FATHER's *heart*) His heart is beating.

FATHER (*recovering consciousness*). Marguerite, I dreamt that Paul . . . (*He feels the* STRANGER's *hand.*) Paul—Paul! Give me something to drink, Marguerite. (MARGUERITE *exits.*) And where do you come from, you rogue?

STRANGER. Where do I come from?

FATHER. Yes, where have you come from?

STRANGER. I have walked a long way. (MARGUERITE *returns with a cup of water.*)

MARGUERITE. Father, can't you see . . .

FATHER. Do you have to remind me that I can't see him? Don't you think my heart is heavy enough—I can hear him talk but I can't see him.

MARGUERITE. I only wanted to say . . .

FATHER. What?

MARGUERITE. That he looks tired. (*She gives him the water.*)

FATHER. You have suffered, have you?

STRANGER. Yes.

FATHER. And why didn't you write? (*The* STRANGER *looks at* MARGUERITE.)

MARGUERITE. I am sure he will tell us everything when he has rested. (*She puts the cup on the mantelpiece.*)

FATHER. Do you find your Marguerite changed?

STRANGER. No.

FATHER. What about me?

STRANGER. Not much.

FATHER. So you have suffered a lot?

STRANGER. That, yes.

FATHER. Was it in the China Seas that you were able to save yourself?

STRANGER. China? That's funny. China.

FATHER. Was it or was it not in China?

STRANGER. Yes, it was in China.

FATHER. Are you still a drunkard?

STRANGER. Yes.

FATHER. And the day your ship sank, you were as drunk as a lord?

STRANGER. No.

FATHER. Then why did you sink your ship? (MARGUERITE *and the* STRANGER *look at each other perplexed.*) Why did you sink your ship?

STRANGER. Such things happen when one sails.

FATHER. Marguerite, give me some more water.

MARGUERITE (*taking the cup from the mantelpiece to the* FATHER). Paul, tell your father to go to bed.

FATHER. No, Paul shall not give the orders here—not until I am dead. Can you see that I am blind?

STRANGER. No.

FATHER. Have I the same eyes?

STRANGER. Yes.

FATHER. My eyes are dead, and tomorrow everything will be dead. Marguerite used to tell me that my eyes had not changed. I believe you. (*to* MARGUERITE) Has he changed? Tell me what he looks like.

MARGUERITE. I'll tell you tomorrow.

FATHER. Why tomorrow?

MARGUERITE (*with an effort*). He is clean-shaven.

FATHER. Why did you shave your beard?

STRANGER (*glancing at* MARGUERITE). Because it had to be done one day.

FATHER. On the way back, did you have to hide?

STRANGER. Something like that.

FATHER. Did you play the fool?

STRANGER. I haven't had an easy time.

FATHER. You haven't played the fool in this country?

STRANGER. No, not here. Far away.

FATHER. In China? If it was in China, I don't mind. Tell me, son, tell me everything.

STRANGER. It was circumstances, events pulling one this way, one that way.

FATHER. You were never very talkative. (*He puts his hands out.*)

STRANGER. Yes?

FATHER. I want to touch your face with my hands.

STRANGER (*taking a pace back*). No, I don't want you to.

FATHER. But I can't see you . . .

STRANGER. No, I won't have you putting your hands on my face.

FATHER. But I'm your father.

STRANGER. My father? You, my father?

FATHER. Yes, your father.

STRANGER. I've had enough. (*He turns to go.*)

MARGUERITE (*softly*) Paul—Paul . . . (*The* STRANGER *looks at her.*)

STRANGER. All right, but first I'm hun-gry.

MARGUERITE. I've some cold meat, bread . . .

FATHER. No! I have waited for him for three years, now I have to talk to him. When I have talked to him, then he'll eat. Leave us, Marguerite.

STRANGER. I could eat and listen at the same time.

FATHER. Leave us, Marguerite, tomorrow I shall be dead, but tonight I am still alive and still the master.

(MARGUERITE *moves away, opens and closes the door, but remains to help the* STRANGER *to answer questions.*)

FATHER (*to the* STRANGER). Sit down. (*The* STRANGER *moves the chair out and sits left of the table.*) Are you sitting?

STRANGER. Yes.

(*The* FATHER *gets up and checks that the* STRANGER *is sitting.*)

FATHER. Good. Do you plan to go away again?

STRANGER (*after looking at* MARGUERITE). No.

FATHER. Good. (*He sits again.*) This farm is run as well as it can be by an old man who is ill and a girl who is not very strong. It's your turn to look after it now.

STRANGER. Yes, I should like that.

FATHER. So I have done well in waiting. I shall now die in peace. I should not worry about the grass that grows on the ground when I shall be underneath it, but I do.

(MARGUERITE *sits right of the table.*)

STRANGER (*laughing*). Yes, it's rather odd.

FATHER. You, who have been like the dead, and who have come back, you should explain that to me.

STRANGER. One thinks one has an answer, and then one hasn't.

FATHER. When you were thrown into the sea, did you think you would ever get out or did you think you would drown?

STRANGER. When that happened, I couldn't think straight, I don't know.

FATHER. Explain.

STRANGER. But what can I explain?

FATHER. You wanted to live, didn't you?

STRANGER. I wanted to be on land. (*ironically*) When everything collapses around you, you know that on land you've got the earth under your feet, you know that doesn't collapse.

FATHER. If I had not been here waiting for you, I should have wanted you to drown. I've suffered waiting for you, hour by hour. An hour is not long, it's not much in a day, but there are many hours in a day, there are many days in a month, and many months in a year.

STRANGER. You know, I am hungry.

FATHER. You'll eat when I tell you. Now tell me about Marguerite.

STRANGER. What do you want me to tell you?

FATHER. Do you love her?

(*The* STRANGER *looks at* MARGUERITE).

STRANGER. She is beautiful.

FATHER. Beauty is nothing. An illusion. We think about beauty when we should be at work.

STRANGER. Work, what work?

FATHER. Did you become a sailor to get out of working on the land?

STRANGER. I didn't say so. Yes, she is beautiful.

FATHER. She is beautiful! What happiness is there in beauty?

STRANGER. Happiness. My mother used to say, happiness is not in this world.

FATHER. Your mother said that? She never said that to me. Poor woman! Happiness is not of this world, she said? Why was she complaining? Do you hear me complain because you left me for three years? There is a lot to be done in the house and you will have to do it. In the past you never spoke to me about Marguerite, but then I had my eyes. And you loved her as one should love one's wife. And now?

STRANGER. And now what?

FATHER. Are you jealous?

STRANGER. Jealous of what, jealous of whom?

FATHER. When you were at the bottom of the sea what did you think of?

STRANGER. When I was at the bottom of the sea?

FATHER. Yes.

STRANGER. And you, what are you thinking about at this very moment?

FATHER. What do you mean?

STRANGER. Aren't you at the bottom of the sea?

FATHER. The sea? For the last three years

I have hated the sea. When I die, I shall be under the ground and I shall care nothing. But when I think of the bottom of the sea, I suffocate. I suffocate because of you.

STRANGER. And I have had enough. I don't like talking about the dead.

FATHER. Why?

STRANGER. I'm jealous of you. I long to . . .

FATHER. You long to what?

STRANGER. I was hungry when I came here, and I am still hungry. Well, I want to eat, and I want to die.

FATHER. If I keep you waiting for food, I have my reasons—but you want to die, at your age?

STRANGER. Why not? Were you happy at my age?

FATHER. Happiness—what does that mean?

STRANGER. To be happy like everybody else.

FATHER. You're a fool. Think of today and think of tonight, and you will be happy.

STRANGER. I arrived here tonight. You know nothing about me.

FATHER. No, I can't even look into your eyes to see what your words mean.

STRANGER. No more than those one says to anybody.

FATHER. We never had much to say to each other, you and I. I didn't like that.

STRANGER. No?

FATHER. I can just see you—you had just been born. You weren't a day old; you hadn't even lived a day. Your mother was resting—be that as it may—she might have said happiness is not of this world, I would not have thought it then. I took you in my arms and I walked round the farm with you. I introduced you to the animals. I had an old horse whose name . . . Oh, well, no one will ever know what we called that old horse. You were only as big as my fist—and I was proud. "Look at our apple trees, look at the lovely oats, look at the dogs and the cats and the fat pig grunting." The sun shone. And now I can't see any more. All my days have been long and my life has passed quickly. But you are here, so I wanted to tell you. Marguerite . . .

(*There is silence for a moment.*)

STRANGER. What about Marguerite?

(MARGUERITE *rises*.)

FATHER. We quarreled one day, you and I, because of her. That was the only time you mentioned her. Do you remember?

STRANGER. I can't say I do.

(MARGUERITE *moves away*.)

FATHER. Of course you remember. Your eyes were strange that day. You said to me: "Marguerite is the only one in the world who counts." So I said to you: "Now that you are married, why don't you stay on the farm?" "Because I know she will be able to wait for me," you said. "But if you love that woman so much, why do you want to leave her?" "I want to breathe the air," you said, "but when I am far away I am still near her. I never forget her. If I go away," you said, "I can think of her more often, and then I shall come back to look at her. I am here, then I'm gone—it's like the night and day of my love, but it's always my love."

STRANGER (*sadly*). Did I say that?

FATHER. Yes. The day—the night—it's always my love. And then you give three years to them Chinese women. This time the night has been long.

(MARGUERITE *starts to cry, then decides to open and close the door so as to pretend she has entered*.)

FATHER. Is that you, Marguerite?

MARGUERITE. Yes, Father.

FATHER. And the boy?

MARGUERITE. Asleep.

FATHER. Don't you think you can wake him the day his father comes back from the sea bed?

MARGUERITE. It is better to let him sleep.

FATHER. I talk to her always of my son, blessed Paul, but she couldn't care less about my son. She only cares for hers . . .

MARGUERITE (*to herself*). That's true.

FATHER. Go and see him.

STRANGER. Me?

FATHER. Yes, you.

STRANGER (*rising*). I can't go and see him now.

FATHER. Why not? He's in his room. The one you painted all in white. You sang that day. Do you remember, Marguerite? Go on, upstairs. I let you. I shall stay alive till you come down again. Marguerite, you stay here near me.

(MARGUERITE *and the* STRANGER *exchange glances. The* STRANGER *exits*.)

FATHER. Well, Marguerite, are you proud of yourself now that Paul is back?

MARGUERITE (*sitting below the fire*). If only you would keep quiet.

FATHER. I have said nothing to Paul—not for your sake, but for his. There have been hours when I needed my wife. Not often, but at times when she was necessary.

MARGUERITE. I beg of you to be quiet.

FATHER. So you are begging me now? You're frightened I'll tell Paul everything. Aren't you ashamed, you with your little doctor?

MARGUERITE. You are very foolish, Father.

FATHER. If it is the truth, Marguerite, and I learn about it—even dead and buried—I'll climb out of my grave and strangle you.

(*There is a silence, then the* DOCTOR *enters quietly. He sees the* FATHER *up and about, and speaks*.)

DOCTOR. What are you doing up and about? I told you to stay in bed.

FATHER. What's the matter?

MARGUERITE (*rising*) It's the doctor.

DOCTOR. I said you had to stay in bed. Come on, what are you doing?

FATHER. And you?

DOCTOR (*putting his bag on the table*). I was passing. I saw a light on. Give me your hand. (*He takes the* FATHER's *pulse*.) Yes, of course.

FATHER. Of course, what?

DOCTOR. I've told you a hundred times, you've got high blood pressure. You must learn to control yourself. And you are not being reasonable.

FATHER. What about you?

DOCTOR (*bewildered*). What about me?

FATHER. Give me your wrist. (*He seizes the* DOCTOR's *arm*.) Where do you feel for the heartbeat?

DOCTOR. What do you want to take? My pulse or my temperature?

FATHER. I feel nothing, but perhaps I shall feel something now Paul has come back.

DOCTOR (*unbelieving*). Paul has come back? What are you saying?

FATHER (*triumphantly*). Yes, my son has come back!

DOCTOR (*trying to humor him*). Yes, one day he will come back. So you must look after yourself so as to be well and fit for when he gets here.

FATHER. Well and fit for *when* he gets here! He is here, Doctor, but you're not one of those who believed that he would come back.

DOCTOR (*to* MARGUERITE). Marguerite?

FATHER. Tell him, Marguerite. He is not content to bury his dying patients, he wants to bury the living.

MARGUERITE (*quietly*). It's true.

FATHER. He pushed open the door and came in.

MARGUERITE. Yes.

FATHER. So you and I have nothing else to say to each other and everything to understand. It wasn't you who kept me alive—it was I, I who wanted to live for him.

DOCTOR. All the same, you must listen to me and keep calm.

FATHER. No, illness and doctors go together like priests and funerals. One believes in them or one doesn't. I now wait for the priest.

DOCTOR (*moving back to the table to pick up his bag*). If you won't listen to me, you will kill yourself.

FATHER. I have the right to, now. Paul has come back. (*The* DOCTOR *looks at* MARGUERITE, *but she dare not look at him. The* STRANGER *returns.*) Is that you, Paul? (*The* DOCTOR *moves away and looks questioningly at* MARGUERITE) Paul, you have eyes. There's the doctor. He's settled in the neighborhood since I have been ill. He thought he would look after me, but he has no longer the right to come here. I'm finished, I don't want to drag on any longer and be a nuisance to you. I'd forgotten. How did you find your son? Come here . . . (*The* STRANGER, *who is terribly moved, comes close to the* FATHER, *who touches him.*) You have been crying?

STRANGER. Yes.

FATHER. What did the boy tell you?

STRANGER. Nothing. He slept.

FATHER. Didn't you wake him?

STRANGER. No, I watched him as he slept. He is as beautiful as his mother.

FATHER. And what about you? Doesn't he look like you?

STRANGER. Kids always look like their mother at the beginning.

FATHER. Bring him up as I did you—to be strong. Well, Doctor, what do you think of my Paul?

DOCTOR (*unable to understand any longer*). As a doctor, I repeat it would be wise to go and rest.

FATHER. Soon I'll have time enough to rest. Paul, Marguerite has got your black suit ready. And on the day of the funeral don't get drunk. And don't spend too much on the priest—no money spent like at your wedding. Doctor, if you could have seen their wedding. How beautiful you were, Marguerite, that I can tell you tonight. I gave her my arm, and my! how proud I was. They loved each other. Paul, tell the doctor how you loved each other so that he can understand.

STRANGER. So that he can understand what?

(MARGUERITE, *beginning to cry, moves between the* DOCTOR *and the* STRANGER.)

FATHER. You know, Doctor, I had forbidden them to go away on their honeymoon. Why? Because I didn't like the idea—I don't know why. Well, seeing them embracing the way they did, my heart warmed, and I told them in the middle of the wedding breakfast: "My children, take the horse and cart and come back in a fortnight." Just like that. Just like that. Do you remember, Marguerite?

MARGUERITE. Yes.

FATHER. And you had suddenly gone, without even swallowing another mouthful, you in your white dress. Paul, you never wanted to tell me where you went.

MARGUERITE. We went to Cambreville, a small village where I had spent my holidays when I was twelve years old.

FATHER. The whole fortnight?

MARGUERITE. Yes, the village was full of roses and our window box full of geraniums.

FATHER. And then?

MARGUERITE. In the afternoon we used to go for walks in the forest.

FATHER. Fine. Oh, I understand well. Into the forest. Blessed Paul.

MARGUERITE (*softly crying*). Paul, Paul, Paul.

FATHER. Go on, take her in your arms. (*The* STRANGER *and the* DOCTOR *look at each other.* MARGUERITE *opens her arms between the two men and embraces herself.*) Well, my children, when I am gone, I want you to go back there for another fortnight.

MARGUERITE. Yes, I swear to you I'll go.

FATHER. How well I've done to fight to live on, now the time has come for me to bow out. They all saw you floating among the fishes and seaweed, living in the sand beneath the rocks like a drowned man. But you came back. I said you would. You came back walking on the land. (*He slumps into his chair. The* DOCTOR *crosses quickly to him.*) It's nothing, nothing at all. (*rising, to the* STRANGER) Give me your shoulder, son, and we'll go.

STRANGER. Where to?

FATHER. Into my room.

MARGUERITE. At the end of the passage. (*The* STRANGER *supports the* FATHER.)

DOCTOR. And this time, you stay in bed.

FATHER. Peace. (*to the* STRANGER) I'll be fine in my bed, falling asleep near you.

MARGUERITE. I'll go on ahead.

FATHER. Stay here. Paul knows the way.

STRANGER. Shall we go?

(*He helps the* FATHER *and opens the door.*)

FATHER (*in the doorway*). Good night, Doctor. And don't forget that Paul is waiting for you, Marguerite.

(*The* STRANGER *and the* FATHER *exit.*)

DOCTOR. Who is that man?

MARGUERITE. I don't know.

DOCTOR. Where does he come from?

MARGUERITE. I don't know.

DOCTOR. Did he know Paul?

MARGUERITE. I don't think so, no.

DOCTOR. Then how was this organized?

MARGUERITE. It just happened.

DOCTOR. But how could you let this man pretend to be your husband?

(*He moves toward her.*)

MARGUERITE. Don't touch me!

DOCTOR. Marguerite . . .

MARGUERITE. You don't understand! Paul could have opened that door tonight and walked in.

DOCTOR. Come on, are you going mad, too? Paul can't come back, you know that as well as I do.

MARGUERITE. But what I didn't know was that if he opened that door and came in, I would throw myself into his arms and ask for his forgiveness. That's what I didn't know. And he would still want me in his arms.

DOCTOR. What's the good of excusing yourself to a man who can't come back?

MARGUERITE. I thought him dead, and I love no one but him. What else can I do but feel ashamed?

DOCTOR. But he would leave you for months on end.

MARGUERITE. I know why, now.

DOCTOR. Why?

MARGUERITE. So as to think better of me. He loved me better than the whole world.

DOCTOR. You're fooling yourself. If he came in through that door, he'd be drunk, you told me so yourself.

MARGUERITE. And I, what could I tell him?

DOCTOR. You beat me. You know very well that he can't come back—that he is dead.

MARGUERITE. Then if he is dead, you can't do anything against him. It's only those who are alive who change. They become bad, they get old, but Paul will always be as young and gentle as the day he left.

DOCTOR. Marguerite, really, you know that is not even sense.

MARGUERITE. No, people who are alive get old and die, but the dead never grow old.

DOCTOR. And are always alive?

MARGUERITE. Maybe you're sad; but could you take me in your arms again, knowing that if Paul came back I would push you away and throw myself at his feet?

DOCTOR. Paul can't come back!

MARGUERITE (*turning away*). Forgive me, Paul, for having been unfaithful to you—with a man I did not love. It's you I love, you, my husband, and I beg you to keep me near you so that at least I can serve you.

(*The* STRANGER *enters.*)

DOCTOR. Oh, there you are.

STRANGER (*sitting.*) Give me something to drink.

DOCTOR. You've done a lot of harm, haven't you?

STRANGER. I want a drink.

(MARGUERITE *goes to the dresser, takes out a bottle of wine and a glass, and pours.*)

DOCTOR (*aggressively*). First of all, where do you come from?

STRANGER. I've told enough stories for

one night.

DOCTOR. Where do you intend to go now?

(MARGUERITE *returns to the table and hands the* STRANGER *the glass.*)

STRANGER. Thank you. I came in here because I was hungry.

MARGUERITE. I'll make you something, and if you've nowhere else to go I ask you to stay here.

STRANGER. Me stay here? Oh, no!

DOCTOR. You're right.

STRANGER. It's not because I want to give you joy that I'm going.

DOCTOR. Then why do you want to go?

STRANGER (*rising*). Is there an inn in the neighborhood? And with a hundred francs do you think I could eat and sleep in a bed with sheets and have breakfast tomorrow morning before leaving?

DOCTOR. With a hundred francs, amply.

STRANGER. Then tell her to give me a hundred francs.

MARGUERITE. If you'll not go away tomorrow without seeing me.

STRANGER. No, I want a change of air. I came in here for a bit of bread. You've been very generous—you gave me a whole family, even a son. The old man was reminded of his son; and your only thought was helping the old man like a woman expecting a child. What about me? Did you think? Did you stop to ask if I had or did not have a father, a wife, a family? Eh, Marguerite?

MARGUERITE. What if tomorrow he asks for his son?

STRANGER. Don't worry about the old man, he is quiet forever. He died in my arms, calling me his son. (MARGUERITE *prays, standing by the table, turned away.*) Maybe he is looking at the three of us now, his last look before the last climb. I won't tell you my life, that only concerns me, but tonight I would like to be in the place of the old man, or his son at the bottom of the sea. Maybe the dead have troubles of their own, but at least they're something different. (*bitterly*) He didn't even know how to die. I don't know how to live.

MARGUERITE. What can I do for you?

STRANGER (*crossing to the door*). Let me go and eat and sleep. I'll feel better then. (*to the* DOCTOR) I'll tell them at the hotel that I've been sent by the doctor. (*He opens the door.*) Good-bye, Marguerite. Marguerite, wife of one evening.

(*The* STRANGER *exits, closing the door*).

DOCTOR. He's right. It's all very well to help the dying to die, but one also has to help the living to live.

MARGUERITE. I'll wait for Paul, just as his father waited for him. And when he comes back . . .

DOCTOR. But he won't come back!

MARGUERITE. How do you know? (*A train whistles in the distance.*) How do you know? If the old man could still talk, he would tell you that Paul has already come back. (*calling softly*) Paul . . . (*She falls to her knees.*) Paul—Paul . . .

CURTAIN

BERMONDSEY

John Mortimer

IRIS PURVIS
ROSEMARY

BOB PURVIS
PIP LESTER

ONE OF BRITAIN's leading contemporary writers, John Mortimer has divided his professional career into four equally successful component parts: dramatist, novelist, scenarist and barrister. The son of a barrister, he was born in Hampstead, London, in 1923, and was educated at Harrow and Brasenose College, Oxford. While working at the bar he wrote a number of novels and a play for radio, *The Dock Brief* (1957), which won for him the Prix Italia and brought him to the theatre when, in the following year, it opened on a double bill with his domestic comedy, *What Shall We Tell Caroline?* at the Lyric Theatre, Hammersmith, and later transferred to the Garrick in the West End. (The 1957–58 London season was a notable one for having introduced six important new dramatists to the theatre: Harold Pinter, Robert Bolt, N. F. Simpson, Ann Jellicoe, William Golding and Mr. Mortimer.)

The Dock Brief, a study of the underside of the law, went on to international success and was performed in dozens of countries, including the United States (on stage and television), Italy, France, Yugoslavia, Germany, Poland, Sweden, Spain and Belgium. As the author himself has noted, *"The Dock Brief* was first written as a play for sound radio. It was later performed on television, then in the theatre and was made into a film. It has not been danced or done on ice. It has, I think, been performed in most countries of the world and I last heard of it being done by two men under life sentence in San Quentin jail in America. I don't know why it has met with such a universal response, unless it expresses some feeling deep in everyone. I believe that we all hold the law in some contempt, and realize, in our hearts, that barristers, judges, and all the elaborate pageantry of the law, are dependent on the hardworking criminal for their existence. In a sense, the lawyers are the criminal's servants . . . As King Lear said, 'Handy-dandy, which is the Justice, which the thief?' That is the feeling I hope this short play releases."

The Dock Brief was followed by a full-length work, *The Wrong Side of the Park* (Cambridge Theatre, 1960) and in 1961, the author returned to the short play form with *Lunch Hour* in the triple bill, *Three,* that also included plays by Harold Pinter and N. F. Simpson. The production originated at the Arts Theatre and subsequently moved to the West End with a cast headed by Emlyn Williams, Wendy Craig and Alison Leggatt.

In 1966, Mr. Mortimer scored an enormous success with his adaptation of Georges Feydeau's French comedy, *A Flea in Her Ear,* mounted by Britain's National Theatre Company with Albert Finney and Geraldine McEwan at the helm of a sparkling troupe.

"Comedy," Mr. Mortimer has said, "is, to my mind, the only thing worth writing in this despairing age, providing it is comedy on the side of the lonely, the neglected and unsuccessful."

His "elegant, witty dialogue and as sharp an eye as any in the theatre for manners, morals, and pleasures of modern Britain" again were manifested in *Come As You Are!,* a quartet of short plays dealing with a common theme, extramarital relationships, and set in four different districts of London. Starring Glynis Johns, Denholm Elliott and Joss Ackland, *Come As You Are!* opened on January 27, 1970, at the New Theatre, and ran for almost a year.

It drew much praise from the press. In his coverage for *The Manchester Guardian,* Philip Hope-Wallace wrote, "The plays are genuinely theatrical in their trick of exciting surprise: with the wit of the dialogue and the deftly managed stroke of sentiment, they earn their time on the stage and keep us amused and involved." Herbert Kretzmer (*The Daily Express*) described the plays as "not only funny, but witty and caring as well," a pronouncement echoed by the *Evening Standard*'s Milton Shulman who concluded that "they are replete with acute comic observation and sharp, witty lines."

Bermondsey, one of the four plays that comprise *Come As You Are!,* was regarded as "comic and tragic at once, and piercingly truthful . . . a perfectly told tale that handles its subject with generosity and concern." The play is published for the first time in the United States in this anthology.

John Mortimer's other recent works for the theatre include *A Voyage Round My*

Father, a reconstruction of incidents in the author's early life and memories of his father who suddenly went blind in middle age. The play originally opened in 1970 at the Greenwich Theatre, then was brought to London in August, 1971, with Sir Alec Guinness in the leading role. During that same year, Mr. Mortimer's new version of Carl Zuckmayer's 1931 satire, *The Captain of Köpenick*, was presented by the National Theatre Company with Paul Scofield as star; and in 1972, the author once again was represented on the London stage with *I Claudius*, based on Robert Graves' modern classics, *I Claudius* and *Claudius the God*.

In addition to his plays, Mr. Mortimer has written and published six novels, a book on travel, and numerous screenplays.

SCENE. *The living room behind the bar in the Purvis' pub—The Cricketers, Bermondsey.*

TIME. *Christmas Eve, after closing time.*

The Purvis' living room, behind the bar of the "Cricketers" in Bermondsey. Peeling three-piece suite, wallpaper with pattern of Windsor Castle, ashtrays and calendar advertising "Take Courage". Christmas decorations. In the centre of the room, a Christmas tree, trimmed. The presents are set round: boxes in gold paper, unexpectedly large and lush. Christmas drinks: large selection on a table. Upright piano with carol book on it, open. When the curtain rises, the stage is empty. Sound of voices, children being put to bed upstairs. A young girl, blonde, mini-skirted and carrying a tray with two children's mugs on it comes in from the kitchen. She looks calm, in control, unhurried when a voice calls at her from upstairs.

———

IRIS. Rosemary? . . . Rosemary?

ROSEMARY. Yes, Mrs. Purvis?

IRIS. Got the kids' hot drinks, have you?

ROSEMARY. Just coming.

BOB (*ad lib—off*). Good-night. Happy Christmas, etc.

(BOB PURVIS *walks in from the bar. He's big, handsome, about thirty-eight. His life in the pub is starting to make him overweight.*)

ROSEMARY. Don't know what your wife thinks she is—Shah of bloody Persia.

BOB (*ignoring this*). Taking that up to the kids, are you?

ROSEMARY. When're you going to tell her, Bob?

BOB. After Christmas. I'll tell her after the holiday.

ROSEMARY. Boxing day. Promise you'll tell her . . . ?

(*She starts to go upstairs.*)

BOB. Of course I promise. After the holiday.

(*She goes.*)

(PIP LESTER *comes in from the empty bar. He's thin, sharp featured, grey round the temples, rather high upperclass voice, pianist's hands and gestures, dressed with perpetual undergraduate untidiness. Shapeless grey trousers, tweed coat with leather patches, old khaki shirt, straying lock of hair, slightly lop-*

ing walk. He looks after ROSEMARY, *doubtful and suspicious.*)

PIP (*feeling his arm*). I'm out of practice, pulling beer handles.

BOB. Why not open the shampoo, boy? That's what you're used to.

(PIP *moves to the drinks table, opens champagne.*)

PIP. Children gone to bed, have they?

BOB. Iris never gets them off till past closing time—not on Christmas Eve.

PIP. Care for a glass of the old shampoo? (*He pours himself a drink.*)

BOB. Go ahead. I'll stick to the Mother's Ruin. Shampoo gets my gut.

PIP (*the cockney phrase carefully mixed with the upper-class accent*). Iris likes a drop of the old shampoo.

(*He pours a gin for* BOB.)

BOB. Yes, Iris likes it.

PIP. The kids look smashing. (*He takes* BOB *his gin, then he looks at the big boxes round the tree.*) I hope my presents'll be a success.

(*noise from above*)

BOB. Cheeky little buggers. They're playing up.

PIP (*pats wrapped presents*). One junior road-scorcher two-wheel Fire-Fly for Ronnie—and a rather impertinent looking person called "Miss Isobel" who brings up her own wind for Carol Anne.

BOB. You spoil them!

PIP. Nonsense. I'm spoiling myself. Trying to make up for what I've missed.

(*He goes back to the table—takes his champagne.*)

BOB. You've not missed a thing. Iris says she can't switch on Late Night Line Up but you're chatting away about Brahms, or whatever . . .

(*pause.* PIP *drinks, looks at* BOB.)

PIP. Bob?

BOB. Yes?

PIP. Do you know how long it's gone on?

BOB. Since I married Iris? I was trying to reckon the other day. Ronnie's just eleven . . .

PIP. No. I mean . . . *it.*

BOB. Oh, "it". "It's" what you're talking about.

PIP. Eighteen years!

BOB. You're joking!

PIP. Eighteen years exactly. Since we

stood on that horrible Parade Ground . . . with Dulcie Dubbin screaming her head off at us.

BOB. Our camp sergeant! (*remembering, imitating shrill sergeant's voice*) "When I say 'Fix'—yer don't fix!"

PIP (*same imitation—not so good*). "But when I says 'Bayonets'—yer pops them off and yer whops them on!"

BOB. When we was on an exercise near this bloody great castle, and Dulcie says "This here's the property of Lady Thaxted. Mind your fairy footprints on the turf, you clumsy bastards." And you said —"Sergeant—she's my mother, and she'd like you all to come in to Christmas dinner."

PIP. My mother's splendid, in National emergencies. She spent the war preparing an icy calm welcome for the German Commandant who never turned up.

BOB. Bit of an anti-climax then, a peace time invasion of National Service jobs . . .

PIP. That was the first time I ever played the piano to you. Remember, when Mother got the other on to Animal Grab . . . ?

BOB. You dragged me off into the music room. I thought you'd never stop. I thought, how the shit do I ask him to belt up, and then we got started on the whisky and the Christmas carols . . . Is that eighteen years, honestly . . . ? Well, I'll say this, Pip. You've done all right for yourself since then, boy.

PIP. Not really. You've had all the great events . . .

BOB (*sarcastic*). Oh, yes! We just live on excitement here in the Cricketers. Do you know what happened? Just in the last three months?

PIP. I haven't been down. Not since Iris' birthday.

BOB. Was that when you brought her— a bottle of pong from the both of us?

PIP. Giant-sized Balmain "Jolie Madame". With a joke card from you to put your name to . . .

BOB. You see! Things only happen when you call on us! Since then, well, since then . . . We had Iris' Mum for one God awful weekend. Carol Anne got a pain in her gut which let everyone down by not being appendicitis . . . And oh, young Rosemary came to help Iris out. Ex-National Service Corporal Robert Purvis— This is your bleeding existence . . .

(*He drinks . . .* PIP *laughs, drinks to him.*)

PIP (*a little anxious*). Yes. Well, about . . . Rosemary?

BOB. Iris needed someone to help out.

PIP. Did she?

BOB. She's not a bad young girl. Had some trouble at home. Of course, Iris has to show her everything.

PIP. I noticed that.

BOB. But we do a lot more trade since her mini-skirt erupted in the saloon . . . (*pause. He goes on, more confidential.*) Also, she's set me thinking . . .

PIP (*laughs at him*). Sounds bad!

BOB. No! No, it's been so long since I got talking to anyone as young as that—I don't count the kids, of course.

PIP. Of course.

BOB. And she got me thinking. Well, I'm in a bit of a rut here, quite frankly, Pip. I mean, it's no use waking up and finding you've missed the bus, is it?

PIP. What bus exactly?

(*He goes to the piano and starts to play "The Holly and the Ivy". He's playing standing up and sings.* BOB *moves and stands close to him.* PIP *plays.*)

BOB (*puts a hand on* PIP's *shoulder.*) Wasn't that the bloody tune?

PIP. . . . Remember?

BOB. Your Mum brought up Scotch in a decanter. She shoved it on the piano.

PIP. You've got a retentive memory!

BOB. We got pissed out of our minds, and sung that bloody thing all the way back to barracks. You're right, boy. It's retentive all right.

(PIP *suddenly stops playing. The two men face each other, move closer—*BOB's *hand still on* PIP's *shoulder.* PIP *speaks very quietly.*)

PIP. It's only eighteen years.

(*At the same moment they lean forward and kiss each other on the mouth. Sound of a door banging and* IRIS' *voice on the stairs*)

IRIS. Quiet now, kids. Or Santa's not going to come. Not ever.

(*The men move apart, not hurriedly.* IRIS *comes in. She's the perfect pub wife: sensible, still attractive, tired from an evening in the bar and putting the kids to bed. She hardly looks at the men, but goes to the tree and straightens the silver ornament on the top of it.*)

IRIS. Can't ever get that old fairy to stand upright.

BOB. Stuff a twig up her.

(*pause. Sound of children upstairs*)

IRIS (*hearing it*). That girl's useless with the kids.

(PIP *pours a glass of champagne and brings it to her.*)

PIP. Shampoo, love?

BOB (*casual*). Rosemary—still up there, is she?

IRIS. Putting her eyelashes on. Apparently there was an accident in the bar. She left her other pair in an empty glass, and Mrs. Beasley poured in a port and lemon and drank them down.

BOB. Silly old fool . . .

PIP. How revolting!

IRIS. I said what do you want to take them off in the bar for anyway, and she said—they get so heavy. After a long evening. She doesn't care if our regular barmaid gets a hairy lining to her stomach.

BOB. She's all right. She had a bit of trouble at home.

IRIS. I said, I should think they do get heavy, I said, with all that fluttering you do. She's hopeless with the kids.

BOB. Ronnie likes her.

IRIS. Carol Anne can't stand the sight of her.

BOB. Well, then—Carol Anne's a woman, isn't she?

IRIS. She's six!

BOB. It doesn't matter she's six. She's still a woman, isn't she? She's jealous. That's all. She's jealous of a bit of mini-skirt.

IRIS. Is that what I am! Jealous of *her*.

BOB. I should rather think so. The way you're criticizing.

IRIS. It's just that she's meant to be helping me out.

BOB. Oh, for God's sake, girl. Where's the spirit of Christmas . . . ?

IRIS. Drunk up by you, I should imagine. You must've got through one bottle of Gordon's since we opened.

BOB. I've been working . . .

IRIS. What do you think I've been doing? And trailing round after a girl who's got no more sense than to let our

bar parlour staff drink down parts of her anatomy . . .

BOB. Give it a rest, Iris. Pip's here.

IRIS. Of course. Pip's here. Pip's always here! Christmas, birthdays. One of the family!

(*She empties her glass.*)

BOB. Well, be grateful. You're swigging down his shampoo.

IRIS. Oh, Pip understands. You understand how it is, don't you, Pip?

PIP (*crosses to* IRIS. *Fills her glass again. Looks at* BOB). Yes, dear. Of course, I understand.

IRIS. And what do *you* think of Miss Mini-Skirt exactly, Pip?

BOB. She's just a young kid—that's got into a bit of trouble at home . . .

IRIS. No. What do *you* think of her, Pip?

PIP (*pauses. He's in difficulties, he answers with tact*). Charming. She's just not —my type exactly . . .

(*crash from upstairs*)

BOB. I'd better go up, before the kids commit murder.

(*He goes.* IRIS *shrugs her shoulders.*)

IRIS. What do we do now? Sit in suspense until she drops the other eyelash?

(*She drops into a chair, kicks off her shoes. Drinks.* PIP *comes over and fills her glass.*)

PIP. You're tired.

IRIS. Bloody fed up.

(PIP *goes to the piano. Starts to play "The Holly and the Ivy" quietly through this dialogue*)

IRIS (*after a pause*). How's your mother?

PIP. Indestructible!

IRIS. Shouldn't you be with her at Christmas? Isn't that your place—in the Castle?

PIP. Rheumatism Towers . . .

IRIS. Doesn't she miss you?

PIP. She's happy as a sandboy. She's sitting in front of a roaring electric fire, wrapped in two cardigans, fur boots, and the sari they wove for her in Delhi, playing consequences with the local M.P. "Malcolm Muggeridge met Diana Dors in the Sauna Bath at the Vatican and the consequence was . . ."

IRIS. Is that what they play . . . ?

PIP. My mother always loved paper games with politicians . . .

IRIS. Your old mum. She's certainly

part of history. Something like the Bloody Tower. (*long pause*) Of course, I know really—why you want to come here.

(*He stops playing abruptly. Listens, tense*)

PIP. Why?

IRIS. You're a bit of a snob, aren't you?

PIP (*gets up, puzzled, offended, but relieved*). Me! A snob.

IRIS. Take a trip round the stately pubs of Jamaica Road. Pay your half-crown and catch a glimpse of the "real people."

PIP. Iris, that's not fair!

IRIS. Oh, I've seen you. When Carol Anne puts sauce on her bread, your eyes light up as if you'd had a personal invitation to watch the Duke of Edinburgh eat his cucumber sandwiches . . .

PIP. Iris, that's just not true!

IRIS. I know what you say about Bob. "Salt of the earth. No nonsense. Real true person." I don't know what you thought you'd met. Jesus Christ, just because he'd never seen a pair of pyjamas till he did his National Service . . .

PIP. It's *all* of you. This family . . . In the world I live in, there's no real feeling of a family anymore . . .

IRIS. That's a load of cobblers . . . You don't think we're more real, do you, just because we have to make do with an Anglia instead of an Aston Martin, and vinyl instead of wall to wall carpeting? Just because we go on holiday in Hayling Island instead of borrowing old Lucy So-and-so's bloody Greek island?

PIP. Personally—yes, I do.

IRIS. Why?

PIP. You're tired . . .

IRIS. *Why?* Tell me why—what's so good about us you have to drive down here with champagne and Paris perfume, and walking, talking, peeing dolls? Just as if you were the Three Wise Men and I was the blessed virgin.

PIP (*trying to explain*). It's because . . . Honestly, it's because you're simple.

IRIS. Thank you very much!

PIP. I mean, you don't make great demands on life . . .

IRIS (*She gets up, impatient and restless*). What? Can't you hear? Bob's shouting all the time to be the twenty-five-year-old millionaire owner of the fifty-story de luxe Happy-Home holiday hotel, Tor-

quay. You don't think the poor fact he's thirty-eight, and the tenant of a small tied house in the Jamaica Road makes any difference to what he's demanding, do you?

PIP. What about you?

IRIS. Oh, what I'm asking for's much more ridiculous.

PIP. What?

(*pause*)

IRIS. Love.

(*pause*)

PIP. You've got so much.

IRIS. Have I?

PIP. You've got Bob and . . .

IRIS. Have I got him?

PIP. And the children . . .

IRIS. Is that what you care about?

PIP. My godchildren? Yes. Yes, of course. I mean, they must be very satisfying.

IRIS. A couple of accidents! If you want to know the truth.

PIP. Iris. I always thought of you as a perfect mother . . .

IRIS. That's what perfect mothers get landed with. Accidents.

PIP. I'm afraid I don't know much about it.

IRIS. That's not an area of scientific knowledge that really appeals to you, is it?

PIP. Perhaps not.

IRIS. I bet your greatest nightmare's being stuck here one weekend when I suddenly gave birth, and you have to rush in with boiling water.

PIP. Look, Iris. I don't want to seem old-fashioned. But it's Christmas Eve. We've decorated the tree. The children are asleep upstairs, and I personally thought we should practise the carol for tomorrow . . .

(*He goes back to the piano, and standing plays a few bars of "The Holly and the Ivy".*)

IRIS. Kids! They don't need us. You know what I seem to hear those kids saying all the time? "We're just an excuse for you, aren't we? All you need us for is to keep your mind off the real trouble."

PIP (*stops playing again*). What's that? (*pause*) What's the real trouble?

IRIS. Naturally, it's Bob.

PIP. What's the matter with Bob?

IRIS. What's the matter with *you?* You

know what's going on . . .

PIP. He just seems a bit restless.

IRIS. Restless! Look—(*She stands looking at him.*) You love him, don't you?

(*long pause*)

PIP. I've always been very fond of Bob.

IRIS (*impatient*). Why can't you tell the truth sometimes?

PIP. Well, I do love him—naturally. As a friend . . .

IRIS. Oh, yes, like you love your mum. Like you love me. Like you're going to put "With loads of love from Uncle Pip" on Ronnie's two-wheeler.

PIP. Well . . . Perhaps not exactly like that.

IRIS. How?

PIP. Well . . .

IRIS. Go on, say it. How?

PIP. Well, I suppose . . .

IRIS. Oh, for God's sake. Do me the credit!

PIP. What?

IRIS. I'm not a complete bloody idiot. I mean I've got some idea—what's going on. He's your boy friend, isn't he?

(PIP *does a dramatic gesture, his head in his hands.*)

PIP. What do you mean exactly?

IRIS. I never know . . . quite how to describe it.

PIP. I'm sorry.

IRIS. Look. It seems perfectly natural to me. It's the people that don't fancy him, I can't understand.

PIP. I won't come again.

IRIS. You've got to.

PIP. I'll stay away.

IRIS. I don't think we could do without you.

PIP. What're you talking about?

IRIS. The way I look at it is—you've kept this family together.

PIP (*incredulously*). *I* have?

IRIS. You've kept Bob steady. (*losing patience*) Do you think I'd've had a peaceful home to bring up the children and a good husband and holidays, if Bob hadn't had you as well to keep him feeling young and handsome as a boy of twenty?

PIP (*pauses. He looks at her.*) When did you work it out?

IRIS. Oh, I've known ever since you first took us out. Remember you got seats for the Victoria Palace? You said, "May I say

how greatly I admire your hat?"

PIP (*desperate, embarrassed*). Look, Iris, my car's outside. On second thoughts, Mother may be feeling a bit low this Christmas, and I really think I should . . . (*turns on her, anxious*) How could you tell?

IRIS. You were so polite to me.

PIP. Just because I happened to appreciate your hat . . .

IRIS. Do you imagine any of the other men we'd known'd say "I greatly admire your hat?" They'd pile beside me in the back of the Anglia and try for a quick grope any time Bob had his eye on the road.

(*She drinks.*)

PIP. What I can't understand is, why didn't you object before?

IRIS. Why should I object? I tell you. I knew what Bob was like. I chose him like that, didn't I?

PIP. And I don't make you jealous?

IRIS. You're not jealous of me, are you?

PIP (*thinking it over*). No. I'm grateful to you, for looking after him.

IRIS. Well, I think you make a nice day out for Bob like going to the dogs, but less expensive . . .

PIP. Thank you very much. But . . . Why suddenly . . . bring it up?

IRIS. Have some sense! Can't you see what's happening to Bob? . . . I thought you loved him?

PIP. You know that, apparently . . .

IRIS. But you don't, do you? He's just the little bit of rough trade you took in to show round the Castle.

PIP. Iris, please!

IRIS. All right. If you care about him, why don't you put up a bit of a fight then?

PIP. Against you?

IRIS. Against her.

PIP. Her?

IRIS. Little Miss Eyelashes.

PIP. You're jealous of her. I believe you're jealous.

IRIS. Of course, I'm bloody jealous!

PIP. Why?

IRIS. Because she's a woman. And because she's nothing to do with Bob. She's not part of him. She's all in his mind, like the girls he gets on the brewery calendar, unzipping their jeans on black leather sofas. It's all a great big dream, and they'll take on a pub they can't afford, and put on dinners she can't cook and get brewery bills they can't pay, and it wouldn't be one bottle a day—but two and a treble before breakfast and you've got to put a stop to it. You've got to break it up, Pip dear. Before that girl takes my husband off both of us.

PIP. How can I?

IRIS. Tell her! Tell her he's queer.

ROSEMARY (*off*). 'Night, 'night, Ronnie. (PIP *is stunned by this suggestion, when* ROSEMARY *comes in downstairs. She's put on enormous eyelashes and she's changed her clothes. She's carrying the emptied children's mugs on the tray.*)

ROSEMARY. I'm not butting in, am I Mrs. Purvis?

IRIS. Not if I can help it, dear. Everything all right up there, then?

ROSEMARY. Oh, yes. Mr. Purvis was telling the kids a story. It was a scream. Shall I rinse these out under the tap?

IRIS. That's very sweet of you, dear. (ROSEMARY *goes.*) You see? In eleven years, he's never told those kids a bedtime story. It's got serious . . .

PIP. Bob wouldn't be thinking of—leaving home, would he?

IRIS. If he does, I don't see her having you down for the holidays. (*She looks at him.*) Of course, we could always spend our Christmases together. Just you and me and the kids.

PIP. Perhaps . . . You're right.

IRIS. She's got to be told . . .

PIP. Then, shouldn't you tell her?

IRIS. She'd never believe me. I'm just the old jealous cow, that's all I am. You see that, don't you, Pip dear? She'd never believe me.

(BOB *comes down the stairs, his hair brushed neatly.*)

BOB. Well, got that lot into bed at last.

IRIS. Including our little Rosemary?

BOB. Sorry, Pip, the kids were just that bit excited.

IRIS (*exasperated*). What did you do? Calm them down with the one about the poor girl who lost her eyelashes dancing with Prince Charming who whipped her out of the Public Bar and made her sweetheart of the Forces.

BOB. I'm sick and tired of that.

IRIS. What exactly?

BOB. You getting at me. That's all you do now. Just get at me.

PIP (*embarrassed*). Isn't this the time we always have our Irish coffee? Christmas Eve.

IRIS. She won't know how to do Irish coffee—not that plastic daffodil out there. Most she knows is how to open crisps.

PIP (*anxious to escape*). Shall I go and do it? Shall I go and do it?

IRIS. Why not. You could probably tell her quite a lot . . . About the way we do things here.

(PIP *goes.*)

IRIS (*to* BOB). You want to leave us, don't you?

BOB. I was going to tell you, after the holiday.

IRIS. Why not now?

BOB. I didn't want to spoil your Christmas.

IRIS (*seriously*). Thank you.

BOB (*collects himself for an outburst, and then explodes*). I want a different sort of place, that's all. By the river, where I could put on prawn cocktails, and charcoal grills and not just rest content with meat pies and cheese biscuits. Somewhere you could put on a dinner dance—for the younger marrieds. I'm getting on, Iris, I'm thirty-bloody-six. Well, don't I deserve it?

IRIS. You weren't thinking of including me? Not in the move?

BOB (*weak and apologetic*). I want a bit of something young around me.

(*pause*)

IRIS. Thirty-eight.

BOB. What?

IRIS. You're thirty-eight.

BOB. You see, I'm not getting any younger.

IRIS. Neither am I.

BOB (*guilt making him angry*). Oh, don't try that. I can see that coming. Bloody blackmail. So I've got to stay because I feel sorry for you, is that it? You want me to pity you?

IRIS. No.

BOB. What?

IRIS. Have a bit of pity on yourself.

BOB. I'm no good. I know that.

IRIS. Yes, you are then.

BOB. What?

IRIS. Good. That's why we both love you.

BOB. You and Rosemary . . . ?

IRIS. No. You know I don't mean *that*. Me and Pip! We've got good taste—both of us. We like you as you are. If you'd been meant as the guv'ner of a dinner dance country club, that's what you'd be by now.

(*The door opens.* ROSEMARY *comes in; she looks extremely puzzled.*)

ROSEMARY. 'Ere, he wants the Irish whisky. Where is it, Bob?

BOB. Top shelf—up with the liqueurs and specials.

ROSEMARY. He says he's about to do miraculous things, with cream and Irish whisky.

(*She goes off into the bar.*)

IRIS. It's too late, Bob. You can't go back and have it all different . . .

BOB. Keep me down! All right! Just keep me down all the time! Can't I have a bit of ambition?

IRIS. If anyone's achieved their ambitions I'd say it was you.

BOB. Gordon—Bennett! I've had less out of life than anyone.

IRIS. At a modest estimate. I'd say you've had—about twice as much.

(ROSEMARY *comes back from the bar carrying the Irish whisky. She speaks to* BOB, *nods towards the kitchen.*)

ROSEMARY. Who is he, Bob?

BOB. Just an old friend, that's all.

ROSEMARY. He said you had a whole lot of laughs when you were in the army together. He called your sergeant Dulcie Dubbin.

BOB. Old Pip—he'd come out with anything.

ROSEMARY. Do you like him at all?

BOB. Pip? I've known Pip for years.

ROSEMARY. I dunno—he seems funny to me.

(PIP *comes in with the coffee tray. Puts it down and takes the whisky bottle from* ROSEMARY. *Speaks in a stage Irish accent*)

PIP. A little drop of something to lift us all into Christmas Day.

(*He starts pouring whiskey and cream over a spoon.*)

IRIS (*to* PIP). Bob's thinking of taking a new place.

PIP. I hope not. (*pouring cream*) I like

it here best.

IRIS. Apparently he's fed up with S.E. 16. He fancies a business more in the Thames Valley.

ROSEMARY. Or Marlow! Marlow's lovely. lovely.

IRIS (*to* PIP). He thinks he'll get a better class of young customer up there. He fancies facilities for dancing.

ROSEMARY. And a grill. Charcoal grill's nice.

IRIS (*to* PIP). And putting on dinners. With prawn cocktail. Rosemary's got all the ideas. Bob thinks she's got a sharp little nose for business.

PIP (*suddenly positive*). I think it sounds revolting. Here you are, love. (*He hands her a cup.*)

BOB. What sounds revolting?

PIP. The Thames Valley. And the local Young Conservatives' annual do. Throwing bread rolls and gobbling down scampi and selections from Sound of Music and Pimms No. 1 and stripping off in Punts. (*He gives coffee to* ROSEMARY.) Coffee, love?

ROSEMARY (*angry*). I'm not your love!

IRIS. And overdrafts and dud checks and ten barmaids—all with eyelashes.

PIP. I don't think that's the sort of place I would want to visit.

(*He gives coffee to* BOB.)

BOB (*puzzled*). Thanks, Pip.

ROSEMARY. Well. No one's asking you. (*Silence.* BOB *and* IRIS *are looking at* ROSEMARY. PIP *goes to the piano stool. Sits on it quite still.* ROSEMARY *repeats, with extra courage*) No one'll be asking you for Christmas. Not necessarily.

(BOB *moves over to* PIP *as if to protect him: but he doesn't say anything. He puts his coffee down on the piano.*)

PIP. No. I suppose they won't.

ROSEMARY. I mean, I'm not exactly sure. Are you the kids' uncle?

PIP. I'm just someone who comes for Christmas.

BOB (*protecting*). You'll be welcome, Pip, wherever . . .

ROSEMARY. Who is he? I'd like to know that first. Before we start extending invitations.

(*Puts down her coffee and moves towards* PIP)

BOB. He's an old family friend, that's who he is, Rosemary.

ROSEMARY. Yes, I can tell he's old.

BOB. This'll interest you. His mum inhabits a castle.

ROSEMARY. Well, why don't he go to *her* for Christmas?

PIP. It's a question everyone seems to be asking.

BOB. Because he always stays with me.

ROSEMARY. Always?

BOB. That's what I said.

ROSEMARY. Why—is he your long lost cousin, or something?

BOB. He's no relation.

ROSEMARY. Then who is he?

IRIS (*to* PIP). Why don't you tell her who you are?

(*But* PIP *ignores this. He looks at* BOB. *Lifts his hands to the piano and plays, singing.*)

BOB (*to* PIP). Is that the one we're going to do?

PIP. We ought to start practising it.

BOB. How's it go?

PIP. The descant?

BOB. Yes. How's it go?

(PIP *plays the descant.* BOB *sings, looking at the sheet of music.*)

ROSEMARY. What's going on?

IRIS (*as* PIP *goes on playing, she puts down her coffee*). It's a practice, Rosemary . . . It's gone on since the three of us got to know each other. It started for ourselves, really; although now we do it for the children. Christmas Night when we never open—we sing them a carol. And Mr. Lester, that's Pip, him being musical, he insists on a practice and a proper performance. The kids don't care much, quite frankly, but we enjoy it. (*She goes over to the piano, looks at the sheet of music. To* PIP.) Which is my verse?

IRIS (*sings*).

The Holly bears a prickle
As sharp as any thorn
And Mary bore sweet Jesus Christ
To be a Saviour.

ROSEMARY. I think it's bloody ridiculous!

PIP. Why? Bob's got a modest baritone and Iris might be described as a plucky soprano. It's not good, but it's not ridiculous.

ROSEMARY. I don't know why you don't open Christmas Day, and give a party, or have a dance or something for God's sake. Why just sit around singing hymns! I still don't know who he is. Anyway, I don't know why we need to have him every Christmas. (*to* BOB) You're not married to the man, are you?

(*long pause.* IRIS *looks round.*)

IRIS. I think it's time someone told her.

PIP (*looks back at* IRIS). Someone?

(*They both look at* BOB; *he takes a deep breath.*)

BOB. A long time ago. Eighteen years to be precise. Pip and I met as we was placed under the care of a maniac—sergeant named by him "Dulcie"—and we spent long, pointless days stamping on a dreary bit of parade ground near a dump called Bishop's Stortford. Well, one Christmas Eve a change came. Pip took me into his mother's house and played the piano in a high room with walls the colour of old birthday cake and we drank whisky from a decanter while we got pissed bloody senseless. On the way home we climbed into a haystack that was all hard with frost, and we saw each other's breath in the moonlight. And suddenly, for no good reason, we grabbed each other like we were both drowning and proceeded to have it away as if all that side of life had just been invented. I regret to tell you, Rosemary, it didn't stop then. It's been going on ever since. So that's why Pip here's kept up with the family, and why he often brings the odd present at Christmas.

(ROSEMARY *has been listening with growing incredulity. At the end of the speech, she looks at the three of them grouped, silent, dignified round the piano. Her hand covers her mouth as if she's not sure whether to break into a scream or giggles. Then she turns and runs away through the kitchen. We can hear the back door slam after her, when everything is quiet.*)

IRIS. We do this bit together, don't we?

PIP. Oh, yes.

(PIP *plays. They all sing together.*)

The Holly and the Ivy
When they are both full grown
Of all the trees that are in the wood
The Holly bears the crown.

The rising of the sun
And the running of the deer.
The playing of the merry organ,
Sweet singing in the choir.

CURTAIN

LARRY PARKS' DAY IN COURT

A Short Documentary Drama

Eric Bentley

INVESTIGATOR	THE CHAIRMAN
MR. PARKS	SIX COMMITTEE MEMBERS
MR. MANDEL	

From *Are You Now or Have You Ever Been: The Investigation of Show Business by the Un-American Activities Committee, 1947–1958* by Eric Bentley.
© 1972 by Eric Bentley. All rights reserved.
Reprinted by permission of Harper & Row, Publishers, Inc.

A DISTINGUISHED AUTHOR, drama critic, adaptor and translator (notably, of the works of Bertolt Brecht and Luigi Pirandello), editor, and anthologist, Eric Bentley also has served successfully as director and as performer with his poetry readings and recordings. His widely read books include: *What Is Theatre?, The Theatre of Commitment, The Life of the Drama, The Dramatic Event, In Search of Theatre, Bernard Shaw, The Playwright as Thinker, A Century of Hero Worship,* and, most recently, *Thirty Years of Treason* and *Theatre of War.*

Larry Parks' Day in Court is a segment from Mr. Bentley's full-length documentary drama, *Are You Now or Have You Ever Been,* which was given its premiere by the Yale Repertory Theatre on November 10, 1972. A searing example of Theatre of Fact, the play was termed by the reviewer for *Variety* as "an exceptional documentary . . . a work of stark authenticity, with every line of dialogue researched from the pages of the Congressional Record" and a dramatic event that "provides a meaningful look, in retrospect, as to what the 1947–58 House Committee on Un-American Activities' investigation was all about."

Born in England in 1916, educated at Oxford and Yale (where he received a doctorate in comparative literature), the author has taught at the University of Minnesota, was Charles Eliot Norton Professor of Poetry at Harvard; and for almost twenty years has been Brander Matthews Professor of Dramatic Literature at Columbia University.

In addition to *Are You Now or Have You Ever Been,* Mr. Bentley also is the author of the following plays: *A Time to Die and A Time to Live; The Red, White and Black;* and *The Recantation of Galileo Galilei.*

March 21, 1951. Room 226, Old House Office Building, Washington, D.C. The Un-American Activities Committee is in public session, and there is a large audience on this day as the witness is a film star. Six Committee members (here labeled CM 1, CM 2, etc.) are present, along with their Chairman and Investigator. Confronting them is Larry Parks (the star of two then recent movies, The Jolson Story *and* Jolson Sings Again), *accompanied by his attorney. A public-address system is in use, and each participant is equipped with a microphone.*

MORNING

INVESTIGATOR. The Committee on Un-American Activities has succeeded in exposing Communists' infiltration into labor organizations, with the result that the organizations have rid themselves of Communist domination, and that the Congress has been informed of important facts as the basis for legislative action. The testimony of Matthew Cvetic virtually destroyed the power of the Communist Party in western Pennsylvania. Then there have been many witnesses who have told how they were duped into joining the Party, the activities they observed as members, and their reasons for breaking. They have performed a service of inestimable value to their country and should receive the plaudits of their fellow citizens. The hearing today is the first of a series designed to accomplish the same results in the entertainment field. It is hoped that any witness who made the mistake of associating himself with the Communist Party will have sufficient courage and loyalty to make an honest disclosure of all he knows. I would like to call, as the first witness, Mr. Larry Parks. Are you represented by counsel, Mr. Parks?

MR. PARKS. Yes, I am.

INVESTIGATOR. Will counsel identify himself?

MR. MANDEL. Louis Mandel, 1501 Broadway, New York City. Mr. Parks has prepared a statement. It will be enlightening to the Committee as his testimony unfolds. May he read that statement?

THE CHAIRMAN. At the conclusion of his testimony.

MR. MANDEL. In fairness to the witness, I would urge that he be permitted to read the statement now. There is a connecting link to what he will testify.

THE CHAIRMAN. Proceed, Mr. Tavenner.

INVESTIGATOR. Mr. Parks, when and where were you born?

MR. PARKS. I was born on a farm in Kansas. The closest town would be Olathe.

INVESTIGATOR. Will you relate the details regarding your educational background?

MR. PARKS. I moved when quite small to Illinois, attended the high school in Joliet, graduated from the University of Illinois, where I majored in chemistry and minored in physics. I sometimes wonder how I got in my present line of work!

INVESTIGATOR. Mr. Parks, there has been testimony regarding a number of organizations in Hollywood, such as the Actors' Laboratory Theater. Have you been connected with any of those?

MR. PARKS. I have.

INVESTIGATOR. Will you state their names? I will hand you the list.

MR. PARKS (*looking at sheet of paper*). Well, I'm familiar with the Actors' Laboratory.

INVESTIGATOR. Did you hold any position in that organization?

MR. PARKS. For a time I was sort of honorary treasurer. (*He reads the list in silence.*)

INVESTIGATOR. Proceed.

MR. PARKS. I was a member of the Hollywood Independent Citizens Committee of the Arts, Sciences, and Professions.

THE CHAIRMAN. We will have to ask the photographers not to block the view.

INVESTIGATOR. Now, referring back to the Actors' Laboratory, of which you were treasurer?

MR. PARKS. In name, yes.

INVESTIGATOR. "In name"?

MR. PARKS. My job was to sign a batch of checks, and that's the extent of my knowledge of the money matters.

INVESTIGATOR. Will you tell the Committee whether or not there were Communists in these various organizations?

MR. PARKS. I can say yes to that.

INVESTIGATOR. Well, who were these Communists?

MR. PARKS. I don't know. There were

Communists attached to the Lab. But this was not a Communist organization in any sense of the word!

INVESTIGATOR. Well, were there Communists attached to these other organizations you say you were a member of?

MR. PARKS. I don't know.

INVESTIGATOR. But do you recall that, at the Actors' Laboratory, there were members of the Communist Party?

MR. PARKS. That's true.

INVESTIGATOR. Did those Party members endeavor to obtain control?

MR. PARKS. No, the Lab was a school for acting and sort of a showcase for actors.

INVESTIGATOR. Well, what was your opportunity to observe that there were Communists in that organization?

MR. PARKS. I knew them as Communists.

INVESTIGATOR. Well, what had been your opportunity to know them as Communists?

(*pause*)

MR. PARKS. In my opinion, there is a great difference between being a Communist in '41 and being a Communist in '51. (*pause*) I was a member of the Communist Party in '41.

INVESTIGATOR. Tell the Committee the circumstances under which you became a member of the Communist Party; and, if you left the Party, when you did and why.

MR. PARKS. Being a member of the Party fulfilled certain needs of a young man who was liberal in thought, idealistic, who was for the underprivileged, the underdog. I felt it fulfilled these needs. Being a Communist in '51, in *this* situation, is a different kettle of fish. A great power is trying to take over the world. This is the difference!

INVESTIGATOR. You didn't realize that the purpose of the Communist Party was to take over other segments of the world in '41? But you do realize that in '51?

MR. PARKS. This is in no way an apology for anything I've done, you see, because I feel I have done nothing wrong, ever. In '41 the purposes, as I knew them, simply fulfilled—at least I thought they would fulfill—a certain idealism, a certain feeling of being for the underdog, which I am today, this minute. This didn't work out . . . I wasn't particularly interested

after I did become a member—I attended very few meetings and petered out the same way I drifted in. I petered out in '44 or '45.

INVESTIGATOR. Your Communist registration card for the year 1944 bore the number 46954 and for the year 1945 the number 47344. Does that refresh your recollection?

MR. PARKS. No, sir, it doesn't. Because I never had a Party card.

(*pause*)

INVESTIGATOR. Now, do I infer that by '46 you had broken with the Party?

MR. PARKS. Correct.

INVESTIGATOR. Will you state to the Committee where you first became a member of the Party?

MR. PARKS. Hollywood, California.

INVESTIGATOR. Who recruited you into the Party?

MR. PARKS. A man by the name of Davidson, I believe.

INVESTIGATOR. What was Davidson's first name and position?

MR. PARKS. I don't remember his first name. I haven't seen him for ten years. And I don't know what his position was.

INVESTIGATOR. Where did he live?

MR. PARKS. I have no idea.

INVESTIGATOR. What was his occupation?

MR. PARKS. I don't know either.

INVESTIGATOR. Can you give us some descriptive data on the individual?

MR. PARKS. Average-looking, young, dark hair.

(*pause*)

INVESTIGATOR. Well, what were the circumstances under which you met?

MR. PARKS. This is hard for me to recall, too.

INVESTIGATOR. Was it at a meeting in your home or where?

MR. PARKS. I *really* don't remember. I'm being as honest as I know how!

INVESTIGATOR. I just wanted you to give the Committee what information you recall about how you got into the Communist Party.

MR. PARKS. I was a good deal younger then—about twenty-five—with certain liberal tendencies, idealism.

INVESTIGATOR. Did you seek this individual out, or did he seek you out?

MR. PARKS. I certainly didn't seek *him*

out. It's hard for me to say whether he sought *me* out.

INVESTIGATOR. Did others counsel you in regard to your uniting with the Communist Party—before you were recruited by this Davidson?

MR. PARKS. No, I did it of my own volition.

INVESTIGATOR. Were you assigned to a Party cell?

MR. PARKS. I was.

INVESTIGATOR. What was the name of that cell, and where was it located?

MR. PARKS. Well, it had no name that I know of.

INVESTIGATOR. Well, now, you were a member of that group from '41 to '45?

MR. PARKS. That's correct.

INVESTIGATOR. Will you tell us what you know about the organization of the Communist Party during that time?

MR. PARKS. Well, I was a pretty bad member by their lights. Didn't attend too many meetings—maybe ten, twelve, fifteen. What I know about the Communist Party is very little.

INVESTIGATOR. Do you know whether the writers and actors in Hollywood were members of any particular branch or group of the Communist Party?

MR. PARKS. I know that certain actors were a group that met. The other things I do not know.

INVESTIGATOR. Well, were there several groups to which the actors belonged, depending upon the geographical location of the actor?

MR. PARKS. I wouldn't say for certain. I'm not under that impression.

INVESTIGATOR. Well, who was the chairman of the group?

MR. PARKS. It had no chairman that I know of.

INVESTIGATOR. Well, who was the secretary?

MR. PARKS. I don't recall. I don't know if there were any actual officers.

INVESTIGATOR. Well, to whom did you pay your dues?

MR. PARKS. This is hard for me to answer, too, because the few times I paid dues were to different people.

INVESTIGATOR. Well, was Communist Party literature distributed to the members?

MR. PARKS. Certain pamphlets were available if you wished to buy them.

INVESTIGATOR. Who had charge of the distribution or sale?

MR. PARKS. Well, this I don't know either. The pamphlets were there. You could buy them if you wished.

INVESTIGATOR. Well, was there any secret about who was handling the literature of the Party?

MR. PARKS. No.

(*pause*)

INVESTIGATOR. What was the total membership of this cell?

MR. PARKS. I would say it went up to maybe, oh, possibly ten or twelve.

INVESTIGATOR. Did the personnel change between '41 and '45?

MR. PARKS. I attended rather irregularly, and at some of the meetings I would see someone I didn't recognize, and I would never see them again.

INVESTIGATOR. Did Party organizers appear before your group from time to time —people from the East, let us say?

MR. PARKS. No, I don't recall ever seeing any big shot.

INVESTIGATOR. You are acquainted with V. J. Jerome?

MR. PARKS. I don't believe I've ever seen him.

INVESTIGATOR. Are you acquainted with Lionel Stander?

MR. PARKS. I've met him.

INVESTIGATOR. Have you ever attended a Communist Party meeting with him?

MR. PARKS. I don't recall ever attending a Communist Party meeting with Lionel Stander.

INVESTIGATOR. Do you know whether he's a Party member?

MR. PARKS. No.

INVESTIGATOR. Are you acquainted with Karen Morley?

MR. PARKS. I am.

INVESTIGATOR. Is she a member of the Communist Party?

(*pause*)

MR. PARKS. Well, counsel, these—I would prefer not to mention names. I don't think it's fair to people. I've come to you at your request. I'll tell you everything I know about myself, because I feel I've done nothing wrong, and I'll answer any question you'd like to put to me about myself.

I would prefer not to mention other people's names.

CM 1. Do you take the same position with respect to the leaders of the Communist movement?

MR. PARKS. I do, because I don't know the leaders of the Communist movement.

CM 1. You know who was active in the movement in California?

MR. PARKS. I only know the names of people who attended certain meetings. These were not leaders of the Communist Party.

CM 1. Who directed the meetings you attended?

MR. PARKS. The meetings consisted mainly of—we were in a war then—discussions of how the war was going, current events, problems of actors in their work. Does that answer your question, Congressman?

CM 1. It's an answer.

MR. PARKS. Hmm?

CM 1. It's an answer.

MR. PARKS. I'd like to answer your question . . .

CM 1. Who directed the activities this group were engaged in?

MR. PARKS. No one to my knowledge *directed* activities.

CM 2. Who would call the meetings together?

MR. PARKS. Well, I don't really know.

CM 2. Did you have a set, scheduled meeting once every week, or was it upon the call of some individual?

MR. PARKS. Various individuals would call. I don't believe there was any set—

CM 2. Certainly it wasn't run by mental telepathy!

MR. PARKS. No. I didn't say that. I say certain individuals would call, and, to the best of my knowledge, there was no set schedule.

CM 2. Somebody had to issue a call?

MR. PARKS. That's correct.

CM 2. Did *you* ever issue a call?

MR. PARKS. No.

CM 2. Then, somebody would have to tell you when and where the meetings would take place, is that not true?

MR. PARKS. I would get a call from a member of the group and they would say, "Let's have a meeting tonight, tomorrow night."

CM 3. Were the meetings always held at the same place?

MR. PARKS. No.

CM 3. Were they held in halls or in your own homes?

MR. PARKS. These were held at homes.

CM 3. Did you ever have meetings at *your* home?

MR. PARKS. Never.

CM 3. Where were some of the meetings held?

(*pause*)

MR. PARKS. These were people like myself, small-type people, no different than myself in any respect at all, no different than you or I.

CM 3. Where were some of the meetings held?

MR. PARKS. As I say, in various homes in Hollywood.

CM 3. Can you name some?

(*pause*)

MR. PARKS. Well, if you will allow this, I would prefer not to mention names. These were people—like myself—who have done nothing wrong, ever. I mean, along this line. I'm sure none of us is perfect. Again, the question of judgment certainly is there, but these are people—

THE CHAIRMAN. Just a moment. Do you entertain the feeling that these parties you were associated with are likewise guiltless of any wrong?

MR. PARKS. This is my opinion: that these are people who did nothing wrong, people like myself.

THE CHAIRMAN. Mr. Parks, in what way would it be injurious to them to divulge their identities when at no time did they do wrong?

(*pause*)

MR. PARKS. If you think it's easy—I've worked hard in my profession, climbed up the ladder a bit—if you think it's easy for me to appear before this Committee and testify, you're mistaken. This is a very difficult job for me. One of the reasons is that, as an actor, my activity depends a great deal on the public. To be called before this Committee at your request has a certain inference, a certain innuendo that you're not loyal to this country. This is not true. I am speaking for myself. This is not true. But the inference, the innuendo is there as far as the public is concerned.

Also, as a representative of a great industry —as an actor who is fairly well known, in that respect I am a representative . . . This is a great industry! At this time it is being investigated for Communist influence—

THE CHAIRMAN. Don't you think the public is entitled to know about it?

MR. PARKS. Hmm?

THE CHAIRMAN. Don't you feel the public is entitled to know about it?

MR. PARKS. I certainly do, and I'm opening myself wide to any question that you can ask me. I'll answer as honestly as I know how. And at this time, as I say, the industry is—it's like taking a potshot at a wounded animal, because the industry is not in as good a shape as it has been— economically, it's been pretty tough. This is a great industry! And I don't say this only because it has been kind to *me*. It has a very important job to do, to entertain people, in certain respects to call attention to certain evils, but mainly to entertain, and I feel they've done a great job. When our country has needed help, the industry has been in the forefront of that help!

INVESTIGATOR. You are basing your reluctance to testify on the great job that the moving-picture industry is doing?

(*pause*)

MR. PARKS. On naming names, it is my opinion that the few people I could name, these names would not be of service to the Committee: I am sure you know who they are. These people are like myself, and I have done nothing wrong. I also feel that this is not—to be asked to name names like this is not—in the way of American justice as we know it. We as Americans have all been brought up to believe it's a bad thing to force a man to do this. I've been brought up that way, I'm sure you have . . . This is not the American way!

THE CHAIRMAN. Well, I'm glad to give considerable leeway to the range of your statement, because I'm curious to understand what your reasons are for declining to answer the question.

MR. PARKS. I'm not declining. I'm asking you if you would not press me on this.

THE CHAIRMAN. I'm not going to press the point unless other members of the Committee wish to.

CM 2. Are any of the members of your cell still active in the Communist Party?

MR. PARKS. I can't say this, Congressman. I divorced myself completely. I know what I *think*: that ninety-nine percent of them are not.

CM 2. If you knew people in Hollywood that were identified with the Party *then,* would you be reluctant to cite their names if they were active members *at the present time?*

MR. PARKS. I would be reluctant on only one score: that I don't think it's good for an American to be forced to do this. But I feel that the people I knew are *not* members of the Communist Party at the present time. If they are, they shouldn't be!

CM 2. If you had knowledge of a man who committed murder, you wouldn't be hesitant to give that information to the proper authorities?

MR. PARKS. That is correct.

CM 2. I assume you share our belief that an active member of the Communist Party believes in overthrowing our Government by force and violence. Now, if you would give information concerning a man you know has committed murder, wouldn't you give information of a man you knew to be working to overthrow our Government by force and violence?

MR. PARKS. If I knew a man who committed murder, which is against the law of our land, I would name him immediately. The other thing—well, even now it is *not* against the law of our land. (*pause*) You understand the difference I mean?

CM 2. So when we are drafting men to fight Communist aggression, you feel it is not your duty as an American citizen to give the Committee the benefit of what knowledge you might have?

MR. PARKS. I think there is a difference, Congressman, between people who would harm our country and people like myself, who, as I feel, did nothing wrong—

CM 2. I'm not questioning the point when you say people like you may be misguided or were members of the Party because of faulty judgment, but you don't believe that anyone can be naive enough to be an active member of the Communist Party *today* and not know what he's doing?

MR. PARKS. That's correct.

CM 2. For that reason I can't see your consistency in saying you won't name someone you know, today, who is an active member of the Party.

MR. PARKS. But I don't know *anyone* today who is an active member of the Party.

CM 2. If you did know, you would tell?

(*pause*)

MR. PARKS. Yes, I think I would.

(*pause*)

INVESTIGATOR. Mr. Parks, your argument is that this Committee should investigate Communism but should not find out who is a Communist.

MR. PARKS. No, this is not my argument at all!

INVESTIGATOR. You are taking the position that it is not important to find out who may be in Communism in Hollywood—

MR. PARKS. No.

INVESTIGATOR. —rather than for this Committee to determine what its obligations are under the statute which created it to investigate Communism?

MR. PARKS. No, counsel, I didn't say *this!*

INVESTIGATOR. But isn't it the result of your argument?

MR. PARKS. No, counsel, what I say is that the few people I knew are as loyal to this country as you.

INVESTIGATOR. And if every witness were permitted to take that position, the extent of the investigation would be *limited* by the attitude of the witness, wouldn't it?

MR. PARKS. But I told you the circumstances surrounding my small activity with the Communist Party, and this makes a difference.

INVESTIGATOR. In your judgment?

MR. PARKS. Not only in my judgment. I know these people were like me, and the most you can accuse them of is a lack of judgment. I say none of this in apology for what I did, because a young man at twenty-five, if he's not a liberal, if he's not full of idealism, is not worth his salt. If you make a mistake in judgment like this, I don't believe it is serious!

INVESTIGATOR. Yes, but if every witness would be the final judge of when a thing was serious and when it was not, how could the Committee carry out its statutory duty?

MR. PARKS. I'm asking that—

INVESTIGATOR. And I'm asking that you see the other side.

MR. PARKS. I do see the other side.

INVESTIGATOR. Now, Mr. Parks, you have placed Hollywood on a very high pedestal.

MR. PARKS. I have.

INVESTIGATOR. But there has been testimony involving the scientific professions, persons in government, persons in numerous industries, and I take it no preference should be allowed to *your* profession over any other calling?

MR. PARKS. That is true. I was probably the poorest member of the Communist Party that has existed, and the few people I knew, you probably know their names! I can see no way this would be of help to the Committee. If it were really consequential, I would do it. But you must realize—

INVESTIGATOR. Pardon me?

MR. PARKS. You must realize that, inconsequential as I was, the few people I knew . . . it's *distasteful* to me to be forced into this position!

INVESTIGATOR. It is a distasteful position to be in.

MR. PARKS. And I—

INVESTIGATOR. You understand the purposes of this organization. If you would be equally frank with regard to other people who are connected with this organization, the Committee would be permitted to function. And, therefore, I am going to ask you who acted as secretary of this group.

MR. PARKS. And I can honestly say I do not know.

(*pause*)

INVESTIGATOR. Do you know Elizabeth Leech?

MR. PARKS. I don't recall an Elizabeth Leech.

INVESTIGATOR. Do you know a person by the name of Elizabeth Glenn?

MR. PARKS. To the best of my knowledge, I do not.

INVESTIGATOR. Do you know a person by the name of Marjorie Potts?

MR. PARKS. I do not. I don't recall ever meeting these people!

INVESTIGATOR. Now, do you know Karen Morley?

(*pause*)

MR. PARKS. I do.

INVESTIGATOR. Was Karen Morley a member of this group with you?

MR. PARKS. And I ask you again, counsel, to reconsider forcing me to name names. I told you I was a member only for a short time, and I don't think this is American justice, to force me to do this, when I have come three thousand miles and—

CM 1. Mr. Chairman, may I ask counsel a question? (*to the* INVESTIGATOR) How can it be material to this inquiry to have the names of people, when we already know them? By insisting that this man testify as to names, aren't we overlooking the fact that we want to know what the *organization* did, how it attempted to influence the thinking of the American people through the arts?

MR. PARKS. May I answer your question?

CM 1. No.

INVESTIGATOR. Some of these individuals have evaded service of process, so we cannot bring them here. That is one point. Another is that this Committee ought to receive *proof* of information which it has in its files. There would be no way to investigate Communist infiltration into labor without asking who *are* Communists in labor.

CM 1. But isn't it more important to learn the extent of the activity, and the purpose of the organization, than to get a list of names of bleeding hearts and fools and suckers?

INVESTIGATOR. As to organizations, that *was* the subject of much testimony.

CM 1. May I ask the witness a question, Mr. Chairman?

THE CHAIRMAN. Yes, Mr. Walter.

CM 1. Were you instructed to influence the thinking of the American people through stage or screen?

MR. PARKS. I was never instructed to do this, and I think it is evident that this was not done.

CM 1. Was it talked about? Was it the purpose of the Communist organization to set up a hard core in Hollywood that would slant pictures and performances?

MR. PARKS. First of all, it's impossible to do this as an actor. I was never asked to.

THE CHAIRMAN. Wouldn't the *writer* be in a position to very decidedly slant—

MR. PARKS. A script passes through too many hands. It is my opinion that this is an impossibility.

THE CHAIRMAN. And didn't happen?

MR. PARKS. I don't believe that this ever happened.

THE CHAIRMAN. Now, you're leaving an impression there was nothing off-color about the people in your group. How then could it reflect against the members of this group for the names to be known— any more than if they belonged to the YMCA?

MR. PARKS. I feel as I do because I think I am a good example. As I said, it's not easy for me to be here. Anybody who thinks it is out of their mind. It is doubtful whether, after appearing before this Committee, my career will continue, it is *extremely* doubtful . . . For coming here and telling you the truth! There were other things open to me, but, feeling that I have not done anything wrong, I will tell you the truth.

CM 4. Mr. Parks, have you any knowledge of the efforts of the movie industry to clean out subversive influence?

MR. PARKS. This is common knowledge.

CM 4. Is it *your* knowledge?

MR. PARKS. When I say "common knowledge" I mean mine, yours, everybody's. (*pause*)

CM 4. A few minutes ago, you said you were honorary treasurer. Your duty was to sign a batch of checks.

MR. PARKS. That's right.

CM 4. To whom were those checks written?

MR. PARKS. Well, these were to pay the office help, the secretaries, the clean-up man, the teachers, electric company . . .

CM 4. How many secretaries and what office help for what organizations?

MR. PARKS. For the Actors' Lab.

CM 4. How many secretaries?

MR. PARKS. It varied. From none to three or four.

CM 4. Was this one cell limited to members of the actors' profession?

MR. PARKS. I believe it was.

CM 4. And you had a social affair? Did you have refreshments?

MR. PARKS. Yes. Coffee. (*laughter*) I'm serious when I say that! Coffee! Doughnuts!

CM 4. Did the cell have dues?

MR. PARKS. It did.

CM 4. How much were the dues?

MR. PARKS. Well, I couldn't have contributed more than fifty, sixty dollars.

CM 4. You were connected with this cell from '41 to '45, yet you only paid a total of fifty or sixty dollars?

MR. PARKS. Well, the dues, as I recall, when you weren't working, were about seventy-five cents a month, and if you were working I think you paid some percentage. I didn't.

CM 4. You were idealistic, liberal, progressive at the age of twenty-five, and that is perhaps one reason you joined the Communist Party—

MR. PARKS. No, that is *the* reason.

CM 4. Didn't that cell make efforts to increase its own membership in Hollywood?

MR. PARKS. I personally never made such an effort.

CM 4. No, but you heard reports of what was being done by the cell?

MR. PARKS. That's correct.

CM 4. Well, what reports were given?

MR. PARKS. I don't remember. It's been a long time.

CM 4. Well, now, you notice, Parks, at this time I'm deliberately avoiding asking you names!

MR. PARKS. Yes.

CM 4. I am assuming you want to be helpful to the Committee and tell the activities of the cell!

MR. PARKS. That's correct, and I'm doing this.

CM 4. Now, manifestly, the cell was trying to increase its membership, wasn't it?

MR. PARKS. That's correct.

CM 4. You testified that you heard reports—

MR. PARKS. Well, as I say—

CM 4.— of what the cell was doing to increase its membership.

MR. PARKS. Well, you're really going a bit further than I said, Congressman.

CM 4. Well, you go as far as you honestly can and tell us what activities the cell participated in to increase its membership.

MR. PARKS. Well, I think certain members of the group approached people about becoming a member of the Communist Party. I myself never did this.

CM 4. Well, names of prospective members were read off in your presence, or possibilities were read off, weren't they?

MR. PARKS. It's possible that this was done.

CM 4. Well, *was* it done?

MR. PARKS. As I say, it's been a long time.

(*pause*)

CM 4. Was any difference in philosophy between Communism and our form of government ever discussed in the cell? (*silence*) What *did* you discuss, besides drinking coffee?

MR. PARKS. We didn't discuss drinking coffee! The war was going on, and this was the major topic of conversation. The discussions also had to do with actors—how we could get more money, better conditions.

CM 4. Well, was it discussed among you that you could get more money as a member of the Communist Party than as a plain Democrat or Republican?

MR. PARKS. No, this was never discussed.

CM 4. Why did you join? What was membership in this cell going to do for you in Hollywood?

MR. PARKS. As a man of twenty-five, with ideals and a feeling for the underdog, I felt this was a legitimate party. Like the Democrats or Republicans. I felt this was the most *liberal* of the parties . . . I was a registered Democrat. I still am. From that time and before, I've voted the straight Democratic ticket! This was the practical thing to do. The other was an idealistic thing . . .

CM 4. How many years were you in that cell before you began to be disillusioned?

MR. PARKS. Well, "disillusion" is not the word I would choose.

THE CHAIRMAN. Do I understand, sir, that you are *not yet* disillusioned?

MR. PARKS. No, no. Don't bend it! It was a question of lack of interest, of not finding the things that I thought I would find.

CM 4. Did it come clearly to you that the Communist Party was part of an international conspiracy against our form of government?

MR. PARKS. No.

CM 4. Did you come to the conclusion that the Communist Party program was aimed at world domination?

MR. PARKS. Not at that time.

CM 4. When did you come to that conclusion, if at all?

MR. PARKS. Well, the way most everybody has: with recent events in the history of our country and the world.

CM 3. Were there members of the Communist Party who spoke to your group?

MR. PARKS. There was one instance.

CM 3. Can you give his name?

(*pause*)

MR. PARKS. Again I wish you would not press me.

CM 5. Mr. Parks, do you know that, at the time you belonged to the Communist Party, it was a subversive organization?

MR. PARKS. A great change has occurred.

CM 1. You feel that the "do-gooders" have gotten out of it and there is nothing remaining except the hard-boiled politicians?

MR. PARKS. I agree.

CM 5. Mr. Parks, how could you know how *other* members of your cell felt about the Party?

MR. PARKS. Well, during the war a common purpose united all the people of this country . . .

CM 5. I don't think you're answering my question, Mr. Parks. I realize your reluctance in telling the membership of your organization.

MR. PARKS. Would you repeat the question then?

CM 5. We had a witness down here last year, Lee Pressman, who was likewise reluctant to answer questions concerning his association with a Communist Party cell, but eventually he did, and it did the Committee good. I *understand* your reluctance, but the Committee is legally organized and has a function.

MR. PARKS. I agree.

CM 5. As such it has the right to inquire as to the names of members of the Communist Party.

MR. PARKS. That is your right.

INVESTIGATOR. Mr. Parks, you are no doubt acquainted with Samuel G. Wood, producer and director? (PARKS *nods*.) Sam G. Wood testified as follows: "The Laboratory Theater is under the control of the Communist Party. Any kid that goes in there with American ideals hasn't a chance in the world." Do you agree?

MR. PARKS. I disagree.

INVESTIGATOR. You agree that Mr. Wood is a man of honor?

MR. PARKS. But I disagree with *this*.

INVESTIGATOR. But, in light of that testimony, do you still feel *you* should be the judge as to whether or not you should testify—

MR. PARKS. At no time did I say I was the judge. I am a witness. I am asking you gentlemen to be the judge!

INVESTIGATOR. But there is a vast difference, apparently, between your opinion of . . . that organization and the opinion of others.

(*pause*)

THE CHAIRMAN. We are going to take a recess for lunch.

AFTERNOON

THE CHAIRMAN. The Committee will be in order.

MR. MANDEL. Mr. Chairman, Mr. Parks would like to talk about naming names.

THE CHAIRMAN. He expressed himself pretty fully this morning. Counsel has a few more questions. Maybe they will bring out what he wants to say.

MR. MANDEL. What he has to say is very pertinent *at this point*. I don't think we can judge it till he says it. It will take him three minutes. In view of the fact that he has cooperated so completely with the Committee, I think he should be granted three minutes!

THE CHAIRMAN. Make it as brief as you can, Mr. Parks.

MR. PARKS. I will. (*pause*) Mr. Chairman, to be a good actor, you must experience from the top of your head to the tip of your toes what you are doing . . . As I told you, this is probably the most difficult morning and afternoon I have ever spent, and I wish that, if it were at all possible, . . . You see, it's a little different to sit *there* and to sit *here,* and if you could transfer places with me, mentally, and put yourself in my place . . . My people have a long heritage in this country. They fought in the Revolutionary War to make this country, to create the government of which this Committee is a part . . . I have two boys, one thirteen months, one two weeks. Is this the kind of heritage I must hand down to them? Is this the kind of heritage you would like to hand down to your children? For what purpose? . . . Children as innocent as I am or you are, people you already know . . . I don't think I would be here today if I weren't a star, because you know as well as I, even better, that I know *nothing* that would be of great service to this country. I think my career has been ruined because of this, and I would appreciate not having to—Don't present me with the choice of either being in contempt of this Committee and going to jail or being forced to crawl through the mud and be an informer! For what purpose? I don't think this is a choice at all. I don't think this is sportsmanlike. I don't think this is American. Something like that is more akin to what happened under Hitler, and what is happening in Russia. I don't think this is American justice for an innocent mistake in judgment, if it was that, with the intention behind it only of making this country a better place in which to live . . . It is not befitting to force me to make this kind of a choice. I don't think it is befitting to *the purpose of the Committee* to do this. This is probably the most difficult thing I have ever done, and it seems to me it would impair the usefulness of this Committee . . . God knows it is difficult enough to come before this Committee and tell the truth . . . There was another choice open to me. I did not choose to use it. I chose to come and tell the truth. If you do this to me, it will make it almost impossible for a person to come to you, as I have done, and tell the truth . . . I beg of you not to force me to do this!

INVESTIGATOR. Mr. Parks, there was a statement you made this morning which interested me a great deal. You said: "This is a great industry. It has an important job to do: to *call attention to certain evils,* but mainly to entertain." Now, do you believe that persons who "call attention to certain evils" ought to be dedicated to the principles of democracy as we understand them in this country?

MR. PARKS. I certainly agree!

INVESTIGATOR. Do you believe, on the other hand, that persons in those positions should be *antagonistic* to the principles of democracy, be members of a conspiracy to *overthrow* our Government?

MR. PARKS. Most assuredly I don't!

INVESTIGATOR. Then what is your opinion as to whether members of the Communist Party should be in positions of power in the various unions which control the writing of scripts, the actors, and so on?

MR. PARKS. I do *not* believe those people should be in *any* position of power!

INVESTIGATOR. Then we will ask your cooperation, before this hearing is over, in helping us ascertain those who are, or have been, members of the Communist Party. (*pause*) Now, Mr. Parks, tell us what you know of the methods by which money was raised for the Party.

MR. PARKS. I don't recall. (*pause*) I'm not trying to avoid the question!

INVESTIGATOR. I have no trick question here through which I am attempting to lead you into denial of something we know about!

MR. PARKS. I have been as aboveboard as I can! I think the testimony will bear me out! I am willing to help you, if you could be more specific! (*pause*) I have appeared at many benefits over many years—

INVESTIGATOR. Were any of these for the benefit of the Communist Party?

MR. PARKS. I don't recall any.

INVESTIGATOR. You have said you were subpoenaed because you were a star. Mr. Parks, you were subpoenaed because the Committee had information that you had knowledge about Communist activities.

MR. PARKS. All I meant was that I know nothing of any conspiracy to overthrow this Government. And my point was that, if I were working in a drugstore, I doubt whether I would be here!

INVESTIGATOR. We have had many people before this Committee who have been engaged in very menial forms of making a livelihood.

MR. PARKS. Please don't take that in the wrong spirit!

INVESTIGATOR. I didn't fully understand your reference to the possible destruction of your career. You didn't mean to infer that this Committee was bringing you here *because* of any effect it might have on your career?

MR. PARKS. No. What I said was that, because of this, I have no career left.

INVESTIGATOR. Don't you think that question might be influenced by the fullness of the cooperation you give the Committee?

MR. PARKS. I have tried to cooperate, but I think the damage has been done.

CM 6. Don't you think the damage occurred when you became a member of an organization which advocates the overthrow of every constitutional form of government in the world? Is the Committee more to blame than your own act in affiliating with that organization? This Committee is an expression of the will of the American people.

MR. PARKS. As I told you, Congressman, when I was younger than I am now, I felt a certain way about things. I felt strongly, and I still do, about the underdog, and it was for these reasons that . . . this organization appealed to me. I later found it would not fulfill my needs. At that time, I don't even believe this was a mistake in judgment. It *may* have been. This is debatable. But my two boys, I would rather have them make the same mistake I did than not feel like making any mistake at all and be a cow in the pasture! If a man doesn't feel that way about certain things, he is not a man! I do not believe I did anything wrong!

CM 6. Mr. Parks, upon what do you base the opinion that the people whose names you have in your possession have probably severed their relations with the Communist Party?

MR. PARKS. The few people I knew are people like myself and feel the way I do.

CM 6. Well, of course, that is *your judgment* of the matter. Have you discussed Party affiliations with those with whom you were affiliated in the Party?

MR. PARKS. I have not. But these people I knew, and this is my honest opinion. And *you* know these people as well as I do.

(*pause*)

CM 6. In a recent case here in Washington, some of the highest officials in government testified that a man with whom they had been associated had never been a member of the Communist Party and in no way constituted any threat to our institutions. Every man who reads the newspapers now knows how fallacious that opinion was!

MR. PARKS. You know who the people are. I don't think this is American justice, to make me choose whether to be in contempt of this Committee or crawl through the mud for no purpose!

CM 6. That is problematic, Mr. Parks. I "know who they are"—*maybe* you are right, but I still think it's within the province of the Committee to determine how far they will go.

MR. PARKS. I am not setting myself up as a judge. I am asking the Committee not to make me do it.

CM 5. I think you are wrong in assuming we know all the activities you engaged in and all the people you engaged in them with. Possibly you could furnish us with a lot of information we do not have. I feel sure you'd be willing to do that to serve the best interests of the United States.

MR. PARKS. I have told you of my activities to the best of my ability.

(*pause*)

THE CHAIRMAN. We will at this time make a break in the testimony. After we resume, the witness will be advised what the disposition of this Committee is with reference to his apparent disinclination to answer questions.

EVENING

The audience present during the morning and afternoon sessions is now absent. Present are only the Committee, the Investigator, Parks, and Parks's attorney.

THE CHAIRMAN. Mr. Parks, we are going to seek your cooperation in a closed session for testimony that will not be publicized until such time, if at all, as the Committee itself may deem expedient. (*pause*) Counsel will now propound additional questions.

MR. MANDEL. Is it the intention of the Committee, unless he answers these questions in private, to cite him for contempt?

THE CHAIRMAN. The Committee makes no threats.

MR. MANDEL. Just to clear his thinking, so he is fully informed of the consequences . . .

THE CHAIRMAN. If Mr. Parks placed himself in the position of being in contempt of Congress, it is possible that the Committee may request a citation. On the other hand, it may not. Does that answer your question?

MR. MANDEL. I would like to spend another minute on it. In view of Mr. Parks's cooperative attitude—and everyone here understands what is motivating him—he feels so bad about what he has to do, and if he thought there were any chance you would elicit information that was important, he would give it to you . . . It is only saving that little bit of something that you live with. You have to see and walk in Hollywood with that. You have to meet your children and your wife with it, your friends . . . It is that little bit that you want to save. Although I don't ask the Committee to commit itself, in fairness to Mr. Parks . . . he may have to sacrifice the arm with gangrene in order to save the body! He will walk around the rest of his life without an arm! I realize the purposes of this Committee, and our attitude has been one of cooperation: we want to go right through with that. Now, if this is the penalty he will have to pay, I have to urge him a different way . . . His opinion is that what he is going to give you will only eat up his insides and you will get nothing.

THE CHAIRMAN. Mr. Attorney, the Committee is not responsible for the position he finds himself in; we are responsible for the position we find *ourselves* in.

(*short pause*)

INVESTIGATOR. Mr. Parks, who were the members of the cell of the Communist Party to which you were assigned?

(*pause*)

MR. PARKS. This is what I've been talking about. This is the thing. I am no longer fighting for myself . . . I tell you frankly, I am probably the most completely ruined man you have ever seen. I am fighting for a principle, I think, if Americanism is involved in this case . . . This is what I have been talking about. I do not believe it befits this Committee to force me to do this. I do not believe it befits the Committee or its purposes to force me to do this. This is my honest feeling about it. I don't think it's fair play. I don't think it's in the spirit of real Americanism. They are not a danger to this country, gentlemen, the people I knew: they are people like

myself.

INVESTIGATOR. Mr. Chairman, if the witness refuses to answer the question, I see very little use in my asking him about *other* individuals.

THE CHAIRMAN. The witness has got to make up his mind. It isn't sufficient, as far as this Committee is concerned, to say that, in your opinion, it is unfair. Or un-American. The question is: Will you answer?

MR. MANDEL. I would like to ask the Chairman whether he is directing the witness to answer.

THE CHAIRMAN. The witness has been asked. He must answer or decline to answer.

MR. MANDEL. I think a little more is needed. He must be *directed* to answer, and if he refuses, just merely asking him and not going beyond, under law, is not sufficient. I think he has to be told, "You've *got* to answer."

THE CHAIRMAN. I don't understand any such rule, but, to avoid any controversy, I direct the witness to answer the question.

(*pause*)

MR. PARKS. I do not refuse to answer the question, but I feel that this Committee is doing a really dreadful thing! I don't believe the American people will look kindly on it!

CM 6. Mr. Parks, we are, each one of us, responsible to the American people. I, for one, resent having my duties pointed out to me!

MR. PARKS. I am not pointing your duty out.

CM 6. The inference is that we are doing something un-American. That is a personal opinion of yours. We have accountability for which we must account!

THE CHAIRMAN. The witness has said he doesn't *refuse* to answer. So I assume he is *ready* to answer.

MR. MANDEL. I think the members of the Committee are all seeking to do the right thing. No question about that. In the same spirit, no one, with the heritage that Mr. Parks has to uphold, can think that he isn't as loyal as any member of this Committee. He has to do the right thing as we Americans do in our elections! Of course, when the final gong goes down, he intends to respect the will of this Committee. But he reserves the right to talk to you gentlemen and possibly *persuade* you to think differently.

THE CHAIRMAN. The Committee took the view, sir, that there might be some merit in your contention if we were still in an open hearing. But we are not.

MR. MANDEL. This is a private session, which is very considerate of the Committee, and I want to thank you . . . (*pause*) May I have a minute to talk to Mr. Parks?

THE CHAIRMAN. Yes.

MR. MANDEL. I make this request of the Committee: I want no promise from you, just a sportsmanlike attitude, so what he gives you will not be used if it can be helped, to embarrass people in the same position he finds himself in today . . .

THE CHAIRMAN. Nobody on this Committee has any desire to smear anyone's name.

MR. MANDEL. In the internal struggle that Mr. Parks is going through, I think it would go a little lighter, having a statement from you . . .

(MANDEL *and* PARKS *confer inaudibly. When they stop conferring*:)

INVESTIGATOR. If you will just answer the question, please. The question was: Who were the members of the Communist Party cell to which you were assigned?

(*a long silence*)

MR. PARKS. Morris Carnovsky—

INVESTIGATOR. Will you spell that name?

MR. PARKS. I couldn't possibly spell it. Morris Carnovsky, Joe Bromberg, Sam Rossen, Anne Revere, Lee Cobb—

INVESTIGATOR. What was that name?

MR. PARKS. Lee Cobb. Gale Sondergaard, Dorothy Tree—

INVESTIGATOR. What was the name of Dorothy Tree's husband? Michael Uris?

MR. PARKS. Yes.

INVESTIGATOR. Was he a member of the cell?

MR. PARKS. Not to my knowledge.

INVESTIGATOR. Do you know whether Michael Uris was a member of the Communist Party?

MR. PARKS. I don't know.

INVESTIGATOR. Can you recall other members of that cell?

MR. PARKS. That's about all.

INVESTIGATOR. Was Howard Da Silva a member?

MR. PARKS. I don't believe I ever at-tended a meeting with Howard Da Silva.

INVESTIGATOR. Was Howard Da Silva a member of the Communist Party?

MR. PARKS. Not to my knowledge.

INVESTIGATOR. Was Roman Bohnen a member?

MR. PARKS. Yes.

INVESTIGATOR. He is now deceased, I believe.

MR. PARKS. He is dead.

INVESTIGATOR. Was James Cagney a member of the cell?

MR. PARKS. Not to my knowledge.

INVESTIGATOR. Was he a member of the Communist Party?

MR. PARKS. I don't recall ever hearing that he was.

INVESTIGATOR. Sam Jaffe?

MR. PARKS. I don't recall ever attending a meeting with Sam Jaffe.

INVESTIGATOR. Was he a member of the Communist Party?

MR. PARKS. I don't recall that Sam Jaffe was ever a member of the Communist Party.

INVESTIGATOR. John Garfield?

MR. PARKS. I don't recall ever being at a meeting with John Garfield.

INVESTIGATOR. Do you recall whether John Garfield ever addressed a Commun-ist Party meeting?

MR. PARKS. I don't recall any such occa-sion.

INVESTIGATOR. Marc Lawrence, was he a member of that cell?

MR. PARKS. I believe he was.

MR. MANDEL. May I suggest to counsel, in view of the feeling of the witness—I don't mean to rush you, but this whole thing being so distasteful—I wonder if we can proceed a little faster so he doesn't suffer so much . . .

INVESTIGATOR. I want him to be accurate. I purposely don't want to rush him in matters as important as these.

MR. MANDEL. I am just trying to be con-siderate of the man's feeling, doing some-thing that—

INVESTIGATOR. I asked you this morning about Karen Morley. Was she a member of the Communist Party?

MR. PARKS. Yes.

INVESTIGATOR. Was she in this particular cell?

MR. PARKS. Yes.

INVESTIGATOR. Were lectures given in which persons outside of your cell took part?

MR. PARKS. The only one I recall was a talk by John Howard Lawson.

INVESTIGATOR. Georgia Backus, was she a member of this group?

MR. PARKS. The name doesn't ring a bell.

INVESTIGATOR. Meta Reis Rosenberg?

MR. PARKS. I don't believe I know the lady.

INVESTIGATOR. Robert Rossen?

MR. PARKS. No.

INVESTIGATOR. Philip Loeb?

MR. PARKS. I don't recall the gentleman.

INVESTIGATOR. Lloyd Gough?

MR. PARKS. Yes, I believe he was a—I saw him at a couple of meetings.

INVESTIGATOR. Sterling Hayden?

MR. PARKS. I don't recall ever being at a meeting with Sterling Hayden.

INVESTIGATOR. Will Geer?

MR. PARKS. I don't recall ever being in a meeting with Will Geer.

INVESTIGATOR. Victor Killian, Sr.?

MR. PARKS. Yes, I recall that he attended at least one meeting.

INVESTIGATOR. Victor Killian, Jr.?

MR. PARKS. I don't believe I am acquainted with the gentleman.

INVESTIGATOR. Lionel Stander?

MR. PARKS. I've met him. I don't recall attending a meeting with him.

INVESTIGATOR. Andy Devine?

MR. PARKS. I don't recall ever attending a meeting with Andy Devine.

INVESTIGATOR. Edward G. Robinson?

MR. PARKS. I don't recall ever attending a meeting with Edward G. Robinson.

INVESTIGATOR. Madeleine Carroll?

MR. PARKS. I don't recall ever attending a meeting with Madeleine Carroll.

INVESTIGATOR. Gregory Peck?

MR. PARKS. I have no remembrance of attending a meeting with Gregory Peck.

INVESTIGATOR. Humphrey Bogart?

MR. PARK. I don't recall a meeting with Humphrey Bogart.

CM 1. I think you could get some comfort out of the fact that the people mentioned have been subpoenaed. If they do appear here, it won't be as a result of anything you have testified to.

MR. PARKS. It is no comfort whatsoever.

INVESTIGATOR. Do you know of any other person whose name comes to your recollection?

MR. PARKS. I don't recall anyone else.

INVESTIGATOR. That is all, Mr. Chairman. (*pause*)

CM 2. I'd like to say, Mr. Chairman, that Mr. Parks's testimony has certainly been refreshing!

CHAIRMAN. We appreciate your cooperation, Mr. Parks. You are excused.

NIGHT

Two years later, July 15, 1953, Larry Parks addressed the following letter to the Committee:

Dear Chairman Velde:

In rereading my public testimony before the House Committee on Un-American Activities, I am now convinced that it improperly reflects my true attitude. Perhaps some of the confusion in my testimony can best be explained by the fact that I was the first cooperative witness from Hollywood to appear before your Committee and at the time I was under strain. Upon reflection, I see that I did not adequately express my true beliefs—beliefs which have been even deepened and strengthened since my appearance. I wish to make it clear that I support completely the objectives of the House Committee on Un-American Activities. I believe fully that Communists and Communist intrigues should be exposed. Liberals must now embrace the cause of anti-Communism with the same dedication and zeal as we once did that of anti-Nazism. To assist your Committee in obtaining full information about the Communist Party is the duty of all who possess such evidence. If I were to testify today I would not testify as I did in 1951 —that to give such testimony is to "wallow in the mud"—on the contrary, I would recognize that such cooperation would help the cause. My statement about not wanting my sons to become "cows in the pasture" needs clarification. I want my sons to participate in the search for democratic answers to the threat of totalitarianism. I hope the Committee will publish the statement of my militant anti-Communist beliefs at the earliest possible date.

If there is any way in which I can further aid in exposing the methods of entrapment and deceit through which Communist conspirators have gained the adherence of American liberals, I hope the Committee will so advise me.

Sincerely,
Larry Parks.

THE SAFETY MATCH

Norman Ginsbury

(Based on the short story by ANTON CHEKHOV*)*

TCHUBIKOV, *the Police Inspector*
DYUKOVSKY, *his assistant*
YEVGRAV KUZMITCH, *the policeman*
PSYEKOV, *manager of Mark Ivanovitch Klyauzov's estate*
YEFREM, *the gardener*
NIKOLASHKA, *valet to Mark Ivanovitch Klyauzov*

MASHENKA
AKULKA
MARYA IVANOVA, *sister to Mark Ivanovitch Klyauzov*
MAID
OLGA PETROVNA, *the policeman's wife*
MARK IVANOVITCH KLYAUZOV

The play is set in Russia and the time is the past.

A BRITISH dramatist of international stature, Norman Ginsbury was born in London in 1903. His initial success in the theatre came with the West End production of *Viceroy Sarah* in 1934.

An exceptionally perceptive and accomplished dramatic interpreter of historical characters and events, Mr. Ginsbury achieved his finest hour with the London presentation of *The First Gentleman,* in which Robert Morley scored a tremendous personal success. The drama opened at the New Theatre in 1945, and it ran there and at the Savoy for nearly two years. The play was honored on V-E night by no less a personage than Sir Winston Churchill. As Mr. Morley recalls the notable occasion: "In a speech at the end I told the audience that the 'First Gentleman of Europe' was in the stalls. Churchill asked the manager to tell me that he had appreciated my words. 'But what,' I asked, 'did he say about my performance?' 'Nothing whatever,' came the reply. We have to remember that Churchill, first and foremost, was a politician, not a diplomat."

Nonetheless, Mr. Morley's portrayal of the Prince Regent in Mr. Ginsbury's drama still is regarded as one of his finest performances. (*The First Gentleman* opened at the Belasco Theatre, New York, in 1957, with Walter Slezak in the title role. The production was directed by Sir Tyrone Guthrie.)

Mr. Ginsbury's own plays (as well as his translations and adaptations from other sources: Ibsen, Chekhov, Strindberg) consistently have been magnetic lures for players of the front rank. Perhaps the most luminous company of all appeared in his version of Ibsen's *Peer Gynt* as presented in 1944 by the Old Vic Theatre Company. The roster of performers who participated in the Tyrone Guthrie production indeed reads like a *Who's Who* of the British Theatre: Lord (Laurence) Olivier, Sir Ralph Richardson, Dame Sybil Thorndike, Margaret Leighton, Joyce Redman, Nicholas Hannen, Harcourt Williams, George Relph and George Rose, among others. The Old Vic's memorable London season (which also included Shakespeare's *Richard III* and Bernard Shaw's *Arms and the Man*) was followed by a continental tour which ended at the Comédie Française at the invitation of the French Government.

In 1960, Mr. Ginsbury's version of *Peer Gynt* was presented in New York by the Phoenix Theatre with a cast headed by Fritz Weaver and Inga Swenson; and in 1972 it was chosen to open the new Crucible Theatre in Sheffield, England.

The author's many produced and published stage works also include: *Walk in the Sun, The Firstcomers, School for Rivals, The Happy Man, Portrait by Lawrence* (in collaboration with Maurice Moiseiwitsch), *Ladies for You,* and new translations of Ibsen's *Ghosts, An Enemy of the People, A Doll's House, Rosmersholm, The Pillars of Society,* and *John Gabriel Borkman.*

In 1966, his new version of Strindberg's *The Dance of Death* was produced at the Tyrone Guthrie Theatre, Minneapolis.

Norman Ginsbury (who resides in Eastbourne, a seaside resort in Sussex, England) has made the initial dramatizations of a number of popular Chekhov short stories including *The Safety Match* which appears in print for the first time in this volume.

SCENE. *Mark Ivanovitch Klyausov's bedroom. Door, back. Window, right. The furniture is good but the room is in a muddled state. The bed is unmade, a pillow on the floor. One boot is under the table, drawers are half-open and there is a general air of untidiness.*

Before the curtain rises, there is a noise of battering at the door. Excited voices accompany the battering. Then the door bursts open and DYUKOVSKY, *his assistant, and the policeman,* YEVGRAV KUZMITCH. TCHUBIKOV, *the police inspector, is about sixty years old.* DYUKOVSKY *is under thirty and the* POLICEMAN *about forty.*

TCHUBIKOV (*turning*). No one else! The rest of you can wait outside! If I need anyone else I'll send for him. Close the door! (*The* POLICEMAN *closes the door. Then the three men look round the room. There is no sign of an occupant.*) He's not here. That's obvious.

DYUKOVSKY. Under the bed?

(*The* POLICEMAN *goes to the bed and looks under it. He begins to draw out various items.*)

POLICEMAN (*drawing out a straw hat*). One straw hat. (*He draws out some empty bottles.*) Twenty-three bottles. (*looks at them*) Empty! (*He smells one.*) Beer. (*draws out a flagon*) One flagon. (*opens it*) Vodka! Half full!

TCHUBIKOV. Give it here.

(*He takes the flagon and puts it on the table.*)

DYUKOVSKY (*taking a boot from under the table*). One boot.

TCHUBIKOV. The ruffians!

DYUKOVSKY. Here's one of Mark Ivanitch Klyausov's boots but where's Mark Ivanitch Klyausov?

TCHUBIKOV. Don't ask idiotic questions. Examine the floor. (*DYUKOVSKY drops on his knees and starts looking about him. In the meantime, the* POLICEMAN *places various objects on the table.*) This is the second case in my experience, Yevgrav Kuzmitch. (*He is speaking to the* POLICEMAN) I had a similar case eighteen years ago. Do you remember? Portretov, the merchant? He was murdered, too. Exactly the same as this! The swines murdered him and then heaved the body through the window.

POLICEMAN (*shaking his head sadly*). Tt! Tt! Tt!

(*TCHUBIKOV goes to the window, draws the curtain aside and pushes open the window.*)

TCHUBIKOV. It opens easily enough. Hm! There are clues on the window sill. Do you see? It looks like the impression of someone's knee. Someone's climbed out of this window. We'll have to go into this thoroughly.

DYUKOVSKY. There's nothing of interest about the floor. No stains, no scratches! The only thing I've found is a match. (*He holds it up.*) But it's a very important match.

TCHUBIKOV. What's so important about it?

DYUKOVSKY. It's a safety match. Mark Ivanitch hardly ever smoked but when he used a match it was an ordinary match, not a safety match. This ought to be a valuable clue.

TCHUBIKOV. Instead of chattering on and on about unimportant trifles like safety matches, why don't you go and do something? Examine the bed. (*He turns to the* POLICEMAN *while* DYUKOVSKY *approaches the bed.*) Who was it who reported the murder?

POLICEMAN. Psyekov, the manager of the estate.

TCHUBIKOV. Mark Ivanitch's manager?

POLICEMAN. Yes.

TCHUBIKOV. Ha!

POLICEMAN. You know him?

TCHUBIKOV. I've seen him.

POLICEMAN. And Yefrem, the gardener, came with him to make the report.

TCHUBIKOV. Call them in.

(*POLICEMAN goes to the door, opens it a few inches and calls.*)

POLICEMAN. Psyekov, Yefrem, come here! (*He ushers them in and closes the door.* PSYEKOV *is about twenty-five,* YEFREM *is an old man with white hair.*)

TCHUBIKOV (*looking at the young man*). You are Psyekov?

PSYEKOV. Yes.

TCHUBIKOV. I want you to tell me everything you know. Don't try to hide anything because I'll catch you out. Now! How did you discover that Mark Ivanitch had been murdered?

PSYEKOV. I didn't. Yefrem was the one who first mentioned it. We'd never have suspected anything if it hadn't been for Yefrem. "What's the matter with the master?" he said, "No one could go on sleeping as long as that. He's been shut up in that bedroom of his for a week now." The moment he said it I realized how true it was. I hadn't seen him since last Saturday week. He'd had his drunken orgies before but they'd never lasted as long as this. "It's not funny," I said to myself. So I went to his room to see what had happened to him. The door was locked and we couldn't get it open and there was no answer when we called. After that, I thought I'd better go for the police.

TCHUBIKOV. That was a sensible thing to do.

POLICEMAN. Poor Mark Ivanitch! I warned him he'd come to a sticky end. I warned him but would he listen to me? Oh, no! All he had time for was beer and vodka! Such a nice chap, too.

TCHUBIKOV. Cultured!

PSYEKOV. A gentleman, if ever there was one.

POLICEMAN. And so good-natured!

YEFREM. And generous!

POLICEMAN. He was a man apart. But a devil with drink! "It'll lead to worse things," I warned him. And now he's gone!

DYUKOVSKY (*near the bed*). There are no telltale clues or anything else.

TCHUBIKOV. What about the sheets? Are they torn?

DYUKOVSKY. No, but there are teeth marks on the pillow and a stain on the quilt.

YEFREM. Blood!

DYUKOVSKY. No. Beer!

TCHUBIKOV. How do you know?

DYUKOVSKY. It still smells of beer. The state of the bed gives the impression that there was a struggle.

TCHUBIKOV. I know there was a struggle. You don't have to tell me that. Instead of wasting my time telling me what I know, why don't you . . .

DYUKOVSKY. There's only one boot here. The other's disappeared.

TCHUBIKOV. Well, what do you deduce from that?

DYUKOVSKY. It means that they must have smothered him while he was in the act of taking his boots off. He was just taking the second boot off when . . .

TCHUBIKOV. What makes you think he was smothered?

DYUKOVSKY. The teeth marks on the pillow of course! The pillow was all ruffled and I found it yards away from the bed.

TCHUBIKOV. Talk, talk, talk! Go out in the garden and see what you can discover there. I don't need you fiddling about here. I can do all the fiddling that's necessary myself.

(DYUKOVSKY *goes*.)

YEFREM. Oh, dear, dear! Trouble, trouble, trouble!

POLICEMAN. What's the matter with you?

YEFREM. The Serbians!

POLICEMAN. What about them?

YEFREM. They're in trouble again. I can't make out what they want. But it's the fault of the Austrians.

TCHUBIKOV. Never mind the Serbians and never mind the Austrians. We're looking for the murderer of Mark Ivanitch and we're going to find him here, not in Serbia or Austria. (*He calls out of window.*) Anything down there?

DYUKOVSKY (*calling back*). The grass here has been trampled all over.

TCHUBIKOV. What's the good of telling me the grass has been trampled all over? As though I couldn't see that! Have you discovered anything, that's what I want to know?

DYUKOVSKY. There are some strands of wool, dark blue wool, clinging to the nettles.

TCHUBIKOV. Well, uncling them, then.

DYUKOVSKY. Ask them the color of the suit Mark Ivanitch was wearing last Saturday week.

TCHUBIKOV (*to* PSYEKOV). What color was the suit Mark Ivanitch was wearing last Saturday week?

PSYEKOV. A sort of fawn linen.

TCHUBIKOV (*repeating it through the window*). Fawn linen.

DYUKOVSKY. Then it must have been one of the murderers who was wearing dark blue.

TCHUBIKOV. Cut off the nettles with the strands of wool, wrap them up in clean paper and bring them back here.

DYUKOVSKY. There's a great big stain on the grass.

PSYEKOV. A stain?

TCHUBIKOV. What is it?

DYUKOVSKY. Blood!

TCHUBIKOV. Blood?

DYUKOVSKY. Yes.

YEFREM. Blood!

TCHUBIKOV. Sure it's not beer?

DYUKOVSKY. It's blood. It stretches from the window to the lilac bush.

TCHUBIKOV. If it's blood he couldn't have been smothered. Take some of the grass, wrap it up in clean paper and bring it here for analysis. I'll take it with me when I leave. (*leaves the window*) What powers of deduction he's got! Everything fits in pat. Theories, theories, theories!

YEFREM. Oh, dear, dear!

POLICEMAN. Now, what's the matter?

YEFREM. If the Austrians could only see that . . .

TCHUBIKOV. I don't want any theories from you, especially political ones. It doesn't seem possible, gentlemen, it doesn't seem possible, does it? Mark Ivanitch murdered! No, it doesn't seem possible.

POLICEMAN. It doesn't—but there it is!

TCHUBIKOV. I saw him only the Friday before last. At the fair at Tarabankovo. We had a glass of vodka together. And now! . . . Mark Ivanitch has a sister. We must send for her.

POLICEMAN. His sister is Marya Ivanovna. She's a holy woman.

TCHUBIKOV. That's neither here nor there. Go and bring her here.

POLICEMAN. Yes, sir.

(*He goes.*)

YEFREM. In my opinion . . .

TCHUBIKOV. Never mind about your opinion! I've got more important things to think about than the Serbians.

YEFREM. It's not the Serbians. It's . . .

TCHUBIKOV. All right then, the Austrians! (DYUKOVSKY *returns.*) Ah, here you are at last! Have you got those specimens?

DYUKOVSKY. Yes, here. (*He hands over two little packages. In his other hand he is holding a boot.*) Here's the other boot. I found it near the lilac bush.

TCHUBIKOV. Put it down. There's no sense in holding it. (DYUKOVSKY *puts it down.*) You said there was blood near the lilac bush, didn't you?

DYUKOVSKY. Yes.

TCHUBIKOV. He couldn't have been smothered if there's blood there.

DYUKOVSKY. He was finished off in the bedroom, dragged into the garden and stabbed with a sharp weapon just to make sure. The stain under the bush indicates that they left him lying there while they were thinking how they could get him out of the garden.

TCHUBIKOV. And the boot? What about the boot?

DYUKOVSKY. That boot confirms my theory that he was finished off while he was taking his boots off just before going to bed. One boot was off already, and the other one, this one, was only half off when he was attacked. It came off by itself while they were dragging him in the garden.

TCHUBIKOV. Theories, theories, theories! One day, you'll learn to keep your theories to yourself. (*turns away and goes to table*) His watch and money are here. So are his other effects. It's as plain as a pikestaff that robbery wasn't the motive.

DYUKOVSKY. And it wasn't committed by a peasant.

TCHUBIKOV. What makes you say that?

DYUKOVSKY. The safety match. The peasants round here don't use safety matches. The only people likely to use them are the gentry, or anyway, people who are a cut above the peasants.

TCHUBIKOV. Any other conclusions?

DYUKOVSKY. Yes. He was murdered by three people at the very least. Two of them kept him pinioned while the third did the smothering. Mark Ivanitch was a very strong man and the murderers knew it.

TCHUBIKOV. If he was asleep, his strength wouldn't help him, would it?

DYUKOVSKY. The murderers attacked him while he was taking his boots off. If he was taking his boots off, he couldn't have been asleep, could he?

TCHUBIKOV. Don't be impertinent! You're just inventing things. You think you sound very clever but you don't.

YEFREM. As I see it, sir, this crime was committed by Nikolashka, and no one else.

PSYEKOV. That's more than likely.

TCHUBIKOV. Who's Nikolashka?

YEFREM. The master's valet. If it's not Nikolashka, who else could it be? Nikolashka's a blackguard and a drunk. (*to* PSYEKOV) Isn't he?

PSYEKOV. And a rake, too.

YEFREM. He's the man who used to get the vodka for Mark Ivanitch. He used to put him in bed, too. What's more, he was heard boasting in the inn, not more than a month ago, that he was going to finish his master off.

TCHUBIKOV. What?

YEFREM. It's true! It was all because of Akulka.

TCHUBIKOV. Akulka?

YEFREM. Yes. Her husband's a soldier somewhere. Nikolashka took up with her and then, one day, Mark Ivanitch met her and he took up with her, too. And after he took up with her he took her up to bed, and when Nikolashka heard about it— well, he took on. He's staggering about the kitchen now crying his eyes out pretending he's so upset about the master.

PSYEKOV. Anyone might get upset about losing Akulka. She's only an ignorant peasant, but there's something about her. Mark Ivanitch used to call her Nana, Nana of the Boulevards, you know, and well— he was right.

TCHUBIKOV (*blowing his nose*). I think I know the woman. (DYUKOVSKY *coughs. To the* POLICEMAN, *as he returns*) Bring in Nikolashka. (*The* POLICEMAN *hastens out.* TCHUBIKOV *turns on* DYUKOVSKY.) Well, any new theories from you?

DYUKOVSKY. What about?

TCHUBIKOV. Nikolashka or anything else.

DYUKOVSKY. Let me hear his evidence first. He's sure to have thought up an alibi of some sort.

TCHUBIKOV. It'll have to be a very subtle one to take me in. (*He ruminates.*) Poor Mark Ivanitch! Murdered by his own valet! All over a woman!

(*He shakes his head. He is almost in tears. The* POLICEMAN *returns with* NIKOLASHKA, *a tall young man with a sunken chest. He is slightly drunk and bows low to* TCHUBIKOV.)

TCHUBIKOV. So you're Nikolashka, are you?

NIKOLASHKA. Yes, sir.

TCHUBIKOV. Find out if we have any information about him. (POLICEMAN *goes.*)

Where's your master?

NIKOLASHKA. Murdered.

(*He begins to cry.*)

TCHUBIKOV. We know he's murdered but where's his body?

NIKOLASHKA. It was pushed through the window and buried in the garden somewhere.

TCHUBIKOV (*triumphantly*). Aha!

NIKOLASHKA. I heard it in the kitchen.

TCHUBIKOV (*deflated*). So the results of our inquiries are known in the kitchen already, are they? Now then, my man, where were you the night your master was murdered? Last Saturday week!

NIKOLASHKA. I can't say truthfully. I was so drunk I don't remember.

DYUKOVSKY. The alibi!

TCHUBIKOV. Why is there so much blood under your master's window?

(NIKOLASHKA *ponders.*)

DYUKOVSKY. Hurry up man, answer!

NIKOLASHKA. It's not my master's blood.

TCHUBIKOV. Whose is it then? Yours?

NIKOLASHKA. A hen's.

TCHUBIKOV. What?

NIKOLASHKA. I killed a hen.

TCHUBIKOV. You killed a hen, did you?

NIKOLASHKA. I cut her throat and she fluttered away.

TCHUBIKOV. So she fluttered away, did she?

NIKOLASHKA. Yes. That's the hen's blood.

TCHUBIKOV. Did anyone see you kill the hen?

NIKOLASHKA. I don't know. I kill a hen every evening.

TCHUBIKOV. Does anybody ever see you kill a hen?

NIKOLASHKA. The gardener sees me sometimes.

TCHUBIKOV (*to* YEFREM). Is that true?

YEFREM. Yes, sir. I frequently see him kill a hen.

TCHUBIKOV. Does he do it every evening?

YEFREM. Yes.

TCHUBIKOV. But *you* don't see him do it every evening?

YEFREM. No, sir.

TCHUBIKOV. Did you see him kill this particular hen he's talking about?

YEFREM. No, sir, I can't say I did.

TCHUBIKOV. So you didn't see it flutter away?

YEFREM. No.

DYUKOVSKY. A stupid alibi, in my opinion.

TCHUBIKOV. Have you ever slept with Akulka?

NIKOLASHKA. Yes. I'm a sinner.

TCHUBIKOV. And your master took her away from you?

NIKOLASHKA. He certainly did not. It was Mr. Psyekov here, who took her away from me. The master took her from Mr. Psyekov. And that's the truth, the whole truth, and nothing but the truth.

(*All eyes are turned on* PSYEKOV *who is looking very embarrassed and starts to rub his left eye.* DYUKOVSKY *is staring at him with eagle eyes. For the first time, he has noticed that* PSYEKOV *is wearing dark blue trousers, the same color as the blue strands found on the nettles.*)

TCHUBIKOV. All right, you may go. Wait outside.

(NIKOLASHKA *scuttles out.* TCHUBIKOV *takes the strands of dark blue wool from one of the packages that* DYUKOVSKY *has brought in.*)

TCHUBIKOV. What color are your trousers, Mr. Psyekov?

PSYEKOV (*looking down at them*). I suppose you'd call them dark blue.

TCHUBIKOV (*getting up, going over to* PSYEKOV *and speaking with heavy sarcasm*). I suppose I would. I suppose everyone else would, too. (*He holds the strands against* PSYEKOV's *trousers, matching the color. Everybody's eyes are on* PSYEKOV's *trousers.* PSYEKOV *looks ready to faint.*) And now, Mr. Psyekov, I must ask you one or two questions. (*pause*) You were in the house here, weren't you, last Saturday week.

PSYEKOV. Yes. I had supper with Mark Ivanitch.

TCHUBIKOV. What time was that?

PSYEKOV. Ten o'clock.

TCHUBIKOV. And afterwards?

PSYEKOV (*confused*). Afterwards . . . afterwards . . . Well, it's difficult to say. I had had a lot to drink. Everyone does who has supper with Mark Ivanitch. I can't even recall what time I went to bed. Why are you all staring at me like that? Anyone would think *I* killed him.

TCHUBIKOV. That's what we're going to find out. When you woke up, where were you?

PSYEKOV. In the servants', kitchen. On the stove. They saw me there. I don't know how I got there but that's where I was!

TCHUBIKOV. Don't worry your head about it. You know Akulka, don't you?

PSYEKOV. Yes, I do. I've made that clear already. But I don't know her as well as you seem to think.

TCHUBIKOV. And she gave you up for Mark Ivanitch, didn't she?

PSYEKOV. Yes.

(*There is a long pause during which they all stare at* PSYEKOV. *Suddenly, the door opens and the* POLICEMAN *returns with* MARYA IVANOVNA. *She is a spinster of forty-five and is dressed in black.* TCHUBIKOV *and* DYUKOVSKY *stand to receive her. She is attended by her maid-servant.*)

MARYA. What *is* all this? Why have you sent for me? This man interrupted me at my prayers.

POLICEMAN. I did apologize, madame. It's the last thing in the world I wanted to do. To interrupt a lady in her devotions—

TCHUBIKOV. I apologize too, madame, but necessity, as you must realize, knows no law.

MARYA. Law? What have I to do with the law?

TCHUBIKOV. Nothing, madame, we hope, but there are one or two questions I must ask you. First of all, Psyekov and Yefrem wait outside. (*They go.*) You've heard, no doubt, that your brother . . . that there's a possibility that your brother has, somehow or other, been murdered. It is God's will. (*profoundly*) No one can escape death, not the peasant nor the magistrate nor the Tsar himself. There's absolutely nothing we can do about it. Now, is there anything you can tell us, anything that will help us to track down your brother's murderers?

MARYA (*covering her face with her hands*). Don't ask me! I know nothing, nothing. Don't ask me anything about my brother. Not a word! I'd rather die than discuss him.

TCHUBIKOV. But don't you want us to apprehend the murderers?

MARYA. I don't want anything. I don't want anything, least of all to be reminded of him! My brother was an atheist. I won't discuss him with anybody.

TCHUBIKOV. Well, if you won't . . .

MARYA. I won't!

(TCHUBIKOV *nods to the* POLICEMAN *who takes her out. They are followed by the maid who gives the two men a most inviting look as she goes. The men react.*)

DYUKOVSKY. The woman's a demon! (*hastily*) Marya Ivanovna, I mean. Did you see how white she went when you mentioned her brother?

TCHUBIKOV. Yes.

DYUKOVSKY. I suppose she thought she'd get some sympathy by telling us he was an atheist.

TCHUBIKOV. A murderer's a murderer even if his victim is an atheist. Besides, everyone knew Mark Ivanitch was an atheist.

DYUKOVSKY. Whatever she knows she's keeping her mouth shut—and she certainly knows *something*. And that maid of hers, too, with her extraordinary smile. Did you notice it?

TCHUBIKOV. Of course I noticed it!

DYUKOVSKY. How would you describe it?

TCHUBIKOV. Inscrutable.

DYUKOVSY. That's it! Inscrutable! But they won't pull the wool over our eyes. I'd like to find out how well in they are with that Nikolashka. He's in it up to the hilt. *Non dubitandem est.* One look at his face and you know what *he* is! That alibi! If anything gave him away, that did! But I don't think he was the master-mind. No, he was just the hired tool, the idiot! But a willing tool! Do you agree?

TCHUBIKOV. No.

DYUKOVSKY. You do. You must. And Psyekov? His role isn't a trivial one, either. He wore blue trousers! Exactly the same color as the strands on the nettles. And his confusion! I've never seen a man look so guilty. And why was he lying there on the stove? I'll tell you. Panic! And his alibi? Weak! And that little hole-in-the-corner business with Akulka! What do you make of that?

TCHUBIKOV. Carry on, carry on! You're in your element, aren't you? If you ask me, Nikolashka isn't the only idiot in this affair. You seem to think that everybody who knows Akulka is the murderer. Well, you had your eye on Akulka, too, at one time. Does that mean you're an accomplice, too?

DYUKOVSKY. I'm not forgetting that Akulka used to be cook in your house. But we'll let it pass. On the Saturday night when Mark Ivanitch disappeared I was playing cards with you, otherwise we'd suspect each other. But Akulka isn't the pivotal point in the matter. No! It's the mean, cheap, revolting emotions that were aroused—they're the pivotal point. That's why the murder was committed. The discreet Psyekov didn't relish the idea of being jilted. Not he! Did you take a look at his mouth? Sex personified! Did you notice how it watered when he compared Akulka to Nana of the Boulevards? He's on fire with lust for the girl, and where there's pride and unrequited lust, there you have murder, too. We've got two of them but where's the third? And who's the third? Nikolashka and Psyekov held him down but who smothered him? Psyekov hasn't the courage to do it and Nikolashka wouldn't use a pillow to finish off his victim. A pickaxe or a hammer is more in his line. So someone else must have smothered him. Who was it?

TCHUBIKOV. I'm waiting for you to tell me.

DYUKOVSKY. All right then, I'll tell you. It was a woman.

TCHUBIKOV. Who? Akulka?

DYUKOVSKY. No. Marya Ivanovna.

TCHUBIKOV. What? The murdered man's sister? You've got a screw loose, my friend.

DYUKOVSKY. You saw her confusion, didn't you? And why did she refuse to discuss him? Because she might have given herself away. She said it was because he was an atheist. He *was* an atheist. That's why she resented him so much. She's a religious fanatic—and he was a profligate and an atheist. Why, only a few weeks ago she told someone he was a messenger from Hell.

TCHUBIKOV. Well?

DYUKOVSKY. She murdered him because she's a religious fanatic. She thinks she's saved the world from anti-Christ. Inwardly, she must be glorying in her achievement. You know what those maiden ladies are! If you don't, read Dostoevsky.

She's the murderer, I tell you. Mr. Tchubikov, my dear man, let me handle the case for you.

TCHUBIKOV. For Heaven's sake . . .

DYUKOVSKY. My dear friend, I've begun it. Let me finish it, let me finish it.

TCHUBIKOV. I know I'm getting on and perhaps I've passed my prime but I'm still capable of doing my job, despite complications, so shut up. And let me give you a piece of advice. Don't push yourself. Let others do it for you. If I thought you were capable of handling this case on your own I'd say "All right, go ahead with it." But I don't think you're capable of doing it despite all your talk. Your job is to write down what *I* dictate to you. Just remember that.

DYUKOVSKY (*subdued*). Very well.

TCHUBIKOV. You're too hasty, too excitable, and too clever by half. When you've learned to control yourself and to take a less rosy view of your own talents you might begin to get somewhere. Till then . . .

(*The* POLICEMAN *returns.*)

POLICEMAN. Here's Nikolashka's police record.

TCHUBIKOV. Ah! (*takes the papers*)

POLICEMAN. And there's a girl outside who says she's got some evidence.

TCHUBIKOV. Who is she?

POLICEMAN. She calls herself Mashenka. She works in the laundry.

TCHUBIKOV. I'll see her.

(POLICEMAN *opens door and beckons her in.*)

DYUKOVSKY. Have you searched Psyekov and Nikolashka?

POLICEMAN. Yes.

DYUKOVSKY. Did either of them have a box of matches?

POLICEMAN. No.

TCHUBIKOV. Finished?

DYUKOVSKY. Yes.

TCHUBIKOV (*sarcastically*). Thank you. (POLICEMAN *goes.* TCHUBIKOV *turns to* MASHENKA. *She is a burly type, about twenty-one.*)

TCHUBIKOV. So you're Mashenka?

MASHENKA. Yes, sir.

TCHUBIKOV. What have you got to tell me?

MASHENKA. Well, last Saturday week, late at night, I was going home. I'd just left my friend and we'd both drunk a bit too much so, after I left him, I thought I'd cool off in the river. Well, while I was there, what do you think I saw?

TCHUBIKOV. Well, what *did* you see?

MASHENKA. I saw two men crossing the bridge carrying something black. "Co-oo," I called out. They were so frightened they ran off to the Makarev vegetable plot. But I saw who it was they were carrying.

TCHUBIKOV. Who?

MASHENKA. Mark Ivanitch Klyauzov.

TCHUBIKOV. You're sure?

MASHENKA. Absolutely positive.

TCHUBIKOV. But it was dark.

MASHENKA. Not so dark that I couldn't see.

TCHUBIKOV. And you were drunk.

MASHENKA. Not so drunk that I couldn't see straight. The man they were carrying was Mark Ivanitch Klyauzov.

TCHUBIKOV. I see. Thank you for coming. Wait outside. (*He rings his bell.* POLICEMAN *enters.*) Put a guard on Psyekov and Nikolashka and then get a team to start digging in the Makarev vegetable allotment. That's where you might find the body.

POLICEMAN (*wide-eyed*). The body? Mark Ivanitch's body?

TCHUBIKOV. Yes.

(POLICEMAN *goes with* MASHENKA.)

DYUKOVSKY. You know as well as I do that Psyekov and Nikolashka are guilty. Then why won't you believe that Marya Ivanovna, that holy woman, had a hand in it?

TCHUBIKOV. Because there's no evidence, that's why. It's just theory. Religious fanaticism and so on.

DYUKOVSKY (*impatiently*). You're never satisfied unless there's a pickaxe somewhere and bloodstained sheets. I see the psychological motives. If you won't see it, I'll prove it to you. If theories aren't good enough I'll produce something substantial.

TCHUBIKOV. What are you talking about now?

DYUKOVSKY. The safety match. Have you forgotten? I'm going to find out who struck that match in the murdered man's room. When Nikolashka and Psyekov were searched, there were no matches on either of them. That match was struck by Marya Ivanovna. I'm going to find out.

When I come back, I'll have proof, what's more.

(*He runs to door.*)

TCHUBIKOV. Send Nikolashka in here before you start on your voyage of discovery.

DYUKOVSKY. All right. And I'll come back with your problem solved for you. I'll have the laugh on you, my friend. Just you wait!

(*He goes.* TCHUBIKOV *touches his forehead and gives a gesture of despair.* NIKOLASHKA *enters.*)

TCHUBIKOV. Stand there. (NIKOLASHKA *takes his stand.*) Now then! (*He rustles papers.*) Eight years ago, you were convicted for theft and sent to prison for three months. Is that so?

NIKOLASHKA (*frightened*). Yes, sir, it is.

TCHUBIKOV. Five years ago, you were condemned for theft again. You went to prison for six months. Well, am I right?

NIKOLASHKA. Yes, sir.

(*He breaks down.*)

TCHUBIKOV. There's nothing we don't know about you. Bear that in mind when you come up for trial for the murder of Mark Ivanitch Klyauzov. That's all! Now stop blubbering and wait outside. Send in Psyekov. (NIKOLASHKA *goes, terrified.* TCHUBIKOV *shakes his head sadly.*) Poor Mark Ivanitch! Poor Mark Ivanitch! I was drinking with him the day before it happened. And now he's dead! Murdered by his own servants! (PSYEKOV *enters.*) Stand there! (PSYEKOV *stands where he is told.* TCHUBIKOV'*s voice is very stern.*) I hope you're not going to be stupid. By that, I mean I hope you'll stop lying. You say that you had nothing to do with the murder of your employer but the evidence against you is piling up. Confession makes a man less guilty. Confess now or it may be too late. Now . . .

PSYEKOV. I know nothing about any murder and I know nothing about the evidence you have against me.

TCHUBIKOV. All right, then, I'll tell you how the crime was committed, step by step. On the evening of last Saturday week, you were in this room here drinking beer and vodka with Klyauzov. Nikolashka was looking after you. Between twelve and one, Mark Ivanitch told you he was going to bed. While he was taking his boots off and giving you his orders about the estate, you and Nikolashka, at a previously arranged signal, seized hold of him. He was drunk, and you threw him down on his bed. One of you held on to his feet, and the other held on to his head. While you were holding on, the lady—you know whom I'm referring to —the lady in the black dress, came into the room. Her part in the murder had been arranged beforehand. She took hold of the pillow and started to smother Mark Ivanitch. While he was fighting for his life, the lamp went out. The woman took out a box of safety matches and lit a candle. (*He stops.*) Your face is giving you away, Psyekov. You see, there's nothing you can hide from us. Well, after she'd suffocated him, you and Nikolashka pushed him through the window onto the nettles just underneath. Then, in order to make sure, one of you struck him with a sharp weapon. Then between you, you carried him to the lilac bush. You stopped to regain your breath and then you lifted him over the fence and dragged him along the road to the bridge. At the bridge you were scared stiff by a girl who called out to you from the river. What's come over you, Psyekov. You look like a ghost.

(PSYEKOV *jumps up.*)

PSYEKOV. That's what you want to believe so you'll believe it! All right then! But let me get outside. I'll suffocate in here. Let me go! Let me go!

(TCHUBIKOV *rings.* POLICEMAN *enters.*)

TCHUBIKOV. Let him wait outside—with the guard.

POLICEMAN. Akulka is here. Shall I send her in?

TCHUBIKOV. Yes. (POLICEMAN *goes with* PSYEKOV. TCHUBIKOV *talks to himself.*) Psyekov didn't confess. Not quite. But he let the cat out of the bag. (*smiles to himself*) Rather subtle, the way I trapped him! (AKULKA *comes in. She is twenty-four, a fair, brazen Slav peasant.*) Now, Akulka—that is your name, isn't it?

AKULKA. Of course it is! You know that as well as I do.

TCHUBIKOV (*ignoring it*). What do you know of this business?

AKULKA. Me? What should *I* know about it?

TCHUBIKOV. Nikolashka was your— friend, shall we say?

AKULKA. Friend? We used to say "good night" and "good morning" to each other. We were as friendly as that.

TCHUBIKOV. You said "good night" when you went to bed with him and "good morning" when you woke up by his side. (*He laughs.*)

AKULKA. I've got a bit more conversation than that—as you well know!

(TCHUBIKOV *does a double take.*)

TCHUBIKOV. All right then, Nikolashka wasn't your friend. But Psyekov was, wasn't he?

AKULKA. Psyekov?

TCHUBIKOV. Don't pretend you don't know him.

AKULKA. He was as much my friend as Nikolashka was.

TCHUBIKOV. And Mark Ivanitch Klyauzov? Was he your friend?

AKULKA. No.

TCHUBIKOV. It's no good lying. Psyekov enticed you away from Nikolashka and Mark Ivanitch enticed you away from Psyekov. Isn't that right?

AKULKA. No, it's not right. They all wanted to sleep with me but I wouldn't let them. I never slept with any of them. (*shouting at him*) The only man I've ever lived with is *you*!

(DYUKOVSKY *rushes in.*)

DYUKOVSKY. *Veni, vidi, vici.*

(*He stops dead.*)

TCHUBIKOV. Wait outside, Akulka.

(*She tosses her head and goes.*)

DYUKOVSKY. What did she have to say?

TCHUBIKOV. Nothing. She knows nothing.

DYUKOVSKY. I don't believe she does. But I know someone who knows a lot.

TCHUBIKOV. You do, do you?

DYUKOVSKY. I've sent for Olga Petrovna, the policeman's wife.

TCHUBIKOV. Yevgrav Kuzmitch's wife? What's come over you?

DYUKOVSKY. Send Yevgrav Kuzmitch away. (*urgently*) Please! He mustn't be here when we interview his wife.

TCHUBIKOV. Where can I send him?

DYUKOVSKY. Anywhere, anywhere, but get him away from here!

TCHUBIKOV (*ringing bell*). If this is another of your mad theories . . . (*The* POLICEMAN *enters.*) Yevgrav Kuzmitch, my good friend, I want you to go and super-

vise the digging in the Makarev allotment. I want you to go at once. Later on, I may come over and join you myself.

POLICEMAN. I ought to be there when the body's dug up, oughtn't I, if only to identify it? I might even do some digging myself if only to pay my respects to poor Mark Ivanitch. Yes.

(*He nods his head and goes.*)

TCHUBIKOV. Now, tell me, what's all this nonsense about?

DYUKOVSKY. Do you know, I'm beginning to believe in my own genius. Sit up and listen! There's another woman in the case. Another murderess! And what a woman! I'd have given ten years of my life just to slide my fingers over one of her shoulders.

TCHUBIKOV. Get on with it, will you!

DYUKOVSKY. Well, I drove over to the village. I'd made up my mind to try the shops and the inns where they sold matches. There aren't many, fortunately, and I didn't have to go far. There's only one shop in the village where they sell safety matches. The shop had eleven boxes. One had been sold last Saturday week! "Who bought it?" I asked. "Olga Petrovna, the policeman's wife," the shopkeeper told me. Olga Petrovna, the policeman's wife! So now we know! And we know because of me! Because *I* made up my mind to find out. What can be done by a man of determination, even if he was expelled from school, is beyond anyone's comprehension. I've grown to have a great regard for myself, Mr. Tchubikov.

TCHUBIKOV. You need to, because no one else has. Your theories are crazy!

DYUKOVSKY. Think it out! Think it out then! First of all, Olga Petrovna smokes like a chimney, the only woman in the district who does. Secondly, she was madly in love with Mark Ivanitch. Everyone knew it except her husband. He wouldn't have anything to do with her because of Akulka. A woman spurned! Now do you understand? I remember seeing them once in Mark Ivanitch's kitchen. She was cursing him right and left and he was smoking her cigarette and blowing the smoke in her face.

TCHUBIKOV. The more I hear of your theories the more I'm convinced you're not all there. Olga Petrovna's an honest, respectable woman.

DYUKOVSKY. Honest, respectable, my foot! If only for the sake of justice I demand that you see this woman.

TCHUBIKOV. Now, don't you start demanding anything, young man. You're getting beyond yourself.

DYUKOVSKY. Then I appeal to you! This is going to be the case of the century. You'll be famous all over Russia. So will I!

(*knock at the door*)

TCHUBIKOV. Who's there?

(*The door opens.* YEFREM *appears.*)

YEFREM. Sir, it's Olga Petrovna, the policeman's wife. She says you sent for her.

(TCHUBIKOV *glares at* DYUKOVSKY.)

TCHUBIKOV. Where's the guard?

YEFREM. They're keeping an eye on Psyekov and Nikolashka.

TCHUBIKOV. Well, send the woman in then.

(YEFREM *goes and* OLGA PETROVNA *enters. She is a ripe twenty-three with black eyebrows and full red lips.*)

OLGA. You sent for me?

TCHUBIKOV. Yes.

OLGA. Here I am. What do you want?

DYUKOVSKY. Madame, will you please tell us where Mark Ivanitch is? You murdered him so you ought to know.

OLGA. I *what?* I murdered him? What are you talking about?

DYUKOVSKY. In the name of the law, I demand to know what you have done with Klyauzov. We know everything, so you'd better tell us the truth.

TCHUBIKOV. Come, madame, tell us, otherwise we might have to resort to different methods.

OLGA. I don't know what you're talking about.

TCHUBIKOV. Oh, yes, you do. And unless your looks belie you, you know very well where his body is to be found. You're trembling all over. Mark Ivanitch has been murdered, yes, murdered—by you and others. We know everything, I tell you. Your accomplices have given you away.

OLGA. My accomplices! (*She seems shattered.*) Very well then, I can see I'll have to tell you everything. Until half an hour ago, I hid him in my bathhouse. But don't breathe a word about it to my husband.

It would kill him.

TCHUBIKOV. No doubt about that! From what you say, I conclude that the body is no longer there. Where is it now?

OLGA. Outside.

TCHUBIKOV. Outside the bathhouse?

OLGA. Outside this room.

TCHUBIKOV. How did you manage . . . ? You mean to say you brought the body here with you?

OLGA. Yes. It's outside now.

TCHUBIKOV. Are you telling us . . .

(OLGA *leans forward and rings* TCHUBIKOV'S *bell.*)

OLGA. Here's the body! (MARK IVANITCH *totters in.*) It's got nothing in its head except a few gallons of beer and vodka. Keep it! I'll be glad to get rid of it. A week of him is enough for any woman.

(*She goes. The others are staring at* MARK IVANITCH, *amazed. He puts his fingers to his lips and goes to the door to make sure she has gone. He returns.*)

KLYAUZOV. That terrible woman! She's gone! She's gone! I hope I never see her again. We'll have to send the policeman to another part of the country.

DYUKOVSKY. But, Mark Ivanitch, tell us . . .

KLYAUZOV. No. You tell me. What are you all doing in my bedroom?

TCHUBIKOV. You disappeared. We were investigating . . .

KLYAUZOV. Disappeared?

TCHUBIKOV. We all thought you were . . . Your manager, Psyekov, reported that . . .

KLYAUZOV. Disappeared, did I? I went to stay with Olga Petrovna and you call that disappearing? We didn't want her husband to find out so I hid in the bathhouse. I only came out when he was on duty. Olga Petrovna gave me lots to eat and just enough to drink but I was beginning to feel I'd outstayed my welcome. Criticizing me all the time! Never a stop for breath even! I drink too much, I snore, I'm a lout, what does Akulka mean to me? I was thinking of moving on when you sent for her. When I heard you were here in my house I made up my mind to come, too.

DYUKOVSKY. It's incredible!

KLYAUZOV. What's incredible?

DYUKOVSKY. We all thought . . . How did your boot get in the garden?

KLYAUZOV. What boot?

DYUKOVSKY. We found one of your boots in the bedroom and the other in the garden.

KLYAUZOV. Why should I tell you? It's none of your business. There's some vodka in that flagon. Let's have a drink. (*He takes a swill and hands the flagon to* TCHUBIKOV *who puts it aside*.) As a matter of fact, that boot could tell quite an amusing story. You see, I didn't really want to go to Olga's. I had too much respect for the policeman, her husband. Very conscientious fellow! She planted herself under that window there scolding me and cursing me, so I flung my boot at her. I only did it because I was drunk. What did Olga do? She climbed in through the window and gave me a damned good hiding. I was too drunk to do anything about it. Well, I'm back now and I'm back for good. Why should I stay there hiding in someone else's bathhouse? I can get everything I want here. Not that I want much! Love and vodka! That's all I want! And beer, too. (*He sounds almost tearful*.) And you all thought I was murdered! They told me outside.

TCHUBIKOV. Well, what else . . . ?

KLYAUZOV. You'd better release Psyekov and Nikolashka. They might sue you for wrongful arrest. Psyekov knows everything there is to be known about the law. By God, he does!

TCHUBIKOV. So does Dyukovsky. Don't you, Dyukovsky?

(DYUKOVSKY *looks away*.)

KLYAUZOV. I'm going out to stop the digging—before they come across my body. (*He totters out.* TCHUBIKOV *glares at* DYUKOVSKY. *He is about to speak when* YEFREM *comes in*.)

YEFREM. Oh, dear, oh, dear, the things that are happening! (*They both look at him inquiringly*.) The Austrians have started all over again . . . and so has Gladstone . . . if you stop to think about it . . .

TCHUBIKOV (*shouting*). For God's sake shut up, you old idiot! (YEFREM *jumps with fright*.) I'm not interested in your politics. Get out of here! (YEFREM *scuttles out.* TCHUBIKOV *turns on* DYUKOVSKY.) As for you . . . (*He shakes his fist at him*.) I'll never forgive you, you . . .

DYUKOVSKY (*excited*). Why not? Why not? I was right about the safety match, wasn't I? I found out who struck it, didn't I? I was right about . . .

TCHUBIKOV (*shouting him down*). Get out of here before I strike you! Get out of here! And set a light to yourself with your damned safety match!

(DYUKOVSKY *goes hurriedly.* TCHUBIKOV *takes a long swill at the vodka. The* POLICEMAN *comes running in*.)

POLICEMAN. He's here, he's here! Mark Ivanitch is alive!

TCHUBIKOV (*putting down the flagon*). I know.

POLICEMAN. But where was he? Where's he been hiding?

TCHUBIKOV. He was living with another man's wife.

POLICEMAN. Another man's wife! Would you believe it? Mark Ivanitch with another man's wife! I warned him again and again that all that drinking would lead to worse things. And so it has! Again and again, I warned him! And he wouldn't listen! Another man's wife! (*He shakes his head sadly*.) Tt! Tt! Tt!

CURTAIN

MARGARET'S BED

William Inge

ELSIE   BEN

WILLIAM INGE began his reign as one of America's foremost dramatists in 1950, when the Theatre Guild introduced his compelling drama, *Come Back, Little Sheba,* to Broadway audiences. In 1953, he scored again with Joshua Logan's staging of *Picnic* and, although the author personally was discontented with the compromissary "romantic" ending, the play won him both the New York Drama Critics' Circle Award and the Pulitzer Prize. At its Broadway opening, critic Richard Watts, Jr., wrote: "William Inge's new work revealed the power, insight, compassion, observation and gift for looking into the human heart that we had all expected in him. . . . Here is a dramatist who knows how to set down how people behave and think and talk, who can create the feeling of a small Kansas town, and is able to write dramatic scenes that have vitality, emotional power and heartbreak. There is a true sense of the sadness and wonder of life in this new dramatist."

In 1955, Mr. Inge added another link to his chain of successes with *Bus Stop* and, two years later, *The Dark at the Top of the Stairs*—a revision of his very first play, *Farther Off From Heaven,* which Margo Jones produced in 1947 at her Dallas Theatre —was hailed by press and public as an exceptionally poignant study of family relationships. Although the latter was admittedly autobiographical, the author transferred the locale of the drama from his native Kansas, where he was born on May 3, 1913, to Oklahoma.

Rated as one of the mid-century's most perceptive and sensitive dramatists, Mr. Inge's close affiliation with the theatre originated with his tenure as stage and screen reviewer for the *St. Louis Star-Times.* In addition to the aforementioned plays, his other produced stage works include: *A Loss of Roses, Natural Affection,* and *Where's Daddy?* Though none of these was successful in New York, the author, in a letter to this editor, wrote: "God knows, neither *Natural Affection* or *Where's Daddy?* ever won any kind of award. But *Natural Affection* was the first *black* comedy and no one knew how to react to it. I still feel that these two plays represent the best of my work. . . . "

Mr. Inge also has written a number of short plays, the most recent of these being *Don't Go Gentle* (introduced in *Best Short Plays of the World Theatre: 1958—1967* under the title of *The Disposal*), *The Call, Midwestern Manic, A Murder, The Killing,* and *Margaret's Bed,* which appears in print for the first time in this volume.

The author, who now makes his home in California, has published two novels, *Good Luck, Miss Wyckoff* and *My Son Is a Splendid Driver,* and in 1962 was the recipient of an Academy Award for his screenplay, *Splendor in the Grass.*

(Note: William Inge died at his home on June 10, 1973.)

SCENE: *A small, compact apartment in a housing complex on New York's upper West Side. It is inhabited by two young women, and so is feminine in its decor. But the decor is not frilly or pretentious. Rather, it looks as if it might be the domicile of two female students, which it is.*

The time is midnight. The apartment is empty and dimly lighted by one small lamp left burning on a table.

After several seconds, two young people, a man and a woman, enter from the corridor. The woman is in her early twenties. The man is close to thirty. They are an attractive couple, well dressed, looking as if they had just come from a concert, and they have. They are talking about it as they enter.

ELSIE. I still just can't get used to Schönberg.

BEN. He's one of my favorites.

ELSIE. Honestly?

BEN. Why should I lie?

ELSIE. Oh . . . I just think that some people like to claim they have modern tastes when actually they don't know what they're listening to. The same is true with movies. Did you like *Blow-Up?*

BEN. Loved it.

ELSIE. Did you *really?*

BEN. Of course. I think it's one of the greatest movies I ever saw.

(ELSIE *turns on more lights. We can see into the bedroom now and observe that there are twin beds.*)

ELSIE. Then maybe I'm just stupid.

BEN. I wouldn't let it give me an inferiority complex.

ELSIE. Well, it does. Margaret . . . that's the girl I share this apartment with . . . she's always bragging about what a wonderful movie *Blow-Up* was . . . *is* . . . and she's always claiming it's one of the greatest movies ever created . . .

BEN. Well, it's one of the best movies *I* ever saw.

ELSIE. You, too! Then what's wrong with *me?* I left the movie absolutely infuriated because it never told me who killed that poor man in the park.

BEN. But, you see . . . that's the point in a way. I mean . . . Well, life is full of mysteries, isn't it?

ELSIE . . . Yes.

BEN. Mysteries that we never find the answer to. I think that's what the picture was about: the mystery of life and all the evil deeds that are done and never accounted for.

ELSIE. Well . . . that makes sense. Margaret never says *why* she thinks it's so wonderful. She just blabs on and on about it so everyone will think she's very *avant-garde.*

BEN. Is she a student at Columbia, too?

ELSIE. Yes. Only she's working on her Ph.D., and I'm just working on my Master's. You see, her family lives over in Trenton. So she goes home every Saturday morning, and . . .

BEN. You're working on a Master's?

ELSIE. In Library Science. Doesn't that sound dull?

BEN. You *make* it sound dull. Is it?

ELSIE. Oh, maybe not. Maybe I'm just not interested in my work. Do you want a drink?

BEN. I don't think so. You go ahead.

ELSIE. Oh, I really don't want one, either. (*She laughs.*) But that's how I got you to come home with me, isn't it?

BEN. How do you mean?

ELSIE. I mean, I suggested very politely that we both come to my place for a drink. And now, neither of us wants a drink.

BEN. I guess we both know why we came here, don't we?

(*He takes her in his arms and kisses her. She doesn't respond. He is baffled.*)

BEN. *Don't* we?

ELSIE. Oh, yes, of course.

BEN. Then give a little. Here, let's try again.

(*He kisses her again but still she fails to respond.*)

BEN. Hey! What's the matter with you?

ELSIE. What are you talking about?

BEN. You're kissing me like a clam.

ELSIE. Here. I'll try to do better.

(*She offers herself again to be kissed.*)

BEN. Forget it.

ELSIE. Oh, I'm sorry.

BEN. Tell me. Why *did* you want me to come here?

ELSIE. Because I liked you.

BEN. Really?

ELSIE. Of course.

BEN. Then why can't you kiss me like you enjoyed it?

ELSIE. I don't know. I *tried*.

BEN. But you acted like you couldn't wait to get me here. *Why?*

ELSIE. Well . . . I'm terribly afraid to be out by myself late at night.

BEN. I see. You wanted my protection.

ELSIE. Oh, please don't feel insulted. After all, I did flirt with you at intermission, didn't I? I wouldn't have tried to pick you up if I hadn't thought you were very attractive. I mean . . . I'd even have gone home alone rather than let *some* men escort me.

BEN. Now that I'm here?

ELSIE. Well . . . we were having a very stimulating conversation, weren't we?

BEN. Yes, but I didn't bring you home for conversation.

ELSIE. No . . . I don't suppose you did.

BEN. Do you want me to go now? Do you want to get rid of me?

ELSIE (*anxiously*). Oh, no! Please don't go.

BEN (*stifles a yawn*). Well, to tell the truth, I don't think I'm up to much more of this stimulating conversation.

ELSIE. You came here expecting to do the sex thing, didn't you?

BEN. I don't mean to offend you, but you gave me the very firm impression of expecting the same.

ELSIE. Yes. I guess I did.

BEN. And you don't feel like . . . carrying through. Is that it?

ELSIE. Well, not really.

BEN. Then I can only say I'm glad to have been of help, escorting you home, protecting you from possible attackers, and say good-night and . . .

ELSIE (*very anxious*). Oh, please don't go!

BEN. I don't understand.

ELSIE. Please stay.

BEN. But whatever for?

ELSIE. Oh, we could have a wonderful talk. We could tell each other all about each other, and discuss music and . . . science, and . . .

BEN. I don't think I'm up to it.

ELSIE. But we could really get acquainted. We don't even know each other's name, and I don't even know what you do.

BEN. My name is Ben Masters. I'm interning at Presbyterian.

ELSIE. Oh, that's fascinating. Ben. I love the name *Ben*. It's so . . . so *trustworthy*. My name is Elsie Hogan. I come from Iowa. You already know my status as a graduate student.

BEN. I'm from Texas originally. But it's been quite a few years since I've been back.

ELSIE. Whereabouts in Texas?

BEN. Lubbock.

ELSIE. Lubbock! That sounds like a name you'd call someone to insult him. Like *Hey, you Lubbock you!*

BEN (*bored*). Funny!

ELSIE. Oh, I didn't mean to insult you.

BEN. You didn't.

ELSIE. Won't you sit down and . . .

BEN (*irate*). No. I won't sit down. It's time I was getting back to my room.

ELSIE (*sounding very much in need*). Oh, please don't go! I beg you, don't go off and leave me.

BEN. I'm beginning to think you're about the biggest kook I ever met, and believe me, I've met some oddballs in my life. But never did I meet an attractive girl who expected a guy she has picked up . . . Yes! You picked me up. You can't deny it . . . to sit down and spend the night with her, *talking*.

ELSIE. I suppose.

BEN. Do you expect the two of us to sit here together all night and just *talk?*

ELSIE. It could be fun.

BEN. You're a weirdo.

ELSIE. Am I?

BEN. You are in *my* book.

ELSIE. Sorry. I feel now I've brought you here under a false impression.

BEN. You have.

ELSIE. Please forgive me.

BEN. I forgive you. But you've got to pardon me if I leave now.

ELSIE. Oh . . . don't! Please don't leave me here all alone.

BEN. Look! I have to get home and get some rest.

ELSIE. Tomorrow's Sunday. Do you work on Sunday?

BEN. Yes.

ELSIE. Oh!

BEN. So I'll say *good-night* now, and . . .

ELSIE. Look! Why don't you stay here and sleep in Margaret's bed?

(BEN *stands looking at* ELSIE *for several*

moments.)

BEN. Are you serious?

ELSIE. Yes. It's a very good bed. I'd promise to get you up in the morning and fix you a lovely breakfast and send you off to work.

BEN. But what is the point in my staying here and sleeping in Margaret's bed?

ELSIE. Well, you see, I . . .

BEN. And besides, I get up at five in the morning to start making my rounds at six.

ELSIE. Oh, I'd get up at five.

(*Again he stares at her inquisitively.*)

BEN. Do you have some kind of a problem?

ELSIE. Why do you ask that?

BEN. Because, I somehow believe you're sane, but you make the most insane requests I ever heard of. How can you possibly expect a young man of normal impulses to spend the night sleeping in the same room with you in a separate bed?

ELSIE. Well, I . . .

BEN. Don't you know what a man is *like*? What a man is *made* of?

ELSIE. Maybe I don't. I'm sorry. I guess maybe I do sound sort of crazy.

BEN. Well, we all have problems.

ELSIE. Look, you can sleep with me, if you like. It's just a single bed, but . . .

BEN. I don't believe I've ever had such a tempting proposition.

ELSIE. I'm serious.

BEN. I *know* it.

ELSIE. And if you really want the sex thing, it's all right with me.

BEN. Somehow now, you've made the whole idea very resistible.

ELSIE. Well?

BEN. And you'd be compliant and allow me to perform the act of fornication just because you don't want me to say goodnight.

ELSIE (*nodding her head*). Uh—huh!

BEN. Now I call that a rare example of feminine magnanimity.

ELSIE. I'll do my best to make you enjoy it, but . . .

BEN. Look! Are you a virgin or something?

ELSIE. I should say not! I'm just as normal as any girl my age.

BEN. Then why are you putting up such

resistance?

ELSIE. Because I . . .

BEN. Let me remind you again that you did flirt with me during intermission . . .

ELSIE. I've already admitted that.

BEN. You've admitted you found me somewhat attractive.

ELSIE. Oh, *very!*

BEN. So what is the problem?

ELSIE. I just can't enjoy intercourse unless I know the man better.

BEN. So you want to sit up and talk all night so we'll know each other well enough in the morning to enjoy sex!

ELSIE. No. I want you to stay with me because . . . Oh, it's so embarrassing to admit.

BEN. Go on. Let's have it.

ELSIE. Well, you see, I've always been afraid to sleep alone at night. I don't mean that I have to have someone sleep with me, but just in the same house, or apartment.

BEN. Oh!

ELSIE. So you see, every weekend when Margaret goes home, and leaves me alone, I'm terrified.

BEN. I see.

ELSIE. I know it's childish of me.

BEN. I'd say the answer to that problem is a good lock on the door.

ELSIE. It doesn't matter how secure the locks are, I'm still afraid.

BEN. So you go cruising on Saturday nights to find some guileless guy to come home and sleep in Margaret's bed.

ELSIE. Well, sometimes one of the boys in the Library School comes to stay with me.

BEN. To sleep in Margaret's bed?

ELSIE. Lots of the boys in the Library School are not very virile. They don't mind.

BEN. A new insight into the ecology of homosexuals.

ELSIE. It's very sweet of them.

BEN. But they failed you this weekend! (ELSIE *nods.*) Well, I'm sorry, but I'm not like the boys at the Library School. Did you think I was when you saw me at the concert?

ELSIE. Oh, no! Honestly! I never once thought that.

BEN. But you're expecting me to act like them.

ELSIE. Not really.

BEN. Then tell me, what did you take me for when you first smiled at me so coyly across the vast foyer of the concert hall?

ELSIE. I took you for a gentleman who happened to be very good-looking.

BEN. Tell me. Do you make a habit of cruising the concert halls to find young men to bring you home and spend the night talking?

ELSIE. Tonight's the first time I've ever done it. But I just couldn't face spending the night here alone.

BEN. How come an attractive girl like you doesn't have a steady boyfriend who can save her from these acts of desperation?

ELSIE. I'm engaged. But he's in Alaska. He's an engineer. He likes Alaska. He wants me to join him there. But I don't think I'd like it at all.

BEN. Are you faithful to him?

ELSIE. I try to be. But once or twice I've failed.

BEN. Once? . . . *or* twice?

ELSIE. Twice.

BEN. You really should be careful, you know.

ELSIE. I suppose.

BEN. For all you knew when you brought me home with you, I could have been a mad rapist, or a homicidal maniac.

ELSIE. I'm a better judge of character than that.

BEN. Undoubtedly, many ravished young women have made the same boast.

ELSIE. Well, I'm certain that rapists and murderers don't go to the symphony on Saturday night.

BEN. Why? They can like music the same as anyone else.

ELSIE. But I just *knew* you were nice. You couldn't act like you do and not be.

BEN. I'm beginning to think I must have looked to you like a sap.

ELSIE. Oh, no. Really! You looked like someone I'd really like to know.

BEN. Like the boy next door, maybe?

ELSIE. The boy who lived next door to me in Iowa tried to seduce me when I was twelve years old.

BEN. Did he succeed?

ELSIE. No. But he did when I was seventeen.

BEN. That's diligence, I'd say.

ELSIE. We went together all through high school. We were madly in love.

BEN. What happened?

ELSIE. Oh, we went away to different colleges and forgot each other.

BEN. Just a youthful romance, huh?

ELSIE. Oh, we're still friends.

BEN. That's nice. Well . . . I'll be going now.

(*He starts for the door. She runs to intercept him.*)

ELSIE. Oh, you mustn't go. Please!

BEN. Look. Be realistic. I can't spend the night here talking to you, or sleeping in Margaret's bed.

ELSIE. I told you I'd sleep with you.

BEN. But I take no pleasure in screwing a young woman who's not enjoying it.

ELSIE. But I'll try. Really, I'll be the sexiest thing you ever experienced.

BEN. Women who have to try to be sexy somehow turn me off. I'd rather sleep in Margaret's bed.

ELSIE (*sounding desperate*). But I'll do anything, *any*thing, if you'll stay.

(*He studies her.*)

BEN. Look, what is your problem?

ELSIE. I told you. I'm afraid to sleep in this apartment alone.

BEN (*seriously*). I see.

ELSIE. I'm more than afraid. I'm terrified.

BEN. I can see. You're even trembling.

ELSIE. You don't know some of the things that happen in this building. I never use the elevators. A woman never knows what's going to happen to her if some man finds her in the elevator alone. That's why I live on the second floor. I can walk up. I won't get into the elevators.

BEN. Yes. Life is pretty scary these days.

ELSIE. In the eight months I've lived here, there've been two murders, three rapes, I don't know how many robberies, and the police are always here arresting someone for dope possession. Oh, it's an inferno!

BEN. But you've got a thick, strong door with a good lock. I don't see how anyone could possibly get in here. You could take a sleeping pill and forget all about it.

ELSIE. I don't have any sleeping pills.

BEN. I could call in a prescription to

that little drugstore across the street and maybe they'd deliver.

ELSIE. A sleeping pill can't take the place of a good, strong man.

BEN. Look, are you neurotic, or something?

ELSIE. If it's neurotic to be afraid of being alone, I am.

BEN. Have you ever talked to a psychiatrist?

ELSIE. Yes.

BEN. What did he tell you?

ELSIE. He didn't tell me much of anything. I told him, all the facts of my life I could remember. And he just sat there nodding his head.

BEN. I'm just an M.D., but I know that these traumatic phobias have their cause in some childhood happening or situation.

ELSIE. Well, you see I was the youngest of three children.

(*There is a silence.* BEN *waits to hear more.*)

BEN. Go on.

ELSIE. And Mama would always send me up to bed first.

BEN. I see.

ELSIE. I can't tell you how terrified I was, in that black room, all alone in bed.

BEN. You thought the bogeyman would get you!

ELSIE. Yes.

BEN. But don't you realize by now that there is no bogeyman?

ELSIE. Yes, there is.

BEN. Well, I've never met him.

ELSIE. Don't you feel he's around, when the lights are off and the dark is filled with mystery and suspense? Don't you feel there's something waiting there in the dark to grab you and . . .

BEN. And what?

ELSIE. I don't know. I never figured out what he'd do after he grabbed me. But he'd do something horrible.

BEN. Are you sure?

ELSIE. Yes. Otherwise I wouldn't be afraid.

BEN. He might just grab you and kiss you.

ELSIE. I don't want to be kissed by a bogeyman.

BEN. I doubt if you ever will be.

ELSIE. Why did you say that?

BEN. Because, I promise you, there *is*

no bogeyman.

ELSIE. No. I suppose there isn't. What *am* I afraid of? Do you know?

BEN. The unknown.

ELSIE. Is the unknown so terrifying?

BEN. You seem to find it so.

ELSIE. Oh, I wish I were normal like other girls and could go to bed at night all by myself without being scared. Honestly, I lie there under the covers simply trembling.

BEN. I'm sure lots of girls suffer the same fear. Probably lots of men do, too.

ELSIE. Really?

BEN. Of course.

ELSIE. But I feel so humiliated by my fear, as if I were the only person in the world who felt it.

BEN. I promise you, you're not.

ELSIE. Are you certain?

BEN. Of course.

ELSIE. But I'm not afraid of *anything* if there's another human soul in the apartment with me.

BEN. All right. I'll stay.

ELSIE. Oh! Will you *really*?

BEN. Yes, I'll sleep in Margaret's bed.

ELSIE. Oh, you're the most wonderful man I ever met!

(*She throws her arms around him and kisses him. But* BEN *is indifferent to the kiss.*)

ELSIE. And I promise to get up at five o'clock and fix your breakfast.

BEN. All I want is coffee, and some juice if you have it.

ELSIE. I'd gladly fix you bacon and eggs.

BEN. Never eat them.

(*He sheds his coat and loosens his tie.*)

ELSIE. You can undress in the bathroom and hang your clothes there.

BEN. Okay.

(*He starts for the bathroom.*)

ELSIE. And I'll undress in a hurry and holler when I'm in bed. Then you can come out and I'll keep my eyes closed until you're in bed.

BEN. Anything you say.

(*He enters the bathroom.* ELSIE *undresses hurriedly and slips into a dainty nightgown. Then she gets into bed and lies with her face hidden.*)

ELSIE. The coast is clear now!

(BEN *enters from the bathroom, wearing only his shorts. He pulls down the covers on Margaret's bed and slides in, turning off the lamp on his bedside table, leaving the room in darkness.*)

BEN. Everything okay?

ELSIE. Yes. I feel very comfy.

BEN. I'm glad.

(*There is a long silence.*)

ELSIE. You're not really bothered by the sex thing, now, are you?

BEN (*sleepily*). Hmmmm?

ELSIE. Oh, I woke you. I'm sorry.

BEN. What'd you ask me?

ELSIE. I said, you're not really bothered now by the sex thing, are you?

BEN. No.

ELSIE. If you are, you can get into bed with me. Really. I promise to do my best.

BEN. I'm okay, thanks.

(*There is another silence.*)

ELSIE. Don't you have a steady girl?

BEN (*still sleepy*). . . . . Hmmmm?

ELSIE. Oh, I woke you again.

BEN. What is it this time?

ELSIE. I said, don't you have a steady girl or someone you're engaged to?

BEN. What do *you* care?

ELSIE. I just wondered.

BEN. No.

ELSIE. How come?

BEN. I *was* engaged but I'm not anymore.

ELSIE. Oh! That's too bad.

BEN. Good-night.

ELSIE. What happened, Ben?

BEN. Look, I think we both should be getting to sleep.

ELSIE. I've got to know. What happened?

BEN. Well . . . she turned me down. That's what happened.

ELSIE. Really?

BEN. Yes. Really. Now good-night.

ELSIE. It makes me furious to think she turned you down. You're too nice a man to be treated that way. Why did she do it?

BEN (*sits up and turns on the bedside lamp*). Look, do we *have* to go into all this?

ELSIE. I've got to know.

BEN (*wearily*). All right, then. She wasn't willing to wait for me to finish my internship. So she married someone else.

ELSIE. Oh, that's selfish of her. I mean,

that's *really* selfish of a girl not to be willing to wait . . .

BEN. It's all in the past now.

ELSIE. Really?

BEN. Of course.

ELSIE. You mean, you don't feel bad about it anymore?

BEN. I don't let myself think about it anymore.

ELSIE. But did it hurt?

BEN. I said, I don't think about it anymore.

ELSIE. How long ago did it happen?

BEN. What does that matter?

ELSIE. I'm curious.

BEN. She called it off several weeks ago. She was married last week. My mother sent me the clipping.

ELSIE. In Lubbock?

BEN. Yes.

ELSIE. Oh, Ben, I'm so very sorry.

BEN. Let's both go to sleep now. Whatta ya say? (ELSIE *slips out of her bed and hurries over to him.*) Hey! What *is* this?

ELSIE. I want to kiss you.

(*She wraps her arms around him and they kiss.*)

BEN. What was that for?

ELSIE. It just occurred to me, you were cruising at the concert, too.

BEN. I guess I was.

ELSIE. I should have guessed.

BEN. Why?

ELSIE. Because, it's just not natural for a man as attractive as you to be at a concert all alone.

BEN. It's not natural for a girl as attractive as you . . .

ELSIE. But I explained about me.

BEN. Now we know about each other.

ELSIE. Mmmmmmm.

(*They kiss. But* BEN *seems strangely indifferent.*)

BEN. Why did you do that?

ELSIE. I just wanted to.

BEN (*in surprise*). What's happened to you?

ELSIE. What do you mean?

BEN. I mean, all of a sudden you kiss me with a feeling that I'd call close to rapture.

ELSIE. Is it so different from the way I kissed you before?

BEN. Yes. Now why couldn't you have kissed me that way before?

ELSIE. Because I didn't know enough about you then.

BEN. And what precisely do you know about me now?

ELSIE. I don't know. I guess it's probably knowing that you've been hurt, too.

BEN. Oh! So you make love to me out of pity.

ELSIE. No . . . really. It's not pity I feel for you.

BEN. What is it, then?

ELSIE. It's just that you seem more human to me now.

BEN. Because you find out that I've been jilted?

ELSIE. But honestly, I don't *pity* you. But I think that I know you now so much better.

BEN. I still could be a bogeyman.

ELSIE. No, you couldn't.

BEN. Oh, yes, I *could*!

ELSIE. Well, I don't care. Even if you are a bogeyman, you wouldn't frighten me.

BEN. I wouldn't?

ELSIE. No.

BEN. Why not?

ELSIE. Because I'd understand you.

BEN. But I could still be a bogeyman and do violence to you, whether you understood anything about me or not.

ELSIE. I know.

BEN. But you wouldn't be afraid?

ELSIE. Not a bit. It's like a dog I once had, named Barnie, and he bit me once when I accidentally touched a bruise he had. I understood it. And it didn't make me afraid of him afterward.

BEN. So you think you've touched one of my bruises?

ELSIE. Well . . . maybe

(*silence*)

ELSIE. Have I?

BEN. Oh, I don't know.

ELSIE. Didn't it bruise you when the girl you were engaged to married someone else?

BEN. I guess so.

ELSIE. That's all I mean when I say I *understand you better*. It doesn't mean that I *pity* you. It only means that I know you're human and vulnerable like anyone else.

BEN. You mean, you want to know that I *can* be hurt.

ELSIE. Well, of course. You wouldn't be human if you couldn't be hurt. (*silence*) If you're a doctor, you should know that people *grow* with their suffering, that without suffering, we never do become human . . . do we?

BEN. I guess not. But . . .

(*silence*)

ELSIE. But *what*?

BEN. Well . . . a person can still have personal little . . . quirks and eccentricities that may not make him a bogeyman, or even inhuman, but still affect his . . . his personal make-up.

ELSIE. Oh, of course. We all have our quirks and eccentricities. But they just don't matter. Please. Kiss me again.

(*He politely takes her in his arms and kisses her, but the kiss doesn't last long.*)

ELSIE (*with surprise*). What's the matter?

BEN. What do you mean?

ELSIE. You don't kiss me now with any feeling at all.

BEN. I'm sorry.

ELSIE. Am I no longer attractive to you?

BEN. Look, please let's just forget the whole thing, shall we?

ELSIE. I don't understand.

BEN. If you want me to, I'll stay here and sleep in Margaret's bed, but . . . I'll sleep alone.

ELSIE (*hurt*). But what have I done?

BEN (*irate*). I said let's forget it!

ELSIE. But tell me *why*.

BEN. Because, regardless how you deny it, you pity me for being jilted.

ELSIE. No. I don't. Honestly, I don't *pity* you.

BEN. Oh, yes, you do. That's all you've been doing since we got here, is to probe inside me until you found some reason you could feel sorry for me.

ELSIE. That's not so. That's just not so.

BEN. I think it is.

ELSIE. Honestly, I was just trying to get to know you better. That's all.

BEN. And to know is to understand is to feel sorry for. No thanks. I don't need it.

ELSIE. I'm no longer attractive to you, am I?

BEN. I think you're a nice kid, but that's as far as it can go now.

ELSIE. I've made you mad.

BEN. Now look, I'll stay here and sleep

in Margaret's bed, but I'll sleep alone.

ELSIE (*sobbing a little*). No, don't bother.

BEN. But I could still keep the bogeyman from your door.

ELSIE. But now . . . if you slept in Margaret's bed . . . *I'd* be wanting *you.*

BEN. I'm sorry.

ELSIE. That's just the way I am.

BEN. But I am absolutely impotent with any woman who feels sorry for me.

ELSIE. But I don't feel sorry for you, *really!* It's just that you've become more human to me now.

BEN. It's the same thing.

ELSIE. Not really.

BEN. The way you mean it, it is.

ELSIE. It is *what?*

BEN. Pity. This understanding bit. This being-human bit. All it amounts to is you're wanting to feel sorry for me. Oh, yes. Once you feel sorry for me, you can make love and feel righteous, like you're doing your good deed for the day. But I don't want it.

ELSIE. I'm sorry.

BEN. Quit feeling sorry.

ELSIE. I think you've got some neurosis about women feeling sorry for you.

BEN. Maybe I do. As I said before, we all have our little quirks and eccentricities.

(*Irate, he enters the bathroom.*)

ELSIE. Are you going?

BEN (*off*). Why not? It's obvious I can't stay here.

ELSIE. No. I suppose you can't.

BEN (*off*). So I'll just have to leave you here for the bogeyman.

ELSIE. I've faced him before. I can face him again.

BEN (*off*). That's the spirit.

ELSIE. I've always thought that love required human understanding.

BEN. More often it is destroyed by human understanding.

ELSIE. That's cynical.

BEN. Maybe it is.

ELSIE. *I'm* not cynical, and you're not much older than I am.

BEN. A few years can make a big difference.

ELSIE. I guess so. (*silence*) I just can't enjoy the sex thing unless it's with someone I really know and can feel chummy with.

BEN. I like going to bed with a woman who's a total mystery to me, inscrutable and intriguing.

(BEN *enters now from the bathroom. His shirt collar is open, and he carries his coat.*)

ELSIE. Maybe it's a fault of mine, wanting to feel *chummy* with everyone.

BEN. Well, I'll be going now.

ELSIE. And I'll always feel we could have been such wonderful lovers.

BEN. I guess it just wasn't meant to be.

ELSIE (*standing*). Well . . . good-bye, Ben.

BEN. Good-bye, Elsie. And let me warn you again about picking up men, even at the symphony.

ELSIE. I don't know if any man could hurt me more than you.

BEN. You'll get over it.

ELSIE. I suppose.

BEN (*at the door*). Good-bye again.

ELSIE. . . . Good-bye.

(BEN *leaves.* ELSIE *closes the door behind him. She returns to bedroom and kneels beside her bed and prays.*)

ELSIE. "Now I lay me down to sleep. I pray the Lord my soul to keep. If I should die before I wake, I pray the Lord my soul to take."

(THE CURTAIN SLOWLY FALLS DURING HER PRAYER)

THE WAITING ROOM

John Bowen

HARRIET   A CLEANING WOMAN
A MAN   ATTENDANT
PAUL

BORN IN 1924 in Calcutta, India, John Bowen was reared by "various relatives in various parts of England." He returned to India in 1940, served in the Indian Army during the war, and was demobilized in 1947. He obtained a place at Pembroke College, Oxford, where he studied modern history as an undergraduate; graduated and was awarded the Frere Exhibition in Indian Studies by the University; and from there went on to do postgraduate work at St. Anthony's College.

He was in the United States from the fall of 1952 to 1953, "partly teaching Freshman English at Ohio State University, partly hitch-hiking and partly on a scholarship to the Kenyon School of Letters at the University of Indiana." He returned to Oxford, promptly ran out of money, and took a job as assistant editor with a fortnightly magazine, *The Sketch*. To augment his income, he also worked at intervals in advertising, as an actor, and reviewed ballet for the British Broadcasting Corporation. ("After a while I couldn't think of anything more to say.")

Mr. Bowen has written six novels, of which four—*After the Rain, The Centre of the Green, The Birdcage,* and *A World Elsewhere*—have been published in the United States.

His first play, *I Love You, Mrs. Patterson,* was produced at St. Martin's Theatre (London) in 1964. As the author recalls the event, "It was sort of Ibsenish, about marriage. It ran for five weeks—in a heat wave."

His second work for the stage, *After the Rain,* was decidedly more impressive. A "very free adaptation" of his novel of the same title, the drama originally was presented in 1966 at the Hampstead Theatre Club, then transferred to the Duchess Theatre in the West End. It was highly praised by the press and *The Daily Express* cited it as "the most fascinating new play in London."

After the Rain opened on Broadway (with Alec McCowen repeating his London role) in the fall of 1967 and although it ran for only sixty-four performances, the New York first-night jurors hailed both author and play for "providing theatregoers with the first solid food for thought of the season." A French translation subsequently was performed at the Théâtre de l'Athénéé, Paris, and a German one in the Kammerspiele, Frankfurt.

In 1968, Mr. Bowen once again was represented on the London stage with *Little Boxes,* a double bill comprised of *Trevor* and *The Coffee Lace.* Its success was immediate and engendered further critical approbation for the author. Harold Hobson wrote in *The London Sunday Times* that "a major talent, disturbing, brooding and despite its humour, essentially tragic, has come into the British theatre," while the correspondent for *Plays and Players* magazine declared: "Mr. Bowen seems to me to belong with Peter Shaffer and Robert Bolt as one of the best dramatists we've got writing within the inherited tradition of the well-made play." The New York premiere took place on December 3, 1969, but the production didn't measure up to its London counterpart.

After launching *Little Boxes,* Mr. Bowen made a "piratical raid" into the texts of the various Medieval Mystery Plays, selecting and adapting to create a work entitled *Fall and Redemption* which he directed at the London Academy of Music and Dramatic Art and later at the Pitlochry Festival Theatre. This was followed by *The Corsican Brothers* (based on the Alexandre Dumas novel) written specially for the new Greenwich Theatre; a segment of *Mixed Doubles* (Comedy Theatre, London); and *The Disorderly Women,* presented at the Hampstead Theatre Club.

The Waiting Room, here published in an anthology for the first time, opened at the Soho Theatre, London, on July 7, 1970. The production, under the direction of the author, was described in *The Sunday Telegraph* as "exemplary of its genre: a mysterious, compelling situation, with tension created by the gradual revelation of character and a chilling surprise ending." The reviewer for *The London Sunday Times* was equally impressed and underscored "the value of Mr. Bowen's sympathetic understanding of aspects of human nature rarely dealt with on the stage with such comprehension. It is not often that such depth of emotion is united with such deftness of plot."

When queried about plays of ideas, the author observed: "Plays are concerned with action, ideas are expressed in action. You must bring people who have ideas and moral principles into conflict to have a play of ideas. But every *good* play *is* a play of ideas."

John Bowen also has written extensively for television and is a frequent contributor to several major British publications.

SCENE. *An anonymous waiting room, and the corridor outside it. The waiting room itself is a depressing room of an official sort. Brown pictures of a military nature in dark frames. Brown walls. Benches along two walls. They are covered with leatherette and stuffed with horsehair. A center table with magazines, all old, all of an unreadably technical nature. A heavy wooden door. Three leatherette-covered solid chairs at the table. Window gives on to a blank wall. Single overhead light. Central heating by metal radiator.*

After a moment, HARRIET *comes along the corridor with a* MAN *in a dark suit.* HARRIET *is in her mid-thirties, expensively dressed, clearly rich. The* MAN *shows her into the waiting room.*

MAN. In here, please.

HARRIET (*surprised*). Here?

MAN. If you wouldn't mind waiting here. It's a waiting room.

HARRIET. Yes, I see it is. It's been waiting some time, by the look of it.

MAN. I beg your pardon.

HARRIET. Time.

MAN. Yes?

HARRIET. Has passed it by.

MAN. Please make yourself comfortable. We shan't keep you long. (*He goes. She is alone.*)

HARRIET. No jokes. Avoid little jokes. (*She looks about her. She tries the window. It won't open.*) Comfortable! (*Examines one of the pictures—a portrait—and it stares back at her. She runs her finger along the top of the back of a bench, and it comes away very dusty. She picks a magazine off the table, and shakes the dust off it. It is a technical journal and doesn't interest her. She looks rapidly at the others, and they are all similar. She looks about her for something to do, returns to the picture, and begins to play noughts-and-crosses on the dusty glass. The same* MAN *ushers in* PAUL, *who is in his late twenties but not rich.* PAUL *wears his work suit and tie and white shirt. As* HARRIET *hears them coming, she turns to watch.*)

MAN. In here, please.

PAUL (*surprised*). Here?

HARRIET. It's a waiting room.

PAUL. Oh!

HARRIET. They don't like you making jokes about it.

MAN. Please make yourself comfortable. We shan't keep you long. (*He goes.*)

HARRIET. You'd think he's human, wouldn't you? But he's not.

PAUL. What?

HARRIET. He's a robot. There's a transistor in his adam's apple. It keeps saying, "In here, please," and "Make yourself comfortable." It's all on magnetic wire. I expect you noticed a tiny clicking sound as you walked down the passage. Robots are very expensive to produce, but it saves on the Selective Employment Tax. (PAUL's *hands are sweating. He wipes them on his handkerchief.*) I'd take your jacket off if I were you. The window won't open.

PAUL (*gives her a look, and goes to try it*). No, it won't.

(*Pause. He is about to sit on a bench.*)

HARRIET. Wait! (*runs her finger along the top of the back, and shows him*) Better not.

PAUL. No . . . No. Thank you.

HARRIET. Do you come here often? (*He looks at her.*) Sorry. I was being flippant. I do get rather flippant, I'm afraid. Specially when I'm nervous. I mean, that man's not really a robot. I expect you guessed.

PAUL. That's alright. (*Pause. He examines a magazine.*)

HARRIET. *The Journal of Creative Management.* Rather an old copy. And there's something for stamp collectors further down.

PAUL. *The Philatelists' Weekly?*

HARRIET. Ah, you know it.

PAUL. I used to know someone who ran a magazine for stamp collectors. He was an actor. He did it when he was out of work. It appeared at frequent intervals.

HARRIET. Very good.

PAUL. Thank you. (*pause*) Have you been here long?

HARRIET. Not long.

PAUL. I wondered how long they . . .

HARRIET. Keep us here? I've no idea.

PAUL. I have to get back to work, you see.

HARRIET. Did you tell the robot?

PAUL. I didn't like to.

HARRIET. I'll tell him when he comes back, then, if you're embarrassed. I'm in no hurry. At least, I don't have anywhere particular to go.

PAUL. I shouldn't think it'd be to do with us. I mean, if *we're* in a hurry or not. I should think it's when they're ready. They call you.

HARRIET. Then why tell me one forty-five if they're not going to be ready at one forty-five?

PAUL. It's like hospitals, isn't it? You get an appointment, but you don't see the doctor for at least a couple of hours. You have to keep moving from one bench to another.

HARRIET. When's *your* appointment?

PAUL. One forty-five. (*pause*) I don't know why. I thought it might be different here. I thought maybe I'd go straight in.

HARRIET. Oh, they like you to wait, I suppose. We should have remembered. There'd be no pleasure in the public service if one couldn't keep people waiting around.

PAUL. You're very hard on them.

HARRIET. They're being rather hard on us at the moment. Cooping us up in this tomb.

PAUL. Yes, you'd think they'd keep it dusted. (*pause. He pulls out a chair from the table, and dusts the seat with his handkerchief.*) If you would like to sit down . . .

HARRIET. No, I'm restless by nature. Can't settle.

PAUL. Yes, you said. Nerves.

HARRIET. What?

PAUL. Sorry. I didn't mean to be personal.

HARRIET. Don't apologize. I wasn't snapping at you. I just didn't hear what you said.

PAUL. I said, "Nerves." What they call "nervous tension." I mean, you said earlier on you were nervous, and I made the connection.

HARRIET. Oh, nerves. Yes, that's certainly it. Nerves. I'm not sure it explains much, but that's certainly it.

PAUL. I used to suffer a lot from my nerves when I was younger. But you make adjustments, you know what I mean? You settle down as you get older.

HARRIET. You find that?

PAUL. Yes.

HARRIET. Lucky you. I find that getting older just makes me more neurotic. Do you play noughts-and-crosses?

PAUL. I have done.

HARRIET. I was just starting a game on the picture when you came in. (*He goes over and looks at it.*) Your turn. (*Her X has been in the middle square. He puts in an O. They finish the game, while:*)

PAUL. They have three-dimensional noughts-and-crosses nowadays. Colored glass balls in a perspex rack. It looks like modern sculpture. Still, it's more interesting, I suppose. Forty-nine and six.

HARRIET. Why more interesting?

PAUL. You can win. I mean, ordinary noughts-and-crosses, you always draw.

HARRIET. I've won.

PAUL. Should we rub it out?

HARRIET. Good God, no! Leave it. It's a criticism. Do you want a cigarette?

PAUL. I don't smoke.

HARRIET. I do. (*Takes a cigarette from the packet in her bag, and gives him matches so he can light it. While:*) It's funny. I'm sure I've met you somewhere before. You're not famous, by any chance?

PAUL. No.

HARRIET. It's television makes things so confusing. I once passed David Frost in the Bayswater Road, and said "Hullo" without thinking.

PAUL. I've never been on television.

HARRIET. Never mind.

PAUL. I used to work in a department store.

HARRIET. Maybe that's it.

PAUL. Behind the counter. I still work there.

HARRIET. You sold me something.

PAUL. I shouldn't think so. I was in Men's Casuals. I'm the buyer there now.

HARRIET. But I must have been in Men's Casuals at some time. I mean, I must have had some occasion to go.

PAUL. We don't get women as a general rule. The kind of women who buy their husband's clothes don't take them to Men's Casuals.

HARRIET. But that's ridiculous. What about Christmas presents? Sweaters? Silk ties?

PAUL. The kind of men who shop in my department don't wear sweaters bought by women.

HARRIET. You're not telling me you never

see women in your department?

PAUL. We do see them.

HARRIET. And don't they buy?

PAUL. For themselves mostly. I'd remember you if you'd come into the department.

HARRIET. Women are that rare? You really mean it?

PAUL. No. I'd remember *you.*

(*pause*)

HARRIET. I must have seen you somewhere else, then. We must have met somewhere else. Wherever it was.

PAUL. I've been looking about for an ashtray, but there doesn't seem to be one.

HARRIET. I'll drop the ash on the floor. It's not as if they were house-proud.

PAUL. What time is it now? I think I'm slow.

HARRIET (*watch*). Five to two.

PAUL (*watch*). Mine needs cleaning. I said I'd be back by two forty-five.

HARRIET. How strange! Your watch is just like mine.

PAUL. It was a present. It's French.

HARRIET. Swiss. Is that what you call it —Men's Casuals? I thought the more swinging department stores went in for special names. Like "Full Steam Ahead" or "Lord Cardigan's Jumper."

PAUL. That's right. We're trying to think of one.

HARRIET. You're a bit slow off the mark.

PAUL. We have to be.

HARRIET. Why?

PAUL. If we were quick off the mark, we'd frighten off the account customers. Most of our account customers are old ladies, you see, but they keep dying off. And their shares go down too, of course, so they can't buy as much as they used to. Three years ago, Mr. Harness—that's the store manager: he's very modern-minded —he called all the buyers together. "We've got to update our image," he said, "to attract the modern generation, particularly young marrieds." So he split Men's Outfitting right down the middle, and gave me half of it, and that's what we call Men's Casuals. It took me a year to get rid of what the old buyer had bought, but I've got some nice stuff now. I was in right at the beginning of the angora boom, *and* I got out of it again in time.

HARRIET. And the new name?

PAUL. Mr. Harness says I'm to move up-stairs, right away from the Outfitting, and take over "For the Modern Miss." (HARRIET: *surprised expression*) Amalgamate them with Men's Casuals—just make one department of it with pop records and Danish open sandwiches—and we'll have a new name altogether, but nobody can think of one. I mean, there's something called Unisex, but it sounds a bit medical.

HARRIET. Drop the "Men's." Just call it "Casuals."

PAUL. Mr. Harness says that's not modern enough.

HARRIET. What about "Mr. Dish"?

PAUL. I thought, "Tomorrow's Teen-ager."

HARRIET. Oh, no!

PAUL. They've all been used, that's the trouble; all the good names. (*watch*) It's two o'clock.

HARRIET. You're a very *old* young man, aren't you?

PAUL. I'm not young.

HARRIET. Oh, surely!

PAUL. I'm twenty-nine. Nearly middle-aged.

HARRIET. I'm thirty-three, and I'm not *nearly* middle-aged.

PAUL. It's different for women.

HARRIET. You're married, you mean? So you can safely go to seed.

PAUL. No, I'm not married.

HARRIET. You've not gone to seed either.

PAUL. Thank you.

HARRIET. I wish I knew where we'd met before.

(*pause*)

PAUL. It's odd that there's nobody else here.

HARRIET (*thinks and agrees*). Yes, it is.

PAUL. .Funny! Talking to you, I'd forgotten why—

HARRIET. So had I. (*looks around*) One wouldn't expect a queue of people, but if you and I are both here, they obviously arrange it so as to have everyone together, on any particular day, and get it all over.

PAUL. It?

(*pause*)

HARRIET. Damn! I've been heartless, have I? I'm sorry.

PAUL. No, it's alright. I mean, you could just as well say *I've* been heartless. One gets talking. Playing noughts-and-crosses.

HARRIET. I asked you to play.

PAUL. Maybe you and I are the only people called for today.

HARRIET. Maybe.

PAUL (*watch*). I wouldn't worry, but I'm rather short-staffed at the moment.

HARRIET. High Gear.

PAUL. What?

(*Absorbed in what she is saying, she sits down on a dusty chair.* PAUL *tries to draw her attention to this throughout the following speech.*)

HARRIET. That's your name for the new department. "High Gear." "Gear" for obvious reasons; it's what they wear—lots of shops must have gear in the title. But "High" makes it interesting. You know—associative. "High Camp"—which is what the clothes should be. "High Fashion." Then the suggestion that they're expensive—high in price—because nobody wants cheap clothes. And of course, "high" also means drugs which is a very teenage thing. And "high" and "gear" together gives you fast cars and a rackety life. And the gear lever's a good phallic shape. It's got everything. Can't miss.

PAUL. (*pointing*). Er . . .

HARRIET (*notices, gets up*). Oh, fuck!

PAUL. I don't think Mr. Harness would like the bit about drugs.

HARRIET. Don't tell him. He'll never work it out for himself. My name's Harriet, by the way.

PAUL. Mine's Paul.

HARRIET. Paul . . . (*tasting it*) No.

PAUL. Hatcher.

HARRIET. What?

PAUL. Paul Hatcher. It's my name.

HARRIET. You said that as if you thought we had met each other.

PAUL. We haven't.

(*pause. She is puzzled. He looks at his watch.*)

HARRIET. Five past.

PAUL. I wonder if there's a phone anywhere.

HARRIET. They won't give you the sack just because you're late back from lunch.

PAUL. They don't like it. I was in groceries the other day—and it was in my lunch hour, because I have to shop in the lunch hour if I want anything to eat when I get home—you can't keep eating out: it's too expensive. Anyway Mr. Bullmore came by. He's the Group Manager: he's above

Mr. Harness; I don't like him; nobody does. "Nothing better to do, Mr. Hatcher?" he said. I said, "Lunch hour shopping, sir." He said, "Lunch hours are for lunch, Mr. Hatcher, not for gossiping in other departments." I felt like falling through the floor.

HARRIET. You mean, you put up with that?

PAUL. You have to. Working in a shop you've got no option. You put up with anything.

HARRIET. You've got a union, surely?

PAUL. There is one, but nobody belongs to it. Anyway, the customers are worse. Italians!—they try on every bit of cashmere you've got, and then ask for a discount. Australians!—you take your eye off *them* for two minutes, and half your stock's gone. And most of them are bored, or frustrated, or they just want someone to hurt for the pastime. They think as long as they're buying something, they can take it all out on you.

(*pause. They look at each other.*)

HARRIET. But I've not been into your department.

PAUL. No, you've not.

HARRIET. And what were *you* buying? For your supper?

PAUL. Baked beans and sausages.

HARRIET. It's iniquitous.

PAUL. No, it's all you feel like. If you've had a hard day, you don't feel like cooking. I just open a tin of beans and watch the television. And I have an orange for breakfast because of the vitamins.

HARRIET. But you don't *have* to be a shop assistant.

PAUL. Buyer.

HARRIET. You don't have to do it.

PAUL. What else would I do?

(*pause*)

HARRIET. It's not well paid.

PAUL. I started behind the counter five years ago. They gave me twelve pounds a week. And one per cent commission.

HARRIET. Badly paid, then.

PAUL. You could say that.

HARRIET. You could earn more on a building site.

PAUL. I'm not cut out for it.

HARRIET. In a factory.

PAUL. I've no trade.

HARRIET. This is a ridiculous conversation. Why should I care what you do for a living?

PAUL. It passes the time, I suppose.

HARRIET. There is no reason on earth why any passably intelligent, passably presentable young man should be a shop assistant in 1971.

PAUL. Somebody has to.

HARRIET. That's not an answer. You tell me yourself that the customers push you around because that's what you're paid for, and your employers push you around because you've got no union. You work—what?—a six-day week—

PAUL. Five and a half.

HARRIET. Overtime?

PAUL. No. If there's a sale or anything you just stay on. They don't pay overtime.

HARRIET. Exactly. You work ludicrous hours for very little money. A bus conductor gets more. Someone making motor cars on an assembly line in Coventry gets three times more.

PAUL. I wouldn't want to live in Coventry.

HARRIET. You don't even get luncheon vouchers. What's wrong with Coventry?

PAUL. There's nothing wrong with it. I'm used to London.

HARRIET. I said it was iniquitous, and it is.

PAUL. I don't see why you're so worked up about it.

HARRIET. I'm not. I have an abstract interest, that's all.

PAUL. You've got to do something. I mean everyone has.

HARRIET. You're thirty, you said?

PAUL. Twenty-nine.

HARRIET. And you started five years ago. You were twenty-four. Wasn't that rather late to start a job?

(*pause*)

PAUL. I don't think that's any of your business.

(*pause*)

HARRIET (*watch*). Ten past.

PAUL. I'd go if I could. Out of this room. Leave.

HARRIET. I . . . have to stay.

PAUL. Well, so do I really.

HARRIET. I'm sorry . . . I was . . .

PAUL. Nervous. You said.

HARRIET. No, concerned. Just for a moment, I was concerned. I don't know why.

I don't know you. I thought for a while we'd met, but I don't know you. And waiting here, together, both of us waiting for—waiting for them to call us—maybe because of that, because we are both under some strain, I suppose I found I was concerned and went too far. But it's nothing to do with me. I haven't, after all, asked you why you're here. I suppose I should have done so if we'd gone on talking. Two people shut up together. It does make a sort of bond.

PAUL. I went out to work because the man I was living with left me.

(*pause. She looks at him.*)

HARRIET. Paul Hatcher. Paul . . . Paul . . .

PAUL. And what do you do?

HARRIET. I think you know.

PAUL. No. I know who you are. I've known that almost since I walked through the door. I don't know what you do.

HARRIET. I'm rich. I don't do anything.

PAUL. I'm sorry.

HARRIET. I get into conversation with strange men in strange rooms and then regret it. (*pause*) Perhaps I should have guessed from the watches being the same. He never had any imagination. He remembered birthdays because he'd write them down in the diary, well ahead of time. Then he'd spend a month wondering what to get.

PAUL. That's right. It wasn't imported.

HARRIET. He bought it for you in Paris.

PAUL. That shop in the Rue de Bac.

HARRIET. And you stayed . . . ?

PAUL. Yes.

HARRIET (*angry*). Don't say "Yes." You don't know what I'm going to ask.

PAUL. If we'd stayed in the same hotel. Well, whoever it was with, he'd stayed there before.

HARRIET. It was our honeymoon. He had no right to take you there.

PAUL. I didn't know.

HARRIET. They probably gave you the same room. (*pause. Then she goes angrily to the door, opens it and goes out into the corridor, where an old* CLEANING WOMAN *is at work with a pail and revolting rag. Maybe she was there from the beginning of the play.*) Is anybody here? (WOMAN *looks up*) Is there anybody around here at all?

WOMAN..Well, I'm here, aren't I? Cleaning.

HARRIET. Is there anybody else here? Anybody with responsibility? Where can I find somebody?

WOMAN. That depends, doesn't it? Depends who you want.

HARRIET. I've been waiting twenty minutes in that room.

WOMAN. You're in the waiting room, are you?

HARRIET. I said so.

WOMAN. I don't do the waiting room today. I don't get round to it.

HARRIET. I want to know how much longer I'm expected to stay there.

WOMAN. I may get round to it tomorrow. I'm a thorough worker. I've had compliments for it. Compliments. Paid. "You're a very thorough worker; you don't skimp" is what they have said to me. I may get round to it tomorrow.

HARRIET. I want to know how long . . .

WOMAN. They'll come for you when they're ready. You can't hurry them. (*She continues her work. Pause. Then* HARRIET *returns to the waiting room, where* PAUL *is standing by the table, looking at a magazine. He looks up at her as she enters, and there is a silent exchange of looks. He looks away. Pause. She goes to the table, selects a magazine, shakes out the dust, and opens it. Pause. He looks at his watch. Pause*)

HARRIET. You say you knew who I was.

PAUL. I'd seen you.

HARRIET. When?

PAUL. He went back to you, didn't he? I used to walk past the house often, and just look at it. Sometimes I'd wait up the street by the telephone kiosk, pretending I wanted to make a call. Or at the bus stop, and I'd let the buses go on by. I'd just wait there. That's where you've seen me before. Waiting at the bus stop outside your house. You passed me more than once. And I'd go to some of the places we used to go to eat, wondering if he'd be there with you. He was very habitual.

HARRIET. I know.

PAUL. I couldn't afford it. And most of those places they don't really like you to eat by yourself. You're taking up a table. They don't make you welcome when you're on your own.

HARRIET. It wasn't my fault.

PAUL. It took a long time before I got used to living—well, at a new rate. I didn't get into debt, though. There was nobody to borrow from. I just used to run out of money early in the week, and not eat for a bit. I did get behind on bills. Telephone, gas, electricity, rates, the rent wasn't much because he'd bought the lease and there was still two years to go on it. When they threatened to cut the phone off, I wrote to him at the office. I had to have the phone in case he was to ring.

HARRIET. And did he pay?

PAUL. Yes. He always was generous with money: you know that. I only asked the once anyway.

HARRIET. I said it wasn't my fault. You mucked up my life; I didn't muck up yours. (*he looks at her. Pause*) You had no rights. I had the rights. I was his wife. We were happy until you came along. We were very happy.

PAUL. I didn't "come along." He picked me up in Piccadilly.

HARRIET (*disgust*). Oh, God!

PAUL (*angry*). It wasn't like that. It wasn't like what you think.

HARRIET (*angry*). I don't think anything. It's not my business.

PAUL (*angry*). Yes, you do. You know what you think. And it wasn't like that.

HARRIET (*angry*). I don't care.

(*pause*)

PAUL. I'd been to a film at the London Pavilion. It was a fine night. I had a room in Pimlico then, not far from Victoria Station. I was walking back along Piccadilly. There was this white sports car with the top down, kept level with me. I knew he was interested, but I was a bit frightened. I thought if I turn down Duke Street, and he still follows, I'll stop. (*pause*) He said he was a married man, and we went back to my place. He wasn't drunk or anything. I didn't expect to see him again.

HARRIET. He gave you money?

PAUL. He would have. He was talking round it. I wasn't experienced then, so I didn't know what he meant.

HARRIET. You were experienced enough to—

PAUL (*angry again*). I was twenty-one, and I didn't know what he meant. I'd been in London six weeks. I wasn't on the game: I was lonely, and I . . . I didn't know very much. (*pause*) He said he couldn't stay the night, and he took the number of the phone in the hall.

HARRIET. You don't pretend it was the first time?

PAUL. Not for him.

HARRIET. You don't pretend he seduced you?

PAUL. No. I don't pretend that. But I'd been brought up in a small town in Norfolk. There hadn't been that many times before. I'd never met anybody like him.

HARRIET (*sarcasm*). You fell in love?

PAUL. Didn't you?

(*pause*)

HARRIET. Not immediately. I was courted for some time first.

PAUL. So was I.

HARRIET. I didn't love him when I married him.

PAUL. I didn't love him when he left you.

(*pause*)

HARRIET. What?

PAUL. When he left you and came to live with me, I didn't love him.

HARRIET. But you'd . . . he'd been . . . it'd been months. *I'd* known for two months.

PAUL. I didn't love him. I liked him. I was fond of him. I could talk to him; he was interested. He'd been good to me. I didn't love him. If I had, he'd never have left you, would he?

(*pause*)

HARRIET. You know him very well.

PAUL. I should think we both do. (*looks at his watch*)

HARRIET. Quarter past.

PAUL. I don't really need to stay. The way they're messing us about, there's no obligation.

HARRIET. Why did he come back to me, do you think?

PAUL. He went off me.

(*pause*)

HARRIET. I hated you.

PAUL. I hated *you*. Anyway you won in the end.

HARRIET. Do you think so?

PAUL. Yes. Whatever happened, you won. Because I improved myself, you see. It'd taken me all that time to get away from home, and get to art school. I'd done a lot of jobs—I've *been* a bus conductor as a matter of fact. But my mother died, and I got away from home, and if I hadn't met him, I suppose I'd have finished up as a sort of commercial artist, doing lettering and captions and that sort of thing. And I wouldn't have minded. But living with him was a great opportunity for me. It taught me I had no talent, except for making a home. So I gave up art school, and made a home for him, and after three years he went back to you.

HARRIET. You're sorry for yourself.

PAUL. Yes.

HARRIET. I knew for two months. I lived with him, knowing.

PAUL. But he was seeing you, wasn't he, all the time he was living with me?

(*pause*)

HARRIET. He had to. There were business matters. The house.

PAUL. Four years! It didn't take you four years to settle about the house. You used to meet for lunch twice a week. (*pause*) And he used to go back to your place sometimes, didn't he?

HARRIET. Sometimes.

PAUL. Did you . . . ? (*silence. She looks away*). Well, I thought as much.

HARRIET. I was still his wife.

PAUL. He had to keep proving something. If it hadn't been you, it would have been someone else.

HARRIET. I never divorced him. I was still his wife.

PAUL. Marital rights?

HARRIET (*angry*). Yes.

PAUL. Anyway you couldn't divorce him. Not on my account. A scandal like that. It'd have been in all the papers.

HARRIET. It could have been done by consent, but he never asked for it.

PAUL. And if *I'd* wanted him to divorce you? (*She won't reply.*) Do you think I couldn't have made him ask? At the beginning when he'd have done anything I wanted. (*still no answer*) You'll give me credit for that, I hope. (*no answer*) You talk about knowing for two months. I knew the whole time nearly that he was still seeing you. *And* going back to your place. *And* . . .

HARRIET. You couldn't have known we made love.

PAUL. I did know.

HARRIET. You don't understand. When you've been married . . . it's a hunger. I was hungry for him.

PAUL. You think I wasn't?

HARRIET. It's not the same.

PAUL. It *is* the same.

(*pause*)

HARRIET. You did hate me, then?

PAUL. Did?

HARRIET. Do. Well, I hated you too all these years. I was very curious about you, but I did hate you.

PAUL. Did?

(*pause*)

HARRIET. Yes. Did.

PAUL. That's right. He went back to you.

HARRIET. Try not to be stupid. You're not stupid.

PAUL. You were curious?

HARRIET. I didn't understand why. Why he was like that. Why he left me, when I said I'd try to understand it, and live with it. The books I read! (*pause*) Then when he had left, and I only saw him at those *arranged* times, I was very reproachful. He didn't enjoy those lunches, certainly not at the beginning when I was difficult; it was only guilt made him go on seeing me.

PAUL. Not only.

HARRIET. Mainly guilt. One reason he was glad to come to the house was because he never knew when I was going to start crying. We'd sit there with him picking at the tablecloth and me dripping tears into the oysters, and oh, the waste, Paul! The waste of all that expensive food and lovely wine! (*pause*) And I used to drink too much, of course, and go home all muzzy with a headache. I once pressed my leg against a young man in the bus all the way from Shaftesbury Avenue to Knightsbridge after one of those lunches, because I wanted to get back at him.

PAUL. What happened?

HARRIET. With the young man? He got off when I did.

PAUL. And?

HARRIET. I was frightened. So I ran into Harrods, and bought some rather expensive bath oil. Now you must admit *that's* more easy for a man. If you wanted revenge like that. Just picking someone up, and having it off.

PAUL. Yes, it's so easy, I was arrested by a plainclothes policeman in a public lavatory.

(*pause*)

HARRIET. Point to you.

PAUL. Thank you. (*looks at watch*) This is no good, is it?

HARRIET. It might be good for us. "Getting things out," as they say. Did you know when he left me again?

PAUL. No.

HARRIET. Did you know he had?

PAUL. I guessed he might. I knew when I saw you here. (*pause*) Who for?

HARRIET. Nobody.

PAUL. Nobody? But he always needed somebody.

HARRIET. I threw him out. Well . . . asked him to go. (*pause*) I'm sorry if that hurts.

(*pause*)

PAUL. It does a bit.

HARRIET. More than a bit, I see. I'm sorry. That wasn't the intention. Not to hurt you. Unthinking, if you like. I said "did hate," remember, not "do hate."

PAUL. I know.

HARRIET. I think—if it's not an impertinent thing to say—I think I'm beginning to like you. I do like you.

PAUL. I never really believed he'd come back to me once he left. Well, I suppose I hoped a bit at the beginning. But he'd lost interest. I don't know if it would have made any difference if I'd had any talent.

HARRIET. No.

PAUL. No?

HARRIET. He didn't want talent in other people. At least he did in a way, but half his pleasure was in killing it.

PAUL. But he encouraged me. We went to galleries. I met people I'd never have met. He bought me paints. Oil paints are very expensive; I couldn't afford them myself.

HARRIET. Only you stopped painting.

PAUL. I wasn't any good.

HARRIET. If you hadn't known that, you might have gone on. Think of all the people who do go on because they never find out they're no good. And some of them get good. Or at least not bad.

PAUL. Not bad's not good enough.

HARRIET. *He* said that, did he?

(*pause*)

PAUL. He never meant . . .

HARRIET. No. It just happened. And then he left you.

PAUL. Not immediately.

HARRIET. No, he had a lot of guilt. He always knew what he *ought* to do, so it just took him longer to do what he *wanted* to do—which is what in the end he always did do.

PAUL. And you threw him out?

HARRIET. I'd had enough. He wasn't going to change. During those four years he was with you, I suppose I'd got stronger. Cried myself into strength. Sulked myself into it, I'd had so many conversations with him inside my own head—long hostile conversations, questions and answers, recriminations, justifications, oh, everything! . . . All the things I didn't say at those lunches, I said to him afterwards inside my head. Real conversations with him were rather dull after that. And when he came back to me after about two or three months, of course there was a little episode, and I looked at him and thought, "It's going to be like this all your life. Back and forward, to and fro, deception and guilt. I don't have to put up with it. I've learned to live alone. I don't enjoy it, but I can do it. You keep this up, my lad, and out you go." And he did keep it up, and he did go. As it happened, there wasn't anybody for him to go to. In fact, *I* went. I left him the house. He sold it. I took a flat, and started using my maiden name again. It was a sort of gesture.

PAUL. I don't see how you manage without anything to do.

HARRIET. I managed through four years.

PAUL. I'd have gone mad.

HARRIET. You find things that want doing. I couldn't very well work in a shop. I help out at a clinic. I visit . . . (*catches the irony of it*) I visit lonely people.

PAUL. You could visit me.

HARRIET. I will if you like. (*pause*) He really was a bastard.

PAUL. No, he was kind. But you couldn't depend on him.

HARRIET. An undependable bastard.

PAUL. He *was* very selfish.

HARRIET. Yes, he was.

PAUL. I mean, it's true, the things *he* did, there were vast sums involved. Important considerations. There was a cabinet minister came to dinner.

HARRIET. Roger?

PAUL. Yes.

HARRIET. Pathetic old thing! Did he squeeze your leg?

PAUL. Up to a point.

HARRIET. Usually farther. What happened at the art school?

PAUL. They said I didn't have any creative imagination. And he was disappointed, but it was because . . .

HARRIET. *His* plan had gone wrong.

PAUL. He couldn't help it. He was like that.

HARRIET. Did you make any friends of your own when you were living with him?

PAUL. I never had any to start with.

HARRIET. But you made some?

PAUL. He had so many. I never met anyone who wasn't a friend of his.

HARRIET. Not even at art school?

(*pause*)

PAUL. I don't make friends easily. And living with him, I couldn't go to student parties.

HARRIET. Exactly.

PAUL. And you?

HARRIET. I had friends of my own before I married him. I lost touch with them afterwards.

PAUL. When he left, I rang up some of the people who'd been our friends. He always called them "our" friends. They weren't rude, but they were always busy. Except for one or two of the older ones, and all *they* wanted was . . .

HARRIET. Same with me.

PAUL. People don't like failure.

HARRIET. He did.

(*pause*)

PAUL. You're rather like me, in a way.

HARRIET. Yes, we're the type he went for.

(*The* MAN *has returned.*)

MAN. Would you follow me, please. We're sorry to have kept you waiting.

(*In the corridor, the* CLEANING WOMAN *is still at it.* HARRIET *and* PAUL *look at her.*)

WOMAN. It's no good you looking. I tell you now, I shan't get round to that room today.

(*They go down the corridor. A stretcher with a body is pushed in by an* ATTENDANT. *The body is covered with a sheet. Its feet protrude. Pause. The* MAN *draws back the sheet, so that they can see the corpse.* HARRIET *feels sick and looks away at once.*)

PAUL. There was a small brown birth-mark by the left nipple.

MAN (*looks*). Yes. (*pause*) Can you make an identification?

PAUL. Yes, I can.

MAN. Madam?

HARRIET (*makes herself look*). Yes.

MAN. Thank you.

(PAUL *and* HARRIET *look at each other. Then they walk away. The* MAN *draws cloth back over the face of the body.* HARRIET *and* PAUL *start to leave. She puts out a hand. He takes it. As they go:*)

THE LIGHTS FADE

THE HOLY GHOSTLY

Sam Shepard

ICE   THE WITCH
POP   THE CORPSE
THE CHINDI

In LESS THAN a decade, Sam Shepard has won a considerable international following, mainly with his numerous and highly regarded short plays. A dramatist of considerable inventiveness, "he dispenses verbal and visual images that tell their own story and unravel in their own private world." As Clive Barnes of *The New York Times* has said, "He writes mythic plays in American jazz-poetry. His command of language is daring and inventive" and in his own imaginative way he deals with "metaphors, symbols and confrontations."

The author was born in Fort Sheridan, Illinois, on November 5, 1943. He attended Mt. San Antonio College in California, where he acted in student productions. After completing two semesters, he came to New York as an actor in 1963, performing with The Bishop's Company, a troupe that traveled by bus and performed in churches and schools. Shortly thereafter, he turned to playwriting and his first production was the double bill, *Cowboys #2* and *The Rock Garden,* presented at Theatre Genesis in St. Mark's in the Bowery. This was followed by a number of plays produced at such pioneer Off-Off-Broadway playhouses as Café La Mama, Judson Poets' Theatre, Caffe Cino and the Open Theatre, firmly establishing him as one of the leading dramatists working in that area.

His initial play to reach Off-Broadway was *Up to Thursday,* presented in 1965 on a triple bill at the Cherry Lane Theatre. Two years later, Mr. Shepard's first full-length work, *La Turista,* was produced at the American Place Theatre and in 1969 it was given in London under the auspices of the Royal Court Theatre.

A winner of multiple "Obie" Awards for distinguished playwriting, Mr. Shepard's other plays include: *Chicago, Icarus's Mother, Fourteen Hundred Thousand, Forensic and the Navigators, Melodrama Play, The Unseen Hand, Red Cross, Shaved Splits, The Mad Dog Blues, Back Bog Beast Bait,* and *Operation Sidewinder,* presented at the Vivian Beaumont Theatre, Lincoln Center, in March, 1970.

One of his most recent works is *The Tooth of Crime* which had its American premiere at the McCarter Theatre, Princeton, in November, 1972. The play, in a new production, opened Off-Broadway in March 1973, and Clive Barnes wrote that "*The Tooth of Crime* confirms all of the playwright's promise and establishes him as a major theatre figure."

The author also contributed material to the revue, *Oh, Calcutta!* and collaborated on the screenplay for Michelangelo Antonioni's film, *Zabriskie Point.*

SCENE. *The desert at night. A large campfire glows in the center, the audience seated around it in a circle.* POP, *in his late fifties, is sleeping face up with a hat over his face in a sleeping bag.* ICE, *his son in the twenties, is crouched on his hips by the fire roasting marshmallows. He wears a hat, blue jeans, boots, vest, and a blanket thrown over his shoulders. Around the fire are various cooking utensils, packs, and empty cans. It looks as though they've been living there for a while. Blue light fades up slowly.*

ICE. (*singing softly*)
Oh, didn't he ramble. Rambled all around.
Rambled 'round the town. Oh, didn't he
    ramble. Rambled all around.
Rambled 'round the town. Oh, didn't he
    ramble. Rambled all around.
Rambled 'round the town. Oh, boy, didn't
    he ever ramble.
Rambled 'round the town. Rambled all
    around. That boy sure did ramble.
Rambled all around. Lookin' at the
    ground. Oh, didn't he ramble
Rambled all around. Rambled 'round the
    town. Oh, didn't he ramble.
Rambled all around. All around the town.
(*He takes the marshmallow out of the fire and tests it with his tongue then sticks it back into the fire.*)
Oh, didn't he ramble. Rambled all around.
    All around the town.
Oh, didn't he ramble. Rambled all around.
    All around the town.
(POP *sits up fast, pulling a gun out from under his pillow and aims it at* ICE *who sits there coolly.*)
ICE. I've been trying to get that particular toasty golden brown that you like, Pop, but it sure takes a long time. So much easier just to stick it directly in the flames and let her burn.

POP. What do ya' think I am, a cannibal or somethin'? I like 'em cooked proper or not at all.

ICE. Well, you just lay back there and take a load off and I'll let you know.

POP. You seen the Chindi?

ICE. Now if I had, do you think I'd be sitting here toasting marshmallows and worrying whether or not they're getting too brown or too black?

POP. Just don't go gettin' confident on

me. He's a sneaky devil.

ICE. Go to sleep.

POP. I have an idea you probably think yer old man's teched in the head. You probably do.

ICE. Go to sleep.

POP. You do, don't ya? Don't ya?

ICE. If I did do you really think I'd have dropped everything I had going for myself in New York City, grabbed the nearest Greyhound bus and wound up out here in the Badlands with you?

POP. All what you had going in New York City? All what? My ass! You were just another bug in the rug, boy. Gimme that marshmallow and stop playin' with it. (*He reaches over and grabs the marshmallow off the end of the stick. He pops it in his mouth.* ICE *takes another one out of a bag and puts it on the stick.*) Now listen to me. I couldn't care less whether or not you believe in ghosts and phantoms. The reason I asked ya' out here weren't for sympathy and it sure as hell weren't for yer instincts. Lord knows those a' been shot to shit in that damn city. I plain and simple need an extra gun.

ICE. Then why didn't you hire one?

POP. Not to be trusted! None of 'em! Get an old man like me out here in the desert alone and right away they'd take me for everything I got.

ICE. Which is exactly what? Let me see. A fishing knife, a John B. Stetson circa 1890, a Colt 45, a Browning over-and-under—

POP. Yer so smart! Yer so goddamn smart! Look at ya'! Just look at ya'!

ICE. Spittin' image of his old man. Yessir. Why if it weren't for the age separatin' 'em you'd think they was the same person.

POP. Ye'r no son a mine. No son a' mine woulda' gone and changed his name and dressed his self up like a hillbilly.

ICE. Well, I didn't know we were in a fashion show.

POP. Yer so goddamn smart, aren't ya'.

ICE. Well, I had me some good teachers. Sheep ranchers and horse thieves and what-all. Taught me everything I know.

POP. I'm tellin' you boy, you don't know what fear's all about. You ain't even begun to taste it.

ICE. How's the marshmallow?

POP. Fair to middlin'.

ICE. They say men make better cooks than women.

POP. Do they now?

ICE. Why don't you stop coming on like a hard-on. I'm the only company you've got.

POP. That's what you think. That's really what you think, ain't it? What if I was to tell you there was a Chindi out there with more faces and more arms and legs than the two of us put together? You really think we're alone, don't ya,' boy. You think we're just a settin' out here in the starry night passin' the time a' day and roastin' marshmallows like a couple a Boy Scouts away from their mothers.

ICE. You told me he looked just like you.

POP. Who?

ICE. The Chindi.

POP. Sometimes he does. Sometimes he does that just to trick me. Trick me into believin' it's all a figment a' my imagination. But I know better. I know he's out there waitin'. Waitin' for me to make a wrong move. Biding his time. Smellin' my campfires. Pushin' his toe into the holes my body made when it was asleep.

ICE. Listen, I got an idea. You say he's out there waiting for us and we're here waiting for him. Right?

POP. That's about the size of it.

ICE. Then why don't we push him. Lean on him a little. Ghosts don't count on that. They count on fear. We might scare the shit out of him if we went after his ass.

POP. And how do you figure on trackin' him, smart boy? Ever seen a ghost make tracks?

ICE. We could pretend we were leaving. He'd come after us and then we'd get him. If we split up, one of us behind, me behind and you in front. We'd get him in the middle.

POP. Go to sleep.

ICE. Look, Pop, I gotta get back to the city. All my friends are there. I can't be diddling around here in the desert forever.

POP. Important business. Big man. Big important man. Go ahead then! Go on! Go off and leave yer old dad. Go ahead!

(*He rolls back into the sleeping bag and puts the hat back over his face.*)

ICE. Will the radio bother you? Pop?

(*No answer from* POP. ICE *takes a transistor out of his bedroll and turns it on softly to a rock station.*)

POP. I'm not in show business, ya' know. There's some people likes to sleep at night. I need my rest. Ice? I said this ain't goddamn New York City where ya' can be playin the radio at all hours of the goddamn day. Ice!

(*A shrieking, screeching howl is heard. They both jump to their feet with their guns out. Silence. Except for the radio*)

POP. He's there!

ICE. Come on. Now's our chance.

(ICE *goes running off.* POP *stays frozen.*)

POP. Ice! Ice! Come back here, boy! Come back here! Ice! (*He goes to the radio and shuts it off. He turns in a tight circle with his gun out, looking into the night.*) I ain't afraid to die. I just want ya' to know that much. I ain't afraid. I had my day. (*The sound of bells jingling on someone's ankles as they walk.* POP *starts in the direction of the sound.*) I hear ya'. Now look. I don't rightly know what this is all about. I really don't. I figure that somewhere in yer mind you got this idea that I done somethin' to deserve yer comin' after me and torturin' me and maybe killin' me or somethin' but—

(*The voice of the* CHINDI *is heard in the dark. He moves onto the stage slowly. A tall figure dressed in black blankets with bells around his ankles, eagle feathers around the wrists, neck, and coming out of his head. The face is all white, the rest of the body jet black.*)

CHINDI. You're already dead, Mr. Moss.

POP. How do you know my name?

(*The* CHINDI *darts across the stage behind* POP. POP *wheels around and fires. The* CHINDI *sways from side to side and clacks his teeth.*)

CHINDI. Did you change it?

POP. No, I didn't change it. *I* got some pride in tradition. That's my son yer thinkin' of. Ice. He changed his name to Ice. What do ya' think of that? From Stanley Hewitt Moss the Seventh to Ice. What do ya' think a' that? It's him yer thinkin' of. Maybe it's him yer after? Is it him yer after?

CHINDI. I'm not after nobody, Mr. Moss.

(*The* CHINDI *darts again to another part*

of the stage. POP *wheels and fires twice. The* CHINDI *shakes his feet and slaps his hands on his thighs.*)

POP. I done nothin' to deserve this. What've I done! I got a right to live out the rest a' my life in peace. Lord knows I've had a struggle.

CHINDI. The Lord knows nothin', Stanley.

(*The* CHINDI *darts again.* POP *fires. The* CHINDI *smacks his lips.*)

POP. Don't go givin' me none a' yer highfalootin esoteric gobbledygook, Buster Brown. Just 'cause ya' struck off fer the big city on yer own and made a big splash when ya' was just a whippersnapper don't mean ya' can humiliate an old man.

CHINDI. Why don't you face up to it, Mr. Moss. You're dead.

POP. Get away from me! Stand back! Stand back or I'll blow ya' to kingdom come!

CHINDI. Come with me, Stanley.

(*The* CHINDI *reaches out his hand for* POP. POP *fires. The* CHINDI *darts to another part of the stage and blows on the back of his hand.*)

POP. I don't know what you think you're trying to prove, Ice, but I ain't fallin' for it. Cheap theatrics. That's all! That get-up don't fool yer old dad for a minute. I suppose ya' thought I'd drop over dead out a' sheer fright. I suppose ya' thought that. You'd like that, wouldn't ya'! Wouldn't ya'! Then with yer old man out a' the way you could step right in and take over the ranch lock, stock, and barrel. All six hundred acres and the sheep to boot. Well, I ain't fallin' for it! Ya' hear me! You hear me, boy!

CHINDI. You're a fool, Mr. Moss.

(*The* CHINDI *darts offstage and leaves* POP *standing there.*)

POP. Now you come back here! Ice! Come back here, ya' damn ingrate! This here has gone further than far enough! I'm yer pa! There's no reason we can't see this thing out eye to eye! All right! All right, you asked for it. There ain't been any feudin' in the family since 1884 but if that's the way you want it that's the way you'll get it.

(POP *goes to the sleeping bag and pulls it away. Underneath is a bazooka. He hoists it up on his shoulder and takes*

it over near the campfire. He sets it down and goes back to the sleeping bag and pulls out some shells. The sound of an Indian drum steadily beating is heard offstage. POP *looks out.*)

POP. Ice? (*He goes to the bazooka and loads a shell in it. The drum keeps drumming.*) ICE! You damn fool! They won't even be able to tell the difference between you and the sand if this thing goes off. Listen to reason, boy. (*He mounts the bazooka up on his shoulder and gets it ready to fire.*) I always liked to think of the two of us as blood brothers. Ya' know what I mean? Not father and son, but brothers. I mean ever since you was old enough to learn how to shoot a thirty thirty. The way we used to go out in the jeep late at night and flash the headlights on them jackrabbits. Blastin' them damn jackrabbits all up against the cactus. Remember that, Ice? Them jackrabbits was as big as puppies. Not enough left to even make a decent stew out of by the time we was through. And that old gun. The way that old Winchester used to kick ya' so hard it'd throw ya' right into the back seat. Yessir. Shadow Mountain that was. Those was rich days, boy. We was close as sticky socks back then. (*The drum gets closer.*) What do ya' want to throw all that away for, Stanley? I know ya' set out to hurt me. Right from the start I knowed that. Like the way ya' changed yer name and all. That was rotten, Stanley. I give ya' that name 'cause that was my name and my Pappy gave me that name and his Pappy before him. That name was handed down for seven generations, boy. Now ain't no time to throw it away. What's gonna happen when you have yerself a son? What's gonna happen to him with a name like Ice? He'll get laughed right out a' school. How's he gonna play football with a name like that? You gotta think on the future, son. (*The drum gets closer.*) I know ya' probably think I was rough on ya' and the truth is I was. But I tried to show ya' the ropes. Tried to give ya' some breaks, too. Me, I never had no real breaks. My old man was a dairy farmer. Started hittin' the bottle and lost the whole farm. Things started goin' downhill from that point on. Next thing he got himself a job sellin'

Hershey bars door to door. Never saw much a' pa then. Travelin' all around. Chicago, Detroit, Des Moines, Tucumcari, Boise. Then we found out that Pa got his self so drunk in a hotel room that he fell asleep with a cigar burning in his hand. Burned the whole hotel right to the ground with him in it. So I had to go to work. Support the whole family. (*The drum continues through the speech.*) Then my brother Jaimie comes home one day complainin' of a bad pain. Take him to the doctor and come to find out he's got himself a case a polio and they're gonna have to take his leg off. The whole damn leg from the hip down. That was right around the time a' the Great Depression. 'Course you don't remember them days. So me, I'm workin' night and day in Macy's, downtown Chicago, and bringin' home the bacon once a week so Ma can buy the groceries. By the time Jaimie gets old enough to work I'm startin' to think on marrying yer mother. 'Course Jaimie was a cripple but strong as an ox from the waist up. That come from hoistin' himself up and down stairs since he was just a squirt. So right away Jaimie goes out and decides he wants to become a truck driver. Yessir. That old boy had some real spunk. Walks right up to Bekins Van and Storage and asks 'em fer a job. Well, they could see right off that he only had but one good leg and the other one wood but he figured he was just as good as the next man. So they sent him to a special school where he learned how to use that wooden leg a' his. First thing ya' know he's out there in the real world drivin' a goddamned Bekins truck with a wooden leg. So me, I get myself hitched to yer mother and get all set to take off fer college and get myself a diploma so's I could make me a heap a' money, when lo and behold if old Uncle Sam don't decide it's come my time to serve my country. So off I goes to learn how to fly B-24s and B-17s, drop bombs and whatall. Italy, Holland, Germany, England, the whole shebang. Then I come back with nothin' to show for it but some Jap rifles and Kraut helmets and little red bombs cut on my leather jacket with a Gillette Blue Blade. Each one showing mission accomplished. Each one showin'

I got back alive. But I was feelin' all right 'cause about that time I got myself somethin' to look forward to Stateside. I'm comin' home to my little woman in Rapid City, South Dakota, and she's got one hell of a package waitin' fer me. She's got me a son. A son with my name and my eyes and my nose and my mouth. My own flesh and blood boy. My son, Stanley Hewitt Moss the Seventh.

(ICE *appears. He has white war paint stripes on his face and an Indian drum in his hand which he beats in a slow steady rhythm.*)

POP. Don't call me none a' yer family names.

(ICE *stops beating the drum.*)

ICE. I saw the Chindi, Pop.

POP. I'll bet you did. I'll bet you could tell me exactly what he looks like, too. What he has for breakfast and which side of his crotch he hangs his dick on.

ICE. When are you going to stop talking like a dirt farmer? You're an intelligent, mature adult with a lot of potential. Stop putting yourself down.

POP. Ya' see this here.

ICE. The bazooka?

POP. It ain't no bazooka. It's a rifle grenade. Made it myself.

ICE. Nice work.

POP. Thanks. I was gonna blow yer damn head off fer pullin' that stunt on me, but now I figure it's all fer the best. Ya' helped bolster my courage for when the real thing comes.

ICE. You know what he told me. He told me that you were dead and you don't even know it.

(*He sits and plays the drum softly with his hands.*)

POP. Now we've carried this damn fiasco far enough, boy! I don't know what kind a' fool plan you've got in yer head but if yer tryin' to scare me yer gonna have to go—

ICE. Go fuck yourself, you old prick! I'm going back to New York and you can stay here and jerk yourself off forever on this desert!

(ICE *starts to leave,* POP *jumps up and grabs* ICE *around the shoulders.* POP *drops his accent.*)

POP. All right. All right, Stanley, look—

ICE. My name's Ice.

POP. All right. OK, Ice. Look, we don't have to fight. We really don't. We can be calm and sensible. But all these games you've been—

ICE. What games! You call me up person-to-person collect and I can barely understand you because you're so hysterical, and you tell me there's a ghost after your ass and I believe you although it seems a bit farfetched and I drop everything and come whaling out here to meet you and pull you together and now—

POP. I was kidding though. Just kidding around. I mean—

ICE. Kidding?! I should blow your head off right here and now!

POP. Wait a minute, Stanley!

ICE. GODDAMNIT! You make that mistake again and I'll cut you in half!

POP. I'm sorry! I'm sorry! I just haven't gotten used to it. The sound of it. It doesn't make any sense to me. I'm an old man, son. I'm not used to—

ICE. Well, get used to it! Get used to another thing too while you're at it. For eighteen years I was your slave. I worked for you hand and foot. Shearing the sheep, irrigating the trees, listening to your bullshit about "improve your mind, you'll never get ahead, learn how to lose, hard work and guts and never say die," and now I suppose you want me to bring you back to life. You pathetic creep. Hire yourself a professional mourner—I'm splitting!

POP. No! No, Stanley!

ICE. That's it! That's it. I told you. One more time, old man.

(ICE *starts stalking* POP.)

POP. Now wait a minute, son.

ICE. I'm no son a' yours. Remember? You better go for yer gun, boy. I'm gonna kill you once and fer all. The difference this time is that you'll know that you're dead.

POP. Ice! Don't be a fool! I always taught you never to play around with a weapon. You have to have respect for a gun!

ICE. Draw, old-timer.

POP. Ice! Have you lost your good sense! I'm your father! Your own flesh and blood!

ICE. Abandon the creeping meatball!

POP. You can't turn against your own

kind! We're civilized human beings! Just because we don't see things eye to eye on certain political opinions—

ICE. Pop, the oppressor's cherry!

POP. I always saw to it that you had a hot meal on the table and a roof over your head. It's just that I'm lonely, Ice. I missed you. Ever since your mother passed on, I've had the most terrible nightmares. Visions of demons and goblins chasing me and taunting me.

ICE. Poor baby. Does him do do-do and pee-pee in hisum's bed, too?

POP. And you know about my stomach. Ever since the war. I keep seeing slanty-eyed faces of faces I never saw. Any minute it could burst and eat into the intestines and then I could die.

ICE. You're already dead, dope. You're a ghost.

POP. Be kind, Ice. It's not asking much.

ICE. It's asking too much. It's asking the world, Bozo, and I ain't got it to give.

POP. Let's just be friends. Let bygones be bygones, son. Why can't we be friends? (*A white* WITCH *appears with* POP's CORPSE *on her back, carrying it piggyback style. The* CORPSE *is dressed exactly the same as* POP, *and has a chalk white face. The* WITCH *is dressed in white robes with black feathers on her wrists, neck, and coming out of her head. Her face is painted black, with long black hair. She sets the* CORPSE *down near the fire facing the flames and warms herself by the flames. The* CORPSE *is in a squatting position.*)

WITCH. Lovely evening.

ICE. Yeah. Howdy.

POP. Who are you?

WITCH. I'm the Chindi's old lady. And you're Bozo the clown.

(*She cackles and laughs like the witch in* The Wizard of Oz.)

POP. What's that thing? It's disgusting. It gives off a stench.

WITCH. That's your body, Bozo.

POP. Stop calling me that! My name's Stanley Hewitt Moss the Sixth.

WITCH. Far out.

POP. Would you kindly warm yourself up and then remove that stinking mound of flesh and be on your way.

WITCH. Didn't you tell him, Ice?

ICE. I didn't get a chance to. We started

arguing.

WITCH. That's a drag.

POP. What in God's name is going on here? Do you two know each other?

ICE. More or less.

WITCH. Your son's a ballin' fool, Mr. Moss.

POP. Is this another part of your scheme to scare me into admitting I lied to you, Ice? I already admitted that. What more do you want?

ICE. To admit that you're dead.

POP. But I'm not dead! I can see! I can touch! I can smell! I can feel! I'm alive!

WITCH. The Chindi is coming back for you, Mr. Moss.

POP. Well, that's nice. And what am I supposed to do when he comes?

WITCH. You're to go with him. He'll take you away.

POP. And what if I don't want to go!

ICE. You got no choice, Pop. Finally you've got no choice.

WITCH. You're a ghost, Mr. Moss. Do you know what a ghost is?

POP. I don't know and I don't care! I've never been inclined toward hocus-pocus and I'll be damned if I'll start now.

WITCH. A ghost is one who has died without finishing what he had to do on earth. Sometimes because they were cut short, like baby ghosts. Sometimes because they never found out what they were here for, like you, Mr. Moss. A ghost is hung up between being dead and being alive because he doesn't know where he's at. We're here to show you exactly where you're at.

POP. You presumptuous little bitch! I have a good mind to take you over my knee and spank you.

WITCH. Try it.

POP. I'm not a man of violence. I never have been.

ICE. Never?

POP. Well, not when I could help it. I was only doing my job. You can't hold that against me.

WITCH. The Chindi asked me to tell you that you have a certain amount of time between now and when you're going to have to reckon with him. That time is going to be measured by this body, Mr. Moss. Your own body. Which you left and abandoned and tried to get back inside of. By the time rigor mortis completely sets into the body, by the time the body stiffens out straight as a board, the Chindi will be back to take you with him.

POP. And where are we supposedly going?

WITCH. To a place you'll never come back from.

ICE. Never?

WITCH. Not this time. He had his chance.

ICE. Looks like curtains, Pop.

WITCH. It's better this way, Mr. Moss. Imagine hanging around for eternity in the state of mind you're in now. Strung out between right and wrong, good and evil, the right and the left, the high and the low, the hot and the cold, the old and the young, the weak and the strong, the body and the spirit. You're a fucking mess! We're going to put you back together again. A whole man. One whole thing. How about it! You'll never be the same again.

POP (*He goes back into accent.*) No soap, Snow White. And you can tell your Chindi friend that he'd better bring a six-shooter if he's aimin' to bring in Stanley Hewitt Moss the Sixth!

WITCH. Well, thanks for the fire, Ice.

ICE. 'Bye.

(*The white* WITCH *disappears into the night.* POP *is back into his dirt farmer image.*)

POP. Well, least we know where we stand now, boy. Least we know who the enemy is. Better dig yerself in there, boy. They'll be a' comin' before long. (*He goes back to the bazooka and lies down behind it, mounting it on his shoulder and trying to dig in like a marine, using the pack and sleeping bags as a foxhole.* ICE *sits by the fire and starts beating on the drum. He stares into the eyes of the* CORPSE. *The* CORPSE *from this point on, almost imperceptibly stiffens from a sitting position to lying straight out on the ground on his back. Something like a slow-motion self-immolation*) Thing I couldn't get straight was whether or not it was real or not. Know what I mean, boy. Like whether I was just scarin' myself fer no good reason. Hallucinatin' and what not. Well now we know, I guess. Don't we? I mean now we know it's real. The ghost. Stop playin' that damn fool drum and talk to yer pa!

(ICE *keeps playing the drum. When he talks to* POP *he directs it to the* CORPSE.)

ICE (*his voice changes to a little boy's*). You're the one who taught me, Daddy. You said practice, practice, practice. That's the only way to be the best.

POP. Well, that's right. It stands to reason. Just look at Gene Krupa, Buddy Rich, how do you think they got where they are today?

ICE. Well, look at Sonny Murray, Keith Moon. What about them?

POP. Never heard of 'em. Upstarts. The whole bunch. It takes more than gull-danged imagination to be a great drummer. It takes guts. That's the thing you never learned. You gotta build up your strength. You gotta work on that left hand so hard you can do a triple paradiddle with yer right hand tied behind yer back. Ya' gotta get yer right foot so strong it's like steel. Work with that ankle so hard that it feels like it's gonna break off. Then when ya' reach that point where ya can hardly stand the pain of it—that's when you start yer real practicin'. That's when yer work begins. Separate all the pieces. Two arms, two hands, two wrists two legs, two ankles, two feet. Everything in pairs. Break it all down in pairs. Make the pairs work together, with each other. Then make 'em work against each other, independent. Do some cymbal work, just use the ride, then the sizzle, then the splash, then yer high hat. Feel out all the sounds you got at yer disposal, all the tones in a good set a' tubs. Yer high toms, yer lows.

ICE. What about cowbells?

POP. Well, if you go fer that Latin hand-drum sound that's all right, too. Congas and bongos and timbals . . . All them catchy calypso, mambo, cha-cha-cha rhythms they got. Helps ya' keep on yer toes. Teaches ya' a lot about what's behind a rhythm structure. Offbeats and such. That offbeat stuff. Course all the technique in the world ain't gonna mean yer a genius. No, sir. Ya' can only go so far with learning the essentials then the rest is up to you and God.

ICE. Were you a genius, Pop?

POP. Me? Naw. Damn good though.

One of the two or three fastest in the country. 'Course them were the days of Dixieland and Cajun music. Don't hear much a' that anymore. Mind if I turn the radio on?

ICE. I'm not asleep.

POP. I know. But ya' always ask me before you turn it on so I thought I'd extend ya' the same courtesy.

(*He turns the radio on softly.*)

ICE. It's just that I know how you hate rock and roll.

POP. Now that ain't true, boy. Not a bit. That kinda' music come out a' good roots. Rhythm and blues and country music, western music. Them's good roots. My gripe was and always has been that it got into the wrong hands. A bunch of teen-age morons. That's all. All that "doo-wa, doo-wa, doo-wa, ditty, talk about the girls from New York City." Stuff like that. Like a bunch a' morons. Grates against a man's ears who's played with the best. Why if I was young today I'd probably be playin' rock and roll myself, right along with the rest of 'em. Can't say's I'd go in fer all this transvestite malarkey that's been goin' on though. I'd keep my self-respect. But I'd probably figure in the picture somewhere.

ICE. You probably would.

POP. Ya' sound far away, boy. What're ya' thinkin'?

ICE. Just dreamin' on the fire. You can see the whole world in a fire.

(*Pause.* POP *sings. During the song he becomes like a little boy.* ICE *becomes like his father.*)

POP (*singing*).

A beautiful bird in a gilded cage
A beautiful sight to see
You may think she's happy and free from care
She's not though she seems to be.

She flew from the hills at a tender age
She flew from the family tree
You may think she got to the promised land
But she's not where she wants to be.

POP. Ice?

ICE. Yeah.

POP. Ice, could you tell me a story. I feel lonely.

ICE. Sure. Turn the radio off and come

on over here.

(POP *turns off the radio and crawls over to* ICE *and curls up in his lap.* ICE *strokes his forehead and tells him a story. He stops beating the drum. The* CORPSE *keeps stiffening through all this.*)

ICE. Once upon a time millions and millions of years ago, before man was ever around, there was a huge, huge fiery ball of fire.

POP. Like the sun?

ICE. Sort of—but much huger and hotter than our sun. A Super-Sun. At the same time, somewhere in space, there was a giant planet made out of cosmic ice.

POP. What's cosmic mean?

ICE. Of, or pertaining to, the cosmos.

POP. What's the cosmos?

ICE. Everything.

POP. Then what happened?

ICE. For millions of years the Super-Sun and the giant ice planet traveled through space, spinning and spinning and spinning. Then one day they collided with each other and the giant ice planet penetrated deep inside to the center of the Super-Sun and buried itself. For hundreds of thousands of years nothing happened until one day suddenly the accumulating steam from the melting ice-planet caused an enormous explosion inside the Super-Sun. Fragments of the sun were blown out into outer space. Other fragments fell back on the ice planet. Still other fragments were projected into an intermediate zone.

POP. What's intermediate?

ICE. Something in between. These intermediate fragments are what we call the planets in our system. There were thirty fragments which gradually became covered with ice. The Moon, Jupiter and Saturn are made out of ice. The canals on Mars are cracks in the ice. The only fragment that wasn't completely ice was the one we're riding on right now. The earth. Ever since then the earth has been carrying on a constant struggle between fire and ice. At the same time as this great explosion, at a distance three times that of Neptune from the earth, there was an enormous band of ice. It's still there and you can see it tonight.

POP. Where?

ICE (*pointing to the sky*). Right up

there. Astronomers call it the Milky Way because stars shine through it from the other side.

POP. It must be really cold up there.

ICE. It is.

POP. But we're nice and warm.

ICE. Well, we're by the fire.

POP. Won't the ice ever melt though?

ICE. Sometimes it does. That's why it rains. Look at the moon.

POP. It seems really close.

ICE. It's getting closer all the time. One day it's going to collide with the earth and another battle will go on between fire and ice. It's happened before.

POP. With the moon?

ICE. Not this moon but other ones. Three other moons came before this one. And three times the earth was destroyed and made over again.

POP. And it's going to happen again?

ICE. Yes.

(POP *jumps up and goes to the bazooka.*)

POP. Bull pukey! You really expect me to believe that hocus-pocus?

(*He switches on the radio again.*)

ICE. No.

POP. The earth ain't no more made out a ice than the sun is. Who filled yer brain with that hogwash anyhow? I'll tell ya' who's gonna make and break this planet, boy. *We* are! You and me and nothing else! We're gonna set this world on fire, boy. Soon's we blow up this Chindi fella and that two-bit whore a his, we'll be on our way. I'll show ya' a thing or two about fire and ice. I'll show ya' how to make the world spin!

ICE. How're you gonna blow him up, Pa?

POP. You'll see. Soon's he sets foot in this camp he's a dead man.

ICE. But he's already dead and so are you. You can't kill a dead man.

POP. More hogwash! Fairy tales! What's real is real and there ain't no way around it.

ICE. You won't even see him this time. He'll just come for you and take you away and you won't even know he's there.

POP. Why don't you go down by the crick and wash that damn makeup off yer face! If ya' weren't my own son I'd say you was a sissy.

(ICE *stands up.*)

ICE. I think I will. I think I'll walk to the crick and keep right on walking.

POP. No! Ice! You can't leave me now. There's not much more time. Look at that corpse. It's gettin' stiffer by the minute.

ICE. Tell you what. As soon as you blow up the Chindi come straight to Rapid City and we'll meet up there.

POP. No! I need your help!

ICE. Really? What for? To load your bazooka?

POP. There must have been some time once when you needed me and I helped you out.

ICE. There must have been.

POP. Well, now you can pay me back.

ICE. Right.

(*He draws his gun and shoots* POP *in the stomach, then walks off.*)

POP. Ice! Ice! Stanley! (*He grabs his stomach and staggers around the stage. The* CORPSE *is almost completely stiffened out by now.*) Stanley! You can have the ranch! The sheep! The station wagon! The Dodge half-ton! The spring-tooth harrow! The barbeque pit! The house! You can take it! Take it! I'm not kidding, Stanley! This is no way to leave yer Pa after all these years! (*to himself*) The moon's getting closer. I can make out the craters. All of the craters. It's a marvelous thing, Stanley! This is a remarkable time we're living in when a man can look from behind the moon, over his shoulder, past the ice and see that warm, greenish blue planet spinning around and around with its cargo of little people. Don't you think? I agree with you, Stanley! I agree with your philosophy and your political point of view only don't leave me now! We can argue! That's part of the fun. Ya' can't expect to make an omelette without breaking a few eggs! Conflict's a good thing! It keeps ya on yer toes! Stanley! Yer pa is dying! (*again the screeching howl. The bells of the* CHINDI *are heard as before, getting louder and louder. The* CORPSE *is completely stiff.* POP *stops and listens; he runs to the radio and shuts it off.*) So yer really gonna try it after all! Yer really gonna try bringin' in Stanley Hewitt Moss the Sixth! Well, come on! Come on then! (*He goes to the bazooka and mounts it on his shoulder. More bells are heard*

from other parts of the theatre. It should be a live sound, not recorded.) Come on ya' weasely little no-count! Sneakin' around in the dark. I can remember the time when wars was fought out in the open field. Hand-to-hand combat. Teddy Roosevelt style. None a' this sneaky guerrilla stuff that's come into fashion. Hit-and-run perverts! Throw a grenade and run the other way. Never even see the faces of the dead. Well, I got one shot and I'm gonna make it count. Stanley! That old Chindi thinks he's come to take a patsy off! (*He pulls his hand away from his stomach and looks at it. It's dripping with blood.*) Wait a minute! Wait a darn minute. (*He crawls over to the fire on his hands and knees. He holds his hand up to the flames so the light shines on it.*) If that don't beat all! (*He rubs his stomach again and holds his hand to the light.*) No blood. A bloodless critter. Not a speck a blood. They was right the whole time. Wait a minute! Stanley! You was right! (*He pulls up his sleeve and slowly, carefully sticks his whole arm into the flames and holds it there.*) No pain. There's no pain! (*He breaks into loud laughter and jumps up. He dances in circles and shouts.*) No pain and no blood! No pain and no blood! No pain and no blood! No pain and no blood! (*He stops for a second and looks into the fire. The sound of the drum starts up again. More bells all over the house in a steady rhythm. In the* CORPSE's *face:*) You're a dead man, Stanley. You're a dead man. (*He looks at the* CORPSE.) A dead body. (*He walks into the center of the campfire and laughs. He dances in the fire.*) Oh, didn't he ramble. Rambled all around. All around the town. Oh, didn't he ramble. Rambled all around. All around the town. He sure did ramble. Rambled all around. All around the town. Boy, didn't he ramble. (*He stops and runs out of the fire. He goes to the bazooka and lifts it up, then throws it into the fire. He keeps up the talk as he goes around the stage throwing everything into the fire: sleeping bags, cans, blankets, guns, hats, radio. He leaves the* CORPSE *for last. As he throws more and more things into the fire the flames grow higher and spread outside the circle. This could be done with a projector and film loop above the audience.* POP *is in a manic state. He talks to the*

CORPSE, *himself, an imaginary* ICE *and ghosts he doesn't see.*) Boy, if my boy could see me now! If my boy Stanley was here to see me now! He wouldn't believe it. The change in his old man. A changed man. Believe you me, Stanley, he wouldn't believe it! Imagine me, crawlin' off into the badlands like an old alley cat, knowin' he's dyin', dyin' alone. Tryin' to save pain. Save face. Keep the family calm. No sense in them seeing their man at the house in his last moment on earth. It's a long moment, Stanley! Boy, don't you know if there was a phone booth out here I'd sure make a collect call to that boy and have him high-tail it out here to see his old man now! Yessir! That boy would be so proud! He'd fall on his knees to kiss the earth my boots stomp on. It's been a long time. A long, long time. Wonder what he's lookin' like now? A grown man. My boy, a grown man. And his old man, a boy. You're as old as ya feel, Stanley! And I feel as old as forever! I've never been more alive in my life, son! Never been more full a' fire and brimstone. All that useless fear. All them years yelpin' like a pup, afraid to look the eagle in the eyeball. It's never like ya' think it's gonna be, Stanley!

Never! Never endless and lonely and no end in sight. Just goin' on and on without a stop. It's right here, boy, in the fire. Ya' take the fire in yer hand, boy, in both hands. And ya' squeeze it to death! Ya' squeeze the life out of it. Ya' make it bleed! Ya' whip it and make it dance for ya'. Ya' make it do its dance. Ya' make it scream like a woman with the pain and joy all wrapped up together! Ya' send it beyond fear, beyond death, beyond doubt. There's no end to its possibilities. (*He looks the* CORPSE *in the eye. To* CORPSE) And what're you doin'?

CORPSE. Nothin'.

POP. Don't do nothin' in the Kingdom a' God! Burn! Burn! Burn! Burn! Burn! Burn! Burn! Burn! (*He picks up the* CORPSE, *holds it over his head and spins him around in circles, then throws him into the fire. The drums and bells increase, the flames flicker all over the audience. The whole theatre is consumed in flames as* POP *screams over and over and dances in the fire*) BURN! Burn! Burn! Burn! Burn! Burn! Burn! Burn!

BLACKOUT

THE LENNON PLAY: IN HIS OWN WRITE

Adrienne Kennedy, John Lennon, Victor Spinetti

ME	RADIO ACTORS 1, 2 AND 3
TEACHER	MRS. SUTHERSKILL
TV STORYTELLER	MAMMY
ACTORS 1, 2 AND 3	TV COMMÈRE
USHERETTE	THE REVEREND FELIX HYACINTH SMYTHE
PRIEST	MR. WABOOBA
DEAF TED	SHAMROCK WOMLBS
DANOOTA	OXO WHITNEY
MUM	MARY ATKINS
DAD	SYDNEES
GREAT MAN	INSPECTRE BASIL
PALS, BUDDIES AND MATES	JOCK THE CRIPPLE
MONSTERS	GREAT LADY
OFFICER	FIGUREHEAD
FAMILY SOLICITOR	POLICEMAT
UNCLE	TV CAMERAS 1 AND 2
AUNT	TV FLOOR MANAGER
FATTY	CONSPIRATORS 1 AND 2
SCRUDDY	STAGE MANAGER
NARRATOR	A KING

THE LENNON PLAY: *In His Own Write,* adapted from John Lennon's two popular books, *In His Own Write* and *A Spaniard in the Works,* was first presented by Britain's National Theatre for a Sunday night performance in 1967. A revised and expanded version (which appears in this anthology) went into the National Theatre's repertory on June 18, 1968, as part of *Triple Bill.* The play was directed by Victor Spinetti and featured Ronald Pickup as Me.

Adrienne Kennedy, who initiated the dramatization, was born in Pittsburgh, Pennsylvania, in 1931, and grew up in Cleveland, Ohio. She attended Ohio State University but found the social structure there so opposed to black people that she did little academic work and started writing at twenty.

In 1964, her drama, *Funnyhouse of a Negro,* opened at the East End Theatre and promptly garnered an "Obie" Award as the most distinguished Off-Broadway play of the year. In *Funnyhouse of a Negro,* as with much of her work, Miss Kennedy is concerned with the problems of identity and self-knowledge and her writing is pervaded by powerful imagery and an intense desire to unite a self fragmented by opposing forces.

Miss Kennedy's other plays include: *A Lesson in Dead Language, A Rat's Mass, The Owl Answers,* and *A Beast's Story.* The latter two were presented as *Cities in Bezique* (described as "two journeys of the mind in the form of theatre pieces") at the New York Shakespeare Festival's Public Theatre in 1969. Gerald Freedman, the play's director, wrote in a program note: "Adrienne Kennedy is a poet of the theatre. She does not deal in story, character and event as a playwright. She deals in image, metaphor, essence and layers of consciousness." And it was on that same occasion that Richard Watts, Jr., of the *New York Post* declared: "Adrienne Kennedy is a remarkable writer who may well possess a touch of genius . . . "

One of the author's most recent works, *Sun,* was commissioned and presented by the English Stage Company in London, and she currently is working on a dance scenario for Alvin Ailey and on an opera libretto.

A recipient of a Rockefeller Foundation grant and an award from the New England Theatre Conference, Miss Kennedy acknowledges Edward Albee as a major influence in her career. In 1962, she joined his playwriting workshop at Circle-in-the-Square where she received much encouragement from him.

John Lennon, of course, was a member of the fabled Beatles, the quartet from Liverpool, England, that sprang to phenomenal success and worldwide prominence in the early 1960s. Born in Liverpool on October 9, 1940, Mr. Lennon has been writing, mainly for the delectation of himself and friends, ever since he was fourteen. In 1964, he published his volume of "nonsense verse and prose," *In His Own Write.* A critic for the London *Times Literary Supplement* found the book "worth the attention of anyone who fears the impoverishment of the English language and the English imagination." His second book, *A Spaniard in the Works,* was published in 1965 and, like its predecessor, it soon climbed onto the best seller list. Referring to critics who have noted influences of James Joyce, James Thurber, and Lewis Carroll in his writings, Lennon has said: "I love the hellish compliments I get from these intellectuals but I'd keep writing whether I got them or not."

Victor Spinetti was born in Cwm., Monmouthshire, Wales, on September 2, 1933. He studied for the stage at the College of Music and Drama in Cardiff and since he began his career in 1953, he has performed in dozens of plays and musicals in London. He also has been seen in the United States in *The Hostage, Oh, What a Lovely War!* (for which he received an Antoinette Perry "Tony" Award), *Skyscraper,* and *La Grosse Valise.*

Mr. Spinetti has appeared in many films and, in addition to *The Lennon Play: In His Own Write,* he has directed a number of productions including several foreign editions of the musical *Hair.*

FOREWORD

This play is about the growing up of any of us: the things that helped us to be more aware. We used John's poems and stories to show "the influences upod us," such as the reading of comic books, going to school, a first visit to the theatre, visits to the cinema, going to church, and the effect of all the things that pour into a home via the TV and radio.

We invented a family who were confirmed TV addicts, rarely speaking to ME, the central character, so he created his own fantasy world and spoke to his own familiars.

After John came to the first rehearsal he commented that the play took him back to his childhood and he remembered the things that he thought about when he originally wrote the books.

The staging was very simple. ME had a bedroom onstage right, and the family had a kitchen onstage left. The large centre area became, with the aid of back-projected slides, a schoolroom or a church or a theatre, and the rest of the cast sat along benches at the back and leapt in and out to play, amongst other things, TV cameras, Monsters and TV personalities.

The play became a kind of journey, a journey of growth: about the beginning of things, childish at first and then more serious as ME began to appreciate the wonder of words and of himself.

All the things we used were based on things that children use when they play at "dressing up"; for instance, a pair of high-heeled shoes means to a little girl that she could play at being Her Majesty the Queen, and a piece of string tied to a tea-strainer becomes a microphone through which a little boy could "talk" to the world.

In rehearsal the play expanded and grew as we worked along the lines of children's games; indeed, the kids around the area of the rehearsal rooms at the National Theatre had many a preview as we invited them in to watch and sometimes take part in rehearsals. The fact that they joined us, and played too, was our greatest compliment; their criticisms were our most important reviews.

VICTOR SPINETTI

Overture.

ME *standing downstage centre, left of gramophone. Rest of company on rostrums upstage centre.*
Overture ends.

ME.
I was bored when I
Believe the nasties were
Still booming us led by
Madolf Heatlump (who only
Had one)
Anyway they didn't get me.

I WANDERED

On balmy seas and pernie schooners
On strivers and warming things
In a peanut coalshed clad
I wandered happy as a Jew

To meet good Doris King
Past grisby trees and hulky builds
Past ratters and bradder sheep
In a resus baby stooped
I wandered hairy as a dog
To get a goobites sleep.
(*Family move to positions at table centre stage left.*)

Down hovey lanes and stoney claves
Down ricketts and sticklys myth
In a fatty hebrew gurth
I wandered humply as a sock
To meet bad Bernie Smith.
(ME *picks up gramophone, places it next to bed, centre stage right, sits on bed, reads comic. Jungle noises*)

ON SAFAIRY

(*company to positions around bed*)
In the jumble . . . the mighty jumble
. . . Whide Hunter sleeps tonight.

At the foot of the bed, Otumba kept wogs for poisonous snacks such as the deadly cobbler and apply python.

Little did he nose that the next day in the early owls of the morecombe, a true story would actually happen.
(*company back to rostrums.* ACTORS *act situations (i), (ii), (iii) and (iv).*)
(*i*) Otumba awoke him with a cup of teeth, and they lit up towards the jumble.
(ii) "Ain't dat Elepoon Pill?" said Wipe Hudnose, "wearing his new Basuti?"

(iii) "Could be the Flying Docker on a case."

(iv) "No, he's walking," said Otumbad in Swahily which is not arf from here as the crow barks. All too soon they reached a cleaner in the jumble and set up cramp.

(*school bell, rung by member of company.*)

(*Two members of company carry blackboard centre stage and take their places with* ME *and two others sitting downstage of blackboard, facing* TEACHER *at blackboard.*)

ALL ABORD SPEECHING

TEACHER. 1. Speak you Clear and Nasal, for distance. "Ron cordially begs to inform Mam all is forgiver." Many peoble express great height with the word Mam.

2. Sing you with long voice for discharge. Deep breathing is Nescafe for a dark voice, deep breeding and in haley is very impotent for broadcastle and outlaying ariels, visibility nil in Rockall and Fredastaire Practice daily but not if your debb and duff.

3. For sample, the word frenetically wrote, must be charged grammatically with bowel pronounced strangely, e.g. "While talking on you my Ivans are getting cold, and you know as well as I do, that we must strive the Ivan while it is hat." Regarth in Oxfam they speak "Aivan" but in Caimbilge "Ovian"—the bowel thus strethed pronuned— piglo.

Practice davy but not if you're Mutt and Jeff.

(*School bell, rung by member of company. Members of company return to rostrums.* ME *goes to chair at family table.*)

ME.

I strolled into a farmyard

When no one was about
Treading past the troubles
I raised my head to shout

"Come out the Cow with glasses,"
I called and rolled my eye
It ambled up towards me,
I milked it with a sigh.

"You're just in time," the cow said,
Its eyes were all aglaze,
"I'm feeling like an elephant
I aren't been milked for days."

"Why is this?" I asked it,
Tugging at its throttles.
"I don't know why, perhaps it's 'cause
MY milk comes out in bottles."

"That's handy for the government,"
I thought, and in a tick
The cow fell dead all sudden
(I'd smashed it with a brick).

TV *introduction music.* TV STORYTELLER, *two* TV CAMERAS (*played by company*) *and* FLOOR MANAGER *with chair move to downstage of bed.*

TV STORYTELLER. Good afternoon children. Are you all sitting comfortably? Good, then I'll begin.

It was little Bobby's birthmark today and he got a surprise. His very fist was jopped off (the War) and he got a birthday hook!

All his life Bobby had wanted his very own hook; and now on his thirty-ninth birthday his pwayers had been answered. The only trouble was they had sent him a left hook and ebry dobby knows that it was Bobby's right fist that was missing as it were.

What to do was not thee only problem: Anyway he jopped off his lest hand and it fitted like a glove. Maybe next year he will get a right hook, who knows?

(*Music. Company return to rostrums.* ME *sits downstage centre.*)

ME.

I SAT BELONELY

I sat belonely down a tree,
humbled fat and small.
A little lady sing to me
I couldn't see at all.

I'm looking up and at the sky,
To find such wondrous voice.
Puzzly, puzzle, wonder why,
I hear but have no choice.

"Speak up, come forth, you ravel me,"
I potty menthol shout.
"I know you hiddy by this tree."
But still she won't come out.

Such softly singing lulled me sleep,
an hour or two or so
I wakeny slow and took a peep
and still no lady show.

Then suddy on a little twig
I thought I see a sight,
A tiny little tiny pig,
that sing with all its might.

"I thought you were a lady"
I giggle—well I may,
To my surprise the lady,
got up—and flew away.

(*School bell*)

School outing to theatre.
ME *goes to rostrums and sits on top with three other members of company.* STAGE MANAGER *places throne centre stage and calls "Beginners." Upstage curtain falls in front of rostrums.* CONSPIRATOR 1 *takes position at throne.* CONSPIRATOR 2 *enters centre stage right.*
Curtain rises.
All action is played upstage to rostrums.

BERNICE'S SHEEP

CONSPIRATOR 1. This night I lable
    down to sleep
With hefty heart—

CONSPIRATOR 2. and much saddened
With all the bubbles of the world
Bratting my boulders
O dear sheep

(KING *enters downstage left, moves centre stage.* CONSPIRATORS *break to stage left and stage right.*)
KING.
    I slapter counting one be one
    Till I can cow nomore this day

Till Bethny hard aches leave we
Elbing my ethbreeds
Dear Griff's son

What keeps me alberts owl felloon
That is earl I ask from anybotty
That I grape me daily work
Cronching our batter
My own bassoon.

Can I get a gribble of me
Should I heffer alway sickened
Should you nabbie my furbern
Wilfing their busbie
Oh dear me.

No! I shall streze my eber-teap!
With lightly loaf and great larfter
With head held eye and all
Graffing my rhimber
Oh dear sheep.

(KING *sits at throne.* ACTOR 2 *enters downstage centre, moves centre stage.*)
ACTOR 2 (HAMLET). I can't not believe this incredible fact of truth about my very body which has not gained fat since mother begat me at childburn.
Yea, though I wart through the valet of thy shatowy hut I will feed no norman. What grate qualmsy hath taken me this into such a fatty harbuckle.
Twelve inches more heavy, lo! but am I not more fatty than my brother Geoffrey whose father Alex came from Kenneth— through Leslies, who begat Arthur, son of Eric, by the house of Ronald and April—
CONSPIRATOR 1. Keepers of James of New Castle—
CONSPIRATOR 2. Who ran Madeline at 2 to 1 by Silver Flower (10 to 2), past Wot, to-wot at 4/3 and a pound?
(ACTOR 3 *enters downstage right, moves centre stage.*)
ACTOR 3 (OPHELIA).He is putting it lithely when he says
    Quobble in the Grass,
    Strab he down the soddieflays
    Amo Amat amass;
    A monk a mink a minibus,
    A marmylaidie Moon,
    A mikky mendip multiplus
    A mighty midgey spoon.

KING.
And so I traddled onward
Careing not a care
Onward, Onward, Onward.
Onward my friends to victory and
   glory for the thirtyninth.
(CONSPIRATOR 2 *stabs* KING *and* HAMLET
[ACTOR 2]. CONSPIRATOR I *stabs* CONSPIRA-
TOR 2. ACTOR 3 *falls on top of bodies. All*
ACTORS *take curtain calls. Applause*)

ACTORS *clear stage.* STAGE MANAGER *takes
throne off stage.* PRIEST *stands on rostrums
facing downstage. Rest of company, including* AUNT, *file into church and kneel facing* PRIEST. *Organ music. Cathedral.
Family exit downstage left as* AUNT *goes
to church.*

THE FAULTY BAGNOSE

PRIEST.
Softly, softly, treads the Mungle
Thinner thorn behaviour street.
Whorg canteel whorth bee asbin?
Cam we so all complete,
With all our faulty bagnose?
OMNES.
With all our faulty bagnose.
PRIEST.
The Mungle pilgriffs far awoy
Religeorge too thee worled.
Sam fells on the waysock-side
And somforbe on a gurled,
With all her faulty bagnose!
OMNES.
With all our faulty bagnose.
PRIEST.
Good Mungle blaith our meathalls
Woof mebble morn so green the wheel
Staggaboon undie some grapeload
To get a little feel
of my own faulty bagnose.
OMNES.
With all our faulty bagnose.
PRIEST.
Its not OUR faulty bagnose now
Full lust and dirty hand
Whitehall the treble Mungle speak
We might as wealth be band
Including your faulty bagnose.
OMNES.
With all our faulty bagnose.
PRIEST.
Give us thisbe our daily tit

Good Mungle on yer travelled
A goat of many coloureds
Wiberneth all beneath unravelled
And not SO MUCH OF YER FAULTY BAG-
NOSE!
OMNES.
And not SO MUCH OF YER FAULTY BAG-
NOSE!
(*Organ music ends. Company file out
of church.* ME *goes to bed, reads comic.
Jungle noises under following speech*)
ME. Jumble Jim, whom shall remain
nameless, was slowly asking his way
through the underpants. He spotted Whit
Monday and the Barking Doctorine shoot-
ing some rhinostrils and hippoposthumous
and Otumbark. "Stop shouting those ani-
moles." Bud it hab no inflience upod them.
They carried on shotting alligarters, wild
boats, garriffes. lepers and Uncle Tom
Cobra and all . . . Old Buncle Ron Gobble
and all . . . Bold Rumple, Bom Dobby and
all . . . Bad Runcorn, Sad Toddy and all.

CINEMA, WESTERN

USHERETTE *appears upper stage left,
flashes torch at* ME *who goes up to her and
follows to centre stage.* ME *sits centre stage
facing downstage.* DEAF TED *enters down-
stage right. This scene is played down-
stage left and downstage right of* ME.
   Characters: DEAF TED, DANOOTA, ME.
   CHARACTERS. Thorg hilly grove and burly
      ive,
         Big daleys grass and tree
         We clobber ever gallup
         Deaf Ted,
   (DANOOTA *enters downstage left.*)
DANOOTA. Danoota,
ME. and me.
CHARACTERS. Never shall we partly stray,
      Fast stirrup all we three
      Fight the battle mighty sword
      Deaf Ted, Danoota,
ME. and me.
CHARACTERS. With faithful frog beside
   us,
Big mighty club are we
The battle scab and frisky dyke
Deaf Ted, Danoota,
ME. and me.
CHARACTERS. We fight the baddy baddies,
For colour, race and cree
for Negro, Jew and Bernie

Deaf Ted, Danoota,
ME. and me.
CHARACTERS. Thorg Billy grows and
Burnley ten,
And Aston Villa three
We clobber ever gallup
Deaf Ted, Danoota,
ME. and me.
CHARACTERS. So if you hear a wonderous
    sight,
Am blutter or at sea,
Remember whom the mighty say
Deaf Ted,
(DEAF TED *shoots* DANOOTA, DANOOTA
shoots DEAF TED.) Danoota,
ME. and me.
(sometimes we bring our friend, Mal-
colm)
(*Fade out music as they ride off into
the sunset.*)
(ME *goes to chair at table.*)
ME.

THE FAT BUDGIE

I have a little budgie
He is my very pal
I take him walks in Britain
I hope I always shall.

I call my budgie Jeffrey
My grandad's name's the same
I call him after grandad
Who had a feathered brain.

Some people don't like budgies
The little yellow brats
They eat them up for breakfast
Or give them to their cats.

My uncle ate a budgie
It was so fat and fair.
I cried and called him Ronnie
He didn't seem to care

Although his name was Arthur
It didn't mean a thing.
He went into a petshop
And ate up everything.

The doctors looked inside him,
To see what they could do,
But he had been too greedy
He died just like a zoo.

My Jeffrey chirps and twitters
When I walk into the room,
I make him scrambled egg on toast
And feed him with a spoon.

He sings like other budgies
But only when in trim
But most of all on Sunday
That's when I plug him in.

He flies about the room sometimes
And sits upon the bed
And if he's really happy
He does it on my head.

He's on a diet now you know
From eating far too much
They say if he gets fatter
He'll have to wear a crutch.

It would be funny wouldn't it
A budgie on a stick
Imagine all the people
Laughing till they're sick.

So that's my budgie Jeffrey
Fat and yellow too
I love him more than Daddie
And I'm only thirty-two.

TV XMAS PARTY—FAMILY GATH-ERING

*Family enter downstage right and go to
table. Play tiny Xmas party noises as
family watch TV.*
ME. Hee! hee! hee!
    Hee! hee! hee!
    Hee! hee! hee!
I bet nobody knows why I am always
larfing. They would dearly love to know
why I am always larfing like this to my-
selve privately to myself. I bet some
people would really like to know.
MUM. What canon I do that would
quell this mirth what is gradually drying
me to drink, have I not bespoken to him
often, betting him to cease, threatling—
cajolson—arsking, pleases stop this larftor.
I am at the end of my leather—my cup
kenneth connor.
AUNT. We will ask the Vicar, surely
he can exercise it out of him. Surely the
Vicar can do it if anybotty can.
MUM. He just keeps larfing fer no a
parent season. Morning noon and nige

always larfing like a mad thin.

DAD. Something will have to be done about that boy larfing all the time. It's not right.

ME. I really doughnut see that it is any concervative of thiers whether i larf or nament. The trifle with the peomle around here is that they have forgoden how, I repeat, how to larf, that's what I think anyhow.

GREAT MAN (*recorded voice of any country's Great Man.*) The Nazis were still booming us. Anyway they didn't get me. How many body people wash: Pentle and Plaices? In a recent Doddi potliddy Poll a roaming retriver intervened asking—Do you like Big Grunty better more than Gray Bush?"

To these questionings many people answered:

"On the other hand, who are we to judge? I mean who are we?"

ME (*moves downstage centre*). It's Crisbus time but I'm alone. Where are all my good pals, Bernie, Freba, Viggy, Nigel, Alfred, Clive, Stan, Frank, Tom, Harry, George, Harold? Where are they on this day? I can't understand being so aloneley on the one day of the year when one would surely spect a pal or two.

(*A knock at the door.*)
Who but who could be a knocking at my door?

(*A knock at the door.*)
Who but who could be a knocking at my door?

(ME *moves to downstage centre and "switches on laboratory." Science Fiction noises start.*)

SCIENCE FICTION SEQUENCE

ME. Come on in old pals, buddies and mates.

(*Four* PALS, BUDDIES *and* MATES *appear on stage and become* MONSTERS.)
Come on in old pals, buddies and mates.
Come on in old pals, buddies and mates.

(MOSTERS *kill* ME, *downstage right.*)

MONSTERS. We never liked you all the years we've known you. You never really one of us you know, soft head.

(MONSTERS *pick up* ME *as music starts, carry him in military style and place him*

centre stage. MONSTERS *stand to attention. State Funeral music.* OFFICER *crosses downstage centre, salutes on Last Post. After Last Post and salute* PALS *and* BUDDIES *say their goodbyes.*)

PALS. Merry Chrustchove Randolf old pal buddy!
Merry Chrustchove Randolf old pal buddy!
Merry Chrustchove Randolf old pal buddy!
Merry Chrustchove Randolf old pal buddy!

(MONSTERS *and* OFFICER *return to rostrums. Family move to* ME. UNCLE *stands at head of* ME. MUM, DAD *and* AUNT *stand upstage of* ME.)

FAMILY SOLICITOR (UNCLE): Last Will and Testicle. I, Barrold Reginald Bunker-Harquart being of sound mind you, limp and bodie, do on this day the 18 of September 1924th, leave all my belodgings estate and brown suits to my nice niece Elsie. The above afformentioned hereafter to be kept in a large box untit he is 21 of age, then to be released amongst a birthdave party given in his honour. He will then be wheeled gladly into the Great Hall or kitchen, and all my worldly good heaped upon him in abundance. Thus accordian to my word will this be carried out as I lie in the ground getting eaten.

ME. Are you sure I have to stay in the box?

DAD. Yer not deaf are yer? Yer 'eard the familias solister as good as we, didn't yer?

ME. I was only making conversation.

MUM. Children should be seized and not hard.

UNCLE. Every clown has a silver lifeboat.

AUNT. He didn't even eat his cake.

ME. Never mind. We'll give it to the dog, he'll eat anything.

UNCLE. You can't have your cake and eat it. Statistics state that ninety percent of more accidents are caused by burning children in the house.

AUNT.
However Blackpool tower maybe,
In time they'll bassaway.
Have faith and trumpand BBC—
Griff's light make bright your day.
AMEN.

MUM AND UNCLE (and mickaela dentist).

(*Family return to table.* PALS, BUDDIES *and* MATES *move downstage centre and sing carol to* ME.)

PALS, BUDDIES AND MATES.
>We never liked you all the
>>years we've known you.
>You were never really one
>>of us you know, soft head
>Merry Christhive Randolf,
>>Old pal buddy
>We have smited you to the
>>ground dead
>Merry Christhive Randolf,
>>Old pal buddy.

(PALS, BUDDIES *and* MATES *return to rostrums.* ME *goes to chair at table.*)

TV DISCUSSION PROGRAMME

FATTY, SCRUDDY, FLOOR MANAGER (*with two chairs*) *and two* TV CAMERAS *move to downstage of bed.* TV COMMÈRE *stands in front of* FATTY *and* SCRUDDY *who adopt Ventriloquist and Dummy positions.* TV ANNOUNCER *introduces programme and returns to rostrum.*

TV COMMÈRE. Good evening, viewers. Tonight we have an absolutely Super Smashing Fantastic Live Discussion for you. Ladies and Gentlemen—The Trade Union and its place in Britain today.

FATTY. It's harf parst three, Taddpill, and the men haven't done a strike. Why can't we settle this here and now without resorting to a long union discussion and going through all that bit about your father.

SCRUDDY. Why don't yer shut yer gob yer big fat get or I'll kick yer face in. Yer all the same you rich fat Bourgies, workin uz poor workers to death and getting all the gelt and going to France for yer 'olidays.

FATTY (*going all red and ashen*). But listen Taddpill you're only working two hours a day now, and three days a week and we're losing money as it is, and here you are complaining again about screw screwing and I'm trying to help you. We could have built our factory somewhere else where men like to work, but ho no here we are government-sponsored and all that.

SCRUDDY. Why don't yer shut yer gob yer big fat get or I'll kick your face in. Yer all the same you rich fat Bourgies, workin' uz poor workers to death and getting all the gelt and going to France for yer 'olidays.

(ME *moves to front of* FATTY *and* SCRUDDY *who change positions.*)

ME. Haddy Grimmble
>Merry Christhive
>Randolf old pal buddy.
>Dad Harry, I want to be a golfer.

(ME *returns to chair at table.*)

FATTY. We could have built our factory somewhere else where men like to work, but ho no here we are government-sponsored and all that.

SCRUDDY. Why don't yer shut your gob yer big fat get or I'll kick your face in. Yer all the same you rich fat Bourgies, workin' uz poor workers to death and getting all the gelt and going to France on yer 'olidays.

(*All return to rostrums as music plays out.*)

DANCE HALL—NEVILLE CLUB

"*Come Dancing*" music.

INTRODUCTION. Hello South-East—well, we really have something for you tonight as we up North in The Neville Club give you the Winnie and Dokey Dave Formation Team's version of The Military Samba.

(*After introduction, company execute ballroom formation dancing routine.* ME *interrupts routine and dancers fall in 'hubbered lumps.'*)

ME. Dressed in my teenold brown sweaty I easily micked with crown at Neville Club a seemy hole. Soon all but soon people accoustic me saying such thing as

"Where the charge man?" All of a southern I notice boils and girks sitting in hubbered lumps smoking Hernia taking Odeon and going very high. Somewhere four foot high but he had Indian Hump which he grew in his sleep. Puffing and globbering they drugged theyselves rampling or dancing with wild abdomen, stubbing in wild postumes amongst themselves.

They seemed olivier to the world about them. One girk was revealing them all over the place to rounds of bread and applause. Shocked and mazed I pulled on my rubber stamp heady for the door.

"Do you kindly mind stop shoveing," a brough voice said.

"Who think you are?" I retired smiling wanly.

"I'm in charge," said the brough but heavy voice.

"How high the moon?" cried another, and the band began to play.

A coloured man danced by eating a banana, or somebody.

I drudged over hopping to be noticed. He iced me warily saying "French or Foe."

"Foe" I cried taking him into jeapardy. (ME *returns to table as dancers finish routine.*)

UNCLE. Ai was always thinking on you Razebeem my own.

DAD. She shouldn't see me like this—not all fat on her thirty-second birthday.

(ME *moves downstage centre.*)

ME. They all jumbled on me and did smite me with mighty blows about my head: They killed me you know at least I didn't die alone, did I? Merry Christ-hive Randolf, old pal buddy. But there are no flies on Frank this morning, after all why not? I'm a responsible citizen with a wife and child aren't I? It's a typical Frank morning. Dad Harry, I want to be a golfer. 'Tis nothing but worth have gained but twelve inches more tall heavy than at the very clock of yesterday at this time—am I not the most miserable of men? Suffer ye not to spake to me of I might thrust you a mortal injury: I must traddle this trail alone?

(ME *goes to bed, switches on radio. Radio music.* MUM *exits downstage right as music starts.* RADIO ACTORS *move to centre stage around microphone.*)

NARRATOR. This is the BBC Third Programme.

Pope Dat Barge, A play for Radio.

He looks sadly but sadly at his wife, walking slowly but slowly towards her, he took her head in his hands and with a few stiff blows clubs her to the ground, dead.

Flies descend on Frank's dead wife. Flies buzz.

Two (or is it three) weeks later.

RADIO ACTOR 1. Still no flies on me. No flies on this Frank boy.

NARRATOR. There are a lot of flies on his wife who is still lying on the kitchen floor. Flies fill the air.

RADIO ACTOR 1. I carn't not partake of bread and that with her lying about the place I must deliver her to her home where she will be made welcome.

NARRATOR. He gathered her in a small sack (for she was only four foot three) and headed for her rightful home. Frank knocked on the door of his wife's mother's house. She opened the door.

RADIO ACTOR 1. I've brought Marion home. Mrs. Sutherskill.

NARRATOR. He opens the sack and places Marion on the doorstep.

Mrs. Sutherskill shuts the door, shouts:

MRS. SUTHERSKILL. I'm not having all these flies in my home.

RADIO ACTOR 1. She could have at least offered me a cup of tea.

NARRATOR. Thought Frank lifting the problem back on his shoulders.

Enter Mammy, Fatty.

Scruddy sits at desk. Mammy unloads a bundle from her back on top of the desk.

RADIO ACTOR 2. What is it Mammy, can't you see I'm having a problem with Tadpill and you come in here all black and singing. And get that bundle of rubbish away from my big desk.

MAMMY. O.K. Kimer sahib fwana nassa.

NARRATOR. She lifts the bundle and eats it.

MAMMY. Sho' was naice.

RADIO ACTOR 2. Anyway what was it, Mammy?

MAMMY. Dat was yer little daughter, by yo second wife Kimu Sahib.

RADIO ACTOR 2 (*colouring*). But I'm not married, old Mammy!

NARRATOR. Mammy clasps her hands to her head horrified.

MAMMY. Oh, Lord, I've jus eaten a bastard!

NARRATOR. She runs around the room crossing herself and singing another verse. Scruddy stands up, replacing his cap firmly on his head. Walking towards the door, he half turns like in films and shakes his fist.

RADIO ACTOR 3. Get this black woman out of this factory before the men find out, yer'll 'ave a strike on yer fat Bourgie 'ands. I'm telling yer that fer nothing yer old bum!

NARRATOR. Scruddy walks out of the room leaving Fatty, Mammy and fourteen little Jewish children all singing together a kind of hymn.

VOICES. Hello, hello, hello.

(*Fade out radio music.* RADIO ACTORS *return to rostrums.* ME *moves to downstage centre.*)

ME. I might as welsh mak me a cooper tea, I night as welp hev a chocolush birskit as well, wile I do noddy. What!—bat noo warty. Goob heralds! what's all of thiz goinge awn? Doe mein ice desleeve me? Am I knot loofing at me owen singunice, and there be know warty?

Oh deally meat! oh woe isme, wart canada, ther are nay werters toe mick a caper tay, ange me moover she arther cooming ferty too. I shall heave two gough nextador, perhats they might hall hefty.

Goody Griff, which artery in HEFFER harold be thy norm! Is these not thet enid of the worm? Surely to goosestep I am nit that larst man on earn?

I wilf give of awl my wordy posesions, awl me foren stabs, awl me classicow rechords, awl me fave rave pidgeons of Humpty Littlesod thee great nothing. All these oh wondrouse Sailor up above, I offer ye if only yer will save me!

(MUM *enters upstage left, moves to centre stage.* ME *gets chair from table, places it centre stage and* MUM *sits on it.* ME *kneels left of* MUM.)

MUM. My dear NORMAN! Wart in Griff's nave are you doing, why are you carroling on this way? Police don't garry-on like this, my son, tell Muddle werts the metre.

ME. Carrot you see, Mubber, Griff have end the worled. I only went to guess sam warty, and then it dibble wirk, so I went to go necktie to a nebough and I saw wit had happened—GRIFF had ended the worl. I saw nothing—every where there where no neybers. Oh mather, wet is happening?

MUM. My Golf! Norman wit are you torking about turn? Donald you member thet there have been nobody's livfing here ever? Remumble whensday first move in how you say, "Thank Heavy there are no peoplre about this place, I want to be aloof?"

(MUM *exits upstage left.*)

ME. Muther, thou art the one, the power ov atterny, for heavan sakes amen. Thank you dear Mether, I had truly forgot. I am a silly Norman! Fancy me ferbetting that no bottle lives roynd here mother! Fantasie forgetting thet!

(ME *takes chair back to table and sits.*)

VIEW POINT

REV., MR. WABOOBA, *two* TV CAMERAS, FLOOR MANAGER (*with chair*) *and* TV ANNOUNCER *move to downstage at bed.* REV. *sits on chair.* MR. WABOOBA *sits on floor on his left.*

TV COMMÈRE. Hello again viewers. Tonight we've really got a fabulous live discussion on the Racial Problem. In the studios tonight we have two smashing people—The Reverend Felix Hyacinth Smythe and Me Aka Wulla Wabooba from Clapham East. We are very proud to present, I Believe BOOT—I Believe BOOT—fantastic.

(TV ANNOUNCER *returns to rostrum.*)

REV. A man came up to me the other day and said—"Tell me Vicar—tell me the deafinition of sin"—and you know, I couldn't answer him! Which makes me think—do you ever wonder (and what do we mean by the word wonder?) what an ordinary man (and what do we mean by an ordinary man?) who works in an office or factory—goes to church on Sunday (what exactly do we mean by Sunday?) who is also a sinner (we are all sinners). People are always coming up to me and asking "why—if Griff is so good and almighty—why does he bring such misery into the World?"—and I can truthfully say St. Alf—Ch. 8 verse 5—page 9, "Griff walks in such mysterious ways his woodwork to perform" (what do we mean by perform?) Which leads me neatly I feel, to our next guest for tonight—A man who is stickle trodding the pathways to our beloved Griff—slowly but slowly I am here to help with the bridges he must surely cross. Welcome to our studios tonight, Mr. Wabooba (a foreigner).

MR. W. Hellow you Rev, boy.

REV. Well, Mr. Wabooba—may I call you Wog? What is the basic problem you are facing? (*He smiles.*)

MR. W. You, you white trash Christian boy!

REV. Hmn! Can you hallucinate?

MR. W. I can.

REV. Well?

MR. W. Wot ah want to know, man—is why almighty Griff continooally insists on straiking my fellow blackpool inde fayse?

REV. A man travelling—like you or I—to Scotland, had two or two bad eggs in his pocket—and you know—no one would sit by him.

MR. W. But ah don't see dat, yo' christship. Ah mean, ah don't see the relevence.

REV. Well, Wabooba—let me put it this way. In Griff's eye, we are all a bunch of bananas—swaying in the breeze—waiting as it were, Wabooba—to be peeled by his great and understanding love—some of them fall on stonycroft and some fall on the waistcoat.

MR. W. Well, yo' worship, ah says dat if de Griff don't laike de peoples in de world starfing an' all dat c'n you tell me why dat Pope have all dem rich robesan' jewelry and big house to live—when ma people could fit too tousand or mo' in dat Vatican Hall—and also the Archbitter of Canterbubble—him too!

REV. Ai don't think that the Archbishoff would like to live in the Vatican with that many people, Mr. Wabooba—besides, he's C. of E.

MR.. W. Ah don't mean dat, you white trash christman imperialist!

REV. No one has ever called me a Christmas imperialist before, Mr. Wabooba.

MR. W. Well, ah have.

REV. You certainly have, Mr Wabooba. (*He turns other chin and leans forward slowly looking at* MR. W. MR. W. *leans forward and they both kiss.*)

MR. W. Ah forgive you in the name of Fatty Waller de great saviour of ma people.

REV. Ai too am capable of compassion, dear Wabooba—and in the name of the Fahter, Sock and Michy Most, I forgive you, sweet brother. Good night.

(*They rise, embrace. All except* MR. WABOOBA *and* REV. *return to rostrums.*)

REV. Have you ever been to Brighton, Mr. Wabooba?

(MR. WABOOBA *and* REV. *return to ros-* trums. ME *goes to bed, writes in book.*)

THE SINGU LARGE EXPERIENCE OF MISS ANNE DUFFIELD

All characters appear on cue around bed and play out situations.

ME (*writing*). I find it recornered in my nosebook that it was a dokey and winnie dave towart the end of Marge in the ear of our Loaf 1892 in Much Bladder, a city off the North Wold. Shamrock Womlbs had receeded a telephart.

(SHAMROCK *appears.*)

WOMLBS. Ellifitzgerrald, my dear Whopper. Guess whom has broken out of jail, Whopper.

ME. "Eric Morley?" I ventured. He shook his bed.

WOMLBS. No, my dear Whopper, it's OXO WHITNEY.

ME. At that precise morman a tall rather angularce tall thin man knocked on the door.

(OXO *appears and knocks on door.*)

WOMLBS. By all accounts that must be he, Whopper.

ME. In warped the favourite Oxo Whitney none the worse for worms.

OXO WHITNEY. I'm an escaped primrose, Mr. Womlbs.

ME. He grate darting franetically about the room. "Calm down, Mr. Whitney!" I interpolled, "or you'll have a nervous breadvan."

OXO WHITNEY. You must be Doctored Whopper.

ME. My friend was starving at Whitney with a strange hook on his eager face, that tightening of the lips, that quiver of the nostriches and constapation of the heavy tufted brows which I knew so well. He gave me no sign except a slight movement of his good leg as he kicked Oxo Whitney to the floor. "What on urn are you doing, my dear Womlbs?" Limply; "nay I besiege you, stop lest you do this poor wretch an injury!"

WOMLBS. Shut yer face yer blubbering owld get.

(MARY ATKINS *appears.*)

ME. Mary Atkins pruned herselves in the mirage, running her hand wantanly through her large blonde hair. Her tight dress was cut low revealingly three or four blackheads, carefully scrubbed on her chess. She addled the final touches to her makeup and fixed her teeth firmly in her head.

MARY ATKINS. He's going to want me to-night.

ME. She thought. She picked up the paper and glassed at the headlines, but it was the Stop Press which corked her eye. "JACK THE NIPPLE STRIKES AGAIN." She went cold all over, it was Sydnees and he'd left the door open.

(SYDNEES appears.)

SYDNEES. Hello, lover.

MARY ATKINS. Oh, you did give me a start, Sydnees.

SYDNEES. I always do, my love.

WOMLBS. Jack the Nipple . . . is not only a vicious murderer but a sex meany of the lowest orgy.

ME. But how do you know, Womlbs?

WOMLBS. Alibabba, my dead Whopper, I have seen the film.

ME. I knew him toby right for I had only read the comic. That evening we had an unpeckled visitor, Inspectre Basil.

(INSPECTRE BASIL appears.)

WOMLBS. Ah, Inspectre Basil, mon cher amie. What brings you to our humble rich establishment?

INSPECTRE. I come on behave of thousands.

ME. The Inspectre said sitting quietly on his operation.

WOMLBS. I feel I know why you are here, Basil. It's about Jock the Cripple, is it not?

ME. How did you guess? I inquired all puzzle.

WOMLBS. Alecguiness, my deep Whopper, the mud on the Inspectre's left, and also the buttock on his waistbox is misting.

ME. The Inspectre looked astoundagast.

INSPECTRE. You neville sieze to amass me, Mr. Womlbs.

(JOCK THE CRIPPLE enters upstage and crosses to downstage centre.)

ME. Meanwire in a ghastly lit street in Chelthea, a darkly clocked man with a fearful weapon, creeped about serging for revenge on the woman of the streets for giving him the dreadfoot V.D. (Valentine Dyall).

JOCK THE CRIPPLE. I'll kill them all, womb by womb.

ME. He muffled between scenes. His minds wandered back to his childhook.

JOCK THE CRIPPLE. I'm demented.

ME. He said checking his dictionary.

JOCK THE CRIPPLE. I should bean at home on a knife like these.

(JOCK THE CRIPPLE exits downstage right.)

ME. He turned into a dim darky and spotted a light. With a carefree yodel Mary Atkins slept into the street and caught a cab to her happy humping grounds.

MARY ATKINS. That Sydnees's nothing but a pimple living on me thus. Lazing about day in day off, and here's me plowing my train up and down like Soft Arthur and you know how soft Arthur.

ME. She got off as uterus at Nats Cafe and took up her position.

MARY ATKINS. They'll never even see me in this fog.

(POLICEMAT appears.)

ME. Just then a blasted Policemat walked by.

MARY ATKINS. Blasted Policemat.

ME. She shouted, but luckily he was deaf.

MARY ATKINS. Blasted deaf Policemat. Why don't yer gerra job!

(INSPECTRE BASIL exits downstage right to reenter as JOCK THE CRIPPLE.)

ME. Little did she gnome that the infamous Jack the Nipple was only a few streets away.

MARY ATKINS. I hope that blasted Jack the Nipple isn't only a few streets away —he's not right in the heads.

(JOCK THE CRIPPLE appears.)

JOCK THE CRIPPLE. How much, lady?

WOMLBS (as MARY ATKINS). More than you bargained for Nipple, the game's up!

JOCK THE CRIPPLE. It's a fair cop, Womlbs, but tell me how did you know it was me?

WOMLBS. Halitosis, my dear Inspectre.

JOCK THE CRIPPLE. Curse you, you devilish swine, you'll never get me alive.

WOLMBS. Yes, I will.

JOCK THE CRIPPLE. No, you won't. (takes poison) Argh!

ME. What happened?

WOMLBS. Euthanasia, my dear Whopper. Now my dear Whopper, back to Bugger Street.

ME. For a gottle of geer, three eggs with

little liars on, two rashers of bacon, a bowl of Rice Krustchovs, a fresh grapeful, mush-rides, some freed tomorrows, a basked of fruits and a cup of teens.

(*All characters exit downstage right as* ME *goes to table. Continues writing and says as imaginary characters disappear*) To be continued . . .

MUM. Something will have to be done about that boy, writing all the time. It's not right.

AUNT. We will ask the Vicar, surely he can exercise it out of him. Surely the Vicar can do it if anybotty can.

UNCLE. Aim home Rosebeen from the war, you know. Anyway they didn't get me—and now on my thirty-ninth birth-day my prayers have been answered.

DAD (*long pause, looks at audience*). Brummer Striving is a fast dying trade.

(ME *moves downstage centre.*)

ME. I hate that table.

Damn that clock in my house.

Don't like that chair one bit.

How can I but garry on? How?

I'm going to sell this daft shed and you too as well, also Mummy.

(ME *goes to bed. Company, as reception committee, escort* GREAT LADY *to centre stage.*)

GREAT LADY. My housebound and eyeball take great pressure in denouncing this loyal ship. Britain sends forth a mighty queen in the tradition of Drake and Drake's drum in the blue corner at three stones two ounces I name this ship God bless her and all who sail in her.

(*Company return to rostrums.* GREAT LADY *goes to foot of bed and becomes* FIGUREHEAD. ME *stands on bed.*)

ME. I want to be a golfer, Dad.

DAD. You're a Brummer, son, so get it straight.

ME. I want to be a golfer, Dad.

FIGUREHEAD. Amo amat amass
          Amonk Amkin a minibus.

ME. Amarmylaidie Moon.
          Hello, hello, hello.

EPILOGUE

DAD. Henry, it is time for you to leave school and go into your father's business of Brummer Striving.

ME. But Brummer Striving is a fast dying business, Father.

DAD. None of thy nonsense, Henry. All thy fathers before have and before even that before me were Brummers and that's a fact.

ME. Tell me again, Father, about how you got those prize stumps, was it not with a Brummer Towdry?

DAD. Why do you always ask about my stumps, son?

ME. Because it's a story I love to hear—and besides it's not every one what has a real cripple for a father.

(ME *and* FIGUREHEAD *move bed centre stage, facing upstage right.* ME *collects gramophone and places it at foot of bed.*)

And so I traddled onward.
Caring not a care
Onward Onward Onward
Onward, my friends to victory and
glory for the thirtyninth.

VOICES (ME'S). Hello, hello, hello, hello.

(MUM *moves downstage centre.* ME *and* FIGUREHEAD *sit on bed.*)

MUM. Henry was his father's son and it were time for him to leave school and go into him father's business of Brummer Striving. It wert a fast dying trade which was fast dying.

(MUM *returns to table.* ME *collects radio, etc. and places with bed.* FIGUREHEAD *stands.*)

ME. Am I not the most miserable of men?

I must traddle this trial alone.

I'm going to sell this daft shed and you too as well, also Mummy.

(MUM *moves downstage centre.* ME *and* FIGUREHEAD *sit on bed. Pause.*)

MUM. Henry was his father's son and it were time for him to leave school and go into him father's business of Brummer Striving. It wert a farst dying trade which was fast dying. The Nazis were booming. And Brummer Striving is fast dying trade.

(*Pause.* MUM *returns to table.*)

ME. Hello. Hello. Hello. Hello.

UNCLE. At least she could have offered me a cup of tea.

(ME *moves between bed and table.* FIGUREHEAD *stands.*)

ME. I want to be a golfer.

DAD. Henry it is time for you to leave school and go into your father's business of Brummer Striving.

ME. But Brummer Striving is a fast dying business, Father.

DAD. None of thy nonsense, Henry. All thy fathers before have and before even that before me were Brummers and that's a fact.

ME. Tell me again, Father, about how you got those prize stumps, was it not with a Brummer Towdry?

DAD. Why do you always ask about stumps, son?

ME. Because it's a story I love to hear, Father—and besides it's not every one what has a real cripple for a father.

DAD. There's something in what you say, my son.

ME. I want to be a golfer, Dad.

DAD. You're a Brummer, son, so get it straight.

(DAD *exits at centre stage left.*)

ME. It seems I'm a born Brummer like Dad Harry says I am. Well, I will not be seen or heard about this quaint little slum.

(ME *stands on table.*)

Amo Amat Amas . . .

(FIGUREHEAD *throws kitbag to* ME. MUM *moves downstage centre, mimes digging.*)

I wonder what she's digging—the old wretch keeps digging. It can't be sounds, man. And also singing to herself a song you don't hear nowadays.

Mother, Mother, it's me. I'm home. Mother, Mother, it's me.

I wonder what she's digging. Mother, Mother.

MUM. Can't you see I'm burying Soft Harry, your father?

(MUM *returns to table.*)

ME.

The best of luck to you old Dad,
We said with slight remorse,
You'll dig it in the Workhouse, man
(He wouldn't though of course)

Ah well he's gone and that's a fact,
We muttered after lunch,
And hurried to the room in which
He used to wash his hunch.

We never heard from Dad again
I 'spect we never shall
But he'll remain in all our hearts
—a buddy friend and pal.

They all jumbled on me and did smite
me
with mighty blows about my head.
They killed me, you know,
at least I didn't die alone, did I?

All I wanted was a civil answer.

I was born on the 9th October, when the Nazis were still bombing us, led by Adolf Hitler, who only had one.—Anyway they didn't get me.

God help and breed you all.

(ME *moves downstage centre.*)

I remember Kakky Hargreaves
As if 'twer Yestermorn'
Kakky, Kakky Hargreaves
Son of Mr. Vaughan.

He used to be so grundie
On him little bike
Riding on a Sundie
Funny little tyke

Yes, I remember Kathy Hairbream
As if 'twer yesterday
Kathy, Kathy, Hairbream
Son of Mr. May

Arriving at the station
Always dead on time
For his destination
Now he's dead on line
(Meaning he's been got by a train or
something.)

And so we growt and bumply
Till the end of time,
Humpty dumpty bumply
Son of Harry Lime.
                    (Thank you.)

(ME *walks upstage as rest of company stand.*)

CURTAIN